Java™ Programming

Making the Move from C++

Joe Wigglesworth
IBM Toronto Lab

Paula Lumby
IBM Toronto Lab

COURSE
TECHNOLOGY

ONE MAIN STREET, CAMBRIDGE, MA 02142

an International Thomson Publishing company I(T)P®

Cambridge • Albany • Bonn • Boston • Cincinnati • London • Madrid • Melbourne • Mexico City
New York • Paris • San Francisco • Singapore • Tokyo • Toronto • Washington

Java™ Programming: Making the Move from C++ is published by Course Technology.

Managing Editor	Kristen Duerr
Product Manager	Cheryl Ouellette
Production Editor	Catherine G. DiMassa
Project Manager	Cindy Johnson
Developmental Editor	Kathleen Habib
Text Designer	Kim Munsell
Cover Designer	Efrat Reis
Cover Illustrator	Douglas Goodman

For more information contact:

Course Technology
One Main Street
Cambridge, MA 02142

International Thomson Editores
Seneca, 53
Colonia Polanco
11560 Mexico D.F. Mexico

ITP Europe
Berkshire House 168-173
High Holborn
London WCIV 7AA
England

ITP GmbH
Königswinterer Strasse 418
53227 Bonn
Germany

Nelson ITP, Australia
102 Dodds Street
South Melbourne, 3205
Victoria, Australia

ITP Asia
60 Albert Street, #15-01
Albert Complex
Singapore 189969

ITP Nelson Canada
1120 Birchmount Road
Scarborough, Ontario
Canada M1K 5G4

ITP Japan
Hirakawacho Kyowa Building, 3F
2-2-1 Hirakawacho
Chiyoda-ku, Tokyo 102
Japan

ISBN 1-85032-922-2

Printed in the United States of America

1 2 3 4 5 6 7 8 9 10 BH 02 01 00 99 98

Preface

Welcome to *Java Programming: Making the Move from C++*! This book was written for C++ programmers who, after investing time and effort in learning C++, are hearing much about the potential of the Java programming language. In particular, they are hearing about the power this new language brings to programming for the Internet and for platform-independent programs. The Java programming language has made such a dramatic entrance into the world of software development that qualified Java programmers are sure to be in great demand. This book will allow you to leverage your C++ skills to quickly develop Java skills, at least to the level of Certified Java Programmer as defined by the Sun Certified Java Programmer Examination.

C++ will not disappear. C++ is an important development language and will continue to be the best vehicle for many forms of software development. There are likely to be demands for programmers that know both the C++ and Java programming languages. The syntax of the Java programming language bears a strong resemblance to the syntax of C++. Therefore, C++ programmers have some advantage over those who do not know C++ when they learn the Java programming language. The Java programming language is also object-oriented and incorporates many object-oriented concepts found in C++. The approach of the authors in this book answers the question, "What does a C++ programmer need to know to take full advantage of the Java language?"

The early chapters of this book describe the basics of the Java language. The middle chapters move through the essential and powerful programming techniques supported by the Java language, including:

- extending existing classes
- implementing interfaces
- exception handling
- multithreading
- cloning objects
- run-time type information
- advanced language constructs such as inner classes

Much of the latter half of this book gives overviews of the packages provided by the Java platform. These packages are analogous to C++ class libraries, but have the great advantage of being available and standard on all implementations of the Java platform. The classes in these packages support:

- stream I/O and random-access file I/O
- networking
- collection classes
- programming graphical user interfaces for applications
- creating applets
- internationalizing programs

This book includes two special sections that introduce integrated development environments (IDEs). In Chapter 1, step-by-step instructions walk the reader through introductions to IBM VisualAge for Java and Sun Java WorkShop. In Chapter 12, the reader can design a class visually with IBM VisualAge for Java. Each of these IDE sections is set off from the rest of the chapter with a shaded background and can be skipped without missing any of the important Java programming concepts presented in the chapter.

This book also includes a chapter that introduces JavaBeans. To create JavaBeans is to create reusable software components that can be input directly into a number of rapid application development (RAD) tools.

Organization and Coverage

Java Programming: Making the Move from C++ is designed to provide the necessary skills to pass the Sun Certified Java Programmer Examination. The following table is organized by the certification topics listed in the Objectives of the Sun Certified Java Programmer Examination for JDK 1.1, available from the Sun certification Web site (URLs are provided in Appendix D). The organization of this book is different from the organization of the Sun objectives. This table will help you locate the section of this book corresponding to a particular Java programming skill.

Certification Exam Topic	Chapter
Language fundamentals	1, 2, 3, 4
Operators and assignments	2, 3
The **java.lang** package	2, 3
Declarations and access control	2, 4
Flow control and exception handling	2, 6
Garbage collection	3
Overloading, overriding, runtime type, and object orientation	4, 5, 7, 9
The **java.io** package	8, 16
Threads	11
The **java.awt** package—layout	12, 13
The **java.awt** package—components and facilities	12, 13, 14
The **java.awt** package—event handling	13
The **java.awt** package—painting	13

Features

Java Programming: Making the Move from C++ is an exceptional book because it also includes the following features:

Read This Before You Begin Page This page appears at the beginning of the first chapter and is consistent with Course Technology's unequaled commitment to helping instructors introduce technology into the classroom. Technical considerations and assumptions about hardware, software, and default settings are listed in one place to help instructors save time and eliminate unnecessary aggravation.

Objectives The Objectives call out the main concepts that will be presented in the lesson. There are two levels of objectives:

- General Java programming objectives

and

- Objectives for the Sun Certified Java Programmer Examination

Syntax Language constructs, class and member declarations, and the like are presented in clearly marked Syntax windows so that the reader can easily identify them. These windows dissect the syntax and provide a complete description of the semantics of new keywords and constructs as they are introduced.

Code examples In addition to code examples included with the syntax, source code for working programs is included to provide additional examples of a concept or illustrate common and preferred usage. All the code examples that appear are provided on the CD-ROM in the java4cpp.jar file so that you do not need to type any of the examples that appear in the book.

Sample code Sample code appears as `int i=3`.

Keywords Keywords appear as int.

Program names Program names appear as **javadoc**.

New terms New terms appear in **boldface**.

Step-by-step instructions In Chapters 1 and 12, special sections on using integrated development environments (IDEs) include text and step-by-step instructions that constantly guide readers, letting them know where they are in the process of completing the task. Numerous illustrations include labels that direct the readers' attention to what they should look at on the screen.

Performance Tip Performance Tips provide information about a procedure or technique to help improve your program's performance.

Programming Tip Programming Tips provide additional information about a procedure or technique.

Moving from C++ tip Moving from C++ tips highlight differences between the C++ and Java programming languages, and subtleties that might create problems if you assume that the two languages work exactly alike.

Version Watch This book was developed using Java version 1.1.5. All example code was tested and all programming exercises can be completed with version 1.1.5 of the JDK. The Java language is still evolving and has undergone changes since it was first announced. Version Watches provide information on changes to the Java platform that have been announced for Java 1.2 and developments that are expected in future versions of Java.

Some features have been deprecated, that is, they are no longer recommended for use in Java 1.1.5, because the same functionality is provided by new and improved features. Generally, the Java platform continues to accept and run programs that contain deprecated features. However, you should not use them when you create new code. If you look at programs written for early versions of Java and see constructs that do not agree with the current description of the language or standard classes, look in boxes such as this one. You may find that the old code is using a deprecated feature.

This book makes no pretense at being able to predict all future developments in the Java platform. However, important features that are likely to be available in the near future are mentioned.

Mini Quiz Mini quizzes appear throughout each chapter as a way for readers to check that they understand the concepts presented up to that point. The answers to the mini quizzes appear at the end of the book, following the appendices.

Summary Following each chapter is a synopsis highlighting the programming concepts and constructs covered in the chapter.

Questions Each chapter concludes with meaningful, conceptual Questions that test readers' understanding of what they've learned in the chapter. Types of questions include true/false, fill-in-the-blank, short answer, multiple choice, and other appropriate methods of self-testing to evaluate comprehension of the subject. The short answer questions are similar in form and nature to the questions on the Sun Certified Java Programmer Examination.

Exercises The Questions are followed by hands-on Exercises that test readers' programming skills. The best, and perhaps only effective, way to learn a programming language is to write programs. Three kinds of Exercises appear at the end of each chapter: Debugging, Complete the Solution, and Discovery Exercises (Programming Problems). These Exercises provide readers with additional practice of the skills and concepts they learned in the chapter. The Exercises encourage readers to challenge and independently develop their own programming skills while exploring the capabilities of their new programming language.

The Supplements

Instructor's Manual The Instructor's Manual has been written by the authors and has been quality assurance tested. It is available in printed form and through the Course Technology Faculty Online Companion on the World Wide Web. (Call your customer service representative for the URL and your password.) The Instructor's Manual contains the following items:

- Answers to all of the Questions and suggested solutions to all of the Exercises.
- Chapter Notes, which contain background information from the author about the chapter and the instructional progression of the chapter.
- Technical Notes, which include troubleshooting tips.

Course Test Manager Version 1.2 Engine and Test Bank Course Test Manager (CTM) is a cutting-edge Windows-based testing software program, developed exclusively for Course Technology, that helps instructors design and administer examinations. This full-featured program allows readers to generate practice tests randomly that provide immediate on-screen feedback, and detailed study guides for questions that were incorrectly answered. Instructors can also use CTM to create printed and online tests. You can create, preview, and administer a test on any or all chapters of this book entirely over a local area network.

CTM can grade the tests readers take automatically at the computer and can generate statistical information on individual as well as group performance. A CTM test bank has been written to accompany this book and is included on the Instructor's CD-ROM. The test bank includes multiple-choice, true/false, short answer, and essay questions.

- **Solution Files** Solution files contain every file that readers are asked to create or modify in the chapters and Exercises.
- **Sample Programs** Sample programs, containing all of the source code that readers will use and see in the chapters and to complete the exercises are provided through Course Technology's Online Companion, as well as on CD-ROM. See the inside front cover of this book and the Read This Before You Begin page before Chapter 1 for more information on sample programs.

CD-ROM The *Java Programming: Making the Move from C++* CD-ROM contains the Java Development Kit (JDK) 1.1.5 Release, IBM VisualAge for Java 1.0, Sun Java WorkShop 2.0, the JavaBeans Development Kit (BDK) 1.0, and the source and compiled code for all the sample programs in this book. The code files are combined in a Java archive (JAR) file, java4cpp.jar. For further instructions on copying these files to your computer, refer to the Help file on the CD-ROM. You can view the Help file using a text editor. For more information on the CD-ROM, refer to the Read This Before You Begin page before Chapter 1.

Acknowledgments

We are grateful to the reviewers for taking the time to thoroughly review our manuscript: Jeff Scott, Blackhawk Technical College; Milton Luoma, University of Wisconsin-Superior; James Kolasa, Lexington Community College; Bill Morrison, Foothill College; Mark Raynes, Bloomsburg; Marvin Solomon, University of Wisconsin-Madison; Susan Horwitz, University of Wisconsin-Madison; Gordon Hirsch, JavaSoft; Vijay Srinivasan, JavaSoft; and John Wegis, JavaSoft. Their contributions certainly improved the quality of the final version. We would especially like to thank Marvin Solomon for his extremely thorough review and many corrections and suggestions, and for going above and beyond his duties as a reviewer by submitting many interesting and useful sample programs.

We also appreciate the feedback and guidance that Graham Lovell, Sun Microsystems; and John Soper, New Paradigms Marketing Group have provided throughout the development of this book. We gratefully acknowledge the role that Sheila Richardson, IBM Toronto Lab, played as Consulting Editor.

Joe Wigglesworth thanks his wonderful wife, Maria, for all her patience and understanding throughout the long process of creating and editing the manuscript. Without her support, this project would not have been possible.

Paula Lumby expresses her gratitude to her children, Joy, Alison, and Thomas, for surviving with a distracted and over-busy mother while this book was being written. These three wonderful young people have contributed enormously to the completion of this book.

Joe Wigglesworth

Paula Lumby

Contents

Read This Before You Begin

To the Reader

CD-ROM

The *Java Programming: Making the Move from* C++ CD-ROM contains the Java Development Kit (JDK) 1.1.5 Release, IBM VisualAge for Java 1.0, Sun Java WorkShop 2.0, the JavaBeans Development Kit (BDK) 1.0, and the source and compiled code for all the sample programs in this book. The code files are combined in a Java archive (JAR) file, java4cpp.jar. For further instructions on copying these files to your computer, refer to the Help files on the CD-ROM or Chapter 1. You can view the Help files using a text editor.

Using Your Own Computer

If you are going to work through this book using your own computer you need:

- **Computer System** Microsoft Windows 95 or Microsoft Windows NT 4.0 (or later), and the Java Development Kit (JDK) 1.1.5 Release must be installed on your computer. This book assumes a complete installation of the JDK from the Developer's Resource Kit CD-ROM.
- **Sample Programs** The source and compiled code for all the sample programs in this book are provided on the CD-ROM supplied with this book.

  The programs are combined in a Java archive (JAR) file, java4cpp.jar. The JAR file contains one Java package, java4cpp, that has the same name as the file. The classes are divided into subpackages:

applet	classes	errors	inheritance	network	rtti
basic	cloning	exceptions	inner	observe	threads
beans	collections	i18n	io	questions	windows

  The package "questions" contains the code that appears in end-of-chapter exercises. This package is further broken down, by chapter number, into subpackages c1, c2, c3 and so on. The package "errors" contains classes that appear in the book with deliberate errors in them, and therefore cannot be run. The other packages roughly correspond to the major topics covered in this book.

  For your convenience, you should copy the JAR file onto your hard disk. You can create a subfolder for JAR files. On Windows-based platforms, if your CD-ROM is on drive G, and you want to set up a folder named "jars" to contain your JAR file on the D drive, issue the following DOS commands:

  ```
  D:
  md jars
  cd jars
  copy G:\java4cpp.jar
  ```

  Please substitute the correct drive letter of your CD-ROM for G, and your choice of destination drive and subfolder for D:\jars.

  For further instructions on copying these files to your computer, refer to the Help file on the CD-ROM or Chapter 1. You can view the Help file using a text editor.

Java Development Kit 1.1.5 Release

The Java Development Kit (JDK) 1.1.5 Release contains a suite of command-line tools. These tools are adequate to complete all of the programming exercises in this book. The JDK lets you write programs and applets for the Java programming language. The JDK for the Windows platform is included in the JDK 1.1.5 folder on the CD-ROM, along with a Help file containing installation instructions.

IBM VisualAge for Java 1.0.1 Professional Edition

IBM VisualAge for Java is a true rapid application development (RAD) tool. The Professional Edition is the full software package. Version 1.0.1 includes several fixes to the initial version 1.0. A unique and popular feature of VisualAge for Java is the visual Composition Editor. With the Composition Editor, you can rapidly create GUIs for applets and applications, and integrate the GUI components of your program with other Java code. The product provides a fully integrated IDE, a true incremental build, and a good debugger. It generates 100% Pure Java code. VisualAge for Java can also create and consume JavaBean components. Versions are available for OS/2 and Windows platforms. The Full Professional Version of VisualAge for Java for Windows is included in the VisualAge for Java folder on the CD-ROM, along with a Help file containing installation instructions.

Sun Java WorkShop 2.0

Sun Java WorkShop has an easy-to-use programming environment. Its IDE provides a debugger, fast compiler, and performance profiler. This product also has full support for JavaBeans. The Sun Java WorkShop promotes and supports Java platform and JavaBean standards. Versions are available for Windows and Solaris platforms. A trial version of Sun Java WorkShop for Windows is included in the Java WorkShop 2.0 folder on the CD-ROM, along with a Help file containing installation instructions.

JavaBeans Development Kit 1.0

The JavaBeans component model provides a framework for creating reusable, embeddable software components. The JavaBeans Development Kit (BDK) 1.0 for Windows is included in the BDK 1.0 folder on the CD-ROM, along with a Help file containing installation instructions.

Visit Our World Wide Web Site

Additional materials designed especially for users of *Java Programming: Making the Move from C++* and other Course Technology products are available on the World Wide Web. Go to **http://www.course.com.**

To the Instructor

The Java source and compiled code for all the example programs in this book are provided on the Developer's Resource Kit CD-ROM. They may also be obtained electronically over the Internet. See the inside front cover of this book for more details.

The code files are combined in a Java archive (JAR) file, java4cpp.jar. Please refer to the "Using Your Own Computer" section for information on working with the JAR file.

The solution files are combined in the file solution.jar. The JAR file contains one package, "java4cpp," that has one subpackage, "answers." The package "answers" is further broken down, by chapter number, into subpackages c1, c2, c3 and so on.

On Windows-based platforms, if your CD-ROM is on drive G, issue the following DOS commands:

```
D:
md jars
cd jars
copy G:\solution.jar
```

Please substitute the correct drive letter of your CD-ROM for G, and you choice of destination drive and subfolder for D:\jars.

Course Technology Data Files

You are granted a license to copy the data files to any computer or computer network used by readers who have purchased this book.

CHAPTER

1

Introduction

objectives

In this chapter you will:

- Gain some insight into the nature and goals of the Java programming language.
- Review the historical context in which Java technology was developed.
- Preview many of the features of Java technology that later chapters of this book describe in depth.
- Be introduced to the tools provided by the Sun Java Development Kit (JDK) and two proprietary Java application development products.
- Make sure you are set up to run the example programs and complete the programming exercises in this book.
- Build and run a simple program written in the Java programming language.
- Learn to insert comments in javadoc format and automatically generate program documentation from them.
- Learn to use standard javadoc format documentation to identify and use variables and methods in classes.
- Use javadoc documentation to identify variables and methods that are inherited from a superclass.

As an experienced programmer, you may be eager to start experimenting with Java technology. Therefore, a large part of this chapter takes you through the development process for some small, but complete, applications. Use the first program as an example of how to code a simple Java program[1]. Some of the Java statements[2] in the first program may look familiar, because designers of the Java programming language borrowed from C++ for many syntactic constructs. On the other hand, you may notice a number of constructs that are not available in C++. The first program can give you some sense of context for many language elements that are covered in the following chapters of this book.

This chapter also takes you through entering and running a program. Follow the scenarios for an introduction to Java development environments[3], and to make sure that you are set up to start programming.

You may be able to combine what you discover in this chapter with your knowledge of C++ and start programming. Experimenting is the best way to learn. However, you should return to the following chapters of this book for a precise description of the Java programming language syntax.

Overview of the Java Platform

What makes the Java programming language so appealing? The answer is largely that Java technology is more than just a programming language; it is also a platform. The designers of Java program-development software considered not only the question of how to write code, but also the problem of how to run code on different hardware and software configurations. The Java programming language is the first language to provide integrated support for features such as multitasking and networking at the language level. These have typically been relegated to hardware or operating system dependent libraries that bound programs to the specific hardware or operating system. The Java platform provides these features through its language and its APIs.

When you install Java technology, you mount the Java platform on your system. The Java platform includes the Java Virtual Machine (JVM) and a number of packages that support the compiler, interpreter, and run-time environment for the Java programming language. In the language, a package is analogous to a library of predefined classes or functions in C++. Such a package contains reusable classes that programmers can access in their programs. The classes that make up the packages provided by the Java platform are called the **core classes**. All core classes are grouped into packages. Some of the packages are further divided into subpackages, which are simply packages within packages.

You have a choice of Java application development tools. You can use the Sun JDK, which is available for free for Windows and Solaris environments. Ports of the JDK are also available on many other platforms from other vendors.

[1]We use the term *Java program* in place of *program for the Java programming language* throughout this text.

[2]We use the term *Java statement* in place of *statement written in the Java programming language* throughout this text.

[3]We use the term *Java development environment* in place of *development environment for the Java programming language* throughout this text.

You can use an integrated development environment (IDE) with a graphical user interface (GUI) by acquiring products such as the Sun Java WorkShop or IBM VisualAge for Java. The CD-ROM that accompanies this book includes the JDK versions of both the Sun Java WorkShop and IBM VisualAge for Java.

Applications and Applets

You can write many kinds of programs in the Java programming language—everything from giant order entry systems running on mainframes to a personal assistant running within a piece of jewelry. In this book we will focus our attention on two kinds of programs: applications and applets[4].

- Applications are the kind of program that you write in C++ or most other general-purpose languages. Applications can run stand-alone on a workstation and can be any size, from large suites of programs to very small programs. They can run from the command line or have a GUI. Whether applications include interfaces to connect to networks, databases, or any other applications depends on the set of application programming interface (API) functions that the application uses. Java applications differ from applications written in C++ and other languages in that they run only in the JVM. Java applications are compiled not for a particular processor instruction set or operating system API, but for the Java platform.
- Java applets are programs that can be embedded in HTML documents. **HTML** stands for HyperText Markup Language and is the coding used by Web pages. HTML has tags specifically designed for Java applets. Applets, unlike applications, can be downloaded along with the Web page in which they reside, and can be run by Web browsers that support the Java platform. Therefore, applets tend to be small, GUI-oriented programs. Chapter 14 of this book is devoted to applets.

You use the same Java platform and tools to develop both applets and applications, with two provisos:

- You cannot use all the features of the Java platform in applets. For security reasons, applets cannot perform the full range of input/output (I/O), system interrogation, and network operations.
- To run applets, you must use an applet viewer tool or a Web browser. All Java application development software, including the JDK, includes an applet viewer.

Version 1.2 of the Java platform brings a new concept: the servlet. Servlets extend the function of a server in a the way that is analogous to applets extending the function of a Web browser. The Java Servlet API is one of the first manifestations of a Java Standard Extension that provides capabilities beyond those of the core classes.

[4]We use the term *Java applet* in place of *applet written in the Java programming language* throughout this text.

What Is Java?

Just what did Sun Microsystems present to the world with the release of the Java programming language? Mainly, Sun developed a language and development paradigm that is intended to be truly platform-independent and, with the Internet in mind, secure. Sun has composed a more comprehensive definition of Java in a white paper, *The Java Language, An Overview*:

> Java: A simple, object-oriented, network-savvy, interpreted, robust, secure, architecture-neutral, portable, high-performance, multithreaded, dynamic language.

Sun Microsystems is the authoritative source on the Java programming language. The Sun definition crams a lot of adjectives into one sentence, but the company boldly presents the Java programming language for the world to evaluate. Here, each adjective is considered in turn.

Java Is Simple The Java programming language is simpler than C++ because it does not include the more complex features available in C++. For example, in the Java programming language you cannot use templates, overload operators, or perform pointer arithmetic. The language has no pointer syntax. The Java programming language does use object references, which have some characteristics similar to C++ references and pointers, to access objects. But you cannot manipulate object references as you can C++ pointers. For example, there is no way to add one to an object reference, and find the location of the next object in storage.

Designing a language that has innovative features, such as the ability to produce both applications and applets, without creating complexity was an impressive achievement for the developers of the Java programming language. On the other hand, the language is evolving and new versions tend to add complexity.

The Java platform includes an ever-growing set of features that were not present in the original version. In later chapters of this book, you encounter additions to the original language, such as inner classes and the reflection API, that undermine the simplicity of the Java programming language.

Java Is Network-Savvy The Java platform includes a package called java.net that supports network programming. In the sense that using the core classes in java.net makes network computing simple, the Java platform is network-savvy. This feature relies not on the language itself, but on packages provided by the Java platform.

Java Is Interpreted The Java platform has a compiler that translates Java source code[5] into a form called bytecode. **Bytecode** is an architecturally neutral representation of code written in the Java programming language. The bytecode, rather than Java source

[5]We use the term *Java source code* and *Java code* in place of *source code written in the Java programming language* throughout this text.

code, is interpreted when you run a Java program. Just to say that the Java programming language is interpreted is misleading. The compilation step is crucial. During this step, the compiler identifies and eliminates many errors and can optimize the bytecode.

Java Is Robust and Secure The Java programming language lends itself to programming for the Internet and the World Wide Web. Therefore, robustness and security are essential. Some features of the language support both robustness and security:

- The Java programming language forces you to work within certain bounds by not providing any facility for pointer arithmetic. The JVM automatically checks array bounds at run time so that programs never intentionally or mistakenly access memory outside the space reserved for the array.
- The language controls casting very carefully. This control has ramifications, especially if you are used to playing tricks with casting data in C++. For example, you cannot overlay a data structure in the system with your own structure and then modify it.
- Bytecode loaded from an untrusted source, such as an unknown server on the Internet, is verified before it is executed. The verifier is a safety mechanism for code that you access with a Web browser. The verifier makes sure that bytecode files are structurally correct by performing checks. One such check is making sure that every instruction has a valid operation code. However, this mechanism is bypassed if you are running bytecode from a file that resides on your local file system.
- There are strict limits on what a Java applet downloaded from an unknown source can do. For example, such an applet cannot write to local files, directly access native code on the local system, or read certain systems properties. Like the bytecode verifier, this safety mechanism does not apply to bytecode that resides on your local file system.

The last two safety features depend upon the ability of the JVM to differentiate between code originating from trusted and untrusted sources.

Java Is Architecture-Neutral and Portable The Java programming language really does provide architecture neutrality. The language allows for no implementation-defined features. For example, the size of a variable of type `int` in C++ is determined by the target processor and the C++ compiler, but is fixed by the Java platform for all implementations on all target processors. All Java programs must be compiled into bytecode before the JVM can run them. Portability comes with architecture neutrality. The bytecode is portable because it runs on all implementations of the JVM. The JVM can run any valid Java program regardless of whether its bytecode was produced on a different implementation of the Java platform.

There is a price to be paid for portability. Architecturally neutral code cannot take advantage of the latest and greatest features of any one platform. There is always a trade-off among features, performance, and portability.

Java Is High-Performance The performance of Java programs can be surprisingly good compared to other interpreted languages. This claim is strengthened by the availability of just-in-time (JIT) compilers. A JIT compiler is a platform-specific program that plugs into the JVM, and that transforms the architecturally neutral bytecode into platform-specific object code. When you run Java programs compiled by a JIT compiler, you bypass the bytecode interpreter. The benefit is a performance boost. Programs that contain many loops can run much faster if compiled with a JIT compiler than if bytecode must be reinterpreted on every pass through every loop.

Java Is Multithreaded The Java platform includes classes specifically to support multithreaded programs. You can use classes from the base language package `java.lang` to create and manage threads. These classes and some Java programming language keywords support interthread communication. When you use core classes to build a GUI, the resulting program is implicitly multithreaded. In addition to the threads that you control, one thread is dedicated to the paint operations that display the visual components of the GUI, and another thread contains an event loop to monitor user activities.

The Java Programming Language Is Dynamic The word *dynamic* may mean different things:

- At run time, the JVM loads classes dynamically as they are required. The JVM does not load a class until the first time the code references the class. There is no requirement that all classes be loaded or even exist before a program begins execution.
- In the object-oriented sense, the Java programming language has dynamic binding.
- The software development process itself has a dynamic quality. You can incrementally build up the set of the classes that make up your program, test them, and combine them in different ways.

A Brief History of Java Technology

The history of Java technology is not very long. The story starts at the beginning of the 1990s, when Sun Microsystems was working on consumer electronics. The primary objective of consumer electronics is to keep the price down. Software for consumer electronics is developed to run on the cheapest chips available. If prices change so that a different chip set becomes cheaper, the developers have to switch to that chip. Sun pursued the goal of creating software that was portable so that it could be switched quickly to new hardware.

A project at Sun was to create an experimental, hand-held computer called the *7, intended for controlling home appliances. James Gosling was the technical leader of the project, and currently oversees and guides the Java technology developments at Sun. Many other people were also involved, but the name James Gosling, more than any other, is to Java technology what the name Bjarne Stroustrup is to C++.

The *7 never became a product. No consumer ever bought such a device to control home appliances, nor now have one gathering dust in a cupboard. Nevertheless, the developers at Sun began to see that the computer language they developed for the *7 could be very useful in other ways. The team realized that it could apply to the Web, where compactness and simplicity are important requirements, and decided to take the language in a new direction. Subsequently, uses of Java technology as a strategic technology for embedded systems in electronic appliances to enterprise-wide applications became more apparent.

At first, the language was called Oak, supposedly in honor of a tree that grew outside Gosling's window. When the development team learned that there was already a computer language called Oak (which is now known mainly because of the loose association that its name has with that of the Java programming language), Gosling and the team had to change the name. They found a much better name, Java, perhaps in recognition of the role caffeine plays in software development. A pleasing side effect is that, when it comes to coining derivative names, such as "latte," "cafe," "espresso," and "beans," Java may have more potential than Oak.

The announcement of the Java programming language generated an unprecedented amount of interest in the software development world. The official history is very short:

- The Java programming language was officially announced in May, 1995. Before that date, alpha and beta versions were available so that programmers could play with the language and start to apply and master it.
- Version 1.1 of the Java platform became available in 1997. This version added some features to the actual Java programming language and significant additions and modification to the set of packages that make up the Java platform.
- Version 1.2 is expected in 1998.
- Since the announcement of the Java programming language, a number of companies have announced Java application development and related products. A Java programmer certification program is available from Sun. IBM also has a certification program for its VisualAge for Java product. The IBM program uses the Sun Certified Java Programmer examination.

Java Tools

The Sun JDK includes the minimal set of tools you need to develop Java programs. Version 1.1.5 of the JDK for Windows and Solaris environments is included on the CD-ROM that accompanies this book. You can also download the latest release of the JDK from the World Wide Web. For a list of sites from which you can get implementations of Java technology for a variety of platforms, as well as a great deal of information about Java technology, see the list of Uniform Resource Locators (URLs) in Appendix D, "Java Resources on the World Wide Web." Alternatively, you can work with the version included on the CD-ROM that accompanies this book.

The tools in the JDK are fairly rudimentary programs that run only in a command-line window. Nevertheless, they are quite suitable for the job of developing Java programs. The Sun Certified Java Programmer examination assumes you are using the standard tools from the JDK.

A number of Java IDE products are available from IBM, Sun, Symantec, and other companies. Versions of IBM VisualAge for Java and the Sun Java WorkShop are also included on the CD-ROM that accompanies this book. These products provide tools for rapid application development, such as visual programming aids or packages that provide connectivity to other proprietary software.

You can complete all the programming exercises in this book with the JDK tools described in this section. This section does not provide a comprehensive list of the programs in the JDK, because it omits some tools that are not required by any example programs in this book. For example, the JDK includes tools for remote method invocation (RMI). You use these tools only when your development environment is distributed over a network. Detailed descriptions of the JDK tools in this book apply to the Sun Windows implementation of JDK. Most of the conventions are cross-platform. However, there are some differences related to file systems and processor invocation on different operating systems. You can find any differences for Solaris by reviewing the documentation on the CD-ROM. If you are using a JDK for another platform, refer to the instructions provided with the specific implementation.

The following are some of the tools in the JDK:

- **javac** is the Java compiler[6]. Run **javac** to create the bytecode for applications and applets. Supply as input a Java source file with the file extension .java. The output is one or more source files with the file extension .class.

  The Java platform has strict naming conventions for files and classes. If the class can be run as an application or used by other classes that are not in the same package, you must give the name of the file that contains the source the same name as the class. Names used in the Java platform are case-sensitive, even on operating systems on which filenames are not case-sensitive, and filenames must match class names exactly, including uppercase and lowercase. You can include the absolute path to find the file. Otherwise, the compiler assumes the filename is relative to the current folder. You must include the file extension .java. For example, to compile the file that contains the class `MyClass`, the command is

  ```
  javac MyClass.java
  ```

- **java** is the Java interpreter[7]. To run an application, you must supply the name of a class that contains the entry point of the application. Enter the **java** command followed by the name of the class you want to run and then by any command-line arguments you want to pass to the program. Do not include the file extension because you are supplying not a filename but a class name. The class name is case-sensitive. For example, to run the class `MyClass`, the command is

  ```
  java MyClass
  ```

[6]We use the term *Java compiler* in place of *compiler for the Java programming language* throughout this text.

[7]We use the term *Java interpreter* in place of *interpreter for the Java programming language* throughout this text.

Conforming to the filenaming conventions is very important because the interpreter loads the file with the extension .class and with the case-sensitive base filename that matches the class name. If the class is in a package, the package must be in a folder that has the same case-sensitive name as the package. You must specify the package name in the **java** command, but you separate the package name and class name with dots instead of the character your operating system uses to indicate subfolders. For example, if `TestClass` is a class in a package called testing, and testing is a subfolder of the current package, the commands to compile and run `TestClass` on Windows-based platforms are

```
javac testing\TestClass.java

java testing.TestClass
```

- **jre** is also a Java interpreter, but it is packaged separately from the JDK. It provides a run-time environment so that developers can include it with their application code without requiring users to install the complete JDK. It is used in the same way as the **java** command.
- **appletviewer** is a utility that runs applets outside a Web browser. Supply the name of an HTML file that contains an applet. The appletviewer tool discards all text on the HTML page except the HTML tags that point to an applet. The tool then opens a window and runs the applet in the viewer window. The command-line arguments for appletviewer are one or more URLs for HTML documents. For an HTML file that resides on the local file system, the URL is the same as the filename. Specify the path relative to the current folder. A separate window displays each applet referenced in the HTML files. For example, to view the applets embedded in the local file mypage.htm, which is in a subfolder of the current folder called myweb, on Windows-based platforms the command (entered from the folder that contains myweb) is:

  ```
  appletviewer myweb\mypage.htm
  ```

  For the **appletviewer** command, whether filenames are case-sensitive depends on your browser and the native operating system. You still have to be careful about filenames because the tags in the HTML page give the location of the .class file for the applet relative to the current folder when you issue the **appletviewer** command.

  On OS/2, the name of this command is truncated to **applet** for compatibility with the file allocation table (FAT) file systems, which restrict filenames to eight characters for the base name and three characters for the extension. For more notes on working with FAT file systems, see Appendix C.
- **javah** generates the C header files needed for linking Java classes[8] with C code. You can call functions generated from source code in other languages by using native methods. A **native method** is an interface from a Java class to a dynamically loadable module that resides on the native file system outside

[8]We use the term *Java class* in place of *class for the Java platform* throughout this text.

the JVM. The most common use of native methods is to link to C functions. Appendix A shows how to make a Java class link to a C function in a dynamic link library in the Windows operating system.

- **jdb** is the Java debugger[9]. This debugger has limited functionality; the proprietary Java application development products use more sophisticated debuggers.
- **javadoc** generates sets of HTML files that make up online documentation for packages of classes. One of the popular and innovative features of Java technology is the ability to generate online user documentation for your classes automatically using this tool and a unique format for comments in your code. The "Doc Comments" section of this chapter describes how to insert the tags that this tool recognizes into your Java source code, how to run the **javadoc** tool, and how to use the output.
- **native2ascii** is a useful tool if you are developing programs for the international market. In the Java platform, all characters are stored in the international character set called Unicode. This tool converts files from the character sets that are commonly used in North America and Western Europe into Unicode. For more information about Unicode and internationalizing a program, see Chapter 16.
- **jar** combines several files into a single Java archive (JAR) file. A JAR file is like a zip file, except that the data is not always compressed. JAR files are useful for combining files such as graphics, sound clips, and executable code that together form an applet. Downloading one JAR file is much more efficient than downloading related files separately.

  The **java** command can find .class files in a JAR file, and most Java development environments can load a JAR file.

  All the example programs in this book are available in one JAR file on the CD-ROM that accompanies this book. See the instructions for using the JAR file in the "Before You Begin" section in the preface of this book.

All the JDK tools have options that you can specify on the command line. A full description of the tools is beyond the scope of this book but is provided by the JDK documentation.

How the JDK Finds Files

Filenames are very important in Java technology. Filenames are case-sensitive in the Java platform. Programs consist of classes, at least one of which must be public, which means accessible from outside the package that contains the class. A file that contains the source for a public class must have the same name as the class. There can be other classes defined within the same file, but they cannot be public. All classes and subpackages in a package must reside in the folder that has the same name as the package.

The commands that take class names as arguments, such as **java**, must find the file that contains the bytecode for the class. The filename is the same as the class name, and the file extension is .class. But where does the search for the class begin in

[9] We use the term *Java debugger* in place of *debugger for the Java programming language* throughout this text.

the local file system? On platforms that support environment variables, the search path is stored in an environment variable called **CLASSPATH**. When you install the JDK, **CLASSPATH** is set by default to search the following folders in order:

1. The current folder.
2. The folder X:\jdk\classes, where X:\jdk is the full path of the folder in which you installed the JDK.
3. The file X:\jdk\lib\classes.zip, where X:\jdk is the full path of the folder in which you installed the JDK. The core classes are stored in the file classes.zip. The Java platform uses this trick so that the Java programs can run on FAT file systems that do not allow long filenames.

You can add other folders to the **CLASSPATH**, or alter the **CLASSPATH**, using the DOS command **SET** on Intel-based platforms. For example, if you want the JVM to find compiled classes stored in the package `java4cpp`, and that package resides in the folder D:\java4cpp, issue the following command:

```
set classpath=%classpath%;D:\java4cpp
```

Java programs are usually built from many classes. What does the compiler do when the source it is processing calls another class? All classes are accessed the same way, regardless of whether they are core classes, your own classes, or third-party software from other sources. The **javac** compiler searches the folders in the **CLASSPATH** for bytecode for the called class, using the class name to identify the file. What if there is no .class file but there is a .java file? What if there is a .class file but its modification timestamp is earlier than that of the .java file? In either case, the .java file is compiled to create an up-to-date .class file. If there is neither a .java file nor a .class file, the compiler reports an error.

The default behavior of the **javac** compiler is to check the validity of .class files automatically. To take advantage of this feature of the compiler, keep .class and .java files with the same names and for the same classes together in the same folder. A side effect of this mechanism is that you can run **javac** against one class and have the compiler inform you if there is an error in another class in a different file. If you find these error messages annoying, try to avoid this situation by making sure all referenced classes are compiled first.

Like the compiler, the **java** command locates bytecode files by class name. It can dynamically load classes that your class calls while your program is running. To find the referenced class, the command searches the folders listed in the **CLASSPATH**. If the JVM cannot find the .class file, it terminates your program with an error message.

Your First Java Program

It is time to start programming. Here is a small but complete Java program. The program reads a number of student IDs and marks, and outputs the IDs of the students who have the highest three marks.

```
package java4cpp.basic;
import java.io.*;
import java.util.*;
```

```
/** A simple Java starter program
  */
public class FirstProgram {
   /** A first program to read a list of IDs and marks.
     * It prints the IDs for the three highest marks.
     * @param args[0] the name of an optional input
     *    file.
     * @exception java.io.IOException
     *    An I/O failure can occur.
     */
   public static void main( String [] args )
                            throws IOException {
      // input file may be supplied in the first
      // argument
      InputStream istream;
      if ( args.length > 0 ) {
         File inputFile = new File( args[0] );
         istream = new FileInputStream( inputFile );
      } else {
         // if no filename, use standard input stream
         istream = System.in;
      }
      // use a buffered reader for line-at-a-time
      // reading
      BufferedReader lineReader;
      lineReader = new BufferedReader(
                   new InputStreamReader( istream ) );
      // arrays record the top three student IDs
      // and marks
      String[] studentID = { "", "", ""};
      float[] marks = { 0, 0, 0};
      // read one line at a time
      String line;
      while ( (line = lineReader.readLine() ) != null ) {
         // student ID and mark are two tokens in
         // a line
         StringTokenizer tokens
            = new StringTokenizer( line );
         String student = tokens.nextToken();
         float mark
            = ( new Float( tokens.nextToken() ) )
              .floatValue();
          // see if the mark is in the top three so far
          for ( int i = 0; i < 3; i++ ) {
             // handle a tie by appending IDs at a rank
             if ( mark == marks[i] ) {
```

```
                    studentID[i] += " " + student;
                    break;
                }
                if ( mark > marks[i] ) {
                    // insert a higher mark than is now in
                    // the top three; the core method
                    // arraycopy shifts entries.
                    System.arraycopy( marks, i, marks,
                                      i+1, 2-i );
                    System.arraycopy( studentID, i,
                                      studentID,
                                      i+1, 2-i);
                    marks[i] = mark;
                    studentID[i] = student;
                    break;
                }
            }   // end of for loop to compare marks
        }   // end of while loop to read input lines
        // print the IDs of the top three students
        for ( int i = 0; i < 3; i++ ) {
            System.out.println( ( i + 1 ) + ": "
                                + studentID[i] );
        }  // end of for printing loop
    }  // end of main
} // end of class
```

Some of the statements in this class may look familiar to C++ programmers, especially in the latter half of the program. However, you may be puzzled by some constructs, such as the use of public in the first line, the complex-looking declaration of main, and many of the types used in the declarations. The following dissection of this piece of code may dispel some of the mystery.

Breakdown of the FirstProgram Class

This program is contained inside a class called `FirstProgram`. Every executable unit of code in the Java programming language must be within a class. This class contains one method, called main. Even the main method has to belong to a class, but not every class must have a method named main. `FirstProgram` is a very simple class that has a main method so that it can be used as an application.

Moving from C++

A C++ program consists of a set of classes and functions. A Java program consists only of classes. A method is the Java programming language's equivalent of a C++ member function. The Java programming language has no equivalent of nonmember functions.

```
package java4cpp.basic;
```

The source code for this example is included in the package `java4cpp` on the CD-ROM that accompanies this book. This program is in the subpackage `basic` within the package `java4cpp`. The structure of packages mirrors the file system, so you will find this source code in the java4cpp\basic subfolder of the folder in which you unpacked the JAR file java4cpp.jar. The name of a source file always matches the name of the public class that it contains, so this source code is found in the file FirstProgram.java. If you enter this code for test purposes, you can omit the package statement. If you run the supplied example code, the package statement tells the Java interpreter where to find the class.

```
import java.io.*;
import java.util.*;
```

This class uses core classes in the packages java.lang, java.io, and java.util. The package java.lang is implicitly imported because it supports the Java programming language itself. The reason for explicitly importing the other two packages is to allow the code to refer to names in those packages without qualifying them with the package name. For example, the class StringTokenizer is a utility class in the package java.util. The `FirstProgram` class can reference it by the name StringTokenizer. If you delete the second import statement, you must modify the code to refer to classes in java.util always by their full names, such as java.util.StringTokenizer.

The import statement looks quite similar to the C++ include preprocessor directive, but it is very different. No code is copied into the `FirstProgram` source. All that these import statements let you do is refer to the classes in the two packages without including the package name every time you use the class name.

```
/** A simple Java starter program
  */
```

The next lines are a comment. Comments in the Java programming language can be block comments enclosed in /* and */ characters, or single-line comments that begin with // and run to the end of the line. This comment is a doc comment because it starts with the sequence /**. The Java compiler treats doc comments as block comments. Doc comments are used with the **javadoc** tool to generate user documentation, and are discussed later in this chapter. The rest of the comments in this program are omitted from this discussion.

Moving from C++

The Java compiler treats comments exactly like a C++ compiler:

- **Block comments can span lines and are delimited by /* and */.**
- **Single-line comments begin with //.**

C++ has no equivalent of doc comments.

```
public class FirstProgram {
```

The definition of the `FirstProgram` class starts here. The first keyword, public, indicates that this class can be used from anywhere. A class that is not public can only be used by the other classes that are in the same package. In the Java programming language, you have two choices:

- Declare a class public to make it accessible from everywhere.
- Omit the keyword public to limit access to within the package that contains the class.

Moving from C++

The closest C++ equivalent to a non-public class is a class declared at a namespace scope other than global namespace scope. In C++, you never apply the keyword public to a class. However, C++ compilers that support namespaces, which are a fairly recent addition to the C++ language, let you declare a class inside a named namespace so that the class name is visible only within the enclosing namespace scope.

The Java programming language allows only one public class in a file, and the filename must match the name of the public class. Therefore, this class declaration tells the compiler to store the bytecode for this class in the file FirstProgram.class. If you include the package statement, you must put the .class file in a folder named basic, which in turn must reside in a folder named java4cpp.

Moving from C++

Unlike C++, the Java programming language is quite strict about the use of filenames. C++ is a language only. The Java programming language, however, is part of the Java platform. Different proprietary application development environments manage file and folder names for you. But when you use the JDK, you must conform to the filenaming conventions when you create your source code.

```
public static void main( String [] args)
                          throws IOException {
```

The main method is the entry point of a program. When you run the java command and provide a class name, the JVM starts execution by calling the main method of that class. In this case, the entire program is contained in main.

The Java programming language is very strict about the form of the method main:

- In the Java programming language, you specify the access for every member of a Java class separately. You must explicitly declare the main method public.
- The keyword static declares that the method applies to the whole class rather than to a particular object. The main method must be static so that it can be called when no object of the class has been created.

- The return type must be void because main does not return a value to the JVM.
- The method main must have one argument, and it must be an array of String objects. Strings are not primitive types in Java. String is one of the core classes provided by java.lang. Giving the String array the identifier `args` is a convention, not a rule. Command-line arguments are passed to main through this array.
- The words following the argument list are a throws clause. Not every main method has a throws clause, but this one must because it calls methods that can throw exceptions and it does not handle them. The program performs I/O, and file operations can fail for a number of reasons. In the Java platform, all run-time errors are manifested as exceptions. The Java programming language has a rule that if an exception can occur during execution of a method, the method must take steps either to recover or list the exception in a throws clause.

A class can have a method called main that does not conform to these rules, but such a method is not recognized as an entry point for an application.

Moving from C++

Both C++ programs and Java applications start execution with a method called main**. But the similarity goes little further.**

- **In C++,** main **is not a member function. Therefore, the keywords** public **and** static **are never appropriate.**
- **In C++, the** main **function can have the return type** int **or** void**. The most common reason to return a value in C++ is to indicate success or return an error code to the calling process. If you want to terminate and return a value in the Java programming language, you can call the method** System.exit (int *return_code*)**.**
- **The argument list has a similar purpose in C++ and the Java programming language. However, it contains a different number of arguments, partly because arrays are implemented very differently in C++ and the Java programming language.**
- **In C++, the argument for the array of strings has type** char** **or** char[ ] [ ]**. In the Java programming language, you cannot use the form** char****, because the language does not include contents-of** (*) **and address-of** (&) **operators. You cannot use the form** char[ ] [ ] **because strings used in the language are not just arrays of characters. The Java programming language, like recent versions of C++, has a standard class for strings. As with the new C++ standard template class, the class is called** String**. In the argument of** main**, C++ still uses the legacy form inherited from the C language.**
- **The throws clause is analogous to a C++ exception specification, except that providing a C++ exception specification is always optional. Including an exception specification in a C++** main **function is not incorrect, but is unusual.**

```
InputStream istream;
```

This program reads from an input stream. This statement is the declaration of an InputStream object named `istream`. All of the core stream classes, including InputStream, belong to the package java.io.

Moving from C++

The stream I/O in the Java platform is conceptually very much like C++ stream I/O. However, the class names and implementations differ. The InputStream class is analogous to the C++ class istream.

```
if ( args.length > 0 ) {
```

This if statement tests the argument `args` of main to see whether the array contains at least one element. Every array has a field called length that records the number of elements in the array. A field is a member of an object that holds data. In other words, this statement determines whether any command-line arguments have been passed to main.

Moving from C++

The if **statement demonstrates a number of differences between C++ and the Java programming language.**

- if **statements are almost identical in the two languages. The only difference is that the conditional expression must evaluate to** true **or** false **in the Java programming language. The condition cannot have an integral value. The Java programming language is unlike C++ in that zero is not equivalent to** false, **and nonzero is not equivalent to** true.
- **Unlike C++ arrays, Java arrays are objects in their own right. Java arrays have members, like classes. You can always determine the length of a Java array by interrogating the field** length. **Therefore, you do not need a separate argument of** main **to indicate the number of elements in the array argument.**
- **A field in the Java programming language is the equivalent of a C++ data member.**
- **The command-line arguments passed to the C++ function** main **include the program name. Therefore, a C++** main **function always receives at least one element in the array. In the Java programming language, the class name is not passed and the array is empty if the user supplies no command-line arguments.**

```
File inputFile = new File( args[0] );
```

The program expects the first argument passed to main to be a filename. This statement creates an object of the core class File to represent the file, and declares an object reference `inputFile` with which the program can access the file. The construct that actually creates a new object is the keyword new followed by an explicit call of a constructor of a class. Constructors are a special method of classes that prepare new objects for use. They always have the same name as their class. They can optionally have arguments. In this case, the argument is the name of the file to encapsulate in the File object.

In the Java programming language, the syntax `File inputFile =` gives the appearance that `inputFile` is the identifier of the File **object. Actually, `InputFile` is an object reference, a separate entity that is used to access the** File **object. Unlike C++, the Java programming language does not have different ways of accessing objects. You cannot create objects, pointers to objects, and references the way you can in C++. In the Java programming language, you can access objects of class types only through object references. The language has no pointer syntax, but object references are implemented like pointers behind the scenes.**

```
istream = new FileInputStream( inputFile );
```

To be used as an input stream, the file must be accessed as an object of the core class FileInputStream. The expression on the right of the assignment operator creates a FileInputStream object for the file. This new object is assigned to the InputStream object reference `istream`. The assignment is valid because classes InputStream and FileInputStreams are related. A FileInputStream object is a kind of InputStream object. Upon successful completion of this statement, the file is open for reading.

Moving from C++

In C++ terms, FileInputStream **is a derived class and** InputStream **is the base class. The core class** FileInputStream **is analogous to the C++ class** ifstream.

```
} else {
   istream = System.in;
}
```

If the user supplies no command-line arguments, this program takes its input from the console. For console input, use the predefined InputStream object System.in. The System class is defined in the package java.lang, and contains a number of useful objects, including standard streams for input, System.in, and output, System.out.

Moving from C++

The Java programming language, like C++, has standard streams for console input and output. System.in **is analogous to** cin **and** wcin, **and** System.out **is analogous to** cout **and** wcout. **In both C++ and the Java programming language, you can perform stream I/O on the standard streams or on files.**

```
BufferedReader lineReader;
lineReader = new BufferedReader(
                new InputStreamReader( istream ) );
```

These two lines wrap two more core classes around the InputStream object `istream`. Each class filters, or processes, the input in a specialized way. The class InputStreamReader converts characters in the native character set of the operating system to Unicode. The BufferedReader class can buffer the input so that the program receives one line at a time.

Moving from C++

The stream classes do not map directly onto the C++ iostream classes. In particular, C++ has a different set of complications when it comes to reading characters that are encoded in different ways. The Java programming language always uses Unicode internally and has filter classes to translate characters as required during input and output. The current standard for C++ defines two types of characters, char and wchar_t, and defines all the iostream classes to be template classes.

Using all these classes may seem a complicated way of setting up streams for input. The Java programming language does not have a direct equivalent to the input and output operators >> and <<. This program takes the common approach of using filter classes to read one line at a time as a string.

```
String[] studentID = { "", "", ""};
float[] marks = { 0, 0, 0};
```

The program must record the top three marks and the IDs of the students who achieved those marks. These two statements create and initialize an array to hold the marks and a parallel array for the student IDs.

Moving from C++

The declaration and initialization of arrays are similar in the Java programming language and C++. You cannot use pointer notation, but you can use a form that looks exactly like that of C++:

```
String studentID[] = { "", "", "" };
float marks[] = { 0, 0, 0 };
```

Placing the square brackets before the identifier is preferred to emphasize that an array is a type in the Java programming language.

Both C++ and the Java programming language can deduce the size of the array from the number of elements in the initializer list.

```
String line;
```

The local variable `line` is an object reference for a String. It is used for the input lines. No String object is created yet.

```
while ( ( line = lineReader.readLine() ) != null) {
```

The BufferedReader class provides the method readLine. Notice that the dot operator connects the object reference `lineReader` with the method that operates the object. If successful, the method creates the String object and returns an object reference for it, which is assigned to `line`. If no more data can be read, readLine returns a null object reference.

If you run this program and enter the input on the console, press Ctrl+Z to indicate the end of file. On Solaris and other Unix platforms, use Ctrl+D, not Ctrl+Z.

Moving from C++

Object references in the Java programming language are quite distinct from C++ pointers or references. The syntax is very different, but the purpose is similar. In the Java programming language, when you call a method with an object reference, you always use the dot operator. The language has no -> operator.

```
StringTokenizer tokens
   = new StringTokenizer( line );
String student = tokens.nextToken();
float mark
   = ( new Float( tokens.nextToken() ) )
     .floatValue();
```

The next three statements extract one student ID and one mark from the current input line. The utility class StringTokenizer has a method nextToken that returns the tokens one at a time. Each token is a String object.

- The first of these lines creates the StringTokenizer object `tokens` to process the current input line.
- The second line extracts the first token and assigns it to the variable `student`.
- The third line not only extracts the second token, but converts it to a float value before assigning the value to the variable `mark`. The Float class is in the package java.lang and supports conversions on floating-point values. The expression `(new Float(tokens.nextToken()))` creates a Float object from the next token in the input. The method floatValue of the Float class returns the value as a float.

```
for ( int i = 0; i < 3; i++ ) {
```

The next step is to compare the student mark with the three highest marks found so far. A for loop is appropriate here.

```
if ( mark == marks[i] ) {
   studentID[i] += " " + student;
   break;
}
```

If two or more students have the same mark, they are tied. This program concatenates the names of all students who tie, and records the mark only once. The + operator, when applied to String objects, appends the second string to the end of the first string. Notice that to separate the strings with a space, you must explicitly concatenate the space first.

After finding a tie, this program should do no more processing for this student record, and the break keyword transfers control out of the loop.

```
      if ( mark > marks[i] ) {
         System.arraycopy( marks, i, marks,
                           i+1, 2-i );
         System.arraycopy( studentID, i,
                           studentID,
                           i+1, 2-i );
         marks[i] = mark;
         studentID[i] = student;
         break;
      }
   } // end for loop
} // end while loop
```

If the current record has a mark that is higher than one of the recorded marks, this student takes his or her rightful place in the top three. The logic here is to shift the remaining marks and student IDs over one position in the arrays, and then insert the ID and mark from the current record. The System class has a static method arraycopy that can be used to duplicate whole arrays. The method can also copy portions of arrays and move elements within an array. These lines call arraycopy to update both arrays. Then they insert the current student ID and mark in the arrays, and use break to leave the loop because there is no more to do for this student.

The static method call has the form System.arraycopy, not System::arraycopy, even though this is a static method. The Java programming language does not have the scope operator, ::. In the Java programming language, use the dot operator to call both static and nonstatic methods.

If the current mark is less that the recorded mark on record, the for loop continues to the next mark in the array. If the current mark is less than all of the top three, the for loop completes all three passes and ends.

The while loop repeats until the input stream is exhausted.

```
for ( int i = 0; i < 3; i++ ) {
   System.out.println( ( i + 1 ) + ": "
                    + studentID[i] );
}   // end of for printing loop
```

Finally, the program prints the IDs of the top three students. Another for loop steps through the StudentID array. This time, the body of the loop is one method call. Coding the output is more straightforward than coding the input because no filtering or file operations are involved. The standard output stream object out is a predefined object of type OutputStream and is defined in the System class. Notice the class, object, and method names are all connected with dots.

This println method has one argument, a String that contains the contents of the entire line. The expression `(i + 1) + ": " + studentID[i]` constructs the output line. The first part is the rank, which is equal to the array index plus one because array indexes in the Java programming language start at zero. The rank is calculated, then converted to a string automatically. Next a colon and space are appended to the string, followed by the student ID.

Moving from C++

In C++, you could produce the output using cout **or the** printf **function. With** cout, **the equivalent code is**

```
cout << i+1 << ": " << studentID[I] << endl;
```

The printf **function may be a closer analogy to** println, **but the equivalent code still looks very different:**

```
printf("%d: %s\n", i+1, studentID[i]);
```

Entering and Running a Program

A brief introduction to three different Java application development environments is presented here:

- The JDK contains a suite of command-line tools. The Sun Certified Java Programmer examination requires some familiarity with these tools, but tests your knowledge of the Java programming languages and core classes rather than any development environment. These tools are adequate to complete all the programming exercises in this book.
- IBM VisualAge for Java is a true rapid application development (RAD) tool. A unique and popular feature of VisualAge for Java is the visual Composition Editor. With the Composition Editor, you can rapidly create GUIs for applets and applications, and integrate the GUI components of your program with other Java code. The product provides a fully integrated IDE, a true incremental build, and a good debugger. It generates 100% Pure Java code. VisualAge for Java can also create and consume JavaBean components. Versions are available for OS/2 and Windows platforms.
- Sun Java WorkShop has an easy-to-use programming environment. Its IDE provides a debugger, fast compiler, and performance profiler. This product also has full support for JavaBeans. The Sun Java WorkShop promotes and supports Java platform and JavaBean standards. Versions are available for Windows and Solaris platforms.

Running the First Program with the JDK

To prepare the source file:

1 Open the command-line window and create a working folder. For example, if you want to work on your D drive in a new folder called myJava, type

```
D:
md myJava
cd myJava
```

You are now in your new myJava folder on the D drive. You can extract the source file directly from the CD-ROM.

2 Substitute the drive letter of your CD-ROM for "G" and enter the following commands:

```
jar -xf G:\java4cpp.jar java4cpp\basic\FirstProgram.java
```

The jar command displays messages only when errors occur. So if it appears that nothing has happened, the command has most likely succeeded.

The JAR file mirrors the structure of packages and folders. The jar command with option -xf extracts files from a .jar file. Here, it has created a folder java4cpp and a folder basic within java4cpp, and copied the file FirstProgram.java into java4cpp\basic. The Java platform is case-sensitive. If your files did not extract, double-check your use of uppercase and lowercase letters and try again.

If the jar command was successful, you are ready to compile the program. If you cannot extract the source file from the JAR file, you can enter the source code manually. First, set up the folders with the following commands:

```
md java4cpp
cd java4cpp
md basic
cd basic
```

Now, open any text editor and create a file named **FirstProgram.java.** (The default DOS editor cannot handle this long filename.) Type in the code for the class `FirstProgram` exactly:

```
package java4cpp.basic
import java.io.*;
import java.util.*;
/** A simple Java starter program
  */
public class FirstProgram {
   /** A first program to read a list of IDs and marks.
     * It prints the IDs for the three highest marks.
     * @param args[0] the name of an optional input
     *    file.
     * @exception java.io.IOException
     *    An I/O failure can occur.
     */
   public static void main( String [] args )
                           throws IOException {
      // input file may be supplied in the first
      // argument
      InputStream istream;
      if ( args.length > 0 ) {
         File inputFile = new File( args[0] );
         istream = new FileInputStream( inputFile );
```

```
} else {
   // if no filename, use standard input stream
   istream = System.in;
}
// use a buffered reader for line-at-a-time
// reading
BufferedReader lineReader;
lineReader = new BufferedReader(
             new InputStreamReader( istream ) );
// arrays record the top three student IDs
// and marks
String[] studentID = { "", "", ""};
float[] marks = { 0, 0, 0};
// read one line at a time
String line;
while ( ( line = lineReader.readLine() ) != null) {
   // student ID and mark are two tokens in
   // a line
   StringTokenizer tokens
      = new StringTokenizer( line );
   String student = tokens.nextToken();
   float mark
      = ( new Float( tokens.nextToken() ) )
        .floatValue();
   // see if the mark is in the top three so far
   for ( int i = 0; i < 3; i++ ) {
      // handle a tie by appending IDs at a rank
      if ( mark == marks[i] ) {
         studentID[i] += " " + student;
         break;
      }
      if ( mark > marks[i] ) {
         // insert a higher mark than is now in
         // the top three; the core method
         // arraycopy shifts entries.
         System.arraycopy( marks, i, marks,
                           i+1, 2-i );
         System.arraycopy( studentID, i,
                           studentID,
                           i+1, 2-i );
         marks[i] = mark;
         studentID[i] = student;
         break;
```

```
            }
        }   // end of for loop to compare marks
    }   // end of while loop to read input lines
    // print the IDs of the top three students
    for ( int i = 0; i < 3; i++ ) {
        System.out.println( ( i + 1 ) + ": "
                            + studentID[i] );
    }   // end of for printing loop
  }  // end of main
}  // end of class
```

Return to the **myJava** folder.

You are ready to compile the source file.

To compile the source file:

1 Type

`javac java4cpp\basic\FirstProgram.java`

You see no messages unless the compiler finds an error. Because you copied a working program, there should be no errors.

If you had to enter the program manually and did get error messages, check for typing mistakes. The error messages should help you locate the error. Suppose, for example, that you deleted the semicolon from the end of the following line:

```
lineReader = new BufferedReader(
                 new InputStreamReader( istream ) );
```

Such errors are reported for the next Java statement, line 31 in this case. The first error message reported for line 31 is:

```
java4cpp\basic\FirstProgram.java:31: ';' expected
      String[] studentID = { "", "", "" };
               ^
```

When the class compiles successfully, you can run it.

To run the class:

1 Enter the **java** command and supply the class name qualified by the package names by typing the following:

`java java4cpp.basic.FirstProgram`

Nothing appears to happen because the program is waiting for input. The program does not prompt you because it can accept input from a file.

2 Enter some lines of input on the console. Type a string and a number on each line, ending with Ctrl+Z (Ctrl+D on Unix-based platforms) to indicate the end of file. For example, you can enter the following:

```
a 6
b 3
c 4
d 5
e 6
f 9
g 2
Ctrl+Z
```

The output for this input is as follows:

```
1: f
2: a e
3: d
```

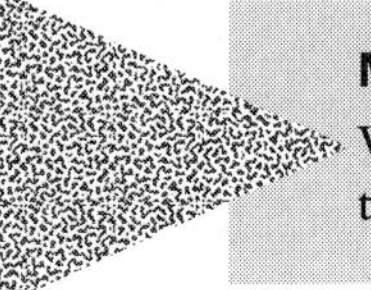

Mini Quiz 1-1

What happens when you enter bad data? Try including a blank line, a line with only one token, a line with two strings that are not numbers, or less than three lines of data.

You can also try running the program on data in a prepared input file.

To create a data file with which to run the program:

1 Using a text editor, create a data file called **students.dat** and put the sample data, with the exception of the end-of-file character, from Step 2 above into the file.

2 Run the program with the following command:

```
java java4cpp.basic.FirstProgram students.dat
```

IBM VisualAge for Java

VisualAge provides a very powerful development tool for the Java platform, and has many features that this scenario does not exercise. Nevertheless, you can use VisualAge to create a very simple class, as well as to build large applications or packages of classes. The hub of the VisualAge for the Java development environment is called the Workbench. You can use the Workbench directly, or add or modify classes and methods using SmartGuides. SmartGuides are tools that automatically set up your classes or packages based on options you select. The scenario you are about to follow demonstrates a bit of both approaches. You can incrementally compile, debug, and run a program without closing the Workbench.

Before you can use VisualAge for Java, you must install it, or have access to a machine on which it is installed.

To start VisualAge for Java on Windows platforms:

1 Click **Start**, point to **Programs**, then **IBM VisualAge for Java for Windows**, then click **IBM VisualAge for Java**.

The VisualAge Quick Start window appears as shown in Figure 1-1.

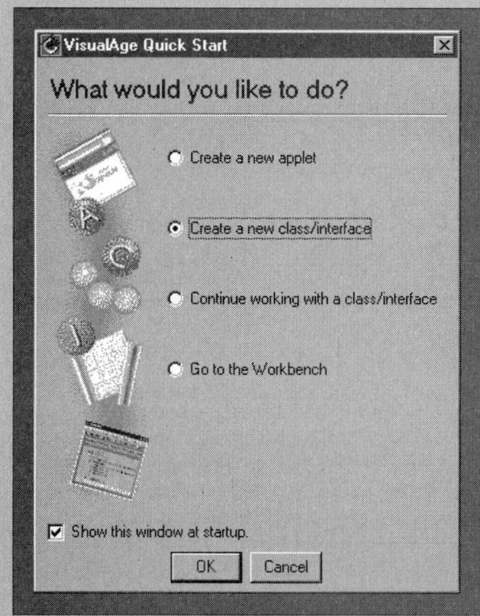

Figure 1-1: VisualAge Quick Start window

Use the Quick Start window to select the SmartGuide for the task you want to complete. You must click one of the following four buttons:

- The **Create a new applet** button starts the SmartGuide to create a new applet.
- The **Create a new class/interface** button starts the SmartGuide to create a new class or interface. Interfaces are used to define the behaviors that some classes must provide.

- The **Continue working with a class/interface** button opens a dialog box in which you select an existing class or interface with which you can work. If you return later to the sample class you are about to create in this exercise, you can click this button to reopen the class.
- The **Go to the Workbench** button opens the Workbench, bypassing the SmartGuides.

To start creating the new class:

1 Click the **Create a new class/interface** button, then click **OK**.

The Create Class or Interface SmartGuide window appears, as shown in Figure 1-2.

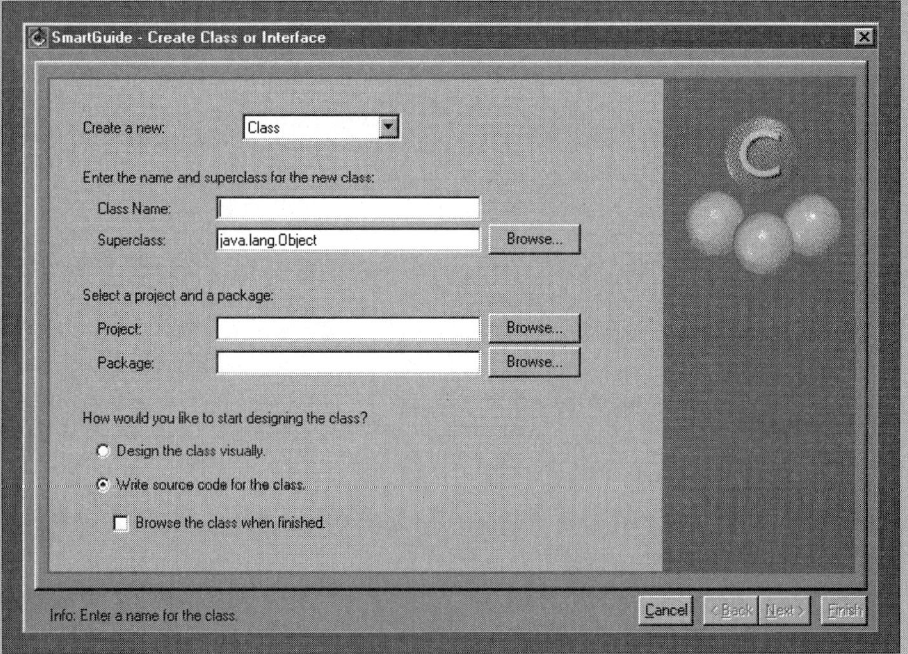

Figure 1-2: Create Class or Interface window

2 Fill in this panel as follows: In the Create a new list box, enter **Class**. In the Class Name text box, enter `ShortProgram`. In the Superclass list box, enter `java.lang.Object`.

If a Java class is to be an extension of an existing class, the Superclass text box displays the name of the existing class. All Java classes are directly or indirectly based on a core class called Object, which is provided by a package called java.lang.

You can give a project any name you choose. VisualAge for Java organizes your work into projects and stores them in an internal repository. Active projects are kept in an area called the **workspace**. The examples in this book are gathered into a project called `java4cpp`. Within a project, classes can be further grouped into packages. To use the same name and organization as is used in this book, the new class belongs in the project `java4cpp` and in the package `basic`.

3 Enter **`java4cpp`** in the Project text box. Enter **`basic`** in the Package text box.

4 Make sure that the **Design the class visually** radio button is not selected.

This option starts the Composition Editor and is used in an example in Chapter 12, where you use VisualAge to create a GUI.

5 Make sure that the **Write source code for the class** radio button is selected. This option is the alternative to designing the class visually with the Composition Editor.

6 Make sure that the **Browse the class when finished** radio button is not selected.
This feature is useful for classes that have many members. For the `ShortProgram` class, this feature is not necessary.

7 Click the **Next** button to create the class `ShortProgram`.

Because you have not worked with this project or package before, a window appears with the message "Package Basic does not exist, VisualAge will create the package for you. Do you want to continue?"

8 Click the **Yes** button.

A message box appears to inform you that VisualAge is preparing the project and package. Then the Attributes SmartGuide appears, as shown in Figure 1-3.

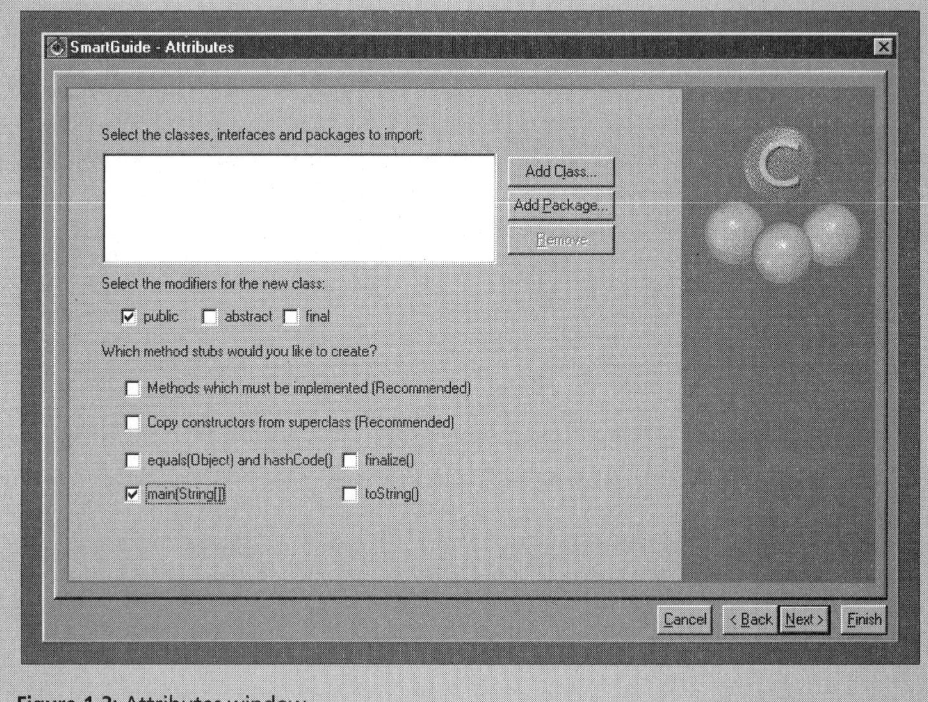

Figure 1-3: Attributes window

The Attributes SmartGuide controls what code is generated for you to make up the skeleton definition of the new class.

To make the selections for the ShortProgram class:

1. Make sure the Add Class and Add Package buttons are not selected and leave the associated text box empty. These buttons generate import statements that make it convenient for the new class to use the imported classes or classes in imported packages. The `ShortProgram` class uses no other classes except the core class System, which is always available by default.
2. Click the **public** check box, if it is not already checked.

   A public class can be accessed from any other class of any package. The modifiers abstract and final determine whether another class must or can extend your class. Only public applies to the `ShortProgram` class.
3. Click the **main(String[])** check box. Make sure a checkmark appears in this box.
4. Make sure the **Methods which must be implemented** option is not selected. You may have to click in this box to remove the check mark.
5. Make sure the **Copy constructors from superclass** option is not selected. You may have to click in this box to remove the check mark.

The SmartGuide can include the stub, or skeleton definition, of a number of methods. The only method in the class `ShortProgram` is `main`. The other options apply to classes that are implementing interfaces or have a superclass other than `java.lang.Object`.

You have now specified everything that is required for the SmartGuide to create the project, package, and class.

6 Click the **Finish** button.

A message box appears to tell you the class is being created. Then the SmartGuide closes and the Workbench reappears on your screen, as shown in Figure 1-4 (your list of projects may differ from Figure 1-4).

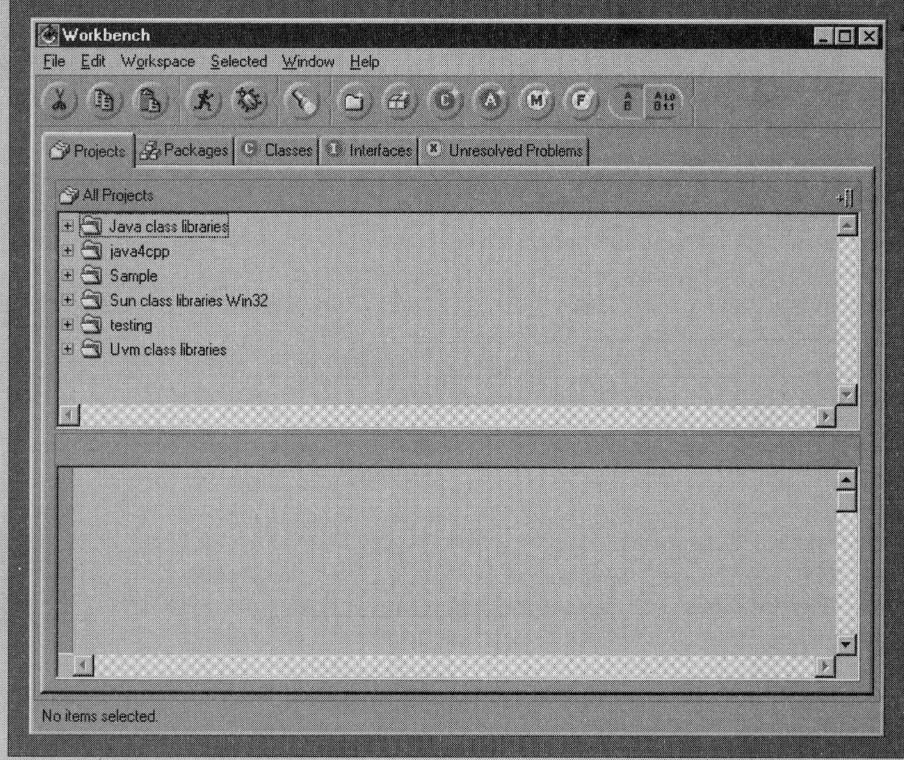

Figure 1-4: VisualAge Workbench

You see the main Workbench window. The Workbench has a menu bar and a toolbar for quick access to the most common actions, such as cut, copy, paste, run, and debug. There is a tab for each of the main pages of the Workbench. The pages give you a variety of ways of navigating the projects, packages, and classes stored in your workspace.

- In the **Projects** page, you can select an existing project with which to work. The page features a list of the projects and the packages in each project. From this panel, you can delete projects, create new projects, add packages to projects, and much more.
- In the **Packages** page, you can locate packages and work with them. The page features a list of the packages that are available, and you can click a package to see the classes and methods it contains. You can delete and add packages, add classes to packages, and much more.
- In the **Classes** page, you can get a more detailed look at classes and the methods one class contains. You can modify source code and perform add, search, compare, and delete operations on classes.
- In the **Interfaces** page, you can navigate interfaces rather than classes.
- In the **Unresolved Problems** page, you can investigate any classes that have unresolved problems. You can click any error message to bring the code in which the problem is detected into an editable panel.

Feel free to explore the Workbench before returning to complete the `ShortProgram` class.

The Workbench is open at the Projects page, which lists all the projects stored in VisualAge for Java. One of the projects is `java4cpp`. The workspace also includes the core Java packages, and the list you see may not exactly match the list in Figure 1-4.

To complete the code for the ShortProgram class:

1. If `java4cpp` is not highlighted in the top panel Projects page, click it. If there are many projects already in the workspace, you may have to scroll down the top panel to find java4cpp. VisualAge lists projects in alphabetic order.
2. When `java4cpp` is highlighted in the Projects page, click the **Classes** tab.

   The Classes page opens and displays the classes in the `java4cpp` project. This page of the Workbench is divided into three panels, as shown in Figure 1-5.

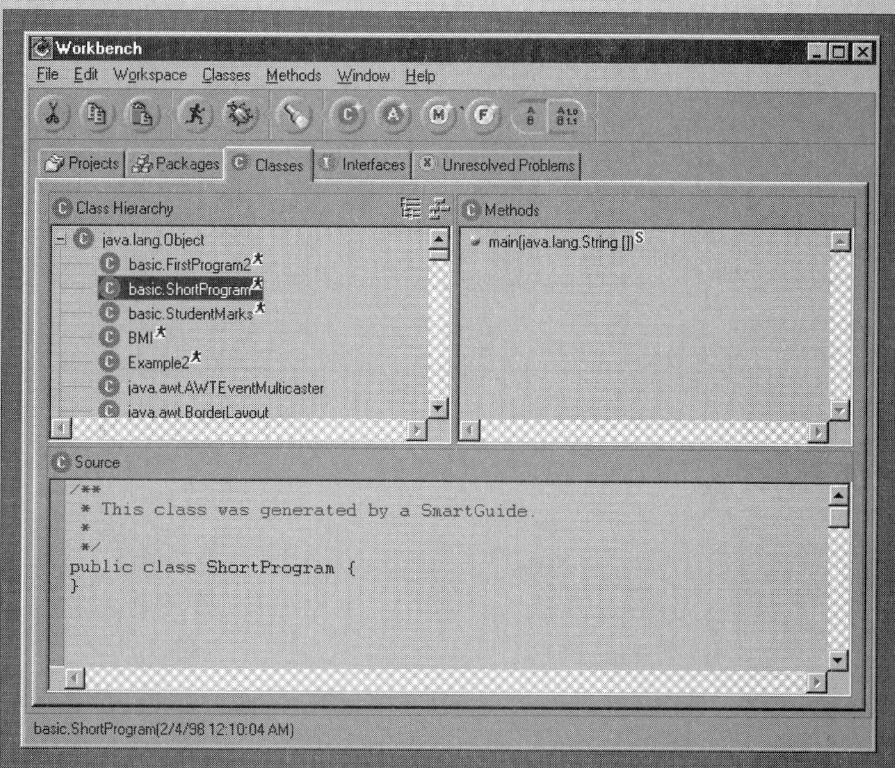

Figure 1-5: Classes page of Workbench

The Class Hierarchy list shows all classes in the VisualAge workspace, including the core classes. The list of classes you see may not be exactly the same as the list of classes in Figure 1-5.

3. If the class name `basic.ShortProgram` is not highlighted in the Class Hierarchy panel in the upper-left corner, click `basic.ShortProgram` to select it. You may have to scroll within the Class Hierarchy window to find `basic.ShortProgram`. The classes are listed in alphabetic order, including the package name. When the `ShortProgram` class is selected, the top-right panel lists the methods, and the bottom panel shows the class definition generated by the SmartGuide. The next task is to insert the body of the `main` method.

4. Click **main** in the upper-right panel, where it is the only method listed. The bottom panel now contains the source code for the main method, as shown in Figure 1-6.

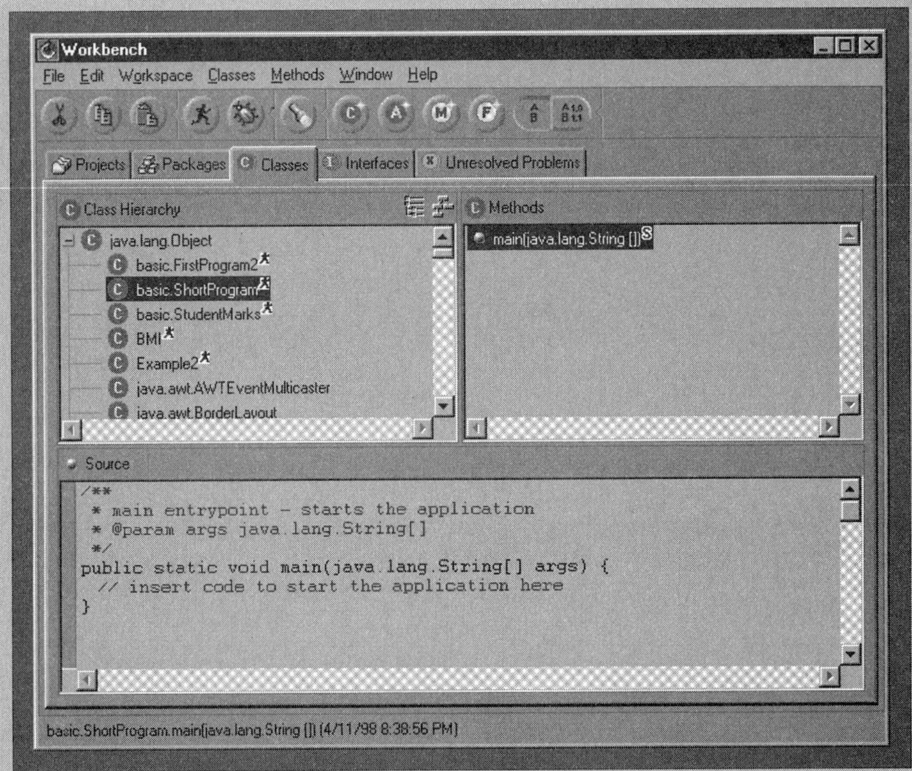

Figure 1-6: ShortProgram class

You must enter the body of the main method.

5 Type in the rest of the method, entering the lines shown in bold:

```
/**
 * main entrypoint - starts the application
 * @param args java.lang.String[]
 */
public static void main(java.lang.String[] args) {
   //insert code to start the application here
   int a = 57;
   int $b = 1024;
   System.out.println("1024/57 = " + ( $b/a) );
}
```

6 At any point, you can save your work. The updates to the class you are editing are saved automatically when you run your program, but if you want to save everything you have done so far explicitly, click **File** on the menu, then click **Save Workspace**, then click **OK**.

The ShortProgram class is now ready to test.

To run the first program in VisualAge:

1 Click the **Run** button .

VisualAge gives you an opportunity to enter arguments that you would enter on the command line if you were running this program with the **java** command of the JDK. The window in Figure 1-7 appears.

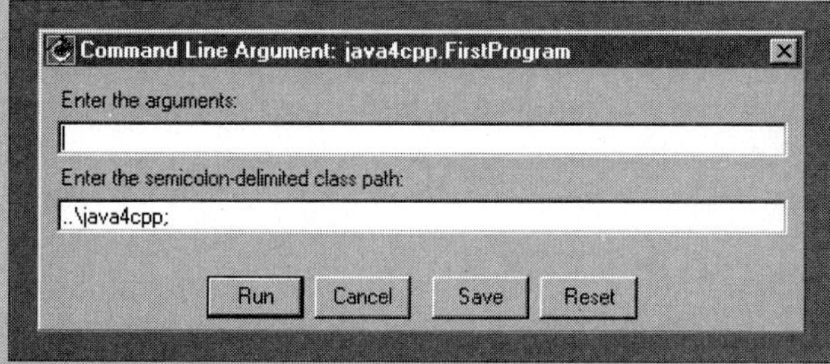

Figure 1-7: Command Line Argument window

This program ignores command-line arguments, so you can leave the Enter the arguments text box empty. Programs that use command-line arguments receive whatever is entered into the first entry field in this window as arguments of the main method.

The entry field Enter the semicolon-delimited class path specifies the internal path to the class within VisualAge for Java. Do not change this field.

2 To run the program, click **Run**.

Because this program uses only console I/O, VisualAge for Java displays the output in a console window. In a windowing program, the program's window automatically appears, but you may have to manually open the console window to see console I/O.

3 Click **Window** on the menu bar, then click **Console**.

Figure 1-8 shows the Console window.

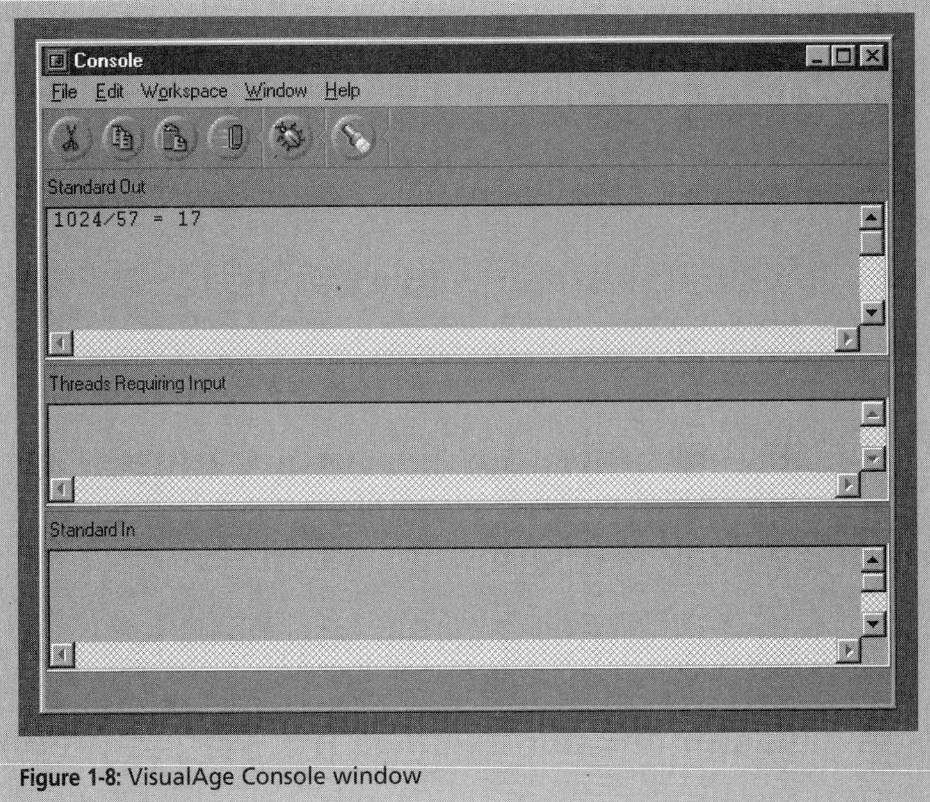

Figure 1-8: VisualAge Console window

The Console window has three panels. The top panel contains output to the standard output stream. For programs that take command-line input, you use the bottom panel for standard input. For this program, no further action is required. The middle panel indicates whether the program is waiting for input. If your screen looks like Figure 1-8, the `ShortProgram` class has run successfully.

There is a lot more you can do in a VisualAge for Java. The debugger is quite easy to use and is one of the strong features of VisualAge for Java. The debugger is beyond the scope of this book, but the online help describes the debugger well. You can also export projects, packages, and classes from VisualAge for Java so you can deploy them outside the Workbench.

To close VisualAge for Java:

1 Click **File** on the menu bar, then click **Exit VisualAge**. A window opens to tell you that your workspace is being saved automatically.

Now that you have run `ShortProgram` in VisualAge, you can experiment with Sun Java WorkShop, or you can continue with Chapter 1. You can run many of the sample programs in the following chapters in VisualAge using these steps as a guide.

Sun Java WorkShop

Sun Java WorkShop is a complete, visual development tool that provides a fully integrated graphical toolset. This toolset allows programmers to design, edit, compile, debug, and tune Java applets and full-scale, client/server Java applications. Applications developed using Java WorkShop are 100% Pure Java and run on any computer system with a JVM. Applets developed with it run using one of the many 100% Pure Java-certified browsers and the JavaBean components it creates can be used by most Java language development products, including Java WorkShop.

Java WorkShop includes a project wizard to aid in the creation of applets, applications, packages, and JavaBeans components; a fast Java compiler (based on **javac** from the JDK); a JIT compiler already built into the JVM; and a visual GUI builder that lets you quickly design the look and feel for your application and, when it is ready to be compiled and run, automatically generates the Java programming language code.

A full version of Java WorkShop 2.0 with a 30-day trial license is included on the CD-ROM that accompanies this book. Version 2.0 of Java WorkShop generates code compatible with JDK version 1.1.3.

Before you can use Java WorkShop, you must install it or have access to a machine on which it is installed. Hardware requirements and instructions for installing Java WorkShop are included in the ReadMe file in the JWS folder on the CD-ROM. Read these instructions before you continue.

The following discussion explains how to use Sun Java WorkShop to enter and run a small program. The full capabilities of this application development tool are not explored fully here, only the basics that enable you to create a simple class.

To start Java WorkShop:

1 At a command-line interface, run **jws.exe**.

The license window opens.

2 Click the **30-day trial** button. Click **Enter** then **Accept** and then **Not Now** to skip the registration process. (You can register later.)

The License window closes and the Startup window opens as shown in Figure 1-9.

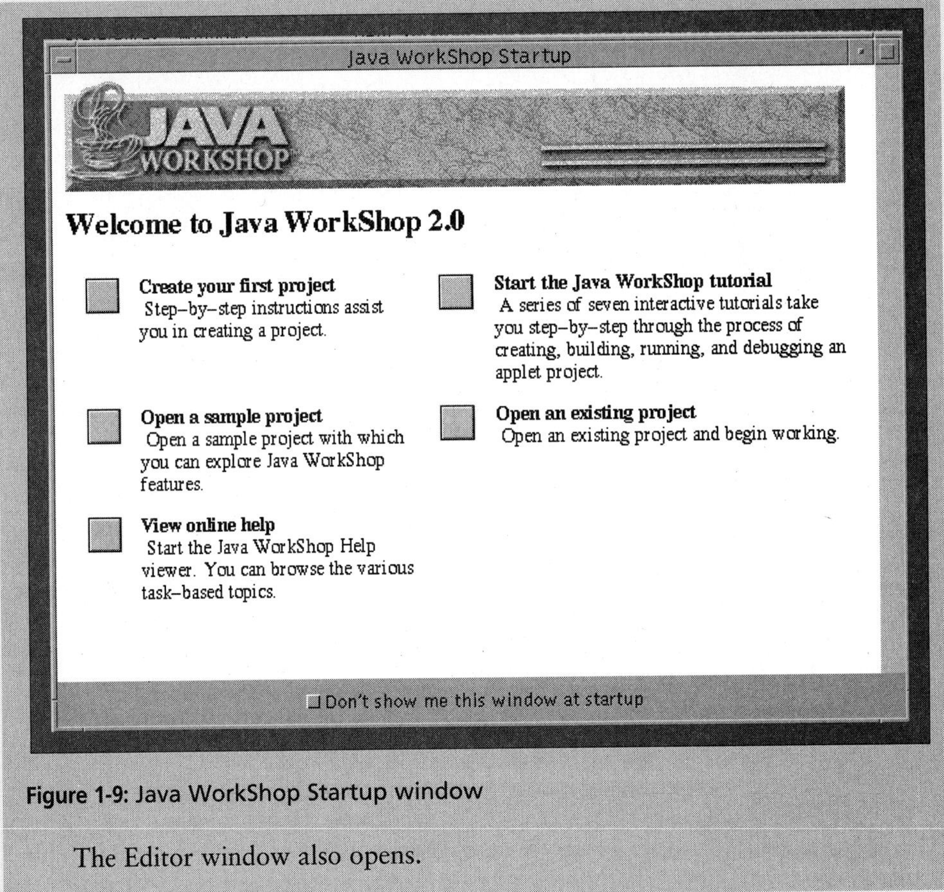

Figure 1-9: Java WorkShop Startup window

The Editor window also opens.

The Startup window guides you through your early stages of learning Java WorkShop by allowing you to select existing programming examples and tutorials. You may wish to explore more of the possible selections later.

To start creating the new class:

1 Click the **Create your first project** button.

The Create Project window appears as shown in Figure 1-10.

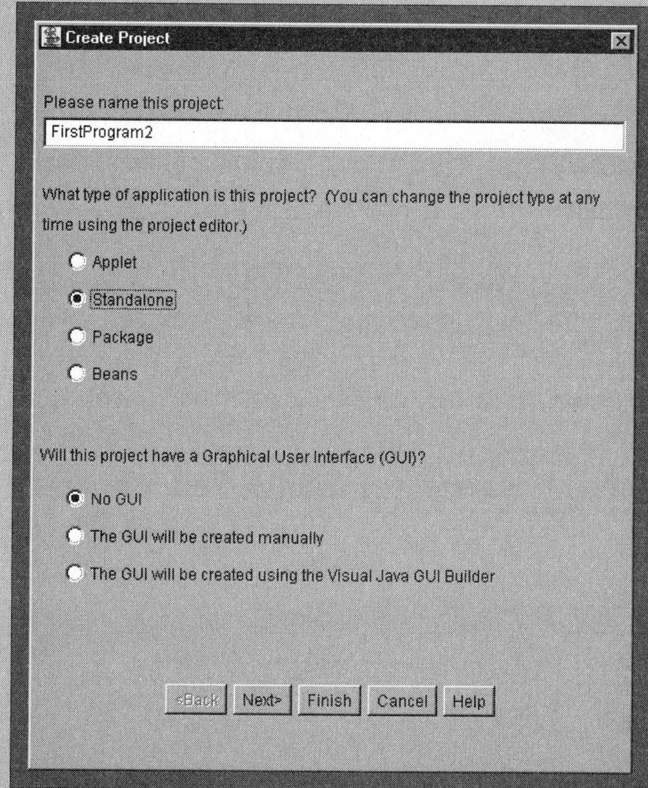

Figure 1-10: Create Project window

2. Type **FirstProgram2** in the Please name this project text box.
3. Click the **Standalone** and **No GUI** radio buttons.
4. Click the **Next** button.

   A new Create Project window appears which shows a default location for the project files.

5 Type **D:\jars\java4cpp\basic** as shown in Figure 1-11. This file and path name assume you followed the instructions on the Read This Before You Begin pages to load the sample programs from the CD-ROM. If you expanded the file java4cpp.jar into a different folder than D:\jars, substitute the full path to the folder you used instead of D:\jars.

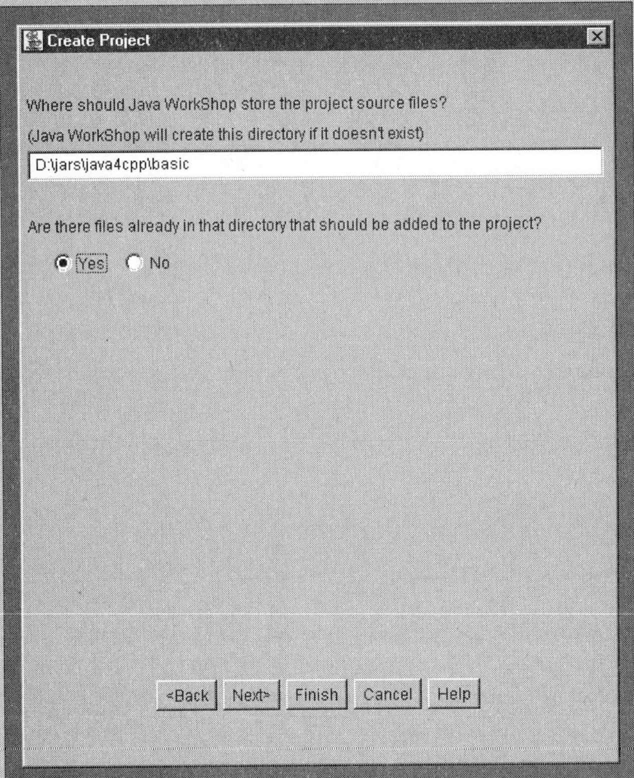

Figure 1-11: Entering a default location for the project files in the Create Project window

6 In response to the question, "Are there files already in that folder that should be added to the project?," make sure that the **Yes** radio button is selected.

7 Click the **Next** button.

To load the appropriate classes into your project:

1 Click the **Add All in Directory** button. Your window then looks like Figure 1-12 (your list of projects may differ from Figure 1-12).

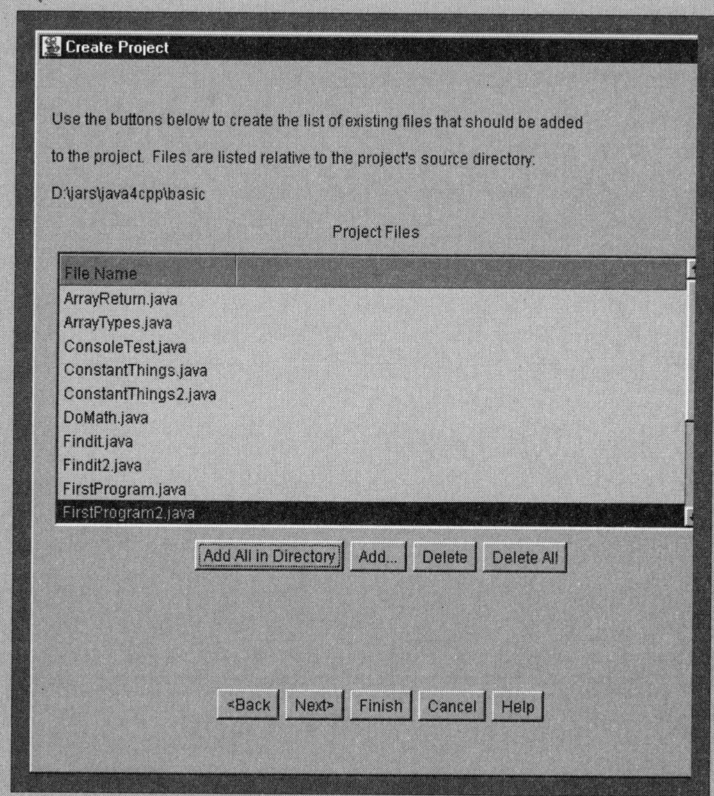

Figure 1-12: Loading classes in the Create Project window

2 Select **FirstProgram2**, then click **Next.** The Create Project window appears as shown in Figure 1-13.

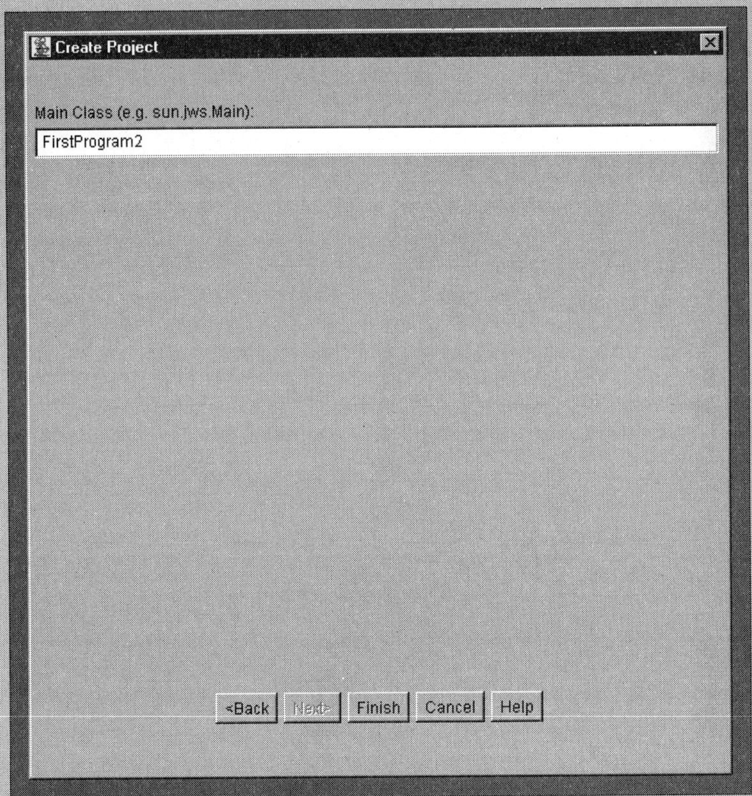

Figure 1-13: Naming the main class for a project

3 Click **Finish,** The project files have been created. The Editor window opens, showing the code from the file `D:\jars\java4cpp\basic\FirstProgram2.java`, as shown in Figure 1-14.

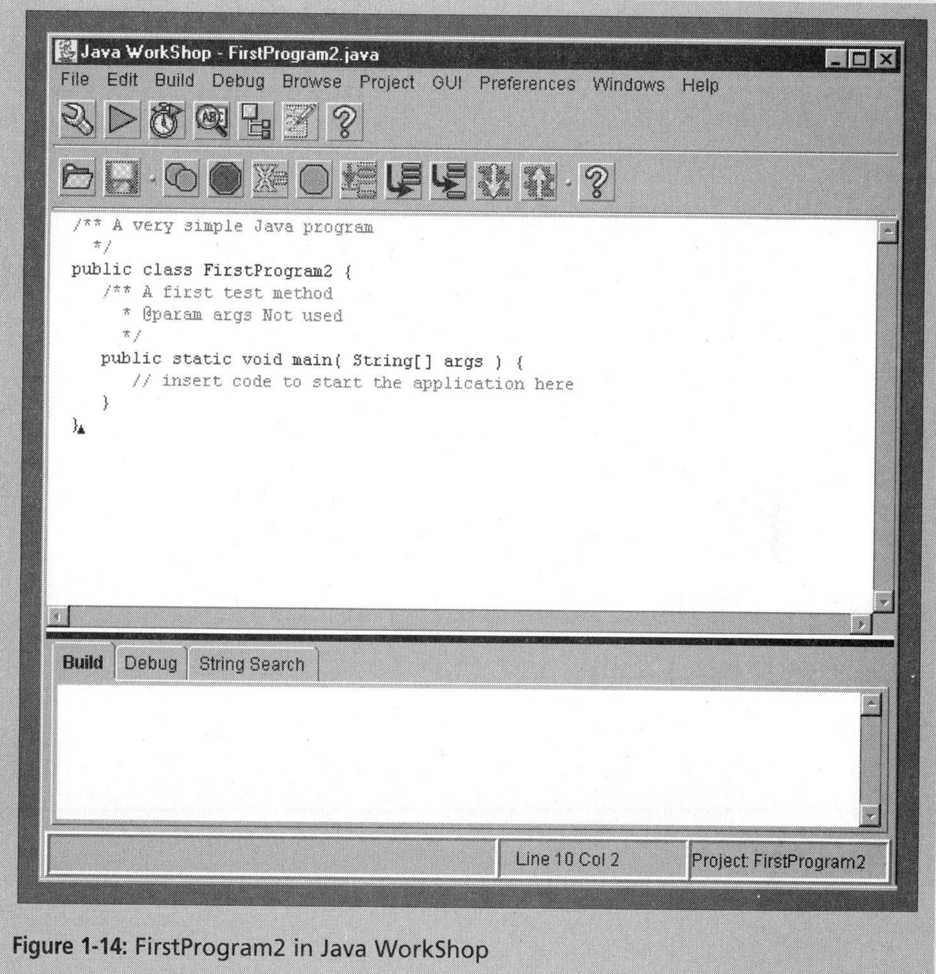

Figure 1-14: FirstProgram2 in Java WorkShop

The create the class by entering code directly into the Editor window.

To create the FirstProgram2 class and complete the code:

1 In the Editor window, type the following code shown in bold:

```
// insert code to start the application here
int a = 57;
int $b = 1024;
System.out.println( "1024/57 = " + ( $b/a ) );
```

2 Click the **Build** button. The editor saves the edits automatically. When the bottom panel has been enlarged to show all messages, the Editor window looks like Figure 1-15.

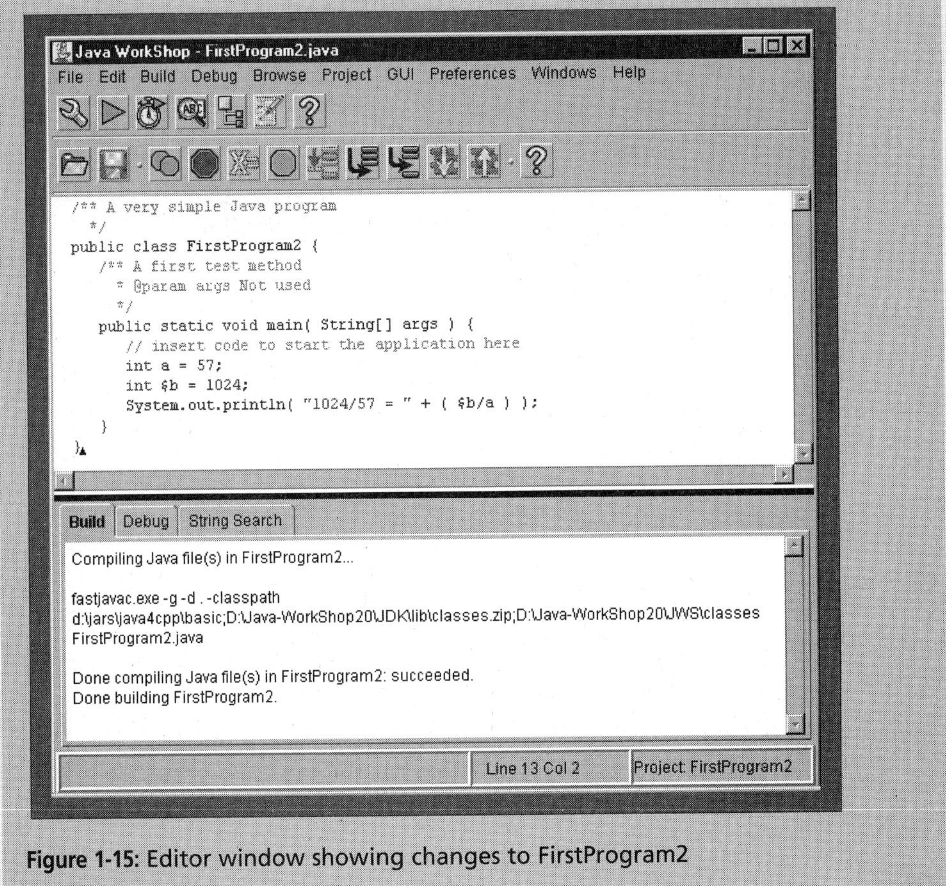

Figure 1-15: Editor window showing changes to FirstProgram2

The `FirstProgram2` class is now ready to test.

To run FirstProgram2 in Java WorkShop:

1 Click the **Start** button ▷ on the toolbar. The Java Console window appears as shown in Figure 1-16. When the console window looks like Figure 1-16, the `FirstProgram2` class has run successfully.

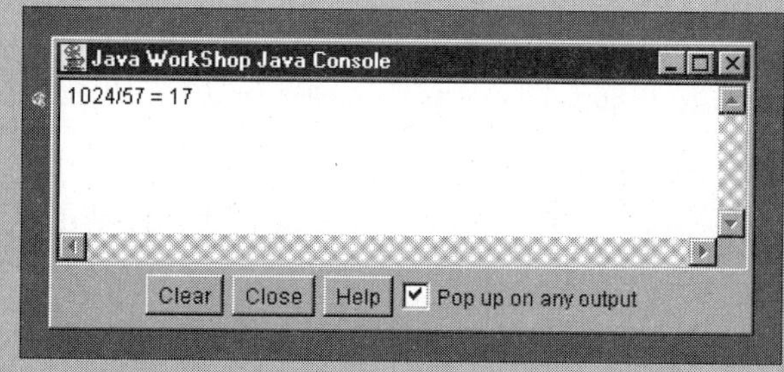

Figure 1-16: Java WorkShop Java Console window

The Java Console window records all execution attempts, which can be both useful and confusing. If you get errors, you might want to clear them using the Clear button after each execution to avoid confusing clean program runs with previous error-ridden ones.

There is a lot more you can do in a Java WorkShop. The visual tools and tutorials are easy to use and are strong features of Java WorkShop.

To exit Java WorkShop:

1 Click **File** on the menu bar, then click **Exit.** If you have any unsaved edits, a message box appears and gives you the option to save them and exit.

Now that you have run `FirstProgram2` in Java WorkShop, you can run any of the sample programs in the following chapters in Java WorkShop using these steps as a guide.

Comments in the Java Programming Language

The Java programming language recognizes three kinds of comments:

- Single-line comments start with a double slash, //, and continue to the end of the line of source code.
- Block comments start with a slash and an asterisk, /*, and terminate with an asterisk and a slash, */. They can start anywhere in a line, span several lines, and stop anywhere.
- Doc comments start with a slash and two asterisks, /**, and terminate with one asterisk and a slash, */. Because doc comments conform to the syntax of block comments, the compiler can treat both types of comments the same.

Moving from C++

For compilation, comments in the Java programming language are identical to C++ comments. The third form of comment, doc comments, is processed by a separate tool, and treated like a block comment by the compiler. In one instance, the Java compiler does look at doc comments: It produces a warning if the code it is compiling uses a class, interface, or method that is marked as deprecated.

Doc comments do serve a special purpose for which there is nothing similar in C++.

Use single-line comments whenever possible. You cannot nest block comments, so they can be a source of errors. It is a good idea to reserve block comments for the sole purpose of commenting out large chunks of code. You can then nest single-line comments within a block comment.

Doc Comments

In the Java programming language, you can insert into your source code textual information from which user documentation can be automatically generated. This textual information takes the form of doc comments.

Java development environments provide a utility for generating HTML documentation directly from Java source code. In the JDK, the **javadoc** tool does this job. A good example of extensive HTML documentation created by **javadoc** is the Core API component of the online documentation for the JDK. When run on a suite of packages, the **javadoc** tool creates a web of HTML pages. The web has a page for each class that lists all methods and fields in the class, and much more. The web includes pages that show all classes in a hierarchy diagram, list all packages, list all classes in each package, and provide an index of fields and methods in all classes. All these pages are created from the declarations in the Java source code, regardless of whether the source code contains doc comments.

Use the doc comments to insert descriptive text into the HTML documentation web.

Unlike the other kinds of comments, doc comments are meaningful only when placed before declarations. Misplaced doc comments are ignored. You can put doc comments before the declarations of classes and members, but not before executable statements within methods. Generally, you provide doc comments for the elements of Java code that are important to the users of the code. For example, you usually describe the arguments of a method and what the method returns. Doc comments can appear before the following kinds of declarations:

- Class
- Interface
- Method
- Field

All the constructs that doc comments can describe are covered in the early chapters of this book. The example programs use doc comments from the very beginning. For example, in the `FirstProgram` class, doc comments precede the declaration of main:

```
/** A first program to read a list of IDs and marks.
  * It prints the IDs for the three highest marks.
```

```
* @param args[0] the name of an optional input
*     file.
* @exception java.io.IOException
*     An I/O failure can occur.
*/
 public static void main( String[] args )
                          throws IOException {
```

To parse a doc comment, **javadoc** looks at the characters that come after /** and before the matching */. It discards the * characters at the start of each line. For all but the first line, **javadoc** also ignores blanks and tabs preceding the initial * characters.

The remaining text is incorporated into the HTML documentation. A doc comment should start with a one-sentence overview of the item being documented. Because the text is inserted into HTML documents, you can include HTML markup. Avoid using HTML tags for headings, because the tool generates its own headings. You may have to experiment to find out which tags are safe. As a rule of thumb, HTML tags that change the font or highlight characters work well, but HTML tags that alter the structure of an HTML document may conflict with **javadoc** presentation. Here is a doc comment that uses HTML tags `<code>` and `</code>` to highlight a name:

```
/** Method to write X to <code>System.out</code>.
  */
```

Using javadoc Tags

In addition to including HTML tags, you can include **javadoc** tags in your doc comments. Use them to generate subheadings such as "Parameters," "Returns," and "See Also" in the description of classes, interfaces, and methods. All javadoc tags start with an @ character. Each tag must start a new line. Whether the tag is appropriate depends on what it precedes. The **javadoc** tags and the headings that they produce are listed here, in the order that they usually appear in source code:

To create a heading "Author," insert the following tag:

```
@author author_name
```

You can put this tag before a class or an interface. The name can be any string. This tag is ignored unless you include the `-author` option when you run **javadoc**.

To create a heading "Version," insert the tag:

```
@version text
```

You can put this tag before a class or an interface. Often the version text follows a numerical pattern such as 1.1 or 3.0.2. This tag is ignored unless you include the `–version` option when you run **javadoc**.

To create a heading "Parameters," insert the following tag:

```
@param variable_name description
```

This tag goes before the definition of a method. It gives the name of one argument of a method followed by a description. If the method has more than one argument, provide a `@param` tag for each argument. You should group these tags together.

To create a heading "Returns," insert the following tag:

```
@return description
```

Put this tag before a method definition to describe the return value of a method.

To create a heading "Throws," insert the tag:

```
@exception fully-qualified_class_name description
```

Put this tag before a method definition to list and describe an exception that the method can throw. The fully qualified class name is a hypertext link to the exception class. If the method can throw more than one type of exception, provide an `@exception` tag for each exception class. You should group these tags together.

To create a heading "See Also," insert one of the following tags:

```
@see class_name
@see class_name#field_name
@see class_name#method_name(argument_list)
```

Use this tag in any doc comments to insert cross-references in the HTML documentation. This tag creates a hypertext link to another class or member. You can include any number of `@see` tags for one declaration. If possible, group them together.

To create a heading "Since," insert the following tag:

```
@since text
```

You can use this tag to inform the user when the class, interface, or member became available.

To create a heading "Deprecated," insert the following tag:

```
@deprecated text
```

Typically, you use the `@deprecated` tag for a class or method that is legacy code from an earlier version. If you cannot delete old code because others still depend on it, this tag gives you an opportunity at least to inform users that the class or method may not be available in the future. The text should include either "Replaced by. . ." or "No replacement."

The compiler looks at doc comments as it is compiling a class and sets an attribute on the .class file for any deprecated class, method, or interface that it finds. Whenever a class is compiled, the **.class** file attributes of the classes, methods, and interfaces it uses are checked to see if they are deprecated. The compiler prints a warning when asked to compile code that uses a deprecated class, interface, or method.

Version Watch

The javadoc tags have been modified in small ways since the original version. Two tags, `@deprecated` and `@since`, were introduced in version 1.1 of the Java platform. The first version of the Java platform had no use for these tags because there was no need to indicate deprecated or new features until there had been changes.

Version 1.2 of the Java platform will introduce the concept of javadoc doclets. You can use a doclet to customize the content and format of the output generated by the javadoc tool.

Creating HTML from javadoc

Application development packages for the Java platform can automatically create an HTML documentation web from Java source files. The JDK provides the **javadoc** tool for this purpose. The **javadoc** tool is a command-line program.

Syntax **javadoc [options] package_or_class_names**

Dissection

- The most commonly used options of the **javadoc** tool are listed below. You can supply one or more class names or package names separated by spaces.

Options

- **-author**
  Specify the **author** option to tell javadoc to process **@author** tags, which are ignored by default.

- **-d** *folder_name*
  If you want to place the HTML output files in any other folder than the current folder, specify a destination with the **d** option. The folder must already exist.

- **-nodeprecated**
  Specify **nodeprecrated** to exclude sections marked with the **@deprecated** tag.

- **-noindex**
  Specify **noindex** to tell javadoc not to output the index page, which javadoc creates by default.

- **-notree**
  Specify **notree** to tell javadoc not to output the class hierarchy page, which javadoc creates by default.

- **-package**
  Specify **package** to include all classes and members except those with private access. The default is **protected**.

- **-private**
  Specify **private** to include all classes and members. The default is **protected**.
- **-protected**
  Specify **protected** to include protected and public classes and members. This is the default.
- **-public**
  Specify **public** to include only public classes, interfaces, and members. The default is **protected**.
- **-version**
  Specify **version** to tell javadoc to process @version tags, which are ignored by default.

Code Example

```
javadoc -d docs monit.gain monit.loss
```

Code Output

```
Loading source files for monit.gain
Loading source files for monit.loss
Generating package.html
Generating documentation for class monit.gain.Windfall
...
Generating documentation for class monit.loss.Storm
Generating documentation for class java4cpp.loss.Rates
Generating index
Sorting 33 items...done
Generating tree
```

Code Dissection

The output listed here appears on the console when you run **javadoc**. Of course, the output you really want is the set of HTML files: packages.html, tree.html, AllNames.html, and the files for the individual classes.

To document packages, the current folder must contain the top-level package, and you must list all subpackage names explicitly.

To document classes, the current folder must contain the source files for the classes. Specify the .java file extension with each class name.

The resulting files use a number of graphic images, or .gif files. These files are not automatically copied into the destination folder. If you have installed the JDK documentation on your system, you can copy the images from there.

If you followed the instructions in "Read This Before You Begin" to extract the files from the JAR file, the set of packages containing the example programs from this book reside on your system in the folder D:\jars. If you have not created the HTML documentation yet, you can do so now. Go to the folder D:\jars or the folder name you used instead of D:\jars. Enter the following command:

```
java4cpp\buildHTML
```

This batch file contains the following two commands:

```
mkdir docs
javadoc -d docs -version -author java4cpp.basic
java4cpp.classes
     java4cpp.inheritance java4cpp.inner
     java4cpp.exceptions java4cpp.cloning java4cpp.rtti
     java4cpp.io java4cpp.network java4cpp.observe
     java4cpp.collections java4cpp.threads
     java4cpp.windows java4cpp.applet java4cpp.beans
     java4cpp.i18n
```

The documentation is now complete, except that the HTML files use images that are not yet available. You can use the files in their current state. If you have installed the JDK documentation, you can improve the appearance of the HTML files by copying the images from the JDK documentation. Find the folder docs\api that contains the JDK documentation. Usually it is in the same folder as the JDK itself. Substitute the name of that folder for D:\jdk and issue the following commands, starting in the D:\jars folder:

```
cd docs
md images
cd images
copy d:\jdk\docs\api\images\*.gif
```

Now you can look at the documentation you just created. Because the files are HTML files, use your Web browser. Open the Web browser and one of the files created by **javadoc**: D:/jars/docs/packages.html. Your display should look very similar to Figure 1-17.

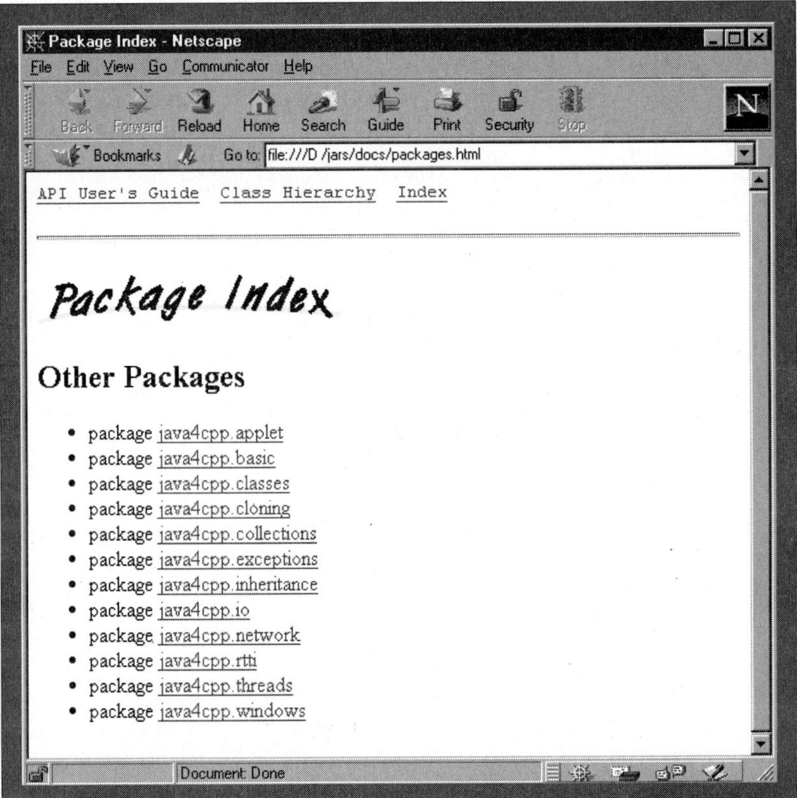

Figure 1-17: Viewing jars/docs/packages.html in Netscape

The file packages.html lists all the packages documented in this HTML web. Each package name is a hypertext link to a page containing a list of classes in that package. To see the effects of the doc comments in `FirstProgram`, click `package java4cpp.basic` to bring up a list of the classes in the `basic` package. Click `FirstProgram` in that list to display a page that is similar to Figure 1-18 and Figure 1-19.

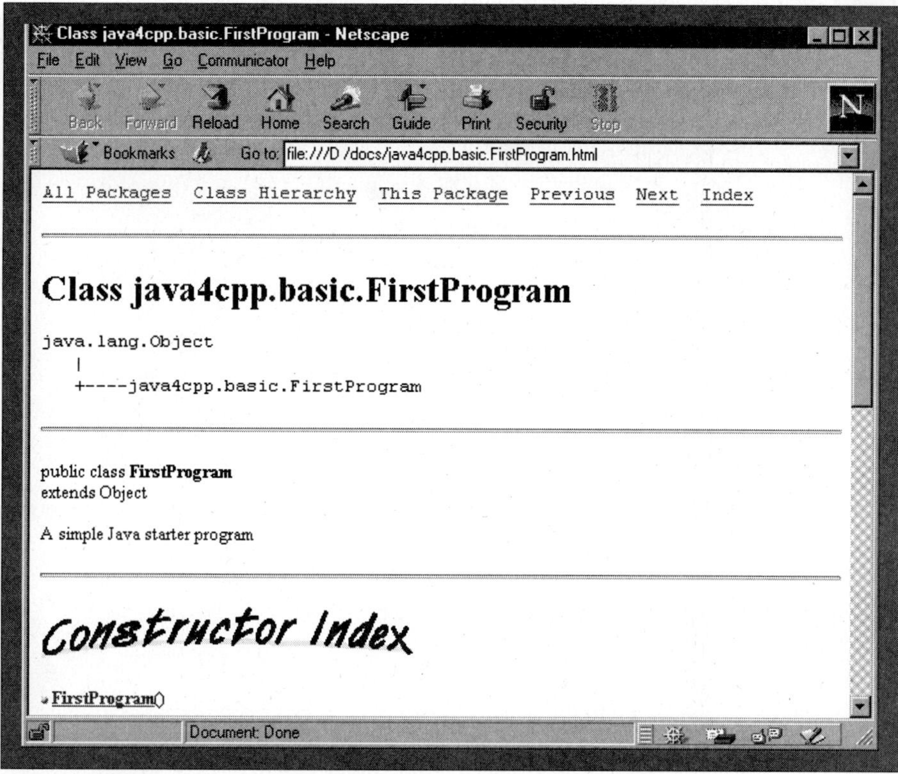

Figure 1-18: javadoc generated documentation for class java4cpp.basic.FirstProgram

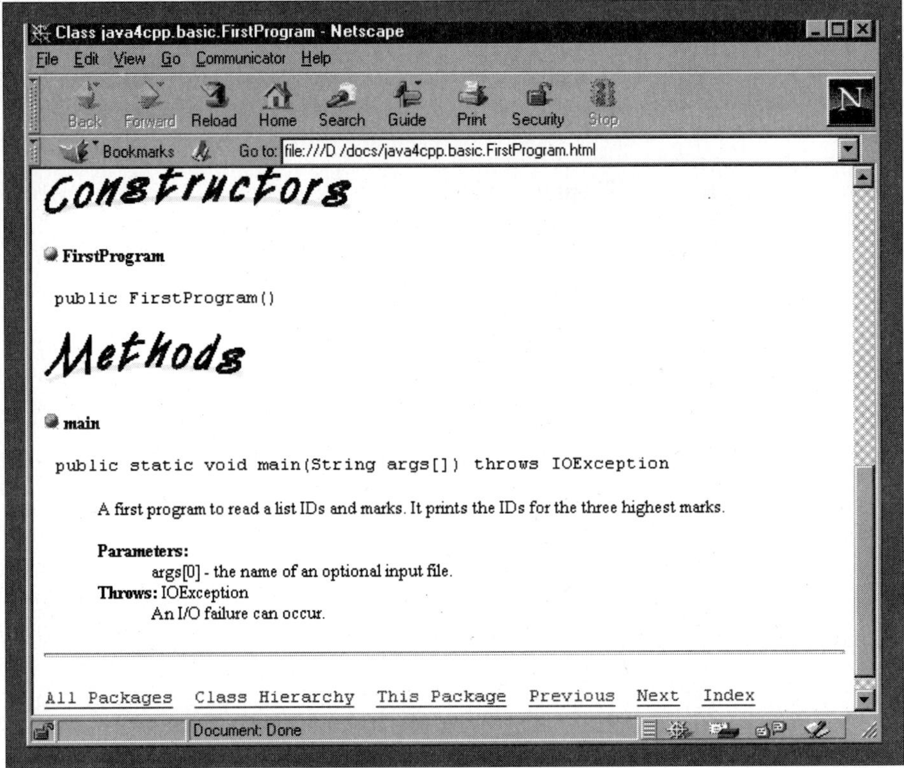

Figure 1-19: documentation for class java4cpp.basic.FirstProgram, continued

Notice that the description of the class and the description of method main use the text from the doc comments in the source file. The **javadoc** output includes a lot of useful information, such as the class relationship diagram at the top of the page that describes each class. There is also an index page, Allname.html, that lists all fields and methods in alphabetic order and has links to each one. Note that there is a link to the index at the top of the `FirstProgram` page, as well as a link to a Class Hierarchy page, tree.html. The Class Hierarchy page lists every class in the packages, with links.

Only one link in the web does not work. At the top of the All Packages page, there is a link to the API User's Guide, API_users_guide.html. The developers of the classes have not yet written the User's Guide.

SUMMARY

The Java programming language is one component of the overall Java platform. Sun Microsystems officially announced the Java programming language in 1995, and gave the world a new programming paradigm with the potential that programs can be written only once, and then run anywhere. The language is designed to work with the Internet, the World Wide Web, and can be used in anything from the smallest embedded systems to the largest enterprise-wide applications.

You install the Java platform, which contains the language, a number of packages that contain the core classes, and the JVM. The JVM gives the Java platform its architecture-neutral development and run-time environment. The JVM translates Java source code into a platform-independent form called bytecode. For faster execution, JIT compilers are available.

With the Java programming language, you can write standalone applications that run in the JVM, or applets that are embedded in Web pages and run by Web browsers that support the Java platform. One set of tools and one language support both kinds of programs. For security reasons, restrictions apply to what applets can do.

A variety of application development tools are available. The JDK is available for free from Sun Microsystems for Windows and Solaris platforms, and from other vendors for a wide range of other platforms. The JDK provides a suite of command-line tools. For an IDE with a GUI, you can acquire products such as the Sun Java WorkShop or VisualAge for Java from IBM.

- If you use the JDK, you compile Java source code into bytecode with the following command:

  ```
  javac filename
  ```

- You load and run classes with the following command:

  ```
  java classname
  ```

- To run applets, you must load the HTML document that contains the applet into a Web browser or an applet viewer.
- To generate HTML documentation from the source code, use the following command:

  ```
  javadoc [options] class_or_package_names
  ```

- There are strict rules for naming files and folders. The JVM depends on these rules to locate classes, so that they can be dynamically loaded as required at run time:
- A source file can contain only one public class, and must have the same name as the class. The extension for a source file is .java.
- The compiler creates files that also have the same name as the class, but the extension is .class.
- If classes are collected into a package, they must reside in the one folder, and the folder name must be the same as the package name.
  If subpackages are collected into a package, they must reside in the one folder, and the folder name must be the name of the containing package.
- The JVM searches the paths stored in the `CLASSPATH` environment variable for packages and classes to load. By default, the current folder and the zip file that contains the core classes are stored in the `CLASSPATH` environment variable.

The Java programming language itself is object-oriented. The syntax bears a strong resemblance to C++, and many of the object-oriented features of C++ are present. Several C++ constructs are not allowed in the Java programming language, including pointer arithmetic, templates, and the ability to write functions that do not belong to a class. In the Java programming language, everything is a member of a class, and a program is a collection of classes.

The executable code in classes makes up the methods of the class. A class can also store data in fields. Methods and fields are the members of a class. To be usable as an application, a class must have a `main` method.

Many of the features of the Java programming language are provided not just by the language, but also by the core classes. The core classes in the package `java.lang` support the language. Java programs make extensive use of the core classes.

One of the innovative features of the Java programming language is doc comments. The **javadoc** tool can parse Java source code and generate an HTML documentation web. You use doc comments to provide the text in the HTML pages. Doc comments begin with `/**` and end with `*/`. You can include HTML tags to format the text in doc comments, and **javadoc** tags to add subtitles for specific information.

QUESTIONS

1. True or False: The JDK contains only the class libraries needed for developing Java programs, and you must purchase development tools separately.
2. True or False: The **appletviewer** program is an extremely simple Web browser that only knows how to display Java applets.
3. If you issue the command `javac MyClass.java`, and `MyClass` uses the public class `HerClass`, which in turn uses the public class `HisClass`, which of the following statements accurately describe what source files are compiled? Select the best answer.
   a. The files MyClass.java, HerClass.java, and HisClass.java are compiled immediately.
   b. The files MyClass.java, HerClass.java, and HisClass.java are compiled only if the modification timestamp is more recent than the .class bytecode file with the same base filename.
   c. The file MyClass.java is compiled immediately, but HerClass.java and HisClass.java are compiled only when a statement that uses them is executed, and only if the modification timestamp is more recent than the .class bytecode file with the same base filename.
   d. The files MyClass.java and HerClass.java are compiled if the modification timestamp is more recent than the .class bytecode file with the same base filename. File HisClass.java is not compiled because MyClass.java does not have any direct dependency on it.
   e. File MyClass.java is compiled immediately. HerClass.java is compiled if the modification timestamp is more recent than the .class bytecode file with the same base filename. The file HisClass.java is compiled if HerClass.java is compiled and if the HisClass.java modification timestamp is more recent than its .class bytecode file.

4. True or False: You can put only one class definition in a single .java source file.

5. On an operating system that treats filenames as case-sensitive, which of the following declarations are valid for a class for which the source is stored in the file Fred.java? Select as many as apply:

a.
```
package myPackage;
public class Fred {
    static void main( String[] args ){
        /* body of Fred.main */
    }
}
class Joe {
    // body of class Joe
}
```

b.
```
package myPackage;
public class FRED {
    // body of class FRED
}
```

c.
```
static class Fred {
    // body of class Fred
}
```

d.
```
public class Fred {
    int month = 1;
    int day = 21;
}
```

e.
```
static void Fred.main( String[] args ){
    // body of Fred.main
}
```

6. What is allowed as a return type of the main method that is the entry point of a Java application? Select all that apply.
   a. int
   b. No return type may be specified
   c. void
   d. Any integral type, including char
   e. int or void
   f. Any defined type

7. How do you distinguish a **javadoc** comment from other comment styles?

8. Which of the following are special tags recognized by the **javadoc** tool? Select all that apply.
   a. @param
   b. @exception
   c. @obsolete
   d. @returns
   e. @author

9. True or False: **javadoc** comments are recognized wherever they are placed within a source file.

10. What kinds of HTML tags should not be used within **javadoc** comments?

11. What **javadoc** tag is used to create a hypertext link to another class or method?

EXERCISES

Debugging

1. Correct the error in the following program:

```
package java4cpp.questions.c1;
public class Debug1_1 {
   public static void main( String[] args ) {
      int a = 6;
      // now output the result of doubling the
      variable a //
      System.out.println( "The answer is " +  a*2 );
   }
}
```

2. Correct the error in the following program:

```
package java4cpp.questions.c1;
   public class Debug1_2 {
   public static void main( String[] args ) {
      /* declare a variable
      int a = 6;
      /* output its square root
      System.out.println( Math.sqrt( a ) );
   }
}
```

3. Correct the following program:

```
package java4cpp.questions.c1;
int a = 0;
int z = 20;
public class Debug1_3 {
   public static void main( String[] args ) {
      for ( int b = a; b < z; b +=2; )
      System.out.println( b );
   }
}
```

Complete the Solution

1. Add a statement to the following program so that it outputs the result of dividing the variable z by the variable y:

```
package java4cpp.questions.c1;
public class Complete1_1 {
   public static void main( String[] args ) {
      int y = 6;
      int z = 12;
      // insert statement here
   }
}
```

2. Add javadoc comments to the following program:

```
package java4cpp.questions.c1;
public class Complete1_2 {
   public static void main( String[] args ) {
      int a = 1;
      int b = 2;
      System.out.println( "Variable a is " + a );
      System.out.println( "Variable b is " + b );
   }
}
```

Discovery

1. Alter the sample program that contains the class `FirstProgram` that reads student records so that the program calculates the average mark from all of the students.
2. Add additional **javadoc** comments to the `FirstProgram` application and then run the **javadoc** utility against it to create user documentation.
3. Complete the following application. The program calculates a person's body mass index (BMI) by applying the following formula:

   BMI = weight_in_kilograms / height_in_meters2

   You can work in metric measure or use conversion formulas such as the following:
   1 kilogram = 2.2 pounds
   1 meter = 39.36 inches

   Values in the range 20 to 27 are considered compatible with good health, with 22 to 25 being the ideal range for average body types. The output from the program should be the BMI value calculated. Optionally, also print a warning message if the BMI is too high or too low. To test the program, use the fact that a large person who is 2 meters tall and weighs 100 kg has a BMI of 25. Here is some code to get you started:

```
import java.io.*;
import java.util.*;
public class BMI {
   public static void main( String[] args )
                                    throws IOException {
```

```
      float height, weight;
      // the following lines wrap a line-oriented
      // input stream around the standard input
      // stream
      InputStreamReader isr =
         new InputStreamReader( System.in );
      BufferedReader br = new BufferedReader( isr );
      // prompt for height
      System.out.println(
         "Enter your height in meters" );
      // the following lines read one number from an
      // input line
      String line = br.readLine();
      if ( line != null ) {
         StringTokenizer st
            = new StringTokenizer( line );
         height
            = ( new Float( st.nextToken() ) )
              .floatValue();
      }
      // insert code to complete the application here
   }  // end of main
}  // end of class
```

CHAPTER

2

Elementary Programming Concepts

objectives

In this chapter you will:

- Begin to learn syntax and semantics of the Java programming language.
- Distinguish between legal and illegal identifiers.
- Identify keywords in the Java programming language.
- Determine the result of the + operator applied to a combination of variables or constants of any type.
- Determine the result of applying the == operator to any two objects of any type.
- Determine the result of applying the >>, >>>, and << operators to an int value specified as a bit pattern.
- State, in an expression involving the operators &, |, &&, and ||, which operands are evaluated and determine the resulting value of the expression.
- Determine the effect of assignment and modification operations upon variables of any type.
- Write code to demonstrate the use of methods of the java.lang.Math class in an expression: abs, ceil, floor, max, min, random, round, sin, cos, tan, and sqrt.
- Construct literal numeric values using decimal, octal, and hexadecimal formats.
- Construct a literal value of char type using the Unicode escape format for a specified character code.
- Write nested conditional code using the if, else, and switch constructs.
- Identify the allowed type of expression for the arguments of if and switch statements.
- Write nested loops to iterate blocks with specific values in loop counter variables.
- Demonstrate the use of both the labeled and unlabeled versions of the break and continue keywords to modify normal loop behavior.
- State the correct declaration for a main method.
- Select specific elements from the command-line arguments passed to main, by using the correct array subscript value.

Introduction

All programs in all languages contain a repertory of statements with which you build your code. Procedures or subprograms combine statements into functional units. Expressions within statements are evaluated while the program is running. This chapter covers these common elements in the Java programming language, and some features that are specific to this new language. To a large extent, this chapter covers constructs that the Java programming language and C++ have in common. But do not skip this chapter. Read it to build a solid foundation in the Java programming language. This chapter highlights many differences between C++ and the Java programming language that can give you grief if you code with the assumption that all constructs that are similar in both languages work in exactly the same way.

Using just the constructs described in this chapter, you can write real programs that perform console I/O. Of course, if you were to do so, you would be as limited as a C++ programmer who cannot define a class. However, from the point of view that you are learning a new programming language from scratch, in this one chapter you achieve much toward the goal of writing working programs.

Variables and Identifiers

All variables have both a type and an identifier. The type determines the nature of a variable, and the identifier is its name in the Java code. Variables can be categorized by type:

- **Primitive types** are predefined types for single data items such as numbers, characters, or boolean values.
- **Reference types** are aggregates, including classes and arrays. There are many predefined core classes, and you can also define your own classes.

A declaration associates a name with a type, and defines a new variable for the Java code to use. The simplest form of declaration is that of a variable inside a method.

Syntax ***type identifier [= initializer];***

Dissection

- The *type* is any type or class name recognized in the Java programming language. If the type is a class, the variable is an object that instantiates that class.
- The *identifier* can be any legal name except keywords and the reserved literals **true, false,** and **null.** The Java keywords are listed in Figure 2-1.

- Including an *initializer* is optional, but the Java compiler flags as an error any attempt to access the value of an uninitialized variable.

Code Example

```
int AOK;
float blossom;
char c = 'c', d2;
boolean flag = true;
String greeting = "Hello";
Dog phydoux = new Dog( "poodle" );
```

Code Dissection

The first four declarations create variables of primitive types.

Strings are not primitive types. They are provided by the core class **String**.

The last of the declarations creates an object called `phydoux` for which the type is a user-defined class, `Dog`.

A variable that is declared inside a method is local to the method. You can define local variables anywhere within a method body. You can add them as you need them, or to follow the convention of declaring them only at the start of blocks. Variables have scope that determines when the identifier is visible and usable by the code. The scope of a local variable extends from its declaration to the end of the immediately enclosing block, with the one exception that the scope of variables defined in the initialization of **for** loops is the body of the **for** loop.

Variables that are declared outside methods are called **fields.** Fields, like methods, are members of the class in which they are declared. Their scope is the class in which they are declared. Chapter 4 explains how the fields and methods declared in a class make up the behavior and attributes of the class. The declaration of a field is a little more complicated than the declaration of a method.

Syntax

[access_specifier] [qualifier] type identifier [= initializer];

Dissection

- Variables that are fields of a class have an access specifier that determines whether other classes can use them. You can specify **public, private,** or **protected**. As with a class, if you omit the access specifier, the field has default access and is accessible only from classes in the same package. Specify **public** to make the field accessible from anywhere. Specify **private** to restrict access to the class in which the field is declared. Use the specifier **protected** with inheritance. Local variables cannot have access specifiers.

- The Java programming language recognizes a number of qualifiers. The qualifier **static** declares a field to be common to the whole class. A static field, also known as a class variable, can be used regardless of whether any variables that instantiate the class have been created. In contrast, every instance of a class has its own copy of the nonstatic variables defined in the class. If you omit the qualifier **static**, the field can be used only with an object of the class. Local variables cannot be static.
- The *type* is any type valid in the Java programming language.
- The *identifier* is any identifier recognized by the Java programming language.
- The *initializer* is optional. If you omit it, the Java programming language automatically assigns a default initial value determined by the type of the field.

Code Example

```
public boolean inStock;
private static int counter = 60;
private String[] message;
Dog chester = new Dog ( "Great Dane" );
```

Code Dissection

The first two fields are of primitive type. The **boolean** `inStock` is implicitly initialized to **false**. Because it is a nonstatic field, `inStock` can be later set to **true** for some instances of the class, and **false** for others. All instances of the class share the same `counter`. If you decrease `counter` for one instance, it decreases for all instances. Indeed, you do not need to have any instances to use `counter`. The field `message` is an array of **String** variables and initially contains no strings. The initial value of every element in `message` is **null**. The declaration of `chester` may be the declaration of a local variable, or it may declare a nonstatic field with default access if it is not inside a method. This declaration creates a new `Dog` object.

You can declare fields before, after, or between method declarations in your class. A common convention is to group the fields by access specifier and put them before the first method in the class definition.

You cannot declare variables or methods outside a class.

Unlike C++, the Java programming language has no concept of just declaring an identifier and later actually allocating storage and creating the object.

The Java programming language's primitive types are similar to the C++ fundamental types. However, there are some important differences, which are described in detail in Chapter 3.

The current C++ standard includes a class String **to support strings. In C++, you now have the choice of using this class, or treating arrays of characters as strings. In the Java programming language, you always use the** String **class.**

The current C++ standard adds type bool **and reserved words** true **and** false **to the C++ language. The Java programming language's type** boolean **is the equivalent of C++ type** bool.

Names in the Java platform are case-sensitive. For variable names, the convention is to use lowercase for letters, except that if the name looks like more than one word, the first letter in all but the first word is often capitalized for readability.

The first character in an identifier must be a letter, an underscore, or a dollar sign. Subsequent characters can be letters, digits, underscores, or dollar signs.

Internally, the Java Virtual Machine (JVM) uses the Unicode character set. This character set supports all alphanumeric characters in the major modern languages, and is far less restrictive than the ASCII character set. For more information about Unicode, see Chapter 16. Any Unicode letter or digit is allowed in an identifier. For example, your identifiers can contain accented characters, symbols, or digits that do not belong to the ASCII set of digits: 0, 1, 2, 3, 4, 5, 6, 7, 8, and 9. The Java programming language follows Unicode rules specifying which character codes are numeric characters and which are alphabetic.

You can enter any Unicode character directly or use a Unicode escape sequence. One reason for using the escape sequence is that you may have no other way of entering or displaying the character. You can use Unicode characters anywhere, not just in strings.

Syntax	\u*XXXX*
Dissection	■ *XXXX* is the four-digit, hexadecimal code for the desired Unicode character.
Code Example	`String delta\u0394 = "deltaδ";`
Code Dissection	This declaration creates a string for which the identifier and value are both `deltaδ`. You can also put the character δ in the identifier name, and the Unicode escape sequence in the literal string.

The Java programming language's identifiers differ from C++ identifiers in two ways:

- **Identifiers can begin with a dollar sign.**
- **Identifiers can include Unicode characters that are not part of the ASCII character set.**

Whether it is wise to take advantage of these features depends upon factors such your local coding conventions and whether you can display or print the characters.

Java Programming Language Keywords

Figure 2-1 lists the Java programming language keywords. These words are reserved for use in constructs of the language, and you cannot use them as identifiers.

abstract	finally	protected
boolean	float	public
break	for	return
byte	goto	short
case	if	static
catch	implements	super
char	import	switch
class	instanceof	synchronized
const	int	this
continue	interface	throw
default	long	throws
do	native	transient
double	new	try
else	operator	void
extends	package	volatile
final	private	while

Figure 2-1: Java programming language keywords

The C++ keywords const, goto, and operator and words byvalue, cast, future, generic, inner, outer, test, and var are reserved, so you cannot use them as identifiers. The Java programming language does not use them. The literals true, false, and null are literals, not keywords. Therefore, they do not appear in Figure 2-1.

In addition to including these reserved words, the Java programming language is rich in the names of packages, classes, and methods that make up the core Java classes. In this book, you can easily spot keywords and the names of the core classes and their methods because they are highlighted with a special font (as in class or void) when they appear in a sentence, unless the word is used in its ordinary English meaning.

For a side-by-side list of the keywords from the C++ and Java programming languages, see Appendix B.

Expressions

Just as in C++, expressions can contain a single variable or constant or they can consist of operators and operands. You use parentheses to group elements, to override operator precedence during evaluation, and to make the expression more readable. An assignment operator in an expression gives values to variables, and an assignment expression is often a complete statement. Here are some expressions that are valid if the variables they use have been defined, have values, and are of appropriate types:

```
a = 2 + 2
( b - 3.3 ) * ( d + 4.175 ) /  sqrt( 5.0 )
t < 32 || t > 212
"carte " + "blanche"
allbits & tflag
5 / 9.0 * ( F - 32 )
```

The operators and operands that make up an expression determine the expression's type. Therefore, the expressions can have types such as char, int, float, double, boolean, and String. Boolean expressions are logical expressions that can have either of two values: true or false. The value of a string expression is an object of the String class.

One type of expression you never use in the Java programming language is a pointer expression. You use the term **object reference** for a Java programming language concept that is similar, but not identical, to C++ pointers or C++ references. Apart from being an operand of an assignment, object references cannot be used in expressions. In other words, the Java programming language allows no pointer arithmetic. That is not to say that you cannot use object references to access the actual objects. You simply cannot manipulate the object references themselves.

Operators

Most of the operators in the Java programming language are the same as their C++ counterparts. Figure 2-2 lists the Java operators, grouped by precedence. The number in the first column indicates precedence; the value has no significance other than to show the order of evaluation when more than one operator appears in an expression. The operators in precedence group 1 are executed before those in group 2, and so on. When precedence does not determine the order of evaluation, expressions are processed from left to right, except that for the right-associative operators, the operand on the right is evaluated first. For example, the assignment operators are right-associative because the operand on the right must be evaluated before its value is assigned to the operand on the left. The first column of Figure 2-2 indicates right-associative operators with a letter *R* following the precedence value.

Precedence	Operator	Description	Moving from C++ Notes
1	[ ]	Array index	Same
1	.	Member	Common, use . instead of C++ scope ::, -> and .->
1	*(argument_list)*	Method call	Same
1	*expression++*	Postfix increment	Same
1	*expression--*	Postfix decrement	Same
2R	++*expression*	Prefix increment	Same
2R	--*expression*	Prefix decrement	Same
2R	+	Unary plus	Same
2R	-	Unary minus	Same
2R	~	Bitwise negate	Same
2R	!	Logical NOT	Same
3R	new	Creation	Common; different usage
3R	*(type) expression*	Cast	Same Alternative C++ forms of an explicit cast are not available
4	*	Multiplication	Same
4	/	Division	Same
4	%	Modulus	Same
5	+	Addition	Same
		string concatenation	not in C++ (except for overloading)
5	-	Subtraction	Same
6	<<	Left shift	Same
6	>>	Right shift with sign propagation	Same
6	>>>	Right shift with zero fill	Not available in C++

Figure 2-2: Operators in the Java programming language

<table>
<tr><th>Precedence</th><th>Operator</th><th>Description</th><th>Moving from C++ Notes</th></tr>
<tr><td>7</td><td><</td><td>Less than</td><td>Same</td></tr>
<tr><td>7</td><td>></td><td>Greater than</td><td>Same</td></tr>
<tr><td>7</td><td>>=</td><td>Greater than or equal to</td><td>Same</td></tr>
<tr><td>7</td><td><=</td><td>Less than or equal to</td><td>Same</td></tr>
<tr><td>7</td><td>instanceof</td><td>Is an instance of</td><td>Not available in C++</td></tr>
<tr><td>8</td><td>==</td><td>Equal to</td><td>Same</td></tr>
<tr><td>8</td><td>!=</td><td>Not equal to</td><td>Same</td></tr>
<tr><td>9</td><td>&</td><td>Bitwise AND</td><td>Same</td></tr>
<tr><td></td><td></td><td>Logical AND without short-circuiting</td><td>Different usage for booleans</td></tr>
<tr><td>10</td><td>^</td><td>Bitwise XOR</td><td>Same</td></tr>
<tr><td>11</td><td>|</td><td>Bitwise OR</td><td>Same</td></tr>
<tr><td></td><td></td><td>Logical OR without short-circuiting</td><td>Different usage for booleans</td></tr>
<tr><td>12</td><td>&&</td><td>Logical AND with short-circuiting</td><td>Same</td></tr>
<tr><td>13</td><td>||</td><td>Logical OR with short-circuiting</td><td>Same</td></tr>
<tr><td>14</td><td>? :</td><td>If ? then : else</td><td>Same</td></tr>
<tr><td>15R</td><td>=</td><td>Assignment</td><td>Same</td></tr>
<tr><td></td><td>+=</td><td></td><td>Common: also for String objects</td></tr>
<tr><td></td><td>-= *= /= %=</td><td></td><td>Same</td></tr>
<tr><td></td><td>>>= <<=</td><td></td><td>Same</td></tr>
<tr><td></td><td>>>>=</td><td></td><td>The Java programming language only</td></tr>
<tr><td></td><td>^=</td><td></td><td>Same</td></tr>
<tr><td></td><td>&= |=</td><td></td><td>Common; usage different for booleans</td></tr>
</table>

Figure 2-2: Operators in the Java programming language (continued)

Among the operators that are common to C++ and the Java programming language, there are some differences:

- The Java programming language allows you to apply & and |, as well as && and ||, to values of boolean type.
- When the operands evaluate to true or false, the difference between & or && and between | or || is whether evaluation of the expression uses short-circuiting. **Short-circuiting** means not evaluating the second operand when the first operand fully determines the result of the operation. For example, (true || *expression*) is true and (false && *expression*) is false regardless of the value of the second operand. Short-circuiting saves execution time, but can cause errors if your code depends on side effects of evaluating the second operand. The Java programming language does not use short-circuiting when & and | are applied to boolean operands, which gives the program a chance to decide whether to use the short-circuiting versions of these operators.

Both C++ and the Java programming language apply short-circuiting to && and ||.

You can use & and | as logical operators in C++ only when the value of each operand is 1 or 0.

The Java programming language supports the comma operator, but only in a for loop to separate subexpressions in the initialization, control, and iteration expressions. Not many programmers use the comma operator in the Java programming language. All it gives you is a way to separate statements to get side effects. For example:

```
for ( int i = 0, j=5; i  < j; i++, j-- )
   System.out.println( "counting: " + i + "-" + j );
```

This line produces the following output:

```
counting 0-5
counting 1-4
counting 2-3
```

The Java programming language has only five operators that do not exist in C++:

- The operators >>> and >>>= perform a logical right shift.
  Because the Java programming language has no unsigned types, you would have no way to do an unsigned shift without this operator. The >> operator repeatedly shifts in a new sign bit. The >>> operator brings in a zero bit regardless of whether the variable has a positive or negative value. This is a logical shift.
  The operators << and >> perform arithmetic shifts. For example, the result of `0xFFFFFF0A >> 4` is `0xFFFFFFF0`, and the result of `0xFFFFFF0A >>> 4` is `0x0FFFFFF0`.

- The instanceof operator provides run-time type information. You can use it to determine whether a variable is an instance of a particular class, or a superclass of that class. In this context, a superclass is a wider type than the particular class, similar to a C++ base class.
- The + and += operators perform string concatenation when used with operands of type String.
  These operators actually create a third string, formed by appending the characters of the second string to the first string. The new string is stored separately from the two input strings, which remain unchanged.

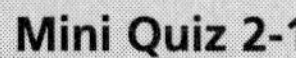

Mini Quiz 2-1

Do you know why a logical left shift is not required?

Moving from C++

From a C++ point of view, you could say the + and += operators are overloaded for class String. They are not actually new operators, just new meanings for the existing addition operators, and they have the same precedence and associativity (left to right) as the numeric addition operators. (The associativity of an operator determines whether it associates with operands to the right or to the left.)

Mini Quiz 2-2

Explain why the output of the following lines of code is `x+y = 12`:

```
int x =1, y =2;
System.out.println( "x+y = " + x + y );
```

Moving from C++

The Java programming language includes some operators that C lacks, but eliminates more C++ operators than it adds to the set. On balance, the Java programming language's set of operators is simpler and the whole topic of operators is smaller. Here are some reasons:

- **The Java programming language does not allow operator overloading. In other words, you cannot redefine the built-in operator symbols to suit your own classes. This is a major simplification from C++.**
- **The following C++ operators either return a pointer or take a pointer as an operand. Therefore, they do not apply in the Java programming language:**
  unary * unary & -> ->* .*
- **In the Java programming language, you cannot apply the arithmetic operators to object references.**
- **The Java programming language has no scope, or double colon, operator. Instead, the language uses the dot notation.**
- **The Java programming language does not support the sizeof operator. This may seem surprising, but is a result of the way that the language stores classes.**

Floating-point Support in the Math Class

The Java platform includes a class called Math. You can use this class like a library of built-in floating-point methods and constants that you can use in arithmetic expressions. For example, the Math class defines the constants Math.PI and Math.E to represent the standard mathematical constants π and *e*. Here, the dot means that the constants PI and E are members of the class named Math. Figure 2-3 lists some of the most commonly used methods of the Math class, along with a brief description of what they do.

Method	Description
int abs(int) long abs(long) float abs(float) double abs(double)	Returns the absolute value of the argument.
double ceil(double)	Returns the smallest double whole number greater than or equal to the argument.
double cos(double)	Returns the cosine of the argument, which specifies radians.
double exp(double)	Returns e^a, where a is the value of the argument.
double floor(double)	Returns the largest double whole number that is smaller than the argument.
double log(double)	Returns $\log_e$ (a), where a is the value of the argument.
int max(int, int)	Returns the larger of the two arguments.
long max(long, long) float max(float, float) double max(double, double)	
int min(int, int)	Returns the smaller of the two arguments.
long min(long, long) float min(float, float) double min(double, double)	
double pow(double, double)	Returns a^b, where a is the first argument and b is the second.
double rint(double)	Returns the closest whole number to the argument. In the case of a tie, returns the even number.

Figure 2-3: Methods in the Math class

Method	Description
double random()	Returns a pseudo random number in the range 0.0 to 1.0.
int round(double)	Returns the closest integer to argument.
long round(float)	
double sin(double)	Returns the sine of the argument, which specifies radians.
double sqrt(double)	Returns the square root of the argument.
double tan(double)	Returns the tangent of the argument, which specifies radians.

Figure 2-3: Methods in the Math class (continued)

All of these methods are static methods of the Math class. You do not have to create an object of a class to use a static method defined in that class.

Syntax

Math.*method*(*argument_list*)

Dissection

- To call *method*, give the class name, **Math**, followed by the dot operator and then the method name.
- If the returned value is assigned to a variable, the variable must have the same type or a type that has a greater range of values. For example, you can assign the return value of type **int** to a variable of type **int**, **long**, **float**, or **double**. Assignment to a variable that has a type with a smaller range of values is an error, unless you explicitly cast the return value to the type of the variable.

Code Example

```
package java4cpp.basic;
/** a class to demonstrate the Math class
  * and working with primitive types */
public class DoMath {
   public static void main( String[] args ) {
      double y = 5.678;
      double x = Math.sqrt( y );
      float a = -4.56F;
      float b = Math.abs( a );
      int r = 56;
      float s = -67.5F;
      int t = (int) Math.max( r, s );
      System.out.println( x );
      System.out.println( b );
      System.out.println( t );
   }
}
```

Code Output

```
2.38285542994115
4.56
56
```

Code Dissection

This program assigns to the variable `y` the value of the square root of the variable `x`. The single argument of **Math.sqrt** has type **double**. If you supply an argument with a numeric type that has a smaller range, such as **float** or **int,** the value is implicitly cast to a **double** when the method is called.

Next, this program assigns to the variable `b` the value of the absolute value of the variable `a`. There are different versions of the **Math.abs** method; this example uses the version that takes an argument of type **float**.

Finally, the program assigns to the variable `t` the value either of `r` or `s`, depending on which is greater. In this case, the method **Math.max(float, float)** is called, and the value of `r` is cast to a **float**. The return value has type **float** and must be explicitly cast to **int** to be assigned to `t`.

Constants

In the Java programming language, you create a constant by specifying the qualifier final in the declaration of a variable. The effect of final is to prevent the value of that variable from changing. You can create constants of any type.

Syntax

[access_specifier] [static] **final** *type identifier [= value];*

Dissection

- The *access_specifier* is optional for fields and not allowed for local variables
- The qualifier **static** is optional for fields and not allowed for local variables.
- The **final** keyword specifies that the value of the variable is constant.
- The *type* is any valid type.
- The *identifier* is any identifier. Following the common convention of using all upper case letters in the names of constants can make your code more readable.
- Usually you assign a value when you declare a constant, even if it is a static field. If you omit the initial value, the constant is called a blank final until it is initialized. A constant cannot be changed after it is initialized.

Code Example

```
public class ConstantThings {
   private static final int ARRAY_SIZE = 57;
   public static void main( String[] args ) {
      String[] stringThings;
      stringThings = new String[ARRAY_SIZE];
      stringThings[0] = "Howdy pardner";
      System.out.println( stringThings[0]) );
   }
}
```

Code Output

```
Howdy pardner
```

Code Dissection

The constant `ARRAY_SIZE` in this class is a **private static** field. Because the field is private, this constant can be used only inside this class. Because the field is static, the **main** method does not have to create a `ConstantThings` object to use the `ARRAY_SIZE` field. The constant represents the integer value 57.

The **main** method creates an array of strings, using the constant `ARRAY_SIZE` to set the number of elements in the array. The rest of **main** puts a string in the first element of the array and then prints that element.

You can also apply final to methods and classes. A final method cannot be overridden. You cannot derive a class from a final class. These applications of the keyword final, as well as the full implications of access specifiers, are explained in Chapter 5. The more general meaning of final is that the behavior of the construct it qualifies cannot be changed. When applied to a field or a variable, final creates a constant.

The value of every constant can be supplied in its declaration. This is simpler than in C++, where you can initialize nonstatic data members only in a constructor and must initialize static data members outside of the class definition. In the Java programming language, you cannot define any variables outside of a class definition.

Usually, constants are static final fields. For example, the Math class contains two constants that are static and final. These constants are also public, so you can use them anywhere:

- Math.E is the closest possible double value to the base of natural logarithms.
- Math.PI is the closest possible double value to the ratio of the circumference of a circle to the diameter.

For example, the following method could be in any class:

```
double area( double radius ) {
    return Math.PI * radius * radius;
}
```

Version Watch

Version 1.1 of the Java programming language was the first version to let programmers use final without static. Earlier versions required that final variables be static fields. Previously, you could not declare nonstatic constants or constants that were local to methods.

As well as removing the restricted use of constants, version 1.1 made it optional to initialize a constant in the same statement that declares it.

Moving from C++

C++ programmers can create constants by specifying the const keyword in the declaration, by using enumerations, or by using #define preprocessor directives. None of these options are available in the Java programming language.

- You cannot use the keyword const in the Java programming language, but declaring a variable final is a close equivalent to declaring a C++ variable const. There are some different rules about initialization. When applied to a method or class, the Java keyword final has a very different meaning than the C++ keyword const.
- The Java programming language does not have a keyword equivalent of enum, so you cannot define enumerations. However, you can declare static final fields with the names that in C++ would be the enumerators in enumerations. For example, consider the following C++ enumeration:

  ```
  enum { animal, vegetable, mineral };
  ```

  In the Java programming language, this enumeration becomes the following:

  ```
  static final int ANIMAL = 0;
  static final int VEGETABLE = 1;
  static final int MINERAL = 2;
  ```

- The Java platform has no preprocessor, and therefore no #define directive.

As a result, constants look very different in the Java programming language than they do in C++.

Blank Final Constants

If you do not assign a value to a constant when you declare it, the constant is known as a blank final. A **blank final** is simply a constant that is given its value separately from its declaration. It takes the first value assigned to it, and then cannot be changed. A statement that initializes blank finals is the only context in which a final variable may appear on the left of an assignment operator.

Here is a class in which main has a constant local variable z, which is created as a blank final.

The structure of packages mirrors the file system, so you will find the source code for this sample in the java4cpp\errors subfolder of the folder in which you unpacked the JAR file java4cpp.jar. The name of a source file always matches the name of the public class that it contains, so this source code is found in the file BlankFinal.java.

```
package java4cpp.errors;
/** A class defined to create
  * intentionally an error with blank finals
  */
public class BlankFinal {
   public static void main( String[] args ) {
      final int y = 6;
      final int z;
      y = 0;           // Error! Value already fixed
      if ( y < 0 ) {
         z = 12;       // Okay. No previous value
      } else {
         z = -12;      // Okay. No previous value
      }
      z = 13;          // Error! Value already fixed
      System.out.println( "The answer is " + z/y );
   }
}
```

In the preceding example, the variables `y` and `z` are local constants because they are declared inside the method main, but only `z` is created as a blank final constant. A useful feature of blank finals is that their value can be computed and fixed at run time.

Here is a simple case where the value is set based on the value of `y`. If you attempt to compile the preceding example exactly as shown, two compiler errors result:

```
BlankFinal.java:5: Can't assign a value to a final
variable: y
                y = 0;          // Error! Value already fixed
                ^
BlankFinal.java:11: Can't assign a second value to a blank
Final variable: z
                z = 13;         // Error! Value already fixed
                ^
2 errors
```

The errors reflect the fact that the value of a constant cannot be changed after it has been set.

Fields can also be blank finals. For example, the `ConstantThings` class can be coded as follows:

```
public class ConstantThings {
   private static final int ARRAY_SIZE;
   public static void main( String[] args ) {
      String[] stringThings;
      stringThings = new String[ARRAY_SIZE];
      stringThings[0] = "Howdy pardner";
      System.out.println( stringThings[0] ) );
      }
    static {
      ARRAY_SIZE = 57;
   }
}
```

A static blank final field must be given an initial value in a static initializer block. The following lines are the static initializer block for the `ConstantThings` class:

```
static {
   ARRAY_SIZE = 57;
}
```

Chapter 4 includes a full discussion of static fields, also known as class variables. What happens when nonstatic fields are blank finals? You can initialize them in either of two ways:

- Assign an initial value in every constructor of the class.
- Provide an instance initializer block. Such blocks are often used in inner classes, and are described in Chapter 10.

Statements

Statements are terminated by a semicolon. You form a block statement by enclosing one or more statements within braces, { and }.

The keywords that can affect the flow of control within methods are listed in Figure 2-4. Many of these keywords are similar or identical to their C++ counterparts. The table's third column summarizes all differences related to these keywords in the Java programming language and C++.

Keyword	Description	C++ Notes
break	Exits an enclosing do, case, for, or while block	Same as C++ except: ■ C++ does not have a labeled **break**
case	Labels a selection in a switch statement	Same as C++
continue	Ends the current iteration of the enclosing do, for, or while block	Same as C++ except: ■ C++ does not have a labeled **continue**
default	Begins the default selection in the switch statement	Same as C++
do	Begins a block that must be executed at least once, and then repeats until the while condition evaluates to false	Same as C++ except: ■ C++ does not have a labeled **break** and **continue** ■ The while condition must evaluate to **true** or **false**
else	Begins a statement or block to execute when the condition of the matching if evaluates to false	Same as C++
for	Begins a counted loop.	Same as C++ except: ■ The termination condition must evaluate to **true** or **false** ■ C++ does not have a labeled **break** and **continue**
		As in the latest C++ standard, the scope of variables declared in the for initialization is the body of the for loop
goto		There is no goto statement in the Java programming language, but goto is a reserved word
if	Controls the conditional execution of a block or statement and of the optional matching else clause	Same as C++ except: ■ The condition for execution must evaluate to **true** or **false**
switch	Begins a block in which the statements following case or default labels are selectively executed	Same as C++
while	Begins a conditional loop	Same as C++ except: ■ The while condition must evaluate to **true** or **false**

Figure 2-4: Conditional and iterative statements

if Statements

Using if statements is the most common way to program conditional execution.

Syntax

if (boolean_expression)
  statement_or_block
[else
  statement_or_block
]

Dissection

- The else clause is optional.
- The statement following the condition or the keyword **else** can be a simple statement ending with a semicolon, or a block enclosed in braces.
- **if** statements can be nested, in which case each **else** is matched with the immediately preceding **if**. The Java programming language follows the same rules of nesting as C++.

Code Example

```
if ( i > j ) {
    i = j;
} else {
    i = 0;
}
```

Code Dissection

This code example works in both C++ and the Java programming language.

Unlike a C++ compiler, the Java compiler rejects if **statements in which the conditional expression has a value of zero, any nonzero integer value,** null, **or any other value than** true **or** false. **You may trip over this rule if you are used to writing C or C++ statements like the following:**

```
if ( x ){/*...*/}.
```

If x **is an integer variable that may have the value 0, this statement is legal and correct in C++. But it is in error in the Java programming language. To get a valid Java statement with exactly the same meaning, rewrite this statement as follows:**

```
if ( x != 0 ){/*...*/}
```

switch Statements

You use the switch keyword to select one or more alternative statements or blocks of code to execute.

Syntax

switch (*integral_expression* **) {**
  case *selector1*:
    statements or blocks
    *[***break;***]*
  *[***case** *selector2*:
    statements or blocks]
  [. . .]
  *[***default:**
  statements or blocks]
}

Dissection

- The expression following the keyword **switch** must have type **byte**, **short**, **int**, **long**, or **char**.
- Any number of **case** labels are allowed. The selector value for each case must be a compile-time integral expression.
- The label **default** is optional. It can be anywhere within the switch statement, but is typically at the end.
- The *integral_expression* is evaluated. Then control goes to the first **case** label for which the value of the selector equals the value of the switch expression. No further matching will be done.
- If none of the **case** labels match the *integral_expression* and a **default** label is present, control passes to the statements following the **default** label.
- Using **break** to exit the switch statement is optional, but very common. Control passes from each case label to the next, including **default**, until a **break** or the end of the switch is encountered.

Code Example

```
char c;
// ...
switch ( c ) {
   case 'a':
   case 'A':
      System.out.println( "You chose a" );
      break;
   case 'b':
   case 'B':
      System.out.println( "You chose b" );
      break;
   default:
      System.out.println( "Default case" );
}
```

while Statements

Use while to program conditional loops. A while loop is most appropriate when you want to repeat some action until a condition occurs. For example, use a while loop to read from a file until you reach the end of the file. You can also set up a while loop to loop indefinitely, if you are sure that some external event will take control out of the loop.

Syntax

while (*boolean_expression* **)**
statement_or_block

Dissection

- The expression is evaluated before the start of each pass through the loop. It must evaluate to **true** or **false**.
- The statement or block following the expression is executed repeatedly as long as the while expression is **true**. It is never executed if the condition is **false** the first time it is evaluated.
- The loop ends when the expression is evaluated and the result is **false**, or when a break statement is encountered in the loop. A continue statement ends the current pass though the loop.

Code Example

```
int i = 0
while ( i <= 5 ) {
   i++;
   System.out.println( "i = " + i );
}
```

do Statements

Use do statements to program conditional loops when you want to force the body of the loop to execute at least once.

Syntax

do
statement_or_block
while (*boolean_expression* **);**

Dissection

- The expression following **while** is evaluated at the end of each pass through the loop. It must evaluate to **true** or **false**.
- The statement or block following the **do** is executed one time, and then repeatedly as long as the while expression is **true**. One pass is guaranteed; the while expression is not evaluated until the end of the first pass through the loop.
- The loop ends when the expression is evaluated and the result is **false**, or when a break statement is encountered in the loop. A continue statement ends the current pass though the loop.

Code Example

```
char c;
do {
  // read a single character into c
} while ( c != 'q' );
```

for Statements

Use for statements for counted loops. A for loop is appropriate when you know in advance how many times to repeat the loop or when you want a counter to be automatically updated on each pass.

Syntax

for (*intialization*; *termination_expression*; *step* **)**
 statement_or_block

Dissection

- If you declare variables in the initialization clause, their scope is the body of the for loop. Usually you set the initial value of a counter in this clause.
- The termination expression is evaluated before the start of each pass through the loop. It must evaluate to **true** or **false**. Usually the value of the counter is a term in this expression.
- The step statement is executed when each pass through the loop ends and before the termination expression is evaluated for the next pass. Usually the step modifies the value of the counter in a predictable way.
- The statement or block is executed repeatedly, as long as the termination expression is **true**.
- The loop ends when the expression is evaluated and the result is **false**, or when a break statement is encountered in the loop. A continue statement ends the current pass though the loop.

Code Example

```
for ( int k = 0; k <= 10; k++ )
   a[k] = k;
```

Code Dissection

This code sets the values of 11 elements in an array of integers. In each pass, the integer k is used as the index of one element in the array, and the value of k is assigned to that element. For example, on the third pass, the element at index **2** in a is given the value **2**.

For this code to work, the **int** array a must be declared before the loop and must have at least 11 elements.

Moving from C++

There are some subtle differences between the Java programming language and C++ that affect the iterative statements while, do, and for:

- The expression that determines whether the loop terminates cannot have an integral value or null. It must have boolean value.
- The C++ standard has changed the rules about the scope of variables declared in the initialization clause of a for statement. The Java programming language rules are the same as the new C++ rules, but different from the rules enforced by many C++ compilers that are still in use. According to the old C++ rules, the scope of the variables extended to the end of the block that enclosed the for statement. Now the scope ends with the for statement. For example, the Java compiler rejects the output statement in the following code because variable p is not defined:

```
{
   long fact = 1;
   for ( int p = 1; p < 9; p++ ) {
      fact *= p+1;
   }
   System.out.println( "factorial " + p + " is " + fact );
}
```

Getting Out of Loops

You can leave loops prematurely with the keywords break and continue. You can put break and continue statements anywhere inside a loop. You can also use break in any enclosing statement, but continue is allowed only in for, while, or do loops.

The simple form of break and continue is identical in both the Java and C++ programming languages. However, the Java programming language does add and remove features for C++ programmers:

- The Java programming language removes the option of using goto to get out of loops. Few C++ programmers use goto statements because they are considered poor style. But goto is tolerated as a way to jump out of loops. The goto statement is the only simple C++ construct that can exit from more than one layer of nested loops in one step. The Java programming language does not support goto statements.
- In the Java programming language, you can break out of several loops at once and go to a specific line of code. For this purpose, the language provides the labeled break and labeled continue. These variations on break and continue do not exist in C++.

The simple form of the break statement does much the same thing in do, for, and while loops that it does in switch statements. It terminates the loop and gives control to the next statement outside the loop.

```
for ( int k = 0; k <= 5; k++ ) {
   if ( k == 3 ) {
      break;
   }
   System.out.println( "loop count " + k );
}
```

The output is

```
loop count 0
loop count 1
loop count 2
```

A **continue** statement terminates the current iteration only, and control passes to the point where the JVM evaluates the **boolean** expression to determine whether to pass through the loop again.

```
for ( int k = 0; k <= 5; k++ ) {
   if ( k == 3 ) {
      continue;
   }
   System.out.println( "loop count " + k);
}
```

The output is

```
loop count 0
loop count 1
loop count 2
loop count 4
loop count 5
```

Both the *break* and *continue* statements can transfer control to locations other than the first statement after the loop. They can transfer control to a labeled **do**, **while**, or **for** statement. Use this construct to get out of nested loops.

Syntax

```
label:
outer_do_while_or_for {
      // ...
      inner_do_while_or_for {
            // ...
            break label;
            // ...
            continue label;
            // ...
      } // end inner loop
      // ...
} // end outer loop
```

Dissection

- A label looks like an identifier, but is followed by a colon that sets it apart from the statement that it labels.
- Inside the loop, you can follow a **continue** or **break** keyword with the name of the label of any enclosing loop. This construct is called a labeled **break** or labeled **continue**.

- A labeled **break** transfers control to the statement following the labeled enclosing block.
- A labeled **continue** transfers control to the point where the decision whether to make another pass through the labeled loop is made.

Code Example

```
package java4cpp.basic;
public class Findit {
   public static void main( String[] args ) {
      int row = 0, col = 0;
      int[][] a = { { 7,4,0 },{ 0,5,0 },{ 2,0,6 } };
      search:
      for ( row = 0; row < 3; row++ ) {
         for ( col = 0; col < 3; col++ ) {
            if ( a[row][col] == 0 ) {
               break search;
            }
            System.out.println( a[row][col]
               + " at (" + row + "," + col + ")" );
         }
      }
      System.out.println( "zero at (" + row + ","
         + col + ")" );
   }
}
```

Code Output

```
7 at (0,0)
4 at (0,1)
zero at (0,2)
```

Code Dissection

The `Findit` class demonstrates a labeled **break**. The **main** method creates a three-by-three array a of type **int** and initializes it. Then **main** searches in a until it finds an element that has the value zero. Two nested **for** loops are used to access each element in turn. When one element satisfies the condition of being equal to zero, the labeled **break** is executed. Here, the third element tested matches zero. At that point, the **break** statement transfers control out of not just the inner loop, but also the labeled outer loop.

Code Example

```
package java4cpp.basic;
public class Findit2 {
   public static void main( String[] args ) {
      int row = 0, col = 0;
      int[][] a = { { 7,4,0 },{ 0,5,0 },{ 2,0,6 } };
      search:
      for ( row = 0; row < 3; row++ ) {
         for ( col = 0; col < 3; col++ ) {
            if ( a[row][col] == 0 ) {
               continue search;
            }
            System.out.println( a[row][col]
               + " at (" + row + "," + col + ")" );
         }
      }
   }
}
```

Code Output

```
7 at (0,0)
4 at (0,1)
2 at (2,0)
```

Code Dissection

`Findit2` is a variation on the `Findit` class. Two lines have changed: The **print** statement outside the loop is gone, and the labeled **break** has been changed to a labeled **continue**. These changes affect the logic considerably. When an element that matches zero is found, the labeled **continue** passes control out of the inner loop to the start of the next iteration of the outer loop. Here, the effect is that the value of every element in a row is printed, until a zero is found in that row. Then the search skips over the rest of the row and starts on the next row.

The labeled break and labeled continue provide an elegant and robust way of getting out of nested loops.

Mini Quiz 2-3

How would you modify the `Findit2` class to print all nonzero elements of the array?

Methods

Every Java method is a member of a class. There are no exceptions, not even the main method. All method declarations include the return type, method name, argument list, and the body of the method.

Syntax

[access_specifiers] [qualifiers] return_type method_name (argument_list)
[throws exception_list]
block

Dissection

- Like every field, every method has its own access specifier. You can specify **public**, **private**, or **protected**, or omit the specifier to accept the default of package access.
- Qualifiers are optional. Include the keyword **static** to make the method usable by any code that has access to the method and the class, regardless of whether any objects of the class have been created. If you omit **static**, the method can be used only with objects of the class. The qualifier **final** determines how the method can be used with inheritance.
- The return type is not optional. Specify **void** if the method does not return a value. A Java method can return any type, including primitive types, class types, and arrays.
- The method name must be a valid identifier. A common convention is to use lowercase letters in method names, except when the name is the concatenation of recognizable words. In such cases, the first letter of all but the first word is capitalized. For example, `myMethod`, `catch22`, and `getMarketShare` are possible method names.
- The parentheses must always be present. They enclose arguments of the method. If the method takes no arguments, just include the empty pair of parentheses. If the argument takes more than one argument, separate the arguments with a comma. In the argument list, you must specify the type of each argument followed by the identifier by which it is known in the method. For example, a method that takes three arguments, two integers, and an array of strings might have an argument list that looks like: `(int first, int last, String[] s).`
- Whether the throws clause is required depends upon what the method does. This clause lists any exceptions that can occur while the method is running and that may prevent the method from returning as expected. Chapter 6 explains that exceptions are a mechanism for handling errors or unexpected situations. For example, a method that performs file I/O may not be able to complete its task because of a problem reading from or a writing to the file. The declarations of methods that work with files may include the clause: **throws IOException**.
- The body of the method is any number of statements enclosed in braces, { and }.

Code Example

```
long setflag( int position, long flag ) {
    long mask = 1;
    return flag | ( mask << ( position-1 ) );
}
```

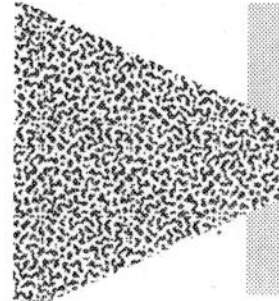

Mini Quiz 2-4

If you delete all parentheses from the following expression, does the value change?

```
flag | ( mask << ( position-1 ) )
```

A method that takes no arguments and returns no value can take the following form:

[access_specifiers] [qualifiers] void method_name () [throws exception_list]
block

Two C++ constructs are not allowed in the Java programming language:

- **In C++ you use the double-colon scope operator to define a member function outside the declaration of a class. Because all Java methods are declared and defined inside a class, there is no need for the equivalent of the C++ syntax:**

  return_type class_name::*method_name* (*arguments*) { *block* }

- **The Java programming language does not let you use the access specifiers as labels for a group of declarations. You must include the access specifier, or accept the default, separately for each Java method. In C++, you can code the following:**

  ```
  public:
     void f();
     void g();
  ```

  But the Java programming language equivalent is:

  ```
  public void f();
  public void g();
  ```

When you call a method that is in another class, use the dot operator. For example, the following line calls a method in the Math class:

```
double d = Math.sqrt( 150.0 );
```

Use the dot notation to call a method with an object of the class, as in the following example:

```
System.out.println( "out is an object declared in class"
                    + " System" );
```

Arguments

All arguments are passed by value in the Java programming language. Some arguments are actual values for primitive types, such as integers and characters, and others are object references for reference types, such as String, the other core classes, or any class that you might define.

The method always receives a copy of the argument. It cannot alter the original value in the calling routine. For example, you cannot write a method like the following to swap the value of integers:

```
public class NoGoodSwap {
   public void swap( int a, int b ) {
      int temp x = a;
      a = b;
      b = temp;
   }
}
```

To be more accurate, you can compile and run such a method, but the altered values are lost when the method returns.

When the argument is an object reference, the fact that the method has a copy of the actual argument is not a problem. A copy of an object reference is just as useful for modifying an object as the original. The reference gives the method access to the actual object so that the method can perform all actions that are valid for that object. Unless the object is immutable, as are some of the objects in the core classes, a method can use the object reference to modify the object. **Immutable objects** are objects that cannot be changed because the class does not give direct access to any fields and provides no methods that can alter the values of fields.

All C++ arguments are passed by value. However, C++ programmers effectively create input and output parameters by explicitly passing pointers or references. C++ references are a syntactic shorthand for pointers. As arguments, object references in the Java programming language work very much like C++ pointers or references, except that the Java programming language has a simpler syntax. The * and & operators are gone, taking with them a common source of errors.

The limitation in the Java programming language stems from the fact that variables of the primitive type do not have object references. Therefore, you cannot do the equivalent of passing a pointer to a variable of type bool, char, int, long, float, **or** double.

You can qualify the argument with the keyword final, much like you can make variables final. A final argument cannot be changed during the execution of the method. The compiler flags any attempt to assign a value as an error. Use final arguments to ensure that the value of an argument remains constant for the duration of the method:

```
public static void f( final int a, final int b ) {
   while ( a < b ) {
      // ...
      a++; // error! can't change a final argument
      System.out.println( "a = " + a );
   }
}
```

If an argument that is an object reference is declared final, the method cannot alter the object reference. The method can still work with the object, but its final object reference cannot be changed to refer to a different object:

```
public static void g( final Dog d ) {
   d.setName("Rover"); // changing the Dog object d is OK
   d = new Dog( "Retriever" ); //error, cannot change d
}
```

Version Watch

Version 1.1 of the Java platform introduced the ability to qualify an argument as final.

When you call a method in the Java programming language, you must provide a value for every argument in the argument list.

Moving from C++

C++ has two features that let you call the same function with different numbers of arguments. Neither feature is available in the Java programming language:

- **In C++, you can declare a function in which the argument list that ends with ..., to indicate that the function has a variable-length argument. This feature depends on the ability to relax the rules of type checking, which the creators of the Java programming language have decided not to do.**

  For an effect similar to that of a variable-length argument list, you can create a method that takes as an argument of type Vector**. The** Vector **class is one of the collection classes described in Chapter 10, and can contain different types of objects.**
- **You cannot specify default values for arguments. Many C++ programmers find the ability to code an assignment right into the argument list of a function definition useful, especially when adding another argument to a function already in use. In C++, you can code the following:**

  ```
  void f( int i, int j = 5 ) { /* ... */ };
  ```

  In the Java programming language, you can get around this restriction by overloading methods, as described in Chapter 4. For example, a way to code the preceding function in the Java programming language is to write two methods:

  ```
  void f( int i, int j ) { /* ... */ };
  void f( int i ) { f( i, 5 ); }
  ```

Return Values and return Statements

A method can return at most one object. A method that is declared to have return type void returns nothing. It can have a return statement but cannot return a value.

A method that has any other return type than void must have at least one return statement.

Syntax return *[expression]*;

Dissection

- The *expression* can be as complicated or simple as you want, but it must evaluate a value than can be assigned to a variable with the return type of the method. It can be a single number or character, **true** or **false**, an object reference, an instance of a class or an array, but must be a single entity.
- The return statement terminates execution of a method. A method can have multiple return statements. Only one return statement is executed for each invocation of the method.

Local Variables

Variables declared within a method are local variables, and the only place local variables can occur is inside a method.

There are some differences between what is allowed for local variables in the C++ and Java programming languages:

- **All local variables must be initialized before they are used. If the Java compiler detects that your code is using a variable that has not been initialized, it gives a compiler error. In C++, you may get a run-time error or, much worse, your code may silently do the wrong thing. Many C++ development tools let you set options for the compiler to print warnings about uninitialized variables, or provide debugging features to detect uninitialized variables. In C++, you cannot prevent this kind of error. The Java programming language does not let errors, such as the following, occur.**

```
void f() {
int i;
j = i * Math.PI;  // error
}
```

- **After a local variable is declared, you cannot redeclare it anywhere in the method, not even in a** for **loop or nested block. For example, in C++ you might have an integer variable** x **with a value of 3 in a block. In an inner block, you could declare** x **again and assign the value 5 to it. While the inner block lasts, the value of** x **is 5 and hides the original** x**. But when the inner block ends,** x **is 3 again because the** x **that was 5 has gone. Confusing? Do not worry, this situation cannot arise in the Java programming language.**

```
public class NestedError {
public static void main( String[] args ) {
   int x = 3;
   {
      int x = 5;   // Error! x is already defined!
      System.out.println( x );
   }
}
}
```

The main Method

The method called main is a very special one. Most sample classes in this book have a main method. That is because these sample programs are small applications that you can run from the command line, or from an icon on your desktop if you take the trouble to create an icon for them. The distinction is between applications that run on their own, and applets that are embedded in HTML documents and started by a Web browser. Applications must have at least one class with a main method.

Any class can have a main method, and more than one class that is used in the same application can have a method named main. You may find it handy to declare a main method for almost every class, so that you can test the class isolated from the larger application.

When you start the JVM by issuing the java command and providing the name of a class, or do the equivalent with an integrated development environment (IDE), the JVM looks for the public class inside the .class file with the same base name as the class. Next, the JVM looks in that class for the method named main. If no such method exists, the virtual machine outputs an error message. If main is found, the JVM passes control to it. In other words, the main method is an entry point into your class.

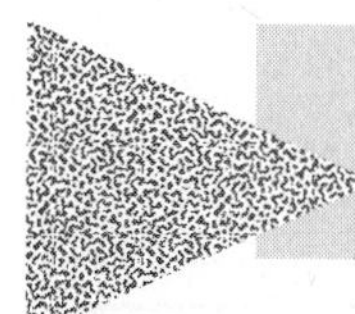

Mini Quiz 2-5

Can there be ambiguity when more than one class contains a method named main?

Syntax	**public static void main(String[ ]** *args* **)** *[throws exception_list]* *block*
Dissection	■ The virtual machine does not recognize **main** as the entry point for a class unless it is static, public, has return type **void**, and has a single argument that is an array of strings. ■ The **main** method must be declared both **static** and **public**. It is **static** because it applies to the whole class, and **public** so that it can be called from outside the class. ■ The single argument of **main** is an array of strings, for which the notation is `String[ ]`. This array contains the arguments supplied when the program is run.

The main method never returns a value, and therefore cannot supply a return code to the JVM . A **return code** is a mechanism by which an application can pass back, to the operating system or parent process, some indication of whether the run completed successfully or terminated with an error code. Because the handling of application return codes is platform-specific, the Java platform isolates the ability to terminate with a return code to the method exit in the standard class System. To terminate with a return code, call System.exit and pass an integer return code as an argument.

Unlike the entry-point method main **of a Java class, the C++** main **method often returns an integer, which is usually ignored or used as a return code.**

The argument list of main **is less similar to its C++ counterpart than it may appear to be:**

- **You cannot use** `args` **as a pointer to the** String **array. In C++, the argument traditionally called** `arg` **is a pointer. In the Java programming language,** `args` **is an object reference.**
- **There is no separate argument to indicate how many strings are in the array, and none is needed, because the length of an array is a field that you can always access.**
- **If the user supplies no command-line arguments, the length of the array** `args` **is zero. The first string in the array is not the name of the program or class. It is the first argument passed to the program. If you need to find out the name of the top-level class for a program from within the code, you can use the run-time type information features described in Chapter 7.**
- **There is no additional argument for environment settings. The Java programming language needs no equivalent for the C++ optional argument** `environ`**.**

Console I/O

Console I/O means input from the keyboard and output to a command-line window on the screen. The Java platform provides basic support for console I/O. The features for developing graphical user interfaces (GUIs) are extensive, and are provided by the Abstract Window Toolkit (AWT) package. Chapters 12 and 13 give an overview of the AWT. Other input- and output-related topics, such as manipulating files, are the subject of Chapter 8.

For simplicity, all sample programs in the early chapters of this book run in command-line mode. This section describes only the simplest—and arguably most useful—features of console I/O. But this discussion should be enough to get you started.

You may find console input and output are also useful in GUI-based programs for inserting debugging output, or for creating program logs. For most applications, the console is unlikely to be your main source for input and destination for output. Most modern applications have a GUI, and few programs— except simple utilities—run in command-line mode.

Simple Stream Input and Output

The Java platform has adopted the same concept of stream I/0 as C++. Three standard streams are defined for input, output, and error output, as shown in Figure 2-5. These stream objects are public, static, final fields of the core class System.

Full name	Type
java.lang.System.in	java.io.InputStream
java.lang.System.out	java.io.PrintStream
java.lang.System.err	java.io.PrintStream

Figure 2-5: Standard Stream objects

In the sample programs, you have already seen a number of statements similar to the following:

```
// prints one line: hello number 2
int id = 2;
System.out.println( "hello number " + id );
```

The PrintStream class provides several methods, including print and println. These two methods have one argument, which can be an object of any primitive or reference type. The difference between them is that print outputs just the argument you pass to it, and println adds a newline character. Use print if you are building up the output line a bit at a time, or use println when each call is to produce a separate line of output.

The most common way to build up the argument to print is to give an argument of type String and use the string concatenation operator, +, to concatenate elements in a string expression. If an item is a number, as `id` is in the preceding line of code, it is converted to a string during the evaluation of the string expression. When you are concatenating numbers, be careful that at least one operand of each + is a String. Otherwise, the + performs arithmetic addition, which may not be what you intend.

```
System.out.println( 1 + 2 + 3 );      // output is 6
System.out.println( "1" + 2 + 3 );     // output is 123
System.out.println( "1" + ( 2+3 ) );    // output is 15
```

Programming console input is more complicated than programming console output. The reason is that you usually want to read a full line at a time, so that you wait for the user to press Enter and let the operating system handle the pressing of Backspace and other inline edits.

Code that reads one line from the console usually is similar to the following lines:

```
java.io.BufferedReader br;
br = new java.io.BufferedReader(
   new java.io.InputStreamReader( System.in ) );
String line = br.readLine();
```

To understand these lines, you must be comfortable with the concept of wrapping an object of one class around an object of another class. Many of the classes in the I/O package, java.io are wrapper classes. A **wrapper class** is essentially a class that provides different behavior for an object than the behavior established by the class of the object. In other words, a wrapper class gives you another way of using the object it wraps. The preceding lines provide a good example of wrapper classes.

For console input, you start with the standard stream object System.in. The first layer of wrapping creates an InputStreamReader object for System.in. The core class InputStreamReader is in the package, java.io. This class implements a character-input stream that reads bytes from a byte-oriented input stream and converts the bytes to characters. For System.in, InputStreamReader converts the input from the character encoding of the native operating system to Unicode. In the following expression, the new keyword creates an InputStreamReader object:

```
new java.io.InputStreamReader( System.in )
```

The next step is to instantiate a BufferedReader object. In other words, the second layer of wrapping creates a BufferedReader object for the InputStreamReader object.

```
java.io.BufferedReader br;
br = new java.io.BufferedReader(
   new java.io.InputStreamReader( System.in ) );
```

The reason for using a BufferedReader object is that the BufferedReader class provides the readLine method, which is the easiest way to read a complete line into a String object. This BufferedReader object is called `br`, and the readLine method returns an object reference for a String, so the following line actually reads the input:

```
String line = br.readLine();
```

All this wrapping of one object inside another may seems like a lot of trouble to go through just to read in a line of text. In Chapter 9, you take advantage of flexibility that such classes as InputStreamReader and BufferedReader bring to the Java platform. These two classes are considered **filter classes** because the bytes from the input stream pass through them and are converted into the format in which the program chooses to receive them.

Console I/O does appear to be more complicated for the Java platform than for C++. The Java programming language lacks any direct equivalents to the C++ << output and >> input operators. The method System.out.println **is analogous to the family of standard functions that includes** printf. **But the structure of the I/O classes and the design of the Java platform do not allow for a direct equivalent of the function** scanf.

Parsing an Input String

The next step after reading a line of input is often to parse it, or break it into separate tokens. A **token** usually consists of a sequence of characters that does not include a space, newline, tab, or other nonprinting characters. These characters are often called whitespace. The following lines show how to extract numbers and words from a string. For demonstration, the first token in this line is to be interpreted as an integer, the second as a floating-point number, and all remaining tokens as one string:

```
java.util.StringTokenizer st
   = new java.util.StringTokenizer( line );
int k = Integer.parseInt( st.nextToken() );
float f = Float.valueOf(
   st.nextToken() ).floatValue();
String s = st.nextToken();
while ( st.hasMoreTokens() ) {
   s += " " + st.nextToken();
}
```

To tokenize a string, you can use the StringTokenizer class provided by the java.util package. Use a StringTokenizer object as a wrapper for a String object. The first of these statements creates a StringTokenizer object called `st` to manipulate an existing String called `line`:

```
java.util.StringTokenizer st
   = new java.util.StringTokenizer( line );
```

By default, a StringTokenizer object interprets whitespace characters as delimiters between tokens. You can call methods of StringTokenizer to customize this behavior. For example, you can specify that the delimiter be a comma.

Class	**java.util.StringTokenizer**
Purpose	This utility class extracts tokens from a string, one by one.
Constructors	■ StringTokenizer(String *s*) StringTokenizer(String *s*, String *delimiter*) StringTokenizer(String *s*, String *delimiter*, Boolean *returnDelimiters*) The constructor builds a **StringTokenizer** for the **String** specified in the first argument. By default, whitespace separates tokens, but you can specify one or more alternative delimiter characters in a second argument of type **String**. If you want each delimiter to be returned as a **String** of length one, set the **boolean** argument to **true**. If this argument is **false** or omitted, delimiters are skipped.

Methods

- **String nextToken()**
  This method returns the next token in the **StringTokenizer** object, or throws an exception if no more tokens are available.
- **boolean hasMoreTokens()**
  This method returns **true** if another token can be extracted from the **StringTokenizer** object, or **false** otherwise. You should call **hasMoreTokens** before **nextToken**, and call **nextToken** only if **hasMoreTokens** returns **true**.

The next three lines perform equivalent tasks for an integer, a floating-point number, and a string. In all three cases, the code extracts the next token from line, by applying the method nextToken to `st`, and converts it to the required type.

- The method parseInt of the Integer class returns the int value represented by a string. The argument is the object returned by nextToken. The Integer class is a wrapper class for the primitive type int, and is described in Chapter 3.

```
int k = Integer.parseInt( st.nextToken() );
```

- Extracting the floating-point number is a two-step process. First, create an object of the class Float from the next token in the line. Float is a wrapper class for the primitive type float, and is also described in Chapter 3. Second, call the valueOf method of the Float class to convert to type float. The syntax of converting to integers and floating-point numbers is not parallel because the Integer and Float wrapper classes do not have parallel sets of methods.

```
float f = Float.valueOf( st.nextToken() ).floatValue();
```

- To get the third token as a string, simply call nextToken. However, building up `s` to contain all the tokens that remain on the input line involves repeatedly calling nextToken until the method hasMoreTokens returns false.

```
String s = st.nextToken();
while( st.hasMoreTokens() ) {
   s += " " + st.nextToken();
}
```

One potential disadvantage of a StringTokenizer is that it folds multiple, adjacent whitespace characters into one delimiter. You cannot use the default delimiter if you want to preserve multiple spaces between words.

Exploring a Console I/O Sample Program

The following program listing does a bit of everything, in terms of simple console input and output. As usual, the program is contained in a public class, this time called `ConsoleTest`.

The main method of this class does all the work. Notice that the declaration of `ConsoleTest.main` contains a throws clause because the java.io package can throw exceptions for certain input and output error conditions.

```
package java4cpp.basic;
/** A class to demonstrate how simple console I/O is used
  */
public class ConsoleTest {
   /** The test method for the class
     * @param args Not used
     * @exception java.io.IOException
     *            Unspecified I/O exception
     */
   public static void main( String[] args )
         throws java.io.IOException {
      int i = 10;
      int j = 20;
      double d = 99.101;

      System.out.print( "Here are some values: " );
      System.out.println( i + " " + j + " " + d );
      System.out.println(
         "Enter an integer, a float, and a string:" );

      java.io.BufferedReader br;
      br = new java.io.BufferedReader( new
         java.io.InputStreamReader( System.in ) );
      String line = br.readLine();

      java.util.StringTokenizer st = new
         java.util.StringTokenizer( line );
      int k = Integer.parseInt( st.nextToken() );
      float f = Float.valueOf(
         st.nextToken() ).floatValue();
      String s = st.nextToken();
      while( st.hasMoreTokens() ) {
         s += " " + st.nextToken();
      }

      System.out.println( "Here's your data: " );
      System.out.println( k );
```

```
        System.out.println( f );
        System.out.println( s );
    }
}
```

The output is

```
Here are some values: 10 20 99.101
Enter an integer, a float, and a string:
13 34.6 Quick brown fox
Here's your data:
13
34.6
Quick brown fox
```

SUMMARY

The Java programming language inherits most of its syntax and many of its concepts—such as scope, classes, and member access control—from C++. You can work from the premise that the Java programming language is very much like C++ for these very basic issues, except for the following differences:

- The rules for valid identifiers are the same as in C++, except that you can start an identifier with a dollar sign and include Unicode characters. Naming conventions for variables, constants, classes, and methods largely carry over from C++.
- Arithmetic expressions look much like C++ arithmetic expressions. However, boolean expressions, also called logical or conditional expressions, can only be true or false. true and false are Java keywords. You cannot treat zero or null as false or any other value than 0 as true.
- Many of the operators are identical in C++ and the Java programming language. The Java programming language adds the following operators:

  Right shift with zero fill: >>> and >>>=
  Is-an-instance-of: instanceof
  String concatenation: + and +=
- The Java programming language has dropped the scope operator, sizeof, and all operators that modify pointers, except assignment operators. There is no explicit address-of or contents-of operator. You cannot overload the built-in operators.
- The core class Math provides many useful mathematical methods, such as abs, sqrt, random, and many more, and the two constants PI and E. These methods and constants are all public and static, so you can use them from anywhere and need not create an object of the Math class.
- Use the keyword final to declare constants. The Java programming language has no preprocessor directives, enumerations, or const keyword. You can initialize constants in their declarations, or create blank finals, which cannot be changed after they are assigned a value.

- The statements that can alter the flow of control in a method contain the following keywords:

break	case	continue	default
do	else	for	if
switch	while		

- The condition in an if statement, and the expression that determines whether to terminate a loop, must be true or false and cannot be numeric.
- The scope of variables declared in the initializer of a for statement is restricted to the for statement itself. The continue and break statements can use labels to jump out of more than one level of nested loops.
- Method declarations take the following form:
  [access_specifiers] [qualifiers] return_type method_name (argument_list)
  [throws exception_list]
  block
- All methods must be members of a class. Every method is declared with an explicit access specifier or is given the default access. The throws clause in a method declaration is similar to a C++ exception specification. Otherwise, the definition of a method looks much like that of a C++ member function. All arguments are passed by value.
- The form of the main method is
  public static void main(String[ ] *args*) *[throws exception_list]*
  block
- More than one class can have a method called main, but only the main method in the public class used to tell the JVM to run is the entry point for an application. It is a good idea to provide a main method as a test method for classes. Applets written in the Java programming language do not have a main method. main never returns a value. The JVM passes command-line arguments to the class, and does not include the name of the program.
- Like C++, the Java platform supports streams for console I/O. The simplest way to output to the console is to call the methods System.out.print and System.out.println. The best way to perform console input is to use the wrapper classes BufferedReader and InputStreamReader to read a line at a time. Use the StringTokenizer class to break the line or any string into individual tokens.

QUESTIONS

1. Which of the following are legal Java identifier names? Select all that apply.

a. `counter1`

b. `$index`

c. `name-7`

d. `Iterator.Class`

e. `array`

2. Examine the following code:

```
package java4cpp.questions.c2;
public class Quiz2_1 {
   public static void main( String[] args ) {
      int a = 8;
      int b = -8;
      System.out.print( a << 2 );
      System.out.println( ", " + ( b >> 1 ) );
   }
}
```

Which one of the following statements correctly describes the behavior when this program is compiled and run?

a. Compilation is successful and the output is `32, -4`
b. Compilation is successful and the output is `16, 4`
c. Compilation is successful and the output is `32, 2147483644`
d. Compilation is successful and the output is `16, 2147483644`
e. The compiler rejects the expression `(b >> 1)` because you cannot use the >> operator with a negative value as the left operand.

3. How is a Unicode escape sequence distinguished?

4. Examine the following set of tokens:

goto	unsigned	class
switch	null	double
label	transient	template

Which of the following statements are true? Select all that apply.

a. template and unsigned are not reserved words.
b. All of the words in the list are reserved words.
c. label is not a reserved word.
d. goto is a reserved word, but its use is not allowed.
e. null is a keyword.

5. What qualifier do you include in the declaration of a variable to prevent its value from being changed after an initial value has been assigned?

6. True or false: The Java programming language does not support the sizeof operator.

7. Examine the following code:

```
package java4cpp.questions.c2;
public class Quiz2_2 {
   public static double foo (  double a, double b ) {
      return( a > b ? a : b );
   }
   public static void main( String[] args ) {
      System.out.println( foo( 3.4, 6.3 ) );
   }
}
```

Which one of the following statements correctly describes the behavior when this program is compiled?

a. Compilation is successful and the output is `6.3`
b. Compilation is successful and the output is `3.4`
c. The compiler rejects the expression `( a > b ? a : b )` because the Java programming language does not support the ? : ternary operator.
d. The compiler rejects the expression `foo( 3.4, 6.3 )` because it does not evaluate to a string value.

8. If the variable t of type short contains the bit pattern `1111 0000 0000 1010`, which of the following statements are true? Select all that apply.

a. The result of `t >> 4` is `0000 1111 0000 0000`.
b. The result of `t >>> 4` is `0000 1111 0000 0000`.
c. The result of `t >> 4` is `1111 1111 0000 0000`.
d. The result of `t >>> 4` is `1111 1111 0000 0000`.
e. The result of `t >>> 4` is `1010 1111 0000 0000`.

9. True or false: The input stream object System.in directly supports the function of reading a String object from the input stream.

10. Examine the following set of operators:

&& || & |

Which of the following statements are true? Select all that apply.

a. All of the operators are logical operators.
b. These operators can be applied only to boolean values.
c. The operator || evaluates its right argument only if the left argument evaluates to false.
d. The operators || and | perform an exclusive OR operation.
e. The operator & evaluates its right argument if the left argument evaluates to true.

11. If `st` is a StringTokenizer object that contains no tokens, which of the following lines fail because they attempt to access an element that does not exist?

a.
```
if ( st.hasMoreTokens() &
    Integer.parseInt( st.nextToken( ) ) != 0 ) { /* ... */ }
```
b.
```
if ( st.hasMoreTokens() &&
    Integer.parseInt( st.nextToken( ) ) != 0 ) { /* ... */ }
```
c.
```
if ( st.hasMoreTokens() |
    Integer.parseInt( st.nextToken( ) ) != 0 ) { /* ... */ }
```
d.
```
if ( st.hasMoreTokens() ||
    Integer.parseInt( st.nextToken( ) ) != 0 ) { /* ... */ }
```

12. Examine the following lines of code:

```
for ( a = 0; a < 3;  a++ ) {
   if ( a == 1 ) continue;
   for ( b = 0; b < 3; b++ ) {
      if ( b == 1 ) break;
      System.out.println( a + ", " + b );
   }
}
```

Which of the following lines are included in the output when the method that contains these lines is run? Select all that apply.

a. `0, 0`
b. `0, 1`
c. `0, 2`
d. `1, 0`
e. `1, 1`
f. `1, 2`
g. `2, 0`
h. `2, 1`
i. `2, 2`

13. Examine the following code:

```
package java4cpp.questions.c2;
public class Quiz2_3 {
    public static void main( String[] args ) {
        int x = 010;
        int y = 0x10;
        int z = 10;
        System.out.println( x + y + z );
    }
}
```

Which one of the following correctly describes the behavior when this program is compiled?

a. Compilation is successful and the output is `30`.
b. Compilation is successful and the output is `36`.
c. Compilation is successful and the output is `34`.
d. The compiler rejects the expression `y = 0x10` because letters of the alphabet are not allowed in numeric constants.
e. The compiler rejects the expression `y = 0x10` because a hexadecimal value cannot be assigned to an `int` variable.

EXERCISES

Debugging

1. Correct all errors in the following code:

```
package java4cpp.questions.c2;
public class Debug2_1 {
   public static void main( String[] args ) {
      int x = 8;
      if ( x = 0 ) {
         System.out.println( x );
      } else {
         System.out.println( x*2 );
      }
   }
}
```

2. Correct all errors in the following code.

```
package java4cpp.questions.c2;
public class Debug2_2 {
   private final int MIN;
   private final int MAX;
   public Debug2_2() {
      MAX = 10;
   }
   public Debug2_2( int input ) {
      MIN = input;
   }
   public static void main( String[] args ) {
      Debug2_2 a = new Debug2_2();
      Debug2_2 b = new Debug2_2( 15 );
   }
}
```

The intended output is:

```
Countdown to 9 from 10
Countdown to 8 from 10
   . . .
Countdown to 0 from 10
```

3. Correct all errors in the following code:

```
package java4cpp.questions.c2;
public class Debug2_3 {
   public static void main( String[] args ) {
      char c = 'x';
      int x = 17;
      double y = 21.4;
      if ( x * y > 400 )
         switch ( c ) {
            case 'a':
               System.out.println( c );
            default
               System.out.println( "Not 'a'" );
         }
         x = 24;
      else {
         x = 25;
      }
   }
}
```

4. Correct all errors in the following code:

```
package java4cpp.questions.c2;
public class Debug2_4 {
   private int x = 11;
   public void main( String args ) {
      Debug2_4 a = new Debug2_4();
   }
   public int getX() {
      return x;
   }
   public void setX( int newValue ) {
      x = newValue;
   }
}
```

5. Correct all errors in the following code. There are semantic errors as well as syntax errors. The purpose of this class is to determine whether the first of the two integer values passed as command-line arguments to the program is a multiple of the second integer value passed as a command-line argument. The class must also print the ratio created by dividing the first value by the second.

```
package java4cpp.questions.c2;
public class Debug2_5 {
   public static int main( String[] args ){
   int num1 = Integer.parseInt( args[1] );
   int num2 = Integer.parseInt( args[2] );
   float x = num1/num2;
   if ( num1 = x * num2 )
      System.out.println( num1, "is a multiple of", num2 );
   else
      System.out.println( "num1/num2 = ", x );
   }
}
```

Complete the Solution

1. Add statements to the following nested loops so that when `j` reaches the value of 7 it will leave the inner loop and go to the next value of `i` in the outer loop.

```
package java4cpp.questions.c2;
public class Complete2_1 {
   public static void main( String[] args ) {
outer_loop:
      for( int i = 0; i < 10; i++ ) {
         for( int j = 0; j < 10; j++ ) {
            //
            // add statements here
            //
            System.out.println( "(" + i + "," + j + ")" );
         }
      }
   }
}
```

2. Add code to the call of the method println in the following class so that the output is a list of the command-line arguments passed to main.

```
package java4cpp.questions.c2;
public class Complete2_2 {
   public static void main( String[] args ) {
      // length returns the number of elements in the array
      for ( int i = 0; i < args.length; i++ ) {
         System.out.println( /* put code here */ );
      }
   }
}
```

3. Add code to the following class to return the absolute value of the field `x`. You must also add a main method to test your solution. The main method should set the value of `x` to the first command-line argument, then print the value of `x` followed by the absolute value of `x`.

```
package java4cpp.questions.c2;
public class Complete2_3 {
   private int x;
   public void setX( int newValue ) {
      x = newValue;
   }
   public int getX() {
      return x;
   }
   public int getAbsX() {
      // your code here
   }
   // insert main here
}
```

4. Add the `FtoC` method to the following class. The method receives an integer number of degrees Fahrenheit to return the equivalent temperature in whole degrees Celsius, using the formula C = (5/9)(F-32).

```
package java4cpp.questions.c2;
public class Complete2_4 {
   // your code here
   public static void main( String[] args ) {
      System.out.println( " 32F = " + FtoC( 32 ) + "C" );
      System.out.println( "212F = " + FtoC( 212 ) + "C");
      System.out.println( "-40F = " + FtoC( -40 ) + "C");
   }
}
```

5. An efficient way to tell if an integer is odd or even is to AND it with the value 1. Add code to print a message saying whether each integer value in the range –2 to 2 is odd or even.

```
package java4cpp.answers.c2;
public class Complete2_5 {
   static public void main( String[] args) {
      boolean isEven;
      //
      // your code goes here
      //
   }
   static String odd = " is an odd number.";
   static String even = " is an even number.";
}
```

Discovery

1. Create a class called `SquaresAndRoots` in which a main method reads a floating-point number from the console and then outputs the square and square root of the number to the console. Code the main method to prompt for input repeatedly until the user enters the end-of-file character used by the native operating system. The program quits in response to end-of-file.
2. Assume your monetary system has only coins called quarters worth 25 cents, dimes worth 10 cents, nickels worth five cents, and pennies worth one cent. A dollar is 100 cents. Write a class called `Coins`. The main method receives as a command-line argument an integer that represents an amount of money, in cents, and prints the number and type of coins required to make up that amount of money using the smallest possible number of coins. If the input value is greater than one dollar, consider only the portion less than one dollar. The output lists types of coins only if at least one coin of that type is required.

   If the input is 70, the output is

   ```
   4 coins required:
   2 quarters
   2 dimes
   ```

   If the input is a multiple of 100 or less than 1, the output is

   ```
   No coins required.
   ```

3. Create a public static method called `gcd` in a class called `Euclid`. This method takes two integers as arguments and returns an integer that is the greatest common denominator of the arguments. The algorithm is based on the following Euclidean principles:

- The greatest common denominator (gcd) of any two integers equals the gcd of the absolute value of those integers.
- The gcd of any integer and zero is the value of the integer.
- The gcd of any two integers x and y is equal to the gcd of y and the value of x modulo y.
- For example, gcd (–20, –8) = gcd (20, 8) = gcd(8, 4) = gcd(4, 0) = 4.

The `gcd` method must be recursive. Write a main method that tests `gcd` with five different pairs of values.

CHAPTER 3

Types

objectives

In this chapter you will:

- **State the range of the primitive data types** byte, short, int, long, **and** char.
- **Construct literal** String **values using quoted format.**
- **Determine the result of applying the** equals **method to any combination of objects of the classes** java.lang.String, java.lang.Boolean, **and** java.lang.Object.
- **Determine whether an assignment is permitted between any two variables of possibly different types.**
- **Determine the effect upon objects and primitive variables of passing variables into methods and performing assignments and other modifying operations in that method.**
- **Declare arrays of any type and correctly initialize them.**
- **Determine the value of an element of an array of any base type, when the array has been constructed but no explicit assignment has been made to the element.**
- **Write code to initialize an array using loop iteration.**
- **Write code to initialize an array using the combined declaration and initialization format.**
- **Identify the earliest point in a method at which, in the absence of compiler optimization, the object referred to by a local variable is definitely eligible to be garbage collected.**
- **Write code to demonstrate the use of the following methods of the** java.lang.String **class:** length, toUpperCase, toLowerCase, equals, equalsIgnoreCase, charAt, concat, indexOf, lastIndexOf, substring, toString, **and** trim.
- **State all operators that are legal in** String **expressions.**
- **Recognize the implications of the immutability rule of the** String **class.**

Introduction

This chapter covers the types provided by the Java programming language and the types you can define yourself. Classes, the cornerstone of object-oriented programming, fall into the latter group. The Java platform provides many classes, known as the **core classes**, and uses many of the core classes to support the Java programming language itself. This chapter discusses a number of core classes that provide specific support for types.

This chapter covers the basics of Java types[1]. Chapters 4 and 5 look in detail at classes and interfaces, a new feature introduced by the Java programming language, and how classes and interfaces can be related in an inheritance hierarchy. Inheritance is the key to powerful object-oriented techniques such as polymorphism.

The Java programming language does not have a primitive type for strings. However, two core classes, String and StringBuffer, support strings. Because string manipulation is a very important programming technique and many programmers consider strings to be, at least conceptually, a fundamental kind of data, this chapter tells you how to use these two classes.

Moving from C++

There are similarities between the Java and C++ types. For example, every class is a type. However, in some major ways, Java types are unlike C++ types:

- **The set of primitive types is different. In both languages, primitive types provide different ways of representing individual data items such as** int, char, **and** float.
- **Arrays are a distinct type, and every array is an object.**
- **The Java programming language does not allow pointers to the primitive types.**
- **The way that you access objects though references or pointers is one of the most striking contrasts between the Java programming language and C++.**
- **There are important differences in the way you can pass variables the various types as arguments of methods.**

C++ is a hybrid language in which you can mix procedural code with classes and object-oriented techniques. As a result, C++ has a fairly complex grammar and its fair share of inconsistencies. Java types should seem simpler. It may be best to approach this chapter with a clear mind. Leverage your conceptual understanding of types in object-oriented programming, but do not expect the Java programming language's syntax to mirror C++ in every way.

Strong Types

The Java programming language is a strongly typed language, just like C++. A **strongly typed** language essentially is one that enforces a comprehensive set of rules about how you use objects of different types. Of course, the traditional purpose of types, to determine how the bits that make up data items should be mapped onto storage, is retained. However, objects in object-oriented languages have behavior as well as data. Strong typing adds restrictions to ensure that objects remain true to their intended behavior. For example, there are limitations about casting, or using an object as though it has a different type.

[1]Throughout this text, we use the term *Java type* rather than *type for the Java programming language.*

In contrast, C has many data types but lets you perform casts and use data of one type as though it were a very different type. C is not a strongly typed language.

Primitive and Reference Types

When you program in the Java programming language, every variable that you declare belongs to one of two categories: primitive types or reference types. In your code, literals, such as numbers and literal strings, are all of primitive type. The types in each category are listed in Figure 3-1.

Type	Category	Description
boolean	primitive	Logical value **true** or **false**
char	primitive	Integral type that holds the representation of a single character
byte	primitive	8-bit signed integral value
short	primitive	16-bit signed integral value
int	primitive	32-bit signed integral value
long	primitive	64-bit signed integral value
float	primitive	Floating-point value
double	primitive	Double-precision, floating-point value
array	reference	Indexed set of elements of the same primitive or reference type
class	reference	Object that can contain data and behavior
interface	reference	Specification of behaviors that a class may implement

Figure 3-1: Java types

You refer to a variable of a primitive type simply by its name. The syntax looks similar for a variable of a reference type, but the identifier is really the name of an object reference through which the object can be accessed. The object itself has no name. The JVM implements object references as pointers to the storage occupied by objects. Object references are entities separate from the objects to which they refer, but the Java programming language does not consider object references to be a separate type.

Version Watch

Upcoming versions of the Java platform will recognize object references to the extent of providing a new core class, Reference, **that programmers will be able to use at run time to access an object reference in its own right, distinct from the referenced object .**

The Java programming language does not have a primitive type for pointers. However, it is not true to say that the language has no pointers. Object references are pointers behind the scenes, but you can use them in specific ways only. You cannot use the values of object references as integral values. You cannot perform arithmetic or bit manipulations on such values.

Moving from C++

Primitive types in the Java programming language closely resemble many of the C and C++ fundamental types, with the following differences:

- boolean, **unlike the C++ type** bool **that is a fairly recent addition to the C++ language, is not an integral type.**
- **The integral types are all signed. C++ supports signed and unsigned integral types.**
- **There is only one character type,** char. **The current C++ standard defines two character types:** char **and** wchar_t. **As in C++,** char **is an integral type. Unlike C++, the Java programming language uses Unicode as the internal representation of all characters.**
- **The Java platform defines the size of the primitive types, and the JVM gives them the same representation on all platforms.**
- **You cannot create variables with reference or pointer types. Therefore, you can refer to a variable of primitive only by its identifier. You do not have the option of accessing the variable indirectly through a pointer or reference. The Java programming language has no unary * or &, operators. Therefore, there is no way to program the equivalent of the following:**

```
int i;            // i is an integer
int *pi = &i;     // not allowed
```

The reference types are what C++ programmers think of as aggregates or user-defined types.

- **Arrays have reference type. This is a radical departure from C++, and has great advantages. Arrays are real objects, not just a fancy syntax for pointers.**
- **The Java programming language has no** struct, enum, **or** union **keywords and does not support structures, enumerations, or unions.**
- **Interfaces are new with the Java programming language. They are analogous to C++ abstract base classes in that they contain declarations of methods that must be defined in classes that implement the interface.**
- **Although object references work like pointers, you do not use the -> operator or any other dereferencing operator with them. The Java programming language does not include the arrow operator.**

The Java programming language does not support typedef **expressions for creating type synonyms. There is no facility for assigning your own names for existing types. The type you see in a declaration is the type you get: You never wonder if a variable really is just an** int **under the covers.**

When you pass variables as arguments to methods, you always pass primitive types by value and reference types by reference. If an argument has a primitive type, a copy of its value is made and the called method works with the copy. As a result, if the value is modified inside the method, the new value is not passed back to the calling routine. When you pass a variable of a reference type, no copy of the object is made and the object reference is passed to the method. The object reference gives the method access to the storage reserved for the object. If the class of the passed object provides the necessary methods, the method can modify the contents of the object permanently.

The boolean Type

A boolean variable can have either of two values, true or false. The boolean literals true and false are part of the Java programming language and are spelled in all lowercase letters.

The most interesting thing about the boolean type is that it is not numeric. You cannot cast true to be an integer, and you cannot cast an integer to be a boolean. The type boolean is a distinct type.

Moving from C++

You cannot treat integral variables as boolean values as you can in C++. For example, you cannot treat any expression that does not evaluate to zero as true; you must be more explicit with your conditions. If you accidentally assign the value zero to a variable instead of comparing the variable to zero, the language produces an error message saying that an integer cannot be cast to a boolean.

Consider the following code:

```
int x;
   // lines of code omitted
if ( x = 0 ) {
   doSomething();
}
```

In C++, these lines compile successfully. However, the function doSomething **is never called because the condition has the value zero, which C++ interprets as false. In the Java programming language, these lines do not compile because the condition does not evaluate to a boolean value. Instead, you have to correct the code to the following, which is probably what was intended in C++ also:**

```
int x;
   // lines of code omitted
if ( x == 0 ) {
   doSomething();
}
```

The char Type

A char variable represents one character, encoded in a platform-independent definition of characters called Unicode. Unicode defines a 16-bit representation of characters. The Unicode character set includes the characters required for most major modern languages and is not limited to the North American or Western European alphabets. The seven-bit industry-standard ASCII character set is a subset of Unicode.

Type char **in the Java programming language is very different from type** char **in C++. In C++, characters of type** char **occupy one byte, and type** char **is often used for a single byte of storage, regardless of the kind of data that is stored there. The sole purpose of the Java type** char **is to contain characters.**

The Java programming language does not have separate types for single-byte and multibyte characters. Because it is a two-byte representation, the type char **is closer to the wide character type,** wchar_t, **of C++ than the single-byte C++ character type,** char. **You cannot, and have no need to, distinguish wide or narrow characters. You just work with the type** char **and automatically use a two-byte representation.**

Because the Java programming language uses Unicode, any particular character is represented by exactly the same bit pattern on all platforms, regardless of the character encoding that the native operating system uses. Therefore, Java programs that manipulate characters can be more portable than C++ programs that manipulate characters.

Strings are not the same thing as arrays of characters. You can declare and use arrays of characters, but the usual way to work with strings is to use the core String **class.**

Character literals are enclosed within single quotation marks. Double quotation marks enclose literal strings.

You can use a char wherever an int is valid without explicitly casting. You can also explicitly cast a character to any size integer and cast an integer to a character. Such casts can lose precision because representation of a character is a 16-bit unsigned value. An int is 32 bits in the Java programming language and can always hold a 16-bit char. However, when you are casting from the int to the char, only the low-order 16 bits are used. Many of the methods of the core classes that operate on characters take an argument of type int. For example, the following line returns the position of the dot character in a String object called `fileName`. The argument of indexOf has type int, so the actual parameter `'.'` is implicitly cast to an int:

```
int suffix = fileName.indexOf('.');
```

Escape Sequences

You can use escape sequences in your code to represent characters that do not display or cannot be easily entered on the keyboard. The term *escape sequences* may be a misnomer because the sequences begin with a backslash rather than the escape control character. Figure 3-2 shows escape sequences used in the Java programming language.

Escape Sequence	Represents
\b	Backspace
\f	Form feed (new page)
\n	New line
\r	Carriage return
\t	Tab
\\	Backslash (\ )
\'	Single quote (')
\"	Double quote (")
\d, \dd, or \ddd	Octal value in the range 0 to 377
\xdd	Hexadecimal value in the range 00 to FF
\udddd	Unicode character value

Figure 3-2: Escape sequences

The set of supported sequences is smaller than in C++. The Java programming language does not recognize the following:

\a	**Alert (bell)**
\?	**Question mark**
\v	**Vertical tab**

You can use Unicode escape sequences for the value of a single character or values of sets of characters in string constants. The representation of a Unicode character starts with \u, followed by four hexadecimal digits. You can put Unicode escape sequences anywhere within a program, even in class names and variable names. For example, you can create a constant called π, instead of `PI` to represent the value 3.14159. Doing this may not be advisable, however, because the character may not be visible when you display the source. Nevertheless, it is important to note that the Java programming language does not require that identifiers contain only ASCII characters.

Unicode escape sequences are processed before the code is compiled. For example, the compiler rejects a literal string that contains the sequence `\u000a`, which becomes a Unicode line-feed character because you cannot include line feed in a string literal.

Integer Types

The Java programming language has four integer types: byte, short, int, and long. All of the integer types are signed. The range of integers is never from zero to some large, positive number. Instead the range is always from a negative number to a positive number. The integer types have fixed sizes on all platforms. Figure 3-3 gives the size and range of the integer types.

Type	Size in Bits	Range
byte	8	-128 to 127
short	16	-32768 to 32767
int	32	-2,147,483,648 to 2,147,483,647
long	64	-9,223,372,036,854,775,808 to 9,223,372,036,854,775,807

Figure 3-3: Integer types

Types byte and short are intended mostly for saving space when storing information. When you perform calculations on variables of type byte or short, they are promoted to type int.

Most hardware currently used is not designed to handle integers that are 64 bits long. If you do not need the extra range, use int instead of long for better performance.

When you supply a numeric literal, the Java programming language assigns type int if the value will fit into 32 bits, or type long if it requires more than 32 bits of storage. You can append the letter L or l to force explicitly the type of the literal to long.

Just as in C++, numeric literals can be decimal, octal, or hexadecimal. The first character in a decimal literal must be one of the digits `1` to `9`, and a decimal integer can contain only the digits `0`, `1`, `2`, `3`, `4`, `5`, `6`, `7`, `8`, and `9`. Do not start a decimal number with a zero, because a leading 0 means octal and a leading `0x` or `0X` indicates hexadecimal. Figure 3-4 presents some example literals.

Type:	int	int	int	long	int
Base:	Decimal	Decimal	Hexadecimal	Decimal	Octal
	`6`	`-1873`	`0xABF8`	`30000000000L`	`0777`

Figure 3-4: Example literals

At first glance, the integer types, with the exception of byte, look deceptively familiar. But there are significant differences between them and the C++ types with the same names:

- The type byte is new for C++ programmers. In C++, char is used for single-byte entities. But in the Java platform, characters are 16 bits and cannot do double duty as bytes. The Java type byte is specifically for the purpose of storing a single byte of information.
- The Java programming language has no keywords signed or unsigned. As a result, you have to take care if you are converting C++ code that uses the values of all the bits, including the bit in the position of the sign bit, or that uses unsigned integers for counters. Watch out for an upper limit that is effectively half of the largest value that can be assigned to an unsigned C++ integer of the same size.
- Unlike their C and C++ equivalents, short and long are complete type names. Do not use the forms short int or long int.

The Java programming language does not support bit fields. Instead, bit evaluation and manipulation is possible through bit-wise operators and masks if necessary.

Floating-point Types

The Java programming language has two floating-point types: float and double. The floating-point types have fixed sizes on all platforms, as shown in Figure 3-5.

Type	Number of Bits	Approximate Significant Decimal Digits
float	32	6 – 7 with a range of ±3.40282347E+38
double	64	15 with a range of ±1.79769313486231570E+308

Figure 3-5: Floating-point types

Floating-point storage conforms to the IEEE 754 standard. It provides distinct values for positive and negative zeros, positive and negative infinities, and a special value called NaN. POSITIVE_INFINITY represents a number that is too large to hold, even as a double, and can be the result of dividing a very large number by a very small number with the same sign. Similarly, NEGATIVE_INFINITY represents a negative number that exceeds the range of a double.

The NaN value is a very interesting constant because its value is "not a number." It can represent the result of a floating-point operation that would otherwise cause an error, such as dividing by zero or calculating the square root of a negative number.

Floating-point literals look exactly as they do in C++. They can contain a decimal point, an exponent, or both. The suffix letters f and F indicate type float, and the suffix letters d and D indicate type double. By default, numbers that contain a decimal point have type double. Figure 3-6 presents some floating-point literals.

float	double	float	double	double	float
67.925f	0.45	5.2e5F	6.73E-6	2.345d	-8.4126f

Figure 3-6: Example floating-point literals

Casting Primitive Types

The rules for casting are simple for the primitive types. You can cast from any type to a type that allows a greater range of values without specifying a cast operator. If you want to cast to a type that has a smaller range of values, you have to use a cast operator explicitly to indicate that you intended the cast to happen. Otherwise, the Java compiler flags a cast that might lose information as an error.

Implicit conversions from integer type to floating-point type are allowed, but the reverse requires an explicit cast. The Java programming language casts a byte to a short, a short to an int, an int to a long, and a float to a double automatically, as required. Any integral type can be cast to float or double without requiring a cast operator.

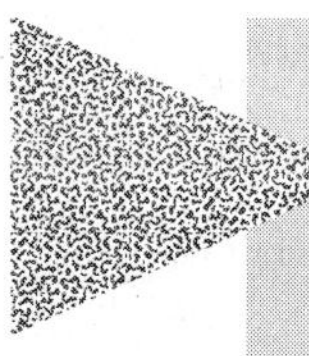

Mini Quiz 3-1

The statement short `x = 123;` compiles successfully. Why does the compiler reject the following statements?

```
int i = 123;
short x = i;
```

A cast in the Java programming language looks like the standard C++ cast notation. Do not use C++ constructor or function notation, as in the following example:

```
long BigNum = 9876543210L;
int aNum,bNum;
aNum = (int)BigNum;
bNum = int( BigNum );     // okay in C++, illegal in
                          // the Java programming language!
```

To make this example work, change the second cast from constructor notation to cast notation, as follows:

```
bNum = (int) BigNum;
```

The Java programming language has no equivalent of the static cast and dynamic cast notation recently introduced into C++:

```
static_cast < type > ( expression )
```

To pass arguments of methods, C++ can perform demotions as well as promotions. In other words, there are occasions when C++ performs implicit casts regardless of whether the range of values in the destination type is greater or smaller than the range of values in the source type. The Java programming language does not do this, so you have to be more careful not to pass a variable of a type with a greater range, such as float, to an argument of a type with a smaller range, such as int.

Object References

Variables of reference types reside in a very different part of storage from variables of primitive types. Variables of primitive types are local, or in C++ terminology, *automatic,* variables. They reside in the stack space for the method to which they belong. Storage for objects of reference types is allocated from the program heap. The **program heap** is that area of memory, also called dynamic memory, from which storage is allocated and freed, independently of the stack, as required during program execution. However, the object references, as distinct from the objects to which they refer, are added to the stack along with the objects of primitive types. In this sense, object references themselves are primitive values. The content of the object reference is the location of an object on the heap.

When used as arguments in method calls, the object references look and behave like C++ references. Object references are also like C++ references in that they are implemented as pointers behind the scenes. But object references are more like C++ pointers in that you can change an object reference to refer to a different object, which you cannot do with C++ references.

When you declare a pointer in C++ and then use the pointer to record the address of dynamically allocated memory, you are creating a situation very similar in the Java platform to that of declaring an object reference and the object to which it refers. The pointer is a local variable on the program stack. The value stored in the pointer is the address of an area in dynamic memory, which is another name for the program heap. The Java programming language gives you no methods to allocate or deallocate storage explicitly on the heap. The JVM manages dynamic memory for you.

Creating Objects of a Reference Type

To create an object of a reference type and to obtain a reference for the object, use the new keyword. The new keyword is very similar to the C++ new operator.

Syntax *ClassName ObjectReference* = **new** *ClassName*(*constructor_arguments*)

Dissection

- The *ClassName* specifies which class the object instantiates. On the left side of the assignment operator, it specifies the type of the object being created, as in any declaration.
- The *ObjectReference* is the identifier for the new variable.
- The expression new *Classname*( ) acquires space on the heap for the new object and calls the constructor of the class that the object instantiates. The constructor is a method that prepares the object for use, and can take arguments. The arguments are enclosed in the parentheses. The parentheses are always required, even if the constructor has no arguments.

Syntax	*ClassName ObjectReference;* *ObjectReference* = **new** *Classname*(*constructor_arguments*);
Dissection	■ You can create an object separately from declaring the object reference, by defining each in separate statements. After you declare an object reference, it has the value **null** until it is assigned an object reference returned by **new**.
Code Example	`SomeType x = new SomeType();`
Code Dissection	This statement creates an object of the `SomeType` class. No input arguments are required to build the object. The object reference for the object has the identifier `x`.

When the type of the object has as a constructor that has no arguments, the syntax is not exactly the same as calling new **in C++. In C++, you omit the parentheses. In the Java programming language, you must always include the parentheses.**

Chapter 9 gives another form for the new keyword that allows an inner class to be defined at the same time that an object of the inner class is created. Inner classes are an advanced programming technique.

Version Watch

Inner classes did not exist when the first version of the Java platform was released. Inner classes and the enhanced syntax of the new **keyword were introduced in version 1.1 of the Java platform.**

Assigning Values to Object References

You can use the assignment operator with object references. Be careful when you assign values to object references. Consider the following lines of code:

```
SomeType a = new SomeType();
SomeType b = new SomeType();
// omitted lines give a and b different contents
a = b;
```

The statement `a = b;` is valid, but is deceptive in its simplicity. This statement does not assign the contents of object `b` to object `a`. This statement assigns the value of the object reference `b` to the object reference `a`, creating a second reference for the object called `b`. Both `a` and `b` now refer to the object created in the second line of the example, and the object created in the first line has one less reference. The Java programming language provides a way to solve the problem of copying object references instead of objects, by introducing a method called clone. In the Java programming language, you clone an object to create an identical copy. Cloning is covered in Chapter 7.

You may be familiar with the problem of mistakenly of assigning pointers instead of the objects to which you intended to point. C++ programmers sometimes call such an assignment performing a *shallow copy.* It is analogous to the common pitfall of attempting to copy the values of strings by assigning pointers instead of calling the standard library function strcpy. There may be less scope for errors with object references in the Java programming language than with C++ pointers, but you should be just as careful when assigning values to object references as you are assigning values to C++ pointers.

Passing Object References as Arguments

When you pass objects of reference types as arguments to a method, you are really passing an object reference, not a copy of the object. This is like passing a pointer into a C++ function. Because object references themselves are primitive types, they are always passed by value. The method gets a copy of the object reference and can modify the copy without changing the original. At the same time, the called method can use the object reference to the object and can make changes to the storage allocated for the object. These changes are not undone when the method returns.

If an argument is qualified with the keyword final, the method cannot change the argument, which is effectively a constant for the duration of the method. What does this mean for reference types? Consider the following method taken from a class that provides some sort of address book objects:

```
public void addEntry( final NameNumber person ) {
    if ( numEntries < MAXENTRIES ) {
       phoneBook[numEntries++] = person;
       person.setIndex( numEntries );
    }
}
```

When an object reference is a final argument, the qualifier final applies to the object reference but not to the actual object. Therefore, you cannot change the object reference in the method. For example, this method cannot change the object reference `person` to refer to a different `NameNumber` object. But the method can modify the object `person` by calling a mutator method of the `NameNumber` class. A **mutator** method is one whose purpose is to set, or change, the contents of fields of a class. Here, the method `NameNumber.setIndex` may record the value of field `numEntries` in a private field of the `person` object. Note that the elements of in the array `phoneBook` are object references, and there is no problem assigning the value of the object reference `person` to one of them.

Deleting Objects of Reference Types

The JVM keeps track of how many object references refer to a particular object. When an object has no object references, your program can no longer access the object. This is correct behavior in a Java program; you are not expected, or even able, to delete objects of reference types explicitly. Instead, you rely on the system to clean up the heap occasionally and to remove all objects you are no longer using.

You can tell the JVM you are finished with an object, but you do not have to do even that. The way to sever the association between an object and an object reference is to assign another value to the object reference. To make an object reference refer to no object, assign the constant null.

Syntax *objectReference* = **null;**

Dissection

- A statement of this form says, "I am finished using the object to which this object reference refers, so I do not mind if the JVM discards the object."

You can also test any object reference to see if its value equals null. You usually do this to determine whether an object has been created, with a statement similar to the following:

```
if ( x == null ) {
   // x does not refer to an object
   // the statement: x.doit(); causes an exception
}
else {
   // x refers to an object that can be used
   // the statement: x.doit(); can run successfully
}
```

Moving from C++

The common C++ idiom of treating null **as** false **and other values as** true **does not work in the Java programming language. For example, if you code the previous** if **statement as follows, the Java compiler rejects the conditional expression:**

```
if ( x ) {  // null is not a boolean expression
         // x refers to an object that can be used
}
```

Collecting Garbage Automatically

A most welcome feature of the Java platform is that the JVM automatically cleans up the heap from time to time. Programmers using the Java platform do not have to keep track of all memory they allocate from the heap and explicitly deallocate it. A garbage collector sweeps through the list of objects periodically and reclaims the resources held by unreferenced objects.

What does garbage collection destroy? All objects that have no object references are eligible for garbage collection. These may be objects for which the references have gone out of scope and no longer exist on the stack, or objects for which you have assigned null. When the count of references for an object drops to zero, the object is eligible for garbage collection.

When does garbage collection occur? This question is hard to answer because the JVM decides when to start the garbage collector. Typically the garbage collector runs only when available memory is becoming low. It may never run at all if your program makes modest demands on memory. The best approach is not to build into your code any dependence on the timing of garbage collection.

You cannot prevent the garbage collector from running, but you can request it to run.

Class	**void java.lang.System**
Purpose	The **System** class provides a number of useful methods. Some are API for the Java platform.
Methods	■ **void gc()** Call the **gc** method to request that the JVM schedule the garbage collector to run soon.

Deliberately starting garbage collection may be appropriate if you can anticipate that the garbage collector is likely to run soon, and your program is at a point where the impact of running the garbage collector is minimal. The use of this method does not force the garbage collector to run; it is only a request.

You have much less control over the heap in the Java programming language than in C++. There is no other way you can use dynamic memory than by creating instances of classes. You cannot put instances of classes anywhere other than in the heap, because the language gives you no other way to create instances of classes than to use new. **The Java programming language has no** delete **operator, so the removing of objects from dynamic memory cannot be brought under program control. You must leave the task of managing memory to the JVM. Unlike a C++ execution environment, the JVM can monitor the status of all objects that your program stores in memory and can automatically delete objects that you can no longer access.**

You can look at this two ways: You have less control over the allocation and deallocation of memory during program execution, but you have less work to do to make sure memory is used properly. One advantage of the Java programming language's approach is that it is less error-prone. You cannot create memory leaks by forgetting to delete objects, or create dangling pointers by deleting objects too early. Because you cannot operate on object references except by performing certain forms of assignment, you have far less scope for creating the wild pointers that can give programs unexpected or unpredictable behavior. Another advantage of the Java programming language's approach is that it makes coding simpler.

The reduction of control and absence of language features could be considered limitations. Garbage collection can affect performance. On the other hand, the JVM performs garbage collection only when it perceives that the heap is close to full or when you explicitly request garbage collection.

Generally, the reasons for explicitly programming the allocation and deallocation of dynamic memory are far less compelling in the Java platform than in C++.

The Object Class

The Object class is the common ancestor class of all classes you can have in a Java program. The name of the class might not be very creative, but it reflects the fact that Object is a superclass of all classes. All variables of reference type are instances of Object, including arrays. Every method of Object is inherited, directly or indirectly, by all other classes. This means that the Object class provides a set of methods that all objects have. Because it is the root of the entire class hierarchy, Object is a common denominator for all objects.

C++ does not have a common base class analogous to Object. In the Java programming language, all classes belong to one inheritance hierarchy with a single root, the Object class. The classes in C++ programs can belong to unrelated inheritance hierarchies. One C++ program may have many hierarchies of different sizes.

The methods in the Object class provide a convenient and standard interface that helps clients of a class work with objects of that class. When you create a new class, you often provide customized definitions of some of these methods so that your class supports a standard set of behaviors in a way that is meaningful for objects of the class.

Class	java.lang.Object
Purpose	The **Object** class is the direct or indirect superclass of all Java classes. All classes can inherit the methods of this class or provide their own implementations. This book refers to the implementations provided by **Object** as default implementations.
Methods	■ **Object clone()** The **clone** method returns a copy of the object for which the method is called. The value of every field is duplicated, regardless of whether the field has a primitive type or is an object reference. The object referred to by a contained object reference is not duplicated. ■ **boolean equals(Object)** The **equals** method returns **true** if two objects are considered equal, and **false** otherwise. The default implementation compares just the object references, and is equivalent to a conditional expression such as `( a == b )`, where `a` and `b` are references for the objects in question. In other words, the base **equals** method returns **true** only when you compare two references for the same object. ■ **void finalize()** The garbage collector calls the **finalize** method before destroying the object. By default, the method does nothing, but you can provide implementations to perform specialized cleanup. ■ **Class getClass()** **getClass** returns an object that can be used to obtain run-time type information about an object.

- **int hashCode()**
  The **hashCode** method returns an integer suitable for determining the hash code for object. Hash codes are used to locate the entries for objects in hash tables. The JVM uses hash tables extensively as a data structure for random access to objects.

- **void notify()**
  void notifyAll()
  void wait()
  You can use **notify**, **notifyAll**, and **wait** in a multithreaded program to perform interthread communication. Signaling and synchronization between threads are essential to ensure that there are no timing or other conflicts when different threads share objects.

- **String toString()**
  The **toString** method returns a printable representation of the object. The **System.out.println** method can output strings and the primitive types. When **println** encounters an object that it does not understand, it calls **toString** and outputs the returned value. The default implementation of this method does not do much; it returns a character string that is the hexadecimal representation of the reference for the object.

You write some of these methods for your own classes for the same reason that you overload some of the standard operators in C++:

- **Implementing** toString **is analogous to overriding the output operator << in C++ so you can output a readable representation of your object.**
- **Implementing** equals **is analogous to overloading the equality operator == in C++.**
- **Implementing** clone **is analogous to implementing a copy constructor in C++.**

Wrapper Classes for Primitive Types

In the object-oriented sense, all variables of the primitive types and reference types are objects, with a lower case *o*. Reference types are also Objects, with a capital O, because they belong to a class that inherits from Object. Being an Object has many advantages. Is there a way to extend the advantages of being an Object to the primitive types? To fill this obvious need, the Java platform includes wrapper classes for all of the primitive types. A **wrapper class** is essentially a class that provides different behavior for a type than the behavior established by the definition of that type. In other words, a wrapper class gives you another way of using the object it wraps. For example, a wrapper for an integer can contain an integer and define methods that are useful for working on integral values.

Wrapper classes encapsulate the primitive types in a class, so that reference semantics apply. Figure 3-7 lists the wrapper classes and their primitive types.

Wrapper Class	Primitive Type
Boolean	boolean
Byte	byte
Character	char
Double	double
Float	float
Integer	int
Long	long
Short	short

Figure 3-7: Wrapper classes

The names of the wrapper classes start with an uppercase letter. Except for Integer and Character, the capitalization is all that distinguishes the wrapper class names from the primitive types.

Version Watch

The original version of the Java platform did not include wrapper classes for the primitive types byte **and** short. **Version 1.1 of the Java platform introduced the classes** Byte **and** Short.

The classes Byte, Double, Float, Integer, Long, and Short derive from a common class called Number, so you can manipulate objects of these types at a more general level. For example, you can call the method byteValue to get the value of the number converted to a single byte. In some cases, the value must be rounded or truncated to fit in one byte, but this method is available for all Number objects.

The Java platform includes constants and utility methods related to the primitive types in the appropriate wrapper class. For example, the Integer class contains the constants Integer.MAX_VALUE and Integer.MIN_VALUE. The Character class defines the methods Character.isDigit and Character.isSpace. By placing these handy constants and methods in the most appropriate wrapper class, the Java platform makes them much easier to locate than they would be if they were all members of some generic utility class. Like the methods in the Math class, these constants and methods are always available, regardless of whether any wrapper classes objects have been created. For example, the following code makes sure no information is lost before casting a long to an int:

```
long l;
int i = 0;
// assign value to l
if ( l <= Integer.MAX_VALUE &&  l >= Integer.MIN_VALUE ) {
   i = (int) l;
}
```

All these wrapper classes directly or indirectly inherit from Object. Therefore, standard methods such as toString, clone, and equals are available. This inheritance is particularly useful when you want to create generic collections of objects. The wrapper classes can participate in such collections, but the primitive types cannot. Chapter 9 describes the collection classes that the Java platform provides.

Unfortunately, the wrapper classes are all immutable. They do not provide mutator methods that allow the programmer to change their values. For example, passing variables of type Integer rather than int does not result in integer input-output method arguments.

Mini Quiz 3-2

What happens when you write and run a swap method such as the following?

```
void swap( Integer a, Integer b ) {
   Integer temp = new Integer ( a.intValue() );
   a = b;
   b = temp;
}
```

You cannot define any classes that inherit from the wrapper classes, because the wrapper classes are declared to be final. In the Java programming language, you can mark a class with the keyword final so that no one can use it as the equivalent of a base class. The creators of the Java programming language clearly thought it best to prevent you from, for example, creating your own kind of number that inherits all the attributes of class Integer and has some special qualities. They imposed this restriction not to create awkwardness, but to enhance security and performance.

Arrays

Arrays are objects of reference type. They can contain a fixed number of elements of any one type. An individual element is identified by the object reference for the array followed by an integral index value enclosed in square brackets, [and]. The individual elements can be used like individual variables. For example, the following statement assigns the value 5 to the third element in an array named a:

```
a[2] = 5;
```

An array variable is really an object reference for the array object. Therefore, only the object reference is on the program stack; the array itself is placed on the heap. This scheme has a slight disadvantage because you lose a little bit of performance compared to storing array elements on the stack.

Moving from C++

Java arrays are very different from C++ arrays. In C++, arrays are really just sets of variables of the same type that are placed in contiguous locations in storage. In C++, accessing elements using index notation is a shorthand for calculating the offset from the first element in the array and performing pointer arithmetic. In C++, you can manipulate the elements, but there is not much you can do with entire arrays.

The syntax of arrays in the Java programming language looks similar to that of C++ arrays, in that the square brackets enclose the index of an element. The big difference is that Java arrays are real objects. As a result, the only way to access an individual element in an array is to use the index notation. The identifier for the array is an object reference for the array as a whole. An advantage is that you can manipulate arrays as a whole.

Object references for array objects are defined quite similarly to other reference types.

Syntax

type[ ] *identifier*;
type identifier[ ];

Dissection

- The two forms are equivalent, but the first is preferable because it gives the full type information first. The second form more closely resembles C++.
- Use the square bracket syntax to declare the object reference, but do not specify a size because size is not part of the array type.

Code Example

```
int[] a;
int a[];
```

Code Dissection

The variable a is an object reference to an array of **int**.

An object reference is not useful on its own, so you must also create the actual array. As with all reference types, you use the new keyword to create an array.

Syntax

type [ ] *identifier* = **new** *type* [*size*];

Dissection

- As with all reference types, you can declare the reference and create the object in one statement or two.

Code Example

```
a = new int[5];
int[] x = new int[5];
```

Code Dissection

In the first statement the existing object reference a is assigned the new array object. In the second statement the variable x is defined to be an object reference for the new array of integers.

You cannot specify a negative size. If you do, a run-time exception of the type java.lang.NegativeArraySizeException is raised. You can create an array with size zero. However, you can use a zero-length array only as a placeholder because you cannot put anything into it!

After the array has been created, you cannot extend it. For example, an array of five integers is always going to be five integers, and you cannot make it hold six or more integers. However, you can use an integer expression for the size of the array, and calculate how many elements to allow at run time. You can also change the object reference to point to a different array. The following two lines of code create two arrays. The first has five elements and the second 10. But the net effect is to replace the five-element array with a 10-element array and continue to use the object reference a.

```
int[] a = new int[5];
a = new int[10];
```

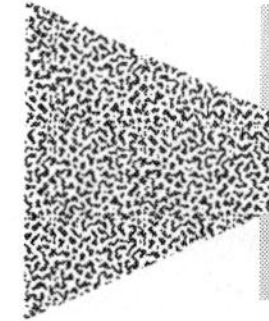

Mini Quiz 3-3

If no other object references refer to the array of five elements in the two previous lines, can you use the array again in your program? If yes, how? If no, what can happen to it?

You can initialize an array when you declare it.

Syntax *type*[] *identifier* = { *initializer_list* };

Dissection

- If you create arrays with objects that already exist, you do not have to use the **new** keyword. Just put the objects in an *initializer_list*. Elements in the list are separated by commas and the list is enclosed in braces.

Code Example

```
double[] x = { 5.67, 4.59, 0.0005, -23455.6 };
String[] light = { "sun", "moon" };
long[] places = { 10, 10*10, (long)Math.pow( 10.0,3.0 )}; };
```

Code Dissection The syntax works for numeric and string literals and arbitrary expressions.

An **anonymous array** is an array object that has no name. This form can be useful when you want to give a new value to an existing object reference. Anonymous arrays are also a handy way to pass an array of known values into a method without creating the array and giving it a name, when you have no other use for the array.

The second of the following lines creates an anonymous array; the right side of the second statement initializes the array:

```
double[] x = { 1.1, 1.2, 1.3, 1.4 }; // initial value
x =  new double[] { 0.1, 0.2, 0.3, 0.4 }; // assign a
                                          // different value
```

Version Watch

When the Java platform was first released, programmers could initialize an array only in the statement that defined it. The ability to use a list of values enclosed in braces to change an object reference became available in version 1.1 at the same time that the platform introduced the anonymous array.

Array Indexes and Lengths

The indexing for arrays is zero-based. **Zero-based indexing** means the first element is at zero. Index values go up in steps of one so that the index of the last element equals the size of the array minus one. In the Java platform, every time you use an array index, it is checked against the array bounds at run time. This safety and security feature prevents you from using the array to access memory outside the storage reserved for the array.

Version Watch

In C++ programs, a common error that can be very hard to debug is that of exceeding array bounds. You can code such an error into a Java program, but in most cases can easily avoid doing so by using a field of the array object that stores the number of elements in the array. The worst-case scenario in the Java platform is far more acceptable than the worst case in C++. The JVM creates an IndexOutOfBoundsException **that halts your program if you use an impossible index. A C++ program may continue to run, and even produce wrong results that give no indication that something has gone wrong.**

You can easily find out the size of the array. Every array stores its size as read-only data in a field called length.

Syntax	*arrayName*.**length**
Dissection	■ You can get size of an array at any time. The field **length** is public, and has type **int**. Because **length** is a field rather than a method, do not follow it with parentheses.

Code Example	`int[] myArray = { 5, 6, 99, -45, 0 };`
	`for( int j=0; j < myArray.length; j++ ) {`
	`   System.out.println( myArray[j] );`
	`}`

Code Output	5 6 99 -45 0
Code Dissection	In these lines, the value of the expression `myArray.length` is 5.

The following class is called **`ArrayTypes`**. It is a public class, and therefore must be in a file called ArrayTypes.java. The structure of packages mirrors the file system, so you will call this source code in the java4cpp\basic subfolder of the folder in which you unpacked the JAR file java4cpp.jar. The class has only one method, the main method, in which it creates, and then works with, two arrays.

```
package java4cpp.basic;
/** A class demonstrating the use of arrays
  */
public class ArrayTypes {
   /** A method that creates and manipulates two integer
     * arrays
     * @param args Not used
     */
   public static void main( String[] args ) {
      int[] a, b;
      a = new int[3];
      b = new int[3];
      for ( int i = 0; i < a.length; i++ ) {
         a[i] = i * i;
         System.out.println( i + " squared is "
                              + a[i] );
      }
      for ( int i = 0; i < b.length; i++ ) {
         b[i] = i * i * i;
         System.out.println( i + " cubed is " + b[i] );
      }
   }
}
```

The output is

```
0 squared is 0
1 squared is 1
2 squared is 4
0 cubed is 0
1 cubed is 1
2 cubed is 8
```

Mini Quiz 3-4

Why is there no problem declaring `i` twice in this example?

Returning an Array from a Method

The return type of a method can have array type.

Syntax *type* **[ ]** *methodName***(** *arguments* **) { }**

Dissection

- The square brackets following the return type indicate that the method returns an object reference for an array.
- No size is specified for the array. Size is not part of the type. It does not matter whether the array contains five elements or a thousand. However, it is important to give the type for the elements in the array.

Code Example

```
package java4cpp.basic;
/** A method demonstrating how arrays can be a
  * return type
  */
public class ArrayReturn {
   /** A method that returns an array object
     * @param flag A boolean value for which
     *              array to return
     * @returns An integer array object
     */
   public int[] returnsArray( boolean flag ) {
      int[] array1 = { 1, 2, 3, 4, 5, 6, 7, 8, 9, 10 };
      int[] array2 = { 10, 20, 30, 40, 50 };
      if ( flag ) {
         return array1;
      } else {
         return array2;
      }
   }
   /** The test method for the class
     * @param args Not used
     */
   public static void main( String[] args ) {
      ArrayReturn x = new ArrayReturn();
      System.out.println( x.returnsArray( true ).length );
      System.out.println( x.returnsArray( false ).length );
   }
}
```

Code Output

```
10
5
```

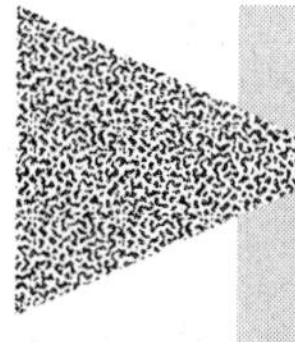

Mini Quiz 3-5

This ArrayReturn program demonstrates a number of Java programming language features. Use it to test your understanding of several topics covered so far:

- Where is the storage for `array1` and `array2` allocated in `returnsArray`?
- Are the boolean expressions true and false passed to `returnsArray` by value or by reference?
- What is the type of `x`?
- What is the type of `x.returnsArray`?
- What does the notation /**, @param, and @returns mean?

Copying Arrays

Because arrays are reference types, you cannot copy the contents of one array into another with the assignment operator. Use the utility method **arraycopy**, which is provided by the **System** class in the package java.lang.

Class	**java.lang.System**
Purpose	The **System** class provides a number of useful methods and objects.
Methods	■ **void arraycopy(Object** *source*, **int** *SourcePos*, **Object** *destination*, **int** *destinationPos*, **int** *number***)** The **arraycopy** method copies the specified number of elements from the source array to the destination array. Specify the first position in the source array from which to take an element, the position in the destination array in which to put that element, and the number of elements.

The arraycopy method copies the specified number of elements from the source array to the destination array. Specify the first position in the source array from which to take an element, the position in the destination array in which to put that element, and the number of elements.

The following class uses the arraycopy method:

```
package java4cpp.basic
/** class to demonstrate method arraycopy
  */
public class MergeArrays {
   public static void main( String[] args ) {
      int[] x = { 5, 4, 0, -2, 53, -3 };
      int[] y = { 100, 101 };
      for( int i = 0; i < x.length; i++ ) {
         System.out.print( " " + x[i] );
      }
      System.out.println();
      System.arraycopy( y, 0, x, 3, y.length );
```

```
        for( int i = 0; i < x.length; i++ ) {
           System.out.print( " " + x[i] );
        }
        System.out.println();
    }
}
```

The output is

```
5 4 0 -2 53 -3
5 4 0 100 101 -3
```

The arraycopy method has some useful features. You can use it to copy a whole array, or just a part of an array. You can even specify source and destination areas that overlap in the same array. Therefore, you can use this method to shift contents within an array. However, you cannot use arraycopy to create a new array. It does not allocate memory. The method fails if the source and destination arrays do not already exist or do not have enough space to perform the copy.

If the elements in the array are object references, the object references are copied, not the referenced objects.

For a different reason, C++ programmers also cannot use the assignment operator to copy a whole array. A common technique in C++ is to program loops that explicitly copy the elements from one array to another, one at a time. An alternative method is to call a library function such as memcpy **to operate on the byte storage occupied by the array. The Java method** System.arraycopy **is analogous to** memcpy**, but more intuitive, and simpler than programming loops.**

Using Multidimensional Arrays

Arrays can be multidimensional. If an array is two-dimensional, it is an array of arrays. Two-dimensional arrays do not have to be rectangular; in other words, the individual inner arrays can have different lengths. When using the length field of a multidimensional array it is important to note that it refers to the length of the first dimension and is not a product of all the dimensions. The Java programming language puts no limit to the number of dimensions that an array must have. The only limit is your ability to visualize the complex data structures that you are creating!

Syntax	**type[][] identifier;**
Dissection	■ The index for each array dimension has its own set of square brackets.

You may find it helpful to visualize the first index as rows and the second as columns in a two-dimensional table. If there is a third index, you can visualize it as depth in a three-dimensional table, and so on. Regardless of how you visualize them, arrays of all dimensions occupy linear areas of storage and you should not be concerned with the placement of individual elements relative to each other.

The example in Figure 3-8 demonstrates a variety of two-dimensional arrays. The array named c is rectangular, two by four, but arrays b and d are jagged in the sense that if you drew a diagram of them, they would look uneven, as Figure 3-8 indicates.

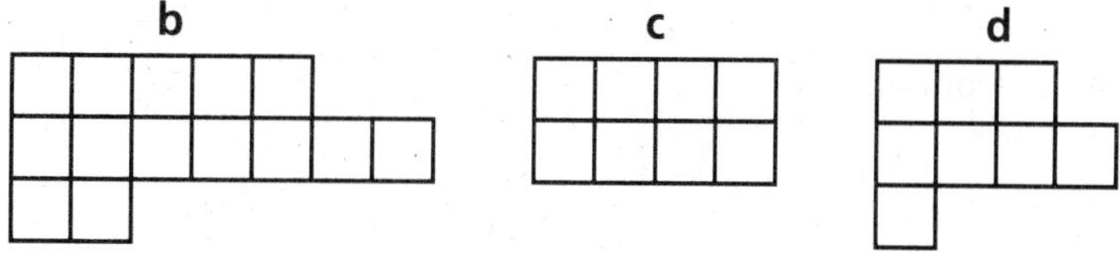

Figure 3-8: Two-dimensional arrays

Because two-dimensional arrays are really just arrays of arrays, accessing an element of a two-dimensional array is twice as expensive as accessing an element of a one-dimensional array. The cost increases proportionally as you add more dimensions. Think twice before using a two-dimensional array. If you can visualize the data structure in some other way than as rows and columns of data, you may be able to use one of the collection classes that are described in Chapter 9 or simplify the data structure enough to use a one-dimensional array.

In the following example, array d contains some integers and is set up by the initializer list. The array d is an array of three arrays. The braces in the declaration of d group the numbers into the three arrays that make up d, and open and close the initializer lists for the three arrays.

Here is an example showing different ways of creating multidimensional arrays:

```
package java4cpp.basic;
/** A class to demonstrate the initialization and
  * use of multidimensional arrays
  */
public class MultDimArrayTypes {
   /** The test method of the class
     * @param args Not used
     */
   public static void main( String[] args ) {
      int[][] b;
      b = new int[3][];
      b[0] = new int[5];
      b[1] = new int[7];
      b[2] = new int[2];
      b[0][4] = 1256;
      int[][] c = new int [2][4];
      c[0][1] = -6754;
```

```
        int[][] d = { { -5,-6,8 }, { -2,11,3456,5 }, { 7 } };
        System.out.println( "b[0][4]=" + b[0][4] +
           " c[0][1]=" + c[0][1] + " d[1][3]=" + d[1][3] );
    }
}
```

The output is

```
b[0][4]=1256 c[0][1]=-6754 d[1][3]=5
```

Note that this example creates d without using the new keyword.

The example uses only integers, but all types work equally well. When you create arrays of reference types, the elements of the arrays actually are references for objects, and each one is initialized to the value null. This is like creating a C++ array of pointers. Because int is a primitive type, the arrays in the example actually contain integer values. If the elements are object references, you must give them values before using them. If you use a null object reference, an exception occurs.

Strings

The Java platform provides two classes for strings in the standard language package, java.lang. The two classes are String and StringBuffer. Therefore, strings are objects of predefined reference types. The String class is the main class for strings. You can use a StringBuffer when you are working within a string. For example, when you are modifying the contents of a string, the StringBuffer class may provide more flexibility than the String class.

String objects are immutable. You cannot change the contents of a string or change its size after storage has been allocated. However, you can concatenate Strings. The JVM implements the string concatenation operators, + and +=, by using StringBuffer objects behind the scenes, so that there is no performance or size penalty in using these operators on String objects.

In most C++ programs, strings are just arrays of characters terminated with a null character. Programming string manipulation in C++ in this way is notoriously awkward. Many C++ class libraries provide a class for strings, but such libraries are proprietary software and most suppliers implement strings differently. The recently published ISO/ANSI standard for the C++ language includes a string class in a standard library. However, few C++ programmers have access to this class yet, and most C++ programmers must find their own solution for handling strings.

In the Java programming language, you should create objects of the String class for strings. If your C++ solution has been to use arrays of type char, you lose the ability to access individual characters in a string directly using array notation. However you gain a standard and generally easier way to manipulate string data. The String class does have a method, charAt, that allows you to access a single character at a specified index.

Working with String Objects

The Java programming language provides a convenient way to create **String** objects.

Syntax

String *identifier* = *"literal string";*
String *identifier* = **new String (** *arguments_ of _constructor* **);**

Dissection

- The object reference for the string is defined and refers to the **String** object constructed to represent the string literal. String literals are enclosed in double quotation marks. Two consecutive double quote characters, "", is a valid string and represents an empty string.
- You can also create **String** objects using the **new** operator and any of the constructors of the **String** class.

Code Example

```
String name = "Joe";
String name = new String( "Joe" );
```

Code Dissection

These two statements are equivalent. The first form is more common because it is simpler.

Many classes provide a method toString that returns a string representation of the information in the class. A very common way to obtain a String object is to call toString or another method that returns an object reference for a String.

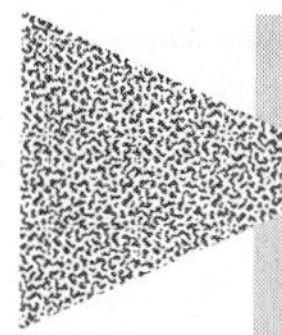

Mini Quiz 3-6

How many objects and object references does the following declaration create? Where are they stored?

```
String[] seasons = { "winter",
                     "spring",
                     "summer",
                     "fall" };
```

Although the declaration of a String **in the Java programming language can look exactly like the declaration of an array of type** char **in C++, Java strings are not arrays. Never use array notation. For example, the following C++ declaration is not valid in the Java programming language:**

```
char name[] = "Joe"; // ERROR, okay in C++
```

To create the equivalent array of characters in the Java programming language, use the following:

```
char[] name = { 'J', 'o', 'e' };
```

All characters in Java strings are stored in Unicode. In C++, the characters have type char **or** wchar_t**, and you can append the letters** L **or** l **to a string literal to indicate the latter type. Do not supply a suffix to Java string literals.**

To access the character at a particular position, use the charAt method of the String class:

```
String jabberwock = "Jabberwock";
char c = jabberwock.charAt(6);      // assigns 'w' to c
```

Use the + or += operators to concatenate strings, as you have already been doing to build up the output line in many code examples. How can these operators work when String objects are immutable? The effect of these operators can be deceptive. Consider the following line:

```
jabberwock += "y";
System.out.println( jabberwock );    // the output is:
                                     // jabberwocky
```

No String objects are changed when the first statement is executed. Instead, a new string is built, the contents of which are the result of concatenating two string objects. The reference `jabberwock` is associated with the new string. The string previously referenced by `jabberwock` has one less object reference, and may have just become a candidate for garbage collection.

If you want to know the length of a string, call the method length. For strings, length is a method. For arrays, length is a field. Therefore, the syntax for determining the number of characters in a string is not consistent with the syntax for determining the number of elements in an array. Notice the difference in these two statements:

```
if ( monthName.length() > 12 )
   { /* the string has more than 12 characters */ }
if ( days.length > 31 )
   { /* the array has more than 31 elements */ }
```

To compare String objects, use the equals method, not the == operator. The == operator just tells you whether the object references are the same.

```
if ( monthName.equals( "January" ) )
   { /* the contents of monthName is "January" */ }
```

If your String objects contain characters other than those used in U.S. English, you may find that equalsIgnoreCase does not work as expected. Different languages and character sets can have different rules for mapping between uppercase and lowercase characters. Locale objects capture national characteristics, and Collator objects apply the rules for comparing strings. The Locale and Collator classes are described in Chapter 16, as part of the discussion of programming for different cultural environments.

The following example demonstrates the difference between the equals method and the ==, or equality, operator:

```
package java4cpp.basic;
/** A class to demonstrate how to define and
  * use String objects
  */
public class StringCompare {
   /** The test method for the class
     * @param args Not used
     */
   public static void main( String[] args ) {
      String s1 = new String( "Hello" );
      String s2 = new String( "Hello" );
      System.out.println( "Comparing references yields "
                          + ( s1 == s2 ) );
      System.out.println( "Comparing using equals() yields "
                          + s1.equals( s2 ) );
   }
}
```

The output is

```
Comparing references yields false
Comparing using equals() yields true
```

If the declarations read `String s1="Hello"` and `String s2="Hello"`, comparing object references would have also yielded true. The JVM stores literal strings in a separate pool and does not make duplicates. Therefore, both references `s1` and `s2` refer to the same object: the string literal object "Hello".

Class	**java.lang.String**
Purpose	The **String** class provides many methods for string manipulation. Only the most frequently used are listed here.
Constructors	■ **String()** **String(String** *s* **)** **String(StringBuffer** *sb* **)** **String(byte[]** *b* **)** **String(char[]** *c* **)** The constructors create **String** objects. You can supply many types of input, not all of which are listed here. The constructor with no arguments creates an empty string. The **String** class is unique in that the JVM creates **String** objects also from statements of the following form: **String** *`identifier = literal_string;`*
Methods	■ **char charAt(int** *position* **)** The **charAt** method returns the character located at the specified position in the string.

- **int compareTo(String** *s* **)**
  Use **compareTo** compare **String** objects. It returns a negative number if the string for which you called the method comes before the contents of the argument in alphabetic order, zero if both strings are the same, or a positive number if the argument string comes first. This method mimics the behavior of the C function **strcmp**.

- **String concat(String** *s* **)**
  Use **concat** to concatenate the specified **String** object *s* to the string for which you called the method. The method returns the resulting string.

- **boolean equals(Object** *o* **)**
  The **equals** method tests for equality. It returns **true** if the object is a string that has the same length and contains the same characters as the string for which the method is called, and **false** otherwise.

- **boolean equalsIgnoreCase(Object** *o* **)**
  This method is like **equals**, except that the comparison of characters treats uppercase and lowercase versions of the same character as matching.

- **int indexOf(int** *character* **)**
  int indexOf(int *character*, **int** *position* **)**
  int indexOf(String *s* **)**
  int indexOf(String *s*, **int** *position* **)**
  Call **indexOf** to locate the first occurrence of the specified character or **String** in the string for which you are calling the method. The method returns zero if no match is found. Note that the argument for a character has type **int**. If you supply a second argument of type **int**, it specifies the start position of the search.

- **int lastIndexOf(int** *character* **)**
  int lastIndexOf(int *character*, **int** *position* **)**
  int lastIndexOf(String *s* **)**
  int lastIndexOf(String *s*, **int** *position* **)**
  This method is like **indexOf**, except that it returns the position of the last occurrence of a character or **String**.

- **int length()**
  The **length** method returns the number of characters in the string.

- **String substring(int** *start* **)**
  String substring(int *start*, **int** *end* **)**
  Use **substring** to extract a **String** from a larger string. The first **int** argument is the position of the first character to extract. The optional second **int** argument is not the position of the last character to extract, but the position following the last character to extract. The next sample program uses this method.

- **String toLowerCase()**
  This method returns a **String** identical to the string for which the method is called, except that all alphabetic characters are forced to lowercase.
- **String toString()**
  This method returns a **String** identical to the string for which the method is called.
- **String toUpperCase()**
  This method returns a **String** identical to the string for which the method is called, except that all alphabetic characters are forced to uppercase.
- **String trim()**
  This method returns a **String** identical to the string for which the method is called, except that it removes all leading and trailing whitespace characters.

Here is an example that uses the substring method:

```
package java4cpp.basic;
/** A class to demonstrate how to use String.substring
  * method
  */
public class SubstringExample {
   /** The test method for the class
     * @param args Not used
     */
   public static void main( String[] args ) {
      String s1 = new String( "The quick brown fox" );
      String s2 = s1.substring( 4, 8 );
      String s3 = s1.substring( 4, 9 );
      System.out.println( "The second word is " + s2 );
      System.out.println( "The second word is " + s3 );
   }
}
```

The output is

```
The second word is quic
The second word is quick
```

Unlike the standard C function substr, **the second argument of** substring **is a character position and not the number of characters to include in the substring.**

Working with StringBuffer Objects

String and StringBuffer are independent classes and are unrelated by inheritance, except that both directly extend the Object class. It is interesting to note that neither of these classes derives from the other, and they have no common methods or fields except the methods that every class inherits from Object. Use the StringBuffer class if you have a string that must change dynamically, and use String in most other circumstances. You can think of the StringBuffer class as the working space for manipulating the characters, and the String class as the place where the final result is put and used.

The methods defined by String and StringBuffer classes give a good indication of how you should use each class. For example, the equals method of the String class is very useful because it overrides the default equals method to compare the contents of Strings. However, StringBuffer uses the default equals method, so equals tests the references rather than the contents of StringBuffer objects.

Class	**java.lang.StringBuffer**
Purpose	The **StringBuffer** class has methods for modifying strings.
Constructors	■ **StringBuffer()** **StringBuffer(int** *size* **)** **StringBuffer(String** *s* **)** If you do not supply an argument to the **StringBuffer** constructor, it creates an empty **StringBuffer** with the capacity for 16 characters. Alternatively, you can specify an initial capacity or string.
Methods	■ **StringBuffer append(String** *s* **)** **StringBuffer append(Object** *o* **)** The **append** method appends a **String** or string representation of an object to the **StringBuffer**, and returns a reference to the modified **StringBuffer**. ■ **StringBuffer insert(int** *position*, **char[]** *characters* **)** **StringBuffer insert(int** *position*, **Object** *o* **)** The **insert** method inserts characters or the string representation of an object into a **StringBuffer** at the specified position. It returns a reference to the modified **StringBuffer**. ■ **void setCharAt(int** *position*, **char** *character* **)** You can replace the character in a **StringBuffer** at the specified position with the character that you specify. ■ **int capacity()** The capacity method specifies the number of characters the **StringBuffer** can hold. The returned value may be more than the number of characters currently stored in the **StringBuffer** object. ■ **void setLength(int** *size* **)** Call this method to truncate or pad the contents of the **StringBuffer** to the number of characters specified in the argument.

■ **int length()**
The **length** method returns the number of characters in the **StringBuffer**.

The String class has a constructor that creates a String from a StringBuffer. A StringBuffer constructor creates a StringBuffer with the same contents as a String. In short, it is easy to convert between String and StringBuffer classes.

Performance ▶ tip

If you are going to append frequently to build up a string in a StringBuffer object, you can increase efficiency by setting an initial size large enough to hold the maximum number of characters expected in the string.

SUMMARY

The Java programming language has primitive types and reference types.

The primitive types are boolean, char, byte, short, int, long, float, and double. The Java platform defines the way that the JVM stores these types, which is independent of the target architecture. This architecture neutrality is a portability feature.

- A boolean can have the value true or false only. The Java programming language does not treat zero or nonzero integral expressions as boolean values, and a boolean is not a numeric type.
- Characters are stored in two-byte Unicode. Character arrays are not strings. Use byte, not char, for single-byte integers.
- The values of variables of types byte and short are cast to int for arithmetic calculations. The advantage of byte and short variables is that they require less memory than int variables. All integer types always hold signed values.
- Casting from one numeric type to another numeric type with a greater range of values is automatic, as required. If the cast converts to a numeric type with a narrower range of values, you must code the cast explicitly.

Arrays, classes, and interfaces are reference types.

- Every object of a reference type has one or more object references. The Java platform allocates storage for the actual object on the heap and maintains a separate local entity, the object reference, to access the object. In your code, you must use the object reference to access the object.
- Use the new keyword to create a variable of a reference type. Always include parentheses, as in the following example:

  ```
  className objectName = new className();
  ```

- You do not have to deallocate storage when you are finished with a variable for a reference type. The Java platform automatically keeps track of object references and knows when an object cannot be used because it has no more object references. Periodically, the JVM automatically performs garbage collection. Garbage collection destroys unreferenced objects so that the storage allocated to them can be reused.

- The Java platform defines a class Object to be the common ancestor for all the reference types. The methods of Object are available to all classes and provide a standard way to work with objects. These methods include clone, equals, and toString.

The Java platform defines wrapper classes for the primitive types. The wrappers are reference-type equivalents of the primitive types. They also provide a number of useful methods and fields, such as Character.isDigit and Integer.MAX_VALUE.

Arrays are variables of reference type. This is very different from C++, where arrays are little more than a notation for pointers to adjacent variables of the same type. You can use the new keyword when you create an array, or when you let an initializer determine the size of the array, as in the following example:

```
int[] x = new int[5];
int[] y = { 3, 5, 8, 13, 21 };
```

A method can return an object reference for an array. You can copy an array as one object by calling the method System.arraycopy, and you can use the length field of an array to determine its size. The Java programming language allows multidimensional arrays.

String is a class for strings. It provides a number of useful methods, such as charAt, equals, substring, indexOf, and compare. The built-in operators + and += perform string concatenation. String objects are immutable; any operation on a String object that seems to be changing the object's value actually creates another String object, which becomes the result of the operation.

If you are composing a string from several other strings, or need to change a string dynamically, you can also use the StringBuffer class.

QUESTIONS

1. Which of the following C++ constructs does the Java programming language support? Select all that apply.
   a. struct
   b. class
   c. union
   d. enum
2. What is the range of values that a short can represent?
   a. 0 to 256
   b. –127 to 128
   c. -2^{15} to $(2^{15}-1)$
   d. 0 to 2^{16}

3. Examine the following code:

```
public class Quiz3_1 {
   public static void main( String[] args ) {
      float x = 2.345;
      double y = 3.14;
      short a = 2;
      short b = 3;
      short c = a * b;
      System.out.println( x );
      System.out.println( a + b + c );
   }
}
```

Which of the following statements are true? Select all that apply.

a. Compilation is successful and the output from running the code is

```
2.345
11
```

b. Compilation is successful and the output from running the code is

```
2.345
236
```

c. The compiler rejects the expression `float x = 2.345;` because of incompatible types.

d. The compiler rejects the expression `short c = a * b;` because of incompatible types.

4. Examine the following code:

```
public class Quiz3_2 {
   public static void main( String[] args ) {
      String a = "Hello ";
      String b = "World!";
      f( a, b );
      System.out.println( a );
   }
   public static void f( String x, String y ) {
      x += y;
   }
}
```

Which one of the following statements correctly describes the behavior when this program is compiled and run?

a. Compilation is successful and the output is `Hello`.

b. Compilation is successful and the output is `World!`

c. Compilation is successful and the output is `Hello World!`

d. The compiler rejects the expression `x += y` because it is not possible to increment the value of a `String` object.

5. Examine the following code:

```
public class Quiz3_3 {
   public static void main( String[] args ) {
      String a = new String( "Hello" );
      String b = new String( "Hello" );
      System.out.println( a == b ? "true" : "false" );
   }
}
```

Which one of the following statements correctly describes the behavior when this program is compiled and run?

a. Compilation is successful and the output is

```
true
```

b. Compilation is successful and there is no output.

c. Compilation is successful and the output is

```
false
```

d. The compiler rejects the expression `( a == b ? "true" : "false" )` because the == operator cannot be used with reference type objects.

e. Compilation is successful and the output is

```
a == b ?
```

6. Examine the following code:

```
public class Quiz3_4 {
   public static void main( String[] args ) {
      StringBuffer sb1 = new StringBuffer( "Hello" );
      StringBuffer sb2 = new StringBuffer( "Hello" );
      boolean result = sb1.equals( sb2 );
      System.out.println( result );
   }
}
```

Which one of the following statements correctly describes the behavior when this program is compiled and run?

a. Compilation is successful and the output is

```
true
```

b. Compilation is successful and the output is

```
1
```

c. Compilation is successful and the output is

```
false
```

d. The compiler rejects the expression `System.out.println( result )` because a boolean value can't be directly written to the console.

e. Compilation is successful and the output is

```
0
```

7. Examine the following code:

```
public class Quiz3_5 {
   public static void main( String[] args ) {
      int[] a = { 0, 1, 2, 3, 4 };
      int b[] = { 10, 11, 12, 13, 14 };
      a = b;
      b = new int[] { 20, 21, 22, 23, 24 };
      for ( int i = 0; i < a.length && i<b.length; i++ ) {
         System.out.println( a[i] + " " + b[i] );
      }
   }
}
```

Which one of the following statements correctly describes the behavior when this program is compiled and run?

a. Compilation is successful and the output is as follows:

```
10 20
11 21
12 22
13 23
14 24
```

b. The compiler rejects the expression `i < a.length && i < b.length` because the parentheses are missing from the calls to the length method.

c. The compiler rejects the expression `int b[] = { 10, 11, 12, 13, 14 }` because the square brackets must follow the array type, not the array name.

d. Compilation is successful and the output is as follows:

```
30
32
34
36
38
```

8. Which of the following is legal syntax for declaring arrays? Select all that apply.

a. `int[] x = { 5 };`

b. `int y[];`

c. `String s[] = "bread", "milk", "chocolate";`

d. `Object[][] theList;`

e. `Object anotherList[][];`

9. Examine the following code:

```
public class Quiz3_6 {                                    // 1
   public static void main( String[] args ) {             // 2
      Integer x = null;                                   // 3
      if ( args.length >= 1 ) {                           // 4
         x = new Integer( args[0] );                      // 5
      }                                                   // 6
      if ( args.length >= 2 ) {                           // 7
         x = new Integer( args[1] );                      // 8
      }                                                   // 9
      System.out.println( x );                            // 10
      x = null;                                           // 11
   }                                                      // 12
}                                                         // 13
```

What is the first line after which the object created on line 5 can be garbage collected?

a. line 6
b. line 8
c. line 9
d. line 11
e. line 13

10. Examine the following variable declarations:

```
String s = "";
float f = 0F;
int i = 0;
```

Which of the following statements are valid? Select all that apply.

a. `s += f;`
b. `f += s;`
c. `i += f;`
d. `i = f;`
e. `f = i;`

EXERCISES

Debugging

1. Correct the following program so that the output prints two lines: "A wild dog is wild" and "A pet cat is tame".

```
package java4cpp.questions.c3;
public class Debug3_1 {
   public static void main( String[] args ) {
      StringBuffer wild = "fox";
      StringBuffer tame = "dog";
      wild = tame;
      tame.setCharAt( 0, 'c' );
      tame.setCharAt( 1, 'a' );
      tame.setCharAt( 2, 't' );
      wild.insert( 1, "wild " );
      tame.insert( 1, "pet " );
      System.out.println( "A " + wild + " is wild" );
      System.out.println( "A " + tame + " is tame" );
   }
}
```

2. Correct all the errors in the following program:

```
package java4cpp.questions.c3;
public class Debug3_2 {
   public static void main( String[] args ) {
      if ( args.length >= 2 ) {
         short x, y;
         x = Short.parseShort( args[0] );
         y = Short.parseShort( args[1] );
         short z = x + y;
         System.out.println( z );
      }
   }
}
```

3. Correct all the errors in the following program:.

```
package java4cpp.questions.c3;
public class Debug3_3 {
   public static void main( String[] args ) {
      if ( args.length >= 1 ) {
         String arg1 = args[0];
         if ( arg1[0] == 'A' ) {
            arg1[0] = 'a';
         }
      }
   }
}
```

4. Correct all the errors in the following program:

```
package java4cpp.questions.c3;
public class Debug3_4 {
   public static void main( String[] args ) {
      String[12] months;
      months = { "Jan", "Feb", "Mar",
                 "Apr", "May", "Jun",
                 "Jul", "Aug", "Sep",
                 "Oct", "Nov", "Dec" };
      if ( args.length >= 1 ) {
         int index = Integer.parseInt( args[0] );
         if ( index > 0 && index < 12 ) {
            System.out.println( months[index] );
         }
      }
   }
}
```

5. Correct all the errors in the following program:

```
package java4cpp.questions.c3;
public class Debug3_5 {
   public static void main( String[] args ) {
      Object[] stuff = new Object[5];
      stuff[0] = "eggs";
      stuff[1] = new StringBuffer( "flour" );
      stuff[2] = 3.56;
      stuff[3] = 'c';
      stuff[4] = 123;
      for( int i = 0; i < stuff.length; i++ ) {
         System.out.println( stuff[i] );
      }
   }
}
```

Complete the Solution

1. Complete the following program by providing implementations for the methods `getCharAt` and `shiftChars`. The method `shiftChars` moves each element in the array the specified number of positions to the right if the argument is greater than zero or to the left is the argument is less than zero. The leftmost element has index value zero. Give empty elements the value '0'.

```
package java4cpp.questions.c3;
 public class Complete3_1 {
   static char[] a = { '1','2','3','4','5',
                       '6','7','8','9' };
```

```
    public static void setCharAt( int index, char c ) {
        if ( index >= 0 && index < a.length ) {
            a[index] = c;
        }
    }
    public static char getCharAt( int index ) {
        // your code here
    }
    public static void shiftChars( int shift ) {
        // your code here
    }
    static public void main( String[] args ) {
        for ( int p = 0; p < args.length; p++ ) {
            int shift = Integer.parseInt( args[p] );
            shiftChars( shift );
            System.out.println( args[p] + " : " + a );
        }
    }
}
```

2. Complete the following class by providing an implementation of the prettyMoney method. This method receives as input an object of type Float and returns a string that represents the value in U.S. or Canadian dollars and cents. For example, if the input is 12345.6789, the output is $12,345.68. For any value less than one penny, return $0.00.

```
package java4cpp.questions.c3;
public class Complete3_2 {
    static String prettyMoney( Float f ) {
        // your code here
    }
    public static void main( String[] args ) {
        int i = 0;
        while ( i < args.length )
            System.out.println(
                prettyMoney( new Float( args[i++] ) ) );
    }
}
```

3. Complete the following program by adding an `asString` method to the class. The `asString` method returns value fields x and y in the following format: (x, y).

```
package java4cpp.questions.c3;
public class Complete3_3 {
    static int x, y;
    static { x = 11; y = -678; }
    // your asString method goes here
    public static void main( String[] args ) {
        System.out.println( asString() );
    }
}
```

4. Add code to the following program to print out the title of the HTML source file whose name is passed as an argument to the main method. An HTML file should have only one title that is enclosed in the tags <title> and </title>. HTML tags are not case-sensitive, and it is possible for an HTML file not to have a title. There are no spaces in <title> and </title>. The title itself can be several words and span lines.

```
package java4cpp.questions.c3;
import java.io.*;
import java.util.*;
public class Complete3_4 {
   public static void main( String[] args )
                              throws IOException {
      // input file may be supplied in the first argument
      InputStream istream;
      if ( args.length > 0 ) {
         File inputFile = new File( args[0] );
         istream = new FileInputStream( inputFile );
      } else {
        // if no filename, use standard input stream
         istream = System.in;
      }
      BufferedReader br
         = new BufferedReader(
           new InputStreamReader( istream ) );
      String Title = "";
      String line;
      boolean found = false;
      while ( ( line = br.readLine() ) != null ) {
         // get token from the file, one at a time
         StringTokenizer tokens
            = new StringTokenizer( line );
         while ( tokens.hasMoreTokens() ) {
            String word = tokens.nextToken();
            // your code goes here
         }
         // you may have to add code here
      }
      if ( Title.length() == 0 ) {
         System.out.println( "HTML file has no title" );
      } else {
         System.out.println( Title );
      }
   }
}
```

5. Complete the method main in the following class so that it determines the type of the command-line argument. Use the wrapper classes for the primitive types boolean, double, and long to print as many of the following statements as apply:

```
The input is true
The input is false
As a real number, the input is ...
As an integer, the input is ...
```

With the wrapper classes, you cannot test whether the input is a valid number, and will have to accept that the try and catch constructions supplied in the code cover that situation:

```
package java4cpp.questions.c3;
class Complete3_5 {
   public static void main( String[] args )
                        throws NumberFormatException {
      if ( args.length == 0 ) {
        System.out.println)
                     "Run again and specify a parameter" );
        return;
      }
      String s = args[0];
      try {
         // your code goes here
      } catch( NumberFormatException e ) {
         System.out.println( "As a string, the input is "
                     + s );
      }
   }
}
```

Discovery

1. Create a class called `HTMLTitle`, starting with your working version of the class Complete3_4. This new class adds enhancements to handle the following situations:
   a. Truncate titles to 80 characters if they are longer.
   b. Print a message if the HTML file has a <title> tag but no following </title>.
   c. Print a message if the HTML file has a </title> tag but no preceding <title> tag.
   d. Print a message if the HTML file has more than one title.
   e. Allow for the absence of a space between the first word of the title and the <title> tag, and between the last word of the title and the </title> tag.
   f. Allow the absence of a space between the <title> tag and the preceding word, and the </title> tag and the following word.

2. Create a class called `BitField` that holds an array of 16 boolean flags in a static field. Write methods that perform the following operations on the array:
   a. Set a flag to `true`.
   b. Set a flag to `false`.
   c. Change the setting of a flag to the opposite of its current setting.
   d. Return the value of a flag.
   e. Return the number of flags set to `true`.

3. Create a class called `Letters` that contains a two-dimensional array of two-by-five integers. One dimension represents the letters A, E, I, O, and U, and the other dimension represents uppercase or lowercase. Read a file line by line into a `String`. Count and record the number of occurrences of each vowel in uppercase or lowercase. When you have finished reading the file, print the following lines, inserting number of appearances of the vowel in lowercase and uppercase, and the total appearances:

```
A: … lowercase, …uppercase, … Total
E: … lowercase, …uppercase, … Total
I: … lowercase, …uppercase, … Total
O: … lowercase, …uppercase, … Total
U: … lowercase, …uppercase, … Total
```

CHAPTER 4

Classes and Packages

objectives

In this chapter you will:

- Design your application to interact with objects.
- Build programs out of multiple classes.
- Build reusable classes.
- Reuse existing classes.
- Collect sets of classes into packages for distribution.
- Define classes, including fields and methods.
- Correctly use the qualifiers static, final, native, and abstract.
- Distinguish between a default and nondefault constructor.
- List the circumstances which govern creation of a default constructor.
- Determine the value of a member variable of any type when no explicit assignment has been made to it.
- State the consequences, in terms of the results of an assignment to a variable, of applying the qualifier static or final to the variable.
- Recognize code that fails to ensure definite initialization before use of local variables, and modify that code to correct the error.
- Distinguish legal and illegal orderings of package declarations, import statements, public class declarations, and nonpublic class declarations.

Introduction

You cannot even begin to program in the Java programming language without using at least one class. This chapter explains how to define and use classes and the members of classes. You will define your own classes and create instances of the classes.

It is possible to program in C++ without using classes, if you limit yourself to the subset of C++ that is essentially C with extensions. To program C++ without classes is to fail to exploit the potential of C++ for object-oriented programming. Classes are the blueprints for the objects in object-oriented programming. Unlike C++, which really is a hybrid language that allows both C-style structured programming and object-oriented programming, the Java programming language forces you to program in a truly object-oriented manner.

In the Java programming language, the usual practice is to collect classes that form logical groupings into a package. **Packages** are collections of classes that the language recognizes. You have already used some packages, including java.lang, to support the basic constructs of the Java programming language, and java.io, for stream input and output. In this chapter, you learn how to store and access packages, and how to create your own packages.

Java Classes

The first step in object-oriented programming is to determine what classes you need. Next, you either find existing classes that you can reuse, or define new ones. Regardless of whether you are creating an application or applet, you must define at least one new class to create a new Java program. You cannot create a program that is not wholly contained in at least one class. In most cases, you define several classes.

Moving from C++

Unlike C++, the Java programming language gives you no choice to make between classes or structures. The Java programming language includes only classes. The one other aggregate type that the language includes is arrays, which are very different from C++ arrays. The C++ keywords struct, union, **and** enum **and the associated types are not available. You can create the equivalent of a structure, by creating a public class in which every member is public, but you must adapt to programming without unions or enumerations. For example, you may have the following structure in C++:**

```
struct Suits {
   char* spades = "Spades";
   char* hearts = "Hearts";
   char* diamonds = "Diamonds";
   char* clubs = "Clubs";
};
```

The following Java class is equivalent to the C++ struct `Suits`:

```
public final class Suits {
   public final static String spades = "Spades";
   public final static String hearts = "Hearts";
   public final static String diamonds = "Diamonds";
   public final static String clubs = "Clubs";
}
```

In both the Java programming language and C++, a class is a distinct type. A class type is as usable as char, Int, and all the other primitive types and core classes provided by the Java platform. The online JDK documentation provides a complete list of the core classes.

For a clear understanding of the underlying concepts, it is important to know the correct terms to describe Java classes and members. A **class** is a type of object, and the objects of a class have both the data and behaviors that the class encapsulates. The data elements and behaviors of a class are the **members** of the class. Members can belong to a class as a whole or to individual objects of the class. The **methods** of a class establish behaviors, and the data is stored in the **fields**.

When created, an object of the class instantiates the class and can therefore be called an **instance** of the class. Instances are most often called **objects** and form the basis of object-oriented programming. However, in some contexts, the term instance is more suggestive of the fact that each instance is built according to its blueprint: the class definition. As you have seen, when an identifier is associated with a reference type, the identifier actually names a Java **object reference**, which is a separate entity from the actual object being referenced. Objects are always accessed through object references and have no identifiers apart from their object references.

The term **variable** is often used loosely. A variable can have primitive type or reference type. A variable can be any entity that has an identifier, regardless of whether the value is indeed variable. The Java programming language has different kinds of variables:

- **Local variables** are declared inside a block, and therefore inside a method.
- **Instance variables** are fields specific to one instance of the class.
- **Class variables** are fields shared by all objects of the class. These are the static fields of a class.

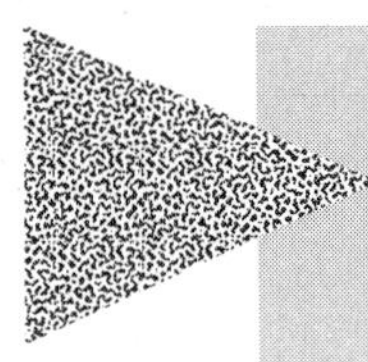

Mini Quiz 4-1

Why is it safe for the Java programming language to drop the qualifier "member" from the terms "function" and "method"? For example, C++ has functions and member functions, but the Java programming language has only methods.

Classes can be independent of each other or related by **inheritance**. The concepts of inheritance in C++ and the Java programming language are very similar, but there are some important differences in implementation. Inheritance is described in Chapter 5. The Java programming language and C++ also use some different words to describe the classes that are related because they belong to the same inheritance hierarchy. If two classes are in a parent-child relationship, in the Java programming language the parent is called the **superclass**, and the child is called the **subclass**.

All classes in this chapter are top-level classes. A **top-level class** may be contained in a package, but not in another class. If a class definition is nested inside another class definition, the contained class is called a **nested class** and may not be a top-level class. In the Java programming language, a class not only can be nested inside another class, but also can be a member of the outer class. Classes that are members are called **inner classes**. Using inner classes is an advanced topic and is covered in Chapter 9.

Both inner classes and nested classes are features added to the Java programming language in version 1.1. In the original version of the language, all classes were top-level classes, and the term "top-level class" was not used.

Moving from C++

Here is some terminology that is a little different from that of C++:

C++ term	Java term
class	class
member	member
member function	method
data member	field
instance or object	instance or object
N/A	object reference
variable	variable, depending on the context: object, local variable, instance variable or class variable
base class	superclass
derived class	subclass
nested class	nested class
N/A	inner class

C++ references are close in meaning to object references, but they are not quite the same things. C++ has nothing like inner classes.

Defining a Class

Java source files contain one or more class definitions. The only statements that can appear outside a class definition are comments, package statements, and import statements.

Syntax

*[***public***]* **class** *class_name* **{**
  // body of class
}

Dissection

- Starting a class definition with the keyword **public** is optional. This keyword is an access specifier that gives all other classes access to the class. If you omit **public**, the class is assigned the default of package access, which means that other classes in the same package can use the class, but that the class is not accessible from outside the package.
- The **class** keyword indicates that the statement is a class definition.
- The *class_name* can be any valid identifier.
- Additional forms that a class definition can take for inheritance are described in Chapter 5, and for inner or nested classes in Chapter 9.
- The body consists of the definitions of the members of the class. It is enclosed in braces, { and }.

Code Example

```
package java4cpp.classes;
/** An introductory class definition
  */
public class FirstClass {
   private int id;
   public void setId( int newId ) {
      id = newId;
   }
   public int getId() {
      return id;
   }
}
```

Code Dissection

The example contains a class is called `FirstClass`. It is a public class, and therefore is found in a file called FirstClass.java. The structure of packages mirrors the file system, so you will find this source code in the java4cpp\classes subfolder of the folder in which you unpacked the JAR file java4cpp.jar.

This example also demonstrates some conventions that are not rules of the Java programming language.

Most Java programmers use both uppercase and lowercase letters in class names, using uppercase for the first letter and the first letter of recognizable words in the class name.

In this example, the programmer declares the field id at the top of class, before methods. This is a convention used in this book, not a rule of the Java programming language. You can declare fields anywhere in the class. Many programmers group fields by their access specifier.

Moving from C++

Class definitions do not end with a semicolon. This is a small difference from C++, but can result in many bizarre error messages if you carry Java programming language habits back into C++. When you come from C++ to the Java programming language, remember to drop the semicolon.

The Java programming language has no features that support parameterized types. There is nothing similar to C++ class templates or function templates. Templates are a powerful feature that C++ programmers may miss. On the other hand, templates have greatly increased the complexity of C++ programming, C++ compiler development, and the standardization of the C++ language. The designers of the Java programming language have omitted templates from the language for reasons of simplicity.

Defining Members

A class definition consists of the definitions of the members of that class. The members can be methods, fields, or inner classes.

Defining Methods

You must define the members of your class completely within the class definitions. Only native and abstract methods can have declarations but not definitions inside the class.

Syntax

*[access_specifier] [qualifiers] return_type method_name***(** *argument_list* **)**
*[***throws** *exception_list]*
block

Dissection

- Every member has its own access specifier. You can begin the declaration of each method with one of the access specifiers **public**, **private**, or **protected**, or you can accept the default of package access. You must not use **package** as an access specifier. You get the package access by omitting the access specifier.

  public access lets all classes use the member.

  protected access is generally used with inheritance.

  Default or package access means that all classes in the same package can use the member, but the member is not available outside the package.

  private access means that the member is available only within the class.

- There are five qualifiers that you can apply to methods:

  The **abstract** keyword creates a method that has no body or implementation. You declare methods to be **abstract** to force all subclasses of your class to override, rather than inherit, the method. Abstract methods are the equivalent to the pure virtual functions of C++.

  The **final** keyword creates a method that cannot be overridden by a subclass. The subclass inherits the method.

  The **native** keyword indicates a method that is implemented in a language other than the Java programming language. Many of the core classes use native methods to provide platform independence. All specific implementations of the Java platform include classes that are written for the native platform on which it is installed. The native methods in the core classes are the interface between the Java platform and the native operating system. You can write your own native methods for your classes. Appendix A gives a brief description and example of implementing a native method in C on Intel platforms.

  The **static** keyword ensures that the method applies to the class. A static method is a class method, and can be used regardless of whether any objects of the class have been created. The core classes provide many class methods. For example, the **java.lang.Math** class provides **sqrt, max, random,** and many more methods that you can use without instantiating the **Math** class.

  The **synchronized** keyword prevents different threads in a multithreaded program from interfering with each other in cases when the method can run on more than one thread. If a method is synchronized, only one thread can use it at a time.

- The **throws** clause in a method declaration lists exceptions that may occur while the method is running and that are not handled inside the methods. You can examine this clause to see what possible abnormal conditions may prevent the method from completing as expected.
- The block is the body of the method and consists of one or more statements enclosed in braces, **{** and **}**.

Code Example

```
public static long factorial( int n ) {
   if ( n < 3 ) return n;
   else return n * factorial( n-1 );
}
```

Code Dissection

This `factorial` method recursively calculates the factorial of the integer value supplied in the argument list.

Moving from C++

The Java programming language does not allow the use of separate header files, and has no scope operator (::). This means you cannot put declarations inside the class and the definitions elsewhere, regardless of the size of the method. As a C and C++ programmer, you may be reluctant to abandon the idea of header files, but as a Java programmer you may come to appreciate the simplicity of the code organization that you use in the Java programming language.

For example, you can declare a method inside a class in C++ code and define it outside:

```
class flower {
   void bloom();  // declaration
}
void flower::bloom() { // no :: scope operator in the
                       // Java programming language
                       // definition
}
```

The Java programming language does not distinguish between the declaration and definition of a method. The equivalent to the preceding C++ code is:

```
class flower {
   void bloom() {
      //  definition
   }
}
```

You cannot group the members and supply the access specifier as a label, as you do in C++. You must either include the access specifier with every member definition, or accept the default access for that member.

Although the keywords public **and** private **specify the same access in the Java programming language as in C++,** protected **is different. In the Java programming language, protected members are accessible by classes in the same package. All such protected members can be inherited by subclasses in any package, and protected methods can be accessed by all subclasses in any package. C++ does not have an equivalent of package access or packages. But C++ does have the keyword** friend**, which is not part of the Java programming language. Java packages serve a similar purpose to C++ friend classes. Members in friend classes are as close as C++ can come to Java methods with package access.**

The throws **clause of a method is similar to an exception specification for a C++ function, except that it begins with the keyword** throws, **not** throw, **and is not optional.**

You cannot create constant methods. The Java programming language does not have the keyword const. **The keyword** final, **when applied to a method, prevents a subclass from overriding the method. When applied to a field,** final **makes the value of the field immutable. However, the Java programming language provides no facility for creating a method that cannot change the object with which it is invoked.**

You cannot indicate that certain methods should be inlined. There is no inline **keyword, and all method definitions must be inside class definitions. Even in C++, you cannot fully control whether the compiler generates code for a function call or inserts the body of the function where it is used. The Java compiler does some optimization and may inline some methods but, unlike the C++ compiler, gives you no way to suggest which methods be inlined.**

Defining Fields

As with methods, fields can have declarations but not definitions inside the class.

Syntax *[access_specifier] [qualifiers] type identifier [= initializer];*

Dissection

- As with methods, every field has its own access specifier. You can begin the declaration of a field with one of the access specifiers **public**, **private**, or **protected**, or you can accept the default of package access.
- There are four qualifiers that you can apply to fields:

  After a field that is declared **final** has been assigned an initial value, that value cannot be changed. Use this qualifier to create constants. If the field is an object reference, declaring it **final** means that the reference cannot be changed to refer to a different object, but the object itself does not become constant.

  As with methods, a field that is declared **static** belongs to the class, and all instances of the class share it. In contrast, every instance of the class has its own copy of instance variables.

  You can declare some fields to be **transient** when you are defining a class with object serialization in mind. Object serialization involves writing a whole object to an output stream and reading it back later. If a field contains temporary information that you do not need to save or has a type that cannot be serialized, you should declare the field to be **transient** to exclude it when the object is serialized.

  If your class may be used in multithreaded programs, consider declaring fields to be **volatile** to prevent situations in which values assigned in one thread may not be picked up in other threads. The keyword **volatile** suppresses optimizations that might effectively discard changes made to the value of a field by a different thread.
- Assigning an initial value to a field in the declaration is optional.

Code Example	`private String message = "Greetings";`
Code Dissection	The field `message` has type **String** and can be directly accessed only by the class in which it is defined. The message is initialized to contain the word `"Greetings"`.

The ability to serialize an object was added to the java.io **package in version 1.1 of the Java platform. Originally,** transient **was a reserved word, but not a meaningful keyword.**

Initializing Fields

You can assign initial values to fields when you declare them. This is much simpler than in C++, where you had to use constructors to assign initial values to nonstatic data members, and use definitions outside the class to initialize static members.

You can initialize a class variable either in its declarations or in a construction called an initializer block. **Initializer blocks** are described with static members in this chapter and inner classes in Chapter 9.

All fields are implicitly initialized if you do not explicitly assign an initial value. Figure 4-1 lists the default initial values for different types.

Field Type	Default Initial Value
boolean	**false**
char	`'\u0000'`
byte, short, int	`0`
long	`0L`
float	`+0.0f`
double	`+0.0d`
reference variables	**null**

Figure 4-1: Default initial value of fields

The Java programming language does not initialize local variables automatically. You must explicitly assign initial values when you declare variables inside a method. For example, the method `convertKilo2lb` in the following class `Metric` contains the local variable `ratio`. The variable is declared and immediately given a value.

```
public class Metric {
   public static float convertKilo2lb( float k ) {
      float ratio = 2.2;
      return k * convert;
   }
}
```

The Java compiler lets you declare a local variable without an initializer, but flags an error if you use a variable before it has been given a value. Unlike fields, local variables do not have default values, and the Java programming language forces you to initialize them.

Using a Defined Class

Because classes are reference types, you use object references to refer to instances of classes. To create references for objects, use the usual syntax to declare fields of any known type.

Syntax	*[access_specifier] [qualifiers] class_name identifier;*
Dissection	■ As with variables of primitive types, you can declare more than one instance of a class by listing identifiers separated by commas. The following statements create two object references for the `FirstClass` class:
Code Example	`FirstClass f1, f2;`
Code Dissection	This declaration is a complete statement. It declares two object references, but does not create the objects.

To create objects of a class, use the new keyword.

Syntax	*object_reference* = **new** *class_name*(*arguments_of_constructor*);
Dissection	■ The **new** keyword calls a constructor, which is a special method that has the same name as the class. Constructors initialize the object. You can pass arguments to the constructor. You must include the parentheses after the constructor name, even if you are using a constructor that has no arguments.

Code Example

```
f1 = new FirstClass();    // parentheses are always required
f2 = new FirstClass();
```

Code Dissection These two statements create two objects and assign the object references to `f1` and `f2`.

You can create the object reference and the instance in one statement.

Syntax *[access_specifier] [qualifiers] classname identifer* = **new** *class_name*(*arguments_of_constructor*);

Dissection

- To pass arguments to the constructor that creates the object, include the arguments between the parentheses following the class name.

Code Example

```
FirstClass f3 = new FirstClass();
```

Code Dissection This statement declares an object reference, creates an instance of `FirstClass`, and sets the value of the object reference.

There are situations where you can use the new keyword without an object reference. For example, you can create an object in the argument list when you call a method. The called method receives a reference from its argument list. The calling method has no object reference and therefore cannot use the object. This is useful when you have no need to refer to an object by name.

Syntax *method_name* (**new** *class_name*(*arguments_of_constructor*));

Dissection

- This statement creates an object inside the expression passed as an argument to use as a term within the expression.

Code Example

```
saw( new Lumber( "hardwood" ) );
```

Code Dissection This statement creates an instance of the class `Lumber`, but does not give the instance a name because the `Lumber` object is used only as an argument of the method **saw**.

Java constructors, like C++ constructors, initialize the object. You can pass arguments to the constructor. Unlike C++, the Java programming language requires you to include the parentheses after the constructor name, even if you are using a constructor that has no arguments.

To call a member method, use the dot operator with the reference for an object. Use object references as though they are the actual objects they represent.

Syntax

class_name.method(*arguments_of_method*)
object_reference.method(*arguments_of_method*)

Dissection

- The dot operator is used to call a method, regardless of whether it is a class method or an instance method.
- You can omit the class name and dot operator when a class method calls another class method of the same class.
- You can omit the class name and dot operator when an instance method calls a class method of the same class.
- You can omit the object reference and dot operator when an instance method calls another instance method of the same class for the same object.

Code Example

```
package java4cpp.classes;
/** Another introductory class definition
  */
public class SecondClass {
   private int id;
   /** Test method for the class
     * @param args not used
     */
   public static void main( String[] args ) {
      SecondClass f1, f2;
      f1 = new SecondClass();
      f2 = new SecondClass();
      f1.setId( 502 );
      f2.setId( 496 );
      int idHolder = f1.getId();
      System.out.println( idHolder );
      System.out.println( f2.getId() );
   }
   public void setId( int newId ) {
      id = newId;
   }
    public int getId() {
      return id;
   }
}
```

Code Output

```
502
496
```

Code Dissection The SecondClass class has a **main** method, so you can test the class with the **java** command. This **main** method creates two instances of SecondClass, sets the id field for each instance, and then prints out the value of the fields. Note that idHolder is a local variable defined in **main** to hold the value returned from getid for f1.

Moving from C++

The syntax used to associate a method or field name with an object is the same as C++, except for the distinction between actual objects and their references. Except for the declaration, an object reference looks more like a C++ reference than a pointer. There is no arrow operator in the Java programming language.

The SecondClass program is also an example of using a main method as a test program for your class. You can write all your class methods without considering whether the class will be the entry point of an application. When you add a main method, your class becomes executable. You can give every class its own entry point, by giving each one a main method with the standard declaration:

```
public static void main( String[] args ) {
   /* . . .  */
}
```

Mini Quiz 4-2

How does the Java platform know where to start when more than one class in an application has a main method?

Using Constructors and Finalizers

Constructors are methods that prepare newly created objects for use. **Finalizers** are methods that perform whatever actions should be completed before the objects are discarded.

In the Java programming language, the most common way to invoke a constructor is through the new keyword, as shown in the preceding section. The java.lang.Class.newInstance method and the new java.lang.reflect.Constructor.newInstance method also invoke the constructor, but they are not commonly used.

Version Watch

Version 1.1 of the Java platform introduced the method java.lang.reflect.Constructor.newInstance **along with the entire package** java.lang.reflect. **This package supports run-time type information and is known as the reflection API.** java.lang.reflect **defines the** Constructor **class.**

All objects of reference types are stored on the program heap. When you are finished with an object, you are not responsible for freeing memory on the heap. Instead, the Java platform automatically performs garbage collection from time to time. Not having to explicitly destroy an object leaves a gap when it comes to performing specialized cleanup before throwing away an object. For example, how do you flush the contents of a buffer to an output file before you destroy the object that contains the buffer? Finalizers perform this function.

As a C++ programmer, you may be wondering why this section is not called "Using Constructors and Destructors." These are familiar concepts from C++. You should fully appreciate the requirement to initialize objects before you use them, and to clean up after you are done. The Java programming language has constructors that look very much like C++ constructors.

However, the Java programming language and C++ destroy objects in very different ways. The Java programming language performs automatic garbage collection, and thus does not provide a delete operator to free the storage occupied by an object and call its destructor. The most common purpose of C++ destructors, to deallocate memory when an object is destroyed, does not apply in the Java programming language. For this reason, the language does not include destructors.

Constructors

You have already seen that when you create an object with the new keyword, you essentially call the constructor. You can include the arguments for the constructor. You must always include the parentheses, even if you are using a constructor that takes no arguments. Here are some statements that construct objects:

```
File outputFile = new File( args[1] );
Fraction third = new Fraction( 1, 3 );
Whatever thing = new Whatever();
```

When you define your Java class, you define constructors much like you define other methods. The rules are as follows:

- Give the constructor the same name as the class name.
- Do not specify a return type, not even void. A constructor cannot return a value.
- You can specify as many arguments as you like. The arguments can have any defined type, including the class of the constructor.

The Java programming language and C++ are alike in that they both provide default constructors if you do not define any constructors for a class. The compiler-generated constructor takes no arguments. All the example programs in this book so far rely on default constructors. If you define your own constructor, the compiler no longer provides a default constructor. Therefore, if you define one constructor, you must define all the forms of constructors that your class needs.

For example, if you define one constructor that has at least one argument, your class does not have a constructor with no arguments unless you also explicitly define one.

Here is an example of a class that has an explicit constructor:

```
package java4cpp.classes;
/** A Java class for text labels of arbitrary
  * length limit
  */
public class LabelText {
   private static final int MAX_TEXT = 20;
   private String label;
   /** Class constructor
     * @param inputText The text to be assigned
     *                  to the label
     */
   public LabelText( String inputText ) {
      System.out.println(
         "Creating a LabelText object" );
      if ( inputText.length() <= MAX_TEXT ) {
         label = inputText;
      } else {
         System.err.println(
            "Input label text is too long!" );
         //NOTE: next line extracts 20 chars at
         //      index 0 to 19
         label = inputText.substring( 0, MAX_TEXT );
      }
   }
   /** Provide the string representation of the object
     * @return The label text
     */
   public String toString() {
       return label;
   }
   /** Method to output the contents of the object
     * to <code>System.out</code>
     */
   public void print() {
      System.out.println( label );
   }
   /** Test method for the class
     * @param args Not used
     */
```

```
    public static void main( String[] args ) {
        LabelText a = new LabelText( "Capital Losses" );
        LabelText b
            = new LabelText( "Really Big Capital Gains" );
        a.print();
        System.out.println( a );
        b.print();
        System.out.println( b );
    }
}
```

The output is

```
Creating a LabelText object
Creating a LabelText object
Input label text is too long!
Capital Losses
Capital Losses
Really Big Capital G
Really Big Capital G
```

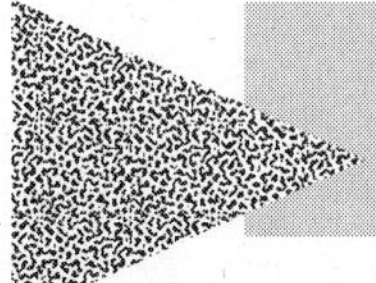

Mini Quiz 4-3

Trace through the code and output to see when the constructors are called.

Finalizers

Because the Java platform frees memory for you when objects are destroyed, you use finalizers less often than you use C++ destructors. Generally, you should use finalizers only for necessary cleanup tasks other than deallocating memory and even then you should use them sparingly. A commonly used alternative to providing finalizers is to define a method called `close` or `dispose` that can be called explicitly as needed. You should not build into your code dependency on the timing of activities of finalizers. Otherwise, you are forced to run the finalizers explicitly before executing the dependent code.

Syntax

protected void finalize() *[***throws Throwable***]*
block

Dissection

- You should declare **finalize** with the access specifier **protected**. A finalizer cannot have private or package access because it overrides a protected method of **Object**. Public access is valid, but giving users of your class access to this method is very dangerous and not recommended.

- The **finalize** method cannot take arguments or return a value. You can include whatever valid code you want.
- Although it is not strictly necessary, you should include the clause **throws Throwable**, to allow for a subclass to include a finalizer that does throw an exception.
- The block is the body of the finalizer method.

Code Example

```
protected void finalize() throws Throwable {
     MyOutputStream.flush();
}
```

Code Dissection

This finalizer flushes any output that remains in a field that is the object reference for an output stream object.

The output of the finalizer consists of whatever data is left in the output stream when the finalizer is run, and the output stream determines the destination of the output.

In inheritance hierarchies, there are additional considerations for finalizers in classes that have superclasses other than Object.

If the class of an object that is destroyed during garbage collection has a finalize method, the finalizer is run before the storage for the object is freed. Therefore, the automatic running of finalizers is tied to garbage collection. Do not rely on garbage collection to run finalizers, because you cannot control when, or even whether, garbage collection occurs. The Java Virtual Machine (JVM) may never perform garbage collection if it does not run low on memory.

You should never call the finalize method directly. Let the JVM decide when the method needs to be run.

Finalizers are like C++ destructors in that you do not call them explicitly. However, the restriction is more severe in the Java programming language than in C++, where you have a delete **operator to destroy objects explicitly and indirectly call the destructor.**

The only way to make sure finalizers run is to call runFinalizersOnExit or runFinalization.

Class **java.lang.System**

Methods

- **void runFinalizersOnExit(boolean *b*)**
  If you call **runFinalizersOnExit** and supply an argument that evaluates to **true**, the JVM guarantees to run the finalizers for all objects some time before program termination. When the argument is **false** or the **runFinalizersOnExit** method is not called, finalizers may run, but there is no guarantee that they will run.

- **void runFinalization()**
  Call **runFinalization** to request that the JVM run finalizers for all objects that have been discarded but for which finalizers have not yet run. There is no guarantee that finalizers will be run as a result of calling this method.

Include the following statement in your program to make sure finalizers are called:

```
runFinalizersOnExit( true );
```

By default, the JVM acts as though runFinalizersOnExit is called with an argument that evaluates to false. You do not need to change this setting if you have no finalizers, or do not care whether your finalizers actually run. Call the method only once, regardless of the number of classes that are in your application. A good position for the call is at the end of main, to avoid the possibility that some other code in the program may undo your setting by calling the method with a value of false.

You can call runFinalization anytime. You should do so only when performing this cleanup is imperative for your application to perform properly.

Version Watch

Version 1.1 of the Java platform introduced the method runFinalizersOnExit. **Previously you had no way to force finalizers to run at the end of a program.**

To make your programs more efficient and easier to maintain, let the virtual machine decide when to finalize objects. The technique of forcing finalization is inefficient.

Here is an example class that has a finalizer and makes sure it runs:

```
package java4cpp.classes;
/** A Java class to demonstrate how a finalizer
  * method is defined and used
  */
public class FinalizerClass {
   private int a, b;
   /** Class default constructor method */
   public FinalizerClass() {
      a = 1;
      b = 2;
      System.out.println( "Constructing an object!" );
   }
   /** Class finalizer method
     * @exception Throwable Any exception at all
     */
   protected void finalize() throws Throwable {
      System.out.println( "Doing object cleanup!" );
   }
```

```
    /** Test method for the class
      * @param args Not used
      */
    public static void main( String[] args ) {
       System.runFinalizersOnExit( true );
       FinalizerClass x = new FinalizerClass();
       FinalizerClass y = new FinalizerClass();
    }
}
```

The output is

```
Constructing an object!
Constructing an object!
Doing object cleanup!
Doing object cleanup!
```

The declaration of `FinalizerClass`.finalize includes a throws clause that allows any exception to be thrown. The throws clause is not required for this class, but including it gives subclasses the opportunity to throw exceptions in their finalizer methods.

Overloading Methods

You can define two or more different methods in the same class and give them the same name. This is called method overloading. Typically, you overload methods because you want different versions of a method to have the same name because they have similar functionality, but to take different inputs. The method name is common, but the argument lists are different. For example, you may want methods to calculate the area of a square given the coordinates of the two corners, the length of one side, or the reference for a square object. You can overload any method, including constructors and main.

You should recognize this technique from C++ as overloading. Overloading methods works in the Java programming language very much like it does in C++. There are two main differences:

- **Overloading operators is not allowed.**
- **In classes that are related by inheritance, you can overload as well as override methods.**

The reasons for overloading are the same in C++ and the Java programming language.

The **signature** of the method consists of the following:

- The name of a method
- The number of arguments
- The types of the arguments

If two methods have different signatures, they are different methods. Two methods are not ambiguous if their argument lists have different numbers of elements or if at least one argument of one method has a different type than the argument in the same position in the argument list of the other method.

The signature does not extend to the return type. You cannot overload a method by defining two versions that differ only in the return type.

To overload a method name, simply define all the versions of that method that you want. Make sure the argument lists are different. The compiler uses a process called name mangling to generate distinct internal names for the method. The **name mangling** process involves adding characters to the function name that represent the encoded argument types. You call an overloaded method exactly like you call any method. Let the compiler determine which argument list is the best match, and then run the correct method.

One feature from C++ that is not available in the Java programming language is the ability to specify default values for arguments. In C++, you can create one function that can be called with different numbers of explicit arguments. If you supply default values for certain arguments, you can omit the arguments from the function call. This mechanism is not as flexible as overloading, but is simpler than overloading and equally effective in some circumstances. For example, suppose that a C++ method has two arguments of types int **and** float**, and both have default values. You can call such a method with an** int **and a** float**, just an** int**, or with no arguments at all, as follows:**

```
// C++ source statements:
void f( int x = 0, float y = 1.0F ) { }
int main( int argc, char* args[] ) {
   f( 2, 3.2 );
   f( 6 );
   f();
}
```

To achieve the same effect in the Java programming language, you must define three overloaded methods: one with two arguments, one with one argument, and one with no arguments.

Consider the following method:

```
void myWay( int ival, float fval ) { /* …*/ }
```

You can call `myWay` with two-argument combinations such as an int and an int, a short and a float, or a char and a long. When you do so, the process you are using is implicit casting, not overloading.

Implicit casting in the Java programming language is more restrictive than C++ automatic type conversions. Casting from a type with a smaller range to a type with a larger range, such as float **to** double**, is the same in both languages. C++ also implicitly converts arguments to types with smaller ranges, such as** long **to** int**, but the Java programming language does not. You cannot pass a** long **and a** float **to** `myWay`**, unless you explicitly cast the** long **to an** int.

Use overloading when you need more than type promotions to provide all required variations on argument lists. Use overloading also if you do not want the type to be cast. For example, if you want the method to do something different when an argument has character type from when the argument has another integral type, overload the method to provide both char and int versions. For example, you can provide, instead of a single method myWay, the following overloaded versions:

```
void myWay( char ival, float fval ) { /* ...*/ }
void myWay( long lval, double dval ) { /* ...*/ }
void myWay( String[] sval ) { /* ...*/ }
```

When you call an overloaded method, the Java compiler first checks whether the types of the arguments in the call exactly match the types of the arguments in the declaration of one of the overloaded methods. If there is a match, that method is called. If not, the Java compiler casts the arguments in the calling statement, following the usual rules that prevent loss of information through implicit casting. The called method casts arguments to types with the closest, but not smaller, ranges compared to the types of the calling arguments.

Here is a simple example of method overloading:

```
package java4cpp.classes;
/** A class definition to show how a method name
  * can be overloaded
  */
public class TelNumber {
   /** Print a telephone number
     * @param s the telephone number as a string
     */
   public static void printTelNumber( String s ) {
      // check for digits only
      for ( int i = 0; i < s.length(); i++ ) {
         if ( ! Character.isDigit( s.charAt( i ) ) ) {
            System.out.println( "Not valid: " + s );
            return;
         }
      }
      // format string into (ddd) ddd-dddd
      StringBuffer sb = new StringBuffer( s );
      while ( sb.length() < 10 ) {
         sb.insert( 0, '0' );
      }
      sb.insert( 6, '-' );
      sb.insert( 3, ") " );
      sb.insert( 0, '(' );
      System.out.println( sb );
   }
```

```
    /** Print a telephone number if it falls within
      * the valid range.  This method will convert
      * the long to a string and then call the
      * printTelNumber method that takes String
      * input
      * @param l the telephone number as a long
      */
    public static void printTelNumber( long l ) {
       if ( l >= 0 && l < 10000000000L ) {
          // convert the number to a string
          printTelNumber( Long.toString( l ) );
       } else {
          System.out.println( "Not valid: " + l );
       }
    }
    /** Test method for the class
      * @param args not used
      */
    public static void main( String[] args ) {
       printTelNumber( "abcdefghij" );
       printTelNumber( "4166448300" );
       printTelNumber( 1234567890 );
       printTelNumber( -5 );
       printTelNumber( 5439432 );
       printTelNumber( "" );
    }
}
```

The output is

```
Not valid: abcdefghij
(416) 644-8300
(123) 456-7890
Not valid: -5
(000) 543-9432
(000) 000-0000
```

In this case, there are two versions of the method `printTelNumber`. One takes a `String` as an argument, and the other takes a long. The main method tests both overloaded `printTelNumber` methods.

In C++, you can use function templates as an alternative to method overloading. This option is not available in the Java programming language, which does not support templates. For example, if you want a method to print a telephone number, regardless of whether the number is input to the method as a String **or a** long**, you cannot use a C++ template to parameterize the type of the telephone number. The Java programming language has no template facility, so the only solution is to overload a method for a** String **argument and for a** long **argument.**

Overloading Constructors

Very often, the method you want to overload is the class constructor. This is because you want to provide alternative ways of creating an object. You may want a default constructor, a constructor that sets initial values, a constructor that copies another object of the same class, or a constructor that converts from another type.

None of these objectives poses any problem. You can overload the constructor just like you overload any other method.

The case of providing a default constructor and a constructor that accepts input values is interesting. For the call, you use the method this.

In C++, you achieve this effect with default arguments by creating one constructor that can be called with zero, one, two, or more arguments. For example, the definition of a class called `Fraction` that has integer fields `numerator` and `denominator` could include the following constructor:

```
Fraction( int n = 0, int d = 1 ) {
   numerator = n;
   if ( d == 0 ) d = 1;
   denominator = d;
}
```

You cannot use default arguments in the Java programming language, but you can do something that is not allowed in C++: You can call one constructor from another. For the call, you use the method this, not to be confused with the this pointer of C++. The keyword this can also be used in a manner similar to this in C++.

In the Java programming language, the this method is a synonym for a constructor. In other words, one constructor can call another constructor.

Syntax **this(** *arguments_of_called_constructor* **);**

Dissection

- Calling **this** is allowed only once in each constructor definition, and the call must be the first line in the constructor. You can chain together any number of constructors in this way. You can use this technique to achieve an effect similar to default arguments for constructors.

Code Example

```
package java4cpp.classes;
   /** A class representing a fraction
     */
   public class Fraction {
      private int num, den;
      public Fraction() {
         this( 0, 1 );
      }
      public Fraction( int initNum ) {
         this( initNum, 1 );
      }
      public Fraction( int initNum, int initDen ) {
         num = initNum;
```

```
        if ( 0 == initDen ) {
           initDen = 1;        // don't allow a zero
                               // denominator!
        }
        den = initDen;
     }
     /** Convert the object to a string
       */
     public String toString() {
        return num + "/" + den;
     }
     /** Test method for the class
       * @param args not used
       */
     public static void main( String[] args ) {
        Fraction a = new Fraction();
        Fraction b = new Fraction( 2 );
        Fraction c = new Fraction( 3, 4 );
        System.out.println( a );
        System.out.println( b );
        System.out.println( c );
     }
}
```

Code Output

```
0/1
2/1
3/4
```

Code Dissection

The constructors are linked in this `Fraction` class so that you can create a `Fraction` in three ways. One constructor with two arguments initializes the numerator and the denominator. The constructor with one integer argument assumes the desired denominator is one. The constructor with no arguments sets a default initial value of 0/1.

When one constructor calls another, the calling constructor is essentially calling another method to operate on the object being created. In this sense, the keyword this is a reference to the current object.

Using this as an Object Reference

In the Java programming language, this can also be a reference for the object for which a method is called. You can use it in any instance method. Class methods apply to the whole class, and instance methods apply to a specific object. The this keyword has no meaning in class methods.

Moving from C++

Instance methods and class methods are the equivalent of C++ nonstatic and static methods. The C++ language also has a keyword this, but it is a pointer. If you are used to using this in C++ with pointer syntax, the constructs involving this look different in the Java programming language. Bjarne Stroustrup would have defined the this pointer to be a reference rather than a pointer, if C++ supported references at the time. In *The Design and Evolution of C++*, he states, "The this pointer is C++'s version of the Simula THIS reference. Sometimes, people ask why this is a pointer rather than a reference and why it is called this rather than self. When this was introduced into C with Classes, the language didn't have references, and C++ borrows its terminology from Simula rather than Smalltalk."

To return a reference to the current object from a method, return this. The return type of the method must be the name of the class, as in the method `setStockNumber` from the next sample program. Returning this facilitates a programming technique that many programmers find advantageous. You can chain together method calls for the same instance using the dot operator, as in the following line:

```
x.setStockNumber( 1235693 ).setPrice( 123.34F );
```

This line of code first calls `setStockNumber`, which can modify the object for reference `x` and returns this. Next, the statement calls `setPrice`, with the `x` returned from `setStockNumber`. Constructions such as this are common in the Java programming language, C++, and other object-oriented languages. Execution moves from left to right. The effect is of compounding operations on the same object.

Three methods in the `MyStock` class also use this to access data files in constructs such as this.`price`. Using this in this way is not required because the fields belong to the current object by default. However, this does emphasize the fact that `price` is a member of the object and is not a class variable, argument, or local variable.

It is also common to use this to select a field that is hidden by a local variable of the same name as in the following method:

```
public MyStock setPrice( float price ) {
   this.price = price;
   return this;
}
```

Here is a class that demonstrates using this as an object reference:

```
package java4cpp.classes;
/** A class definition to demonstrate the use
  * of the this reference
  */
```

```
public class MyStock {
   private int stockNumber;
   private float price;
   public MyStock setStockNumber( int stockNumber ) {
      this.stockNumber = stockNumber;
      return this;
   }
   public MyStock setPrice( float price ) {
      this.price = price;
      return this;
   }
   public int getStockNumber() {
      return this.stockNumber;
   }
   public float getPrice() {
      return this.price;
   }
   /** The test method for the class
     * @param args Not used
     */
   public static void main( String[] args ) {
      MyStock x = new MyStock(), y = new MyStock();
      x.setStockNumber( 1235693 ).setPrice( 123.34F );
      y.setStockNumber( 1234833 ).setPrice( 11.57f );
      System.out.println( x.getStockNumber() + " "
                          + x.getPrice() );
      System.out.println( y.getStockNumber() + " "
                          + y.getPrice() );
   }
}
```

The output is

```
1235693 123.34
1234833 11.57
```

Using Static Members

Static members are class variables and class methods, because they are associated with the class, and not with any particular object or instance of the class. Nonstatic members are instance variables and instance methods.

Class variables are static fields. One use of class variables is to share information among objects of the class. If two or more instances use the same class variable, they are accessing the same location in storage. Each instance has its own storage location for instance variables. In the next sample program, the class variable `count` records the number of objects created for the class `Counted`. Any method of a class, static or nonstatic, can use a class variable.

Moving from C++

The concept of static members of classes is the same in the Java programming language as it is in C++. However, in the Java programming language, static members are often called class variables and class methods.

Defining constants by using the qualifiers final and static is another common use for class variables. The qualifier final ensures that a constant cannot be changed. static ensures that a constant is available regardless of whether any instances of that class have been created. For example, the core class Math defines some useful constants, such as Math.PI. Math.PI is static, final, and also public, so it can always be accessed.

Class methods are static methods. Declare a method to be static if you want it to be available even when no objects of the class exist. You use class methods in many of this book's example programs. All methods of the System class are static. For example, the following statements call class methods of the System class:

```
System.runFinalizersOnExit( true );
System.gc();
```

Moving from C++

The other uses of the keyword static **in C++ do not apply in the Java programming language:**

- **C++ inherited the linkage specifiers** static **and** extern **from C. You can apply these specifiers to functions and variables declared at file scope. However, the Java programming language has no concept of file scope because nothing is declared outside a class, except classes themselves. Therefore,** extern **is not a Java keyword, and** static **does not affect whether code in other files can use a member.**
- **In C and C++, you can declare as** static **any variables that are local to functions so that the variables retain their values between calls of a function. The Java platform has no equivalent feature. You can use fields to store data that is available to methods but is not destroyed when any method ends.**

You can supply either the name of the class or any instance of that class to reach a static member. Use the dot notation with the name of the class just as you do with an instance variable.

Moving from C++

A difference from C++ is that you do not use the double-colon scope with the class name, because the Java programming language has no such operator.

Syntax *class_name.static_member_name*
object_name.static_member_name

Dissection
- When you use the latter form, you use the object name just as an indicator of type. The object name can even have the value **null.** Just as in C++, a class method does not have access to the reference **this** because the method does not apply to an object, regardless of whether an object is named in the method call.

Here is a program that uses a static member to count the number of instances of a class that have been created but not yet destroyed:

```
package java4cpp.classes;
/** A Java class to demonstrate how static members
  * are defined, initialized, and used.
  */
public class Counted {
   private int value;
   private static int count = 0;  // simple init clause
   /** Default constructor method */
   public Counted() {
      ++count;
      System.out.println( "Creating a "
                          + "Counted object" );
      value = -1;
   }
   /** Class finalizer */
   public void finalize() {
      --count;
      System.out.println( "Destroying a "
                          + "Counted object" );
   }
   /** Method to return the number of objects
     * @return The number of existing objects of
     *    the class
     */
   public static int getCount() {
      return count;
   }
   /** Mutator method to set the value of the object
     * @param newValue The new value for the object
     * @return The updated object
     */
   public Counted setValue( int newValue ) {
      value = newValue;
      return this;
   }
```

```
    /** Accessor function to obtain the value of
      * the object
      * @return The value of the object
      */
    public int getValue() {
       return value;
    }
    /** The test method for the class
      * @param args Not used
      */
    public static void main( String[] args )
    {
       Counted a = new Counted();
       Counted b = new Counted();
       Counted c = new Counted();
       System.out.println( "There are "
                          + Counted.getCount()
                          + " Counted objects" );
       Counted d = new Counted();
       System.out.println( "There are "
                          + Counted.getCount()
                          + " Counted objects" );
       a = null;
       System.gc();       // start garbage collection
       System.runFinalization();
       System.out.println( "There are "
                          + a.getCount()
                          + " Counted objects" );
       /* without the next three method calls, the
        * objects b, c, and d would be picked up in
        * the preceding garbage collection
        */
       b.setValue( 1 );
       c.setValue( 2 );
       d.setValue( 3 );
    }
}
```

The output is

```
Creating a Counted object
Creating a Counted object
Creating a Counted object
There are 3 Counted objects
Creating a Counted object
There are 4 Counted objects
Destroying a Counted object
There are 3 Counted objects
```

This example class called `Counted` has a class variable, `count`, and a class method, `getCount`. The initialization of `count` shows the simplest way to initialize class variables. In this case, the initialization is not necessary because it sets the default value, but it is worth including for clarity. The constructor and finalizer apply to instances of the class. In this case, the constructor increments `count`, and the finalizer decrements it. Thus `count` becomes a record of the number of instances created but not yet finalized.

Do you notice that the three calls to `setValue` in main assign values that are never used? In this simple program, these statements do have a purpose other than being representative of a larger application. The Java compiler optimizes code, usually with beneficial effects. In this example, the optimization actually throws away the objects you are counting if the compiler determines that the objects are not used. The three calls of `setValue` access `a`, `b`, and `c` just to prevent the compiler from making them available for garbage collection before the call of println.

Performance ▶ tip

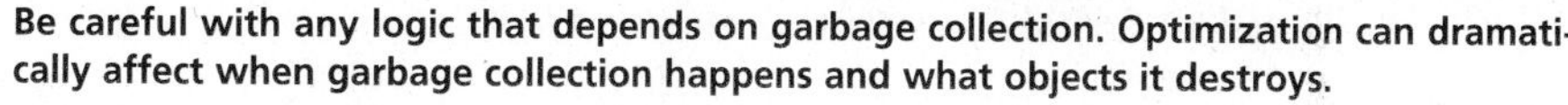

Be careful with any logic that depends on garbage collection. Optimization can dramatically affect when garbage collection happens and what objects it destroys.

Initializing Static Members

You can initialize a class variable in the same way that you can initialize a local variable or instance variable. The Java programming language, unlike C++, lets you assign the initial value in the definition of a class variable.

The Java programming language has another form of initializer for class variables: the static initialization block. A **static initialization block** looks rather like a class method with no return type, arguments, or name.

Syntax

static {
  identifier = *value*; // repeat for as many fields as desired
}

Dissection

- You must declare variables before they are initalized in a static intialization block. Typically, you use a static initialization block when a simple initialization clause is not sufficient to give a field its initial value. In the initialization block, you can create objects, call methods, or include any valid Java code you want. A class can have no static initialization blocks, one such block, or more than one. Initialization occurs when the class is loaded, and proceeds from left to right and top to bottom, through the initialization blocks. Any exceptions that may be generated by statements in a static initialization block must be handled within the block.

Code Example	`static final int FREEZING;`
	`static {`
	`   FREEZING = 32;`
	`}`

Code Dissection	The static initialization block declares and then initializes the constant `FREEZING`.

Here is a program that uses a static initialization block:

```
package java4cpp.classes;
/** A Java class to demonstrate how static members
  * are defined, initialized, and used.
  */
public class StaticNames {
   private static String[] names;
   /** Method to write the list of names to a
     * specified <code>PrintStream</code> object
     * @param s The printstream to which the names
     *          are written
     */
   public static void printNames(
      java.io.PrintStream s ) {
      for ( int i = 0; i < names.length; i++ ) {
         s.println( names[i] );
      }
   }
   /** The test method for the class
     * @param args Not used
     */
   public static void main( String[] args ) {
      printNames( System.out );
   }
   /** Static initializer */
   static {
      names = new String[4];
      names[0] = "Billy"
      names[1] = "Alyssa";
      names[2] = "Amanda";
      names[3] = "Henry";
   }
}
```

The output is

```
Billy
Alyssa
Amanda
Henry
```

The `StaticNames` class contains a static array of `String` objects. The four strings in the array `names` are created and initialized at load time so that the `main` method has only to print elements of `names`.

A static initialization block cannot throw an exception, or call any other method that may throw an exception, unless it handles the exception inside the block.

In C++, you must initialize static members outside the class definition, but no code is allowed outside a Java class definition. Instead, the Java programming language offers two ways to initialize class variables inside the class definition:

- **Include an assignment in the declaration. Unlike C++, the Java programming language lets you initialize class and instance variables the same way.**
- **Use a static initialization block. C++ has no construct that is equivalent to a static intialization block.**

Class Methods and Inheritance

The Java programming language has rules about class methods in classes that are related by inheritance:

- Class methods must be defined in the class nearest the root of the class hierarchy that uses them. A class can call all the static members that are defined in its superclass as though they were defined in the class itself, but cannot redefine them. To express this concept in the correct terminology of inheritance, class methods are inherited, but cannot be overridden. Class methods are implicitly final.
- Similarly, class methods cannot be abstract. An abstract method is one that has an argument list and return type but no implementation in the class. Usually you define an abstract method to force subclasses to override the method with a full definition.

Using Packages

Java classes are grouped into packages. All classes, regardless of whether they are included in the core classes or you write them yourself, belong to a package.

There are several ways programmers decide what classes to put into the same package. The following are three common schemes:

- Categorize classes into logical groupings and make a package for each group
- Build packages that contain sets of classes designed to be used together
- Collect classes together for convenient distribution

You can create packages that serve all of these purposes. Often the best time to decide what packages to create is early in the development cycle, when you are designing your classes and before you create the individual classes. This top-down approach helps you organize your files and is particularly helpful when your classes depend on each other.

Moving from C++

The closest thing that C++ has to packages is namespaces. Both packages and namespaces allow you to group classes together in a common scope. The difference is that only classes can be put in a Java package, whereas C++ namespaces take global functions and identifiers. But this difference is really just a consequence of the fact that everything in the Java programming language must be encapsulated in a class.

Namespaces are a relatively recent addition to the C++ language, and many C++ programmers do not use them. Therefore, you may find it useful to compare Java packages with C++ class libraries. In the loose sense that a package usually includes a collection of classes that together support some functionality, packages do serve a similar purpose to C++ class libraries. But Java packages are more integrated into the syntax of the language than C++ libraries. Package names are also tightly bound to the folder structure and filenames.

By default, members of a C++ class are private, and accessible only within the class. A common technique in C++ is to create helper classes or sets of cooperating classes by declaring the classes involved to be friends of each other. C++ starts with the idea that classes should be self-contained, then bends the rule with the concept of friendship. If one C++ class declares another class to be a friend, it grants the friend class the right to access all its members, including the private members. The Java programming language does not have the friend **keyword or a direct equivalent, but classes in the same package can access each other's members, much like C++ friend classes. A notable difference between friendship and shared-package membership, however, is that friends can access private members while other classes in a package cannot.**

The Java programming language starts with the premise that you are designing classes to work together. Packages embody this premise for top-level classes. Indeed, all classes and members have package access by default. Unless you explicitly set more restricted access on individual members, classes in the same package can call methods and use fields defined in all classes in the same package. In this way, a Java package is like a set of C++ mutual friend classes. Packages can have classes and interfaces that are available only within the package. Package access is more restrictive than public access and less restrictive than private access.

So far, all your classes have been top-level classes, and the only way to group top-level classes is into packages. The Java programming language also supports nested classes and inner classes. Using nested and inner classes is not an alternative to grouping classes into packages. It is a refinement that is appropriate in specific situations.

You can reuse the same names in different packages without causing conflicts. The full name of a class is the concatenation of the package name, with the class name, using the dot operator.

Syntax	*package_name.class_name*
Dissection	■ When you access a class that is in a different package, chain together the name of the package and the name of the class with dots.
Code Example	`trees.Maple`
Code Dissection	If the class `Maple` is in the package `trees`, the full class name is `trees.Maple`.

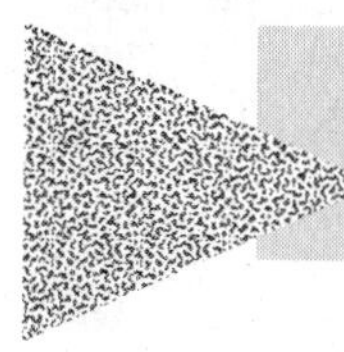

Mini Quiz 4-4

Why does a full class name not use the scope operator, ::?

To avoid name clashes, you need only make sure your identifiers are unique within your package. The full name of a class includes the name of its packages. You never include files or use a class from another package without also specifying the package name, so it does not matter if another package contains a class with the same name as one of your classes.

Membership in a package is established at the file level. All classes in one file must belong to the same package. To include a file in a package, insert a **package** statement as the first noncomment source line in the file.

Syntax	**package** *package_name*;
Dissection	■ If you omit the package declaration, the contents of a file are added to a default, unnamed package. ■ Only comments may appear before a package statement in your source. The compiler outputs an error message if it finds a package statement anywhere else.
Code Example	`package trees;`
Code Dissection	All files that make up a package named `trees` must begin with this statement.

Package Names, File Names, and Folders

You must store a public class in a source file with same name as the class. As a consequence, a .java file can contain only one public class. Similarly, you must store a package in a subfolder with the same name as the package. A package can contain any number of classes, just as a subfolder can contain more files than you should ever want to put there. You can use the following general guidelines to put a class into a package using the JDK:

1. Insert a package declaration at the start of the file containing the Java source code for the class. For example, if your class is called `Maple` and you want to put it in the package called `trees`, use a text editor to insert the following line before the first line of code in your file Maple.java:

   ```
   package trees;
   ```

2. Store the source file in a folder with the same name as the package. For example, put the file Maple.java in a subfolder called trees.
3. Compile the class as usual. If Maple.java is in the current folder, enter the command

   ```
   javac Maple.java
   ```

4. Make sure the parent folder of the package folder is included in the CLASSPATH environment variable so the **java** command can find your class. For example, if the trees folder is in the woodwork folder on the D drive, and the woodwork folder is not on your CLASSPATH, you can add D:\woodwork to your CLASSPATH environment variable on Intel-based platforms by typing the following DOS command in a command-line window:

   ```
   SET CLASSPATH=D:\woodwork;%CLASSPATH%
   ```

5. If the class compiles successfully, you can run it from the command line by entering the following command:

   ```
   java trees.Maple
   ```

Subpackages

You can combine packages into other packages. Looking at the same feature from the top down, a package can have subpackages. For example, the java package has many subpackages, one of which is java.lang. To create subpackages, reflect the package hierarchy in your folder structure. Make the top-level, or most inclusive, package at the root of a subfolder tree. For subpackages, create properly named subfolders. You can further divide the subpackages into more levels, by putting the files into more levels of subfolders.

To access a class in such a hierarchic structure, chain together the subfolder and filenames, using the dot notation. Start with the highest-level, or most inclusive, package.

Here are some facts about a hypothetical public class named `Pine` in a package named `conifers`, where `conifers` is a subpackage of a package named `trees`.

The parent folder of trees is included in the CLASSPATH environment variable. On Intel-based platforms this example would become:

Filename for the source.	trees\conifers\Pine.java
First line in the source.	package trees.conifers;
Command to compile the source when Pine.java is in the current folder. If Pine.java is not in the current folder, you can include an absolute or relative path.	`javac Pine.java`
Command to run `Pine`.main, if such a method exists and trees is the subfolder of the current folder:	`java trees.conifers.Pine`

For example, if the absolute path name and filename are D:\forest\trees\conifers\Pine.java, then the CLASSPATH would have to include D:\forest for the class `trees.conifers.Pine` to be found.

Mini Quiz 4-5

If there is a boolean instance variable in class `Pine` named `alpine`, what is the code to set `alpine` to true from within `Pine`.main, from another class in `conifers`, and from another class in the `trees` ?

Import Statements

You import packages to simplify your code. An import statement merely sets up a shorthand for package and class names. The code for the imported package is not treated as though it appears in the current file.

Moving from C++

At first glance, an import **statement may be confused with an equivalent of a C++** #include **preprocessor directive. However, an** import **statement more closely resembles the C++** using **directive. Just as a** using **directive lets you use the contents of a name-space without specifying the full namespace name, an** import **statement lets you use the classes in a package without specifying the full package name.**

You do not have to import a package to use it. You can always use and access any public class or interface that is in another package. You can use them simply by supplying the fully qualified name. For example, to use the StringTokenizer class of the java.util package, it is sufficient to declare a StringTokenizer object as follows:

```
java.util.StringTokenizer a;
```

Using these long, fully qualified names can quickly become tedious. If you frequently access a particular class or use several classes from certain packages, you can include import statements in the source file for the class.

Syntax

import *package_name.class_name*;
import *package_name*.*;

Dissection

- To import one class from a package, use **import** *package_name.class_name*;. To import all classes in a package, use **import** *package_name*.*;. Place your import statements after your package declaration and before all class or interface definitions in your source file. Include as many import statements as you want. It is considered better style to import individual classes rather than entire packages at once. As a result, your code is more understandable because it lists the origin of each class used. But use common sense. No one wants to wade through dozens of import statements!
- Every Java source file implicitly imports the package **java.lang**. The effect is similar to starting every file with **import java.lang.*;**.
- The package **java.lang** supports the actual Java programming language. All the classes that the example programs in this book use, but which you do not import or specify with fully qualified names, are in the **java.lang** package. Explicitly importing **java.lang.*** does no harm, but is not necessary.

Code Example

```
import java.util.StringTokenizer;
import java.util.*;
StringTokenizer st = new String Tokenizer( s );
```

Code Dissection

If you include one of the two import statements, you can declare a **StringTokenizer** object `st` for a **String** object **s** with the declaration: `StringTokenizer st= new StringTokenizer( s );`.

Code Example

```
java.util.StringTokenizer st =
   new java.util.StringTokenizer( s );
```

Code Dissection

This statement is equivalent to the version you must use if your class does not have either of the two import statements.

Core Java Packages

Figure 4-2 lists the core Java packages and states, very briefly, the features each package supports.

Package Name	Supports
java.applet	Applet programming
java.awt	GUI programming
■ **java.awt.datatransfer**	■ Generic interapplication data transfer and cut-and-paste data transfer
■ **java.awt.event**	■ Event-handling classes
■ **java.awt.image**	■ Manipulating images
■ **java.awt.peer**	■ Platform-specific windowing
java.beans	The component software model introduced in version 1.1 of the Java platform
java.io	Input and output
java.lang	The Java programming language
■ **java.lang.reflect**	■ Information describing classes and interfaces
java.math	Arbitrary precision arithmetic
java.net	Network programming
java.rmi	Invocation of methods on remote objects
■ **java.rmi.dgc**	
■ **java.rmi.registry**	
■ **java.rmi.server**	
java.security	Security interfaces, including digital signatures
■ **java.security.acl**	
■ **java.security.interfaces**	
java.sql	The standard SQL database interface
java.text	Support for creating internationalized programs
java.util	The operating system, random numbers, and other useful classes
■ **java.util.zip**	■ Data compression and decompression

Figure 4-2: Standard Java packages

The core classes that the Java platform provides are organized into packages. These classes compose the API that supports the Java language and the features described in this book.

A full description of the packages, the classes they contain, and all the members that you can use is beyond the scope of this book. Later chapters of this book do discuss many of the packages in more detail. You can find comprehensive and frequently updated documentation for the Sun JDK. To download this documentation from the Web, use the URLs listed in Appendix D.

SUMMARY

In this chapter you explored the heart of object-oriented programming in the Java programming language, classes. Now you can really see the legacy of C++, because much of the syntax and semantics of classes is common to C++ and the Java programming language.

Class definitions look much alike in both languages, except that in the Java programming language, the whole class and every member has a separate access specifier. By default, a class and all its members have package access. For a class, the only alternative to the default is public access. For members of the class, you can also specify private, protected, and public access.

A class contains members. Some members are data and are referred to as fields. Others are methods. You must define all methods inside the class definition. You cannot separate a declaration from the definition, as you can in C++. You can include initializations inside the class, even for static fields. Use static initializer blocks to initialize class variables when your initializations involve more complicated logic than assignment statements. By default, fields are initialized to zero, null, or false, depending on the type of the field. The compiler does not initialize local variables, and considers it an error if you access a local variable that has not been assigned a value.

To access a member of a class from methods that are not members of the class, use the dot notation to connect the class name to a field or method name. The Java programming language has no separate scope operator equivalent to the double colon of C++. If the class is in a package, connect the package name to the front of the class with another dot operator. The syntax can look like the following:

package.subpackage.class.object.method()

You usually create an object, or instance, of a class by using the new keyword and assigning the result to a reference for the object. The new keyword calls the constructor of the class.

Java classes have constructors, but no destructors. Automatic garbage collection is used to free memory when required, so the most common reason for defining C++ destructors does not apply to the Java programming language. You can write finalizers, which are methods that perform other cleanup when an instance is destroyed. You can call System.runFinalizersOnExit or System.runFinalization to ensure that finalizers run, rather than depending on automatic garbage collection.

You can overload methods in the Java programming language, much like you can in C++. The Java programming language does not support default arguments or templates, so you may have additional need for overloading. You cannot overload operators. Overloading constructors is very common. The Java programming language has a feature that is not available in C++: one constructor can call another by using the keyword this as a method call in the first line of the constructor. This is a handy way to consolidate the logic for creating objects, and at the same time give the impression that constructors have default arguments.

Instance methods can refer to the object for which the method is called, by using the reference this. Return this if you want to return the object. You can also refer to another member of the class as this.*member_name* in the method, for clarity.

A method or field that is static applies to the whole class, not an instance. You can use the qualifier static for members in the Java programming language much like you do in C++. Not only can you initialize class variables inside the class, but you can use a new construct, the static initializer block, for that purpose.

Constants always have the qualifier final. Often, constant fields also have the static qualifier, which gives them a scope equal to the entire class. The qualifier final prevents the field from being changed. The Java programming language has no keyword const, and no equivalent to a C++ const function that cannot change the object for which it is called.

In the Java programming language, is it common to group classes into packages. Classes in the same package have special access privileges similar to friend classes in C++. Also, you can reuse the same names in different packages without conflict because the package name is part of the full class name.

You organize classes into packages. The Java programming language has strict rules for your file structure and filenames. Only one public class is allowed in a single source file. If a .java file contains a public class, the file must have the same name as the class. For nonpublic classes, you can put each class into a separate file, combine several in one file, or even include them in a file that contains a public class. The compiler creates a separate .class file for every public and nonpublic class. Therefore, a source file that contains more than one nonpublic class, or at least one nonpublic class in addition to a public class, compiles into more than one .class file.

Classes in the same package must be stored in the same folder, and the folder name must match the package name. You can store subpackages in subfolders. There is a nameless default package for classes that you do not explicitly put in a package.

The first line in source files should be a package statement naming the package to which the class or classes in the file belong. You can put import statements after the package keyword. The import keyword introduces the name of another class or package of classes so that you can use the class names without specifying a fully qualified class name each time it is used.

The Java platform provides many packages. The packages include the core classes that make up a standard API for all programmers on all implementations of the Java platforms.

QUESTIONS

1. Examine the following code:

```
public class Quiz4_1 {
   int x;
   public int increment() {
      return ++x;
   }
   public static void main( String[] args ) {
      Quiz4_1 a = new Quiz4_1();
      System.out.println( a.increment() );
   }
}
```

   Which of the following statements are true? Select all that apply.

   a. The compiler rejects the expression `++x` because `x` is being used before it is initialized.
   b. Compilation is successful and the output from running the code is `1`.
   c. The compiler rejects the expression `a.increment()` because it does not evaluate to a String.
   d. The compiler rejects the expression `new Quiz4_1( )` because parentheses are not allowed when there are no constructor arguments.

2. Examine the following code:

```
public class Quiz4_2 {
   private static final double A = 5.6;
   private double b;
   Quiz4_2( double z1, double  z2 ) {
      b = z1 * z2;
   }
   Quiz4_2( double z ) {
      if ( z > 0.0 ) {
         this( z, 2.0 );
      } else {
         this( z, 1.0 );
      }
   }
   public static void main( String[] args ) {
      System.out.println( new Quiz4_2 ( 4.0, 3.0 ) );
   }
   public String toString() {
      return( "b = " + b );
   }
}
```

   Which one of the following statements correctly describes the behavior when this program is compiled and run?

   a. The compiler rejects the expression `new Quiz4_2( 4.0, 3.0 )` because it is not possible to create an object without a name.

b. Compilation is successful and the output is `b = 12.0.`
c. The compiler rejects the expression `this( z, 2.0 )` because it is not the first statement in the method.
d. The compiler rejects the second definition of the method `Quiz4_2` because the name has already been defined.

3. Examine the following code:

```
public class Quiz4_3 {
   protected void finalize() throws Throwable {
      System.out.println( "object finalized!" );
   }
   public static void main( String[] args ) {
      Quiz4_3 x = new Quiz4_3();
      System.runFinalizersOnExit( true );
   }
}
```

Which of the following statements correctly describes the behavior when this program is compiled and run? Select all that apply.
a. Compilation is successful and the output is `object finalized!`
b. Compilation is successful, but the output is uncertain because it is not possible to be 100% certain whether the garbage collector runs.
c. Compilation is successful, but no output appears.
d. The compiler rejects the expression `System.runFinalizersOnExit( true )` because the variable `true` is undefined.

4. True or False: Assuming `value` is a float instance variable of a class, a class method of the class can output its value with the following statement:

```
System.out.println( this.value );
```

5. Examine the following code:

```
public class Quiz4_4 {
   private static int a;
   private static int b;
   public static void main( String[] args ) {
      System.out.println( a + "  " + b );
   }
   static {
      a = 100;
   }
   static {
      b = 200;
   }
}
```

Which of the following statements correctly describes the behavior when this program is compiled and run? Select all that apply.
a. The compiler rejects the attempt to define a method called `static`.
b. The compiler rejects the attempt to define two static initialization blocks.

c. Compilation is successful and the output is `0 0`.
d. Compilation is successful and the output is `100 200`.
e. Compilation is not successful because the argument of **main** must be `(String[] args)`.

6. Examine the following code:

```
import java.lang.*;
import java.util.StringTokenizer;
package mypackage;
public class Quiz4_5 {
   public static void main( String[] args ) {
      String a = "Hello World!";
      StringTokenizer st
         = new StringTokenizer( a );
      String token1 = st.nextToken();
      System.out.println( token1 );
   }
}
```

Which of the following statements are true? Select all that apply.
a. The compiler rejects the statement `import java.lang.*;` because that package is already implicitly imported.
b. The compiler rejects the statement `package mypackage;` because it is not the first statement of the file that is not a comment.
c. Compilation is successful and the output is `Hello World!`
d. Compilation is successful and the output is `Hello`.
e. The compiler rejects the statement
`StringTokenizer st = new StringTokenizer( a );`
because the class name StringTokenizer is not fully qualified with the name of its package.

7. Examine the following code:

```
public class Quiz4_6 {
   Boolean condition;
   public void testCondition() {
      if ( condition ) {
         System.out.println( "TRUE!" );
      } else {
         System.out.println( "FALSE!" );
      }
   }
   public static void main( String[] args ) {
      Quiz4_6 a = new Quiz4_6();
      a.testCondition();
   }
}
```

Which of the following statements are true? Select all that apply.
a. The compiler rejects the expression `if ( condition )` because **condition** is being used before it is initialized.

b. The value of the variable `condition` is null when it is tested in the first statement of `testCondition`.
c. Compilation is successful and the output from running the code is **`TRUE!`**
d. Compilation is successful and the output from running the code is **`FALSE!`**
e. The compiler rejects the expression `if ( condition )` because it does not evaluate to a boolean value.

8. Which of the following are valid statements for declaring local variables within a method body? Select all that apply.

a. `final int a;`
b. `static int b;`
c. `transient int c;`
d. `volatile int d;`
e. `static final int e;`

9. Which of the following are valid statements for declaring fields of a class? Select all that apply.

a. `final int a;`
b. `static int b;`
c. `transient int c;`
d. `volatile int d;`
e. `static final int e;`

10. Examine the following code:

```
public class Quiz4_7 {
    private int value;
    public Quiz4_7( int input ) {
        value = input;
    }
    public String toString() {
        return String.valueOf( value );
    }
    public static void main( String[] args ) {
        Quiz4_7 a = new Quiz4_7();
        Quiz4_7 b = new Quiz4_7( 42 );
        System.out.println( a );
        System.out.println( b );
    }
}
```

Which of the following statements are true? Choose as many as are appropriate.

a. Compilation is successful and the output from running the code is `42`.
b. The compiler rejects the statement `new Quiz4_7()` because the definition of a no-argument constructor is missing.
c. Compilation is successful and the output from running the code is as follows:
```
null
42
```
d. Compilation is successful and the output from running the code is as follows:
```
a
b
```

11. Examine the following code:

```
import java.util.Date;
// -X-
public class Quiz4_8 {
   // class definition
}
```

Which of the following statements are valid if inserted at the line marked `-X-`? Select all that apply.

a. `import java.util.StringTokenizer;`
b. `package java4cpp.questions.c4;`
c. `class AnotherClass { }`
d. `public class AThirdClass { }`

12. Which of the following qualifiers can be used with members of a class? Select all that apply.

a. static
b. const
c. public
d. private
e. package

EXERCISES

Debugging

1. Correct all errors in the following program:

```
package java4cpp.questions.c4;
public class Debug4_1 {
   public static void main( String[] args ) {
      int x;
      if ( args.length > 0 )
      x = args.length;
      report();
   }
      public static report( x ) {
      System.out.println( x );
   }
}
```

2. Correct all errors in the following program:

```
package java4cpp.questions.c4;
public class Debug4_2 {
   private double x;
   public void Debug4_2( double input ) {
      x = input;
   }
   public String toString() {
      return String.valueOf( x );
   }
   public static void main( String[] args ) {
      Debug4_2 a = new Debug4_2( -7.3 );
      System.out.println( a );
   }
}
```

3. Correct all errors in the following program:

```
package java4cpp.questions.c4;
public class Debug4_3 {
   private double x;
   public Debug4_3( double input ) {
      x = input;
   }
   public String toString() {
      return String.valueOf( x );
   }
   void finalize() throws Throwable {
      System.out.println( "Goodbye!" );
   }
   public static void main( String[] args ) {
      Debug4_3 a = new Debug4_3( -7.3 );
      System.out.println( a );
      System.gc();
      System.runFinalize();
   }
}
```

4. Correct all errors in the following program so that the list displayed contains the numbers 0.1 to 1.0 in steps of 0.1. Do not make any changes to the main method.

```
package java4cpp.questions.c4;
public class Debug4_4 {
   private static double[] a;
   public static void displayList() {
      for( int i = 0; i < a.length; i++ ) {
         System.out.print( a[i] + " " );
      }
      System.out.println();
   }
```

```
    public static void main( String[] args ) {
        displayList();
    }
    {
        a = new double[10];
        for( int i = 0; i < a.length; i++ ) {
            a[i] = (i+1)/10;
        }
    }
}
```

5. Correct all errors in the following program:

```
package java4cpp.questions.c4;
public class Debug4_5 {
    private double x;
    private double y;
    public Debug4_5( double d1, double d2 )
        X = d1;
        y = d2;
    }
    public Debug4_5( double d1 ) {
        this( d1, 0.0D );
    }
    public Debug4_5() {}
    public ~Debug4_5() {}
    public static void displayValues() {
        System.out.println( "Value x = " + x );
        System.out.println( "Value y = " + y );
    }
    public static void main( String[] args ) {
        Debug4_5 a = new Debug4_5( 5.6, 9.345 );
        a.displayValues();
    }
}
```

6. Correct all errors in the following program:

```
package java4cpp.questions.c4;
public class Debug4_6 {
    Debug4_6( int n) {
        String data = new String[n];
        for ( int = 0; i < n; i++ )
        data[i] = args[i];
        int count = n;
    }
    public static void main( String[] args ) {
        int n = args.length;
        if ( n ) {
            Debug4_6 D46 = new Debug 4_6( n );
        }
        System.out.println( n );
```

```
            if ( !n ) return;
               for ( int i = 0; i < D46.count; i++ )
                  System.out.println( data[i] );
         }
      }
```

Complete the Program

1. Complete the following program by providing a main method that constructs an instance of the `Pair` class with a Double object and an Integer object as input and then writes the object to System.out.

```
package java4cpp.questions.c4;
public class Pair {
   private Object item1, item2;
   public Pair( Object o1, Object o2 ) {
      item1 = o1;
      item2 = o2;
   }
   public String toString() {
      return item1.toString() + ", "
               + item2.toString();
   }
   // your main method here
}
```

2. Complete the following program by providing all the missing methods that are needed for the given main method to compile and execute successfully:

```
package java4cpp.questions.c4;
public class Student {
   private String name;
   private int id;
   // Your code here
   public static void main( String[] args ) {
      Student alice = new Student();
      alice.setName( "Alice Smith" );
      alice.setID( 92345602 );
      Student henry = new Student( "Henry Jones",
                                   81047236 );
      System.out.println( alice );
      System.out.println( henry );
   }
}
```

3. Complete the following program by adding a finalize method that prints the final contents of the `Point3D` object to System.out just before the object is destroyed:

```
package java4cpp.questions.c4;
public class Point3D {
   private int x, y, z;
   public Point3D( int x, int y, int z ) {
      x = x;
      y = y;
      z = z;
   }
   // put your finalize method here.
   public static void main( String[] args ) {
      Point3D p1 = new Point3D( 23, -6, 78 );
      p1 = null;
      System.gc();
      System.runFinalization();
   }
}
```

4. The following class calculates the first 25 numbers in the Fibonacci sequence and provides a method to return the value of any particular value in the sequence. Complete the class by providing a static initialization block that calculates the first `MAXFIB` numbers in the sequence. The first two numbers in the sequence are 0 and 1. Every other number in the sequence is the sum of the two numbers that precede it in the sequence. For example, the Fibonacci sequence starts 0, 1, 1, 2, 3, 5, 8, 13 ...

```
package java4cpp.questions.c4;
public class Fibonacci {
   public static final int  MAXFIB = 25;
   private static int[] fibNums;
   public static int getFibonacci( int index ) {
      if ( index >= 1 && index <= MAXFIB ) {
         return fibNums[index-1];
      } else {
         return -1;
      }
   }
   public static void main( String[] args ) {
      System.out.println( getFibonacci( 10 ) );
      System.out.println( getFibonacci( MAXFIB ) );
   }
   // your static initializer goes here
}
```

5. Complete the following class by adding two more constructors to simulate the use of default values. The integer default for the first parameter is 0, and the double default for the second parameter is 1.0. Both of the constructors you add should call the constructor shown in the following code.

```
package java4cpp.questions.c4;
public class Constructors {
   private int count;
   private double multiplier;
   public Constructors( int i, double d ) {
      count = 10 * i;
      multiplier = i * d;
   }
   // Your constructors go here
   public static void main( String[] args ) {
      Constructors a, b, c;
      a = new Constructors( 5, 11.7 );
      b = new Constructors( -337 );
      c = new Constructors();
   }
}
```

Discovery

1. Create a public class called `SentenceFormatter` that takes a **String** object as the single argument of the constructor. The class should have at least one private field, an array of strings in which each element is a token extracted from the **String** passed to the constructor. For simplicity, assume the input consists of a set of words without punctuation. Provide the following instance methods in addition to the constructor:

   - `public int getWordCount()`
     returns the number of words in the string.

   - `public String getWordAt( int position )`
     returns the word in the position indicated by the argument, or null if the index is greater than the number of words in the string or less than 0. The first word is in position 1.

- `public String sentence()`
  returns the string formatted as a sentence. The letter of the first word is capitalized and a period is added to the end.

- `public String heading()`
  returns the string with the first letter of every word capitalized.

- `public String justify( int size, int justification )`
  returns the string truncated or expanded to the number of characters specified in the first argument. If the second argument equals the public field `SentenceFormatter.RIGHT`, the method appends trailing spaces if necessary. If the second argument equals the public field `SentenceFormatter.LEFT`, the method inserts leading spaces if necessary. If the second argument is `SentenceFormatter.CENTER`, the method might add both leading and trailing spaces.

- `public static void main( String[] args )`
  is a test method to exercise every other method.

2. Create a public class called `StringReverser` that takes a String object as a constructor parameter. The class should have one private field of type `SentenceFormatter`, the class you created to answer the previous exercise. Make sure that `StringReverser` and `SentenceFormatter` are in the same package. Provide the following methods:

- A constructor that takes a String object as an argument.

- `String wordsReversed()`
  returns the string with the words in the reverse order.

- `boolean reversible()`
  returns true if the string is the same with the words in the original order and in reverse order, and false otherwise. For example, "all for one and one for all" is reversible but "every man for himself" is not. Consider any one-word string to be reversible.

- `public static void main( String[] args )`
  is a test method to exercise every other method.

3. Create a class called `Inventory` that contains three arrays with elements of type String, int, and float. An element in the String array holds an identifying code for an item that a store might sell. The element at the corresponding index position in the integer array is the number of that item in stock, and the corresponding element in the float array is the retail price. The constructor takes one argument, which is the size of the arrays. The class must have at least the following additional public methods:

- `public int update( String ID, int quantity, float price )` adds or updates a stock item. If an item with the specified ID already exists, the method prints a warning and updates the int and float arrays. Otherwise, the method writes new values into all three arrays. The return value is the number of items recorded in the arrays when the update is complete.

- `public void setQuantity( String ID, int quantity )` changes the recorded number in stock for the item that matches the specified ID. If no items match the specified ID, the method prints a warning.

- `public int getQuantity( String ID )` returns the number in stock for the item that matches the specified ID. If no items match the specified ID, a warning is printed and the return value is zero.

- `public void setPrice( String ID, float price )` changes the recorded price for the item that matches the specified ID to the specified price. If no items match the specified ID, the method prints a warning.

- `public float getPrice( String ID )` returns the price for the item that matches the specified ID to the specified price. If no items match the specified ID, the method prints a warning, and the return value is zero.

- `public void update( String ID, int number )` changes the number in stock for the item whose identifier matches the specified ID to the specified quantity, and adds the specified number to the number in stock. A negative number represents a sale or loss of stock. If no items match the specified ID, the method prints a warning.

- `public void update( String ID, float percent )` increases the price for the item that matches the specified ID by the specified percent. The percentage can be negative to reduce the price. If no items match the specified ID, the method prints a warning.

- `public void stockReport()`
  prints an inventory report in the following format, where a *c* represents a character and a *d* represents a digit:

```
Item cccc: in stock: d price dddd.ddd price: ddddd.ddd
Item ccc: in stock: ddd price dd.d price: dddd.ddddd
Item cccccc: in stock: dd price dd.dd price: dddd.dd
...
Total value of inventory: ddddddd.ddddd
```

- `static public void main( String[] args )`
  is a test method that exercises all the other methods.

Provide as many private methods and fields as you want to simplify coding this class. For this exercise, you can assume the user always supplies sensible arguments. For example, you do not have to check for a negative price or allow for an attempt to create more items than there is room for in the array. However, you may find it interesting to test such situations and see what happens.

CHAPTER 5

Inheritance

objectives

In this chapter you will:

- **Define classes that extend other classes and implement interfaces.**
- **Build and use class hierarchies.**
- **Construct and finalize classes in an inheritance hierarchy.**
- **Understand and use dynamic binding.**
- **Declare classes using the modifiers** public, abstract, **and** final.
- **Declare variables using the modifiers** private, protected, **and** public.
- **State the effects on scope and accessibility of an instance variable or method of these factors:**
  The calling method is a class method.
  The calling method is an instance method.
  The calling method is in the same class as the target.
  The calling method is in a subclass of the class containing the target.
  The calling method is in a class which is in the same package as the class containing the target.
  No special relationship exists between the class of the caller and the class of the target.
  The target declaration is qualified by any of the private, protected, public, static, final, **and** abstract **modifiers.**
- **Write classes that implement object-oriented** ***is-a*** **and** ***has-a*** **relationships.**
- **Distinguish between overloaded and overridden methods.**
- **State legal return types for an overriding method given the original method declaration.**
- **Describe the effect of invoking overridden methods in base and derived classes.**
- **Write code for any overridden method that invokes the parental method, using** super.
- **Write constructor bodies using** this **and** super **to access overloaded or parent-class constructors.**

Overview of Inheritance

One great benefit of classes is that a well-designed class is a reusable piece of code. The Java platform includes several packages of classes that you can reuse in the programs you create. All Java programs consist of a mixture of custom-coded and existing classes.

Much greater flexibility comes with the ability not only to reuse classes, but also to create new classes from existing classes. Creating new classes from existing classes is **inheritance.** With inheritance come a number of concepts that are fundamental to object-oriented programming in the Java programming language.

When you base the definition of one class upon another, the existing class becomes the **superclass.** The superclass is the more general type, and can also be called the **supertype** for objects of the new class. The new class becomes a **subclass,** and defines a **subtype** of the superclass. A subclass inherits all the members of the superclass. A design criterion should be that the subclass has specializations that define a more narrow classification of objects. For example, if you define a superclass `ReadingMaterial`, `Books` and `Magazines` are appropriate subtypes.

You can set up hierarchies of classes that are related by inheritance. In an inheritance hierarchy, any number of classes can be directly or indirectly based on a common superclass. Indeed, every Java class you define belongs to a hierarchy. Unless you explicitly specify otherwise, your classes are direct subclasses of the core class Object. The **Object** class is the common ancestor of all Java classes and is the root of the Java class hierarchy. This is why all Java classes, including those you define yourself, inherit a default set of behaviors from the Object class. You can create your own hierarchies within this all-embracing Java hierarchy.

The concept of inheritance is the same in the Java programming language as it is in C++, and the implementation is similar but not identical. The common ancestor class Object **in the Java programming language is a very fundamental difference. In this respect, the Java programming language is more like Smalltalk than C++. Unlike C++ classes, all Java classes belong to one unifying hierarchy, and a single root class defines the attributes common to all classes.**

The terms **is-a** and **has-a** apply to possible kinds of relationships among class types. An is-a relationship can exist between a subclass and a superclass. For example, if the class `Book` is a subclass of `ReadingMaterial`, a `Book` object is a `ReadingMaterial` object. Its type is `Book`, and its supertype is `ReadingMaterial`. The book may have additional fields, such as `author` and `number_of_pages`, but it also has the attributes of all reading material, such as `language` and `available_online`.

In contrast, the has-a relationship describes containment. Classes can have members that are in themselves objects of other classes. For example, a `Book` object may have an `author` field. The value in this field can be an object reference to a class called `Writer`. The book is not a `Writer` object; the book *has* a `Writer` object.

The process of defining a new class based on an existing class is called **extending** a class. You often add fields or methods to your new subclass to give it additional capabilities, or override methods inherited from the superclass to customize or complete their implementation. A class can extend only one class directly. Therefore, all Java classes have exactly one direct superclass. The superclass can in turn extend another class, and so on, until the superclass is Object.

In object-oriented programming, the interface of a class is a concept that relates to how other code can use the class. The interface includes the fields and methods that are accessible from outside the class, and specifies the behavior of the class, as far as that behavior is detectable from outside. The Java programming language provides a language construct for the specific purpose of defining the behaviors of classes separately from the class definitions. In the Java programming language, an **interface** is a language construct. An interface definition is similar to a class definition in that it includes the definition of methods and fields. But an interface cannot be instantiated.

Just as a class can extend a superclass, it can **implement** an interface. The new class inherits the fields and methods of the interface, but is forced to provide definitions of the methods defined in the interface. The interface specifies what methods the class must provide, but not how they are implemented. The interface that a class implements is not a superclass. One major difference is that a class can implement any number of interfaces. A class can implement one or more interfaces in addition to extending a superclass. Nevertheless, the is-a relationship applies equally to the superclass that a class extends and to all interfaces that a class implements.

You can define classes to be abstract. Like interfaces, **abstract classes** cannot be instantiated, but they can be extended. Like interfaces, abstract classes can contain methods without implementations. But, unlike interfaces, abstract classes can also define methods with complete implementations. The only way to use an abstract class is as a superclass.

There are several differences in the rules of inheritance between the Java programming language and C++:

- **The Java programming language supports single inheritance only. In other words, a subclass cannot extend to more than one superclass. Multiple inheritance, as you know it from C++, is not possible.**
- **The Java programming language has no equivalent to C++ private or protected inheritance. All inheritance in the Java programming language is the same as C++ public inheritance.**
- **Interfaces in the Java programming language provide an elegant alternative to multiple inheritance. Interfaces are analogous to abstract base classes. You cannot instantiate them, but you can derive a class from them and, if you implement all the required methods, you can instantiate that class.**

Extending Classes

In the Java programming language, you achieve inheritance by extending a class. Every Java class implicitly extends Object. To inherit from another class explicitly, use the keyword extends. You can explicitly extend Object using the following form but it is never necessary.

Syntax

[public] [qualifiers] class *class_name* **extends** *superclass_name* {
  /* member definitions */
}

Dissection

- The optional class access specifier must be either **public** or omitted to assign package access by default. You can apply the access specifiers **private** and **protected** to a class that is defined inside another class. Nesting class definitions is described in Chapter 9.
- You can qualify the new class with any of the following optional qualifiers: **final, abstract**, or **static**. Declare a class with **final** or **abstract** to determine whether it can or must be used as a superclass. You can apply the qualifier **static** only to a class that is defined inside another class.
- The keyword **extends** introduces the name of the superclass. You can name only one superclass. If you omit the keyword **extends** from a class definition, the class implicitly **extends java.lang.Object**.

Code Example

```
public class Book extends ReadingMaterial {
   // the members of Book are defined here
}
```

Code Dissection

The class `Book` is a subclass of `ReadingMaterial`. It inherits all methods and fields defined in superclass `ReadingMaterial` and has, in addition, the members and fields defined in the `Book` class definition.

Moving from C++

In C++, you precede the name of the base class with a simple colon, :, where in the Java programming language you use the keyword extends. **For example, the equivalent to the preceding class definition in C++ is as follows:**

```
class Book : public ReadingMaterial {
   // the members of Book are defined here
};
```

In the Java programming language, public inheritance is the only option. The language provides no equivalent to the keywords protected **or** private **when used where** public **appears in this class definition. Whether a subclass in the Java programming language can directly access specific fields and methods of the superclass depends only on the access specifiers assigned to the members of the superclass when the superclass is defined.**

Here is a class that can be used as a superclass. This example contains a class called `HasX`. It is a public class, and therefore is found in a file called HasX.java. The structure of packages mirrors the file system, so you will find this source code in the java4cpp\inheritance subfolder of the folder in which you unpacked the JAR file java4cpp.jar.

```
package java4cpp.inheritance;
/** A Java superclass to demonstrate inheritance
  * concepts
  */
public class HasX {
   private int x;
   /** Method to set the value of the object
     * @param inputX The field's new value
     */
   public void setX( int inputX ) {
      x = inputX;
   }
   /** Method to get the value of the object
     * @return The value of the field
     */
   public int getX() {
      return x;
   }
   /** Method to write X to <code>System.out</code>
     */
   public void showX() {
      System.out.println( x );
   }
}
```

The class `HasX` has a private field `x`, public methods to set and get the value of `x`, and a public method to output the value of `x`. The next class, `HasXY`, extends `HasX`:

```
package java4cpp.inheritance;
/** An example Java subclass used to demonstrate
  * inheritance concepts
  */
public class HasXY extends HasX {
   private int y;
   /** Method to set the object's value
     * @param inputY The field's new value
     */
   public void setY( int inputY ) {
      y = inputY;
   }
```

```
    /** Method to get the object's value
      * @return The value of the field
      */
    public int getY() {
       return y;
    }
    /** Method to write Y to <code>System.out</code>
      */
    public void showY() {
       System.out.println( y );
    }
    /** The test method for the class
      * @param args not used
      */
    public static void main( String[] args ) {
       HasXY obj = new HasXY();
       obj.setY( 20 );
       obj.setX( 10 );
       obj.showY();
       obj.showX();
    }
}
```

The output is

```
20
10
```

The class `HasXY` is a subclass of `HasX`. It has an additional field `y`, methods to get, set, and output `y`, and a main method for testing. The main method creates a `HasXY` object, `obj`. The `obj` object is also a `HasX` object and has all the members of both `HasX` and `HasXY`.

Final Classes

Declare a class with final to prevent it from ever being used as a superclass. This is a way of ensuring that your class is never extended and that its methods are never overridden. Some of the core Java classes are final, including the wrapper classes for the primitive types and String. As a result, you cannot extend Integer to create subclasses such as `EvenInteger` or `PositiveInteger`.

One reason to make a class final is to improve performance. If there can be no method overriding, there is no need for dynamic binding, and the method-call mechanism is quicker. The String class is probably final for this reason alone. Security is another reason for making a class final. You can disallow subclasses to prevent anyone from creating classes that change the implementations of methods you rely upon. You can also declare individual methods to be final, to prevent them from being overridden when you choose not to make the whole class final.

Abstract Classes

Declare a class with abstract if the intention is never to instantiate the class. Do this to design a class for use only as a superclass. You can then extend the class and create objects of the subclasses. The only way to use an abstract class is to extend it.

You can also declare methods to be abstract, but only within abstract classes. Abstract methods have no body, or implementation, and must be overridden in any extending class that is not also abstract.

An abstract class can contain a mixture of abstract methods and fully implemented methods. This is very useful in situations where some of the characteristics of objects can be inherited from the superclass and others depend on which subclass the objects instantiate. Make methods abstract to force the subclasses to provide an implementation.

Here is a variation on the HasX and HasXY classes in which the superclass is an abstract class:

```
package java4cpp.inheritance;
/** A Java superclass to demonstrate inheritance
  * concepts
  */
public abstract class HasX2 {
   private int x;
   /** Method to set the value of the object
     * @param inputX The field's new value
     */
   public void setX( int inputX ) {
      x = inputX;
   }
   /** Method to get the value of the object
     * @return The value of the field
     */
   public int getX() {
      return x;
   }
   /** Method to somehow display the X value
     */
   public abstract void showX();
}
```

The class HasX2 is explicitly declared to be an abstract class. If you remove the keyword abstract before the keyword class, HasX2 is still implicitly abstract, because it contains the abstract method showX. You make the method abstract by explicitly qualifying it with abstract and removing the method body. As a result, each subclass must provide its own implementation of showX. You cannot create a HasX2 object because the class definition is incomplete. The following class definition, HasXY2, extends HasX2 and implements the abstract showX method.

```
package java4cpp.inheritance;
/** An example Java subclass used to demonstrate
  * inheritance concepts
  */
public class HasXY2 extends HasX2 {
   private int y;
   /** Method to set the object's value
     * @param inputY The field's new value
     */
   public void setY( int inputY ) {
      y = inputY;
   }
   /** Method to get the object's value
     * @return The value of the field
     */
   public int getY() {
      return y;
   }
   /** Method to write the value of Y to
     * <code>System.out</code>.
     */
   public void showY() {
      System.out.println( y );
   }
   /** Method to write the value of X to
     * <code>System.out</code>. This is required
     * because this method is an abstract
     * method in the superclass.
     */
   public void showX() {
      System.out.println( getX() );
   }
   /** The test method for the class
     * @param args Not used
     */
   public static void main( String[] args ) {
      HasXY2 obj = new HasXY2();
      obj.setY( 20 );
      obj.setX( 10 );
      obj.showY();
      obj.showX();
   }
}
```

The output does not change as a result of the modifications to the code, and remains the following:

```
20
10
```

Mini Quiz 5-1

Suppose you want to represent birds in an inheritance hierarchy for which the superclass is called `Birds`. You can have subclasses for `SongBirds`, `BirdsOfPrey`, `FlightLessBirds`, `WaterFowl`, and the like. Design a simple class hierarchy. Where do you define the method `fly`?

The Problem of Multiple Inheritance

Inheriting from more than one base class can cause problems. You may be familiar with the problem of multiple indirect base classes, sometimes described as diamond inheritance, as shown in Figure 5-1.

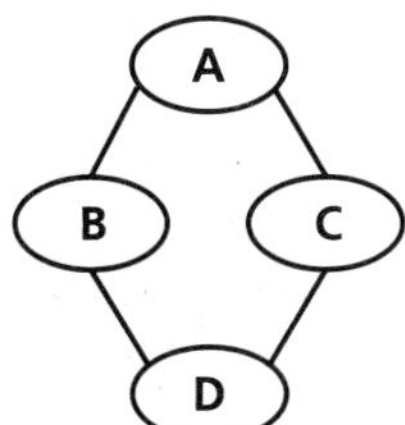

Figure 5-1: Diamond inheritance

In Figure 5-1, class `D` inherits the attributes of `A` through both `B` and `C`, possibly without even knowing that either class derives from `A`. What happens if `A` has a member named `a` and when class `D` accesses `a`? Is it referring to the copy of `a` inherited from `A` through `B`, or to the copy of `a` inherited from `A` through `C`? C++ has a partial solution in virtual inheritance. You can declare the classes as follows:

```
class B : virtual public A {}
class C : virtual public A {}
class D : public B, public C {}
```

In this case, `D` inherits `A` only once. But what if `B` and `C` are existing classes that do not use virtual inheritance and cannot be changed? It is not possible to "retrofit" virtual inheritance, and the only solution is to devise some other pattern of inheritance relationships. In C++, you often can find yourself in this situation. Because it imposes a performance penalty, programmers tend not to use virtual inheritance unless forced to do so.

In the Java programming language, there is no multiple inheritance. In its place, the language provides a new way to encapsulate methods so that they can be implemented in other classes. Interfaces serve this purpose.

Implementing Interfaces

An interface is like a design document for the external features of a class. To define an interface is to establish what public methods must be provided by classes that implement the interface. An interface defines public methods that are abstract and have no implementations. It can have fields, but they must be static and final.

Interfaces provide a mechanism for a subclass to define the behaviors from sources other than the direct and indirect subclass's superclasses.

In C++, you used multiple inheritance to derive a class from more than one base, and you created an abstract base class to contain pure virtual methods that a derived class must override. An abstract base class consisting of only pure virtual methods and static const **data members is the closest C++ equivalent of an interface in the Java programming language.**

C++ provides no mechanism other than programmer discipline to make sure nothing else is included in a class designed for use as an interface. The Java programming language ensures that interfaces contain neither method implementations nor nonconstant

The Java platform provides a number of interfaces that are covered in later chapters of this book. One of these is Runnable from the package java.lang. The Runnable interface defines the behavior of being capable of running as a separate thread in a multithreading program. Threads are separate paths through one program that can be executing at the same time. All threads must have a method run, which acts like the main method for the thread. One way to define a class that can run as a thread is to define it to implement Runnable. This interface includes the method run.

You can design your own interfaces, much like you can define your own classes. Use the keyword interface in the definition rather than the keyword class.

Syntax

*[*public*]* **interface** *interface_name [*extends *interface_name]* **{**
    / declaration of members */*
}

Dissection

- Like a class, an interface can have public access or the default package access.
- An interface can extend another interface. In this way, you can accumulate the behaviors from layers of interfaces into one very powerful or very specialized interface.

- An interface can contain methods, but the following restrictions apply:

  All methods are abstract.

  You cannot define the implementation of methods in an interface.

  You can explicitly include the qualifier abstract in the method declaration, but do not have to because it is implied.

  You cannot include methods that are qualified with the keywords **native**, **static**, **synchronized**, or **final**.

  All methods are public.

  You can explicitly include the access specifier **public**, but do not have to because the default access for methods in an interface is public rather than package.

- An interface can contain fields, but they are all static and final. In other words, the only data items allowed in interfaces are constants. If you omit the qualifiers **static** and **final**, the Java programming language silently provides them for you!

Code Example

```
public interface Artistic {
   public void sketch();
}
```

Code Dissection

The interface `Artistic` contains just one method. The method is implicitly abstract. Any class that implements `Artistic` must provide an implementation of `sketch`.

Mini Quiz 5-2

Why are final and static not allowed as qualifiers for methods in an interface?

Any class can implement one or more interfaces by including the **implements** keyword in its class definition.

Syntax

[public] *[qualifiers]* class *class_name* **implements** *interface_name*
[, interface_name] **{**
   / declaration of members */*
}

Dissection

- As always, a class can have explicit public access or the default package access.

- A class that implements an interface can be **final** or **abstract**, just like any other class.
- The keyword **interface** introduces the name of the interface that the class implements. A class can implement more than one interface. List all the interfaces' names, separated by commas.
- Interfaces in the Java programming language meet most requirements of C++ multiple inheritance.

Code Example

```
public class Painter implements Artistic {
    public void sketch() {
       System.out.println( "pen and ink drawing" );
   }
}
public class Sculptor implements Artistic, Runnable {
    public void sketch() {
       System.out.println( "Charcoal drawing" );
   }
   public void run() {
      sketch();
   }
}
```

Code Dissection

Because the `Sculptor` class implements two interfaces—`Artistic` and the core interface **Runnable**—it must implement methods defined in both interfaces: `sketch` and `run`. When the Java Virtual Machine (JVM) starts this class as a thread, it executes the `Sculptor`**.run** method.

All classes that implement `Artistic` must have a fully implemented `sketch` method. This class can be instantiated. The class can also define new methods.

A class can implement an interface as well as extending another class. Indeed, one of the reasons for implementing the interface Runnable—rather than the core class Thread, which provides a more complete framework for threads—is that your class may already be extending some class other than Object.

Syntax

[public*] [qualifiers]* **class** *class_name* **extends** *superclass_name*
implements *interface_name [, interface_name]* **{**
  / declaration of members */*
}

Dissection

- A class can simultaneously extend a superclass and implement one or more interfaces.

Code Example

```
public class Designer extends Thread implements Artistic {
   public void sketch() {
       System.out.println( "conceptual drawing" );
   }
   public void run() {
      sketch();
   }
}
```

Code Dissection

This class extends **Thread**, perhaps so that it can inherit the full support for threads that the **Thread** class provides. The `Designer` class can do so because it has no other superclass than **Object**. After extending **Thread,** `Designer` still has **Object** as a superclass, but now **Object** is an indirect superclass. The specialized behavior of a `Designer` is specified in the interface `Artistic`.

Like the `Sculptor` class, the `Designer` class implements **run**, but this class is overriding the **run** method of the **Thread** class.

Like the `Painter` and the `Sculptor` classes, the `Designer` class would be rejected by the compiler if the class did not provide an implementation for `sketch`.

When a class implements an interface, objects of that class are also considered to be instantiations of the interface. Using the example classes in this section, a `Designer` is an `Artistic` object as well as a Thread and Runnable object, a `Sculptor` is both a Runnable object and an `Artistic` object, and a `Painter` is `Artistic`.

Mini Quiz 5-3

Why is an interface not allowed to implement another interface or to extend or implement a class?

Here is a file that contains two interfaces and two classes:

```
package java4cpp.inheritance;
interface Inflatable {
   public void inflate();
}
interface Kickable {
   public void kick();
}
class SportsBall {
   public void manufacture() {
      System.out.println( "Making a sports ball." );
```

```
    }
}
public class SoccerBall extends SportsBall
         implements Inflatable, Kickable {
   public void inflate() {
      System.out.println( "Inflating a soccer ball." );
   }
   public void kick() {
      System.out.println( "Kicking a soccer ball." );
   }
   public static void g1( Inflatable x ) {
      x.inflate();
   }
   public static void g2( Kickable y ) {
      y.kick();
   }
   public static void g3( SportsBall z ) {
      z.manufacture();
   }
   public static void main( String[] args ) {
      SoccerBall ball = new SoccerBall();
      ball.inflate();
      ball.kick();
      ball.manufacture();

      g1( ball );
      g2( ball );
      g3( ball );
   }
}
```

The output is

```
Inflating a soccer ball.
Kicking a soccer ball.
Making a sports ball.
Inflating a soccer ball.
Kicking a soccer ball.
Making a sports ball.
```

The class `SoccerBall` acquires the method `inflate` from `Inflatable`, `kick` from `Kickable`, and `manufacture` from `SportsBall`. `SoccerBall` must provide implementations for `inflate` and `kick`, but can simply inherit `manufacture`.

`SoccerBall` also defines methods `g1`, `g2`, and `g3`. These functions give you a sneak preview of dynamic binding in the Java programming language. The `main` method declares the object `ball` to be an instance of the class `SoccerBall`. Because `SoccerBall` extends `SportsBall`, `ball` is also an object reference for the class `SportsBall`, and can be passed into the argument `z` of `g3`. Similarly, `ball` is an `Inflatable` object reference and also a `Kickable` object reference, because `SoccerBall` implements both interfaces. The same mechanism of dynamic binding that lets you pass a `SoccerBall` object to a `SportsBall` argument of `g3` lets you pass a `SoccerBall` object to the `Inflatable` argument `x` of `g1` and to the `Kickable` argument `y` of `g2`. This mechanism is sometimes called **polymorphism.**

Applying Access Specifiers to Members

The full implications of access specifiers become clear only in terms of inheritance. Every member of every Java class, as well as the class itself, has an access specifier. For simplicity, most members of classes declared so far in this book have been public.

The Java programming language uses three access specifier keywords: private, protected, and public. The fourth access type, package, is a default that you cannot specify explicitly.

Like packages themselves, package access does not exist in C++. The usage of the other access specifiers is similar, but not identical, to that in C++.

Figure 5-2 describes the access methods of the Java programming language. The table is quite dense, so some summary statements follow to reiterate the meanings of each access type in more general terms. The more restrictive accesses are to the right, and less restrictive accesses are to the left.

Situation	Public	Protected	Default or package	Private
Accessible to a non-subclass from the same package?	yes	yes	yes	no
Accessible to a subclass from the same package?	yes	yes	yes	no
Accessible to a non-subclass from a different package?	yes	no	no	no
Accessible to a subclass from a different package?	yes	no (fields) yes (methods)	no	no
Inherited by a subclass in the same package?	yes	yes	yes	no
Inherited by a subclass in a different package?	yes	yes	no	no

Figure 5-2: Java access specifiers

Access specifiers establish whether members of a class can be inherited by subclasses or accessed by other classes. The access can depend upon whether the classes are in the same package, or whether the classes are related by inheritance.

- public grants unlimited access to all classes.
- protected gives unlimited access to classes in the same package. It also allows all subclasses to access methods, regardless of whether the subclasses are in the same package. A subclass from a different package can inherit fields but not access them directly. A class that is in a different package and is not a subclass has no access to protected members.
  The next sample program should clarify how subclasses in different packages access protected fields.
- There is no keyword for default access. This access is called **package** access, and applies when the access specifier is omitted. Package access grants unlimited access to classes in the same package, but no access to classes outside the package.
- private allows no access to the member from outside the class.

The main difference between the Java programming language and C++ is that the default access is private in C++ and package in the Java programming language. The access specifiers public **and** protected **have the same meaning in the Java programming language and C++. In the Java programming language, unlike C++, access to protected members depends on whether the classes are in the same package, as well as whether they are related by inheritance. Another important difference is that** private **methods in the Java programming language cannot be overridden. Binding to private methods is not dynamic, unlike virtual private methods in C++.**

An Example of Cross-Package Protected Access

The following program demonstrates how protected access works. The classes Location2D and Location3D are in two packages: `java4cpp.inheritance` and `java4cpp.errors`, respectively.

Here is the definition of the class `Location2D`. It contains protected fields `x` and y.

```
package java4cpp.inheritance;
/** An example point in 2D space
  */
public class Location2D {
   protected int x = 0, y = 0;
   public Location2D( int initX, int initY ) {
      x = initX;
      y = initY;
   }
   public Location2D() {
      this( 0, 0 );
   }
}
```

The class Location2D also uses the this method in the constructor with no arguments, to initialize x and y to zero by default.

Here is the definition of class Location3D. This class extends Location2D. There is a deliberate error in the class Location3D.

```
package java4cpp.errors;
import java4cpp.inheritance.Location2D;
/** A class intended to create an error
  */
public class Location3D extends Location2D {
   protected int z;
   public Location3D( int initX, int initY,
                      int initZ ) {
      x = initX;
      y = initY;
      z = initZ;
   }
   public static void show2D( Location2D p2 ) {
      // The line below results in a compiler error
      // because the data members are not accessible
      System.out.println( "( " + p2.x + ", " + p2.y
                          + " )" );
   }
   public static void show3D( Location3D p3 ) {
      System.out.println( "( " + p3.x + ", " + p3.y
                          + ", " + p3.z + " )" );
   }
   static public void main( String[] args ) {
      Location3D a = new Location3D( 1, 2, 3 );
      Location3D.show3D( a );
   }
}
```

This file begins by importing class java4cpp.inheritance.Location2D so that the file can refer to the class simply as Location2D. The constructor and the method Show3D use x and y correctly. A class can use members it inherits from the superclass just like members it defines for itself. The error is that method Print2D uses x and y as members of Location2D. In other words, the class Location3D is trying to access protected fields of its superclass through an object of the superclass instead of one of its own objects. Because that superclass is in another package, the compiler flags an error.

The class Location3D really does have access to x and y of Location2D through inheritance. The rationale behind protected access is to prevent exactly the situation in method Show2D. A subclass in a different package from the superclass can call methods in the superclass, but accessing data is dangerous and unnecessary.

The Object Reference super

Is it possible for instance methods to call instance methods from other classes in the same hierarchy? The only way to call instance methods is with an object reference, and dynamic binding ensures that the method called for an object is the one implemented or inherited by the class that the object instantiates.

Sometimes it is useful to call the method of the superclass, bypassing any overriding method in the subclass. Therefore, the Java programming language provides an object reference super that refers to the superclass for the current object.

Syntax **super**.*method_name*(*argument_list*)

Dissection

- Any method of a subclass can use **super** to call a method of the superclass, unless prohibited by the access specified for the method.
- You can use **super** as an object reference to chain upward only one level in the class hierarchy. An expression such as the following is not valid:

  super.super.*method_name*(*argument_list*)

Code Example

```
public String toString() {
   return( super.toString() + "Passengers: " +
      passengers );
   }
```

Code Dissection Here, **toString** in a subclass calls the very method that it overrides. The return type of **toString** in the superclass is also **String**, so the value returned by this method is the concatenation of strings.

What if the superclass does not override the called method, but inherits the implementation of its superclass? The expression uses the implementation of the method that the superclass uses, and searches the inheritance hierarchy if necessary to find it. If the superclass does not implement or inherit the method, the compiler rejects the method call, even if the calling subclass does implement the method. In the case of the method toString, an implementation of it is always found even if it is the default inherited from Object. Calling super.toString() in an instance method is never an error.

In C++, a nonstatic method can call a method in a direct or indirect base class using a construct with the following form:

class_name.method_name(argument_list)

In the Java programming language, you cannot call a method at an arbitrary location within the inheritance hierarchy. A Java method cannot get around this rule by referring to another class by name. The keyword super **lets you specify the immediate superclass only, and is the only time that the type of the object reference, rather than the object itself, determines which method is called.**

Constructors and Inheritance

The superclass object is created before the subclass object at every level in the class hierarchy. In other words, the order of construction of objects that are related by inheritance is the same in the Java programming language as it is in C++.

Here is an example based on three related classes: `Bottom` , `Middle`, and `Top`.

```
package java4cpp.inheritance;
/** A class used to demonstrate inheritance
  * concepts
  */
public class Bottom extends Middle {
   public Bottom() {
      System.out.println( "Constructing a Bottom "
                        + "class object" );
   }
   /** Test method for the class
     * @param args not used
     */
   public static void main( String[] args ) {
      Bottom x = new Bottom();
   }
}
/** Example top class in a hierarchy
  */
class Top {
   public Top() {
      System.out.println( "Constructing a Top "
                        + "class object" );
   }
}
/** Example middle class in a hierarchy
  */
class Middle extends Top {
   public Middle() {
      System.out.println( "Constructing a Middle "
                        + "class object" );
   }
}
```

The output is

```
Constructing a Top class object
Constructing a Middle class object
Constructing a Bottom class object
```

The Bottom class extends Middle, which in turn extends Top. When the main method of Bottom creates a Bottom object, the messages printed by the constructors confirm the order in which the constructors are called.

By default, the JVM calls the constructor of the superclass and passes no arguments. Therefore, the superclass should have a constructor that takes no arguments. Also, the superclass is constructed automatically before the subclass. What if the superclass requires some initialization? How can you call a constructor other than the no-argument constructor of the superclass?

The Java programming language addresses the question of initializing the superclass with a special method called super. It works for superclass constructors much like the method this works for constructors of the same class.

Syntax **super(** *arguments_of_superclass_constructor* **);**

Dissection

- A subclass constructor can explicitly invoke a superclass constructor with the **super** method. You must insert the call to **super** only when you want to pass arguments to the constructor of the superclass.
- If you do not explicitly call **super**, the Java compiler calls it for you, with no arguments. This is the mechanism by which superclasses are automatically built first. An error results if the superclass does not have a constructor without parameters.
- The **super** method can appear only in constructors and must be the first line in the constructor.
- The one exception to the rule that execution of a constructor starts with a call to **super** is when the first statement in your constructor is a call to **this**. The default **super** defers to **this**. You are not allowed to call both **this** and **super** from one constructor. But you can chain your constructors together through calls to **this**, until one of the constructors explicitly or implicitly calls **super**.

Code Example

```
package java4cpp.inheritance;
class ReadingMatter {
   boolean available_online;   // false by default
   String title;
   public ReadingMatter() {
      this.title = "TBA";
   }
   public ReadingMatter( String title ) {
      this.title = title;
   }
}
public class Book extends ReadingMatter {
   String author;
   int numPages;
```

```
    public Book( String title, String author,
                 int numPages ) {
        super( title );
        this.numPages = numPages;
        this.author = author;
    }
}
```

Code Dissection

A Book object has four fields: `available_online`, `title`, `author`, and `numPages`, the first two of which are inherited from `ReadingMatter`. The superclass constructor initializes the field `title` and accepts the default value for the field `available_online`. The constructor for `Book` must explicitly call **super** to pass the title of the book on to the superclass constructor before initializing the fields `author` and `numPages`.

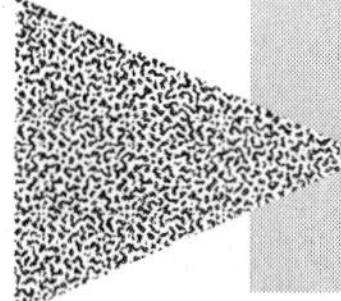

Mini Quiz 5-4

The this pointer of C++ is almost the equivalent of the object reference this of the Java programming language. Why would it be impossible to implement a super pointer in C++?

Moving from C++

The constructs you use in C++ to initialize base classes are very different from the syntax that you use in the Java programming language. In C++, you must use an initializer list to pass arguments to the constructor of a superclass. The arguments passed in such an initializer list entry become the base class arguments to the base class constructor.

C++ also lets you use the initializer list as an alternative to assignment statements in the constructor. For example, a close C++ equivalent to the constructor of the `Book` class is

```
Book::Book( char* st, char* sa, int np )
   : ReadingMatter( st ), author( sa ), numPages( np ) {};
```

The Java programming language has no initializer lists.

Does the Java programming language limit functionality by not allowing initializer lists in constructors? Essentially, there are three reasons to provide an initializer list for a C++ constructor:

- **To initialize a nonstatic constant field.**
  The Java programming language lets you give constant fields their initial values where they are defined. Most constants are initialized this way. If a class has a blank final instance field, the Java compiler requires that the constructor initialize it explicitly. The initialization can happen anywhere within the constructor, if the instance blank final is initialized before it is used.
- **If a member of the class is a C++ reference, to assign an object to the reference.**
  Object references in the Java programming language are not the same as C++ references and cannot be manipulated like C++ pointers and C++ references. While an object is being constructed in C++, references it contains cannot be altered to refer to different objects, and therefore have fixed values just like constants. This use for initializer lists does not apply to the Java programming language.
- **In a derived class, to pass arguments to the constructor of the base class.**
  The super **method provides this functionality.**

An Example of Constructing Related Objects

Here is a set of three classes that demonstrate constructing related objects:

```
package java4cpp.inheritance;
/** A class used to demonstrate inheritance concepts
  */
public class Vehicle {
   private int wheels, range;
   /** Class constructor
     * @param w number of wheels
     * @param r range in kilometers
     */
   public Vehicle( int w, int r ) {
      wheels = w;
      range = r;
   }
   /** Represent the object as a string
     * @return The object as a String
     */
   public String toString() {
      return ( "Wheels: " + wheels
               + " Range: " + range );
   }
}
```

The class `Vehicle` has one constructor with two arguments. Those arguments initialize the fields `wheels` and `range`. The class also provides an implementation of the method toString.

```
package java4cpp.inheritance;
/** A class used to demonstrate inheritance concepts
  */
public class Car extends Vehicle {
   private static final int NUMBER_OF_WHEELS = 4;
   private int passengers;
   /** Class constructor
     * @param p number of passengers
     * @param r range in kilometers
     */
   public Car( int p, int r ) {
      super( NUMBER_OF_WHEELS, r );
      passengers = p;
   }
   /** Represent the object as a string
     * @return The object as a String
     */
```

```
    public String toString() {
        return( super.toString() + " Passengers: "
                + passengers );
    }
}
```

The class Car is a subclass of Vehicle. Because Car extends Vehicle and the only constructor of Vehicle takes two arguments, Car must call super. The Car class adds a third field, passengers, which the constructor initializes after it calls super. Assume that all cars have four wheels, so that a constant fills the parameter of the superclass constructor. Notice that the toString method of the Car class calls the super.toString method to build up the line to output.

The third class is a test class for Vehicle and Car:

```
package java4cpp.inheritance;
/** A class used to demonstrate inheritance concepts
  */
public class VehicleTest {
   /** Test method for the class
     * @param args Not used
     */
   public static void main( String[] args )
   {
      Car c = new Car( 5, 500 );
      System.out.println( "Car: " + c );
   }
}
```

The output is

```
Car: Wheels: 4 Range: 500 Passengers: 5
```

These classes demonstrate the uses of the keyword super:

- The constructor of the class Car calls the constructor of the superclass Vehicle by using the method super.
- Both Vehicle and Car override toString. The toString method of Car uses the object reference super to call the toString method of Vehicle.

Finalizer Methods and Inheritance

An inconsistency exists between object construction and destruction. A constructor for a superclass always runs before the constructor of the subclass, and that pattern repeats as often as required to make sure that an object is built in the proper order. Moreover, the Java platform calls the super constructor implicitly if a call is not explicitly coded.

Finalizer methods of subclasses do not call the finalizers of their superclasses automatically. This may seem to be an omission, but is based on the fact that the finalizer of a subclass overrides, and therefore replaces, the finalizer of its superclass. Only one finalizer is called implicitly for an object. Explicitly calling the finalizer method for a superclass never is an error, because all objects can inherit a default finalize from Object. You may define many classes without a finalizer, but all classes have at least the finalizer method inherited from the Object class.

If you want to chain together the finalizer methods of your subclasses and superclasses, you must do it manually. Fortunately, the Java programming language gives you a simple construct for calling the finalizer of the superclass. Simply add the following statement to the end of your finalizer method.

Syntax **super.finalize();**

Dissection

- This statement should be the last statement in your finalizer so that the superclass is available throughout the execution of the subclass finalizer.
- The only method that should explicitly call a finalizer is the finalizer of a direct subclass.
- Finalizers can take no arguments and have return type **void**.
- You should specify protected access when you define a finalizer method for a class. Include the clause **throws Throwable** in case the method, or a method invoked by the method, can throw an exception.

Code Example

```
protected void finalize() throws Throwable {
   // perform cleanup
   super.finalize();
}
```

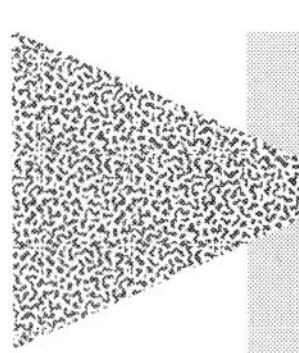

Mini Quiz 5-5

Why is protected the most appropriate access specifier for a finalizer method?

When does the first finalizer in the chain of subclass and superclass finalizers run? How can you ensure that it runs?

Here are two classes that demonstrate chaining finalizer methods. They are stored in the same file.

```
package java4cpp.inheritance;
/** A class used to demonstrate how inheritance
  * influences finalization
  */
public class FinalizerClass extends FinalizerSuper {
   /** Class default constructor method
     */
```

```
    public FinalizerClass() {
       System.out.println( "Constructing the "
                           + "subclass" );
    }
    /** Class finalizer method
      * @exception Throwable any exception at all
      */
    protected void finalize () throws Throwable {
       System.out.println( "Finalizing the "
                           + "subclass" );
       super.finalize();
    }
    /** Test method for the class
      * @param args Not used
      */
    public static void main( String[] args ) {
       System.runFinalizersOnExit( true );
       FinalizerClass fc = new FinalizerClass();
    }
}
class FinalizerSuper {
    /** Class default constructor method */
    public FinalizerSuper() {
       System.out.println( "Constructing the "
                           + "superclass" );
    }
    /** Class finalizer method
      * @exception Throwable Any exception at all
      */
    protected void finalize() throws Throwable {
       System.out.println( "Finalizing the "
                           + "superclass" );
       super.finalize();    // calls Object.finalize()
    }
}
```

The output is

```
Constructing the superclass
Constructing the subclass
Finalizing the subclass
Finalizing the superclass
```

The public class `FinalizerClass` extends the class `FinalizerSuper`. Both classes have finalizer methods that end with the statement super.finalize();. In the class `FinalizerSuper`, the statement runs the finalizer of the Object class, which does nothing.

Overriding Methods

When you create a subclass, that class inherits all the methods of the superclass by default. The subclass can redefine the inherited methods, as well as define new methods. In this way, subclasses can augment and customize the behavior inherited from their superclasses. The process of redefining methods that a subclass would otherwise inherit is called **overriding** methods.

All classes directly or indirectly extend Object, and therefore inherit a common set of methods by default. It is common practice to override the following methods:

- Override toString to provide a string representation of instances suitable for printing.
- If objects may be compared for equality, override equals.
- When you override equals, you should also override hashCode. The JVM uses hash tables to access objects, and the value returned by hashCode locates the entry for an object in a table. If two or more objects are equal, in the sense that the equals method returns true, they should have the same hash code. Hash tables are discussed in Chapter 10.
- If any of the fields are object references, override clone so that the instances can be copied properly. Cloning is discussed in Chapter 7.

When you call an overridden method, the version of the method that is used is determined by the class of the object rather than by the type of the object reference in the calling statement. The following program demonstrates this:

```
package java4cpp.inheritance;
class SuperOverload {
    public String toString() {
       return "superclass";
    }
}
class SubOverload extends SuperOverload {
   public String toString() {
      return "subclass";
   }
}
public class TestOverload {
   public static void main( String[] args ) {
      SuperOverload a = new SuperOverload();
      SubOverload b = new SubOverload();
      // SubOverload.toString
      System.out.println( a.toString() );
      // SuperOverload.toString
```

```
            System.out.println( b.toString() );
            // a is a SuperOverload ref to SubOverload object
            a = b;
            // SubOverload.toString
            System.out.println( a.toString() );
        }
    }
```

The output is

```
superclass
subclass
subclass
```

Overloading methods must conform to the following rules:

- The signature and the return type of the method must be identical in the superclass and the subclass. The signature includes the name of the method, the number of arguments, and the type of each argument. For example, the compiler rejects the following files because the method `f` is overloaded with different return types:

```
package java4cpp.errors;
/** A class used to demonstrate how overloaded methods
must have the exact same return type
*/
public class MisMatch extends SuperClass {
   public MisMatch f() {
      return this;
   }
}
class SuperClass {
   public SuperClass f() {
      return this;
   }
}
```

The output from the javac command is

```
MisMatch.java:7: Method redefined with different return
type: java4cpp.errors.MisMatch f() was java4cpp.errors.
SuperClass f()
public MisMatch f() {
                 ^
```

- A throws clause lists the types of exceptions that can occur during execution of the method, or the methods that the method calls. You cannot add types to the list of exceptions in the overridden method, but you can remove types and make the throws clause more restrictive.

- The access specifier of the overriding method must be the same as, or less restrictive than, the access specifier in the superclass. You may, for example, inherit a protected method and override it with a public method. In a subclass, you can make overriding methods more accessible, but never less accessible, than the methods in the superclass.
- You can override a method with an abstract method, even if the overridden method is not abstract. Do this if you do not want to implement the method, but want to force all classes that extend your class to implement the method.
- You can also override an abstract method with a method that is not abstract.

These rules have implications that you should consider when you define a class that may be extended. When your class becomes a superclass, it imposes limitations on how its methods may be overridden.

- You cannot do much to get around the fact that return types in overriding methods and overridden methods must match. In some cases, returning the type Object is appropriate and can accommodate all the reference types.
- Consider that the overriding methods cannot throw exceptions that you do not allow in your throws clause. The easiest way to let overriding methods throw any exceptions is to specify throws Throwable, which allows all exceptions.
- If you declare a method to be public, you force all overriding methods also to be public.

What happens when the signatures in the superclass and subclass do not match? Of course, if the names are different, the methods are different. If the names are the same but the argument lists differ, a different mechanism comes into play: **overloading.** In the Java programming language, methods in a subclass can both overload and override a method from the superclass. For example, suppose that a superclass defines the following method:

```
void myWay( int ival, float fval ) { /* ... */ }
```

The method definitions in the subclass shown in Figure 5-3 have different effects.

Method	Effect
`void myWay( int ival, float fval ) { // . . . }`	overriding
`void myWay( long ival, double fval ) { // . . . }`	overloading
`void myWay( String[] sval ) { // . . . }`	overloading
`private void myWay( int ival, float fval ) { // . . . }`	error: more restrictive access
`int myWay( int ival, float fval ) { // . . . }`	error: return type mismatch

Figure 5-3: Methods in a subclass

Overriding methods in the Java programming language is very similar to overriding in C++. You do the same thing for the same reasons in almost the same way. The Java programming language differs from C++ in the following ways:

- **In the Java programming language, the return types of overriding and overridden methods must always match. In some situations, C++ accepts return types that differ.**
- **C++ does not have the rule that access specifiers must be the same or less restrictive.**
- **C++ does not allow an overriding method to be abstract.**
- **C++ does not let a derived class overload methods in the base class. Instead a method in the derived class hides all functions in the base class with the same name, even if the argument list is different.**

C++ programmers sometimes take advantage of the hiding rule to make sure that the argument lists of overriding functions match. If argument lists do not match, most C++ compilers give a warning of the form "function x(y) hides function x(z)." If argument lists do not match in the Java programming language, the method is overloaded in your subclass and not overridden.

An Example of Overriding and Overloading a Method

The following program shows how a subclass can overload and override a superclass method:

```
package java4cpp.inheritance;
/** A class used to demonstrate the interaction
  * among methods that are both overridden and
  * overloaded
```

```
  */
public class OverloadOverride {
   /** Test method for the class
     * @param args not used
     */
   public static void main( String[] args ) {
      SubClass1 x = new SubClass1();
      x.chewGum( 2.4 );  //overriding subclass method
      x.walk( 100.345 ); //overloaded superclass method
      x.walk( 89 );      //overloaded subclass method
   }
}
/** An example superclass */
class SuperClass1 {
   public void chewGum( double x ) {
      System.out.println( "SuperClass1.chewGum( double )"
                          + " called" );
   }
   public void walk( double x ) {
      System.out.println( "SuperClass1.walk( double )"
                          + " called" );
   }
}
/** An example subclass */
class SubClass1 extends SuperClass1 {
   public void chewGum( double x ) {
      // override superclass function chewGum
      System.out.println( "SubClass1.chewGum( double )"
                          + " called" );
   }
   public void walk( int x ) {
      // overload superclass function walk
      System.out.println( "SubClass1.walk( int )"
                          + " called" );
   }
}
```

The output is

```
SubClass1.chewGum( double ) called
SuperClass1.walk( double ) called
SubClass1.walk( int ) called
```

Class `SubClass1` extends class `SuperClass1`. The superclass has two methods, `chewGum` and `walk`. This subclass overrides `chewGum` and overloads `walk`. The class `OverloadOverride` calls three different methods—the `chewGum` of `SubClass1`, the `walk` of `SuperClass1`, and the `walk` of `SubClass1`—all for an object of class `SubClass1`.

If you convert this program to C++, you will see that the behavior of the function call `x.walk( 100.345 );` differs in the Java programming language and C++. In C++, the value `100.345` is truncated to an integer and passed to the `walk` of `SubClass1`. You also receive a warning that the `walk` in `SuperClass1` is hidden.

Dynamic Binding

Dynamic binding is a manifestation of polymorphism in the Java programming language. The **polymorphism** of dynamic binding refers to the ability of code to have different behaviors depending on the type of the objects being manipulated, and not on the type of the object references. Other meanings are sometimes associated with the word polymorphism, some of which relate to facilities that are available in other languages but not the Java programming language. The Java programming language supports polymorphism for methods of classes that are related by inheritance. In particular, a method call for an object reference of a superclass type may invoke the method defined in the superclass or an overriding implementation of the method in a subclass. Which method to call is resolved at run time, and depends on the actual class of the object behind the reference.

Dynamic binding is the process of resolving the reference to a method at run time. When you call a method that has been overridden by at least one subclass in an inheritance hierarchy, the JVM determines which version of the method to call. You do not have to do any special coding to take advantage of dynamic binding, because it is automatic. However, you can exert some control over whether dynamic binding occurs with the keywords **abstract** and **final**.

Syntax

[access_specifier] **abstract** *return_type method_name*(*argument_list*) *[*throws *exception_list]*;

Dissection

- Use the keyword **abstract** to indicate that the method has no implementation in the current class.
- An abstract method has no body. Therefore, there is no block of code or **{ }** in the declaration.

Code Example

```
public abstract double profit( Revenue r, Costs c );
```

Code Dissection

The method `profit` is abstract. The declaration specifies that it has two arguments—an object reference to a `Revenue` object, and an object reference to a `Costs` object—and that it returns a value of type `double`. But this declaration gives no indication of how the return value is calculated.

Moving from C++

The equivalent of abstract in C++ is the pure virtual function, as in the following example:

```
double Finance::profit( Revenue r, Costs c ) = 0;
```

In *The Design and Evolution of C++*, Bjarne Stroustrup says, "The curious =0 syntax was chosen over the obvious alternative of introducing a keyword pure or abstract because at the time I saw no chance of getting a new keyword accepted."

When you declare a method to be abstract, you are forcing all subclasses to override the method with a full implementation. Any class that contains an abstract method must also be declared abstract. Including the keyword **abstract** in the declarations of both the class and the method is repetitious, because a class with at least one abstract method is itself abstract. Nevertheless, the repetition is required.

Syntax *[access_specifier]* **final** *return_type method_name* (*argument_list*) *[*throws *exception_list]*

Dissection

- Use the keyword **final** to prevent the method from being overridden in subclasses.

Code Example

```
public final String greeting( String name ) {
   return ( "Hello " + name + "!" );
}
```

Code Dissection The method `greeting` cannot be overridden by a subclass of the class in which this method is defined.

You can also apply the qualifier final to a class definition. The effect of final is to prohibit the overriding of the method or the extending of the class. The effect is to turn off dynamic binding for methods.There are two main reasons for doing this:

- *Security*. When a class is extended, the subclass has an opportunity to change or add behavior. To prevent a subclass from overriding your implementation with something potentially malevolent or simply out of keeping with the intention of your design, declare your class or method final.
- *Performance*. The lookup and dispatch algorithm of dynamic binding imposes some overhead at run time. If you turn off dynamic binding, the method call can be executed a little quicker, and there may be additional opportunities for code optimization.

If you have used the C++ keyword virtual**, you have used dynamic binding in C++. You may be familiar with Virtual Function Tables (VFTs). C++ implements dynamic binding by registering all virtual functions in VFTs, and using the VFTs at run time to locate the appropriate version of the method before passing control to it.**

The Java programming language implements dynamic binding with a mechanism similar to C++ VFTs. The difference is that the default behavior of the Java programming language is to make all non-private instance methods eligible for dynamic binding. C++ does not build an entry for a function in the VFT unless you explicitly declare the function virtual**. In C++, the default is static binding, largely for reasons of compatibility with C code.**

Because dynamic binding is the default in the Java programming language, you do not have to supply a keyword to turn it on, unlike C++, which requires you to use the qualifier virtual**. The Java programming language has no need for an equivalent to the C++ keyword** virtual**. C++ has no equivalent of the keyword** final **in this context.**

The Java programming language also is free from the C++ trap of object slicing, which nullifies dynamic binding. Object slicing occurs in C++ when you pass a derived class object as a base class argument, by value. The called function receives a copy of the object, because it is passed by value. The copy constructor of the base class is used to make the copy. The base class copy constructor does not know about the attributes added by the derived class, and effectively omits them. Often, this situation is the result of programmer error in C++. This is an error you cannot make in the Java programming language, simply because you always pass object references, not the actual objects.

When should you use an interface rather than an abstract superclass? One reason is to let classes that have other superclasses implement the interface. But what if other superclasses are not a factor? As a rule of thumb, abstract classes are more appropriate when some of the behaviors can be implemented in the superclass because they are common to all subclasses. If none of the behaviors can be specified in a way that is useful to all the subclasses, use an interface.

Mini Quiz 5-6

Can you include a main method to test an abstract class?

When you use the object reference super to call a method in a superclass, you are altering how the JVM resolves method calls through dynamic binding. You are explicitly specifying which class in the hierarchy to search first for the method. This is the only exception to the rule that the type of the object alone determines what version of an overridden method is called.

The following program demonstrates the effect of using super to call an overridden method:

```
package java4cpp.inheritance;
/** A class used to demonstrate how dynamic
  * binding can be altered by using the
  * <b>super</b> reference.
  */
```

```
public class AlteredBinding {
   /** Test method for the class
     * @param args not used
     */
   public static void main( String[] args ) {
      D x = new D();
      x.g1();
      x.g2();
   }
}
/** An example superclass */
class B {
   public void f( String caller ) {
      System.out.println( "B.f() called by "
                          + caller );
   }
}
/** An example subclass */
class D extends B {
   public void f( String caller ) {
      System.out.println( "D.f() called by "
                          + caller );
   }
   public void g1() {
      f( "subclass" );         // this will call D.f( )
   }
   public void g2() {
      super.f( "subclass" ); // cannot use B.f() here
   }
}
```

The output is

```
D.f() called by subclass
B.f() called by subclass
```

This example program contains a class `B`, a class `D` that extends `B`, and a class `AlteredBinding` that creates and exercises a `D` object. The method `g2` in `D` calls the method `f` from the superclass. The call takes the form `super.f()` because the syntax `B.f()` is an error in this context.

Dynamic Binding and Superclass Constructors

Dynamic binding always calls the implementation of a method in the class that matches type of the object for which the method is called. The only exception is that if a subclass does not implement the method, the version inherited from its superclass is used. The Java programming language applies this rule even during the construction of the superclass, even before the constructor for the subclass has been run!

A superclass constructor can call a method of a subclass while it is building the superclass portion of a subclass object, if the subclass overrides a superclass method. Therefore, you must be careful when you call methods from constructors. For example, consider the `ReadingMaterial` and `Book` classes from earlier in this chapter. The `ReadingMaterial` constructor may call a `Book` method while it is setting up the fields that a `Book` inherits from `ReadingMaterial`. If that method depends on subclass fields that have not yet been initialized, it uses the default initial value of zero, false, or null, depending on the type of the field. As a result, the method may not work as expected, and the object may not be built properly.

Unlike a constructor in the Java programming language, a C++ constructor always calls methods of its own class, never methods of a derived class.

The safest strategy is to declare any methods used by constructors to be final or private. However, this strategy is not always acceptable, because it prevents the methods from ever being overridden. Some additional logic may be an alternative solution. However, the problem remains, because a class that is not final can never know how future subclasses may extend it.

Here is a sample program that demonstrates a superclass constructor calling a subclass method:

```
package java4cpp.inheritance;
/** A class used to demonstrate how dynamic binding
  * works when superclass objects are constructed.
  */
public class Construction {
   /** Test method for the class
     * @param args not used
     */
   public static void main( String[] args ) {
      SuperClass y = new SuperClass();
      SubClass x = new SubClass();
      x.g();
   }
}
/** An example superclass */
class SuperClass {
   public SuperClass() {
      f();       // which f() will be called?
   }             // SuperClass.f() or SubClass.f()?
   public void f() {
      System.out.println( "SuperClass.f() called" );
```

```
    }
    public void g() {
        f();        // which f() will be called?
    }              // SuperClass.f() or SubClass.f()?
}
/** An example subclass */
class SubClass extends SuperClass {
    public void f() {
        System.out.println( "SubClass.f() called" );
    }
}
```

The output is

```
SuperClass.f() called
SubClass.f() called
SubClass.f() called
```

Class `SubClass` extends class `SuperClass`. Both `SubClass` and `SuperClass` implement method `f`. The constructor of `SuperClass` calls `f`. When the `SuperClass` object `y` is created, the `SuperClass` constructor calls `SuperClass.f`. When the `SubClass` object `x` is created, the `SuperClass` constructor calls `SubClass.f`.

SUMMARY

Support for inheritance is essential in any object-oriented language. The concepts of inheritance, method overriding, constructor chaining, and dynamic binding are quite similar in the Java programming language and C++. However, the implementation details are different.

A class that is based on an existing class is a subclass, and the existing class is the superclass. Subclassing is a technique for defining classes that have additional or more specialized behavior and attributes compared to those of the more general superclass. The subclass extends the superclass with the keyword **extends**, as in the following syntax:

[access] [qualifiers] class *subclass_name* extends *superclass_name* { /*...*/ }

Interfaces are similar to classes except that they are declared with the keyword **interface**. All methods in an interface are implicitly abstract and public. The only fields allowed in interfaces are constants. Interfaces can extend other interfaces. Use interfaces to design but not implement behavior for future classes.

Classes do not extend interfaces, but you can implement interfaces by using the following syntax:

[access] [qualifiers] class *class_name* implements *interface_name { /* ... */ }*

A class that implements an interface must provide implementations for all the methods in the interface. Otherwise, it is an abstract class. Classes can implement one or more interfaces, and can also extend a superclass.

The Java programming language does not allow multiple inheritance. Instead, you use interfaces to specify behaviors that classes can implement. A class can implement any number of interfaces as well as extend one class.

The access specifiers for members are public, private, and protected. The default access, package, does not have a keyword and applies if you omit the access specifier from a member declaration. The specifier private restricts access to within the class. The default gives access to all classes in the same package. Protected access is less restrictive than the default in that it lets subclasses access methods and inherit members regardless of whether the subclasses are in the same package. Public access is wholly unrestricted.

Subclasses can overload methods from their superclass, override them, or inherit them. If the argument lists are different, the method is overloaded. If the signatures are the same, the method is overridden and must comply with a number of restrictions, including the requirement that the return types must match. Methods that are not implemented in the subclass are inherited. Overriding and inheriting methods comprise a very powerful technique that lets subclasses customize and augment behaviors established by the superclass.

You cannot extend a class declared with final, or override a method declared with final.

A class declared with abstract or that contains an abstract method cannot be instantiated. A method declared with abstract has no implementation, and must be overridden by a subclass. Declare a class or method to be abstract to force subclasses to implement methods.

Superclass objects are always created before subclass objects. To pass arguments to a superclass constructor, you must explicitly call the superclass constructor with the super method, using the following syntax:

super(*arguments_of_superclass_constructor*);

By using the keyword super, you can ensure that a subclass can call any superclass implementation of a method. Because the Java programming language does not automatically chain superclass and subclass finalizers, you should do so explicitly, using super.finalize().

The Java programming language dynamically binds all nonprivate instance methods by default. Dynamic binding applies even while constructing the superclass portion of subclass objects. The keyword final turns off dynamic binding for the class or method to which it is applied.

QUESTIONS

1. List all access specifiers that are less restrictive than protected.
2. Examine the following code from a single source file:

```
interface Calculator {
   public void calculate();
}
interface Microwave {
   public void cook();
}
```

```
public class Quiz5_2 implements Calculator,
                                Microwave {
   public void calculate() {
      System.out.println( "calculating" );
   }
   public void cook() {
      System.out.println( "cooking" );
   }
   public static void main( String[] args ) {
      Quiz5_2 x = new Quiz5_2();
      x.calculate();
      x.cook();
   }
}
```

Which of the following statements are true when the code is compiled and run? Select all that apply.

a. The compiler rejects the attempt to implement two interfaces at once.

b. The compiler rejects the definition of the class `Quiz5_2` because it implements two interfaces but does not extend anything.

c. Compilation is successful and the output is
```
calculating
cooking
```

d. The compiler indicates an error because the interfaces and the class are not in separate source files.

e. It is optional for the class `Example` to implement the methods `calculate` and `cook`.

3. Examine the following code taken from a single source file:

```
class Vehicle {
   protected void goSomewhere() {
      System.out.println( "travelling..." );
   }
}
public class Bicycle extends Vehicle {
   public void goSomewhere() {
      System.out.println( "pedalling..." );
   }
   public static void main( String[] args ) {
      Bicycle x = new Bicycle();
      x.goSomewhere();
   }
}
```

Which of the following statements are true when the code is compiled and run? Select all that apply.

a. The compiler rejects the definition of the class `Bicycle` because the keyword **extends** is not appropriate for a superclass and should be replaced by the keyword **implements**.

b. The compiler rejects the definition of `Bicycle.goSomewhere` because its access specifier does not match the access specifier of `Vehicle.goSomewhere`.
c. Compilation is successful and the output is `travelling...`
d. Compilation is successful and the output is `pedalling...`
e. It is optional for the class `Bicycle` to implement the method `goSomewhere`.

4. Examine the following code taken from a single source file:

```
abstract class Barbeque {
   public abstract void ignite();
   public void cook() {
      System.out.println( "put food on the "
                         +"grill and wait" );
   }
}
class GasBarbeque extends Barbeque {
   public void ignite() {
      System.out.println( "turn on gas and "
                         +"light match" );
   }
}
class CharcoalBarbeque extends Barbeque {
   public void ignite() {
      System.out.println( "pour on lighter "
                        +"fluid and light match" );
   }
}
public class Cookout {
   public static void makeDinner( Barbeque b ) {
      b.ignite();
      b.cook();
   }
   public static void main( String[] args ) {
      GasBarbeque gb = new GasBarbeque();
      CharcoalBarbeque cb = new CharcoalBarbeque();
      makeDinner( gb );
      makeDinner( cb );
   }
}
```

Which of the following statements are true when the code is compiled and run? Select all that apply.

a. The compiler rejects the definition of `Cookout.makeDinner` because it is not possible to instantiate the argument `b` of the abstract class `Barbeque`.
b. The compiler rejects the definition of the classes `GasBarbeque` and `CharcoalBarbeque` because they do not implement the method `Barbeque.cook`.

c. Compilation is successful and the output is

```
turn on gas and light match
put food on the grill and wait
pour on lighter fluid and light match
put food on the grill and wait
```

d. The compiler rejects the statements `makeDinner( gb );` and `makeDinner( cb );` because the type of `gb` or `cb` does not match the input type of `Barbeque`.

5. Which of the following are valid class definitions? Select all that apply.

a. `final class A { }`

b. `class B { }`

c. `public final class C { }`

d. `public abstract class D { }`

e. `abstract final class E { }`

6. Examine the following code taken from a single source file:

```
class A {
   protected Integer doSomething() {
      return new Integer( 2 );
   }
}
public class B extends A { }
```

Which of the following methods are valid for class B? Select all that apply.

a.
```
protected Integer doSomething(){
    return new Integer( 3 );
}
```

b.
```
public Integer doSomething() {
    return new Integer( 3 );
}
```

c.
```
Integer doSomething() {
    return new Integer( 3 );
}
```

d.
```
protected Object doSomething() {
    return new Integer( 3 );
}
```

e.
```
protected Number doSomething() {
    return new Integer( 3 );
}
```

7. Examine the following code taken from a single source file:

```
class A {
   protected double d = 3.14;
   public static void f() {}
   public void g() {}
}
class B {
   public void m() {}
}
```

```
class C extends A {
   protected static void s() {}
   void t() {}
}
```

Which of the following methods have direct access to the field `A.d`? Select all that apply.

a. `A.f()`
b. `A.g()`
c. `B.m()`
d. `C.s()`
e. `C.t()`

8. List the Java keyword or keywords that are used to indicate an is-a relationship between two classes.

9. Examine the following code taken from a single source file:

```
class X {
   public X() {
      System.out.println( "Constructing X" ) );
     f();
   }
   protected void f() {
      System.out.println( "X.f()" );
   }
   protected void g() {
      System.out.println( "X.g()" );
   }
}
public class Y extends X {
   public Y() {
      System.out.println( "Constructing Y" ) );
      F();
   }
   protected void f() {
      System.out.println( "Y.f()" );
   }
   public static void main( String[] args ) {
      new Y();
   }
}
```

Which of the following lines appear in the output when the code is compiled and run? Select all that apply.

a. `Constructing Y`
b. `X.f()`
c. `Constructing X`
d. `Y.f()`
e. `X.g()`

10. Which of the following statements correctly declare an abstract method f? Select all that apply.

a. `void abstract f();`

b. `private abstract void f();`

c. `protected abstract void f();`

d. `public abstract void f() {};`

e. `public void f() = 0;`

11. Examine the following class definitions for one file:

```
class B {
    protected long l;
    B( long l ) {
        this.l = l;
    }
    B() {
        l = 99;
    }
}
class C extends B {
    public float f;
    public String s = "hello";
    C ( String s, float f ) {
        this.s += " " + s;
        this.f = f;
    }
    C ( String s ) {
      // -x-
      l = Math.abs( l );
    }
}
```

Which of the following statements are allowed at the line marked `-x-`? Select all that apply.

a. `super( 27L );`

b. `f = 2.75F;`

c. `super( 3L ); this ( s, 0.5F );`

d. `B( 0L );`

e. `this( s, 10 );`

12. Examine the following class definitions:

```
class B {
    int f( int i ) {
        return i + i;
    }
    int f( int i, int j ) {
        return i + j;
    }
    int f( char c ) {
        return c;
    }
```

```
}
public class C extends B {
   int f( int i, int j ) {
      return super.f( i, j );
   }
   int f( int i ) {
      return -i ;
   }
   double f( double d ) {
      return Math.sqrt( d );
   }
   public static void main( String args[]) {
      C c = new C();
      B b = new B();
      System.out.println( c.f( 5, 10 ) + " " +
                          ( ( B )c ).f( 4 ) + " " +
                          c.f( 9D ) + " " +
                          c.f( 'A' ) );
   }
}
```

Which of the following statements are true when the code is compiled and run? Select all that apply.

a. The compiler rejects the method `C.f` because only a constructor can call another constructor.

b. The compiler rejects the method `B.f` because a char cannot be returned as an int.

c. Compilation is successful. Because the Unicode representation of A is the same as the integral value 65, the output is `15 -4 3 65`.

d. Compilation is successful. Because the Unicode representation of A is the same as the integral value 65, the output is `15 8 3 65`.

e. The compiler rejects the call `c.f( 'A' )` as ambiguous between `C.f( int )` and `B.f( char )`.

13. You have acquired some code that you are modifying. The code uses random numbers and calls the method nextGaussian with an object of type java.security.SecureRandom. Because it is a core class, you can look up SecureRandom in the JDK documentation. The method nextGaussian is not described there. Where should you look next? Select one answer.

a. At the comments in the code you are modifying.

b. In the javadoc output for the code you are modifying.

c. In the superclass of the class in which the call to nextGaussian occurs, and then in its superclass, and so on, until you reach the class Object.

d. In the class java.util.Random, which the JDK says is the superclass of java.security.SecureRandom.

e. In any subclasses of java.security.SecureRandom defined in the JDK or in the code you are modifying.

E X E R C I S E S

Debugging

1. Correct the error(s) in the following program:

```
package java4cpp.questions.c5;
class DebugShape {
   public abstract double getPerimeter() {};
   public abstract double getArea() {};
}
public class DebugSquare extends DebugShape {
   private double length;
   public DebugSquare( double l ) {
      length = l;
   }
   public abstract double getPerimeter() {
      return 4 * length;
   }
   public abstract double getArea() {
      return length * length;
   }
}
```

2. Correct the following program so that the `calculate` method in class `Debug5_2` overrides the `calculate` method in the superclass of `Debug5_2`:

```
package java4cpp.questions.c5;
class A {
   double baseValue = 3.14;
   public void setBaseValue( double d ) {
      baseValue = d;
   }
   public double calculate( double x, double y ) {
      return x * y / baseValue;
   }
}
public class Debug5_2 extends A {
   private static final float ALT_BASE = 2.5F;
   float calculate( float x, float y ) {
      return x * y / ALT_BASE;
   }
}
```

3. Correct the errors in the following program:

```
package java4cpp.questions.c5;
class Identifiable {
   private int idNum =  -1;
   public Identifiable( int id ) {
      idNum = id;
   }
   public void setID( int id ) {
      idNum = id;
   }
}
public class StockItem extends Identifiable {
   private double price = 0.00;
   public void setPrice( double p ) {
      price = p;
   }
   public static void main( String[] args ) {
      StockItem s = new StockItem();
      s.setID( 12343567 );
      s.setPrice( 34.67 );
   }
}
```

4. Correct the errors in the following program:

```
package java4cpp.questions.c5;
class Tool {
   private String name = "";
   public void setName( String n ) {
      name = n;
   }
   public String getName() {
      return name;
   }
   String toString() {
      return name;
   }
}
public class Hammer extends Tool {
   private int weight;
   public void setWeight( int w ) {
      weight = w;
   }
   public int getWeight() {
      return weight;
   }
   String toString() {
      return Tool.toString() + " "
             + String.valueOf( weight );
   }
   public static void main( String[] args ) {
```

```
        Hammer sledge = new Hammer();
        sledge.setName( "sledgehammer" );
        sledge.setWeight( 10 );
        System.out.println( sledge );
    }
}
```

5. Correct the errors in the following program:

```
package java4cpp.questions.c5;
interface RiceCereal {
   protected void snap();
   protected void crackle();
   protected void pop();
}
public class Krispies implements RiceCereal {
   protected void snap() {
      System.out.println( "Snap!" );
   }
   protected void crackle() {
      System.out.println( "Crackle!" );
   }
   public static void main( String[] args ) {
      Krispies k = new Krispies();
      k.snap();
   }
}
```

Complete the Solution

1. Complete the following program by creating the `Cat` interface with the methods `eat`, `sleep`, and `play`:

```
package java4cpp.questions.c5;
// interface goes here
public class TabbyCat implements Cat {
   public void eat() {
      System.out.println( "munch munch" );
   }
   public void sleep() {
      System.out.println( "purr purr" );
   }
   public void play() {
      System.out.println( "pull on string" );
   }
   public static void main( String[] args ){
      TabbyCat boots = new TabbyCat();
      boots.eat();
```

```
        boots.play();
        boots.sleep();
    }
}
```

2. Complete the following program by adding the class `Customer`. The `Customer` class extends the `Person` class and adds a field of the type `Purchase`. Add a `main` method to the `Customer` class that creates a `Customer` object.

```
package java4cpp.questions.c5;
class Person {
    private String name;
    private String address;
    public Person( String n, String a ) {
        name = n;
        address = a;
    }
}
class Purchase {
    private String item;
    private double amountSpent;
    public Purchase( String i, double a ) {
        item = i;
        amountSpent = a;
    }
}
```

3. Complete the following program by creating the class Book that extends the abstract class `ReadingMaterial`. Since reading material comes in many forms, the content is the generic type Object. The Book class can use the String class as its content type.

```
package java4cpp.questions.c5;
abstract class ReadingMaterial {
    private String title;
    public String getTitle() {
        return title;
    }
    public void setTitle( String t ) {
        title = t;
    }
    public abstract Object getContents();
    public abstract void setContents( Object contents );
}
```

4. Complete the following interface by adding methods that should be part of the implementation of any stack. A `Stackable` object can have any reference type but must store and retrieve elements on a last-in-first-out basis.

```
package java4cpp.questions.c5;
interface Stackable {
   public void printAll();
   // add your Stack methods here
}
```

5. Write a complete class, `Hand`, that implements the interface `Stackable` from the previous question and that stores a stack of objects. Use the classes `Deal` and `Card` provided in the following listing. The class `Deal` is the public class to test `Hand`, and `Card` is the type of object that `Deal` stores in `Hand` objects.

The class `Deal` does not deal cards in the usual manner. From an unshuffled deck, it gives one card at a time to a player chosen at random. Dealing stops as soon as one player has a full hand. Then the contents of all hands are printed, listing the cards in the opposite order to that in which each player received them.

```
package java4cpp.Questions.c5;
class Card {
   String suit;
   int value;
   Card( int i ) {
      if ( i < 13 ) suit = "Spades";
      else if ( i < 26 ) suit = "Hearts";
      else if ( i < 39 ) suit = "Diamonds";
      else suit = "Clubs";
      value = i % 13 + 1;
   }
   public String toString () {
      return Integer.toString( value ) + " of " + suit;
   }
}
// non-public Hand class to implement Stackable Here
// one constructor that takes one int argument for size of
// Hand
public class Deal {
   private static int nplayers, sizehand;
   static private Card[] deck = new Card[52];
   public static void main( String[] args ) {
      // create a hand for each player
      Hand[] players = new Hand[nplayers];
      //
      // deal the cards: up to sizehand to a player
      for ( int i = 0; i < nplayers; i++ ) {
         players[i] = new Hand( sizehand );
      }
```

```
        int count = 0, whichPlayer = 0;
        for ( int i = 0; i < 52; i ++ ) {
           // see which player gets the next card
           whichPlayer = i % nplayers;
           players[whichPlayer].push( deck_[i] );
           // stop as soon as one player has a full hand
           count++;
           if ( players[whichPlayer].isFull() ) break;
        }
        System.out.println( "Cards dealt: " + count );
        // see which card was last dealt
        System.out.println( "last card dealt: "
           + ( Card ) players[whichPlayer].peek() );
        // now print the hands dealt:
        for ( int i = 0; i < nplayers; i++) {
           System.out.println( " Player " + i + ":" );
           while ( ! players[i].isEmpty() )
              System.out.println( "\t"
                                  + ( Card ) players[i].pop() );
        }
     }
     static {
        nplayers = 5; sizehand = 5;
        for ( int i = 0; i < 52; i++ ) {
           deck[i] = new Card( i );
        }
     }
  }
```

Discovery

1. Create a set of classes representing pieces of a chess set that all implement an interface called `ChessPiece`. This interface defines the behavior that all pieces will implement, such as `getPosition`, `setPosition`, `getPossibleMoves`, and so on. You do not actually have to program a chess game. For simplicity, just create a test class that sets and gets information about the king and pawns.
2. Create a hierarchy of classes for the geometric shapes square, rectangle, circle, right-angled triangle, line, and point. All shapes have an origin, or position. All shapes have a name, such as "line" or "square." All shapes have a method for calculating the area, which is simply to return zero for lines or points. Define an interface with the common methods and fields for shapes. Define classes for at least the six types of shapes mentioned here and any more you can think of. Use inheritance to express relationships such as the fact that a square is a rectangle. Provide a variety of constructors for the different ways of representing shapes. For example, you can construct a square from lower-left and upper-right corners or from origin (lower-left) and length of a side. In the test method, create an array that contains at least two shapes of each type. Then calculate and print the area of each shape in the array.

CHAPTER

6

Exceptions

objectives

In this chapter you learn to:

- Write code to create exceptions when error or unexpected conditions arise.
- Write code to handle exceptions.
- Demonstrate the flow of control that occurs in try, catch, and finally constructions of normal execution, caught exceptions, and uncaught exceptions.
- Write code that correctly uses the throws clause in a declaration for a method that contains code that might throw exceptions.
- State what exceptions may be legitimately thrown from an overriding method in a subclass based on the declaration of the overridden superclass method.
- Understand the difference between checked and unchecked exceptions and know which kind to use.
- Deal with exceptions that are not completely handled when they are first caught.
- Use the finally clause to alter the usual order of execution in the code.

Introduction to Exceptions

An **exception** is a representation of an error condition or any situation that is not the expected result of a method. Exceptions can be divided into two categories:

- Some exceptional conditions are directly related to the functionality of a method. For example, an exception is raised when you try to open a file in read mode, if no file with the specified name is available. Exception handling can provide a recovery mechanism for these sorts of situations.
- You can never predict when some exceptions can occur. Some unpredictable exceptions are the result of logic errors in the code. For example, one of the most common causes is misuse of a null object reference. These exceptions often are unrecoverable errors or conditions that only the Java Virtual Machine (JVM) or operating system can detect. By default, the effect of these exceptions is to terminate the program.

Compared to C++, the Java programming language does eliminate many error conditions that cause programs to terminate abnormally. For example, the Java programming language gives you far fewer opportunities to program access violations. This is a benefit of the limited ways you can use object references. You cannot assign to them addresses of memory locations that your program is not allowed to access.

Nevertheless, there are in both the C++ and Java programming languages many situations in which your code may produce an error that you could not have anticipated.

Exceptions are a mechanism for isolating the code that deals with unusual or error situations from the regular program logic. The act of detecting an abnormal condition and generating an exception is called **throwing** an exception. The exception is represented as an object that encapsulates the unexpected condition. The act of throwing an exception alters the normal flow of control and starts the search for a **handler**, which is code written specifically to recover from the exception. When the handler takes control, it **catches** the exception. When the handler is done, control passes back to the program, but not in the same place where the exception interrupted the program. The whole process is called **handling** the exception.

Exception handling is a very elegant and object-oriented methodology that is packaged with the Java programming language. You should code all your methods to throw exceptions whenever they cannot complete their operation. If you can detect an error or condition for which the only sensible action is to abandon whatever your method is trying to do, throw an exception that encapsulates the problem.

The reason any programming language supports exception handling is to shift the performance penalty of error handling out of the usual path of execution. Code that deals with exceptional conditions is consolidated and removed to a separate error path. As a result, programmers cannot ignore exceptions; the program terminates if exceptions are not handled when they occur.

The concepts and implementation of exception handing in the Java programming language are very similar to exception handling in C++. You use exception handling in similar circumstances in both languages to deal with unexpected conditions that your code can anticipate. The essential difference is that the JVM raises exceptions in all exceptional and error situations. Many of the core classes can raise exceptions, and all programmers using the Java programming language must master exceptions very early in their programming careers.

C++ programmers do not have to incorporate exception handling into their code. They can, and too often do, rely on old C-style techniques or simply let unexpected conditions terminate their programs. In both C++ and the Java programming language, you can continue to use C-style error handling, in which methods return special values to indicate failures and the calling methods perform explicit tests to check for error codes in the returned values. In both C++ and the Java programming language, using exception handling is a more efficient, robust, and elegant technique. Unlike C++, the Java programming language has constructs that ensure the programmer is always aware when exceptions can be thrown. The presence of garbage collection makes exceptions easier to use than in C++. In C++ it can be difficult to determine what memory must be deleted when an exception happens. Therefore, a programmer using the Java programming language has no excuse for not using exception handling.

Encapsulating Exceptions in try Blocks

To program exception handling, you must use **try blocks**. A try **block** is a Java programming language construct that encloses one or more Java statements. Exceptions are thrown by throw statements. You enable exception handling by placing throw statements inside try blocks. Exception handlers take the form of **catch clauses** that follow the body of the try block. If an exception is thrown, the JVM immediately stops executing the Java code, including all methods started but not completed when the exception is thrown, and looks for a handler in the catch clauses in the enclosing try blocks. If no exception is thrown, the compiler runs the statements in the try block as usual and ignores the catch clauses.

Syntax

```
try {
   // statements that are monitored for exceptions
   [ throw exception;                 // statements that throw exceptions ]
   // statements that are monitored for exceptions
}
[catch ( exception_class  object_reference ) {
   // blocks that handle exceptions
}]
[finally {
   // statements always executed at the end of the try block
}]
```

Dissection

- The try block includes any catch clauses that follow the block of statements, and an optional finally clause.

- Usually there is at least one throw statement in a try block. The throw statement may not be visible if it is inside a method that is called by a statement in the try block.
- You can have zero, one, or more catch clauses. Each catch clause catches a different kind of exception object, and is never executed unless it catches an exception. The compiler can execute at most one catch clause each time the try block is run.
- You do not have to match every type of exception that is thrown in the try block with a catch clause. Include a catch clause for the exceptions you want to handle for this try block.
- The finally clause is optional if you have at least one catch clause. If you have no catch clauses, you must provide a finally clause. The compiler always executes the statements inside a finally clause at the end of the try block, regardless of whether an exception is thrown and caught or the entire try block runs without an exception.

You can nest try blocks. When you do so, catch and finally clauses are associated with the closest preceding try block.

When the try block is complete and either no exception is thrown or an exception is thrown and caught, the compiler executes the statements following the block in the usual manner. In this way, exception handling interrupts the regular flow of control when an exception occurs, but does not otherwise affect the flow of control.

If an exception is thrown in the try block and not caught by one of the catch clauses, the exception is an **uncaught** exception. The search for a handler continues to the next enclosing try block, if there is one.

The try block in the Java programming language is very similar to the try block in C++. The C++ try block does not have a finally clause, which is optional in the Java programming language. Without a finally clause, a try block in the Java programming language looks, and works, like a C++ try block.

In the Java programming language, you can include zero or more catch clauses in a try block. C++ requires at least one catch clause because that language offers no alternative like a finally clause.

Exception Handling and the Call Stack

What happens if a method that is called inside a try block throws the exception? The Java programming language keeps a record of the methods that are active at any one time, arranged so that the last method called is always the last method in the list, in what is called the **call stack**. When an exception occurs, the JVM unwinds the call stack until a handler for that exception is found. Stack entries for each method are cleared in turn, just as though the methods are returning normally. Therefore, control can jump back several levels of method calls without corrupting the program stack. If the call stack is completely unwound, the program terminates, and that is what happens when an exception is thrown but never caught.

The Java platform ensures that an uncaught exception is the most likely possible reason for terminating your Java program prematurely. The Java interpreter outputs a stack trace before terminating the program because of an uncaught exception. The stack trace lists all the methods in the call stack when the exception occurred, and makes it easy to determine the origin of the error.

A Java program never ends prematurely without an indication why. This is one of the most popular differences between the Java programming language and C++. There are many possible reasons that a C++ program can fail, and sometimes you can only guess that the cause is an uncaught exception. Under the Java platform, you do not have to guess.

Declaring Uncaught Exceptions

If you throw an exception in a method, you must either catch and handle that exception in the method or list it in the throws clause in the method declaration. The throws clause lists the types of exceptions a method is allowed to transfer, uncaught, to the calling method.

Syntax

[access_specifiers] [qualifiers] return_type method_name(*argument_list*)
*[***throws** *exception_list]*
block

Dissection

- A method definition must include a **throws** clause if any uncaught exceptions can occur while the method is running.
- The **throws** clause need not list exceptions that are thrown and caught inside a method because they have no impact outside the method.
- You can omit the **throws** clause if the method does not throw any uncaught exceptions and does not call any method that throws uncaught exceptions.

Code Example

```
void myMethod() throws IOException {
    // body of method
}
```

Code Dissection

The method `myMethod` or a method that it calls can throw an exception of type **IOException**. This method performs input or output but does not catch exceptions of type **IOException**.

When you are programming using the Java programming language, you can rely on the throws clause to determine, short of bugs, all possible outcomes of a method: it completes successfully or throws one of the listed types of exceptions.

Even the main method must have a throws clause if exceptions may occur during the method's execution and not be caught. In the case of main, the throws clause becomes a list of reasons that the program may terminate prematurely.

Moving from C++

The C++ counterpart of the Java programming language's throws clause is an exception specification. Syntactically, there are two minor differences:

- **The Java programming language begins the clause with the keyword throws, whereas C++ uses throw.**
- **In C++, the list of exception types is enclosed in parentheses.**

More importantly, in C++ the exception specification is optional. A C++ compiler does not check exception specifications, but a Java compiler rejects a method if the throws clause does not list uncaught exceptions. The purpose of the C++ exception specification is the same as that of the Java programming language's throws clause. But the optional C++ exception specification is far less effective than the Java programming language's obligatory throws clause.

The Java compiler verifies the correctness and completeness of the throws clause for every method. Because the compiler is very demanding when it checks the throws clause, coding the exception list requires attention to detail.

You can also use the throws clause to put some restraints on the behavior of the subclasses of your class, because the throws clause limits the types of uncaught exceptions allowed in overriding methods.

An overriding method cannot list more exception types in the throws clause than the overridden method does. However, it can list fewer exceptions. In other words, the method closest to the base of the inheritance hierarchy limits the types of uncaught exceptions that can be thrown by all methods that will ever override that method.

You can list exception classes in the throws clause even if they are not actually thrown from within the method, to allow an overriding method in a subclass to throw objects of the additional exception classes.

C++ has no rules about what exceptions overriding classes can throw. Watch out for this restriction of the Java platform if you are translating hierarchies of classes from C++ to the Java programming language.

Throwing Exceptions

Many of the exceptions that occur in a Java program are thrown by the core classes. For example, many of the methods in the classes that support input and output can throw an IOException. Much like methods in the core classes, your methods can throw exceptions to respond to requests that they cannot complete.

Use a throw statement to throw an exception. You can place a throw statement directly inside a try block. Alternatively, you can wrap a try block around the call to the method that contains the throw statement. If you see a throw statement in the code of a method but no try block, the reason is usually that handling the exception is left up to a calling method.

Syntax	**throw** *[new] exception[(arguments_of_constructor* **)]**;
Dissection	■ The **throw** keyword starts the exception mechanism. ■ The object reference for an exception object is thrown. The object can instantiate one of the exception classes provided by the Java platform or an exception class of your own. ■ The most common coding practice is to create an exception object in the **throw** statement. As always, use the **new** keyword to create the object and include the argument list for the constructor. You can also throw an exception object that already exists.
Code Example	`throw new WrongPasswordException( "Access denied" );`
Code Dissection	A login or user validation method can throw an exception if the user does not enter the correct password. The `WrongPasswordException` class must be defined and accessible to the class that contains this **throw** statement.

All exceptions are objects. The most important concept in mastering the throwing of exceptions is what types of objects a method should throw. The Java programming language does not let you throw primitive values or arbitrary objects. You can throw only objects that directly or indirectly extend the class java.lang.Throwable.

The thrown object carries information about the error condition. Sometimes the type of the object is all that a handler needs. Other handlers can use the fields and methods of the exception object.

A handler can call some very useful methods that are provided by the Throwable class.

Class	**Throwable**
Methods	■ **String getMessage( )** returns a printable message stored in the exception object. ■ **void printStackTrace( )** **void printStackTrace(PrintStream** *s* **)** **void printStackTrace(PrintWriter** *s* **)** print a representation of the call stack at the time the exception object is created. These methods print to the specified stream or, if no stream argument is specified, to the standard stream **System.err**.

Checked and Unchecked Exceptions

The Java programming language has two types of exceptions, **checked** and **unchecked**. Only checked exceptions must be listed in the throws clause, so you usually use only checked exceptions for exception handling. Unchecked exceptions are intended only for severe, unpredictable errors that could happen in any method. Let your code ignore unchecked exceptions, because you gain little by identifying them as potential problems. Examples of unchecked exception situations are NullPointerException and ArrayIndexOutOfBoundsException.

The Java package java.lang contains the core classes Exception, RuntimeException, and Error, all of which extend Throwable. If you want to create your own classes specifically for use as exceptions, the preferred method is to define the classes to extend Exception but not RuntimeException or Error, because objects of type RuntimeException and Error are unchecked exceptions. Objects of classes that extend RuntimeException or Error are also unchecked exceptions.

Figure 6-1 shows the inheritance relationships among all these classes, and how the type of exception you create depends on the choice of superclass. The method's throws clause must list only exceptions that are Exception objects.

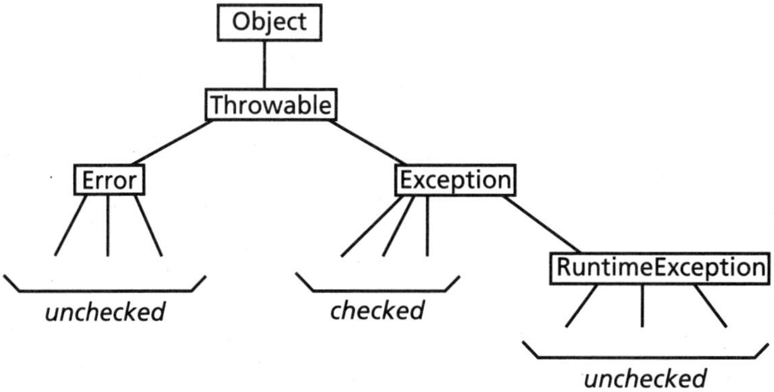

Figure 6-1: Classes of throwable objects

Mini Quiz 6-1

What is the simplest correct and complete throws clause that you can use with all the methods to let them throw any valid object?

Throwing Exceptions in Finalizers

Finalizers are methods that perform cleanup when you have finished using objects. Uncaught exceptions thrown by finalizers are ignored. Therefore, if you throw an exception in a finalizer, you should also catch it. On the other hand, if the application is not affected by uncaught exceptions that leak out of finalizers, simply ignoring them does no harm.

C++ has other techniques that you may find handy to program around error conditions. Some C++ features are legacies from the C language and are not available in the Java programming language:

- **Signals are a C language construct that lets C programs react to some operating system exceptions and some user actions such as pressing the Break or Esc key. Signal handling is also available in C++. The Java programming language has nothing like it. In C++, you can use both C signals and C++ exceptions. Even in C++, such mixtures are not recommended. However, they do occur, especially when C legacy code is involved. The Java programming language offers only exception handling.**
- **Another handy C technique that you may wish you had in the Java programming language is the** assert **macro. This useful macro evaluates a boolean expression and terminates the program with a message if the expression is not true. The Java programming language has no equivalent to the** assert **macro, but you can get the same effect with an if statement and a** RuntimeException**. For example, consider the following C++ statement:**

```
assert ( x != 0 );
```

You can translate this C++ statement into a Java statement as follows:

```
if ( x == 0 ) throw new RuntimeException ( "x == 0" );
```

Catching Exceptions

Throwing an exception is one side of the story. So far you know how to stop the forward momentum of the program when the unexpected occurs. The other side of the story is how to catch the exception and provide a handler.

If an exception is to be handled, as well as thrown, the path through the code must enter a try block before it reaches the throw statement. Catch clauses are exception handlers in the Java programming language. You code the recovery for an exception in a catch clause. The **catch** clause can belong to the **try** block in which the exception is thrown; if you have nested try blocks, the **catch** clause can belong to an outer **try** block.

Syntax

catch (*[*final*] exception_type object_reference* **) {**
  // handle the exception
}

Dissection

- A **catch** clause begins with the keyword **catch**. It looks like the definition of a method named `catch` except there is no return type or access specifier, and no other qualifier.
- A **catch** clause has one argument, which is enclosed in parentheses. The argument must be an object reference for the class **Throwable** or a subclass of **Throwable**.

- Just like the arguments of methods, the argument of a catch clause can optionally be declared **final**. If the argument is final, the catch clause cannot assign another value to the object reference for the exception. However, the contents of the exception may be changed if the exception class provides mutator methods.

Code Example

```
catch ( WrongPasswordException e ) {
   System.out.println( e.getMessage );
}
```

Code Dissection

This **catch** clause can catch an exception of type `WrongPasswordException` or a subclass of `WrongPasswordException` that is thrown in the same **try** block or an inner, nested **try** block. This handler outputs to the standard output stream whatever message is stored inside the exception object.

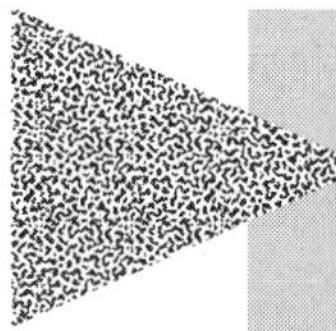

Mini Quiz 6-2

When arguments of methods are declared with final, the value of arguments of primitive type remains constant throughout the execution of the method. Does this rule also apply to final arguments of catch clauses? Why or why not?

The Java programming language's catch clauses are similar to the C++ catch clauses, but not identical. As in C++, a catch clause begins with the keyword catch **and has a block of code that handles the exception. The differences are in the arguments of the catch clause:**

- **A C++ catch clause can catch a type, without a specific object. A catch clause in the Java programming language must receive an object.**
- **A C++ catch clause can catch any type, including the fundamental types. A catch clause in the Java programming language can catch only a** Throwable **object.**
- **C++ has a generic form of** catch(...) **that catches any exception. The Java programming language has no catchall handler. The most general form of** catch **you can code in the Java programming language is** catch(Throwable), **which catches any exception, but** catch(Exception) **is usually preferable because it catches only checked exceptions.**

When an exception occurs, the catch clauses are checked in the following order:

1. The search for a handler starts with the catch clauses for the try block in which the exception is thrown. The type of each catch argument is tested in the order in which the catch clauses appear in the try block. If a catch type matches the exception type, that catch clause is executed. Then control passes to the finally clause, if one is present. If there is no finally clause, control passes to the statement following the last catch clause.
2. If no catch clauses for the try block can catch the exception, the finally clause is executed, if there is one. Then the search moves on to the next enclosing try block. The call stack is unwound as required.

3. Ultimately, there may be no more try blocks and no handler for the exception. The program ends when the call stack is fully unwound. In other words, the default behavior of an exception is to terminate the program.

The Java programming language, like C++, gives you no command to resume execution at the point where the exception was thrown. The end of a catch clause does not work like a return from a method. The call stack has been unwound and execution must carry on from the end of the try block.

Moving from C++

The Java programming language differs from C++ in that the Java compiler rejects all redundant or unreachable catch clauses as errors. C++ is less rigorous in the following ways:

- **In both C++ and the Java programming language, a handler for a superclass, or base class, catches exception objects of related subclasses, or derived classes. In C++, you must make sure that you catch derived classes first, because a catch clause for a derived class that comes after a catch clause for a base class is simply ignored. If a catch clause for a superclass precedes a catch clause for one of its subclasses, the Java compiler flags this as an error. C++ accepts unreachable catch clauses, whereas the Java compiler flags them as errors.**
- **C++ accepts catch clauses for exceptions that cannot occur. The Java compiler checks catch clauses against the possible exception types and forces you to include only catch clauses that can actually be used. In this case, you may find the Java compiler checks restrictive, because you cannot add catch clauses in anticipation of future needs.**

In the next sample program, you see an exception handler that calls one of the methods of Throwable to print the stack trace without stopping the program. The sample contains a public class called `Fraction`. Because it is a public class, it is found in a file called Fraction.java. The structure of packages mirrors the file system, so you will find this source code in the java4cpp\exceptions subfolder of the folder in which you unpacked the JAR file java4cpp.jar. The first files define the exception classes used by the program.

```
package java4cpp.exceptions;
/** Class of objects thrown when a mathematical
  * exception is detected
  */
class MathException extends Exception {}
/** Class of objects thrown when division by
  * zero is detected
  */
class DivideByZeroException extends MathException {}
/** Class of errors thrown when a zero
  * denominator is detected in a fraction
  */
class ZeroDenominatorException extends MathException {}
```

The first three classes define specialized types of exceptions. Classes `ZeroDenominatorException` and `DivideByZeroException` both extend MathException, which in turn extends the core class Exception.

The class `Fraction` uses exceptions to deal with denominators of zero:

```
/** A class to represent mathematical fractions
  */
public class Fraction {
   private int num;   // fraction numerator
   private int den;   // fraction denominator
   /** Constructor without arguments
     */
   public Fraction() {
      num = 0;
      den = 1;
   }
   /** Class constructor for whole numbers.
     * The denominator is set to 1.
     * @param initNum numerator value
     */
   public Fraction( int initNum ) {
      num = initNum;
      den = 1;
   }
   /** Class constructor
     * @param initNum numerator value
     * @param initDen denominator value
     * @exception ZeroDenominatorException
     *            if a zero denominator is
     *            specified
     */
   public Fraction( int initNum, int initDen )
         throws ZeroDenominatorException {
      if ( 0 == initDen ) {
         throw new ZeroDenominatorException();
      }
      num = initNum;
      den = initDen;
   }
   /** Divide one fraction by another
     * @param divisor The divisor fraction
     * @exception ZeroDenominatorException
     *            if a fraction with a zero
     *            denominator is created
     * @exception DivideByZeroException
     *            if the divisor is zero
     */
```

```
    Fraction divideBy( Fraction divisor )
                throws DivideByZeroException,
                       ZeroDenominatorException {
       if ( 0 == divisor.num ) {
          throw new DivideByZeroException();
       }
       return new Fraction( num * divisor.den,
                            den * divisor.num );
    }
    /** The test method for the class
      * @param args not used
      */
    public static void main( String[] args ) {
       try {
          Fraction a = new Fraction( 1, 0 );
       }
       catch( MathException x ) {
          System.err.println( "A math error occurred" );
       }
       try {
          Fraction a = new Fraction( 37, 0 );
       }
       catch( ZeroDenominatorException x ) {
          System.err.println( "A zero denominator " +
                   "was detected" );
       }
       catch( MathException x ) {
          System.err.println( "A math error occurred" );
       }
       try {
          Fraction a = new Fraction( -7, 0 );
       }
       catch( MathException x ) {
          System.err.println( x );
       }
       try {
          Fraction a = new Fraction( -102, 6 ),
               b = new Fraction( 0 );
          Fraction c = a.divideBy( b );
       }
       catch( MathException x ) {
          x.printStackTrace( System.err );
       }
    }
}
```

The annotated output is

- `A math error occurred`
  The first line is output by the handler for `MathException` as the result of the attempt to create the fraction 1/0.
- `A zero denominator was detected`
  The second line is output by the handler for the `ZeroDenominatorException` as the result of the attempt to create the fraction 37/0.
- `java4cpp.exceptions.ZeroDenominatorException`
  The third try block attempts to create the fraction -7/0. This time, a `MathException` is caught, but the handler outputs the contents of the exception object rather than a simple message.
- ```
  java4cpp.exceptions.DivideByZeroException
     at java4cpp.exceptions.Fraction.divideBy
     ( Fraction.java:69 )
     at java4cpp.exceptions.Fraction.main
     ( Fraction.java:107 )
  ```
  The remaining lines of output are a stack trace produced by the handler for the `MathException` which was thrown as a result of the attempt to divide a by b. The trace first prints the contents of the exception, then gives the locations in the call stack where the exception occurred.

The constructor that has two input parameters throws a `ZeroDenominatorException` if the given denominator value is zero. The method `divideBy` can throw either a `DivideByZeroException` directly or a `ZeroDenominatorException` when it creates a new fraction. In this case, the programmer has chosen to place all the try blocks and handlers in the main method, so that each declaration of each `Fraction` in main can demonstrate a different handler for a `MathException`. The main method handles all the exceptions that may occur within it, so main does not require a throws clause of its own.

Incompletely Handled Exceptions

The Java programming language gives you three options for dealing with exceptions in catch clauses:

- You can use a catch clause to catch an exception and handle it.
- You can omit a catch clause for an exception and let the call stack unwind further looking for a handler in an outer try block.
- You can catch the exception and then **rethrow** it. In catch clause, you can throw the exception that has just been caught without completely handling it. For example, you can catch an exception, inspect it, and then determine that this handler cannot completely deal with the situation. The handler can take some actions first, or simply decide to pass the exception further up the call stack immediately. You may also decide to substitute the caught exception with another that is more applicable or understandable.
  ```

To rethow an exception, throw the same object you caught using an ordinary throw statement. Use the argument of the catch clause as the argument of the throw statement.

Moving from C++

In C++, you can rethrow an exception by using the throw **keyword on its own within a catch clause. The Java programming language does not allow this construct. Every throw statement in the Java programming language must throw an object.**

C++ needs a special syntax for rethrowing exceptions to deal with caught exceptions for which the type of the object is not available to the handler. The Java programming language does not need a "rethrow" keyword because it has no catch-all handler equivalent to the C++ construct catch(...).

Here is a simple program that throws and rethrows an exception:

```
package java4cpp.exceptions;
/** A user-defined checked exception class to be
  * used when an illegal integer value is detected
  */
class IllegalValueException extends Exception {
   private int value;
   /** Class constructor
     * @param iv the illegal value that was
     *           detected
     */
   public IllegalValueException( int iv ) {
      value = iv;
   }
   /** Method to get the illegal value
     * @return the illegal value
     */
   public int getValue() {
      return value;
   }
   /** Method to set the illegal value
     * @param iv the illegal value
     * @return the updated IllegalValueException
     *         object
     */
   public IllegalValueException setValue( int iv ) {
      value = iv;
      return this;
   }
}
```

The class `IllegalValueException` defines a throwable type that is a checked exception. An `IllegalValueException` has a field, `value`, to hold an integer, and methods to set and get the value of the integer.

The class ReThrow contains some utility methods to demonstrate the kinds of things you can do with exceptions:

```
package java4cpp.exceptions;
/** A class to demonstrate rethrowing an exception
  */
public class ReThrow {
   /** A utility class method that always throws
     * an exception
     * @exception IllegalValueException For
     *            demonstration purposes
     */
   public static void methodThrowsException()
      throws IllegalValueException {
         throw new IllegalValueException( 150 );
   }
   /** A utility class method that catches, alters,
     * and rethrows IllegalValueException exceptions
     * @exception IllegalValueException An uncaught
     *            exception from a called method
     */
   public static void methodReThrowsException()
         throws IllegalValueException {
      try {
         methodThrowsException();
      }
      catch( IllegalValueException ive ) {
         System.out.println( "Caught illegal value "
                             + ive.getValue() );
         if ( ive.getValue() > 100 ) {
            ive.setValue( ive.getValue() - 100 );
            throw ive;
         }
      }
   }
   /** Test method for the class
     * @param args Not used
     */
   public static void main( String[] args ) {
      try {
         methodReThrowsException();
      }
      catch( IllegalValueException ive ) {
         System.out.println( "Caught illegal value "
                             + ive.getValue() );
      }
   }
}
```

The output is

```
Caught illegal value 150
Caught illegal value 50
```

The method `methodThrowsException` simply creates an `IllegalValueException`, sets `value` to 150, and throws the exception. The method `methodReThrowsException` calls the method `ThrowsException2` and catches the exception. This handler prints a message, subtracts 100 from `value`, and rethrows the exception. The main method contains an outer try block. The catch clause of this outer try block catches the exception when it is rethrown. You can see from the output that the `value` in the rethrown exception has been modified to 50.

Completing a try Block with a finally Clause

Often you want to make sure some code runs at the end of a try block no matter how the block ends. If you find yourself duplicating the same statements that follow the throw statements in a try block in every catch clause, move those statements into a finally clause. The finally clause runs also if control leaves the try block as a result of a return, continue, or break. In all cases, you have a chance to perform cleanup, or do whatever processing you feel should be completed at the end of the try block.

Syntax

try {
   // statements that are monitored for exceptions
}
*[***catch(** *exception_class object_reference* **) {**
   // 0, 1, or more catch blocks]
}
*[***finally {**
   // statements always executed at the end of the try block
}*]*

Dissection

- If a finally block is present, the statements it contains are always executed when control leaves the try block.
- If a finally block is present, the catch clauses are optional.
- The finally block is optional if the try block has at least one catch clause. A try block that has no catch clauses must have a finally clause.

Code Example

```
MyClass temp;
try {
    temp = new MyClass();
    // work with temp
}
finally {
    temp = null;
}
```

Code Dissection The object `temp` is required only inside this try block, so the finally clause sets its object reference to **null**. The object can then be removed from memory the next time the JVM runs garbage collection.

The finally clause records the reason it was entered so that, when it ends, it reinstates the flow of control that it interrupted. Here are some examples:

- If the try block ends normally, the finally clause runs, followed by the first statement after the finally clause.
- If a statement within the try block throws an exception, and a catch clause in the try block catches the exception, the finally clause runs immediately after the catch clause followed by the first statement after the finally clause.
- If a statement within the try block throws an exception, and no catch clause in the try block catches the exception, the finally clause runs before the call stack unwinds further in search of a handler.
- When a break or continue statement transfers control outside the try block, the statements in the finally clause run first.
- If the method ends with a return statement inside a try block, the finally clause runs before the method returns.

Moving from C++

The finally clause has no equivalent in C++. In this case, the designers of the Java programming language looked to sources other than C++ for design ideas.

In the Java programming language, a try block must have either at least one catch clause or a finally clause, and can have both. C++ does not allow a try block with no catch clauses because you cannot complete the try block with a finally clause instead of a catch clause.

What if the finally clause itself changes the flow of control? For example, if a finally clause contains a throw statement, the handling of that exception takes precedence over whatever control flow was in progress when the finally clause was entered. Interrupting exception handling by throwing another exception in a finally clause is possible. However, such logic is not advisable because it creates opportunities for problems. You should either avoid throwing exceptions in a finally clause, or at least arrange to catch them locally. In any event, take care when altering the flow of control in a finally clause.

This sample program uses methods from the input and output package java.io. The program throws and catches IOException objects and demonstrates several features of exception handling.

```
package java4cpp.exceptions;
import java.io.*;
/** A class to help demonstrate how the finally
  * clause can be used with a try block
  */
public class CharCount {
   /** Method to count characters in a file
     * @param args[0] The name of the file to be
```

```
    *                   opened for character counting
    */
   public static void main( String[] args ) {
      if ( args.length == 0 ) {
         System.err.println( "Please provide "
                           + "a file name." );
      } else try {
         FileReader input
            = new FileReader( args[0] );
         int charCount = 0;
         try {
            while ( input.read() != -1 ) {
               charCount++;
            }
            System.out.println( "There were "
                              + charCount
                              + " characters" );
         } catch( IOException iox ) {
            System.err.println( "Exception occurred "
                              + "at character "
                              + charCount );
            System.err.println( iox );
         } finally {
            input.close();
         }
      } catch( IOException iox ) {
         System.err.println( "Error opening or "
                           + "closing the file "
                           + args[0] );
      }
   }
}
```

If this program is run from the folder where CharCount.java is located with the source code for the example as input, the input is

```
java java4cpp.exceptions.CharCount CharCount.java
```

The output is

```
There were 1373 characters
```

If this program is run with a nonexistent file as input, the input is

```
java java4cpp.exceptions.CharCount Eigijiehf.java
```

The output is

```
Error opening or closing the file Eigijiehf.java
```

The purpose of this program is to count and output the number of characters in a file. The local variable `charCount` in `main` is the counter.

The `main` method contains nested try blocks. The outer block opens a file for reading. Opening a file can cause an `IOException`, and the outer try block has a handler to catch that exception. The inner try block reads characters from the file, an operation that can throw a different `IOException`. The catch clause for the inner try block handles an exception caused by reading the file.

The finally clause for the inner try block closes the file, regardless of whether the program is read successfully to the end of the file. The method `read`, which `FileReader` inherits from `InputStreamReader`, returns the value `-1` to indicate that the end of the file has been reached. The inner `try` block reads until either the end of the file or a read error throws an `IOException`.

SUMMARY

The Java programming language provides a number of constructs that you can use when the unexpected happens during execution of your code. Exceptions are objects that encapsulate errors or exceptional conditions. In the Java programming language, all run-time errors are exceptions. Exceptions that are not handled terminate your program. Use exception handling to recover and continue running, or at least to end your program more gracefully than with an abnormal termination.

Generally, you leave severe errors up to the JVM, because your code usually cannot detect them and can take no reasonable steps to recover from them. Use exception handling for conditions that relate to the tasks that your methods are designed to perform and that prevent your methods from completing successfully.

In the Java programming language, you use the following keywords to handle exceptions:

`catch` `finally` `throw` `throws` `try`

Here is the form of the statements that relate to exception handling:

```
[access_specifiers] [qualifiers] return_type method_name( argument_list )
  [throws exception_list]
{
  // statements that are not monitored for exceptions
  try {                                        // start of try block
    // statements that are monitored for exceptions
    [throw exception_object;                   // throw statement]
    // statements that are monitored for exceptions
  }
  [catch( exception_class object_reference ) {  // start of catch clause
    // statements                              // exception handler
    [throw exception_object;                   // throw statement]
  }]
  [finally {                                   // start of finally clause
    // statements always executed at the end of the try block
```

```
  }]
    // statements that are not monitored for exceptions
}
```

Usually, all exceptions for which you use exception handling are checked exceptions. Checked exceptions are instances of the core class java.lang.Exception or a subclass of Exception. The core classes define and use many exceptions. For example, methods in the core classes that perform I/O throw IOException objects if they encounter a problem reading or writing files. You can also define your own exception classes. To ensure that instances of your exception classes are checked exceptions, extend the Exception class or a subclass of Exception rather than RunTimeException.

Instances of the core classes java.lang.RuntimeException and java.lang.Error, and all classes that extend these two classes, are unchecked exceptions.

For each type of checked exception that can occur during the execution of your method, you must do one of the following:

- List the exception class in the throws clause of the method declaration. The throws clause informs calling methods what exceptions may leak out of your method.
- Catch and handle the exception in your method.

Try blocks enclose the statements that are monitored for exceptions or that are involved in exception handling. You can nest try blocks.

A throw statement raises an exception. You can throw only objects that instantiate the core class java.lang.Throwable or a subclass of Throwable. The classes Exception, RuntimeException, and Error all extend Throwable.

When an exception is thrown, the flow of control through the program stops and the search for a handler begins. The JVM looks first at the catch clauses of the immediately enclosing try block, and then works outward, unwinding the call stack as it goes.

A catch clause is exception handler. It has a single argument, which must be an object reference for an exception class. Each catch clause handles a different type of exception that can be thrown in the try block. A throw statement inside a catch clause can rethrow the exception instead of completely handling it.

If there is no catch clause for an exception that occurs, the exception is uncaught. An uncaught exception can be caught by an outer try block. If the exception is never caught, the JVM terminates your program and prints a trace of the call stack at the time the exception was thrown.

A try block must have at least one catch clause if there is no finally clause. A finally clause is optional if there is at least one catch clause.

The statements in a finally clause are always executed at the end of a try block. Regardless of whether an exception has been thrown, all the statements in the try block have completed without interruption, or a return, break, or continue statement transfers control out of the try block. The finally clause gives you an opportunity to perform cleanup in one place for all possible routes out of a try block.

When a try block completes, control passes to the statement following the try block. Control never returns to the point where the exception occurred.

QUESTIONS

1. Objects of which of the following types can be thrown as an exception? Select all that apply.
   a. String
   b. Integer
   c. int
   d. Error
   e. Exception
2. How is a checked exception distinguished from an unchecked exception?
3. Examine the following code:

```
class BinEmpty extends Exception { }
class StockBin {
   private int itemsInBin = 0;
   public StockBin( int initialCount ) {
      itemsInBin = initialCount;
   }
   public void removeFromBin() throws BinEmpty {
      if ( itemsInBin == 0 ) {
         throw new BinEmpty();
      } else {
         --itemsInBin;
      }
   }
}
public class Warehouse {
   public static void main( String[] args ) {
      try {
         StockBin b = new StockBin( 1 );
         b.removeFromBin();
         b.removeFromBin();
      }
      catch( BinEmpty be ) {
         System.out.println( "Oops, no more!" );
      }
      finally {
         System.out.println( "Cleaning up" );
      }
   }
}
```

   Which of the following statements are true when the code is compiled and run? Select all that apply.
   a. The compiler rejects the definition of the method `Warehouse.main` because it does not have a throws clause declaring the exception class `BinEmpty`.
   b. The class `BinEmpty` defines a class of checked exceptions.

c. Compilation is successful and the output is
```
Oops, no more!
Cleaning up
```

d. Compilation is successful and the output is
```
Oops, no more!
```

4. Examine the following code:

```
class E1 extends Exception { }
class E2 extends E1 { }
public class Quiz6_1 {
   public static void f( boolean flag ) throws E1, E2 {
      if ( flag ) {
         throw new E1();
      } else {
         throw new E2();
      }
   }
   public static void main( String[] args ) {
      try {
         f( true );
      }
      catch( E1 e1 ) {
         System.out.println( "Caught E1" );
      }
      catch( E2 e2 ) {
         System.out.println( "Caught E2" );
      }
   }
}
```

Which of the following statements are true when the code is compiled and run? Select all that apply.

a. The compiler rejects the definition of the method `Quiz6_1.main` because it does not have a throws clause declaring the exception classes `E1` and `E2`.

b. The compiler rejects the catch clause for `E2` because it is unreachable.

c. Compilation is successful and the output is
```
Caught E1
Caught E2
```

d. Compilation is successful and the output is
```
Caught E1
```

5. Examine the following code:

```
class E1 extends Exception { }
class E2 extends E1 { }
class SuperQuiz6_2 {
   public void f( boolean flag ) throws E1 {
   }
}
public class Quiz6_2 extends SuperQuiz6_2 {
   // -- X --
}
```

Which of the following function definitions are valid when placed at the line marked `-- X --`? Select all that apply.

a. `public void f( boolean flag ) throws E1 { }`
b. `public void f( boolean flag ) { }`
c. `public void f( boolean flag ) throws E2 { }`
d. `public void f( boolean flag ) throws E1, E2 { }`
e. `public void f( boolean flag ) throws Exception { }`

6. Which class is the superclass of all classes of objects that may be thrown as exceptions?

7. Examine the following code:

```
class E1 extends Exception { }
class E2 extends E1 { }
public class Quiz6_3 extends SuperQuiz6_2 {
   public void f( boolean flag ) throws E1 {
      // -- X --
   }
}
```

Which of the following statements are valid when placed at the line marked `-- X --`? Select all that apply.

a. `throw new Exception( );`
b. `throw new E1( );`
c. `throw new E2( );`
d. `throw new Object( );`
e. `throw new Error( );`

8. Examine the following code:

```
public class Quiz6_4 {
   public static void main( String[] args ) {
      f( false );
      f( true );
   }
   public static void f( boolean flag ) {
      try {
         if( flag ) {
            return;
         } else {
```

```
                System.out.println( flag );
            }
        } finally {
            System.out.println( "Cleaning up" );
        }
    }
}
```

Which of the following statements are true when the code is compiled and run? Select all that apply.

a. The compiler rejects the definition of the method `Quiz6_4.f` because the try block it contains does not have a catch block.
b. The compiler rejects the definition of the method `Quiz6_4.f` because the try block does not contain any statements that may throw an exception.
c. Compilation is successful and the output is `false`.
d. Compilation is successful and the output is
```
false
Cleaning up
```
e. Compilation is successful and the output is
```
false
Cleaning up
Cleaning up
```

9. Examine the following code:

```
class E1 extends Exception { }
class E2 extends E1 { }
public class Quiz6_5 {
    public static void main( String[] args ) {
        try {
            throw new E1();
        }
        // -- X --
    }
}
```

Which of the following statements are valid when placed at the line marked `-- X --`? Select all that apply.

a. `catch ( Exception x ) { }`
b. `catch ( final Exception x ) { }`
c. `catch ( final E1 x ) { }`
d. `catch ( E2 x ) { }`
e. `catch ( ... ) { }`

10. What method of any exception object can be used to display the contents of the program stack at the time the exception occurred?

EXERCISES

Debugging

1. Correct all the errors in the following program.

```
package java4cpp.questions.c6;
class D61_OutOfRangeException extends Exception {
}
public class Debug6_1 {
   public static final int MAX_X = 1000;
   public static final int MIN_X = 10;
   private int x;
   public int getX() {
      return x;
   }
   public void setX( int value ) {
      if ( value >= MIN_X && value <= MAX_X ) {
         x = value;
      } else {
         throw new D61_OutOfRangeException();
      }
   }
   public static void main( String[] args ) {
      Debug6_1 a = new Debug6_1();
      a.setX( 275 );
      System.out.println( a.getX() );
   }
}
```

2. Correct all the errors in the following program without changing the definition of the interface:

```
package java4cpp.questions.c6;
interface IfaceDebug6_2 {
   public void f( int input );
}
class D62_OutOfRangeException extends Exception {
}
public class Debug6_2 implements IfaceDebug6_2 {
   public static final int MAX_X = 1000;
   public static final int MIN_X = 10;
   private int x;
   public void f( int input ) {
      setX( input );
   }
   public int getX() {
      return x;
   }
   public void setX( int value ) {
      if ( value >= MIN_X && value <= MAX_X ) {
```

```
            x = value;
         } else {
            throw new D62_OutOfRangeException();
         }
      }
      public static void main( String[] args ) {
         Debug6_2 a = new Debug6_2();
         a.f( 275 );
         System.out.println( a.getX() );
      }
   }
```

3. Correct all the errors in the following program:

```
package java4cpp.questions.c6;
class D63_E1 extends Exception {
}
class D63_E2 extends D63_E1 {
}
public class Debug6_3 {
   private int x;
   public String toString() {
      return String.valueOf( x );
   }
   public void f( int input ) throws Exception {
      x = input;
      throw D63_E1;
   }
   public static void main( String[] args ) {
      Debug6_3 a = new Debug6_3();
      try {
         a.f( 275 );
      } catch ( Exception e ) {
         System.out.println( e );
      } catch ( D63_E1 e ) {
         System.out.println( e );
      }
      System.out.println( a );
   }
}
```

4. Correct the programming style error in the following program:

```
package java4cpp.questions.c6;
class D64_E1 extends Exception {
}
class D64_E2 extends D64_E1 {
}
public class Debug6_4 {
   public static void g() throws D64_E2 {
      System.out.println( "Processing here" );
      throw new D64_E2();
   }
   public static void cleanUp() {
      System.out.println( "Clean up processing here" );
   }
   public static void main( String[] args ) {
      try {
         g();
      } catch ( D64_E2 e ) {
         System.out.println( e );
         cleanUp();
      } catch ( D64_E1 e ) {
         System.out.println( e );
         cleanUp();
      }
      cleanUp();
   }
}
```

5. Correct all the errors in the following program:

```
package java4cpp.questions.c6;
class TooBigException {
   private double value;
   public TooBigException( double errorValue ) {
      value = errorValue;
   }
   public double getErrorValue() {
      return value;
   }
}
public class Debug6_5 {
   private double pressure = 10.0;
   public void setPressure( double newPressure )
                           throws TooBigException {
      if ( newPressure > 2*pressure ) {
         // pressure must be increased slowly
         throw TooBigException();
      } else {
         pressure = newPressure;
      }
```

```
    }
    public double getPressure() {
       return pressure;
    }
    public static void main( String[] args ) {
       try {
          Debug6_5 x = new Debug6_5();
          x.setPressure( 15.0 );
          x.setPressure( 25.0 );
          x.setPressure( 60.0 );
       } catch ( TooBigException tbe ) {
          System.out.println( tbe.value );
       }
    }
 }
```

Complete the Solution

1. Complete the following program by defining the needed exception class:

```
package java4cpp.questions.c6;
public class Complete6_1 {
   private double volume = 100.0;
   public void setVolume( double newVolume )
                         throws NegativeValueException {
      if ( newVolume <= 0 ) {
         // can't have a negative volume
         throw new NegativeValueException( newVolume );
      } else {
         volume = newVolume;
      }
   }
   public double getVolume() {
      return volume;
   }
   public static void main( String[] args ) {
      Complete6_1 x = new Complete6_1();
      try {
         x.setVolume( 5.0 );
      } catch ( NegativeValueException nve ) {
         System.out.println( "Illegal volume: "
                             + nve.getErrorValue() );
      }
   }
}
```

2. Complete the following program by using the defined `IndexTooBigException` class for cases where the character count requested is larger than the string:

```
package java4cpp.questions.c6;
class IndexTooBigException extends Exception {
   private int value;
   public IndexTooBigException( int newValue ) {
      value = newValue;
   }
   public int getErrorValue() {
      return value;
   }
}
public class Complete6_2 {
   private String name;
   public void setName( String newName ) {
      name = newName;
   }
   public String getBeginChars( int count ) {
      return name.substring( 0, count );
   }
   public static void main( String[] args ) {
      Complete6_2 x = new Complete6_2();
      x.setName( "Bad Bad Leroy Brown" );
      String s = x.getBeginChars( 7 );
      System.out.println( s );
      s = x.getBeginChars( 100 );
   }
}
```

3. Expand upon your answer to the previous question by adding a second exception type, `NegativeIndexException`, that is thrown if a negative count is specified in the method `getBeginChars`.

4. Further expand upon your answer to the previous question by adding a common superclass exception type, `IndexException`, for both `NegativeIndexException` and `IndexTooBigException`. Move the `getErrorValue` method and the `value` field, used by both subclasses for handling the invalid index value, into the superclass. The subclass constructors should use the method super to set the illegal value. Put three catch blocks in the main method: one for the superclass and one for each subclass.

5. Complete the following program by adding a class of exceptions called `AlreadyInSetException`. An object of this class should be thrown if an attempt is made to add a character to a set for the second time. Take advantage of the exception class's superclass constructor to set a message that indicates which character was added in error.

```
package java4cpp.questions.c6;
public class SetOfCharacters {
   private String chars = "";
   public void addChar( char c ) {
      chars += c;
   }
   public boolean contains( char c ) {
      // indexOf will return -1 if the character
      // is not present
      return ( chars.indexOf( c ) >= 0 );
   }
   public static void main( String[] args ) {
      SetOfCharacters soc = new SetOfCharacters();
      soc.addChar( 'j' );
      soc.addChar( 'p' );
      System.out.println( "Set contains 'j': "
                          + soc.contains( 'j' ) );
      System.out.println( "Set contains 'k': "
                          + soc.contains( 'k' ) );
   }
}
```

Discovery

1. Create a class called `Stack` that encapsulates an array of integers and provides methods for pushing a value onto the stack, popping a value off the stack, and for peeking at the value on the top of the stack. There should also be a method, `isEmpty`, that returns a boolean value to indicate whether or not the stack is empty. Since the stack is being built around an array which will have a fixed size, you should add another method, `isFull`, to return a value indicating whether or not there is room for another item on the stack.

   Add exception classes with a common superclass called `StackException`. The subclasses should be `EmptyStackException`, which is thrown when an attempt is made to pop or peek at an empty stack, and `FullStackException`, which is thrown when an attempt is made to push an item onto a full stack. Don't forget to write a main method that tests all of your methods.

2. Add exception handling to the `Inventory` class described in the exercises at the end of Chapter 4. Wherever the program prints a warning, replace that action with a statement that throws an exception.

   Add exception classes with a common superclass called `InventoryException`. Example subclasses that you may choose to create include `ItemNotFoundException`, `NegativePriceException`, and `ArrayOverflowException`. The main method should catch all these exceptions and print error messages.

CHAPTER

7

Cloning Objects and Using RTTI

objectives

In this chapter you learn to:

- **Clone objects so that the result is a deep, rather than shallow, copy.**
- **Use the interface** Cloneable **to control whether instances of a class you define can be cloned.**
- **Use the interface** Cloneable **to control whether instances of subclasses of your class must be, can optionally be, or cannot be cloned.**
- **Determine the effect of assignment and modification operations upon variables of any type.**
- **Determine at run time if an object is an instance of a specified class or some subclass of that class by using the** instanceof **operator.**
- **Investigate the class named** Class, **with which you can get information about a class at run time.**
- **Understand why some casts between class types are safe, whereas others throw an exception, and learn how to handle this exception.**
- **Use the Reflection API to get run-time information about fields, methods, and primitive types.**
- **Call a method or a constructor for a class with the Reflection API.**

Introduction

You have used objects of primitive and reference types, including user-defined classes. This chapter elaborates on two specific facets of classes: cloning, or duplicating objects, and obtaining run-time type information (RTTI) about objects and classes. The package java.lang includes the classes and interfaces that support these two activities. Otherwise, they are quite separate topics. This chapter combines them because both are programming techniques that operate on classes, rather than simply calls to methods of classes to achieve other ends. Learning about these topics can greatly increase your understanding of the nature of classes.

This chapter also serves as a checkpoint indicating that you have fully mastered the previous chapters in this book. To understand how cloning and RTTI work, you must have a solid understanding of Java types, classes, inheritance, and even exception handling.

Cloning Objects

Before long, you are bound to run into the deceptively simple-sounding problem of copying objects. For the primitive types, there is no problem: just use the assignment operator. However, using the assignment operator with object references changes only the references, not the objects referenced.

To copy objects of reference types, you must clone the objects. Cloning involves calling the method clone, which is available for all objects of reference types, including instances of classes and arrays.

Class	java.lang.Object
Purpose	The **Object** class defines methods that are available in all objects of reference types.
Methods	■ **Object clone()** The method **clone** creates a duplicate of the object for which the method is called and returns an object reference to the new object. The returned value must be cast for the actual type of the object.

In the case of arrays, programmers with a C++ background may have to remember that arrays are reference types in the Java programming language. They are true objects, and not just a programming notation for pointers to elements stored in contiguous addresses in memory. Arrays have a clone **method, just like classes.**

The following lines show why using the assignment operator to copy objects may not have the desired effect.

```
Pair x = new Pair( 5, 6 );
Pair y = new Pair( 54, 40 );
x = y;
```

As shown in Figure 7-1, these lines produce two object references, `x` and `y`, for the same object, instead of two object references for separate but identical objects. Also, the object that `x` originally referred to may not be accessible through any object reference and thus become available for garbage collection.

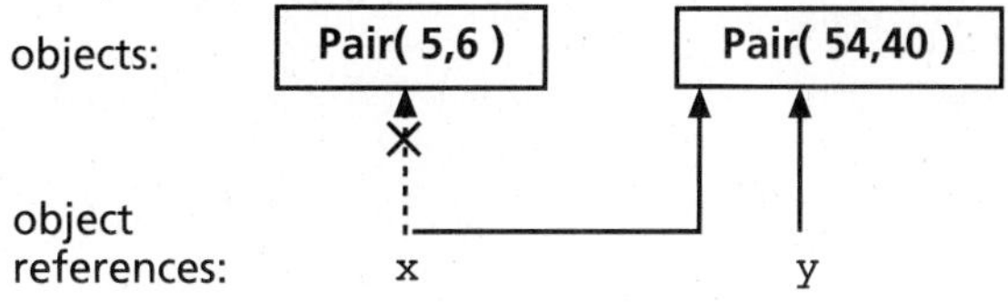

Figure 7-1: Assigning object references

Figure 7-2 shows what happens when this code fragment is rewritten to call clone, as follows:

```
Pair x = new Pair( 5, 6 );
Pair y = new Pair( 54, 40 );
x = ( Pair ) y.clone();
```

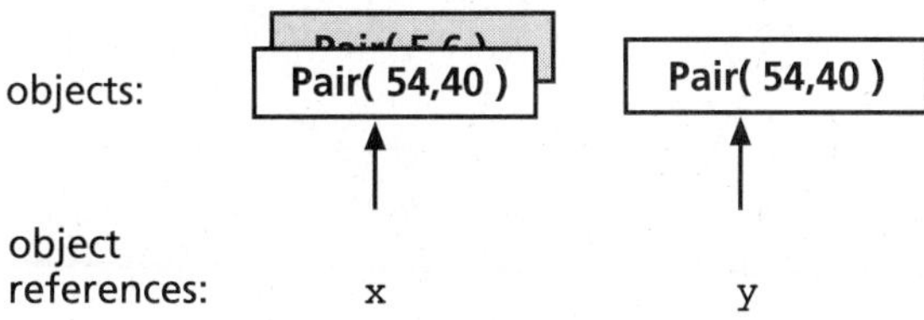

Figure 7-2: Calling Object.clone

Now `x` and `y` are object references for two different objects that are identical to each other.

You must cast the value returned from clone to an object reference for the correct type of object. If you feel this casting is unsafe, rest assured that the Java Virtual Machine (JVM) throws an exception of the type ClassCastException if the cast is inappropriate.

Mini Quiz 7-1

Why must the clone method of all classes return an object reference for an Object?

Moving from C++

C++ has no equivalent of the clone method. Instead, there are two ways of providing a copy feature for a C++ class. They are used in very different circumstances:

- When you define classes in C++, you can overload the assignment operators, and often do overload the = operator to copy an object. The Java programming language has no feature for operator overloading. The following statement does very different things in each language:

```
p = q;  // uses overloaded = operator of a C++ class
        // if one exists, and default = otherwise
p = q;  // assigns value to object reference in
        // the Java programming language
```

  In the Java programming language, you must use the following:

```
p = q.clone();  // makes a copy and assigns it to p
```

- C++ makes extensive use of copy constructors. The C++ compiler even generates a default copy constructor if you create a class without one. In C++, copy constructors are essential to allow objects to be passed by value as arguments to a method. When you pass an object as an argument, C++ makes the copy implicitly, using the copy constructor, and passes the copy to the method. When you pass an object in the Java programming language, its object reference is passed and no copy is made, The JVM never implicitly copies an object.

  In both languages, you can define a constructor that takes as an argument an object of the same class. In C++, the resulting method is a copy constructor and has a special syntax:

```
ThisClass::ThisClass( const& ThisClass object ); // C++
```

  In the Java programming language, the equivalent method is just another constructor and has no special status or syntax:

```
ThisClass( ThisClass object ) // Java language
```

  In the Java programming language, a copy constructor is really useful only when creating a copy of an existing object using the new keyword. It is not used in argument passing and never called implicitly. Therefore, the Java compiler does not generate a default copy constructor and you do not have to provide one unless you use it in your own code. For example, you may have code such as the following:

```
Pair x = new Pair( 5, 6 );
Pair y = new Pair( x );
```

  However, an important advantage that the clone method has over such a constructor is that the clone method uses dynamic binding to make a clone of the actual type that `x` references. The constructor will make a copy of `x` as a `Pair` object, even if `x` refers to an object that is a subclass of `Pair`.

For the reference types, you usually want to make a deep copy rather than a shallow copy of an object. When you create a **shallow copy**, you duplicate the data members of an object regardless of whether some members are object references. A shallow copy makes no attempt to make duplicates of the referenced objects. As a result, the copy and the original can contain object references for the same object. A **deep copy** duplicates the objects referred to by object references, and inserts a new object reference for the duplicate object into the copy. Figure 7-3 illustrates a shallow and deep copy of an object z that contains an object reference for object x.

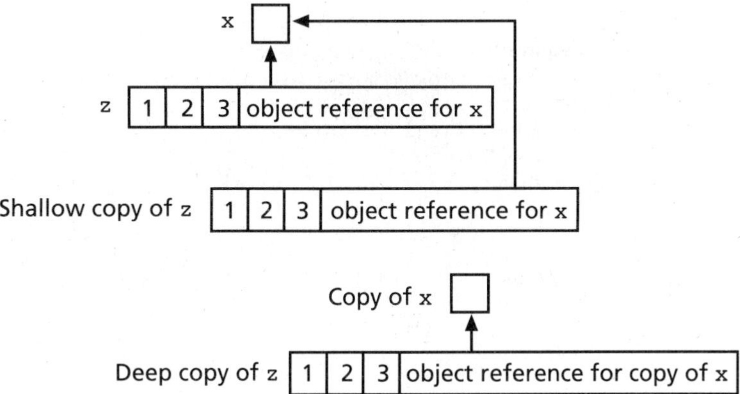

Figure 7-3: Shallow and deep copies

The method Object.clone performs a shallow copy. It copies all fields of the original object to the new object, regardless of whether the fields are primitive types or object references. This works for many, but not all, classes. If a class is mutable and has any fields that are object references to mutable objects of reference type, the class should provide an implementation of clone that returns a deep copy. Alternatively, you may want to prevent an object from being cloned. For example, if instances of a class cannot be duplicated in some safe and meaningful way, the class should not be cloneable.

Next comes the question of how to tell whether the classes of object references that are fields in the class also override the clone method. Often, whether your class is cloneable depends on whether all fields in the class are cloneable. The Java platform includes a core interface called Cloneable for the specific purpose of indicating whether objects are cloneable.

Making Objects Cloneable

One of the cornerstones of the philosophy of the Java programming language is that subclasses inherit no surprising behavior from superclasses. In the case of copying objects, whether cloning works depends upon whether the class is defined to implement the core interface Cloneable. If a class is declared to implement Cloneable, you can assume it is safe to call clone for instances of that class and use the objects produced by the clone method. If you call clone for a class that does not implement Cloneable, the exception CloneNotSupportedException is thrown. This may not be the behavior you want, but it is safer than and preferable to a default clone that gives no outward sign of error and creates a corrupt copy.

If you call clone for an instance of a class that uses the default method Object.clone, you must take one of the following actions:

- Wrap a try block around the call of clone and catch the possible CloneNotSupportedException.
- Add the CloneNotSupportedException exception to the throws clause for the method that calls clone.

The definition of clone in the Object class lists CloneNotSupportedException in its throws clause. When you override Object.clone in your class, you have the option of removing CloneNotSupportedException from the throws clause of your clone method.

The Cloneable interface is an example of a marker interface. **Marker interfaces** have no methods. Note, for example, that the interface Cloneable does not define the method clone. The sole purpose of a marker interface is to attach a piece of type information to a class. In this case, declaring a class with implements Cloneable means that the class supports cloning of its objects. When you define a class, you can use Cloneable like an on-off switch. Implement Cloneable, and the class supports cloning. That is all you have to do to enable the inherited clone method. Do not implement Cloneable, and the clone method throws an exception. Pseudocode for Object.clone is essentially as follows:

```
if the object is an instance of Cloneable
  then make a shallow copy of the entire object
  else throw a CloneNotSupportedException
end if
```

Here is an example class called `Pair`. Because `Pair` is a public class, it is found in a file called Pair.java. The structure of packages mirrors the file system, so you will find this source code in the java4cpp\cloning subfolder of the folder in which you unpacked the JAR file java4cpp.jar. It has only two fields and they are integers. Therefore, the default clone method is adequate.

```
package java4cpp.cloning;
/** An example class used to demonstrate how to
  * enable cloning for a class without fields that
  * contain object references.
  */
public class Pair implements Cloneable {
   private int a, b;
   /** Class constructor method
     * @param a Initial value for the first field
     * @param b Initial value for the second field
     */
   public Pair( int initA, int initB ) {
      a = initA;
      b = initB;
   }
   /** Convert object to String representation
     * @return The value of the array as a String
     */
   public String toString() {
      return "( " + a + ", " + b + " )";
   }
   /** The test method for the class
```

```
     * @param args Not used
     * @exception CloneNotSupportedException
     *            If clone not supported by
     *            inherited clone method
     */
    public static void main( String[] args )
         throws CloneNotSupportedException {
       Pair x = new Pair( 5, 6 );
       System.out.println( x );
       Pair y = ( Pair ) x.clone();
       System.out.println( y );
    }
}
```

The output is

```
( 5, 6 )
( 5, 6 )
```

The method main contains a throws clause because the class inherits Object.clone, which can throw the exception CloneNotSupportedException.

Overriding the Default Clone Method

For objects related by an inheritance hierarchy to be cloned correctly, each class in the hierarchy that has object reference fields must override clone. The reason is that the class at each level of the hierarchy is responsible for cloning the fields it defines, and relies on the clone method of its superclass to copy the fields it inherits. Here are some guidelines for implementing clone:

- If classes outside the package, other than subclasses, are to be allowed to use your implementation of the clone method, declare your method with access specifier public. The Object.clone method is a protected method.
- When you implement clone, it is not necessary to program it to deal with fields of the primitive types. You can leave them for the default clone method to handle.
- Define the clone method to copy objects for all fields that are reference objects. The only exceptions to this rule are object references for immutable objects. For example, objects of classes like String and the wrapper classes for the primitive types such as Integer, Character, and Double cannot be changed. Because the objects are immutable, clones that have references to the same object cannot cause problems. A different complication occurs when one or more fields are object references for classes that do not support cloning. When this happens, then you must fall back on the "brute force" method of creating a new object of the class and then calling public methods to copy the fields one by one.

- To make sure every superclass in the hierarchy has a chance to copy the fields it defines, start your definition of clone with the following statement:

  ```
  super.clone();
  ```

  This statement calls the clone method of the superclass. You should repeat the statement in every superclass until Object.clone initiates the cloning process by making a shallow copy of the entire object. Then, as the call stack retreats, each class should call the clone methods for its object references to mutable objects. In the end, everything is cloned correctly.

Here is an example of a class that inappropriately uses the default clone method:

```
package java4cpp.cloning;
/** An example class used to demonstrate what
  * happens when the default Object.clone method
  * is not overridden in a class with object
  * reference fields.
  */
public class IntArrayShared implements Cloneable {
   private int[] a;
   /** Class constructor method
     * @param size The maximum number of elements
     * @param initValue The initial value given
     */
   public IntArrayShared( int size, int initValue ) {
      a = new int[size];
      for( int i = 0; i < a.length; i++ ) {
         a[i] = initValue;
      }
   }
   /** Obtain the value of an array element
     * @param index the array index of interest
     * @return the value at the specified index
     */
   public int elementAt( int index ) {
      return a[index];
   }
   /** Set the value of an array element
     * @param index the array index to be updated
     * @param newValue the new value given
     */
   public void setValue( int index, int newValue ) {
      a[index] = newValue;
   }
   /** Converts the object into a String
     * @return The value of the array as a String
     */
```

```
    public String toString() {
       StringBuffer sb = new StringBuffer( "[ " );
       for( int i = 0; i < a.length; i++ ) {
          sb.append( a[i] + " " );
       }
       return sb.append( "]" ).toString();
    }
    /** The test method for the class
      * @param args Not used
      * @exception CloneNotSupportedException
      *            The inherited clone method may
      *            throw this exception
      */
    public static void main( String[] args )
          throws CloneNotSupportedException {
       IntArrayShared x = new IntArrayShared( 5, 0 );
       IntArrayShared y = ( IntArrayShared ) x.clone();
       System.out.println( x );
       System.out.println( y );
       x.setValue( 2, 9999 );
       System.out.println( x );
       System.out.println( y );
    }
}
```

The output is

```
[ 0 0 0 0 0 ]
[ 0 0 0 0 0 ]
[ 0 0 9999 0 0 ]
[ 0 0 9999 0 0 ]
```

The reference field a, which is an array of integers, is not immutable. Therefore, the inherited Object.clone method does not properly clone the field. Notice from the output that the clones are not independent.

Here is how the clone method should be written. This method is taken from the example class `java4cpp.cloning.IntArray`. The class `IntArray` is identical to the previous example, `IntArrayShared`, except that `IntArray` overrides the clone method with the following method:

```
/** Provide a clone method specifically for the
     * intArray class
     * @exception CloneNotSupportedException
     *            Superclass may throw this
     * @return A clone of the object
     */
   public Object clone()
         throws CloneNotSupportedException {
```

```
        IntArray newObject = ( IntArray ) super.clone();
        newObject.a = ( int[]) a.clone();
        return newObject;
    }
```

When you use this proper clone method, the output is as follows:

```
[ 0 0 0 0 0 ]
[ 0 0 0 0 0 ]
[ 0 0 9999 0 0 ]
[ 0 0 0 0 0 ]
```

The proper clone method has a number of notable features:

- The return type is Object, because it overrides Object.clone. Therefore, the returned object must be cast to type IntArray.
- It calls super.clone to clone the fields in the superclass. This statement could be omitted in this case, because Object is the direct superclass of IntArray. However, including this statement is never an error and is always the safest approach.
- Next, IntArray.clone calls the clone method for the field a, which is an array. Like any reference object, this array has a clone method. The clone method used by arrays makes a shallow copy, which is adequate in this case. If the elements of the array are themselves reference objects, as in an array of arrays, you have no choice but to clone each element explicitly. Unfortunately, there is no way to override the clone method of an array.

Defining Cloneable Classes

The Cloneable interface gives the creator of the class the responsibility of deciding whether instances of the class are cloneable. Moreover, the decision affects not only the class being defined, but all subclasses that may extend the class in the future.

When you are deciding whether to implement the Cloneable interface, consider the impact on subclasses for which the class is the superclass, as well as on unrelated classes that use the class. Here are five possible approaches you can provide:

1. All objects of the class can be cloned. The simplest option is to support cloning fully, by:

   - Defining the class with implements Cloneable.
   - Inheriting or overriding the default clone method. If you override the method, do not throw any exceptions in your implementation, but do include CloneNotSupportedException in the throws clause.

   This approach provides the most flexibility for any subclasses. A subclass that extends the class has the same options for implementing cloning as the class had.

Example:

```
class SubClass extends SuperClass
                              implements Cloneable {
   // optionally implement clone
   public Object clone()
             throws CloneNotSupportedException {
      // do not throw CloneNotSupportedException
   }
}
```

2. Objects of the class are cloneable only if all contained objects are also cloneable. This is an attractive option for classes that do not have control over what they contain. Collection classes usually use this technique. To support cloning conditionally:

   - Define the class with implements Cloneable.
   - Implement clone. For the fields of reference types, call the clone method of those classes. To give these contained objects an opportunity to throw an exception, include CloneNotSupportedException in the throws clause of the clone method.

   A subclass that extends this class has the same options for implementing cloning as the class.
   Example:

```
class SubClass extends SuperClass
                              implements Cloneable {
   OtherClass fieldName;
   // Implement clone if fields are object
   // references
   public Object clone()
             throws CloneNotSupportedException {
      fieldName = ( OtherClass ) fieldName.clone();
      // do not throw CloneNotSupportedException
   }
}
```

3. Objects of the class are not cloneable, but a subclass can extend the class in such a way that its objects are cloneable. To let subclasses support cloning, but not publicly support cloning in the class:

   - Omit implements Cloneable from the class definition. Leave implementing the interface up to the subclass.
   - Override or inherit the clone method. Even though the class is not cloneable, you should provide a clone method that correctly duplicates the fields defined in the class, for the sake of cloneable subclasses.

   Although this class does not allow cloning, a subclass can implement Cloneable, inherit or override the clone method, and become fully cloneable.

Example:

```
class SubClass extends SuperClass {
   OtherClass fieldName;
   // implement clone if fields are object
   // references
   public Object clone()
             throws CloneNotSupportedException {
      fieldName = ( OtherClass ) fieldName.clone();
      // do not throw CloneNotSupportedException
   }
}
```

4. No object of the class or any class that extends the class can be cloned. Do not support cloning if you are designing a class of objects in which the subclass objects must be unique. For example, it may be a design criterion of the application that only one copy of an object is allowed. To prohibit cloning:

   - Omit implements Cloneable from the class definition.
   - Implement a clone method that always throws a CloneNotSupportedException object.

   Even if a subclass implements Cloneable and overrides clone, the exception is thrown when the subclass calls super.clone for the fields it inherits from your class. Therefore, you guarantee that no subclass can clone an object.

   Example:

```
class SubClass extends SuperClass {
   // implement clone to throw an exception
   public Object clone()
             throws CloneNotSupportedException {
       throw new CloneNotSupportedException();
   }
}
```

5. The class is an abstract class and all subclasses are required to provide a clone method that does not throw CloneNotSupportedException. To force a subclass to support cloning:

   - Optionally add implements Cloneable for clarity.
   - Define a clone method and declare it to be abstract.
   - Omit CloneNotSupportedException from the throws clause of clone.

   Example:

```
abstract class SubClass extends SuperClass {
   public abstract Object clone();
}
```

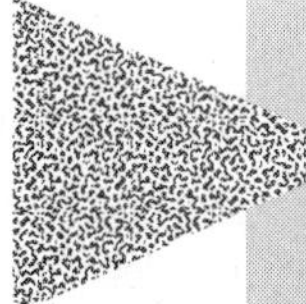

Mini Quiz 7-2

a. Why must a superclass that forces subclasses to implement Cloneable be an abstract class?

b. Why must the class that extends a superclass with an abstract clone method override clone?

c. Why can the overriding method clone not throw the exception CloneNotSupportedException?

Run-Time Type Information

Some programming challenges arise from the environments supported by the Java platform and the very nature of programs that you write in the Java programming language. For example, many programs are driven by a graphical user interface (GUI) or run in a distributed environment. As a result, you may find that your class has to deal with objects for which the type is not known. These objects may be instances of classes created by different programmers, and may even be instances of classes that did not exist when you wrote and tested your class. An important use of RTTI is to access members of classes that you cannot know about when you develop your class. For example, your method may extract information from a database and need the flexibility to display records for which the structure is unknown at development time.

RTTI can also be helpful in debugging the code. For example, one effect of dynamic binding may be that a method can receive a different type of object than it expects. The object received as an argument to a method can instantiate a subclass of the argument type. A good debugger can show you what is happening at run time, or you can use RTTI to determine whether you are operating on the type of object for which the method was designed.

RTTI is a relatively recent addition to the C++ language, and not everyone agrees that C++ even needs such a feature. The argument against RTTI is based largely on the hybrid nature of C++. Some argue that RTTI may give programmers an alternative to taking advantage of dynamic binding and fully using object-oriented programming techniques. With RTTI, you can call a function to get the type of an object, and then use a switch statement with case clauses to select the function to call. This approach may be tempting in C++ because you have to declare explicitly the functions virtual to engage dynamic binding. C++ programmers also may be reluctant accept the performance penalty that is inherent in dynamic binding.

On the other hand, the Java platform always performs dynamic binding, unless you call a method that is explicitly declared with the qualifier final, or a class method. There is no extra coding associated with dynamic binding in the Java platform. Therefore, there is less inducement to misuse RTTI to avoid dynamic binding.

Unlike C++ environments, the Java platform cannot be seriously accused of not needing RTTI. On the contrary, the kinds of environments for which Java technology is best suited introduce real needs for RTTI.

RTTI also helps to make up for the lack of parameterized types in the Java programming language. For example, in an argument list you must specify the type of every argument of every method, and the only flexibility is that dynamic binding lets you specify a superclass when a subclass object may actually be passed. You can pass the most general type, Object, to a method and let the method use RTTI to determine how to use the object.

C++ programmers can use templates for parameterized types. If you are switching from C++, you may miss templates and perhaps criticize the Java programming language for having no analogous feature. On the other hand, the template feature has proven to be one of the trickiest parts of the C++ language to standardize, and attempts by C++ compiler developers to support templates have produced some very complex implementations that are difficult to use.

C++ programmers also sometimes fall back on the technique of using pointers of type void* **and casting, combined with a variety of programming tricks to determine type. This approach is roughly analogous to declaring an argument of type** Object **in a Java method, but far less elegant because it relies on non-object-oriented techniques that are allowed in C++ as part of the legacy of the C language.**

Determining the Type of Objects

Built into the Java programming language is an operator, instanceof, that you can use to ask if an object is an instance of a particular class or any of its subclasses. This operator is useful in situations like the following:

You may be writing a method that receives an object reference, of a type such as `BankAccount`. The superclass `BankAccount` may be extended by the classes `CheckingAccount` and `SavingsAccount`. If the method must handle the different kinds of `BankAccount` subclasses differently, you can use the instanceof operator.

Syntax

object_reference **instanceof** *class_name*
object_reference **instanceof** *interface_name*

Dissection

- The operator **instanceof** returns a boolean value. The result is **true** if the object on the left of the operator is an instance of the class or a subclass of the class on the right of the operator. The result is **false** otherwise.
- You can also use **instanceof** to ask whether the class of the object implements a particular interface. For example, you may want to know if an object is **Cloneable**.
- The **instanceof** operator does not work for the primitive types. The leftmost argument must be an object reference. If the value of the object reference is **null**, **instanceof** returns **false**, regardless of the type of the object reference.
- If the object is an instance of a class that extends the class or implements the interfaces specified by the rightmost argument, the value returned by **instanceof** of is **true**.

Code Example

```
if ( account instanceof CheckingAccount ) {
   // process a checking account
}
else {
   // process all other account types
}
```

Code Dissection

If the account object is a CheckingAccount, it must also be a BankAccount. The operator is most useful when you know the supertype, or superclass, of an object but you want to determine which subclass the object instantiates.

C++ has no operator equivalent to the Java programming language's instanceof **operator, but you can use the** dynamic_cast **operator to make a similar test. The C++** dynamic_cast **operator succeeds in the same situations in which the Java programming language's** instanceof **operator returns** true.

Only C++ compilers that support RTTI recognize the dynamic_cast **operator and the related operators** const_cast, static_cast, **and** reinterpret_cast. **A C++ expression of the following form casts the value of an expression to the type of *T*, where the type of *T* is pointer or reference to a class. If the compiler cannot perform the cast, a** bad_cast **exception is thrown.**

dynamic_cast <T> **(expression)**

Accessing Information about Classes at Run Time

For every class and every instance of a class that a program uses, the JVM creates an object with the type Class. This object contains information about the class, and is itself an instance of a class called Class. The Java platform creates the Class object automatically and stores in it several facts about the class, so that you can access the information at run time.

The class type_info **provides part of C++ language support for RTTI. This class serves a purpose similar to that of the Java platform class named** Class. **However,** type_info **is more limited, and is used in a very different way from the** Class **class. In particular, instances of the** type_info **class store a pointer to type information that is specific to the implementation of C++. The C++ standard specifies only that the instances also store values that can be used to compare types for equality and collating order.**

This class is a good example of a very fundamental difference between the Java programming language and C++. C++ leaves many platform-specific details up to the developers of C++ compilers and development tools. Unlike type_info **of C++, the** Class **class is fully defined by the core classes and is the same on all implementations of the Java platform.**

You can call a method to get the Class object for a class or an instance of a class.

Class	java.lang.Object
Purpose	The **Object** class defines the methods that are available in all objects of reference types.
Methods	■ **Class getClass()** The **getClass** method returns an object reference for a Class object.

The getClass **method is analagous to the C++ operator** typeid. **In C++, you apply the** typeid **operator to a type identifier or to an expression, and the operator returns a C++ reference to an instance of** type_info.

You do not create Class objects, and no constructor for the class Class is available. Instead, use one of the following methods to access the Class object for a class or an object:

- Use the Object.getClass method for any object. All objects of reference type inherit this method. It is public, so you can always use it. Also the method is final so that you cannot override it. For example, the following statement gets the class for an object called `account`:

  ```
  Class classAcc = account.getClass();
  ```

- If you know the name of a class or interface, you can use a class variable that the Java programming language adds to every class automatically. The name of the class variable is class, and it contains a reference to the corresponding Class object. For example, the following statement assigns an object reference for the Class object of the `BankAccount` class to classBankAcc:

  ```
  Class classBankAcc = BankAccount.class;
  ```

- If you know the full name of the class or interface, call the class method Class.forName, passing the fully qualified name of the class as a String argument. For example, the following statement assigns an object reference for the Class object of the `BankAccount` class to `classBankAcc`, if the `BankAccount` class is in the subpackage `Banking` of the package `Financial`:

  ```
  Class classBankAcc =
     Class.forName( "Financial.Banking.BankAccount" );
  ```

  If the named class is not loaded into the JVM, calling this method forces the JVM to load the class. The next sample program uses this method.

Version Watch

The field class **was added after the original version of the Java platform, to simplify the process of accessing the** Class **object when the class name is known. This addition is one of many changes to enhance RTTI support in version 1.1 of the Java platform.**

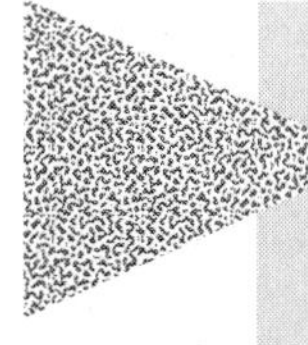

Mini Quiz 7-3

This definition of the class field is

```
public static final Class class;
```

Why is it public, static, and final?

After you have a reference to a Class object, you can call instance methods of Class to ask questions about the class this object describes.

Class	**java.lang.Class**
Purpose	The **Class** class provides run-time information about Java classes.
Methods	■ **Class forName(String** *classname* **)** The **forName** method returns the **Class** object for the given class name. ■ **String getName()** The **getName** method returns the fully qualified name of the class, interface, array, or primitive type. ■ **Class getSuperclass()** The **getSuperclass** method returns a reference to the **Class** object for the superclass of the class. If called for an instance of **Object** or a type that is not a direct or indirect subclass of **Object**, the method returns **null**. ■ **boolean isArray()** The **isArray** method returns **true** if the **Class** object represents an array type, and **false** otherwise. ■ **boolean isInstance(Object** *object* **)** The **isInstance** method returns **true** if the specified object can cast to the type described by the **Class** object, and **false** otherwise. If the argument has the value **null**, this method returns **false**, regardless of the type of the argument. ■ **boolean isInterface()** The **isInterface** method returns **true** if the **Class** object represents an interface, and **false** otherwise. ■ **Object newInstance()** The **newInstance** method creates a new instance of the class and returns an object reference to the new object. You should cast the reference from type **Object** to the actual class of the object. If this method is used with the **Class** object of an interface or an abstract class, an **InstantiationException** is thrown. The noargument constructor of the class is called to create the new instance. If such a constructor does not exist, the program terminates with a **NoSuchMethod** run-time error.

Mini Quiz 7-4

- Under what circumstances can a class not have a no-argument constructor?
- Of the methods listed here, only forName is a class method. Why is forName not an instance method like the others?

Here is a sample program that exercises the instanceof operator and the Class class:

```
package java4cpp.rtti;
/** A class used to demonstrate RTTI concepts
  */
public class CreateByName {
  /** Test method for the class
    * @param args names of classes to be
    *        instantiated
    */
   public static void main( String[] args ) {
      for ( int i = 0; i < args.length; i++ ) {
         try {
            Class x = Class.forName( args[i] );
            Object y;
         try {
            if ( x.isInterface() ) {
               System.out.println( "The class " +
                  x.getName() + " is an interface "
                  + "and can't be instantiated." );
            } else {
               y = x.newInstance();
               if ( y instanceof java.awt.Component ) {
                  System.out.println( "The GUI "
                     + "component class "
                     + x.getName() + " was specified." );
               } else {
                  System.out.println( "The non-GUI "
                     + "component class "
                     + x.getName() + " was specified." );
               }
            }
            } catch( InstantiationException ix ) {
               ix.printStackTrace();
            } catch( IllegalAccessException iax ) {
               iax.printStackTrace();
            } // end inner try
            } catch( ClassNotFoundException cnfx ) {
            System.err.println( "Sorry, the class "
```

```
                + args[i] + " could not be found." );
            } // end outer try
        } // end for
    } // end main
} // end CreateByName
```

Suppose that you run this program with the following command on one line:

```
java java4cpp.rtti.CreateByName java.lang.String
   java.awt.Button java.lang.Gazoom
   java.lang.Cloneable
```

The output is

```
The non-GUI component class java.lang.String was
specified.
The GUI component class java.awt.Button was specified.
Sorry, the class java.lang.Gazoom could not be found.
The class java.lang.Cloneable is an interface and can't
be instantiated.
```

The main method receives the names as arguments. It obtains the Class object for each name supplied. The main method then tests whether the name represents an interface or a class. If it is an interface, main prints a message. Otherwise, main instantiates the class and then determines whether the object is a Component. The class Component is defined in the java.awt package, and Button is a subclass of Component. In all cases, main prints appropriate messages.

The use of java.awt.Component here is incidental. Any class would have served this purpose. The relevant part of this code is the nested try blocks and the catch clauses. When run with the input suggested above, the only exception thrown and caught is a ClassNotFoundException.

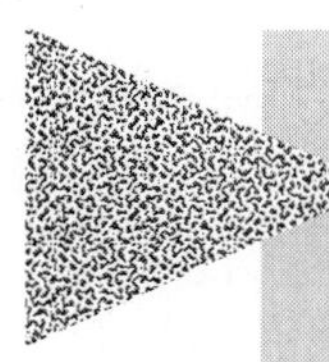

Mini Quiz 7-5

Which of the called methods can throw the exceptions of the following types?

- InstantiationException
- IllegalAccessException
- ClassNotFoundException

Casting Between Types

Whenever you cast between types, the operation may not be safe. In this context, **safe** means that no information can be lost or corrupted as a result of the cast. The JVM ensures that only safe casts are performed. For example, casting from a type with a narrower range of values to a type with a wider range of values, such as from a float to a double or from a subclass to its superclass class, is always safe.

An unsafe cast can be from a wider type to a narrower type or between classes that are not a direct or indirect subclass and superclass of each other. For example, casting from long to short or from String to Exception is unsafe.

In the case of primitive types, the compiler allows explicitly casting as a way for you to indicate that you know a particular cast may not be safe and are aware of the potential problems. For example, you can convert from double to a float if you cast explicitly. Even explicit casting has limits. For example, you cannot cast a boolean to an int.

Moving from C++

The Java programming language allows only one form of explicit cast that looks like the traditional C syntax for casting, as in the following example:

```
int whole = ( int ) 6.75;
```

The C++ language recognizes additional forms of casting. As well as the dynamic_cast **and related operators that were introduced with RTTI, C++ allows function notation casting, as in the following example:**

```
int whole =int( 6.75 );
```

You cannot use this alternative syntax for casting in the Java programming language.

For the reference types, deciding what is safe is not so easy. The compiler can detect casts between types that are not a subclass and superclass of each other, and some unsafe casts from superclass to subclass. When the compiler detects a cast that is definitely unsafe, it outputs an error message. When the compiler cannot tell whether a cast between classes is safe, it assumes the code is correct and leaves the JVM with the job of checking the cast at run time.

Therefore, some unsafe casts can be attempted at run time. When this happens, the JVM throws a ClassCastException. This exception can occur only in casts between subtypes and supertypes, because the compiler always detects other casts as errors.

Moving from C++

The C++ equivalent to ClassCastException **is the exception that is thrown when the** dynamic_cast **operator attempts to cast references that are not compatible. A notable difference between the Java programming language and C++ is that in C++ you must specifically request a safety check by using** dynamic_cast. **By default, the C++ compiler and run-time environment assume that you know what you are doing, and allow an unsafe cast to succeed. The Java platform always performs a safety check. You cannot avoid a** ClassCastException **by coding the cast in a different way.**

The class ClassCastException extends RunTimeException. The reason is that casting exceptions are unpredictable. They can happen anywhere. If it were an Exception, you would have to list ClassCastException in the throws clause of every method that casts classes. You can still catch this exception, as the next sample program does.

Mini Quiz 7-6

A RunTimeException object is an Exception object. Why is it not necessary to list ClassCastException in the throws clause of a method that can throw it but does not catch it?

In this sample program, the abstract class `Animal` is superclass to the classes `Reptile` and `Mammal`:

```
package java4cpp.rtti;
/** Classes to demonstrate a run-time cast error
  */
public class BadCast {
   /** Test method for the class
     * @param args not used
     */
   public static void main( String[] args ) {
      Mammal horse = new Mammal( "horse" );
      Reptile snake = new Reptile( "snake" );
      Mammal mouse = new Mammal( "mouse" );
      horse.categorize();
      snake.categorize();
      mouse.categorize();
   }
}
/** A generic animal class
  */
class Animal {
   protected String name;

   public Animal( String name ) {
      this.name = name;
   }
   public void categorize() {
      try {
         if ( ( ( Mammal ) this ).isRodent() ) {
            System.out.println( "A " + name
                                + " is a rodent." );
         } else {
            System.out.println( "A " + name
                                + " is not a rodent." );
         }
      }
      catch ( ClassCastException ccx )  {
         ccx.printStackTrace();
      }
```

```
        try {
           int legs = ( ( Reptile ) this ).numLegs();
           System.out.println( "A " + name + " has "
                                 + legs + " legs." );
        } catch ( ClassCastException ccx )  {
           ccx.printStackTrace();
        }
     }
  }
  /** The class representing all mammals
    */
  class Mammal extends Animal {
     private static String[] rodents
        = { "rat", "rabbit", "mouse", "beaver" };
     public Mammal( String name ) {
       super( name );
     }
     public boolean isRodent() {
        for ( int i = 0; i < rodents.length; i++ ) {
           if ( name.equals( rodents[i] ) ) {
              return true;
           }
        }
        return false;
     }
  }
  /** The class representing all reptiles
    */
  class Reptile extends Animal {
     public Reptile( String name ) {
        super( name );
     }
     public int numLegs() {
        if ( name.equals( "snake" ) ) {
           return 0;
        } else {
           return 4;
        }
     }
  }
```

The output is

```
A horse is not a rodent.
java.lang.ClassCastException: java4cpp.rtti.Mammal
        at java4cpp.rtti.Animal.categorize
        ( BadCast.java:34 )
```

```
        at java4cpp.rtti.BadCast.main
        ( BadCast.java:13 )
java.lang.ClassCastException: java4cpp.rtti.Reptile
        at java4cpp.rtti.Animal.categorize
        (BadCast.java:46)
        at java4cpp.rtti.BadCast.main
        ( BadCast.java:14 )
A snake has 0 legs.
A mouse is a rodent.
java.lang.ClassCastException: java4cpp.rtti.Mammal
        at java4cpp.rtti.Animal.categorize
        (BadCast.java:31)
        at java4cpp.rtti.BadCast.main
        ( BadCast.java:15 )
```

This program creates objects to represent different animals, each of which can be a `Mammal` or a `Reptile`. Both `Mammal` and `Reptile` classes extend the class `Animal`. The method `Animal.categorize` can receive any kind of animal as an argument. It casts the argument to a Mammal to call the `Mammal.isRodent` method and to a `Reptile` to call the `Reptile.numLegs` method. However, at run time, the `Mammal` objects `horse` and `mouse` cannot be safely cast to `Reptile` objects, and the `Reptile` object `snake` cannot be safely cast to a `Mammal`. When these casts are attempted, the JVM throws the exception ClassCastException.

Using the Reflection API

Sometimes you need to know much more about a type than the information provided by the Class class. For this purpose, you can use the classes in the package java.lang.reflect, otherwise known as the **Reflection API**. This set of classes increases the power and usefulness of the Class class.

The Reflection API supports an activity called **introspection**, which essentially means asking a class to describe itself. JavaBeans technology depends on introspection. In Chapter 15, you learn that JavaBeans are classes that conform to a rigid coding standard, so that they can be used as input for JavaBeans-based development tools. The tools use introspection to analyze the JavaBeans, and then give the developers ways, often through graphical interfaces, of building programs quickly from the JavaBeans.

The Reflection API became available in version 1.1 of the Java platform. The Class **class, as defined in the original Java platform, proved to be very useful. Nevertheless, the** java.lang.reflect **package was added to satisfy requests that the** Class **class be extended.**

One of the most important advances in Java technology since the first release of the Java platform is the formulation of a standard for JavaBeans. Many of the changes introduced in version 1.1 were to convert the core classes into JavaBeans. One very important use of the Reflection API is to support JavaBeans-based tools.

The Reflection API gives an object the ability to reflect upon itself and discover its contents. The package java.lang.reflect defines a number of classes that together give a complete description of an object. Three classes represent the building blocks of classes: Constructor, Method, and Field. The most commonly used methods of these classes are listed in the following.

Class	java.lang.reflect.Constructor
Purpose	Each instance of the **Constructor** class provides information about one constructor of a class, and provides a way for the calling program to create an object using the constructor.
Methods	■ **Class[] getParameterTypes()** The **getParameterTypes** method returns an array of **Class** objects for the arguments of the constructor. Each element of the array is an object reference for the **Class** object of one argument. The order of the elements reflects the order that the arguments are listed in the definition of the constructor. ■ **Object newInstance(Object[]** *args* **)** The **newInstance** method creates an instance of the class and returns an object reference for the new object. The elements in the array of type object **Object** are passed as arguments to the constructor.

Class	java.lang.reflect.Method
Purpose	Each instance of the **Method** class provides information about one method of a class, and provides a way for the calling program to call the method. The method may be a class method or an instance method, and may be abstract.
Methods	■ **Class[] getParameterTypes()** The **getParameterTypes** method returns an array of **Class** objects for the arguments of the method. Each element of the array is an object reference for the **Class** object of one argument. The order of the elements reflects the order that the arguments are listed in the definition of the method. ■ **Class getReturnType()** The **getReturnType** method returns an object reference for the **Class** object of the return type of the method. ■ **Object invoke(Object** *object*, **Object[]** *args* **)** The **invoke** method invokes the method with the object specified in the first argument. For a class method, the first argument has the value **null**. The elements in the array of type **Object** are passed as arguments to the method.

Class	java.lang.reflect.Field
Purpose	Each instance of the **Field** class provides information about one field of a class, and provides the calling program a way to get and set the value of the field. The field may be a class variable or an instance variable.
Methods	■ **Class getType()** The **getType** method returns an object reference for the **Class** object of the field. ■ **Object get(Object** *object* **)** The **get** method returns the value of the field for the specified object. This class has methods to return the value of a field as values of the primitive types. ■ **void set(Object** *object*, **Object** *value* **)** The **set** method sets the value of the field for the specified object to the specified value.

The type of most arguments and many return values of the methods in the Reflection API classes is Object. Therefore, you can actually pass any type of object, and any type may be returned. But what about the primitive types? The Reflection API classes use the wrapper classes for the primitive types. Some of the methods in these classes, such as Field.getType and Method.getReturnType, return an object reference for a Class object. Use the methods in the Class class with these object references to get more information about the returned objects.

The classes Constructor, Method, and Field implement an interface called Member. Therefore, all three classes provide the methods defined in Member.

Interface	java.lang.reflect.Member
Purpose	The class that implements this interface provides identifying information about a member of a class.
Methods	■ **Class getDeclaringClass()** The **getDeclaringClass** method returns an object reference for the **Class** object of the class in which the member is defined. ■ **String getName()** The **getName** method returns the name of the member as a **String**. ■ **int getModifiers()** The **getModifiers** method returns the Java programming language's access specifiers and qualifiers that apply to the member. The return value is encoded in an **int**. Use the **Modifier** class to decode the **int** value.

Two additional classes complete the suite of Reflection API classes: Array and Modifier.

Class	java.lang.reflect.Array
Purpose	The **Array** class provides methods to manipulate a **Field** object as an array. The **Field** class only has methods for getting and setting individual values. Use this class with the **Field** class when the field is an array. To determine whether a **Field** object is an array, call the **Class.isArray** method and pass the value returned by **Field.getType**. Methods include the following:
Methods	■ **Object get(Object** *object*, **int** *position* **)** The **get** method returns an object reference for the element at the specified position in the array. The **Array** class has methods that return the value of individual elements as values of the primitive types. ■ **void set(Object** *object*, **int** *position* **)** The **set** method sets the value of the element at the specified position to the value of the first argument. ■ **int getLength()** The **getLength** method returns the number of elements in the array. ■ **Object newInstance(Class** *type*, **int** *length* **)** The **newInstance** method creates a new array to hold the specified number of elements of the specified type, and returns an object reference for the new array. ■ **Object newInstance(Class** *type*, **int[]** *dimensions* **)** The **newInstance** method creates a new multidimensional array to hold the specified number of elements of the specified type, and returns an object reference for the new array.

Class	java.lang.reflect.Modifier
Purpose	The **Modifier** class contains a number of constants that represent the access specifiers and qualifiers that can be applied to members. It also provides class methods that return **true** if a member has a certain qualifier and **false** otherwise. For example, the method **isStatic(int** *value* **)** returns true only when called for a static member. The constant **STATIC** is an **int** representing the modifier **static**. Call the method **Member.getModifiers** to get the value to pass to the methods in this class.

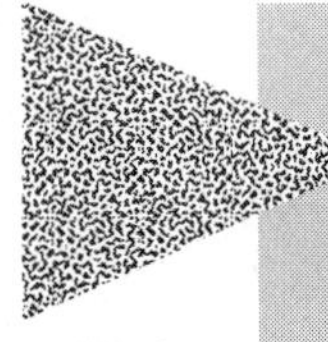

Mini Quiz 7-7

There are 11 constants and 13 methods in the class Modifier, including STATIC and isStatic. The two extra methods are the constructor and toString. Can you guess the names of the other 10 fields and methods?

How can you access the Class object for a primitive type when you cannot invoke a method such as getClass for a primitive type? Each wrapper class for a primitive type has a field called TYPE that is a reference to the Class object for its corresponding primitive type. Just like the field class of all reference types, the field TYPE of wrapper classes is a public, static, and final field. For example, Integer.TYPE is a reference to the Class object for int. Be careful not to confuse Integer.TYPE with Integer.class. The first refers to the Class object for primitive type int, and the second refers to the Class object for the wrapper class Integer.

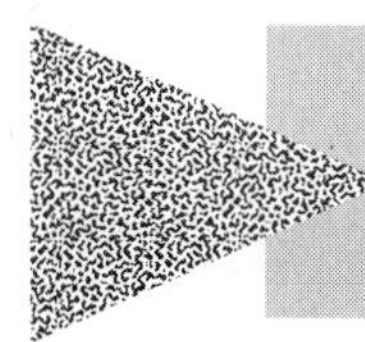

Mini Quiz 7-8

Why is the name of the field TYPE, as in Integer.TYPE, in uppercase, but the name of the field class, as in Integer.class, in lowercase?

What about methods that do not return a value, and have return type void? The package java.lang contains a wrapper class named Void for the primitive type void.

Version Watch

To provide run-time type information about void**, the class** java.lang.Void **was added to the core classes at the same time as the Reflection API. The purpose of** Void **was to contain the** Void.TYPE **field.**

Here is sample program that uses the Reflection API to make a list of the methods in the String class:

```
package java4cpp.rtti;
import java.lang.reflect.*;
/** A class used to demonstrate the use of the
  * Reflection API
  */
public class ListStringMethods {
   /** Test method for the class
     * @param args not used
     * @exception ClassNotFoundException
     *            Thrown if the class being
     *            investigated isn't found
     */
   public static void main( String[] args )
         throws ClassNotFoundException {
```

```
        Method[] ma
           = String.class.getMethods();
        for ( int i = 0; i < ma.length; i++ ) {
           System.out.println( ma[i] );
        }
    }
}
```

The output is a complete list of the methods in the String class, and too long to include here. The first three lines are as follows:

```
public static java.lang.String
       java.lang.String.valueOf( java.lang.Object )
public static java.lang.String
       java.lang.String.valueOf( char[] )
public static java.lang.String
       java.lang.String.valueOf( char[],int,int )
```

In the class ListStringMethods, the main method declares an array of Method objects, ma, which is assigned the object reference obtained by calling the method String.class.getMethods. This one method call acquires a lot of information: Every method in the String class is described in an element of the returned array. The Method class overrides the Object.toString method so you can easily print out all the information about the method, including its access specifier.

Calling Methods with the Reflection API

You can do more with the Reflection API than receive a great deal of useful information about a class. Now you have two ways to execute a method or a constructor:

- Call the method by name or create an object with the new keyword in the usual way. This is the obvious approach to take when you know the name of the method or type of the object when you are entering source code.
- Use a Method object or a Constructor object. This approach works when you must use the Reflection API to discover what methods are available or determine the type of an object.

C++ programmers can use pointers to members to select dynamically what method to call at run time. For example, you may have a function that manipulates data and sorts it. You can try different sorting algorithms by providing a different sort function for each algorithm. If you pass a pointer to one of the sort functions as an argument to the data manipulation function, that function can then call whichever sort function it is given.

You cannot play such tricks with pointers in the Java programming language, but you can use the Reflection API. Instead of passing a pointer, you can pass a Method **object as an argument. However, the recommended and most common way to handle this is to define an interface containing the declaration of the sort method and pass an object that implements the interface.**

To call a method with the Reflection API, use the following instance method of the Method class:

Object invoke(Object *object*, Object[] *args*)

In the first argument of invoke, pass an object reference for the object on which the called method is to run, or specify null for class methods. Create an array of type Object for the arguments of the method and insert an object reference for the first argument of the method into the first element of the array, for the second argument into the second element, and so on. If an argument has a primitive type, wrap it with the appropriate wrapper class and insert the object reference for the wrapper instance in the array. Specify the array as the second argument of invoke.

If the called method returns a value, you retrieve the value through the object reference returned by invoke. If the return type is a primitive type, invoke returns an instance of the appropriate wrapper class.

If the called method does not return a value, invoke returns an object reference of type Void.

To create an instance of a class with the Reflection API, use the following instance method of the Constructor class:

Object newInstance(Object[] *args*)

The only argument of newInstance is an array that contains the arguments for the constructor. Build up this array in exactly the same way you build up the array argument of Method.invoke. The newInstance method returns a reference to the newly created object, which you can cast to the appropriate class type.

The method Constructor.newInstance has one great advantage over the method Class.newInstance: you can pass arguments to the constructor.

Version Watch

In the original Java platform, the only way to call a constructor explicitly was to use the method Class.newInstance**. The Reflection API introduced the method** Constructor.newInstance **with version 1.1. The method** Class.newInstance **still works, but only if the class has a constructor with no arguments.**

Here is an example program that creates instances of classes using Constructor.newInstance:

```
package java4cpp.rtti;
import java.lang.reflect.*;
/** A class defined to demonstrate the Reflection API
  */
class FirstType {
   private String name;
   public FirstType( String name ) {
      this.name = name;
   }
   public FirstType() {
      this.name = "DefaultFirst";
   }
```

```
   public String toString() {
      return ( "A FirstType object named " + name );
   }
}
/** A class defined to demonstrate the Reflection API
  */
class SecondType {
   // explicit constructor needed for Reflection API
   public SecondType() {
      // intentionally left empty
   }
   public String toString() {
      return ( "A SecondType object" );
   }
}
/** A class used to show how the Reflection API can
  * be used to construct objects
  */
public class Construct {
   /** Test method for the class
     * @param args the class name to be constructed
     *    followed by any constructor arguments
     */
   public static void main( String [] args ) {
      if ( args.length == 0 ) {
          System.out.println( " usage: Construct"
                            + " classname"
                            + " [ctor_arg]" );
          return;
      }
      // get the class object for the specified class
      Class classObj = null;
      try {
         classObj = Class.forName( args[0] );
      } catch ( ClassNotFoundException ex ) {
         System.err.println( " Unknown class "
                           + args[0] );
         return;
      }
      // get constructor for class
      Constructor ctor = null;
      Class[] ctorTypes = new Class[args.length -1];
      for ( int i = 0; i < args.length-1; i ++ ) {
          ctorTypes[i] = java.lang.String.class;
      }
      try {
```

```
            ctor = classObj.getConstructor( ctorTypes );
         } catch ( NoSuchMethodException ex ) {
            String msg = "No constructor: ";
            msg += classObj.getName() + "(";
            for ( int i = 0; i < ctorTypes.length; i++ ) {
               msg += ctorTypes[i].getName();
               if ( i < ctorTypes.length-1 ) {
                  msg += ", ";
               }
            }
            msg += " )";
            System.err.println( msg );
            return;
         }
         // build up the array of arguments
         // for the constructor from the
         // commmand-line arguments
         String[] ctorArgs
            = new String[ctorTypes.length];
         System.arraycopy( args, 1, ctorArgs, 0,
                           ctorTypes.length );
         // call the constructor
         Object obj = null;
         try {
            obj = ctor.newInstance( ctorArgs );
         } catch ( Exception ex ) {
            ex.printStackTrace();
            return;
         }
         // print the object created
         System.out.println( obj );
      }
   }
```

This program tried to create instances of either `FirstType` and `SecondType`, depending on which class name is specified in the argument list `Construct.main`. It may be useful to look at the code in more detail.

```
class FirstType {
   private String name;
   public FirstType( String name ) {
      this.name = name;
   }
   public FirstType() {
      this.name = "DefaultFirst";
   }
   public String toString() {
```

```
        return ( "A FirstType object named " + name );
    }
}
```

The class `FirstType` has two constructors: one with no arguments, and one that takes a single String as an argument. This simple class does no more than store either the String supplied to the constructor or a default String in the private field, `name`, and provide a toString method so that the contents of the class can be printed.

```
class SecondType {
    public SecondType() {}
    public String toString() {
        return ( "A SecondType object" );
    }
}
```

The class `SecondType` has only a no-argument constructor and a toString method. If a constructor is not explicitly supplied, the compiler can supply one and this program compiles successfully. However, the Reflection API does not recognize the compiler-supplied constructor and one must be supplied here.

```
public class Construct {
    public static void main( String [] args ) {
        if ( args.length == 0 ) {
            System.out.println( " usage: Construct"
                              + " classname"
                              + "[ctor_arg]" );
            return;
        }
```

The work happens in the main method of the test class `Construct`. This program expects the name of a class and the arguments of a constructor for that class to be supplied as command-line arguments. For simplicity, the program assumes the type of all arguments for the constructor is String. If no arguments are supplied, the program stops with a message.

```
        Class classObj = null;
        try {
            classObj = Class.forName( args[0] );
        }
        catch ( ClassNotFoundException ex ) {
            System.err.println( " Unknown class "
                              + args[0] );
            return;
        }
```

The first step is to determine what kind of class the user wants to instantiate. The Class.forName method loads the specified class into the JVM, and returns the class object for that class. If no such class can be found, the JVM throws a ClassNotFoundException. Because forName expects the full class name, the exception is thrown if the user enters just FirstType, SecondType, or any other unknown class name. For the program to work with the example classes supplied in this file, the user must enter java4cpp.rtti.FirstType or java4cpp.rtti.SecondType.

The exception handler provided by this catch clause for the ClassNotFoundException prints an appropriate message and then terminates the program.

```
Constructor ctor = null;
Class[] ctorTypes = new Class[args.length-1];
for ( int i = 0; i < args.length-1;i ++ ) {
    ctorTypes[i] = java.lang.String.class;
}
```

Having determined that the class exists, the program prepares to call a constructor to instantiate the class. It declares a Constructor object, `ctor`, but needs to look at the argument list before identifying a specific constructor. Therefore, the next step is to build an array of type Class, `ctorTypes`, in which each element encapsulates the type of one argument for the constructor. Here, all arguments have type String and the number of arguments is determined by the command-line arguments entered by the user.

```
try {
   ctor = classObj.getConstructor( ctorTypes );
}
catch ( NoSuchMethodException ex ) {
   String msg = "No constructor: ";
   msg += classObj.getName() + "(";
   for ( int i = 0; i < ctorTypes.length; i++ ) {
      msg += ctorTypes[i].getName();
      if ( i < ctorTypes.length-1 ) {
         msg += ", ";
      }
   }
   msg += " )";
   System.err.println( msg );
   return;
}
```

The purpose of this try block is to get a Constructor object for the required constructor. If such a constructor is available, the getConstructor method returns the Constructor object to `ctor`. Otherwise, the getConstructor method throws a NoSuchMethodException. The catch clause handles this exception by printing a message and terminating the program. In this case, the catch clause builds the message to contain the name of the constructor and the argument list. Notice that the method getName is used to return a printable representation of the type of each argument.

```
String[] ctorArgs = new String[ctorTypes.length];
System.arraycopy( args, 1, ctorArgs, 0,
                  ctorTypes.length );
```

Having determined that the required constructor is available, the program sets up the array of objects to pass to the constructor, `ctorArgs`. In this case, every element in the array is a String.

```
Object obj = null;
try {
   obj = ctor.newInstance( ctorArgs );
}
catch ( Exception ex ) {
   ex.printStackTrace();
   return;
}
```

The variable `obj` is an object reference that will be assigned to the new object after it is created. The call of newInstance that creates the object is enclosed in another try block in case something unanticipated goes wrong while the program instantiates the object. This catch clause catches any checked exception, prints the call stack at the point where the exception occurs, and terminates the program.

```
      System.out.println( obj );
   }
}
```

Ultimately, the program may create a new object. The program announces this success by printing the object.

The output for this program depends on the command-line input. Here are some trial runs. (Some of the messages are split because they are too long to fit on one line in this book.)

- Command-line arguments:

```
java4cpp.rtti.FirstType Hello
```

- Output:

```
A FirstType object named Hello
```

- Command-line arguments:

```
java4cpp.rtti.FirstType one two three
```

- Output:

```
No constructor: java4cpp.rtti.FirstType( java.lang.String,
                             java.lang.String,
                             java.lang.String )
```

- Command-line arguments:

```
java4cpp.rtti.SecondType
```

- Output:

```
A SecondType object
```

- Command-line arguments:

```
SecondType
```

- Output:

```
Unknown class SecondType
```

- Command-line arguments:

```
java.lang.String "Hello World"
```

- Output:

```
"Hello World"
```

SUMMARY

Copying objects is not as simple as it sounds. For the primitive types, you can copy with the assignment operator. For the reference types, the assignment operator alters the value of the object reference so that it points to a different object, but does not make a copy.

The Object class defines a method that you should use to copy objects:

Object clone()

All objects of reference type, including arrays, can use this method. By default it performs a **shallow copy**. In other words, it copies the values of all fields that are contained in the object being cloned, regardless of whether the fields are primitive types or object references. Usually a **deep copy** is preferable. A deep copy duplicates contained objects, creates new object references for the duplicates, and inserts the new object references into the copy of the containing object.

If your classes contain fields that have reference types, you should override the clone method to perform a deep copy, with the proviso that a shallow copy is adequate for immutable, contained objects. You should start the implementation of clone with the statement super.clone() so that every class in the hierarchy can correctly copy the fields it defines.

To be cloneable, an object must be an instance of a class that implements the interface Cloneable. This is a marker interface that indicates whether a class allows cloning. The clone method throws an exception when called for an instance of a class that is not cloneable.

You can define classes that are cloneable or not cloneable. You can force subclasses of your classes to be cloneable, or prevent them from being cloneable. You have great flexibility because you can do the following in different combinations:

- Override or inherit clone
- Optionally define your class to implement Cloneable
- Optionally throw the exception CloneNotSupportedException
- Optionally catch the exception CloneNotSupportedException
- List or omit the exception in the throws clause of the clone method

Run-time type information (RTTI) is particularly important in the Java platform. Your class may be using classes from other sources, such as networks, and you sometimes cannot know the type of objects at development time. RTTI is also useful with dynamic binding.

The simplest form of RTTI involves using the instanceof operator:

object_reference instanceof *class_or_ interface_name*

This operator returns true if the first operand is an instance of the class, a subclass of the class, or a class that implements the interface specified in the second operand. It returns false otherwise.

For every class known to the JVM, an object of type Class exists. Every instance of a class has a field named class that is an object reference to a Class object. The Class class provides several methods that are described in this chapter. You can call these methods to find out, for example, whether a class is an interface, what its name is, and what the name of its superclass is. There are three ways to access the Class object:

- Use the field class
- Call the following method of the Class class and supply the fully qualified class name as the argument:
  Class forName(String *class_name*)
- Call the following method of the Object class for an object:
  Class getClass()

Even the primitive types have Class objects; you access them by using the object reference TYPE that is a field of each wrapper class for the primitive types.

Another form of run-time type information is to be warned when you try to cast class types in an unsafe manner. The compiler rejects casts between classes that are not a direct or indirect superclass and subclass of each other. But some casts from superclass to subclass must be checked at run time, especially when dynamic binding is involved. The JVM throws a ClassCastException if you try performing an unsafe cast at run time.

For more extensive run-time type information, the Java platform provides the **Reflection API**. This API consists of five classes in the package java.lang.reflect (Field, Method, Constructor, Array, and Modifier) along with some other features such as the Class objects for the primitive types. The classes Field, Method, and Constuctor provide many methods that describe the building blocks of classes.

To find out what methods are available for an object at run time, call the following method of the Class class:

Method[]getMethods()

To call a method for which you do not know the name at compile time, use the following method of the Method class:

Object invoke(Object *object*, Object[] *args*)

There are three ways you can create instances of classes:

- Use the new operator in the usual fashion
- If you can use the no-argument constructor, call the following method of the Class class:
  Object newInstance()
- To use any constructor, first get the Constructor object for the constructor by calling
  Constructor getConstructor(Class[] *argtypes*)
  of the Class class and then call the following method of the Constructor class:
  Object newInstance(Object[] *args*)

QUESTIONS

1. Which of the following methods are defined in the Cloneable interface? Select all that apply.
   a. toString
   b. clone
   c. equals
   d. hashCode
   e. finalize
2. Which of the following are references to objects of the class Class? Select all valid answers.
   a. Object.TYPE
   b. StringBuffer.class
   c. Long.TYPE
   d. Class.class
   e. Class.TYPE
3. True or False: The instanceof operator returns true when the class of an object exactly matches the class specified.
4. Examine the following code:

```
public class Quiz7_4 {
   String s = "Good morning!";
   public Object clone()
            throws CloneNotSupportedException {
      Quiz7_4 result = ( Quiz7_4 ) super.clone();
      return result;
   }
   public static void main( String[] args )
          throws CloneNotSupportedException {
      Quiz7_4 x = new Quiz7_4();
      Quiz7_4 y = ( Quiz7_4 ) x.clone();
      System.out.println( y.s );
   }
}
```

Which of the following statements are true when the code is compiled and run? Select all that apply.

a. The compiler rejects the definition of the method Quiz7_4.clone because it returns a reference of type Object, not Quiz7_4.
b. Compilation is successful, but a CloneNotSupportedException is thrown when Quiz7_4.main executes.
c. Compilation is successful and the output is Good morning!
d. Compilation is successful, but the Quiz7_4.clone method does not give a correct result because the field s is not cloned.

5. Examine the following code:

```
public class Quiz7_5 implements Cloneable {
   StringBuffer sb
      = new StringBuffer( "Good morning!" );
   public Object clone()
            throws CloneNotSupportedException {
      Quiz7_5 result = ( Quiz7_5 ) super.clone();
      result.sb = this.sb;
      return result;
   }
   public static void main( String[] args )
         throws CloneNotSupportedException {
      Quiz7_5 x = new Quiz7_5();
      Quiz7_5 y = ( Quiz7_5 ) x.clone();
      x.sb.append( " How are you today?" );
      System.out.println( y.sb );
   }
}
```

Which of the following statements are true when the code is compiled and run? Select all that apply.

a. The compiler rejects the definition of the method Quiz7_5.clone because it returns a reference of type Object, not Quiz7_5.
b. Compilation is successful, but a CloneNotSupportedException is thrown when Quiz7_5.main executes.
c. Compilation is successful and the output is Good morning!
d. Compilation is successful and the output is
Good morning! How are you today?
e. The two Quiz7_5 objects share the same StringBuffer object.

6. Examine the following code:

```
public class Quiz7_6 {
     public static void main( String[] args ) {
      Class c = Integer.TYPE;
      System.out.println( c.getName() );
   }
}
```

Which of the following statements are true when the code is compiled and run? Select all that apply.

a. The compiler rejects Class as an unknown type because the following statement is missing: `import java.lang.reflect.*;`

b. Compilation is successful and the output is Integer.

c. Compilation is successful and the output is int.

d. The compiler rejects the expression `Integer.TYPE` because it is missing parentheses.

7. Examine the following code:

```
class A { }
class B extends A { }
public class Quiz7_7 {
     public static void main( String[] args ) {
      A a = new A();
      System.out.println( a instanceof B );
   }
}
```

Which of the following statements are true when the code is compiled and run? Select all that apply.

a. The compiler rejects the definitions of classes `A` and `B` because they are empty.

b. Compilation is successful and the output is true.

c. Compilation is successful and the output is false.

d. The compiler rejects the following expression because the result of the instanceof operator cannot be printed:
`System.out.println( a instanceof B )`

8. The presence of fields of which of the following types will likely require that a clone method be written for the class if the Cloneable interface is supported? Select all that apply.

a. Integer

b. StringBuffer

c. int

d. String

e. double[ ]

9. Examine the following code:

```
public class Quiz7_9 {
   public static void main( String[] args ) {
      Integer i = new Integer( 6 );
      Long l = new Long( 10000000067 );
      Double d = new Double( 4.567 );
      Number n;
      n = d;
      d = i;
      l = ( Long ) i;
      System.out.println( l );
   }
}
```

Which of the following statements are true when the code is compiled and run? Select all that apply.

a. Compilation is successful and the output is 6
b. The compiler rejects the expression: `n = d`
c. The compiler rejects the expression: `d = i`
d. The compiler rejects the expression: `l = ( Long ) i`
e. Compilation is successful, but a ClassCastException is thrown when the program is run.

10. Which interface is implemented by all of the classes in the java.lang.reflect package that represent the contents of a class definition?

EXERCISES

Debugging

1. Correct all the errors in the following program.

```
package java4cpp.questions.c7;
public class Debug7_1 implements Cloneable {
   StringBuffer sb
      = new StringBuffer( "Sales Report for " );
   public Debug7_1 clone()
            throws CloneNotSupportedException {
      Debug7_1 result = super.clone();
      result.sb
         = new StringBuffer( this.sb.toString() );
      return result;
   }
   public static void main( String[] args )
            throws CloneNotSupportedException {
      Debug7_1 x = new Debug7_1();
      Debug7_1 y = x.clone();
      x.sb.append( "October" );
      System.out.println( y.sb );
   }
}
```

2. The output in the following program should be

```
Inventory count 300
```

Correct all the errors in the program:

```
package java4cpp.questions.c7;
class Debug7_2_Base {
   private int x;
   int getX() {
      return x;
   }
```

```
      public void setX( int newX ) {
         x = newX;
      }
   }
   public class Debug7_2 extends Debug7_2_Base
            implements Cloneable {
      StringBuffer sb
         = new StringBuffer( "Inventory count" );
      public Object clone()
               throws CloneNotSupportedException {
         Debug7_2 result = new Debug7_2();
         result.sb
            = new StringBuffer( this.sb.toString() );
         return result;
      }
      public static void main( String[] args )
            throws CloneNotSupportedException {
         Debug7_2 a = new Debug7_2();
         a.setX( 300 );
         Debug7_2 b = ( Debug7_2 ) a.clone();
         System.out.println( b.sb + " " + b.getX() );
      }
   }
```

3. Correct all the errors in the following program without making any changes to the main method:

```
package java4cpp.questions.c7;
class Debug7_3_Base {
   private StringBuffer name;
   public String getName() {
      return name.toString();
   }
   public void setName( String newName ) {
      name = new StringBuffer( newName );
   }
}
public class Debug7_3 extends Debug7_3_Base
         implements Cloneable {
   private double weight;
   double getWeight() {
      return weight;
   }
   public void setWeight( double newWeight ) {
      weight = newWeight;
   }
   public static void main( String[] args ) {
      Debug7_3 a = new Debug7_3();
      a.setWeight( 11.567 );
      a.setName( "Steel girders" );
      Debug7_3 b = ( Debug7_3 ) a.clone();
```

```
            System.out.println( b.getName() + " "
                                + b.getWeight() );
        }
    }
```

4. Correct all the errors in the following program so that it takes a string from the command line, creates an instance of the class named in the string, and then outputs the class name without directly using the input string:

```
package java4cpp.questions.c7;
public class Debug7_4 {
   public static void main( String[] args ) {
      if ( args.length >= 1 ) {
         Object x = Class.newInstance( args[0] );
         System.out.println( x.getName );
      }
   }
}
```

5. The output for the following program is

```
Name: int is a primitive type.
```

Correct all the errors in the program:

```
package java4cpp.questions.c7;
public class Debug7_5 {
   public static void printClassInfo( Class c ) {
      System.out.print( "Name: " + c.getName() );
      if ( c.isPrimitive() ) {
         System.out.println( " is a primitive "
                             + "type." );
      } else {
         System.out.println( " is not a primitive
                             + "type." );
      }
   }
   public static void main( String[] args ) {
      int x = 1;
      printClassInfo( x.class );
   }
}
```

Complete the Solution

1. Complete the following class definition by adding a clone method:

```
package java4cpp.questions.c7;
public class Complete7_1 implements Cloneable {
   char[] someChars = { 'a', 'x', 'C' , '8' };
   public static void main( String[] args )
         throws CloneNotSupportedException {
```

```
        Complete7_1 x = new Complete7_1();
        Complete7_1 y = ( Complete7_1 ) x.clone();
        x.someChars[0] = 'A';
        System.out.println( y.someChars[0] );
    }
}
```

2. Complete the `Complete7_2` class definition by adding a clone method:

```
package java4cpp.questions.c7;
class MyPoint {
    int x;
    int y;
    public MyPoint( int initX, int initY ) {
        x = initX;
        y = initY;
    }
    public void setPoint( int newX, int newY ) {
        x = newX;
        y = newY;
    }
    public String toString() {
        return "( " + x + "," + y + " )";
    }
}
public class Complete7_2 implements Cloneable {
    MyPoint point1 = new MyPoint( 0, 0 );
    public static void main( String[] args )
            throws CloneNotSupportedException {
        Complete7_2 x = new Complete7_2();
        Complete7_2 y = ( Complete7_2 ) x.clone();
        x.point1.setPoint( -5, -10 );
        System.out.println( y.point1 );
    }
}
```

3. Complete the following program by adding statements to the function `f` that use the instanceof operator to handle two specific subclasses of Number. If the parameter of `f` is an Integer, output the integer value divided by 2. If the parameter of `f` is a Double, output the double value divided by 2.5. Otherwise, do nothing.

```
package java4cpp.questions.c7;
public class Complete7_3 {
    public static void f( Number n ) {
        // your code here
    }
    public static void main( String[] args ) {
        f( new Integer( 23 ) );
        f( new Double( 3.14 ) );
    }
}
```

4. Complete the following program by adding statements to the function `f` that use a try block and a catch block for `ClassCastException` objects to treat one specific subclass of Number differently from all the others. If the parameter of `f` is a Long, output the long value multiplied by 2. If the parameter of `f` is any other subclass of Number, output its value as a double multiplied by 3.

```
package java4cpp.questions.c7;
public class Complete7_4 {
   public static void f( Number n ) {
      // your code here
   }
   public static void main( String[] args ) {
      f( new Integer( 23 ) );
      f( new Long( 2356789 ) );
      f( new Double( 3.14 ) );
   }
}
```

5. Complete the following class definition so that it takes a string from the command line, and prints out a message if the class named in the string has a constructor without parameters.

```
package java4cpp.questions.c7;
import java.lang.reflect.*;
public class Complete7_5 {
   public static void main( String[] args ) {
      // your code here
   }
}
```

Discovery

1. Enhance the `Stack` class from the end of the previous chapter's exercises so that it is an array of Object objects, not integers. Then add a clone method to the new `ObjectStack` class that delegates the cloning of individual stack elements by calling the clone method of each element.

2. Create a class called `PropertyFinder` that has a method that analyzes the method input parameter of type Object. Using the Reflection API, the class will look for method pairs of the form void `setX( T )` and `T getX( )`, where `X` is some arbitrary string and `T` is a type. For every such pair that it finds, the class will write a message saying that the object has a property `X` of type `T`.

CHAPTER 8

Input, Output, and Networking

objectives

In this chapter you will:

- **Perform stream input/output (I/O) with the core classes in the package** java.io.
- **Use the standard streams** System.in, System.out, **and** System.err.
- **Distinguish between byte-oriented and character-oriented streams.**
- **Write code that uses objects of the** File **class to navigate a file system.**
- **Select valid constructor arguments for** FilterInputStream **and** FilterOutputStream **subclasses from a list of classes in the** java.io **package.**
- **Write appropriate code to read, write, and update files using** FileInputStream, FileOutputStream, **and** RandomAccessFile **objects.**
- **Describe the permanent effects on the file system of constructing and using** FileInputStream, FileOutputStream, **and** RandomAccessFile **objects.**
- **Use object serialization.**
- **Perform network I/O using the core classes in the package** java.net.
- **Write programs that establish connections to URLs and perform stream I/O between URLs.**
- **Read and write data to local and remote sites using TCP/IP sockets and datagram sockets.**

How the Java Platform Supports I/O

It is time to return to the matter of input and output, which is generally referred to simply as I/O. The first part of this chapter is about the package java.io, which supports console I/O, file I/O, I/O streams that are designed for bytes, and I/O streams that are designed for characters. The latter part of this chapter looks beyond the local workstation and expands the concept of input and output to making connections and transferring data between workstations on a network.

You can use all the features described in this chapter in applications, but applets are prohibited from some activities, as explained in Chapter 15. For example, an applet can perform file I/O on or establish connections with only the server system from which the applet originates. Default security mechanisms prevent applets from accessing files on the client workstation or connecting to other workstations on the network.

Not all forms of user interaction are considered I/O. For example, a very different mechanism manages graphical user interfaces (GUIs). Chapters 12 and 13 describe how to program a GUI. The java.io package supports data transfer between the program and the console, files, or the network. The package does not provide facilities for drawing or displaying graphical components on the screen. Also, the I/O package does not support the mouse.

The first program in Chapter 1 gave a sneak preview of stream I/O, and most of the sample programs in this book use the stream I/O classes in java.io.

C++ programmers should quickly become comfortable using stream I/O in Java programs because of the many similarities between how both languages support I/O. Both languages direct most I/O through streams. Of course, the actual names of classes and methods are different, and the hierarchies of input and output stream classes contain different classes. Nevertheless, the concepts of streams, buffers, and stream I/O are common to C++ and the Java programming language.

The importance of supporting I/O for characters that occupy more than one byte is increasing with the demand for software that is internationalized not only for the North American and Western European character sets, but also for Asian and other character sets. This chapter describes both byte-oriented and character-oriented I/O streams. Internally, the Java platform has only one type of character set, 16-bit Unicode character set. The character streams support Unicode characters and other recognized character-encoding schemes. Byte-oriented streams are intended for handling noncharacter, or binary, information.

There is an interesting contrast between the way C++ and the Java platform deal with multibyte characters. The 1998 definition of standard C++ has introduced the concept of wide or narrow streams into the C++ language. The new type wchar_t **is designed for wide characters. The type** char **continues to represent one-byte, or narrow, characters. As with all types, the C++ language leaves the internal representation of the type** wchar_t, **or wide characters, up to the particular implementation of C++. As with all types, the Java platform specifies how data is mapped in the JVM. All characters in the Java platform are 16-bit Unicode.**

If you have worked with earlier versions of C++, you have probably used the unofficial industry-standard iostream **class hierarchy. The byte-oriented set of the Java platform's stream classes that has been available since version 1.0 of the Java platform is analogous to the old C++ industry-standard** iostream **classes.**

The latest C++ standard changes the iostream **classes. To accommodate wide characters, the standard redefines** iostream **to contain a set of template classes that can be instantiated for** char **or** wchar_t **characters. This approach is not available in the Java programming language, at least in part because the language does not have templates. Instead, the package** java.io **contains distinct classes for character-oriented streams and byte-oriented streams.**

The Java platform is not only aware of networks, but also claims to make network programming simple. For many programmers, the only network of interest is the Internet. However, programmers can use the classes in java.net for communication between systems connected to any network that supports communication using the common protocols of the Internet: TCP/IP (Transmission Control Protocol/Internet Protocol) sockets and User Datagram Protocol (UDP) sockets, which are often called datagram sockets. Because these are the industry-accepted Internet standards, your network applications can potentially communicate with a limitless number of existing network applications.

The classes in java.net are easy to use. These core classes save you from having to write a lot of low-level code. TCP/IP sockets let you use stream I/O. In a few simple statements, you can make connections, transfer data, and do what in other environments would require considerable knowledge of the internals of network protocols, or of systems programming for the platforms involved.

Moving from C++

All I/O provided by the C++ language is local to the workstation on which a C++ program is running. To program for networks in C++, you usually have to acquire a proprietary class library or write your own code using a system-dependent API. Either way, you lose a measure of portability and must invest extra time or money. One of the most potentially useful and appealing aspects of the Java platform is that it includes core classes that support programming for networks.

Programming I/O

Most I/O in the Java platform operates through streams. In stream I/O, characters or bytes are read or written sequentially. For example, when a file is opened as a stream, all input or output starts at the beginning of the file and proceeds character by character or byte by byte to the end of the file. There is no inherent blocking into records or lines, and no direct access to any locations in the file other than the next byte or character position.

Moving from C++

In C++, you can use either the iostream **classes or the C library functions to perform I/O. The Java platform has no equivalent to the C library, but the classes in** java.io **that support stream I/O are roughly analogous to the** iostream **class hierarchy of C++.**

The core classes do not offer much formatting control for the output streams. If you are writing applets or applications for a graphical environment, you use the Abstract Windowing Toolkit, which is described in Chapters 12 and 13, to draw your output on the screen, so this limitation of the stream classes affects far fewer programs that it may at first seem. Console I/O is often used only for debugging or for quick and simple utilities. Console I/O on the Java platform is not very flexible. You may be disappointed if you want to set the width of fields or precision floating-point numbers when you write to the console or a formatted file.

Moving from C++

The Java platform's stream classes have no equivalent to the C++ I/O manipulators or even the format string of the C printf **function.**

When you program for the international market, you should format numbers, dates, times, and the like according to the local customs of the users. The Java platform includes classes that help you internationalize your program. The package java.text gathers many of the classes and interfaces for handling local customs. Chapter 16 describes the programming techniques and core classes you can use to make your program international.

Moving from C++

You can use the core class DecimalFormat **in the package** java.text **to set up patterns for formatting and parsing numbers. For example, you can specify grouping by thousands with commas as separators, set the minimum or maximum number of digits on either side of the decimal point, provide a different pattern for negative numbers, and specify how to represent percentages. Even if internationalization is not your goal, you may find that the classes in** java.text **can meet your number-formatting requirements.**

Not all I/O in the Java platform is stream I/O. The package java.io includes the core class RandomAccessFile, which you can use to read and write arbitrary locations within a file without first having to read or write all the bytes or characters that precede that location. However, most I/O, including sequential file reading and writing, operates through streams.

The Java platform includes two dual hierarchies of classes that support streams: byte-oriented input and output, and character-oriented input and output. The byte-oriented streams are widely used, partly because they have been available since the original version of the Java platform and partly because they are adequate for the ASCII seven-bit character set used by North American personal computers. The structure of the hierarchy of character-oriented stream classes mirrors that of the stream-oriented classes.

The discussion of streams finishes with a look at object streams, which support object serialization.

The character-oriented streams and object streams became available in version 1.1 of the Java platform. The original version of the Java platform lacked support for I/O to character sets other than ASCII, and had no object serialization.

Version 1.1 of the Java platform also introduced the package java.text **and full support for internationalization.**

Byte-Oriented Stream Classes

The hierarchies of the byte-oriented stream classes have a superclass for output and another superclass for input. All the classes in these hierarchies extend the input and output superclass directly or indirectly, and ultimately extend Object. Figure 8-1 shows the classes that support byte-oriented streams and how they are related. The shaded boxes represent abstract classes.

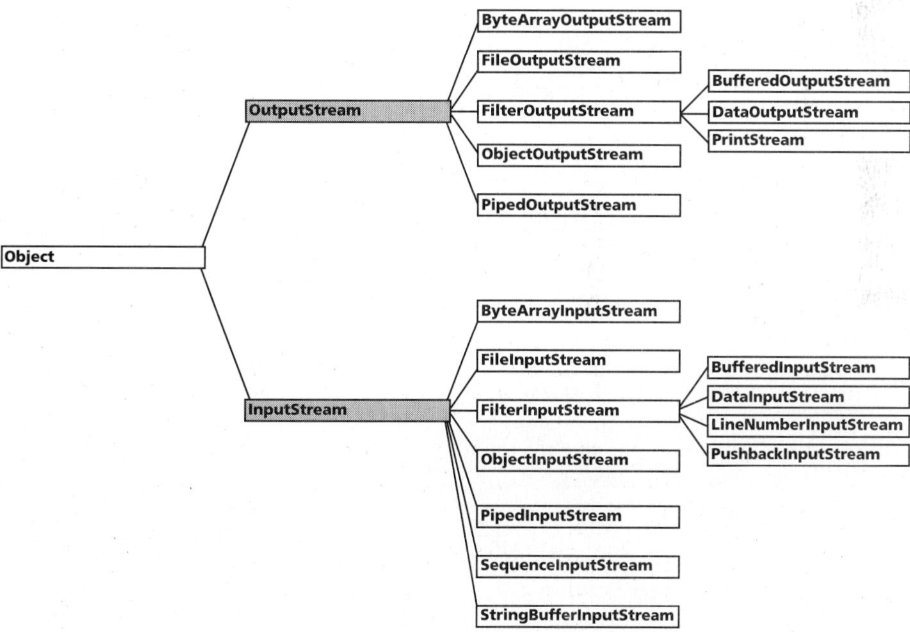

Figure 8-1: Byte-oriented stream classes

The classes java.io.InputStream and java.io.OutputStream are the roots of a dual hierarchy that encapsulates most of byte-oriented I/O. The next sections of this chapter present highlights of the subclasses of InputStream and OutputStream.

Predefined Stream Objects

All Java programs can use three stream objects that are defined in the System class of the java.lang package. These objects are System.in, System.out, and System.err.

Class	java.lang.System
Purpose	The **System** class provides the standard stream objects.
Fields	■ **System.in** The field **System.in** is a **java.io.BufferedInputStream** object. The field is often called the standard input stream. By default, this object encapsulates keyboard input. You can wrap a character-oriented stream around **System.in** to get buffered, character-oriented input from the console. This is desirable, because it gives the user the opportunity to backspace over errors, and relieves you of responsibility for processing every keystroke individually. ■ **System.out** The field **System.out** is a **java.io.PrintStream** object. The field is often called the standard output stream. By default, this object encapsulates output to a command-line window and is used for most command-line mode output. When you run a program with the **java** command, you can use features of your operating system to redirect the output to a file. ■ **System.err** The field **System.err** is a **java.io.PrintStream** object. It is often called the standard error stream. Output sent to **System.err** goes to a command line and can be mixed with output to **System.out**. The difference between **System.err** and **System.out** is that **System.err** is usually reserved for error messages, or log or trace information. Therefore, by directing **System.out** or **System.err** to a file, you can separate the desired program output from other messages.

System.in **is analogous to the C++ stream** cin. System.out **is analogous to the C++ stream** cout. System.err **is analogous to the C++ stream** cerr.

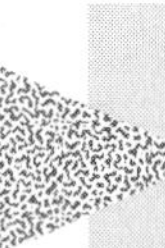

Mini Quiz 8-1

System.in, System.err, and System.out are declared to be static, final, and public. What does this tell you about how you can use them?

Two sets of overloaded methods of the PrintStream class are particularly useful for console output: print and println. Most of the example programs in early chapters of this book use these methods. The difference between them is simply that every println appends a line separator to its argument to produce a complete line of output. The print method does not add the line separator, so you can build up one line of output with several calls of print.

For example, examine the following lines:

```
for ( int i = 0; i < 10; i++ ) {
   System.out.print( '*' );
}
for ( int i = 0; i < 2; i++ ) {
   System.out.println( "one line" );
}
```

These lines produce the following output:

```
**********one line
one line
```

The methods print and println are overloaded to create versions specifically for the primitive types, for char[ ], and for String. All other reference types use the version of print or println that takes an Object as input. This catch-all version essentially calls the toString method for the object and then outputs the resulting String object in the normal way. As a result, you can easily print textual representations of objects of any class that implements toString. Usually, when you anticipate that you will need to display a class in textual format, you implement toString. This conversion of data to text is a form of **filtering**. PrintStream is one of the filtered stream classes.

Input and Output Methods

You perform most byte-oriented I/O operations by calling methods that are defined in the InputStream and OutputStream classes. The subclasses of InputStream and OutputStream add value by overriding and overloading these methods for specific circumstances.

Class	**java.io.InputStream**
Purpose	The **InputStream** class is the superclass of all byte-oriented input streams.
Constructors	■ The constructor of this class, **InputStream()**, takes no arguments.
Methods	■ **int available()** The **available** method returns the number of bytes that can be read without blocking. ■ **void close()** The **close** method closes the input stream and frees the resources it was using.

- **void mark(int *readlimit*)**
  The **mark** method is used to set a bookmark in the stream. You can return to the marked spot until the number of bytes specified in the argument have been read.

- **boolean markSupported()**
  The **markSupported** method indicates whether the stream supports the setting of bookmarks.

- **int read()**
  int read(byte[] *buffer* **)**
  int read(byte[] *buffer*, **int** *offset*, **int** *length* **)**
  The **read** method reads bytes from the input stream. To read one byte, supply no arguments and receive the data in the return value. To read bytes into an array, pass the array as a parameter. No more bytes are read than can be stored in the array, and the return value is the actual number of bytes read. You can also specify as an integer argument the first position in the array to fill, and as a second integer argument the maximum number of bytes to read.

- **void reset()**
  The **reset** method repositions the stream to the bookmark.

- **long skip(long** *bytecount* **)**
  The **skip** method reads but discards up to the number of bytes specified in the argument, and returns the actual number of bytes skipped.

Class	java.io.OutputStream
Purpose	The **OutputStream** class is the superclass of all byte-oriented output streams.
Constructors	■ The constructor of this class, **OutputStream()**, takes no arguments.
Methods	■ **void close()** The **close** method closes the stream and frees the resources it was using. ■ **void flush()** The **flush** method forces any buffered bytes to be written. ■ **void write(int** *b* **)** **void write(byte[]** *bytebuffer* **)** **void write(byte[]** *bytebuffer*, **int** *offset*, **int** *count* **)** The **write** methods write either a single byte or an array of bytes. If you specify an array of bytes, you can optionally specify the first element in the array to write, and the number of bytes to write.

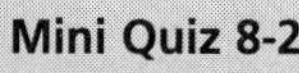

Mini Quiz 8-2

If you call the write method to output a single byte of data, why is the argument of type int instead of type byte?

Filter Streams

A number of classes provide extra functionality in the sense that they add or override methods to preprocess output before actually writing the data, or postprocess input after the data has been read. These are called filter streams. They are provided by a set of classes that extend FilterInputStream or FilterOutputStream.

The class FilterInputStream extends InputStream, and the class FilterOutputStream extends OutputStream. These abstract classes are designed to act as wrappers for the InputStream and OutputStream classes. To use a filter stream, you must first create an InputStream or an OutputStream object. When you create the filter stream object, specify an InputStream object or an OutputStream object as the argument of the constructor, as shown in Figure 8-2.

Filter Streams	Description
BufferedInputStream and **BufferedOutputStream**	These classes provide buffering for input and output operations. Use these classes to increase efficiency. **System.in** is a **BufferedInputStream** object.
DataInputStream and **DataOutputStream**	These classes transmit data of specific types across a stream instead of treating a stream as a sequence of independent bytes. You can also call methods of these classes to read and write the binary representations of the primitive types.
PushbackInputStream	This class maintains a one-byte push-back buffer. With a push-back buffer, you can peek at the next byte in the input stream, and then either treat it as read or push it back into the input stream to be read later.
PrintStream	**PrintStream** implements methods for displaying data types textually. Two familiar methods in this class are **print** and **println**, and two familiar objects are **System.out** and **System.err**. To convert the output into the representation of the characters native to the operating system, use the class **PrintWriter** instead of this class.

Figure 8-2: Byte-oriented filter streams

Other Byte I/O Classes

The java.io package defines many classes. Some extensions of InputStream include the following:

- The class ByteArrayInputStream lets you read an array of bytes as though it is an InputStream object. To create a ByteArrayInputStream object, supply a parameter of type byte[] to the constructor.
- The class SequenceInputStream provides a mechanism for concatenating the data from two or more InputStream objects into a single, seamless stream.
- The class PipedInputStream implements half of a pipe and is especially useful for communication between threads. Chapter 11 tells you how to develop multithreaded programs and shows how you can create a pipe that is an input stream for one thread and an output stream for another.

Some extensions of OutputStream include the following:

- The class ByteArrayOutputStream sends its output into an object of type byte[]. You can use this class to perform your own buffering, or to build an object that another piece of code reads as a ByteArrayInputStream.
- The class PipedOutputStream is the complementary class to PipedInputStream. Together, these two classes comprise a pipe that you can use for communication between threads.

File I/O Basics

Programming stream I/O to and from files is much like programming stream I/O to and from the console. After a stream is established, its usage is the same regardless of whether the ultimate destination is a file or the console.

C++ and the Java platform both implement stream I/O so that files and the console can be used almost interchangeably. This is one of the advantages of stream I/O.

There are some major differences between files and the standard console I/O objects System.in, System.out, and System.err:

- Before you can use a file, you must associate the file with a FileInputStream or FileOutputStream object.
- If you want to access the data in a file in random-access order, you must open it as a RandomAccessFile, not as a FileInputStream.
- In a network environment, the default security restrictions do not let applets do any file I/O on the client workstation. Applets can perform I/O only on files that reside on the server from which the applet originated.

When you perform stream I/O on a file, you are actually manipulating either a **FileInputStream** object or a **FileOutputStream** object. First you must set up the association between the object and the actual file. You can do this in either of two ways:

- You can pass the name of the file, as a **String**, to the constructor of the **FileInputStream** or **FileOutputStream** class.
- You can create a **File** object, passing the name of the file to the constructor of the **File** class. Then create the stream object and pass the **File** object as a parameter of the constructor.

The second method has two steps, which are a little more work. Creating a **File** object has advantages:

- When you create the **File** object, you can perform checks, such as whether an input file exists and is read-only or has read-write capabilities. Use this method if you want to check the status of the file before you open it. If you check the **File** object, as in the following sample code, you may be able to avoid throwing **IOException** objects for reasons such as writing to a read-only file.
- The **File** class provides a level of insulation from platform-dependent conventions such as whether a separator between subfolder names is a forward slash, /, or backslash, \.

Here is a sample program that checks whether a file can be written to. This program defines the class `FileChecking`. Because it is a public class, it is found in a file called FileChecking.java. The structure of packages mirrors the file system, so you will find this source code in the `java4cpp\io` subfolder of the folder in which you unpacked the JAR file `java4cpp.jar`.

```
package java4cpp.io;
import java.io.*;
/** Class used to demonstrate how to find out
  * information about a file
  */
public class FileChecking {
   /** Test method for the class
     * @param args[0] the filename to be used
     */
   public static void main( String[] args ) {
      if ( args.length < 1 ) {
         System.out.println( "Please supply a "
                             + "filename" );
      } else {
         File f = new File( args[0] );
         if ( f.exists() ) {
            System.out.println( f.getName()
                                + " exists:" );
            if ( f.canRead() ) {
```

```
                System.out.println( "\tand can be "
                                    + "read" );
             }
             if ( f.canWrite() ) {
                System.out.println( "\tand can be "
                                    + "written" );
             }
          } else {
             System.out.println( "Sorry, " + args[0]
                                 + " doesn't exist" );
          }
       }
    }
}
```

The two-step method does not give you the ability to reuse a File object for different FileInputStream or FileOutputStream objects unless it is for the same folder and filename. File objects are immutable and cannot be altered to reference another file.

You may be used to closing and reopening files in C++. However, in the Java programming language, you must use a different File object for every FileInputStream or FileOutputStream.

Creating stream objects for file input does not in itself change the status of the files on the native file system. For example, creating and using a FileInputStream object makes no physical change to any data stored on disk. However, creating a FileOutputStream object or writing to a RandomAccessFile object does modify physical storage. A new file is created when you use an output file that did not previously exist. What you write to files is permanently stored on disk, with the exception that if your program ends prematurely some buffered output may be lost if it is still in a buffer when termination occurs.

Here is a sample program that demonstrates file I/O:

```
package java4cpp.io;
import java.io.*;
import java.util.Random;
/** A class used to demonstrate file input and output
  */
public class CaseMixer {
   /** Method randomly sets case of characters in a
     * stream
     * @param args[0] The name of the input file
     *        ( defaults to standard in )
     * @param args[1] The name of the output file
     *        ( defaults to standard out )
```

```
     * @exception IOException
     *             if an error is detected opening or
     *             * closing the files
     */
   public static void main( String[] args )
                            throws IOException {
      InputStream  istream;
      OutputStream ostream;
      if ( args.length >= 1 ) {
         File inputFile = new File( args[0] );
         istream = new FileInputStream( inputFile );
      } else {
         istream = System.in;
      }
      if ( args.length >= 2 ) {
         File outputFile = new File( args[1] );
         ostream = new FileOutputStream( outputFile );
      } else {
         ostream = System.out;
      }
      int c;
      Random mixer = new Random();
      try {
         while ( ( c = istream.read() ) != -1 ) {
            if ( mixer.nextFloat() < 0.5f ) {
               c = Character.toLowerCase( (char) c );
            } else {
               c = Character.toUpperCase( (char) c );
            }
            ostream.write( c );
         }
      }
      catch( IOException iox ) {
         System.out.println( iox );
      }
      finally {
         istream.close();
         ostream.close();
      }
   }
}
```

Suppose the input is as follows:

```
The quick brown fox jumps over the lazy dog.
```

The output may be the following:

```
thE qUiCk BRown FOx JUmPs OVEr tHe lAZY DOg.
```

This code reads characters from an input file, randomly forces each character into either uppercase or lowercase, and prints the result to an output file. The filenames are passed as parameters to main. If the parameters are missing, the program substitutes System.in and System.out for files. The actual input is performed with the method read of the InputStream class, and the output is performed with the method write of the OutputStream class. Notice that read takes no parameters but returns an int, which is stored in the local variable c. The write method has one parameter, which is also of type int. Both read and write can throw an IOException.

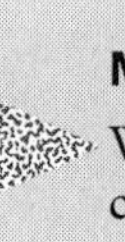

Mini Quiz 8-3

Why does the main function in the preceding example list IOException in its throws clause, as well as contain a catch block for IOException?

File Navigation Methods

The File class gives you more than a way of checking the status of a file before you perform I/O on it. This class provides a number of methods that you can use to navigate the file system on your workstation, or on the server of an applet or application, in a platform-independent manner. It is worth noting that the Java platform does not define a separate class for folders. The File class does double duty as a representative of both kinds of file system objects.

If you have had the experience of programming with the API for different operating systems to perform simple file manipulations or move around the file system on a variety of platforms, you should like the File class.

Syntax	**java.io.File**
Purpose	The **File** class encapsulates most of the platform-dependent complexities of files and path names in a portable manner.
Constructors	■ **File(String** *filename* **)** **File(File** *folder*, **String** *filename* **)** **File(String** *folder*, **String** *filename* **)** You can create a **File** object by specifying only the filename or the filename and the folder in which it resides. You can specify the folder by path name or with an existing **File** object.

- **String getAbsolutePath()**
  The **getAbsolutePath** method returns the platform-specific absolute path to the **File** object for which the method is called.

- **boolean canRead()**
  The **canRead** method returns **true** if the file is readable, and **false** otherwise.

- **boolean canWrite()**
  The **canWrite** method returns **true** if you can write to the file, and **false** otherwise.

- **boolean delete()**
  The **delete** method deletes the file. The return value indicates success or failure.

- **boolean exists()**
  The **exists** method returns **true** if the file already exists on disk, and **false** otherwise.

- **String getName()**
  The **getName** method returns the name of the file. The value returned is the portion of the path that follows the last file separator character.

- **String getParent()**
  The **getParent** method returns the name of the folder in which the file resides, or **null** if the file is in the root folder.

- **boolean isDirectory()**
  The **isDirectory** method returns **true** if the file is a folder and **false** otherwise.

- **boolean isFile()**
  The **isFile** method returns **true** if the file is an ordinary file and **false** if it is a folder.

- **long lastModified()**
  The **lastModified** method returns the system-specific time when the file was last modified.

- **String[] list()**
  String[] list(FilenameFilter *filter* **)**
  If the file is a folder, the **list** method returns an array that contains a list of the names of files that reside in the folder. You can specify an object of a class that implements the interface **java.io.FilenameFilter** to get only filenames accepted by a filter object.

- **boolean mkdir()**
  The **mkdir** method creates a folder with the name of this **File**. The return value indicates success or failure.

Random-Access File I/O

The class RandomAccessFile supports byte-oriented I/O to and from random-access files. Use it to read and write data from or to any specified location within a file. RandomAccessFile objects are not streams. The class RandomAccessFile extends Object, not InputStream or OutputStream.

RandomAccessFile combines input and output operations in one class. It has the same close, read, and write methods as InputStream and OutputStream. In addition, it has the same methods for reading and writing primitive types as the DataInputStream and DataOutputStream classes. The seek method distinguishes this class from the stream I/O classes. The seek method selects the position within the file where the next I/O operation will begin. Another important difference is that you can both read and write a RandomAccessFile unlike any stream which must be either input or output but not both.

Character Streams

The java.io package has classes that are specifically designed to support character streams. You can use them to work with characters, character arrays, and strings. The character streams differ from the byte streams mainly in that they operate on buffered input and output and properly convert each character from the encoding scheme of the native operating system to the Unicode character set used by the Java platform. In contrast, InputStream and OutputStream, and the classes that extend them, operate on bytes and arrays of bytes. The byte-oriented streams correctly handle only seven-bit ASCII characters, which have the same value as the first 128 Unicode characters. Character streams are sensitive to different character-encoding schemes and fully support international applications. Character conversions are described in more detail in Chapter 16.

The hierarchy of classes that support character streams mirrors the structure of the hierarchy of classes that support byte-oriented streams. The superclass of character-oriented input stream I/O is java.io.Reader. The corresponding output stream is java.io.Writer. Like java.io.InputStream and java.io.OutputStream, the Reader and Writer classes are also direct subclasses of Object. Most byte stream classes have a corresponding character stream class. For example, FileReader is the character-oriented counterpart to FileInputStream, and FileWriter is the counterpart to FileOutputStream. Figure 8-3 shows character stream classes and how they are related.

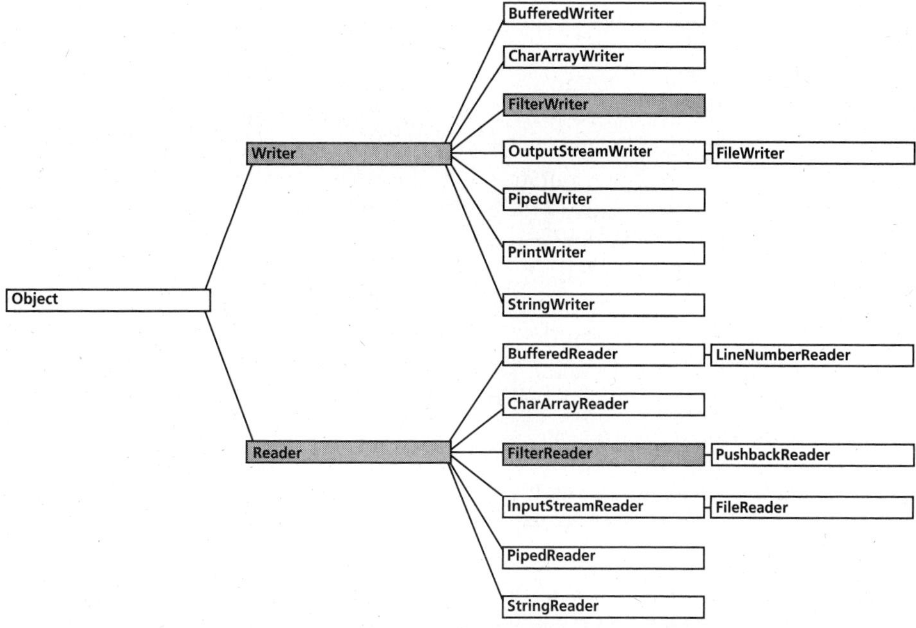

Figure 8-3: Character stream classes

The Java platform did not always support character I/O. The original release had only the byte-oriented streams. Therefore, the release was of limited use outside North America, even though it represented characters internally in Unicode. Version 1.1 of the Java platform added the character streams. The inherent overhead of encoding conversion for character streams is offset by buffering and improved implementation. The character streams can be more efficient than byte-oriented streams.

At the same time, the method DataInputStream.readLine() **was deprecated because it does not properly convert the input characters. You may see this method used in old programs; this method still works, but you should use** BufferedReader.readLine() **instead.**

Just as there are filter-stream classes for the byte streams, there are also character filter-stream classes. The base classes for character filter streams are FilterReader and FilterWriter. Both are abstract classes. Only FilterReader has a subclass that is part of the java.io package. The PushbackReader wraps a Reader object and adds the ability to push characters back into the stream. The size of the pushback buffer is an argument of the constructor parameter and has the default value of one character.

Connecting Byte and Character I/O Classes

The Java platform includes adapter classes that bridge between character I/O classes and the byte I/O classes. These adapter classes are very useful because programs written for old versions of the Java platform sometimes use the InputStream and OutputStream classes for stream I/O.

The InputStreamReader and OutputStreamWriter classes perform the adaptation. For example, you can convert an existing InputStream object, such as System.in, by constructing an InputStreamReader object and passing the object reference for the InputStream object as the argument of the constructor. The resulting object can be used anywhere that a Reader object is required. Chapter 16 contains an example of using an OutputStreamWriter to take advantage of different character encodings when programming for the international market. Similarly, you can adapt the System.err OutputStream object for use as a PrintWriter object by creating an OutputStreamWriter object and passing a reference to the System.err object as an input argument. However, it is worth noting that this adaptation works in only one direction. You cannot create a stream object from a Writer object or a Reader object.

Using Other Character I/O Classes

There are many other classes that extend Reader and Writer besides FileReader and FileWriter. The following are some extensions of the Reader object:

- The class CharArrayReader lets you read an array of characters as though it is a Reader object. To create a CharArrayReader object, supply a parameter of type char[] to the constructor of the object.
- The class StringReader lets you read a String as though it were a Reader object. To create a StringReader object, supply a parameter of type String to the constructor of the object.
- The class PipedReader implements half of a pipe and is especially useful for communication between threads. Chapter 11 describes developing multithreaded programs, and shows you how to create a pipe that is a reader stream for one thread and a writer stream for another.

The following are some extensions of the Writer object:

- The class CharArrayWriter sends its output into an object of type char[]. You can use this class to perform your own buffering, or to build an object that another piece of code reads as a CharArrayReader.
- The class StringWriter lets you write to a StringBuffer as though it were a Writer object. No input is necessary to create the StringBuffer object explicitly. Just construct the StringWriter object. You can accept the default initial size for the buffer, or specify an optional initial size as an argument of the StringWriter constructor. Use the method getBuffer to get the object reference for the StringBuffer object that contains the information that is written.

- The class PipedWriter is the complementary class to PipedReader. Together, these classes comprise a pipe that you can use for communication of character information between threads.
- The class PrintWriter is the character I/O equivalent of the PrintStream class. It has all the same methods as PrintStream, but has the internationalization support that PrintStream lacks. You can easily convert a PrintStream object to a PrintWriter object by constructing a PrintWriter and passing a reference to the PrintStream as the input parameter.

Reading One Token at a Time

The class StreamTokenizer is a utility class in java.io that is not related to any of the other classes by inheritance. It lets you read a file as a sequence of tokens by encapsulating a Reader object and grouping the stream of input bytes into tokens. By default, tokens are delimited by whitespace, but you can call many methods to customize a tokenizing algorithm. **Whitespace** is any combination of space, newline, or tab characters. You can also call a method to find out on what line in the file a token appeared.

To use the StreamTokenizer class, first create a Reader object, and then pass the Reader object as a parameter to the constructor of the StreamTokenizer object.

Mini Quiz 8-4

The current version of the Java platform lets you create a StreamTokenizer object for an InputStream object, but such use of StreamTokenizer is a deprecated feature. Why?

Object Serialization

During the discussion about reading and writing numbers, strings, and the like to and from files, have you been wondering if you can write entire objects to a file so that you can read them back later with their state intact? If so, you have anticipated the requirement to serialize objects. You may want to serialize an object to do the following:

- Transmit objects over a network
- Save objects to files between runs of your program, or perhaps write and then read objects later in the same application

For the primitive types, the byte-oriented filter classes DataOutputStream and DataInputStream provide methods to write and read binary representations of variables of all the primitive types or String objects to and from a file. But what about objects of other types? The simplistic approach of saving to a file on a field-by-field basis requires discipline and constant maintenance. Every time a field is added to the class, the methods for saving and restoring the objects must be updated. What happens when a field that is an object reference field is added? Should just the reference or the whole contained object be saved and restored?

Object serialization is a general solution that lets you write objects to I/O streams and then read them, without defining any additional methods. Object serialization properly handles not only the fields defined in the class, but also inherited fields and any subfields that these fields may have.

The object serialization feature is an important component of the Java Remote Method Invocation (RMI) enterprise API. A full discussion of the RMI is beyond the scope of this book. Essentially, RMI allows an object in the Java programming language on one system to invoke a method of an object in the Java programming language across a network on a different system. You need object serialization to write objects that are arguments to methods to a stream on one system and to read from the stream at the other system. Typically, the data is transferred over a TCP/IP socket.

The original version of the Java platform had no facility for object serialization. Version 1.1 added this much-needed feature. That version also added the RMI API, which depends upon object serialization.

Serializing Objects

Just as not all classes of objects can be cloned, not all classes of objects support serialization. By default, classes are not serializable. To let instances of a class be serialized, define the class with implements Serializable. The Serializable interface, like Cloneable, is a marker interface and contains no methods. Most of the classes in the java.lang package implement the Serializable interface. The only core classes in the java.lang package that do not implement Serializable are Math, Process, Runtime, SecurityManager, System, Thread, ThreadGroup, and Void. These omissions make sense for the following reasons:

- Math and System contain only class methods and variables.
- Void is just a placeholder and is essentially empty.
- The nature of the other classes is incompatible with the rationale for object serialization. The Process, Runtime, SecurityManager, Thread, and ThreadGroup objects are used as a program runs.

Using Object Streams

Two stream classes support object serialization: ObjectOutputStream and ObjectInputStream. The next example program shows how to use them.

ObjectOutputStream is a subclass of OutputStream. To create an ObjectOutputStream, provide an existing OutputStream object as the argument of the constructor. In the upcoming example, the output object is an instance of FileOutputStream that was created in the usual way, but you can use an object of any subclass of OutputStream. For example, if you have established a pipe between two threads, you can use a PipedOutputStream object to send an object from one thread to the other.

ObjectInputStream is a subclass of InputStream. To create an ObjectInputStream, provide an existing InputStream object as the argument of the constructor. In the upcoming example program, the input object has type FileInputStream, but any subtype of InputStream is acceptable.

Suppressing Serialization of Fields

The Java programming language has no requirement that every field in a class be serialized. Some fields may contain sensitive information that should not be transmitted over a network. Others may be references to objects of classes that do not implement Serializable. Also, classes can contain fields for temporary information that never needs to be serialized.

Version Watch

The Java platform will soon extend the flexibility of object serialization by providing a dynamic method for determining which fields of an object should be serialized. A new core class, ObjectStreamField, **is designed to hold information about fields to be serialized. You can create an array of** ObjectStreamField **objects and define the array to be a field for your class called** serialPersistentFields. **If you set up this field, the JVM uses the contents of the array to determine which fields to serialize.**

You can include the qualifier transient when you declare fields to indicate that they should not be serialized with instances of the class. Fields that have the transient qualifier are not output when the object is serialized. When the object is deserialized later, transient fields are given the default value normally used for fields of their type.

Version Watch

The qualifier transient **has been a reserved word in the Java programming language since the original release, but had no use until the Java platform started to support object serialization.**

The support for serialization that is automatically generated for a class is usually totally adequate. However, the designers of the Java platform know that programmers are sure to want some ability to customize serialization for a particular class. Therefore, the designers have given you two additional methods for this purpose: readObject and writeObject. These methods have two unusual characteristics:

- The readObject and writeObject methods are not part of any interface to be implemented or class to be extended.
- Even though the serialization support calls readObject and writeObject, they must be private methods.

You must define readObject and writeObject as in the following lines, which are taken from the next example program. If they are defined properly, the serialization support finds them and can use them.

```
private void readObject( ObjectInputStream ois )
   throws ClassNotFoundException, IOException {
   /* whatever you want */
   ois.defaultReadObject();
   /* whatever you want */
}
private void writeObject( ObjectOutputStream oos )
   throws IOException {
   /* whatever you want */
   oos.defaultWriteObject();
   /* whatever you want */
}
```

Make sure you call the defaultReadObject and defaultWriteObject methods in your customized methods. The defaultReadObject and defaultWriteObject methods do the actual serialization work. If you leave them out, not much happens.

Here is an example that uses object serialization. The class `ObjectToSave` is defined and implements Serializable.

```
package java4cpp.io;
import java.io.*;
/** A class defined to be used in
  * serialization operations.
  */
class ObjectToSave implements Serializable {
   static final long serialVersionUID
      = 7482918152381158178L;
   private int i;
   private String s;
   private transient double d;
   public ObjectToSave( int i, String s, double d ) {
      this.i = i;
      this.s = s;
      this.d = d;
   }
   public String toString() {
      return "i = " + i + ", s = " + s + ", d = " + d;
   }
   private void readObject( ObjectInputStream ois )
      throws ClassNotFoundException, IOException {
      System.out.println( "deserializing..." );
      ois.defaultReadObject();
      System.out.println( "deserialized" );
   }
```

```
   private void writeObject( ObjectOutputStream oos ) {
      throws IOException {
      System.out.println( "serializing..." );
      oos.defaultWriteObject();
      System.out.println( "serialized" );
   }
}
/** A class used to demonstrate serializing objects
  * to and from a file.
  */
public class ObjectSaver {
   private static final String FILE_NAME
      = "objects.ser";
   /** Test method for the class
     * @param args not used
     */
   public static void main( String[] args ) {
      try {
         // create the object to be serialized
         ObjectToSave ots
            = new ObjectToSave( 57, "pizza", 3.14 );
         // create the target File object and erase
         // any already existing file
         File objectFile = new File( FILE_NAME );
         if ( objectFile.exists() ) {
            objectFile.delete();
         }
         // open the file, create the output stream,
         // and write the object
         FileOutputStream fos
            = new FileOutputStream( objectFile );
         ObjectOutputStream oos
            = new ObjectOutputStream( fos );
         oos.writeObject( ots );
         oos.close();
         // reopen the file and retrieve the object
         FileInputStream fis
            = new FileInputStream( objectFile );
         ObjectInputStream ois
            = new ObjectInputStream( fis );
         ObjectToSave retrieved
            = (ObjectToSave) ois.readObject();
         ois.close();
         System.out.println( retrieved );
      }
      catch ( OptionalDataException x ) {
```

```
            System.out.println( x );
            x.printStackTrace();
         }
         catch ( ClassNotFoundException x ) {
            System.out.println( x );
            x.printStackTrace();
         }
         catch ( IOException x ) {
            System.out.println( x );
            x.printStackTrace();
         }
      }
   }
```

The output is:

```
serializing...
serialized
deserializing...
deserialized
i = 57, s = pizza, d = 0.0
```

This code includes its own customized serialization routines that do nothing more than print messages to the console when a serialization operation starts or finishes.

The class `ObjectSaver` does the actual work of creating an `ObjectToSave` object, opening the file, and writing the object into the file. After closing the file, `ObjectSaver` reopens the file and retrieves the object to verify that everything worked correctly.

Notice that when the transient field `d` is restored it receives the default value for a double, which is 0.0.

Specifying the Version Number

In the serialization sample program, did you notice the following unusual field in the `java4cpp.io.ObjectToSave` class?

```
static final long serialVersionUID
   = 7482918152381158178L;
```

Just from looking at the code, you may suspect that this field serves no purpose. However, this field is a unique identifier that specifies the version of the class that was serialized. The version number is saved with the serialized object. When the object is restored, this field serves as a check that the object is being restored by a class definition that matches the version that created it.

You do not make up a version number. The value is calculated using a formula that takes the name of the class and its interfaces, fields, and methods. You can determine the value with the **serialver** tool supplied with the JDK, by entering the following command:

```
serialver class_name
```

For the class `java4cpp.io.ObjectToSave`, the output is:

```
ObjectToSave:
static final long serialVersionUID
   = 7482918152381158178L;
```

You can use cut and paste techniques to edit this number into your class definition. Alternatively, you may prefer not to define a serialVersionUID field and let the JVM generate one for you. The only drawback when the JVM generates the number automatically is that minor changes in the class definition, such as renaming a method or adding a method that does not require any new fields, result in a new version value. Objects serialized before such a change appear to be out of date when really they are not. If the needed version of the class cannot be found, the compiler throws a ClassNotFoundException object.

Programming for Networks

Input and output is not restricted to your workstation or the personal computer that is the host of the Java platform. There is a very high probability that you are connected to a network. If you are not on a local area network (LAN), you may have a dialup connection to the Internet. For many programmers, the need to program for the Internet or Web-oriented HTML browsers is among the main reasons for learning the Java programming language. Unlike C++, C, and most other languages, the Java programming language is designed for use in just such an environment. The JDK includes a package java.net, specifically so that you can make connections and perform I/O to and from other stations on the network.

A program can communicate with another program on the same host or on a different host. Often, the programs have a client-server relationship with each other. For example, if you are reading an HTML document in a Web browser, the system from which the document originates is the server, and your workstation is the client. When you are developing and testing applets written in the Java programming language locally, your workstation is both server and client. Client-server relationships and networking protocols are beyond the scope of this book, but the relationship between the client and server for applets is discussed in Chapter 15.

You can perform network programming at different levels. You can work with URLs and sockets. A **socket** is an abstraction of the end points of connections between processes or applications. The term originated in the UNIX environment, where it applies to communication between unrelated processes. Using the Java platform, you can set up connections and communicate over TCP/IP sockets.

With a little more programming effort, you can send and receive packets of data using datagram sockets.

Most of the classes in java.net can be categorized by whether they support URLs, TCP/IP sockets, or datagram sockets. Some classes are used by all supported protocols. For example, instances of the InetAddress class represent Internet Protocol (IP) addresses. An IP address is a 32-bit binary value that identifies one host on the Internet. To be human-readable, an IP address can be represented as four decimal numbers separated by dots, as in 9.21.105.214, or by a string, such as torolab.ibm.com.

Working with URLs

You are probably used to specifying URLs to your Web browser. As you know, they begin with a protocol specification such as **http** (for Hypertext Transfer Protocol) or **ftp** (for File Transfer Protocol), followed by :// and the host name along with optional file and port information.

The java.net package contains classes that are designed around URLs. The next sample program demonstrates two of these, URL and URLConnection. Use these classes for creating and manipulating URLs. You can get the file associated with a URL and process the contents in any manner in which you choose to program. You can also connect to the host of a URL, and perform more complex operations.

The safest way to communicate with the host of a URL is through a URLConnection. After you connect, you can request and receive information. However, a URLConnection closes after one exchange and you cannot sustain a long-running conversation. You must reestablish the link for every exchange. For a connection that can stay open, you should use a TCP/IP socket.

Here is a simple program that connects to the home page for the IBM VisualAge for Java product:

```
package java4cpp.network;
import java.net.*;
import java.util.Date;
/** An example class to demonstrate the use of URL
  * class objects
  */
public class TryURLObjects {
   /** The test method for the class
     * @param args not used
     */
   public static void main( String[] args ) {
      try {
         URL vajavaPage
            = new URL( "http://www.software.ibm.com"
                       + "/ad/vajava" );
```

```
            URLConnection vajavaConn
               = vajavaPage.openConnection();
            Date lastModified
               = new Date( vajavaConn.getLastModified() );
            System.out.println( vajavaPage
                                + " was last modified "
                                + lastModified );
         }
         catch( Exception x ) {
            System.out.println( x );
         }
      }
   }
```

The output is of the following form:

```
http://www.software.ibm.com/ad/vajava was last modified
Fri Feb 20 15:20:40 EST 1999
```

Notice how easy it is to construct a URL object by passing to the constructor a String containing a URL. To open a connection, you call the method openConnection for the URL object. This method creates and then returns a URLConnection object.

This program simply asks when the page was last modified, by calling getLastModified for the URLConnection. To store the information returned, the program creates a Date object, then prints the date in a readable format by taking advantage of the fact that the Date class overrides the Object.toString method in a meaningful way.

This very simple program demonstrates how easy it is to set up a connection with systems that host URLs. You can do many meaningful activities with URL connections. For example, with just the methods shown in this sample, you could write an application to monitor when URLs on your site are updated. You can also send information to the URL, if the page has a form that has been set up in some other way to receive data.

This program is indeed a very rudimentary Web browser. All that is required to convert it to a useable, though very limited, Web browser is logic to read the page, to interpret and display its contents, and to follow the hypertext links code in the page.

Working with Sockets

Different programs can communicate through communications channels called sockets. You can use sockets to transfer data between unrelated processes that can be running on the same workstation or on different hosts on a network. The concept of sockets originated in UNIX environments but is now supported on a wide range of operating systems. The Java platform supports two types of sockets: TCP/IP sockets and datagram sockets, including multicast sockets.

TCP/IP Sockets A TCP/IP socket is connection-oriented. When you create a socket, you create an endpoint for a connection between two processes. This is analogous to plugging a telephone into a suitable outlet in the wall. The person at the other end of the conversation must also be plugged into a suitable outlet, and the telephone company plays the role of the network by connecting the points. The programs at the two ends of the socket can write to and read from the socket. This is analogous to using a pipe to pass data between streams in a multithreaded program, which you will see in Chapter 11.

You can easily read and write to TCP/IP sockets using stream I/O. All you have to do is set up the socket by creating a Socket object, ask the socket for its input stream and output stream, and use these streams like any other input or output stream. The next example program demonstrates this process.

The ease of use of TCP/IP sockets is one of the most appealing features of network programming in the Java programming language. Because sockets are connection-oriented, you can use them as two-way communication channels over a period of time. If you are sending more than a brief message—for example, if you are transferring a file—you can be sure that no parts of the transmission drop out and fail to reach the destination.

However, TCP/IP sockets impose an overhead that datagram sockets do not have. A connection requires setup time before and shutdown time after you transfer any data. Therefore, delivery of information is slower than datagram sockets, but more reliable.

Datagram Sockets Datagram sockets are not connection-oriented. Instead of establishing a two-way connection, you send self-contained packets of data whenever necessary. Each packet contains information that identifies the network destination in addition to the content of your message. The class DatagramPacket represents these packets. The amount of data transmitted is less than over a TCP/IP socket because TCP/IP sockets transmit additional packets for connection setup and teardown, and also transmit checksum data to detect data corruption. However, while a connection is open, datagram sockets give no advantage in speed. On the other hand, delivery of datagram packets is not guaranteed. The intended recipient might miss a packet due to some network error or congestion, and neither the sender nor recipient may be aware of the loss. The UDP protocol used by these sockets makes no attempt to recover from lost or damaged packets.

Datagram sockets provide an alternative communications interface to TCP/IP sockets. For example, they are used in the Simple Network Management Protocol (SNMP) and are commonly used for playing games across a network. Use datagram sockets, rather than TCP/IP sockets, if your application meets the following criteria:

- You want to avoid the overhead of opening and closing connections.
- The nodes in the network periodically send relatively short messages to each other.
- Losing the occasional packet does not have serious repercussions.

Here is a sample program that creates a TCP/IP socket with a server side and a client side. In this case, the client and server reside on the same host. Nevertheless, they run as separate processes, just like client and server programs on different hosts. The client side has the responsibility of identifying its server, and uses a combination of a server-host name and a port number that make up a unique identifier for the server. The port number must be a different port number for every socket on the server. The server is not hard-coded for a particular port, because the socket is created with the port number as an argument of the socket constructor.

Here is the server class, `AdditionServerThread`. A detailed breakdown of the class follows the code.

```
package java4cpp.network;
import java.io.*;
import java.net.*;
import java.util.StringTokenizer;
/** An example class that uses the server socket class
  */
public class AdditionServer {
   private int port;
   // This is not a reserved port number
   static final int DEFAULT_PORT = 8189;
   /** Constructor
     * @param port The port where the server
     *        will listen for requests
     */
   AdditionServer( int port ) {
      this.port = port;
   }
   /** The method that does the work for the class */
   public void run() {
      try {
         ServerSocket ss
            = new ServerSocket( port );
         Socket incoming = ss.accept();
         BufferedReader in;
         in = new BufferedReader(
            new InputStreamReader(
            incoming.getInputStream() ) );
         PrintWriter out
            = new PrintWriter(
            incoming.getOutputStream(), true );
         String str;
         while ( !( str = in.readLine() ).equals( "" ) ) {
            double result = 0;
            StringTokenizer st
```

```
                    = new StringTokenizer( str );
                 try {
                    while( st.hasMoreTokens() ) {
                       Double d
                          = new Double( st.nextToken() );
                       result += d.doubleValue();
                    }
                    out.println( "The result is "
                                 + result );
                 }
                 catch( NumberFormatException nfe ) {
                    out.println( "Sorry, your list "
                                 + "contains an "
                                 + "invalid number" );
                 }
              }
              incoming.close();
           }
           catch( IOException iox ) {
              System.out.println( iox );
              iox.printStackTrace();
           }
        }
        /** The test method for the class
          * @param args[0] Optional port number in place of
          *        the default
          */
        public static void main( String[] args ) {
           int port = DEFAULT_PORT;
           if ( args.length > 0 ) {
              port = Integer.parseInt( args[0] );
           }
           AdditionServer addServe
              = new AdditionServer( port );
           addServe.run();
        }
     }
```

The following breakdown of the code does not follow the order of statements in the program listing, so that explanation can follow more closely the order in which statements are actually executed.

The constructor of an `AdditionServerThread` object just stores the port number that it receives as an argument.

```
public class AdditionServer {
   private int port;
   static final int DEFAULT_PORT = 8189;
   AdditionServer( int port ) {
      this.port = port;
   }
```

The main method creates a server object, `addServe`, using a port number that can be either supplied as a command-line argument or taken from an arbitrarily chosen default.

The client and server must use the same port, and that post must not be used or reserved by another process. A convention on UNIX and some other operating systems is to reserve port numbers 0 to 1023 for system services. If you run the server and client in separate threads of one multithreaded program, the client thread can create the server thread object and pass the port number to the server constructor. Otherwise, the programmers of the client and server sides must agree on a port number to use.

The main method starts the server by calling the `run` method of this class:

```
public static void main( String[] args ) {
   int port = DEFAULT_PORT;
   if ( args.length > 0 ) {
      port = Integer.parseInt( args[0] );
   }
   AdditionServer addServe
      = new AdditionServer( port );
   addServe.run();
}
```

The `run` method does all the work of this server. It creates a ServerSocket object for the port, and then calls the method accept. This is a very important method defined by the ServerSocket class. The nature of a server is to listen passively to its port. The accept method puts the server into a wait state until input arrives. Then it returns a socket.

```
public void run() {
   try {
      ServerSocket ss
         = new ServerSocket( port );
      Socket incoming = ss.accept();
```

When the connection is established, the server asks the socket for its input stream, by calling the method getInputStream. Notice that here you use buffered, character-oriented input, by wrapping BufferedReader and InputStreamReader around the InputStream object returned by getInputStream. Similarly, on the output side, you ask the socket for its output stream and wrap a PrintWriter object around the OutputStream object returned. The second argument of the constructor for PrintWriter is a boolean set to true when you want every call of println to flush the output buffer.

```
BufferedReader in;
in = new BufferedReader(
   new InputStreamReader(
   incoming.getInputStream() ) );
PrintWriter out
   = new PrintWriter(
   incoming.getOutputStream(),true );
```

After setting up the streams, you can use ordinary stream I/O to and from the socket. All this server does is read and add numbers. It reads from the socket, one line at a time. An empty line indicates the end of the input. The method uses the classes StringTokenizer and Double to extract numbers from the input and convert them to type double, so that it can add them. After handling the last token, the server writes the sum of the numbers to the output stream:

```
String str;
   while ( !( str = in.readLine() ).equals( "" ) ) {
      double result = 0;
      StringTokenizer st
         = new StringTokenizer( str );
      try {
         while( st.hasMoreTokens() ) {
            Double d
               = new Double( st.nextToken() );
            result += d.doubleValue();
         }
         out.println( "The result is "
                        + result );
         }
```

Finally, the server closes the socket. The server also contains handlers for the two types of exceptions that may occur. It has nested try blocks with catch blocks for NumberFormatException and IOException:

```
         catch( NumberFormatException nfe ) {
            out.println ( "Sorry, your list "
                           + "contains an "
                           + "invalid number" );
         }
      }
      incoming.close();
   }
   catch( IOException iox ) {
      System.out.println( iox );
```

```
        iox.printStackTrace();
    }
}
```

Here is the client-side class. Again, the detailed breakdown follows the class:

```
package java4cpp.network;
import java.io.*;
import java.net.*;
/** A client-side class that uses a TCP/IP socket
  */
public class AdditionClient {
   private InetAddress host;
   private int port;
   // This is not a reserved port number
   static final int DEFAULT_PORT = 8189;
   /** Constructor
     * @param host Internet address of the host
     *        where the server is located
     * @param port Port number on the host where
     *        the server is listening
     */
   public AdditionClient( InetAddress host,
                          int port ) {
      this.host = host;
      this.port = port;
   }
   /** The method used to start a client object
     */
   public void run() {
      try {
         Socket client = new Socket( host, port );
         BufferedReader socketIn;
         socketIn
            = new BufferedReader(
               new InputStreamReader(
               client.getInputStream() ) );
         PrintWriter socketOut
            = new PrintWriter(
               client.getOutputStream(), true );
         String numbers = "1.2 3.4 5.6";
         System.out.println( "Adding the numbers "
                             + numbers
                             + " together" );
         socketOut.println( numbers );
         System.out.println( socketIn.readLine() );
         socketOut.println ( "" );
```

```
         }
         catch( IOException iox ) {
            System.out.println( iox );
            iox.printStackTrace();
         }
      }
      /** The test method for the class
        * @param args Optional port number
        *        and host name
        */
      public static void main( String[] args ) {
         try {
            InetAddress host
               = InetAddress.getLocalHost();
            int port = DEFAULT_PORT;
            if ( args.length > 0 ) {
               port = Integer.parseInt( args[0] );
            }
            if ( args.length > 1 ) {
               host = InetAddress.getByName( args[1] );
            }
            AdditionClient addClient
               = new AdditionClient( host, port );
            addClient.run();
         }
         catch ( UnknownHostException uhx ) {
            System.out.println( uhx );
            uhx.printStackTrace();
         }
      }
   }
```

The structure of the client class, `AdditionClient`, is complementary to that of the server. The constructor stores the host address, which is of type **InetAddress**, as well as the port number. The class **InetAddress** is defined in the **java.net** package to represent IP addresses:

```
public class AdditionClient {
   private InetAddress host;
   private int port;
   // This is not a reserved port number
   static final int DEFAULT_PORT = 8189;
   public AdditionClient( InetAddress host,
                          int port ) {
      this.host = host;
      this.port = port;
   }
```

As on the server, let the port number be either a command-line parameter or a stored arbitrary default value. Here the default value is 8189.

Mini Quiz 8-5

Why does the client, but not the server, enclose the body of the main method in a try block and have an exception to catch?

The main method of the `AdditionClient` class gets the IP address for the server host by calling the method InetAddress.getLocalHost to serve as the default value. The user can override this default by specifying a different host address as the second command-line parameter. With these two pieces of information, the main method can create a client object, `addClient`, and then start the client by calling its `run` method:

```
public static void main( String[] args ) {
   try {
      InetAddress host
         = InetAddress.getLocalHost();
      int port = DEFAULT_PORT;
      if ( args.length > 0 ) {
         port = Integer.parseInt( args[0] );
      }
      if ( args.length > 1 ) {
         host = InetAddress.getByName( args[1] );
      }
      AdditionClient addClient
         = new AdditionClient( host, port );
      addClient.run();
   }
   catch ( UnknownHostException uhx ) {
      System.out.println( uhx );
      uhx.printStackTrace();
   }
}
```

Like the server, the client has its work performed by its `run` method. The first job of this method is to create the client end of the socket. Next `run` sets up a BufferedReader object for input and a PrintWriter object for output, much like the server does, except that these objects are associated with the sides of the socket that are opposite those of the server end.

```
public void run() {
   try {
      Socket client = new Socket( host, port );
      BufferedReader socketIn;
```

```
        socketIn
           = new BufferedReader(
              new InputStreamReader(
              client.getInputStream() ) );
        PrintWriter socketOut
           = new PrintWriter(
              client.getOutputStream(), true );
```

The actual processing is trivial. The client writes a textual representation of three numbers to the socket. Then it reads whatever the server sends back, and outputs that line to System.out:

```
     String numbers = "1.2 3.4 5.6";
     System.out.println( "Adding the numbers "
                         + numbers + " together" );
     socketOut.println( numbers );
     System.out.println( socketIn.readLine() );
     socketOut.println( "" );
  }
```

Like the server, the client catches IOException objects that can occur during any kind of stream I/O:

```
     catch( IOException iox ) {
        System.out.println( iox );
        iox.printStackTrace();
     }
  }
```

For this application to work, TCP/IP must be installed and running on your system. A working Internet connection is proof that TCP/IP is running. You must start the server class in one window and then start the client in a different window.

1. Open two command-line windows.
2. If you are running from the jar file that contains all sample programs, go to the folder in which the file java4cpp.jar resides in both windows. Make sure the jar file is part of your path by entering the following command in both windows:

   ```
   SET CLASSPATH=java4cpp.jar;%CLASSPATH%
   ```

3. In one window, start the server by entering the following command:

   ```
   java java4cpp.network.AdditionServer
   ```

4. In the other window, start the client by entering the following command, optionally adding a port number to the end of this command string:

   ```
   java java4cpp.network.AdditionClient [port]
   ```

5. If you run and receive a message saying the connection is refused, try running the client again with a different port number.

If you cannot open a connection successfully, you may have to stop the server by pressing Ctrl+C in the window in which you started the server. If the connection is successful, the output appears in the client window as follows:

```
Adding the numbers 1.2 3.4 5.6 together
The result is 10.2
```

Then both the client and server programs stop.

SUMMARY

Most input to and output from the Java platform is stream-based, regardless of whether your program is communicating with the console, files, or another program running on your network. The notable exception is that random-access file I/O does not use streams.

Support for I/O is provided by the core classes in the package java.io, and for network I/O in package java.net.

The Java platform supports byte-oriented streams that are usually adequate for working in the English language in North America, and character-oriented streams that convert from the native character encoding of the native operating system to Unicode.

For byte-oriented I/O, the two classes InputStream and OutputStream are the abstract classes that are the roots of the input and output class hierarchies, respectively.

The predefined console input stream object, System.in, and the console output stream objects, System.out and System.err, are InputStream and OutputStream objects. You should wrap a character-oriented stream class around System.in to ensure the data is converted correctly to Unicode.

The stream I/O model means that console I/O and file I/O are very similar. FileInputStream and FileOutputStream are the classes used for reading and writing files. Their constructors take either a string containing the filename or an object of the class File.

File objects are constructed by providing a string containing a filename in a platform-independent manner. File objects offer the capability to query the physical file it represents and find out whether it exists, whether it can be read or written, and so on. You can also use a File object to navigate the file system on your host in a platform-independent manner.

Filter stream classes are designed to wrap either an InputStream or an OutputStream class. They build on the base I/O functions and add features such as buffering and data pushback.

Several other classes extend the InputStream and OutputStream classes to provide capabilities such as reading and writing byte arrays, sequencing of multiple streams as a single stream, and reading and writing pipes.

Use the class RandomAccessFile to read and write information at arbitrary locations within a file without first having to read or write information at the preceding locations.

The design of the character-stream class hierarchy is very similar to the byte-stream class hierarchy.

To enable programmers to read and write objects as a whole, the Java programming language provides **object serialization**. Objects are written to and read from ObjectOutputStream and ObjectInputStream objects. Only classes that implement the marker interface Serializable can be serialized. You can exclude individual fields within a class from the serialization operation by applying the transient qualifier. Customizing the serialization methods is supported but not usually necessary.

The Java platform includes core classes with which you can communicate with URLs and create TCP/IP and datagram sockets. You are most likely to use the first two of these three options, because they provide connection-based communication.

Objects of the URL class hold the details of URLs such as the protocol and host. To exchange information with a URL, you must create a URLConnection object. Do this by calling the method openConnection for a URL.

For a connection that remains open, you can connect to a system on your network with a TCP/IP socket. A number of classes, including Socket, support TCP/IP sockets. To perform ordinary stream I/O to and from a TCP/IP socket, use the methods Socket.getInputStream and Socket.getOutputStream.

You can use the ServerSocket class to create the server side of a TCP/IP socket.

You can also use datagram sockets. Some extra programming is required, but may be worthwhile if you intermittently send very short messages, and do not need the reliability of a TCP/IP connection.

QUESTIONS

1. Which of the following classes are subclasses of InputStream? Select all that apply.
   a. SequenceInputStream
   b. File
   c. ObjectInputStream
   d. StringReader
   e. RandomAccessFile
2. Which of the following classes can be passed as a parameter to the constructor of FilterOutputStream? Select all that apply.
   a. PipedOutputStream
   b. BufferedWriter
   c. String
   d. File
   e. ByteArrayOutputStream
3. True or False: The RandomAccessFile class extends neither InputStream nor OutputStream.
4. Examine the following code:

```
import java.io.*;
public class Quiz8_4 {
   public static void main( String[] args )
                                    throws IOException {
```

```
            PrintWriter pr = new PrintWriter( System.out );
            pr.println( "What a lovely day." );
            pr.flush();
        }
    }
```

Which of the following statements are true when the code is compiled and run? Select all that apply.

a. The compiler rejects the expression new PrintWriter(System.out) because it is not possible to construct a PrintWriter object from a PrintStream object.
b. The flush method ensures that the information in the PrintWriter stream is written to the console.
c. Compilation is successful and the output is What a lovely day.
d. The throws clause in main is unnecessary since none of the methods in main throw an IOException.

5. Which class is used to represent a file system folder?

6. Which of the following statements will create a physical file in the file system assuming that the file data1 does not already exist? Select all that apply.

a. `new RandomAccessFile( "data1", "rw" );`
b. `new File( "data1" );`
c. `new FileOutputStream( "data1" );`
d. `new FileOutputStream( new File( "data1" ) );`
e. `new FileWriter( "data1" )`

7. Examine the following code:

```
import java.io.*;
class SaveMe implements Serializable {
   boolean b = true;
   transient String s
      = "Something from the meat case, Linda?";
}
public class Quiz8_7 {
   private static final String FILE_NAME
      = "objects.ser";
   public static void main( String[] args ) {
      try {
         SaveMe sm = new SaveMe();
         File objectFile = new File( FILE_NAME );
         FileOutputStream fos =
         new FileOutputStream( objectFile );
         ObjectOutputStream oos =
            new ObjectOutputStream( fos );
         oos.writeObject( sm );
         oos.close();
         FileInputStream fis =
            new FileInputStream( objectFile );
         ObjectInputStream ois
            = new ObjectInputStream( fis );
         SaveMe retrieved = (SaveMe) ois.readObject();
         ois.close();
```

```
                System.out.println( retrieved.b );
                System.out.println( retrieved.s );
            }
            catch ( Exception x ) {
                System.out.println( x );
            }
        }
    }
```

Which of the following statements are true when the code is compiled and run? Select all that apply.

a. The compiler rejects the method `Example.main` because all possible exceptions have not been handled by a catch clause or been identified in a throws clause.
b. The class `SaveMe` accepts the default value of the field serialVersionUID.
c. Compilation is successful and the output is

```
true
null
```

d. Compilation is successful and the output is

```
true
Something from the meat case, Linda?
```

e. The compiler rejects the definition of the class `Quiz8_7` because it does not implement the Serializable interface.

8. Which of the following classes do *not* implement the Serializable interface? Select all that apply.
   a. Integer
   b. Process
   c. String
   d. Object
   e. Thread
9. Which of the following methods are defined in the Serializable interface? Select all that apply.
   a. serialize
   b. readObject
   c. writeObject
   d. getSerialVersionUID
   e. setSerialVersionUID
10. True or False: A URLConnection object closes after one read/write operation.
11. Which of the following classes can be passed as a parameter to the constructor of Socket? Select all that apply.
   a. InetAddress
   b. URL
   c. URLConnection
   d. ServerSocket
   e. DatagramSocket

12. True or False: TCP/IP sockets have input and output streams that can be used just like any other I/O streams.

13. True or False: Datagram sockets are connection-oriented and guarantee the delivery of all packets sent through them.

EXERCISES

Debugging

1. Correct the following program so that it uses Reader and Writer subclasses for reading and writing characters.

```
package java4cpp.questions.c8;
import java.io.*;
public class Debug8_1 {
   public static void main( String[] args )
         throws IOException {
      InputStream  input;
      OutputStream output;
      if ( args.length >= 2 ) {
         input = new FileInputStream( args[0] );
         output = new FileOutputStream( args[1] );
      } else {
         input = System.in;
         output = System.out;
      }
      int c;
      try {
         while ( ( c = input.read() ) != -1 ) {
            // change blanks to underscores
            if ( c == ' ' ) {
               c = '_';
            }
            output.write( c );
         }
      }
      catch( IOException iox ) {
         System.out.println( iox );
      }
      finally {
         input.close();
         output.close();
      }
   }
}
```

2. Correct all the errors in the following program so that it outputs a message specifying the length of the line read for each line in the input file:

```
package java4cpp.questions.c8;
import java.io.*;
public class Debug8_2 {
   public static void main( String[] args )
          throws IOException {
      if ( args.length >= 2 ) {
         Reader  input;
         Writer output;
         String inputLine;
         input = new FileReader( args[0] );
         output = new FileWriter( args[1] );
         inputLine = input.readLine();
         try {
            while ( inputLine != null ) {
               output.println( "Line length = "
                             + inputLine.length() );
               inputLine = input.readLine();
            }
         }
         catch( IOException iox ) {
            System.out.println( iox );
         }
         finally {
            input.close();
            output.close();
         }
      } else {
         System.err.println( "Usage is <input_file> "
                           + "<output_file>" );
      }
   }
}
```

3. Correct all the errors in the following program so that the StreamTokenizer is used to output each of the tokens in the input file:

```
package java4cpp.questions.c8;
import java.io.*;
public class Debug8_3 {
   public static void main( String[] args )
          throws IOException {
      if ( args.length >= 1 ) {
         Reader  input;
         StreamTokenizer st;
         input = new FileReader( args[0] );
         st = new StreamTokenizer( input );
         try {
            while ( st.moreTokens() ) {
               System.out.println( "token = "
                                   + st.getNext() );
            }
         }
         catch( IOException iox ) {
            System.out.println( iox );
         }
         finally {
            input.close();
         }
      } else {
         System.err.println( "Usage is "
                             + "<input_file>" );
      }
   }
}
```

4. Correct all the errors in the following program:

```
package java4cpp.questions.c8;
import java.io.*;
public class Debug8_4 {
   private static final String FILE_NAME
      = "debug8_4.ser";
   int count = 11;
   Thread t = new Thread();
   String title = "Placeholder";
   public static void main( String[] args ) {
      try {
         File objectFile = new File( FILE_NAME );
         Debug8_4 x = new Debug8_4();
         x.count = 57;
         x.title = "Varieties";
         FileOutputStream fos =
            new FileOutputStream( objectFile );
         ObjectOutputStream oos =
            new ObjectOutputStream( fos );
         oos.writeObject( x );
         oos.close();
         FileInputStream fis =
            new FileInputStream( objectFile );
         ObjectInputStream ois
            = new ObjectInputStream( fis );
         Debug8_4 retrieved
            = (Debug8_4) ois.readObject();
         ois.close();
         System.out.println( retrieved.count );
         System.out.println( retrieved.title );
      }
      catch ( Exception x ) {
         System.out.println( x );
      }
   }
}
```

5. Correct all the errors in the following program so that it returns the type of content located at the specified URL:

```
package java4cpp.questions.c8;
import java.net.*;
public class Debug8_5 {
   public static void main( String[] args ) {
      if ( args.length >= 1 ) {
         URL x = new URL( args[0] );
         URLConnection xConnect = x.openConnection();
         System.out.println( x + " has content type "
                                    + xConnect.getType() );
      } else {
         System.out.println( "Please enter a URL" );
      }
   }
}
```

Complete the Solution

1. Complete the following class definition by finishing the `initialize` method. This method should initialize the character array by reading from the specified file.

```
package java4cpp.questions.c8;
class Complete8_1 {
   char[] someChars;
   public void initialize( String fileName,
                           int maxCharCount ) {
       // Your code to initialize the
       // array goes here.
   }
   public String toString() {
      return new String( someChars );
   }
   public static void main( String[] args ) {
      if ( args.length >= 1 ) {
         Complete8_1 a = new Complete8_1();
         a.initialize( args[0], 100 );
         System.out.println( a );
      } else {
         System.out.println( "A filename is "
                                    + "required." );
      }
   }
}
```

2. Complete the following class definition by finishing the getInt method that reads an integer from the specified starting location within a specified file:

```
package java4cpp.questions.c8;
class Complete8_2 {
   String fileChunk;
   int value;
   public void getInt( String fileName, int start ) {
      // Your code to read the integer goes here
   }
   public String toString() {
      return String.valueOf( value );
   }
   public static void main( String[] args ) {
      if ( args.length >= 1 ) {
         Complete8_2 a = new Complete8_2();
         a.getInt( args[0], 100 );
         System.out.println( a );
      } else {
         System.out.println( "A filename is "
                             + "required." );
      }
   }
}
```

3. Complete the following class definition by adding the methods readObject and writeObject to have them print messages indicating the status of the serialization store and retrieve operations:

```
package java4cpp.questions.c8;
import java.io.*;
public class Complete8_3 implements Serializable {
   private static final String FILE_NAME
      = "debug8_4.ser";
   double price;
   String name;
   public static void main( String[] args ) {
      try {
         File objectFile = new File( FILE_NAME );
         Complete8_3 x = new Complete8_3();
         x.price = 1.29;
         x.name = "Macaroni and cheese dinner";
         FileOutputStream fos =
            new FileOutputStream( objectFile );
         ObjectOutputStream oos =
            new ObjectOutputStream( fos );
         oos.writeObject( x );
         oos.close();
         FileInputStream fis =
            new FileInputStream( objectFile );
         ObjectInputStream ois
```

```
            = new ObjectInputStream( fis );
         Complete8_3 retrieved
            = (Complete8_3) ois.readObject();
         ois.close();
         System.out.println( retrieved.price );
         System.out.println( retrieved.name );
      }
      catch ( Exception x ) {
         System.out.println( x );
      }
   }
}
```

4. Add to the class definition in the previous question by calculating and defining the appropriate serialVersionUID field for the class.

5. Complete the following class definition by finishing the method `waitForMessage`. This method should open a server socket for the port number specified and wait for a connection. When the connection is made, it should read a string from the connection, echo it to the console, and then close the socket.

```
package java4cpp.questions.c8;
import java.io.*;
import java.net.*;
public class Complete8_5 {
   public void waitForMessage( int portNum ) {
      try {
         // your code goes here
      }
      catch( IOException iox ) {
         System.out.println( iox );
      }
   }
   public static void main( String[] args ) {
      Complete8_5 x = new Complete8_5();
      x.waitForMessage( 8000 );
   }
}
```

Discovery

1. Using the classes from the java.io package, create a simple copy utility in a class called `FileCopyUtility` that can copy the contents of an entire folder into a different folder. For an additional challenge, add support to your utility that allows the user to specify an option that will also recursively copy any subfolders of the specified folder.
2. Create a class called `URLMonitor` that can be used to monitor a list of URLs for changes. Objects of this class will provide support to check the modification dates of a list of URLs and print a report of which URLs have changed since the last time they were checked. You will probably find it useful to serialize the `Date` objects collected by the objects to simplify the storing and retrieval of the information for later comparison. The URL list should be read from a file.
3. Create a pair of classes called `ImmediateMessage` and `ImmediateMessageServer`. Objects of the `ImmediateMessageServer` class should listen on a specified port for connection from other systems, and then display the information received on the connection. Objects of the `ImmediateMessage` class will connect to these server objects and send a single message to be displayed at the server system.

CHAPTER

9

Nested and Inner Classes

objectives

In this chapter you will:

- **Define an inner class either in a class or method scope.**
- **Define, in method scope, an anonymous inner class that implements a specified interface.**
- **Write code in an instance method of the outer class to construct an instance of the inner class.**
- **Write code to construct an instance of an inner class where either no** this **object exists, or the current** this **object is not an instance of the outer class.**
- **State which variables and methods in enclosing scopes are accessible from methods of the inner class.**

Introduction

This chapter completes the discussion of classes. A **nested class** is a class that is defined inside the definition of another class. A nested class may also be an **inner class**, depending upon how it is defined. A nested class that is not an inner class is much like the kind of class you have been using so far in this book. The differences relate mainly to scope and accessibility, and not to the nature of the class. Inner classes are very different in nature from other classes. An inner class can be a member of the class that encloses it or can be local to a block of code.

This chapter covers both nested classes and inner classes, to differentiate between these two very different ways of enclosing classes inside other classes. The larger portion of the chapter is devoted to inner classes. To reduce confusion, this book uses the term **enclosed class** for a nested class that is an inner class as well as for a nested class that is not an inner class. A class in which a definition of the enclosed class appears is an **enclosing class**. This book also follows the common convention of applying the term **nested class** to an enclosed class that is not an inner class, and the term **inner class** otherwise.

The ability to define nested and inner classes was not available in the original version of the Java programming language. At that time, only packages could enclose classes, and the only way to group classes was into packages or subpackages. Nested and inner classes became available in version 1.1 of the Java platform.

Between the original version and version 1.1, many features were added to the Java platform. You probably use some of them much more often than you use inner classes, and many changes affect the core classes rather than the Java programming language. However, since the Java platform was first announced, no new feature has had a greater impact on the Java programming language than inner classes.

Some developers welcome inner classes because they complete the language and relax the restrictions on the situations in which classes can be defined. Others are concerned that inner classes push the Java programming language away from its original goal of being simple and easy to use.

You can certainly use the Java programming language without using inner classes. You do not even sacrifice program functionality by deciding not to use them. On the other hand, you can make your code more elegant and greatly improve the structure of your classes by using inner classes.

Nesting classes is an excellent way to collect a group of cooperating classes or interfaces. Packages are a rather "coarse-grained" way to collect classes. Often you combine classes into packages when really the classes have no logical grouping except convenience or the fact that the files reside in the same folder. You can take advantage of inner classes and nested classes to indicate more clearly how classes interact with each other. The enclosing class and all that it encloses still must belong to one package.

As well as grouping classes with a finer granularity than you can usually achieve with packages, you can set up enclosed classes so that they share full access to private members of other enclosed classes within the same enclosing class.

The relationship between an enclosed and enclosing class does not involve inheritance. A completely different set of rules determines the scope and accessibility of members between the enclosing and enclosed class. In fact, you can combine inner and nested classes with inheritance, by defining inner or nested classes that are subclasses and superclasses.

Nested Classes and Interfaces

A class or interface may be nested inside another class or interface. The simplest way to enclose a class inside another class is to nest their definitions one inside the other. It is even possible to nest classes within interfaces, and interfaces within classes.

To define a nested class or interface, you must qualify the enclosed class with the keyword **static**. Do not omit this qualifier because, syntactically, the keyword **static** is all that distinguishes a nested class from an inner class.

Syntax

*[***public***] [qualifiers]* class *enclosing _name* {
    // . . .
    [*access_specifier*] *[qualifiers]* **static** class *enclosed _name* **{**
        // . . .
    }
}

Dissection

- The syntax of the enclosing class or interface definition is like any class or interface definition.
- You can declare nested classes to be **public**, **protected**, or **private**. If you omit an access specifier, the class has the default package access.
- Classes nested within interfaces are implicitly **static**, like fields defined in interfaces.
- The qualifiers **abstract** and **final** have their usual meaning when applied to nested classes.

Code Example

```
public interface outer {
   //. . .
   public static class inner {
      // . . .
   }
}
```

Code Dissection

Here, the class `inner` is nested inside the interface `outer`.

The keyword **static** is very appropriate for nested classes. They are not associated with instances of the enclosing class. It is the classes or interfaces, not objects, which are nested. The term **top-level class** refers to a class that is contained only in packages. Nested classes are top-level classes, just like all the classes you have seen so far in this book. They are enclosed in other classes but are not members of the enclosing classes.

What do access specifiers mean when applied to nested classes? The rules for accessing a nested class are similar to the rules for accessing members of the enclosing class. Only the enclosing class can instantiate a private nested class. All classes in the same package can access a nested class with the default package. Protected nested classes can be accessed by classes in the same package and by classes that inherit from the enclosing class. Public nested classes are always accessible.

A nested class has no special privileges for accessing members of the enclosing class or other enclosed classes in the same enclosed class. It has the same access privileges as any other class in the same package.

Version Watch

The term top-level class was not needed before there were inner classes, and was never used before version 1.1 of the Java platform. The term top-level nested class may sound like an oxymoron, but it is the correct way to specify a nested class that is not an inner class.

Nested classes can extend other classes, and can be extended by other classes.

Moving from C++

The most striking difference is that you use the dot connector in the Java programming language in situations where you would use the double-colon scope operator, ::, in C++. On the other hand, there is no precedent for inner classes in C++. Inner classes are indeed a new kind of class.

The discussion of inner classes should remove any suspicions you may have that the Java programming language is tied to the legacy of C++, or that it is a simplified version of C++ that includes a virtual machine and some core classes.

This form of nesting in the Java programming language is very similar to that of nesting C++ classes, except that in the Java programming language you can nest interfaces as well as classes.

The names of nested classes consist of package names, enclosing class names, and the simple name of the nested class, separated by dots. For example, in the next sample program, the class `Node` belongs to the package `java4cpp` and subpackage `inner`, and is enclosed in the class `Graph1`. The name of the class is `java4cpp.subpackage.Graph1.inner`.

To import all the classes nested within a class, use the asterisk, *, just as you do to import all the classes in a package. For example, you can import all the classes in the `Graph1` class with the following statement:

```
import java4cpp.inner.Graph1.*;
```

Mini Quiz 9-1

Can you tell just from the name `java4cpp.inner.Graph1.Node` whether `Node` is a class or a package?

Here is a small application in which a class called `Node` is nested inside a class called `Graph1`. Because `Graph1` is a public class, it is found in a file called Graph1.java. The structure of packages mirrors the file system, so you will find this source code in the java4cpp\inner subfolder of the folder in which you unpacked the JAR file java4cpp.jar.

```
package java4cpp.inner;
import java.util.Hashtable;
import java.util.Enumeration;
/** Class representing an undirected graph composed
  * of nodes.  The node class is a top-level class
  * nested within the Graph1 class.
  */
public class Graph1 {
   private Hashtable nodeList = new Hashtable();
   /** Add a node to the graph
     * @param x the x coordinate of the node
     * @param y the y coordinate of the node
     */
   public void addNode( int x, int y ) {
      Node n = new Node( x, y );
      if ( ! nodeList.containsKey( n.key() ) ) {
         nodeList.put( n.key(), n );
      }
   }
   /** Get the object as a string
     * @return the object as a string
     */
   public String toString() {
      StringBuffer sb = new StringBuffer( "[ " );
      Enumeration e = nodeList.elements();
      while ( e.hasMoreElements() ) {
         sb.append( e.nextElement().toString()
                    + " " );
      }
      sb.append( "]" );
      return sb.toString();
   }
   /** Test method
     * @param args not used
     */
```

```
   public static void main( String[] args ) {
      System.out.println( "creating the graph" );
      Graph1 g = new Graph1();
      System.out.println( "adding nodes" );
      g.addNode( 4, 5 );
      g.addNode( -6, 11 );
      System.out.println( g );
   }
   /** The class representing nodes within the graph
     */
   private static class Node {
      private int x, y;
      public Node( int x, int y ) {
         this.x = x;
         this.y = y;
       }
      /** Determine the key value for a node
        * @return the key as a String
        */
      public Object key() {
         return x + "," + y;
      }
      /** Get the object as a string
        * @return the object as a string
        */
      public String toString() {
         return "(" + x + "," + y + ")";
      }
   }   // end of Node class
}   // end of Graph1 class
```

You can run this program from the .class files provided in the java4cpp.jar file on the CD-ROM that accompanies this book. You can also compile and run the `Graph1` class using the JDK by entering the following commands:

```
javac java4cpp\inner\Graph1.java
java java4cpp.inner.Graph1
```

If you look at the files produced by the compiler, you notice that the compiler creates a .class file for each class even though `Node` is nested inside `Graph1`. The character $ in a filename separates an enclosing and an enclosed class. The two .class files for this example are the following:

- java4cpp\inner\Graph1.class
- java4cpp\inner\Graph1$Node.class

The output from running the program is

```
creating the graph
adding nodes
[ ( -6,11 ) ( 4,5 ) ]
```

A Graph1 object contains a collection of nodes stored in a hash table. The field nodeList is of type Hashtable. The core class Hashtable is defined in the package java.util and provides hash table objects. In the next chapter, you learn more about using Hashtable and the other collection classes. The first statement in the definition of the Graph1 class declares the nodeList field:

```
public class Graph1 {
   private Hashtable nodeList = new Hashtable();
```

The method addNode uses two methods from the Hashtable class:

- containsKey determines whether an object with a particular key is already stored in the hash.
- put adds a node object to the hash table.

```
   public void addNode( int x, int y ) {
      Node n = new Node( x, y );
      if ( ! nodeList.containsKey( n.key() ) ) {
         nodeList.put( n.key(), n );
      }
   }
```

The method key in the nested class Node generates identifying keys for the node objects. Note that Graph1 has exclusive use of Node because Node is private, and that Graph1 can access the members of Node. The methods addNode and main of Graph1 use Node exactly as they would use any class to which they have access.

```
   private static class Node {
      private int x, y;
      public Node( int x, int y ) {
         this.x = x;
         this.y = y;
      }
      public Object key() {
         return x + "," + y;
      }
      public String toString() {
         return "( " + x + "," + y + " )";
      }
   }
}
```

Inner Classes

Inner classes are very different in nature from top-level classes. The term top-level applies to classes that are the top level of containment, excluding packages, and inner classes are always contained in other classes.

To understand why top-level classes and inner classes are so different in nature, you must consider the **state data** of objects. All instances of classes have state data. For objects of top-level classes, the state data is equivalent to the current instance of the class. The state data for an instance includes all the fields that it contains. The object reference this refers to the state data of one instance. The complicating factor for inner classes is that the object reference this relates not only to the current instance of the inner class, but also to the enclosing instances of all enclosing classes.

Compare what happens with subclasses to what happens with inner classes. An instance of a subclass has an independent copy of all the fields declared in the subclass and of all the fields inherited from its superclass. With inheritance you cannot create two objects that share the same copies of instance variables. If you instantiate a subclass and its superclass, you create two objects that can have some of the same fields, but they have different copies, or instances, of those fields. The superclass and subclass objects are completely separate objects.

In contrast, when you instantiate an inner class and the class that encloses it, the two objects are created with access to the same copies of the fields defined in the enclosing class. In fact, you must have an instance of the enclosing class with which to create the inner class. The inner class state data contains the inner class fields. The enclosing class state data contains the enclosing class fields. The object reference this for the inner class instance refers to both the inner and enclosing state data. In Figure 9-1, the gray boxes are included in the state data of both the enclosing and inner class objects.

This situation is analogous to the way in which all instances of the same class share class variables. Just as all instances of a class have access to the class variables and share a single copy of these fields, all inner class instances that share an enclosing instance have access to the fields of the enclosing instance and share a single copy of them.

In terms of state data, top-level classes are equivalent to all C++ classes. The characteristic of inner classes that may be most foreign to C++ programmers is the ability of one object reference, this, to refer to more than one instance. C++ has nothing equivalent or even analogous to a pointer or reference that gives access to fields that make up the state data of more than one object. The this object reference of an instance of an inner class gives access to the immediate instance of the inner class and all enclosing instances of all enclosing classes.

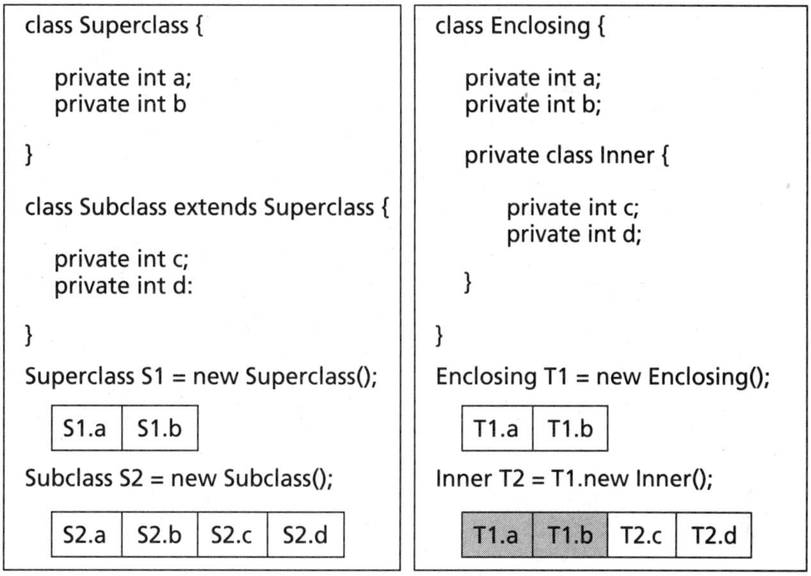

```
class Superclass {

    private int a;
    private int b

}

class Subclass extends Superclass {

    private int c;
    private int d:

}

Superclass S1 = new Superclass();

  | S1.a | S1.b |

Subclass S2 = new Subclass();

  | S2.a | S2.b | S2.c | S2.d |
```

```
class Enclosing {

    private int a;
    private int b;

    private class Inner {

        private int c;
        private int d;

    }

}

Enclosing T1 = new Enclosing();

  | T1.a | T1.b |

Inner T2 = T1.new Inner();

  | T1.a | T1.b | T2.c | T2.d |
```

Figure 9-1: Comparing inner classes to subclasses

There are three kinds of inner classes:

- **Member inner classes** are defined inside another class, at the same level as fields and methods. They are members of the enclosing class.
- **Local inner classes** are defined inside blocks of code. They are local to the enclosing method or block.
- **Anonymous inner classes** are local inner classes that have no name.

Understanding the Reasons for Using Inner Classes

Programming inner classes is an advanced technique, and you may be wondering whether inner classes are worth the complications that they bring to the Java programming language. For example, you must use an expanded form of the new keyword to instantiate anonymous inner classes, and you must learn a new way to use the super method when inner classes have subclasses.

One benefit is the elegant way you can use them to create adapter classes within an existing class. **Adapter classes** are a programming design pattern intended to convert the interface of a class into a different interface that the class does not implement but that the clients of the class expect. When implemented as inner classes, the adapter classes can be defined where they are used. They also have access to the internal variables and methods of the enclosing class or block. The example class `Equation1` later in this chapter demonstrates using inner classes in this way.

An inner class is also handy when a class uses another class for which the sole purpose is to implement interfaces with a single method. This situation is common when you are programming graphical user interfaces. Several frequently used interfaces provided by the Java platform include a single method that reacts to a specific user action. Your source code is tidier if you define an anonymous inner class to implement the interface than if you define and create an instance of another top-level class. This technique of using inner classes to implement one-method interfaces is essentially a way of packaging a block of statements so that it can be passed as an argument. The method that receives the instance of the inner class can then use the instance by calling the method as defined in the interface.

Moving from C++

References to instances of inner classes that encapsulate blocks of statements are similar to function pointers used in other languages like C++.

The impact of inner classes on your code depends very much on how you use them. They are not as critical as inheritance, without which object-oriented programming is severely limited. On the other hand, some techniques that previously were awkward become elegant when implemented with inner classes. You may even be tempted to take advantage of all the nuances of inner classes. If you are, take care not to create programs that are difficult to understand and maintain. If you use inner classes in a straightforward manner and for the purposes for which they were designed, you can reap considerable benefits from minimal effort.

Defining Member Inner Classes

Inner classes are nonstatic members of their enclosing classes. Define a member inner class like you define a nested top-level class, but do not qualify the inner class with the keyword static.

Syntax

```
[public] [qualifiers] class enclosing_class_name {
    // . . .
    [access_specifiers] [qualifiers] class enclosed_class_name {
    // . . .
    }
}
```

Dissection

- The syntax of the enclosing class definition is like any class definition.
- You can declare inner classes to be **public**, **protected**, or **private**, because they are members of the enclosing class. If you omit an access specifier, the class has the default package access.
- The qualifiers **abstract** and **final** have their usual meaning when applied to inner classes, but you cannot use the qualifier **static**. If you declare the enclosed class to be **static**, it becomes a nested class but not an inner class.

Code Example

```
public class Outer {
   //. . .
   private class Inner {
      // . . .
   }
}
```

Code Dissection Here the class `Inner` is an inner class enclosed in the class `Outer`. Only `Outer` and other classes enclosed in `Outer` can access `Inner`, because `Inner` is private.

Every instance of the inner class must exist within an instance of the enclosing class. An inner class cannot be instantiated without an instance of the outer class.

Therefore, you must associate the keyword new with an instance of the enclosing class to create an instance of an inner class.

Syntax *enclosing _instance*.**new** *inner_class*(*arguments*)

Dissection

- The enclosing class instance must be an object reference for an existing object. If you are creating the inner class object in an instance method of the enclosing class, the object reference **this** is implied.

Code Example

```
public static void main( String[] args ) {
   Outer O = new Outer();
   Inner I = O.new Inner();
      // . . .
}
```

The next program is a reworking of the undirected graph classes `Graph1` from the previous example program. This new class is called `Graph2`. The class `Node` is now a member inner class instead of a nested class. The lines that have changed since `Graph1` appear in boldface.

```
package java4cpp.inner;
import java.util.Hashtable;
import java.util.Enumeration;
/** Class representing an undirected graph composed
  * of nodes.  The node class is a top-level class
  * nested within the Graph2 class.
  */
public class Graph2 {
   private Hashtable nodeList = new Hashtable();
   /** Add a node to the graph
     * @param x the x coordinate of the node
     * @param y the y coordinate of the node
     */
```

```
public void addNode( int x, int y ) {
  // the use of "this." is not required here
  this.new Node( x, y );
}
/** Get the object as a string
  * @return the object as a string
  */
public String toString() {
   StringBuffer sb = new StringBuffer( "[ " );
   Enumeration e = nodeList.elements();
   while ( e.hasMoreElements() ) {
      sb.append( e.nextElement().toString()
                 + " " );
   }
   sb.append( "]" );
   return sb.toString();
}
/** Test method
  * @param args not used
  */
public static void main( String[] args ) {
   System.out.println( "creating the graph" );
   Graph2 g = new Graph2();
   System.out.println( "adding nodes" );
   g.addNode( 4, 5 );
   g.addNode( -6, 11 );
   System.out.println( g );
}
/** The class representing nodes within the graph
  */
private class Node {
   private int x, y;
   public Node( int x, int y ) {
      this.x = x;
      this.y = y;
      // the use of "Graph2.this." is not
      // required here
      if ( ! Graph2.this.nodeList
                  .containsKey( key() ) ) {
         nodeList.put( key(), this );
      }
   }
   /** Determine the key value for a node
     * @return the key as a String
     */
   public Object key() {
```

```
            return x + "," + y;
        }
        /** Get the object as a string
          * @return the object as a string
          */
        public String toString() {
           return "( " + x + "," + y + " )";
        }
    }   // end of Node class
}   // end of Graph2 class
```

In this program, a single line determines the nature of the enclosed class **Node**: the start of the class definition. This definition omits the keyword static. Because Node does not have the static qualifier, it is an inner class.

```
private class Node {
```

The method addNode of the enclosing class Graph2 method has changed. Where the method in Graph1 created an object of the nested class Node and then conditionally called method addNode for the nodeList field, the method in Graph2 has just one line:

```
this.new Node( x, y );
```

Because Node is a member of Graph2, its constructor can call addNode for the nodeList field. To create the Node object, you must specify an enclosing instance of the Graph2 class. Here, the object reference this indicates the current Graph2 object. Because addNode is an instance method, the implicit this object reference would have sufficed, but the expression this.new emphasizes the fact that an enclosing instance is being associated with the object being created. The next sample program demonstrates a situation where you cannot omit the object reference this.

Now consider the constructor of the Node class, and consider in particular the use of the this object reference:

```
public Node( int x, int y ) {
   this.x = x;
   this.y = y;
   if ( ! Graph2.this.nodeList
                .containsKey( key() ) ){
     nodeList.put( key(), this );
   }
```

The state data of an inner class object includes current instances of the enclosing class as well as the immediate current instance of the inner class. These lines use two current instances: this and graph2.this.

For the inner class object, this refers to the enclosed instance containing the fields defined in the inner class. Thus, this for a Node object relates to its x and y fields. This constructor passes the current Node object, this, to the put method of the Hashtable class because put must receive the object reference for the object to add to the hash table in its first argument.

You can always access the current instance of an enclosing class with a qualified this object reference. In this constructor, the object reference, called `Graph2.this`, explicitly qualifies the `nodeList` field. In this case, the explicit qualification is not necessary because there is no ambiguity and the conditional expression could read as follows:

```
( ! nodeList.containsKey( key() ) )
```

The only time you must explicitly qualify a member name is when there is a name conflict between a member in an enclosing class and a name inherited from a superclass.

Avoiding Name Conflicts in Inner Classes

The potential for name conflicts is one of the complications inner classes add to the Java programming language. An inner class belongs to two hierarchies: its containment hierarchy and its inheritance hierarchy.

- The containment hierarchy for an inner class is defined as the sequence of classes that enclose it up to and including the top-level class at package scope.
- The inheritance hierarchy is the sequence of superclasses from which it inherits, up to and including the class **Object**.

If your inner class inherits a member with the same name as a member of the enclosing object, the unqualified name of the member is ambiguous. If a method of the inner class uses the member name without qualifying it, a compiler error results. Figure 9-2 demonstrates how name conflicts can arise.

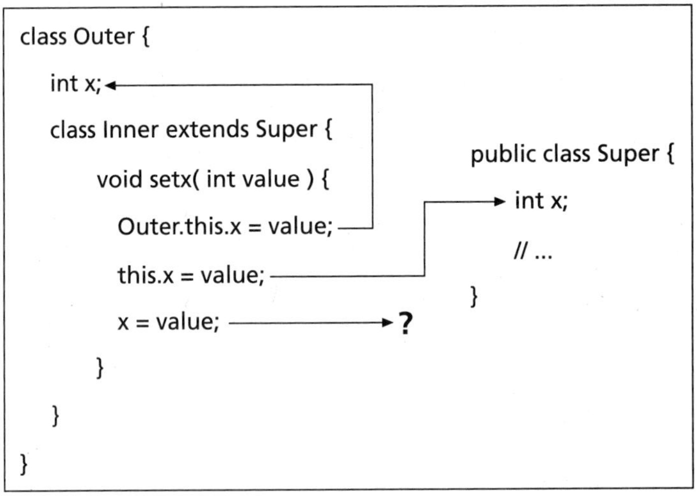

```
class Outer {
   int x;
   class Inner extends Super {                public class Super {
      void setx( int value ) {                   int x;
         Outer.this.x = value;                   // ...
         this.x = value;                      }
         x = value;          → ?
      }
   }
}
```

Figure 9-2: Name Conflicts in Inner Classes

Enclosing Objects of Inner Classes

You have seen what happens when a member inner class is created within an instance method of an enclosing class: the enclosing object defaults to the instance of the enclosing class for which the instance method is run. What happens when an instance of an inner class is created in a class method of the enclosing class? In this case, you must qualify the new keyword with an object reference for the enclosing object. When you create an instance of an inner class in a class method of the enclosing class, the enclosing object can be any instance of the enclosing class.

The state data of an inner class object includes the instance of the inner class, and one instance of the enclosing class for every enclosing level. The fact that inner class objects have more than one instance has the following implications:

- More than one instance of inner classes can share the same enclosing object.
- Inner class objects have access to private members of enclosing classes. The reason is that the members of the enclosing objects are extensions of the states of the inner class objects.
- If an enclosing class has more than one member inner class definition, each of the inner classes has access to the private members of the others.
- Every instance of an inner class is permanently associated with its enclosing instance. You cannot move an inner class object from one enclosing instance to another. The references to enclosing objects are immutable, just as the this reference is immutable. For example, a statement such as the following is not allowed:

```
outer_class.this
   = new outer_class( argument );    // not valid
```

- Inner classes may not contain class methods or class variables. The Java programming language specifies that the keyword static can qualify only the definition of a top-level construct. Because the entire body of an inner class is within the scope of one or more enclosing instances, an inner class cannot contain a top-level construct.

C++ programmers often falsely assume there can be only one-to-one correspondence between the state of an object and an instance of a class. The assumption is true in C++, where all classes are top-level classes. But in the Java programming language, several instances of an inner class can share the same enclosing instance. C++ programmers must make an extra effort to realize that many-to-one relationships between enclosed and enclosing objects can be created with inner classes.

Here is a sample program in which an inner class, `HardDrive`, is instantiated in the main method of a class called `Computer`. Indeed, the `Computer` object `atWork` has two instances of `HardDrive: IDE1` and `IDE2`. Therefore, the two instances of `HardDrive` share the same enclosing object, `atWork`. Notice that the `HardDrive` class can use the private members of `Computer`. Further notes about the code follow the example program.

```
package java4cpp.inner;
/** Class to represent the memory and hard drive
  * information of a computer
  */
public class Computer {
   /** Maximum number of hard drives in a computer */
   public static final int MAX_DRIVES = 4;
   private int installedDrives = 0;
   private HardDrive[] drives
      = new HardDrive[MAX_DRIVES];
   private int memMegs;
   /** Test method
     * @param args not used
     */
   public static void main( String[] args )
                           throws Exception {
      Computer atWork = new Computer( 64 );
      System.out.println( atWork );
      // must specify the enclosing object here
      HardDrive IDE1 = atWork.new HardDrive( 1024 );
      HardDrive IDE2 = atWork.new HardDrive( 2048 );
      System.out.println( atWork );
   }
   /** Construct a Computer object
     * @param memSize the amount of memory in MB
     */
   public Computer( int memSize ) {
      memMegs = memSize;
   }
   /** Provide a string representing the computer
     * @return string representation of the object
     */
   public String toString() {
      StringBuffer sb
         = new StringBuffer( "Memory: " + memMegs
                             + "MB" );
      for ( int i=0; i<installedDrives; i++ ) {
         sb.append( ", Drive" + i + ": " );
         sb.append( drives[i].size + "MB" );
      }
      return sb.toString();
   }
   /** Class representing a hard drive within
     * a computer
     */
   public class HardDrive {
```

```
        private int size;
        /** Construct a hard drive object and add it
          * to the list of installed drives
          * if there is room
          * @param size Size of the drive in MB
          * @exception Exception thrown
          *     if there isn't room for
          *     the hard drive being added
          */
        public HardDrive( int size ) throws Exception {
           this.size = size;
           // add this drive to the enclosing computer
           if ( installedDrives < MAX_DRIVES ) {
              drives[installedDrives++] = this;
           } else {
              throw new Exception( "Sorry, no "
                                   + "more room." );
           }
        }
     }
  }
```

The output is

```
Memory: 64MB
Memory: 64MB, Drive0: 1024MB, Drive1: 2048MB
```

Because the `HardDrive` objects are created in the class method main, the new keyword that constructs them must be qualified with the enclosing object, as in the following lines:

```
HardDrive IDE1 = atWork.new HardDrive( 1024 );
HardDrive IDE2 = atWork.new HardDrive( 2048 );
```

Notice that the constructor of `HardDrive` adds each new `HardDrive` object to an array called `drives`, which is a private field of `Computer`. The array `drives` is an array of object references for the inner `HardDrive` objects that share the enclosing instance. The `HardDrive` constructor freely uses the private members of `Computer`, regardless of whether they are class variables, like `MAX_DRIVES`, or instance variables, like `installedDrives` and `drives`, as in the following lines:

```
if ( installedDrives < MAX_DRIVES ) {
   drives[installedDrives++] = this;
}
```

If you were to add another member inner class, `HardDriveController`, to the `Computer` class, objects of the `HardDrive` class would have access not only to all the members of the `Computer` class, but also to all the members of the `HardDriveController` class. Likewise, objects of the `HardDriveController` class would have access to all the members of the `Computer` and `HardDrive` classes.

Similarly, the enclosing class has access to private members of the inner class. The toString method, which overrides the default toString of the Object class so that you can print out a report on the hard drives, can use the instance variable `size`.

Mini Quiz 9-2

If the enclosing class has full access to all fields in an inner class, why is it necessary to qualify the name of the field `size` in the following statement?

```
sb.append( drives[i].size + "MB" );
```

Working with Subclasses of Member Inner Classes

You can extend a member inner class. Inheritance works in the same way for inner classes as it does for top-level classes, except that some new syntax is required to deal with inner classes. Here is the declaration of a subclass of the `Computer.HardDrive` class defined in the previous example:

```
package java4cpp.inner;
/** A class definition to show how it is possible
  * to use an inner class as a superclass
  */
public class SCSIHardDrive extends Computer.HardDrive {
  private static final int DRIVE_CAPACITY = 512;
  /** Construct a SCSI hard drive object within an
    * enclosing Computer instance
    * @param c the enclosing computer instance
    * @exception Exception is thrown if there is no
    *    room to put the hard drive into the computer
    */
  public SCSIHardDrive( Computer c ) throws Exception {
    c.super( DRIVE_CAPACITY );
  }
}
```

A subclass constructor can explicitly call the constructor of the superclass. If super is not called explicitly, the default constructor of the superclass is called implicitly. Inner classes add a complication: if the superclass is an inner class, an object of the superclass cannot be constructed without an enclosing object. Where should the enclosing object be specified? The most obvious place is within the call to the superclass constructor. The Java programming language puts the onus on you to call super explicitly when the constructor must be qualified or take arguments. Here, the constructor of the `SCSIHardDrive` class calls the constructor of its superclass, the `Computer.HardDrive` class. You qualify the call with the `Computer` object passed as an argument to the constructor of `SCSIHardDrive`, so that the superclass object can be successfully constructed.

Mini Quiz 9-3

Can you instantiate a subclass of a member inner class with a default constructor?

Local Inner Classes

Classes declared inside methods are called **local inner classes**, to distinguish them from **member inner classes**. The only kind of class you can define inside a method is an inner class, and you define it simply by including the definition within a block of code.

Local inner classes are different from member inner classes in the following ways:

- They are private to the blocks in which they are defined, and cannot be declared with the keywords public, private, or protected. For this reason, the names of the classes cannot be used anywhere except in the method where they are defined.
- The methods of a local inner class have access to much more than just the fields defined within them. The state of a local inner class object includes:
  - Its own fields, which cannot be qualified with static
  - All local variables marked final within any enclosing method or local block
  - All arguments of enclosing methods that are marked final
  - One enclosing instance of each enclosing class up to and including the top-level class at package scope
- Objects of a local inner class and all the objects within their extended states live on beyond the scopes in which they are created.

The extended lifetime of local inner classes arises because of the way the Java Virtual Machine (JVM) instantiates local inner classes. The JVM builds all objects of reference types, including instances of local inner classes, not on the stack but in a separate area of memory from which only the garbage collector can remove them. When creating objects of a local inner class, the JVM copies local variables and the method arguments into the object. If the arguments or local variables have reference types, objects of the local inner class hold object references for the arguments or variables and prevent the garbage collector from sweeping the referenced objects away. Therefore, the lifetime of method arguments and local variables continues after the method execution ends.

The compiler for the Java programming language must impose one condition so that instances of local class objects can have this extended lifetime: all arguments and local variables of the enclosing methods that are referenced by a local inner class must be qualified with final. The compiler rejects an inner class that breaks this rule. This restriction is necessary because the inner class object has only copies of the arguments and local variables. If the inner classes could change these copies, the changes would not be properly propagated to the enclosing objects.

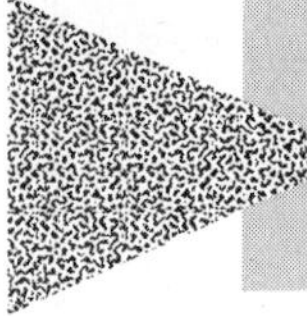

Mini Quiz 9-4

Do arguments and local variables of a method have to be constants if the method has an inner class that refers to them? Consider objects of both primitive and reference types.

Local inner classes can be defined within both class and instance methods. When defined in an instance method, the local class can use all members of the enclosing class. When defined in a class method, the local class can use only class variables and class methods of the enclosing class. In all other ways, it does not matter whether the enclosing method is a class method.

Have you used local classes in C++? If you have, the concept of a class defined within the scope of an enclosing block should be familiar to you. In both C++ and the Java programming language, the declaration of a local class looks like an ordinary class declaration except that it occurs inside a block of code. Of course, in a program written in the Java programming language, the block of code must be within a method and therefore inside a class. The major difference is that in the Java programming language, the local class is an inner class. C++ does not have inner classes or any equivalent feature. Therefore, the nature of local classes in C++ and the Java programming language is very different. In particular, C++ programmers may find quite strange the idea that method arguments and local variables can outlive their enclosing scope. Such a thing never happens in C++, where all objects are destroyed when the scope that contains them ends.

The next sample program demonstrates many of the characteristics of local inner classes. This program consists of a class of which each instance has a method to solve an equation. The actual equation solved in this example is rather silly and not based on any known mathematical formula. The interesting aspect of this class is that the method that returns the solution to the equation has an inner class that implements an interface. Because it implements the interface, the inner class must implement the method defined in that interface, which in this case is the method that solves the equation. Therefore, this example shows how an inner class can be an adapter class by implementing an interface that the enclosing class does not implement.

The following listing is the definition of the class `Equation1`. A top-level interface, `Equation1.Result`, is nested inside `Equation1`. The interface contains one method, `getAnswer`. The method `Equation1.getResult` has an inner class, `MyResult`, that implements `Equation1.Result` and therefore implements `getAnswer`. You look in more detail at some of the interesting constructs in the class, after you see the code for entire program.

```
package java4cpp.inner;
/** A class definition to explore the use of local
  * inner classes
  */
public class Equation1 {
   private int equationInput;
```

```
   /** An interface defining the result from an
     * equation
     */
   public interface Result {
      public double getAnswer();
   }
   /** Constructor method
     * @param ei the equation input
     */
   public Equation1( int ei ) {
      equationInput = ei;
   }
   /** Create the result of the equation for the given
     * input values
     * @param input1 the first equation input
     * @param input2 the second equation input
     * @return the result object
     */
   public Result getResult( final int input1,
                            final int input2 ) {
      final int localVar[] = new int[10];
      class MyResult implements Result {
         private int normalField;
         public MyResult() {
            normalField = 2;
         }
         public double getAnswer() {
           return (double) input1 / input2
                          - equationInput + localVar[2]
                          - normalField;
         }
      }
      return new MyResult();
   }
   /** The test method for the class
     * @param args not used
     */
   public static void main( String[] args ) {
      Equation1 e = new Equation1( 10 );
      Result r = e.getResult( 33, 5 );
      System.out.println( r.getAnswer() );
   }
}
```

The definition of the interface **Result** is nested inside the class **Equation1** so that this example is a self-contained class. If you move the definition of **Result** out of the class and provide it elsewhere in the same package, there would be no impact on the rest of the `Example1` class. The interface `Result` contains one method, `getAnswer`, and all classes that implement this interface must implement this method. `getAnswer` returns a value of type **double**.

```
public class Equation1 {
  public interface Result {
    public double getAnswer();
  }
```

The class `Equation1` has a method, `getResult`, to solve the equation. The actual calculation is performed by the method `getAnswer` of the class `MyResult`, which is a local class defined in `getResult`. Because `MyResult` implements `Result`, the class must provide an implementation of the method `getAnswer`. This particular implementation is interesting because it uses data stored in different places to demonstrate the different kinds of extended state that a local inner class may have.

```
public Result getResult( final int input1,
                         final int input2 ) {
   final int localVar[] = new int[10];
   class MyResult implements Result {
      private int normalField;
      public MyResult() {
         normalField = 2;
      }
      public double getAnswer() {
         return ( double ) input1/input2
                         - equationInput
                         + localVar[2]
                         - normalField;
      }
   }
```

Notice that the five terms in the equation from which the answer is calculated are stored in different ways:

- `equationInput` is a private instance variable of the enclosing class.
- `input1` and `input2` are arguments of the instance method in which the local class is defined.
- `localVar[2]` is an element of an array that is a local variable of the instance method in which the local class is defined.
- `normalField` is a private instance variable of the local inner class.

Notice that the `getResult` method returns an object that it creates. There would be nothing special about such a construct if the type of `MyResult` were defined outside the method:

```
return new MyResult();
```

You must look in the main method to see where the object of the class MyResult is actually used. The main method calls getAnswer and writes the value to the standard output stream. Thus, a MyResult object is actually used long after the end of the scope in which the object is created. The arguments and the local variables of the method are available even though the method has finished.

```
public static void main( String[] args ) {
   Equation1 e = new Equation1( 10 );
   Result r = e.getResult( 33, 5 );
   System.out.println( r.getAnswer() );
}
```

Here, the Java programming language makes a radical break away from C++ traditions: Local inner class objects and all the objects within their extended states live on beyond the scopes in which they are created.

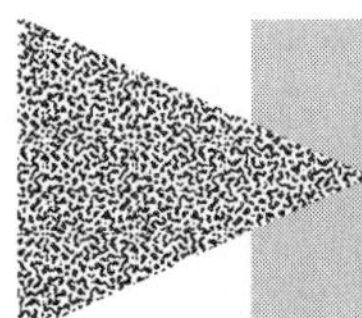

Mini Quiz 9-5

What is the output of this program?

Could you insert assignment statements into the method getAnswer to change the value of the elements of the array localVar, even though the array is a local variable in the method getResult and is declared to be final?

Anonymous Local Inner Classes

The name given to the local inner class in the previous example may seem somewhat pointless. The name of a local inner class cannot be used outside the block in which the local class is defined. As in the Equation1 example, all references to the type of an object of a local class use the name of the interface that the local class implements or the class that the local class extends. If you do not need to refer to a local class by its name inside the method, you can make it an anonymous inner class. Anonymous inner classes are always local to a code block.

Creating Anonymous Inner Classes

Here is another example of inner classes adding complexity to the Java programming language. The new keyword has an enhanced form so that a class definition can follow it. Use the enhanced new keyword to declare anonymous inner classes.

Syntax	new *[class_or_interface_name()]* { *body_of_class* }
Dissection	■ As always, the **new** keyword creates an object and returns the object reference for the new object. An anonymous inner class cannot have a constructor; if you supply arguments with the **new** keyword, they are passed to the constructor of the superclass. ■ The optional ***class_or_interface_name*** is the name of either a class that is extended or an interface that is implemented by the anonymous class being defined. If you omit a class or interface name, the anonymous class extends the **Object** class. ■ The members of the class are defined in the body of the class and enclosed in braces in the usual manner.

Code Example

```
new {
   String msg() {
      return "anonymous inner class";
   }
}
```

Code Dissection This anonymous inner class contains one method that returns a **String**. You can call this method with the object for which the inner class is instantiated.

Before version 1.1 of the Java programming language added inner classes, the name of an interface could never follow the keyword new.

Using Instance Initializers

Anonymous inner classes have no name. How can you define constructors for anonymous classes when constructors must have the same name as their classes? Use an instance initializer. The syntax of instance initializers is very simple.

Syntax

{
initialization_statements
}

Dissection

■ An instance initializer is a nameless block of code surrounded by braces and placed anywhere inside the definition of a class.

■ An instance initializer has the same syntax as a static initializer, but without the keyword **static**.

The use of instance initializer blocks is not limited to anonymous inner classes. You can include an instance initializer block in any class definition, even if you also define one or more constructors. Instance initializer blocks are executed before the constructor, but after the superclass constructor. They provide a very handy way to collect common initialization statements into one place when a class has more than one constructor.

The `Equation1` example program has been reworked to use an anonymous inner class, and the resulting class is called `Equation2`. All the changes required to convert the local inner class from the `Equation1` example to the anonymous inner class of the `Equation2` example are confined to the `getResult` method that follows and are shown in boldface.

```
/** Create the result of the equation for the given
  * input values
  * @param input1 the first equation input
  * @param input2 the second equation input
  * @return the result object
  */
   public Result getResult( final int input1,
                            final int input2 ) {
      final int localVar[] = new int[10];
      return new Result() {
         private int normalField;
         public double getAnswer() {
            return ( double ) input1 / input2
                              - equationInput
                              + localVar[2]
                              - normalField;
         }
         // this is an instance initializer block
         {
            normalField = 2;
         }
      };
   }
```

The definition of the local class is moved into the return statement and combined with the enhanced form of the new keyword.

The structure of `Equation1.getResult` is as follows:

```
public Result getResult( final int input1,
                         final int input2 ) {
   final int localVar[] = new int[10];
   class MyResult implements Result { /*. . . */ }
   return new MyResult();
}
```

The structure of `Equation2.getResult` is as follows:

```
public Result getResult( final int input1,
                         final int input2 ) {
   final int localVar[] = new int[10];
   return new Result() { /* . . . */ };
}
```

The constructor in the local class definition has been dropped:

```
public MyResult (){
   normalField = 2;
}
```

An instance initializer has been added to the body of the anonymous class:

```
{
   normalField = 2;
}
```

Effects on Generated Class Files

How does the file-naming scheme required by the JVM cope with inner and nested classes? A few extra naming rules and conventions apply:

- For the purpose of gaining access from other packages, all classes have either public or package access. If a member class is declared to be protected, its .class file defines it as a public class. If a member class is declared private, its .class file defines it as having package scope.
- Each nested top-level class or inner class is stored in its own .class file.
- The filename generated for .class consists of the enclosing class name followed by a dollar sign character ($) and then the enclosed class name, for every level of nesting.
- An anonymous class is identified by a number.

For example, the Java compiler creates three .class files when it compiles the Equation2.java file:

- `Equation2.class`
  As you probably expect, this file contains the public class `Equation2`.
- `Equation2$Result.class`
  This file contains the nested interface `Result`.
- `Equation2$1.class.`
  This file is for the anonymous inner class.

SUMMARY

A top-level class is a class that is contained only in packages and not in other classes. All classes in C++ are top-level classes, but in the Java programming language classes can also be contained in other classes.

You can define a class inside the definition of another class. The enclosed class is a nested class. Depending on how you define it, the enclosed class falls into one of the following categories:

- Nested top-level classes
- Member inner classes
- Local inner classes
- Anonymous local inner classes

Nested top-level classes are declared with the keyword static. Except for the fact that they are defined within another class, they have the same behavior and characteristics of top-level classes defined at package scope.

Member inner classes are defined inside another class. Their definitions are syntactically identical to those of nested classes except that they are not declared static.

Member inner classes must be instantiated as part of an instance of their enclosing class. Therefore, you can qualify the new keyword with an object reference to specify the enclosing object. You must qualify new if the object of an inner class is created in a class method.

The state data of an inner class object includes the current instance of the inner class and every enclosing object up to and including the enclosing object of the top-level class at package scope. Thus, inner class objects have an extended state compared to top-level class objects. Enclosing objects can be shared by more than one inner class object.

Local inner classes are defined within a method, and their definitions are private to that method. Like member inner classes, local inner classes have state data that extends to include the enclosing object. In addition, the state data includes all method parameters and method local variables that are declared final.

After an object of a local inner class has been created, its lifetime continues even after the scope in which the class is declared ends.

Anonymous inner classes are local inner classes that do not have a name. Objects of such classes are created using an enhanced syntax for the new keyword:

new *[class_or_interface_name()]* { *body_of_class* }

Anonymous inner classes do not have constructors, but you can initialize their fields with instance initializer blocks. You can also use instance initializer blocks within top-level classes.

QUESTIONS

1. Examine the following code:

```
public class Quiz9_1 {
   private int a = 200;
   public static void main( String[] args ) {
      Quiz9_1 x = new Quiz9_1();
      B y = new B();
}
public class B {
   private int b = 100;
   }
}
```

Which of the following statements are true? Select all that apply.

a. The compiler rejects the definition of the `B` class because it is not declared with the static keyword.

b. Compilation is successful.

c. Class `B` is a member inner class.

d. The compiler rejects the expression `new B()` because it does not provide an enclosing instance for the object being created.

2. Examine the following code:

```
public class Quiz9_2 {
   // -- X --
}
```

Which of the following class definitions are valid when placed at the line marked `-X-`? Select all that apply.

a. `public class A { }`

b. `protected class B { }`

c. `public static class C { }`

d. `private static class D { }`

e. `static class E { }`

3. Examine the following code taken from a single source file:

```
public class Quiz9_3 {
   private int x;
   static public void main( String[] args ) {
      class A { };
   }
   protected class B { }
   public int getX() {
      class C { }
      return x;
   }
   private static class D { }
}
class E { }
```

Which of the classes are inner classes? Select all valid answers.

a. `A`

b. `B`

c. `C`

d. `D`

e. `E`

4. Examine the following code taken from a single source file:

```
interface Y {
     public void f();
}
abstract class Z {
     public abstract void g();
     public void h() {
        System.out.println( "Hello!" );
     }
}
public class Quiz9_4 {
     public static void main( String[] args ) {
        // -- X --
     }
}
```

Which of the statements include valid definitions of anonymous inner classes when placed at position -X-? Select all that apply.

a.
```
Object y = new Y() {
   public void f() {
      System.out.println( "Choice a)" );
   }
};
```

b.
```
Z z = new Z() {
    public void g() {
       System.out.println( "Choice b)" );
    }
};
```

c.
```
Object y = new Y, Z() {
   public void f() {
      System.out.println( "Choice c)" );
   }
   public void g() {
      System.out.println( "Choice c)" );
   }
};
```

d.
```
Z z = new Z() {
   public void h() {
      System.out.println( "Choice d)" );
   }
};
```

e.
```
Object z = new Z() {
   public void g() {
      System.out.println( "Choice e)" );
   }
   public void h() {
      System.out.println( "Choice e)" );
   }
};
```

5. Examine the following code taken from a single source file:

```
public class Quiz9_5 {
   public int calculate() {
      return a + b + c + d + e;
   }
   static public void main( String[] args ) {
      class A {
         private int a;
      };
   }
   protected class B {
      private int b;
   }
   class C {
      private int c;
   }
   private static class D {
      private int d;
   }
}
class E {
   private int e;
}
```

Which of the following statements are true? Select all that apply.

a. The compiler rejects the expression `a + b + c + d + e` because the variable `a` is undefined at that place in the file.
b. The compiler rejects the expression `a + b + c + d + e` because the variable `b` is undefined at that place in the file.
c. The compiler rejects the expression `a + b + c + d + e` because the variable `c` is undefined at that place in the file.
d. The compiler rejects the expression `a + b + c + d + e` because the variable `d` is undefined at that place in the file.
e. The compiler rejects the expression `a + b + c + d + e` because the variable `e` is undefined at that place in the file.

6. Examine the following code:

```
public class Quiz9_6 {
   public class C {
   }
}
```

Which of the following statements best describes the type of the class called `C`? Select the best answer.

a. local inner class
b. member inner class
c. member inner class at package scope
d. static member class
e. anonymous inner class

7. Examine the following code taken from a single source file:

```
public class Quiz9_7 {
   static public void main( String[] args ) {
      class A {
         private int a;
      };
   }
   protected class B {
      private int b;
      public int calculate() {
         return a + b + cObj.c + dObj.d + e;
      }
   }
   class C {
      private int c;
   }
   private static class D {
      private int d;
   }
   private D dObj = new D();
   private C cObj = new C();
   private int e;
}
```

Which of the following statements are true? Select all that apply.

a. The compiler rejects the expression `a + b + cObj.c + dObj.d + e` because the variable `a` is undefined at that place in the file.
b. The compiler rejects the expression `a + b + cObj.c + dObj.d + e` because the variable `b` is undefined at that place in the file.
c. The compiler rejects the expression `a + b + cObj.c + dObj.d + e` because the variable `cObj.c` is undefined at that place in the file.
d. The compiler rejects the expression `a + b + cObj.c + dObj.d + e` because the variable `dObj.d` is undefined at that place in the file.
e. The compiler rejects the expression `a + b + cObj.c + dObj.d + e` because the variable `e` is undefined at that place in the file.

8. True or False: When you are creating an instance of any inner class, specifying an enclosing instance is optional.

9. Examine the following code:

```
public class Quiz9_8 {
   public void calculate() {
      // - X -
   }
}
```

Which of the following class definitions are valid when placed at the line marked `-X-`? Select all that apply.

a. `public class A { };`

b. `protected class B { };`

c. `class C { };`

d. `private class D { };`

e. `static class E { };`

10. Examine the following code:

```
public class Quiz9_9 {
   class A {
      // - X -
   }
}
```

Which of the following definitions are valid when placed at the line marked `-X-`? Select all valid answers.

a. `static int v;`

b. `private int w;`

c. `static final int x = 10;`

d. `transient int y;`

e. `final int z = 20;`

EXERCISES

Debugging

1. Correct all the errors in the following program.

```
package java4cpp.questions.c9;
public class Debug9_1 {
   public Debug9_1() {
      class A {
         int a = 6;
      }
      Debug9_1.A x = new Debug9_1.A();
      System.out.println( x.a );
   }
   public static void main( String[] args ) {
      new Debug9_1();
   }
}
```

2. Correct all the errors in the following program:

```
package java4cpp.questions.c9;
public class Debug9_2 {
   A x;
   public static void main( String[] args ) {
      Debug9_2 a = new Debug9_2();
      a.x = new A();
      System.out.println( a.x.getValue() );
   }
   class A {
      private String s = "pork chops and applesauce";
      public String getValue() {
         return s;
      }
   }
}
```

3. Correct the errors in the following program so that the output of the program is as follows:

```
Shopping List:
eggs & cheese
```

Here's the program listing:

```
package java4cpp.questions.c9;
interface ShoppingList {
   public void f();
   public void g();
}
public class Debug9_3 {
   public static void main( String[] args ) {
      ShoppingList y = new ShoppingList() {
         public void f() {
            System.out.println( "Shopping List:" );
         }
      }
      y.f();
      y.g();
   }
}
```

4. Correct the errors in the following program without adding initializers to the definitions of the strings ON_MSG and OFF_MSG:

```
package java4cpp.questions.c9;
interface Switch {
   public void on();
   public void off();
}
public class Debug9_4 {
   public static void main( String[] args ) {
      Switch s = new Switch() {
         public Switch() {
            ON_MSG = "Switch on";
            OFF_MSG = "Switch off";
         }
         public void on() {
            System.out.println( ON_MSG );
         }
         public void off() {
            System.out.println( OFF_MSG );
         }
         final String ON_MSG;
         final String OFF_MSG;
      };
      s.on();
      s.off();
   }
}
```

5. Correct the errors in the following program so that the output, correct to two decimal places, is `148.41`:

```
package java4cpp.questions.c9;
public class Debug9_5 {
   public static double calculate( double x,
                                   double y ) {
      class Helper {
         double doSomething() {
            return Math.sqrt( x ) + Math.sqrt( y );
         }
      }
      Helper h = new Helper();
      return Math.exp( h.doSomething() );
   }
   public static void main( String[] args ) {
      System.out.println( calculate( 4.0, 9.0 ) );
   }
}
```

Complete the Solution

1. Complete the following program by adding a definition of an anonymous class that implements the `TapePlayer` interface. Test your object by invoking each of the four methods against the created object.

```
package java4cpp.questions.c9;
interface TapeRecorder {
   public void play();
   public void stop();
   public void record();
   public void pause();
}
public class Complete9_1 {
   public static void main( String[] args ) {
      // add your anonymous class definition here
   }
}
```

2. Complete the following program by creating four instances of the `Tire` class that all share the object `a` as their enclosing instance:

```
package java4cpp.questions.c9;
public class Automobile {
   public static void main( String[] args ) {
      Automobile a = new Automobile();
      // create 4 instances of the Tire class, each
      // with object a as the enclosing instance
   }
   class Tire {
      private double pressure;
      public void setPressure( double p ) {
         pressure = p;
      }
      public double getPressure() {
         return pressure;
      }
   }
}
```

3. Complete the following class definition by adding a top-level nested class called `StockItem`. Add a statement to the main method to create an object of the class. Your `StockItem` class will need to include the methods required by the main method.

```
package java4cpp.questions.c9;
public class Complete9_3 {
   public static void main( String[] args ) {
      // construct the object x here
      System.out.println( x.getName() );
      System.out.println( x.getColor() );
      System.out.println( x.getIdNum() );
   }
   // Add your nested top-level class
}
```

4. Complete the following class definition by adding a class definition inside the main method. Your class definition should implement both the `Nameable` and the `Identifiable` interfaces provided.

```
package java4cpp.questions.c9;
public class Complete9_4 {
   interface Nameable {
      public String getName();
   }
   interface Identifiable {
      public int getId();
   }
   public static void main( String[] args ) {
      // add your class definition here
   }
}
```

5. Complete the following class definition by completing the body of the `concatenate` method. Your method body should define a class of objects that implements the `Concatenates` interface, create an instance of that class, and use that instance to perform the concatenation operation on the `String` objects in the top-level class.

```
package java4cpp.questions.c9;
public class Complete9_5 {
   String s1, s2;
   interface Concatenates {
      public String concatenate();
   }
   public Complete9_5( String newS1, String newS2 ) {
      s1 = newS1;
      s2 = newS2;
   }
   public String concatenate() {
      // your concatenate method body here
   }
   public static void main( String[] args ) {
      Complete9_5 x = new Complete9_5( "egg drop ",
                                       "won-ton" );
      System.out.println( x.concatenate() );
   }
}
```

Discovery

1. Expand the Graph2 example class in this chapter to include edges as well as nodes, and call the new class EdgeNodeGraph. You can start with the code in the file java4cpp\inner\Graph2.java from the unpacked java4cpp.jar file. In a graph, a start node and an end node define an edge. Create another member inner class called Edge that is nested in EdgeNodeGraph and is a peer of Node. You will need to expand the methods and fields of EdgeNodeGraph to allow the user to create edges and to query edges already in the graph. Add a main method to EdgeNodeGraph that tests the class by adding several nodes and edges.
2. Create a class called MusicCollection. This class must have member inner classes called Artist and Recording. The Recording class must have an inner class called Track that represents a single piece of music within a Recording object. A MusicCollection object must have an array of Artist objects and an array of Recording objects. Recording objects must have a single Artist object, for simplicity, and an array of Track objects. Add a main method to MusicCollection that tests the creation of all of these objects.

CHAPTER 10

Utility and Collection Classes

objectives

In this chapter you will:

- **Look in the package** java.util **for a variety of useful utility classes.**
- **Set up an event notification mechanism using** Observer **and** Observable **objects.**
- **Select the appropriate classes for different kinds of data structures from the core classes that support collections.**
- **Use enumerators to traverse collections.**
- **Define your own collection classes.**

Introduction

In previous chapters, you learned most of the Java programming language and looked at a wide variety of sample programs. You are ready to move on to programming topics such as abstract data structures and more specialized techniques. At this stage, a professional programmer typically looks for ways to leverage existing technology. In an object-oriented environment, this becomes a search for existing code that does what is required and is proven, robust, efficient, and available for reuse in new programs.

The Java platform provides you a core set of classes to support the kinds of applications that programmers are likely to be developing with the Java programming language. You have already seen two of these packages, java.io and java.net, which support I/O programming and programming for the network, in Chapter 8. This chapter covers the package java.util, which provides collections and some other useful classes. One great advantage of programming in the Java programming language is that you can take advantage of the specialized services that are provided by the core classes and ensure that your program is completely portable across all platforms that support the JVM. Moreover, the core classes are relatively easy to learn.

You can use this chapter as a guide to the collection classes that can encapsulate the data structures in your programs. The Java platform supports many kinds of collections, ranging from simple vectors to hash tables and the system property table. Selecting appropriate and efficient implementations of data structures in the form of collection classes can have a major impact on the performance and robustness of your program.

The java.util Package

Many of the classes in java.util support collections, but it would be misleading to present java.util as the collection-class package. Figure 10-1 shows the structure of the classes and interfaces in java.util. The shaded boxes represent abstract classes and the rounded boxes represent interfaces.

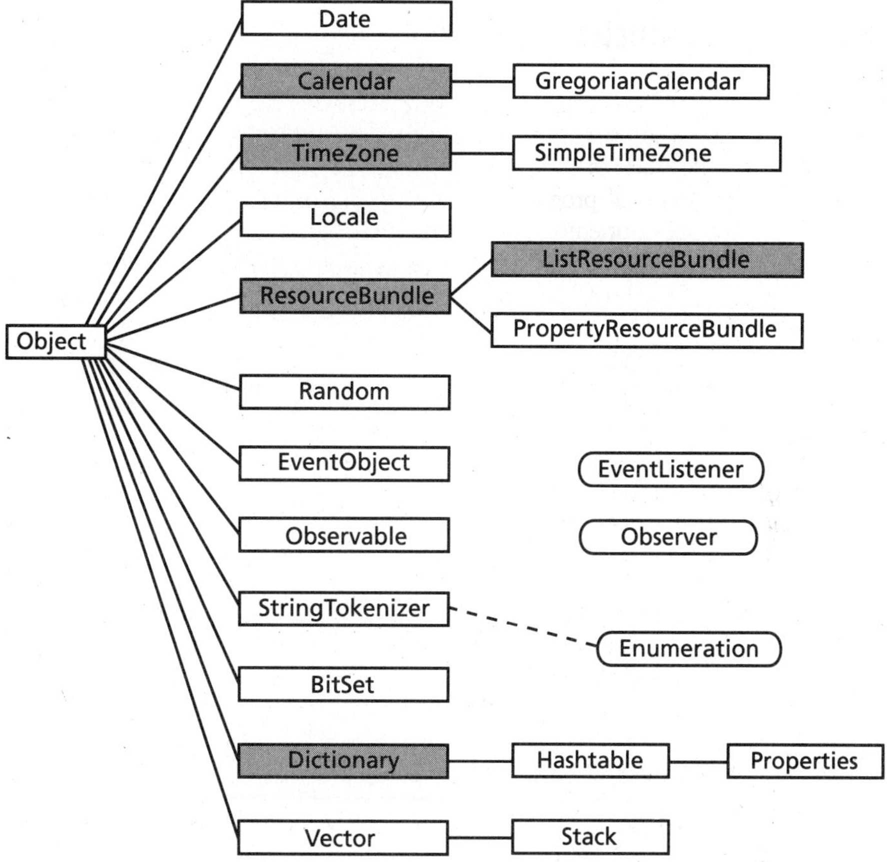

Figure 10-1: Classes and Interfaces in java.util

The collection classes are **BitSet**, **Dictionary**, **Vector**, and the subclasses of those three classes. This package also includes a variety of other useful classes. Figure 10-2 summarizes the classes and interfaces in java.util that are not involved in supporting collections.

Classes and Interfaces	Description
Date **Calendar** **GregorianCalendar** **TimeZone** **SimpleTimeZone**	These classes support dates and times, formatted according to local customs. You can call methods to convert between different date and time representations. If you have not set up a cultural environment, dates and times are formatted according to the default lfor your installation of the Java platform. These classes are described in more detail in Chapter 16.

Figure 10-2: General utility classes in java.util

Classes and Interfaces	Description
Locale **ResourceBundle** **ListResourceBundle** **PropertyResourceBundle**	You use the locales and resource bundles when you are creating an applet or application for use in the international market. These four classes are described in Chapter 16.
Observable **Observer**	Use the **Observable** class and **Observer** interface in combination to set up a notification mechanism between classes.
Random	You can use or extend the **Random** class to generate sequences of pseudorandom numbers if the **random** method of the **Math** class does not meet your requirements. You can call methods to set the **seed**, which is an initial value from which the following numbers are generated. You can obtain uniformly distributed pseudorandom numbers of type **int**, **long**, **float**, or **double**, and Gaussian (normally) distributed numbers of type **double**. The `CaseMixer` example class in Chapter 8 uses the **Random** class.
StringTokenizer	The **StringTokenizer** class is analogous to the **StreamTokenizer** class that is discussed in Chapter 8. This class is frequently used to parse a **String** object or to read a line of data one token at a time, as described in Chapter 2.
EventObject **EventListener**	The superclass for all event object classes is **EventObject**. Classes that act as handlers for these events implement the interface **EventListener**. Programming for events is an essential part of creating GUIs, and is described in Chapter 13.

Figure 10-2: General utility classes in java.util (continued)

Some of the classes in java.util, such as the random number generator, are exactly the tools you need for specialized programming requirements. Other classes and interfaces in this package are used directly by classes in other packages. For example, the EventObject class and EventListener interface form the basis for the classes and interfaces that support user interaction with a graphical user interface (GUI). You can use these classes directly, but are more likely to use the classes in other packages that extend them.

The original release of the Java platform contained the Date class, but none of the other support for internationalization. From its very beginning, the Java platform provided for manipulating date and time data. The original Date class was popular because working with raw date and time data tends to be a very messy programming exercise. The Date class still encapsulates date objects, but the Calendar class is now the focal point of date and time operations.

Observers and Observable Objects

You can set up an event notification mechanism using the Observer interface and the Observable class.

An event can be any change of the state of an object. For example, when a field changes value, it is an event. Many events receive no special treatment and have no impact on the flow of control. But often you want objects to react to events that are external to themselves. How can you create an object that responds to changes in instances of other classes? The Java platform provides the Observable class and Observer interface for that specific purpose.

A different and more comprehensive event-handling mechanism drives GUI-based programs. In Chapter 13, you learn how to create programs that are driven by user-initiated events. The classes upon which user-interface events are based extend EventObject, and objects that handle the events are instances of classes that implement interfaces that extend EventListener.

The Observable class and Observer interface provide a simpler event-notification mechanism. Here, the events are changes in the state data of Observable objects. And objects that are instances of classes that implement the Observer interface can react to these events.

The Observable class drives the event-notification mechanism. If you are defining a class upon which other classes depend, you can define the class to extend Observable. Your program can then notify all the Observer objects that are registered for an Observable object whenever that Observable object changes. You call notifyObservers to alert the observers of possible changes. The notifyObservers method calls the hasChanged method to check if the object has changed. If it has changed, the observers are notified. The object is considered changed if the setChanged method has been called since the last call of the clearChanged method, and not changed otherwise.

Class	java.util.Observable
Purpose	Instances of classes that extend **Observable** are observable objects. In the model-view paradigm where the presentation of data is separated from the data itself, observable objects represent data.
Constructors	■ The no-argument constructor is the only constructor available with this class.

Methods	■ **void addObserver(Observer *object*)** Call **addObserver** to register an object as an observer for this object. ■ **void deleteObserver(Observer *object*)** Call **deleteObserver** to remove the object from the list of observers. ■ **void notifyObservers()** **void notifyObservers(Object *object*)** The effect of calling **notifyObservers** is to call **hasChanged** method and, if the return value is **true**, call the **update** method of all observers. You can optionally specify an object to be passed as an argument to the **update** method. Then the **clearChanged** method is called for the current object. ■ **void setChanged()** Call **setChanged** to set the changed condition for the current object. ■ **boolean hasChanged()** The **hasChanged** method returns **true** if the current object has changed, and **false** otherwise. ■ **void clearChanged()** Call **clearChanged** to clear the changed condition for the current object.

To create an observer, define a class that implements the interface Observer. To register the observer, call addObserver for the Observable object and pass the Observer object as the argument of the method. Because Observer is an interface rather than a class, you can easily adapt existing classes to be observers. The Observer interface contains one method, update, which is called automatically whenever the Observable object for the Observer interface calls notifyObservers.

Interface	**java.util.Observer**
Purpose	Instances of classes that implement **Observer** can be notified of changes in **Observable** objects.
Methods	■ **void update(Observable *object*, Object *argument*)** The **update** method of registered observers is called by **notifyObservers** for the **Observable** object. If an argument is provided to the **notifyObservers** method, it is passed on to the second argument of **update**. Otherwise, the second argument is **null**.

In the following sample program, the class `Pump` encapsulates an application in which a `Valve` is an Observable object, and a `Buzzer` is an Observer object. Because `Pump` is a public class, it is found in a file called Pump.java. The structure of packages mirrors the file system, so you can find this source code in the java4cpp\observe subfolder of the folder in which you unpacked the JAR file java4cpp.jar.

```
package java4cpp.observe;
import java.util.Observable;
import java.util.Observer;
/** Class to demonstrate the use of the Observer
  * interface and the Observable class
  */
public class Pump {
   /** Method for creating a Pump, a Valve, and
     * a Buzzer object and connecting the Valve
     * and Buzzer objects together
     * @param args not used
     */
   public static void main( String[] args ) {
      Pump p = new Pump();
      Valve v = p.new Valve();
      Buzzer b = p.new Buzzer();
      v.addObserver( b );
      v.setPressure( 150 );
      v.setPressure( 200 );
      v.setPressure( 75 );
   }
   /** A class representing a valve in a pump
     * that can be observed by other objects
     */
   private class Valve extends Observable {
      private int pressure;
      /** Method used to set the pressure at
        * the valve.  It notifies its
        * observers of the change
        * @param p Updated pressure value
        */
      public void setPressure( int p ) {
         pressure = p;
         setChanged();
         notifyObservers();
      }
      public int getPressure() {
         return pressure;
      }
   }
   /** Class representing the warning buzzer on a
     * pump.  The buzzer sounds when the pressure
     * of the valve it is observing exceeds the
     * threshold, and goes silent when the pressure
     * drops back below the threshold.
     */
```

```
    private class Buzzer implements Observer {
       private int threshold = 100;
       private boolean buzzerOn;
       /** This method is called whenever the valve
         * being observed changes
         * @param o the object under observation
         * @param arg optional argument, not used
         */
       public void update( Observable o, Object arg ) {
          Valve v = (Valve) o;
          if ( v.getPressure() > threshold
               && buzzerOn == false ) {
              buzzerOn = true;
              System.out.println( "Buzzer on" );
          } else if ( v.getPressure() < threshold
                      && buzzerOn == true ) {
              buzzerOn = false;
              System.out.println( "Buzzer off" );
          }
       }
    }
}
```

The main method of the Pump class creates an enclosing Pump object and the Buzzer and Valve objects enclosed in the Pump object. Next the Buzzer is registered as an observer for the Valve. During execution, the valve pressure is set to three different levels.

Mini Quiz 10-1

Are the classes Buzzer and Value top-level nested classes or member classes?

The setPressure method of the Valve class sets the pressure and then calls two methods that Valve inherits from Observable: setChanged, followed by notifyObservers. The Buzzer class implements the update method of the Observer interface to print the message "Buzzer on" or "Buzzer off," depending on the pressure in a Valve object and whether the buzzer is currently on or off.

Notice that the first argument of update has type Observable, and must be cast to the type of the Observable object. The value of the second argument is null because no explicit object is passed to the call of notifyObservers in setPressure.

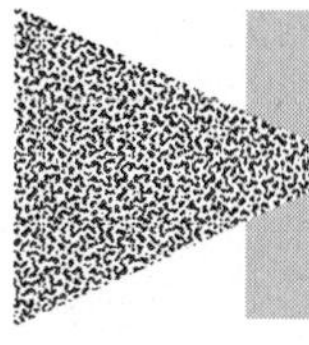

Mini Quiz 10-2

What mechanism calls the Buzzer.update method?

What is the output of this application?

Collection Classes

Classes that support collections make up a large part of the java.util package. Collections are objects created for the sole purpose of holding other objects. Usually, the contained objects are all of the same type or related types. Collections can be organized into abstract structures such as sets, bags, lists, trees, stacks, queues, and hash tables. Arrays are a kind of collection. However, arrays that you declare directly have a very rigid and simple structure.

If your C++ programs require collections, at this point you usually start evaluating class libraries, and you may be facing a difficult decision: What classes should you use? There may be several candidates:

- **Many proprietary class libraries are on the market. One may be packaged with your C++ development software. Some of the popular class libraries are powerful packages. But they are not standard, and using them can build into your code dependence on a particular software supplier. Because these packages tend to be large and complex, you may have to climb a steep learning curve before you can use them effectively.**
- **The recently published C++ standard includes the Standard Template Library (STL). The STL defines a standard set of classes for collections, internationalization, and a number of other purposes. However, the STL is not widely available yet. The STL is also large and may not be easy to learn. The STL includes collection classes, but does not address many common application requirements such as windowing or programming for a network.**
- **You could go back to basic principles and code your own reusable classes for collections and the like. This approach may be acceptable for small jobs, and efficient if you tailor the classes to specific requirements. Usually, you cannot invest the time and effort to take this approach.**

The collection classes in java.util form a compact and basic set of collection classes. The core collection classes hold objects of type Object. Because all classes either directly or indirectly extend the class Object, they hold all of the reference types. All collection classes have methods for adding, removing, and retrieving objects, and for traversing the data structure.

When you extract items from any generic collection class, you receive object references for objects of type Object. Therefore, you must cast the reference returned to the actual type of the object. Without the cast, you can call only the methods of the class Object for objects extracted from a collection.

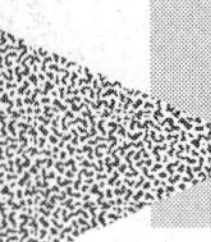

Mini Quiz 10-3

Can you create a collection of int, float, or any of the other primitive types?

The traditional way to program collections in C++ is as class templates. Indeed, the STL is, as its name states, a library of templates. The Java programming language does not support the use of templates, so this approach is not available in the Java platform. On the other hand, C++ has no generic type like Object**. Therefore, the two languages have very different solutions to the question of how to allow for different types of members of collections.**

Traversing Collections

A characteristic of a collection is that you use a separate iterator object to traverse the collection and to visit individual items in the proper order. **Iterators** (also known as **cursors**) are separate objects from the collections, rather than methods of the collection classes. Indeed, a single collection may have several different iterators. In the Java platform, an iterator is an Enumeration object, and is an instance of a class that implements the interface Enumeration. You do not create the iterators for collections yourself. Instead, you call a method of the collection to obtain an iterator.

It is important to note that an Enumeration object does not have its own copy of the collection as it existed at the time the Enumeration object was obtained. If the collection is changed by other methods while the Enumeration object is being used, the results of using the Enumeration object are undefined and difficult to predict.

Interface	java.util.Enumeration
Purpose	This **Enumeration** interface defines the methods you can use to access the objects in a collection.
Methods	■ **boolean hasMoreElements()** Call **hasMoreElements** to determine whether you can extract an object from the collection. The method returns **true** if an object is available and **false** if the collection is empty or has been completely traversed. ■ **Object nextElement()** Call **nextElement** to obtain the next object in a collection. If no object is available, the method throws the exception **NoSuchElementException**. You can prevent the exception by calling **hasMoreElements** first, and then calling this method only if **hasMoreElements** returns **true**.

Other than its name, an Enumeration **object bears no resemblance to the C++ construct defined with the C++ keyword** enum.

Selecting a Collection Class

If you want to use one of the data structures encapsulated by any of the core collection classes, simply create an object of the collection class. The exception is Dictionary, which is an abstract class. You must extend Dictionary or use one of the predefined subclasses Hashtable or Properties. The predefined collection classes are summarized Figure 10-3. After you have created the collection class object, you can use any of the methods of the class. All but BitSet have a method, elements, that you can call to obtain an Enumeration iterator for the collection.

Collection Class	Description
BitSet	Use **BitSet** collections to contain sets of true-false flags. The collection is dynamically sized so you can add elements without worrying about exceeding any limits. Simply setting or clearing a value at an index value that is beyond the current size extends the set. When you extend a **BitSet**, all the added elements are given the default value of **false**. A BitSet never shrinks.
Dictionary	This abstract class defines methods for storing elements of type **Object**, according to key values that are also of type **Object**. It is the superclass of the **Hashtable** and **Properties** classes. You can also extend **Dictionary**, but you cannot instantiate an object of the **Dictionary** class.
Enumeration	The **Enumeration** interface defines the methods used for sequentially accessing the objects in a collection.
Hashtable	The **Hashtable** class extends **Dictionary**. Instances of this class are hash tables. **Hash tables** are a very efficient way of storing large numbers of items that do not naturally lend themselves to storage in a stack, binary tree, or some other specialized structure. In hash tables, objects are put into locations called **buckets**, and each bucket has a unique identifier, or **hash code**. More than one object can fall into a bucket.
Properties	The **Properties** class extends **Hashtable** to create an even more specialized implementation of **Dictionary**. A **Properties** object is a collection of key-value pairs, where each key and each value is a **String** object. The key for an item in the **Properties** table is the name of a property.
Stack	The **Stack** class has methods to add and remove objects according to the last-in first-out rule. The **Stack** class extends **Vector** and adds methods for pushing, popping, and peeking into the stack.

Figure 10-3: Predefined collection classes

Collection Class	Description
Vector	A **Vector** is an indexed list of objects, much like an array. Use a **Vector** when you need greater flexibility than arrays provide. The main advantage is that a **Vector** can grow and shrink in size as required, but an array has a fixed size. The **Vector** class also has several methods that are not available for arrays. Because **Vector** objects are ordered, they are more efficient than **Hashtable** objects for enumeration operations.

Figure 10-3: Predefined collection classes (continued)

Class	java.util.BitSet
Purpose	A **BitSet** contains a number of bits, each of which represents a **true** or **false** value.
Constructors	■ **BitSet()** **BitSet(int *size*)** The constructor creates an empty set. You can optionally specify an initial size.
Methods	■ **void and(BitSet *b*)** The **and** method performs a logical AND on the bits in the current object and specified **BitSet**. ■ **void clear(int *position*)** The **clear** method clears the bit in the specified position so that its value, when returned by **get**, is **false**. ■ **boolean get(int *position*)** The **get** method returns **true** if the bit in the specified position is set, and **false** otherwise. ■ **void or(BitSet *b*)** The **or** method performs a logical OR on the bits in the current object and specified **BitSet**. ■ **void set(int *position*)** The **set** method sets the bit in the specified position so that it its value, when returned by **get**, is **true**. ■ **void xor(BitSet *b*)** The **xor** method performs a logical EXCLUSIVE OR on the bits in the current object and specified **BitSet**.

Moving from C++

Unlike C++, the Java programming language does not have a built-in syntax for creating identifiers for fields smaller than one byte, also known as bitfields. For example, in the following C++ class, the members `oneBit`, `twoBits`, and `fourBits`, occupy one, two, and four bits, respectively, and are packed into one byte.

```
class BitFields {
private:
   unsigned int oneBit: 1;
   unsigned int twoBits: 2;
   unsigned int fourBits: 4;
// . . .
}
```

You cannot declare such a structure in the Java programming language. But, with a BitSet collection, you can approximate sets of bitfields in which each member occupies just one bit.

Class	**java.util.Dictionary**
Purpose	The abstract class **Dictionary** is a superclass for collection classes that contain key-value pairs.
Constructors	■ **Dictionary()** Only a no-argument constructor is available.
Methods	■ **Enumeration elements()** The **elements** method returns an **Enumeration** object to iterate through the values in the dictionary. ■ **Object get(Object *key*)** The **get** method returns the value for the specified key. ■ **boolean isEmpty()** The **isEmpty** method returns **true** if no key mappings are contained in the collection, and **false** otherwise. ■ **Enumeration keys()** The **keys** method returns an **Enumeration** object to iterate through the keys in the dictionary. ■ **Object put(Object *key*, Object *value*)** The **put** method adds a key and value to the dictionary, or updates the value for a key that is already stored in the dictionary. Both arguments must have non-**null** values. The return value is the value that was associated with the key before the method call, or **null** if the key was not previously in the dictionary. ■ **Object remove(Object *key*)** The **remove** method deletes a key and value from the dictionary. The return value is the value associated with the removed key, or **null** if the key was not in the dictionary. ■ **int size()** The **size** method returns the number of entries in the dictionary.

Class	java.util.Hashtable
Purpose	The **Hashtable** class extends **Dictionary**. You can use a **Hashtable** for key-value pairs when the keys are instances of classes that implement the **hashCode** and **equals** methods.
Constructors	■ **Hashtable()** **Hashtable(int *capacity*)** **Hashtable(int *capacity*, float *load*)** When you create an empty **Hashtable**, you can optionally specify a capacity and load factor. The load factor must be a number between 0.0 and 1.0, and is a measure of how full the **Hashtable** is allowed to become. A larger load factor uses memory more efficiently, but can increase the time required to look up keys.
Methods	■ **boolean contains(Object *value*)** The **contains** method returns **true** if a key is stored for the specified value, and **false** otherwise. ■ **boolean containsKey(Object *key*)** The **containsKey** method returns **true** if the specified key is in the **Hashtable**, and **false** otherwise. ■ **Enumeration elements()** The **elements** method returns an **Enumeration** object to iterate through the values in the **Hashtable**. ■ **void rehash()** The **rehash** method rehashes the contents of the **Hashtable** to increase its capacity. This method is called automatically when the number of entries exceeds the value produced by multiplying the capacity and the load factor.

The method hashCode returns an integer that identifies a bucket in a hash table. A default hashCode method is defined in the Object class. If you have a very good hash function, you can override the default hashCode method for objects in your hash table, to increase its efficiency. As a rule of thumb, if you define a class that overrides Object.equals, and if objects of that class may be used in a hash table, you should also override the method Object.hashCode for your class. A correct hashCode method meets the following two criteria:

- The hashCode method must return the same integer value for two objects whenever comparing the two objects with the equals method returns true.
- The hashCode method must consistently return the same value for any particular object during the execution of an application.

If objects that satisfy the equality relationship have different hashCodes, or if the hashCode for an object changes during the execution of a Java application, the Hashtable data structure can become corrupt.

Class	java.util.Properties
Purpose	The **Properties** class extends **Hashtable**. The key and value are both **String** objects, suitable for writing to or reading from I/O streams. A **Properties** object can contain another **Properties** object that gives default values.
Constructors	■ **Properties()** **Properties(Properties default)** When you create a **Properties** object, you can optionally supply another **Properties** object to serve as a table of default values.
Methods	■ **String getProperty(String *key*)** **String getProperty(String *key*, String *default*)** The **getProperty** method searches first the property table and then the default table for an occurrence of the specified key. If it finds the key, the method returns the associated value. Otherwise, **getProperty** returns **null** or the default **String** specified in the optional second argument. ■ **void load(InputStream *in*)** The **load** method reads a property list from an input stream. ■ **Enumeration propertyNames()** The **propertyNames** method returns an **Enumeration** object to iterate through the keys in the **Properties** object. ■ **void list(PrintStream *out*)** **void list(PrintWriter *out*)** The **list** method prints the property list on the specified output stream. ■ **void save(OutputStream *out*, String *header*)** The **save** method outputs to the specified output stream first the header **String** and then the contents of the **Properties** table.

The JVM maintains a Properties collection of system information. You can ask it questions such as "What version of the Java platform is running?" or "What operating system is the JVM running under?" Applets have limited access to this table, but applications can make full use of it.

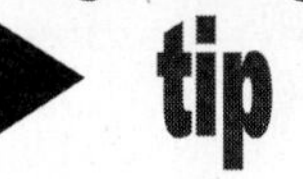

Referring to the values contained in the system Properties **collection is a standard way to determine information about the native system in which your program is running. Call the** load **and** save **methods of the** Properties **class for a straightforward way of saving and restoring program attributes such as the current window size and window position.**

Class	java.util.Vector
Purpose	The **Vector** class supports a dynamically resizable list of object references.

Constructors

- **Vector()**
  Vector(int *capacity*)
  Vector(int *capacity*, int *increment*)
  When you create a **Vector** collection, you can optionally specify an initial capacity, or the number of elements for which to reserve space, and by how much the capacity should be incremented every time the **Vector** must grow. The size of a **Vector** is the number of elements actually contained in the **Vector**. The capacity is always equal to or greater than the size.

Methods

- **void addElement(Object *object*)**
  The **addElement** method adds an object reference to the end of a **Vector**. The capacity of the **Vector** is increased, if necessary.

- **int capacity()**
  The **capacity** method returns the number of elements the **Vector** can hold before it has to grow.

- **void copyInto(Object[] *array*)**
  The **copyInto** method copies into an array the object references stored in the **Vector**. You must supply an existing array for which the number of elements is equal to or greater than the size of the **Vector**.

- **void ensureCapacity(int *capacity*)**
  The **ensureCapacity** method increases the capacity of the **Vector**, if necessary, to make sure it can hold at least the specified number of elements.

- **Object elementAt(int *position*)**
  The **elementAt** method returns the value of the element at the specified position in the **Vector**.

- **Enumeration elements()**
  The **elements** method returns an iterator for the **Vector**.

- **Object firstElement()**
  The **firstElement** method returns the value of the element in the first position in the **Vector**.

- **int indexOf(Object *object*)**
  int indexOf(Object *object*, int *position*)
  The **indexOf** method returns the position of the first occurrence of the specified object reference in the **Vector**. If you supply a position argument, the method returns the position of the first occurrence at or after the specified position. The **equals** method is used to determine matches.

- **void insertElementAt(Object *object*, int *position*)**
  The **insertElementAt** method inserts an object reference at the specified position in the **Vector**. All elements previously in the **Vector** at or after the specified position are moved back by one position toward the end of the **Vector**. The method increases the capacity of the **Vector**, if necessary.

- **Object lastElement()**
  The **lastElement** method returns the value of the element in the last occupied position in the **Vector**.

- **lastIndexOf(Object *object*)**
  lastIndexOf(Object *object*, int *position*)
  The **lastIndexOf** method returns the position of the last occurrence of the specified object reference in the **Vector**. If you specify a position argument, the method returns the position of the last occurrence at or before the specified position.

- **void removeAllElements()**
  The **removeAllElements** method deletes all elements from the **Vector**.

- **boolean removeElement(Object *object*)**
  If the specified object reference is stored in the **Vector**, the **removeElement** method deletes the first occurrence of it, moves all following elements forward one position, and returns **true**. Otherwise, the method returns **false**. The **equals** method is used to determine matches.

- **void removeElementAt(int *position*)**
  The **removeElementAt** method deletes the object reference at the specified position and moves all following elements forward one position.

- **void setElementAt(Object *object*, int *position*)**
  The **setElementAt** method sets the value of the object reference at the specified position.

- **void setSize(int *size*)**
  The **size** method sets the size of the **Vector**. If the **Vector** contains more elements than the specified size allows, the method deletes the elements at positions following the value of the new size.

- **int size()**
  The **size** method returns the number of elements currently in the **Vector**.

- **void trimToSize()**
  The **trimToSize** method trims the capacity of the **Vector** to its current size.

Performance

tip

If you know in advance approximately how many elements will be stored in the Vector, **pass that number as the capacity argument of the constructor. Do this to improve efficiency, especially if the** Vector **grows gradually to a large size. Every time a** Vector **grows, the object references it contains are copied into a new** Vector, **and the old** Vector **space is left for garbage collection.**

Class	java.util.Stack
Purpose	The **Stack** class extends **Vector** and adds methods for last-in first-out behavior.

Constructors	■ **Stack()** The **Stack** class has only the no-argument constructor.
Methods	■ **boolean empty()** The **empty** method returns **true** if the **Stack** is empty, and **false** if at least one element is in the **Stack**. ■ **Object peek()** The **peek** method returns the object reference last added to, but not removed from, the **Stack**. Unlike **pop**, this method does not remove the element from the **Stack**. If the **Stack** is empty, **peek** throws the exception **EmptyStackException**. ■ **Object pop()** The **pop** method returns the object reference last added to, but not removed from, the **Stack**. It also removes the element from the **Stack**. If the **Stack** is empty, **pop** throws the exception **EmptyStackException**. ■ **Object push(Object *object*)** The **push** method adds an element to the **Stack**, and returns an object reference that is passed as an argument. ■ **int search(Object *object*)** The **search** method returns the position of the specified object reference on the **Stack**, or –1 if the object reference is not stored on the **Stack**.

Version Watch

Version 1.2 of the Java platform will introduce a new API for collection classes. The classes in the new collections API will implement one or more of the following interfaces:

- Collection **is the most basic of the interfaces and defines the basic behavior of a group of objects.**
- Set **extends** Collection **and does not allow duplicate elements.**
- List **extends** Collection **and defines methods for positioning elements. Duplicates are generally allowed.**
- Map **provides for a mapping from keys to values. Each key can map to only one value.**

The API will add Iterator **interfaces to complement the** Enumeration **interface that is implemented by all iterators in version 1.1.** Iterator **objects will have greater capabilities than** Enumeration **objects.**

The Collections **interface will define algorithms for sorting, searching, finding the minimum, and finding the maximum.**

Using the Core Collection Classes

The following program demonstrates the Vector class and Enumeration interface. The class Line manipulates a Vector of Point objects. Here is the definition of the Point class:

```
package java4cpp.collections;
/** A simple class that implements a point in
  * two-dimensional space
```

```
  */
public class Point {
   private int x, y;
   public Point() {
      this( 0, 0 );
   }
   public Point( int initX, int initY ) {
      x = initX;
      y = initY;
   }
   public String toString() {
      StringBuffer sb = new StringBuffer( 20 );
      sb.append( "( " + x + ", " + y + " )" );
      return sb.toString();
   }
}
```

The class `Point` stores the x and y coordinates of a two-dimensional point, and implements the toString method to return a textual representation of a point.

Here is the class `Line`, which stores a line as a Vector of `Point` objects:

```
package java4cpp.collections;
import java.util.Vector;
import java.util.Enumeration;
import java.io.PrintStream;
/** A class to demonstrate the use of the Vector and
  * Enumeration classes in the java.util package
  */
public class Line {
   private Vector points = new Vector();
   /** Set the starting point for a line
     * @param p the starting point
     */
   public void setStart( Point p ) {
      points.removeAllElements();
      points.addElement( p );
   }
   /** Set the next point in a line
     * @param p the next point
     */
   public void addPoint( Point p ) {
      points.addElement( p );
   }
   /** Print all the points in a line
     * @param ps the stream where the points
     *           will be printed
     */
   public void listPoints( PrintStream ps ) {
```

```
        Enumeration e = points.elements();
        while ( e.hasMoreElements() ) {
           ps.println( e.nextElement() );
        }
     }
     /** Test method for the class
       * @param args not used
       */
     public static void main( String[] args ) {
        Line x = new Line();
        x.setStart( new Point( 4, 11 ) );
        x.addPoint( new Point( -6, 1 ) );
        x.addPoint( new Point( 2, 3 ) );
        x.listPoints( System.out );
     }
  }
```

The output is

```
( 4, 11 )
( -6, 1 )
( 2, 3 )
```

The main method of the `Line` class creates the Vector. The class provides methods to start a new line with one point (`setStart`), to add a point to the line (`addPoint`), and to print out the points in the line (`listPoints`). The last of these methods uses a PrintStream object, `ps`, to output each point and an iterator e to visit each point in turn.

Do not assume that the declaration of e instantiates Enumeration. Instead, it declares an object reference for an object of unknown type that implements the Enumeration interface. The method Vector.elements creates the object for the object `points`. The actual class of the object returned by Vector.elements is unimportant. All that matters is that it implements Enumeration.

Mini Quiz 10-4

When is the method Point.toString called during the execution of this sample program?

The following program demonstrates the Properties collection class:

```
package java4cpp.collections;
import java.util.*;
/** A class to help demonstrate how to work with
  * system properties
  */
public class SystemProperties {
   /** Display the system properties specified as
```

```
     * input parameters or, if no input is given,
     * all the system properties
     * @param args the list of system properties
     *             to be displayed
     */
   public static void main( String[] args ) {
      if ( args.length > 0 ) {
         // dump selected system properties
         for ( int i = 0; i < args.length; i++ ) {
            System.out.println( args[i] + ": " +
               System.getProperty( args[i],
                                   "not found" ) );
         }
      } else {
         // dump all system properties
         Properties sysProps = System.getProperties();
         Enumeration e = sysProps.propertyNames();
         while ( e.hasMoreElements() ) {
            String propName = (String) e.nextElement();
            System.out.println( propName + ": " +
               sysProps.getProperty( propName ) );
         }
      }
   }
}
```

When there are no input arguments, the output describes the native environment on which the program has run and the implementation of the JVM used. If you run the program, you should see output similar to the following lines, except that several lines have been deleted from this listing and your results will describe your installation of the Java platform:

```
user.language: en
java.home: d:\jdk\bin\..
file.encoding.pkg: sun.io
java.version: 1.1.5
file.separator: \
line.separator:
user.region: US
file.encoding: 8859_1
user.timezone: EST
path.separator: ;
```

You can specify particular properties as command-line arguments. For example, you can enter the following on one command line:

```
java java4cpp.collections.SystemProperties user.timezone
```

If your system clock is set for Eastern Standard Time, the output is

```
user.timezone: EST
```

You can run the program with more than one property name, by entering the following on one command line:

```
java java4cpp.collecions.SystemProperties
     file.encoding not.a.property
```

If your operating system uses the default U.S. character-encoding scheme, the output is

```
file.encoding: 8859-1
not.a.property: not found
```

The bulk of this program is contained in the main method. If the user supplies the name of a system property as a command-line argument, the program prints the name and the value associated with the name in the system property table. The JVM maintains the system property table. The table is available to programs as a Properties collection in which the property names are the keys and the property values contain current settings. The System class provides the method getProperty, which returns the value of the property named in the argument.

When the user supplies no arguments, the program prints the entire system properties table. The method System.getProperties returns an object reference for full system property table, which is assigned here to the local variable sysProps. The main method next calls propertyNames to obtain an Enumeration object, e, to use as an iterator to step through the names of the properties. In the while loop, the program extracts property names one at a time by calling nextElement for e, as long as the method hasMoreElements returns true for e. The program obtains the associated value by calling System.getProperty, and prints each name-value pair.

Mini Quiz 10-5

In this sample program, why is each item in the collection sysProps cast to type String after it is returned from the method nextElement of the Enumeration e?

Writing Your Own Collection Classes

You can write your own generic collections in the Java programming language, if the core classes do not suit your needs. The circumstances for which you need to create your own collection classes are likely to be greatly reduced in a future version of the Java platform, when the new collections API becomes available. But no predefined API can meet all specialized requirements. In the future, as well as now, you may want to code a collection class of your own.

To make the collection truly generic, you must design it to contain objects of type Object. This may be a major limitation, because you can assume only the methods defined in Object are available. Object defines the method equals so you can test for duplicates. However, Object does not have a method for determining if one object has a value greater than or less than another value. Therefore, you cannot build in dependence on methods that perform less-than or greater-than comparisons. As a result, you cannot create a sorted collection, unless you introduce your own nonstandard superclass or interface. Nevertheless, you can create unsorted collections of Objects. The next sample program shows how to create a linked list.

Version Watch

Version 1.2 of the Java platform will introduce a new interface called java.lang.Comparable. This interface has only one method, compareTo, that returns an integer. If you have two objects, x and y, the call x.compareTo(y) will return a negative integer if x is less than or comes before y, zero if x is equal to y, and a positive integer if x is greater than or comes after y. When this interface is available, implementing a sorted collection will become a matter of defining a collection of Comparable objects.

You can also create collections for any defined type. Just substitute the type of the objects in your collection for the generic type Object in the signatures of the methods for the collection. The Properties class is an example of just such a collection. In the case of the Properties class, the elements of the collection are restricted to String objects but all the methods of the String class are available.

To provide a working collection, you must define more than one class. Of course, you need a public class for the externally accessible collection. You must define a second class to implement the Enumeration interface. You may need more helper classes, depending on the structure of your collection. You can combine the public class and the helper classes in one package. A more elegant solution is to define the helper classes as nested or inner classes within your collection class, as shown in the next sample program.

The following sample program implements and exercises a collection object that holds a linked list. Three classes are required to implement a linked list:

- The public class `LinkedList` is a collection of `ListNode` objects. A linked listed is a set of nodes in which each node contains data and a link to the next node. Here, the `LinkedList` is an enclosing class and `ListNode` is an enclosed class.
- The class `ListNode` defines the nodes in a `LinkedList` object. It is implemented as a private top-level nested class because it is a helper class for `LinkedList`.
- The class `LinkedListEnumerator` implements Enumeration and is the iterator for the enclosing `LinkedList` object. It is a private inner class.

Here is the `LinkedList` class:

```
package java4cpp.collections;
import java.util.Enumeration;
/** A class to help demonstrate how to use the Object
  * class to create generic collections.
  * Inner classes are used in the implementation.
  */
```

```
public class LinkedList {
   private ListNode head = null;
   private ListNode tail = null;
   /** Add an element to the list
     * @param newElement the object to be added
     * @return the updated list
     */
   public LinkedList addElement( Object newElement ) {
      ListNode newNode = new ListNode( newElement );
      if ( head == null ) {
         head = newNode;
      } else {
         tail.next = newNode;
      }
      tail = newNode;
      return this;
   }
   /** Remove an element from the list
     * @param unwanted the object to be removed
     * @return whether the removal was successful
     */
   public boolean removeElement( Object unwanted ) {
      boolean result = false;
      ListNode currentNode = head;
      ListNode previousNode = null;
      while ( currentNode != null ) {
         if ( currentNode.contents.equals(
               unwanted ) ) {
            if ( previousNode == null ) {
               head = currentNode.next;
            } else {
               previousNode.next = currentNode.next;
            }
            if ( tail == currentNode ) {
               tail = previousNode;
            }
            result = true;
         }
         previousNode = currentNode;
         currentNode = currentNode.next;
      }
      return result;
   }
   /** Obtain an iterator for the list
     * @return the Enumeration object iterator
     */
   public Enumeration elements() {
```

```
      return new LinkedListEnumerator();
   }
   /** Get the list as a string
     * @return the string representation of the list
     */
   public String toString() {
      StringBuffer sb = new StringBuffer( "[ ");
      Enumeration e = elements();
      while ( e.hasMoreElements() ) {
         sb.append( e.nextElement().toString() + " " );
      }
      sb.append( "]" );
      return sb.toString();
   }
   /** The test method for the class
     * @param args not used
     */
   public static void main( String[] args ) {
      Integer a = new Integer( 5 );
      Double b = new Double( 3.14 );
      String c = new String( "Hello World!" );
      LinkedList list = new LinkedList();
      list.addElement( a ).addElement( b );
      list.addElement( c ).addElement( System.out );
      System.out.println( list );
      list.removeElement( c );
      System.out.println( list );
   }
```

The `LinkedList` class has two private fields:

```
private ListNode head = null;
private ListNode tail = null;
```

All linked lists must have a pointer to the first element. This list also has a pointer to the last element. The pointers are implemented as the private fields `head` and `tail` and are initially set to `null`. Of course, the term *pointer* is used rather loosely here. The methods `addElement` and `removeElement` assign object references to these fields.

The `LinkedList` class has five public methods:

- `addElement` adds a node to the tail, or back, of the list.
- `removeElement` locates a node in the list and removes it. Notice that it uses the equals method to match a node in the list with an object specified as a parameter.
- elements returns an iterator for the list. The name of this method follows the convention established by the JDK core collection classes.

- toString builds a printable String Object that contains a representation of the items in the list. This method creates and uses an Enumeration object to traverse the collection.
- main is a test method that exercises the list.

If you think the closing brace, }, is missing for the `LinkedList` class, do not worry. The top-level nested class `ListNode` and the inner class `LinkedListEnumerator` precede the closing brace. You see these classes, as well as the closing brace, in the next few listings.

Here is the nested class that defines nodes in the linked list, `ListNode`:

```
/** A class representing a node in the list
  */
private static class ListNode {
   final Object contents;
   ListNode next = null;
   /** Construct a list node
     * @param value the object to be put in
     *        the node
     */
   public ListNode( Object value ) {
      contents = value;
   }
   /** Get the node as a string
     * @return the string representation of
     * the node
     */
   public String toString() {
      return contents.toString();
   }
}  // end ListNode
```

This class, together with `LinkedList` and `LinkedListEnumerator`, provide a very traditional implementation of a linked list.

In this example, object references are used as the links between items in the list. In C++, it would be natural to code `next` as a pointer. In the Java programming language, `next` is an object reference to the following `ListNode` object. The field `next` has the value null when there are no more items in the list.

Here is the inner class that implements Enumeration for the linked list, `LinkedListEnumerator`:

```
/** The Enumeration class for the list
  */
private class LinkedListEnumerator
              implements Enumeration {
   private ListNode currentPosition;
   /** Construct the Enumeration for the
```

```
         * enclosing List
         */
       public LinkedListEnumerator() {
          // use field from enclosing LinkedList
          currentPosition = head;
       }
       /** Determine if there are more elements in
         * the list
         * @return whether there are more elements
         */
       public boolean hasMoreElements() {
          return currentPosition != null;
       }
       /** Return the next object in the list or null
         * if there are no more
         * @param the next object
         */
       public Object nextElement() {
          if ( hasMoreElements() ) {
             Object element = currentPosition.contents;
             currentPosition = currentPosition.next;
             return element;
          } else {
             return null;
          }
       }
    }   // end LinkedListEnumerator
}   // end LinkedList
```

Because this is an inner class, the constructor can access the private field `head` of `LinkedList`. It stores a reference to the current node in the linked list in the local variable `currentPosition`. This class must implement the methods hasMoreElements and nextElement. When the list is exhausted, hasMoreElements returns false, and nextElement returns null.

If you run this application, you see output similar to the following lines. The final characters may be different because they represent an address contained in the object System.out and are likely to vary from one implementation of the JVM to another.

```
[ 5 3.14 Hello World! java.io.PrintStream@1cc0ee ]
[ 5 3.14 java.io.PrintStream@1cc0ee ]
```

SUMMARY

The Java platform provides classes that support a variety of data structures, and some other useful features, in the package java.util.

Use the Calendar, Date, and TimeZone classes to store dates and times. With these classes, you can represent and manipulate date and time information as specified by the cultural environment in which your program runs.

If you have classes that depend on, or must react to, changes in the state of some other class, use Observer and Observable to set up an automatic event-notification mechanism. Classes that implement the interface Observer are notified when an object of a class that extends the class Observable changes. The notification takes the form of a call to the method update, which is part of the Observer interface.

If you need a collection, you can use one of the predefined collection classes BitSet, Hashtable, Properties, Vector, and Stack. All these collections are generic because they contain objects of type Object.

- A BitSet stores boolean values.
- Hashtable and Properties extend the abstract base class Dictionary. These kinds of collections are useful when the information has a key and a value.
- Vector and Stack support resizable lists. Stack extends Vector.

All Java platform collections have methods for adding, removing, and extracting items. Every collection class also has a method called elements. To visit the items in a collection, use the object returned by elements. This object implements the interface Enumeration for the collection. Enumeration objects serve as iterators, or cursors, to traverse a collection.

You can write your own collection classes. If you base your collection on the generic class Object, you can use the collection for objects of any reference types, but are then restricted to using only the methods defined in Object. You should also create a class that implements Enumeration, and provide a method in your collection class that returns an Enumeration object.

Collection classes are now a focus of Java platform development, because a new collections API will greatly enhance the set of core collection classes in future versions of the Java platform.

QUESTIONS

1. Which of the following types can be stored in a Vector object? Select all that apply.
   a. Integer
   b. int
   c. boolean
   d. Boolean
   e. String

2. Which of the following are abstract classes? Select all that apply.
   a. Dictionary
   b. Date
   c. Calendar
   d. TimeZone
   e. Observable

3. Which of the following types has a fixed capacity? Select all that apply.
   a. BitSet
   b. Hashtable
   c. int[ ]
   d. Vector[ ]
   e. Stack

4. Examine the following code:

```
import java.util.Vector;
public class Quiz10_4 {
   public static void main( String[] args ) {
      Vector v = new Vector( 100 );
      int x = -34;
      v.addElement( x );
      System.out.println( v.firstElement() );
   }
}
```

   Which of the following statements are true when the code is compiled and run? Select all that apply.
   a. The compiler rejects the expression `new Vector( 100 )` because no constructor parameters are allowed when creating a Vector object.
   b. Compilation is successful and the output is `-34`.
   c. Compilation is successful and the output is `100`.
   d. The compiler rejects the expression `v.addElement( x )` because `x` cannot be converted to the type Object.
   e. The compiler rejects the expression `v.addElement( x )` because Vector objects can contain only string values, not numeric values.

5. Which of the following methods are defined in the Observer interface? Select all that apply.
   a. observe
   b. update
   c. toString
   d. hashCode
   e. equals

6. Which class is the best choice for storing String values that have a String key name?

7. Which of the following methods are defined in the Enumeration interface? Select all valid answers.
   a. hasMoreElements
   b. deleteElement
   c. addElement
   d. nextElement
   e. removeAllElements

8. True or False: If a class definition overrides the equals method, it should not override the hashCode method.

9. Which of the following classes implement the Enumeration interface? Select all that apply.
   a. BitSet
   b. Hashtable
   c. Vector
   d. Properties
   e. Stack

10. Examine the following code:

```
import java.util.StringTokenizer;
public class Quiz10_10 {
   private static final String text
      = "The quick, brown fox";
   public static void main( String[] args ) {
      StringTokenizer st
         = new StringTokenizer( text, "," );
      while( st.hasMoreTokens() ) {
         System.out.println( st.nextToken( " " ) );
      }
   }
}
```

Which of the following statements are true when the code is compiled and run? Select all that apply.
   a. Compilation is successful and the output is:
      ```
      The
      quick,
      brown
      fox
      ```
   b. Compilation is successful and the output is:
      ```
      The quick,
      brown
      fox
      ```
   c. Compilation is successful and the output is:
      ```
      The quick,
      brown fox
      ```
   d. The compiler rejects the expression `new StringTokenizer( text, "," )` because only one String object can be passed as an argument to StringTokenizer constructors.
   e. The compiler rejects the use of the methods hasMoreTokens and nextToken because they are not defined in the Enumeration interface.

EXERCISES

Debugging

1. Correct all the errors in the following program.

```
package java4cpp.questions.c10;
import java.util.Vector;
public class Debug10_1 {
   private static final int SIZE = 100;
   public static void main( String[] args ) {
      Vector v = new Vector( SIZE );
      for ( int i=0; i<=SIZE; i++ ) {
         v.addElement( new Integer( i*i ) );
      }
      Integer x = v.lastElement();
      System.out.println( x.intValue() );
   }
}
```

2. Correct all the errors in the following program so that both output statements print `true`:

```
package java4cpp.questions.c10;
public class Debug10_2 {
   private String name = "";
   public String getName() {
      return name;
   }
   public void setName( String newName ) {
      name = newName;
   }
   public boolean equals( Object other ) {
      return name.equals( ((Debug10_2) other).name );
   }
   public static void main( String[] args ) {
      Debug10_2 x = new Debug10_2();
      Debug10_2 y = new Debug10_2();
      x.setName( "Bono" );
      y.setName( "Bono" );
      System.out.println( x.equals( y ) );
      System.out.println(
            x.hashCode() == y.hashCode() );
   }
}
```

3. Correct all the errors in the following program.

```
package java4cpp.questions.c10;
public class Debug10_3 {
   public static void main( String[] args ) {
      Calendar c = new Calendar();
      Date d = c.getTime();
      System.out.println( d );
   }
}
```

4. Correct all the errors in the following program:

```
package java4cpp.questions.c10;
public class Debug10_4 {
   private static final int SIZE = 3;
   public static void main( String[] args ) {
      BitSet myBits = new BitSet( SIZE );
      myBits.insertElementAt( true, 0 );
      myBits.insertElementAt( false, 1 );
      myBits.insertElementAt( true, 2 );
      System.out.println( myBits );
   }
}
```

5. Correct all the errors in the following program:

```
package java4cpp.questions.c10;
import java.util.Observable;
import java.util.Observer;
public class Debug10_5 {
   public static void main( String[] args ) {
      FireStation fs = new FireStation();
      FireAlarm fa = new FireAlarm();
      fa.addObserver( fs );
      fa.soundAlarm();
      fa.clearAlarm();
   }
   static private class FireAlarm {
      private boolean alarmOn;
      public boolean isAlarmOn() {
         return alarmOn;
      }
      public void soundAlarm() {
         alarmOn = true;
         setChanged();
         notifyObservers();
      }
      public void clearAlarm() {
         alarmOn = false;
         setChanged();
         notifyObservers();
      }
   }
   static private class FireStation
                        implements Observer {
      public void update( FireAlarm fa, Object arg ) {
          if ( fa.isAlarmOn() ) {
             System.out.println( "Go to fire!" );
          } else {
             System.out.println( "Go back to "
                                 + "station." );
          }
      }
   }
}
```

Complete the Solution

1. Complete the following class definition by adding a Vector object to hold the Point objects, and by finishing the methods addPoint and numberOfPoints:

```
package java4cpp.questions.c10;
public class Complete10_1 {
   static public class Point {
      private int x, y;
      public Point() {
         this( 0, 0 );
      }
      public Point( int initX, int initY ) {
         x = initX;
         y = initY;
      }
   }
   public void addPoint( Point p ) {
      // your code here
   }
   public int numberOfPoints() {
      // your code here
   }
   public static void main( String[] args ) {
      Complete10_1 x = new Complete10_1();
      x.addPoint( new Point( 17, 102 ) );
      x.addPoint( new Point( 678, 56 ) );
      System.out.println( x.numberOfPoints() );
   }
}
```

2. Complete the preceding class definition by adding another method called points that returns an Enumeration object that can be used to iterate through the collection of Point objects. Add statements to the main method to test this method and the Enumeration object it returns.

3. Complete the following class definition by providing a correct hashCode function:

```
package java4cpp.questions.c10;
public class Complete10_3 {
   private String name = "";
   private Integer stockNumber = new Integer( -1 );
   private Double price = new Double( 0.00 );
   public Complete10_3( String initName,
                        int initStockNumber,
                        double initPrice ) {
      name = initName;
      stockNumber = new Integer( initStockNumber );
      price = new Double( initPrice );
   }
   // put your hashCode method here
   public boolean equals( Object obj ) {
      Complete10_3 other = (Complete10_3) obj;
      return ( name.equals( other.name )
               && stockNumber.equals(
                  other.stockNumber )
               && price.equals( other.price ) );
   }
   public static void main( String[] args ) {
      Complete10_3 x = new Complete10_3( "wrench",
                                         1239067,
                                         4.99 );
      Complete10_3 y = new Complete10_3( "wrench",
                                         1239067,
                                         4.99 );
      System.out.println( x.equals( y ) );
      System.out.println(
           x.hashCode() == y.hashCode() );
   }
}
```

4. Complete the following class definition by finishing the methods for setting and getting the address and phone number fields. Also, finish the methods that are used for saving the properties to disk and restoring them from disk.

```
package java4cpp.questions.c10;
public class Complete10_4 {
   private Properties objInfo = new Properties();
   private static final String NAME_KEY = "name";
   private static final String ADDR_KEY = "address";
   private static final String PHONE_KEY = "phone";
   public String getName() {
      return objInfo.getProperty( NAME_KEY, "" ) ;
   }
   public void setName( String name ) {
      objInfo.put( NAME_KEY, name );
   }
   public String getAddress() {
      // your code here
   }
   public void setAddress( String address ) {
      // your code here
   }
   public String getPhone() {
      // your code here
   }
   public void setPhone( String phone ) {
      // your code here
   }
   public void saveToFile( String fileName ) {
      // your code here
   }
   public void readFromFile( String fileName ) {
      // your code here
   }
   public String toString() {
      return getName() + " " + getAddress()
             + " " + getPhone();
   }
   public static void main( String[] args ) {
      Complete10_4 x = new Complete10_4();
      x.setName( "Andrew" );
      x.setAddress( "Dublin, Ireland" );
      x.setPhone( "555-1212" );
      x.saveToFile();
      x.readFromFile();
      System.out.println( x );
   }
}
```

5. Complete the following class definition by providing the missing class `Motorist`. This class should be defined as an observer of the `StopLight` class and should respond as the `StopLight` object it observes changes color.

```
package java4cpp.questions.c10;
import java.util.Observable;
import java.util.Observer;
public class Complete10_5 {
   public static void main( String[] args ) {
      Motorist m = new Motorist();
      StopLight sl = new StopLight();
      sl.addObserver( m );
      sl.setLightColor( StopLight.RED );
      sl.setLightColor( StopLight.GREEN );
      sl.setLightColor( StopLight.YELLOW );
   }
   static private class StopLight extends Observable {
      public static final int RED = 0;
      public static final int YELLOW = 1;
      public static final int GREEN = 2;
      private int lightColor = RED;
      public int getLightColor() {
         return lightColor;
      }
      public void setLightColor( int color ) {
         switch ( color ) {
            case RED:
            case YELLOW:
            case GREEN:
               lightColor = color;
               setChanged();
               notifyObservers();
               break;
            default:
               // invalid, do nothing
         }
      }
   }
   // put your class Motorist here
}
```

Discovery

1. The java.util package has a subpackage called java.util.zip that was introduced in version 1.1 of the Java platform. Using the classes provided in this package, write your own unzip utility in the class `JUnzip`. Begin with the class ZipFile and use its methods to obtain an array of ZipEntry objects that represent the contents of the file and the InputStream objects that correspond to each ZipEntry. For simplicity's sake, just unzip the entire file contents in the current folder.
2. Create a collection class called `IntegerSet` that imposes the restriction that all elements in the collection must be integer values, and disallows duplicate values. The `Set` class should have methods for adding and removing values, checking to see if a value is already in the set, removing all values, and returning an Enumeration object for iterating through the set.

CHAPTER

Multithreading 11

objectives

In this chapter you will:

- **Write code to create a new thread of execution, using both the** java.lang.Runnable **interface and the** java.lang.Thread **class.**
- **State the requirements for a concrete class that is declared to implement the** Runnable **interface.**
- **Name the method that provides the starting point for execution of a thread.**
- **Write code to start the execution of a thread.**
- **State and recognize conditions that might prevent a thread from executing.**
- **Write code to use the** synchronized **keyword to require a thread of execution to obtain an object lock prior to proceeding.**
- **Define the behavior of a thread that invokes the** wait **method of an object, and the effect of that method on a lock placed on the object.**
- **Define the behavior of a thread which invokes the** notify **or** notifyAll **methods of an object, and the effect of the method on the object lock flag.**
- **Define the interaction between threads executing the** wait, notify, **or** notifyAll **methods, and the object lock flag.**

Threads and Multithreading

If you draw a line through your code to trace how control moves from statement to statement as your program runs, you are tracing what is called a **thread** of execution. All programs have at least one thread. A **multithreaded** program allows more than one thread to run through the code at once. In some programs, the flow of control splits and executes your program almost as though it were two or more separate processes, rather than sticking to the single sequential order. Multithreaded programs are those that can execute more than one thread at once. All the programs you have seen so far in this book are single-threaded. This chapter describes the features that the Java programming language provides for managing multithreaded programs. Understanding the material in this chapter is essential if you are planning to write multithreaded programs.

Unlike many programming languages, the Java programming language lets you create threads and manage them in a wholly portable way.

When you launch a new path through your code, you start a thread. Typically, you use more than one thread to improve the performance or responsiveness of your application. For example, you can run the graphical user interface (GUI) for your application in one thread and separate processor-heavy tasks or file manipulation into other threads. You may want a separate thread for animation.

If you have created multithreaded programs in other environments, you may be familiar with the complications that multithreading introduces to your code. Threads can interfere with each other, especially when two or more threads that can run concurrently operate on the same variables or objects. At times, you must synchronize your threads so that they do not write to the same storage or contend for the same resources. You want to eliminate the potential for threads to corrupt the values of objects for other threads, or go into deadlock when they all wait on the same condition or for each other. In short, you need a way for your threads to communicate with each other.

The Java programming language includes features for multithreading. You do not have to call an operating system API to manage threads or use platform-dependent features for interthread communication. The close connection between the Java virtual machine (JVM) and the Java programming language breaks down traditional borders between the programming language, supporting libraries, and system APIs.

C++ has no support for threads. Often C++ programmers have to rely on operating system APIs to manage multithreaded programs. At best, in C++ you can use C++ classes that are really are wrappers for operating system APIs. As a result, porting multithreaded C++ applications to different platforms can involve an extensive rewrite.

Even if you are familiar with the concepts of multithreading and have created multithreaded programs in other environments, you should read this chapter carefully. The Java platform provides a comprehensive set of services for managing threads that may be unlike operating system APIs or class libraries you have used in the past. The Java platform also introduces a feature that you may not have encountered before: You can gather threads into groups and operate on all threads in a group with a single method call.

The Life Cycle of a Thread

Threads can come into being, start running, pause, and resume any number of times, and finally stop dynamically during program execution. One thread, the main thread, is launched by the JVM when you run an application or by a Web browser when it starts an applet. But how do other threads that you define in your Java source code come into being, start running, share the processor, and finally stop? The bulk of this chapter discusses the constructs in the Java programming language and core classes that you use to manage threads. Before looking into the details, you may find it helpful to see an overview of the life cycle of threads.

After a single-threaded program starts, it has sole control of the process in which it runs until it ends. It may wait from time to time for user input or some I/O operation to complete, but no other activities occur in the JVM, with the possible exception of some internal operations, such as garbage collection, that run on other threads behind the scenes. This situation is represented by the left side of Figure 11-1. Your program can explicitly create one or more objects that can run as separate threads. After an object capable of running as a thread is created, your program can call a method to start it running. Your threads can also launch other threads. Your program can consist of several threads, all sharing the JVM.

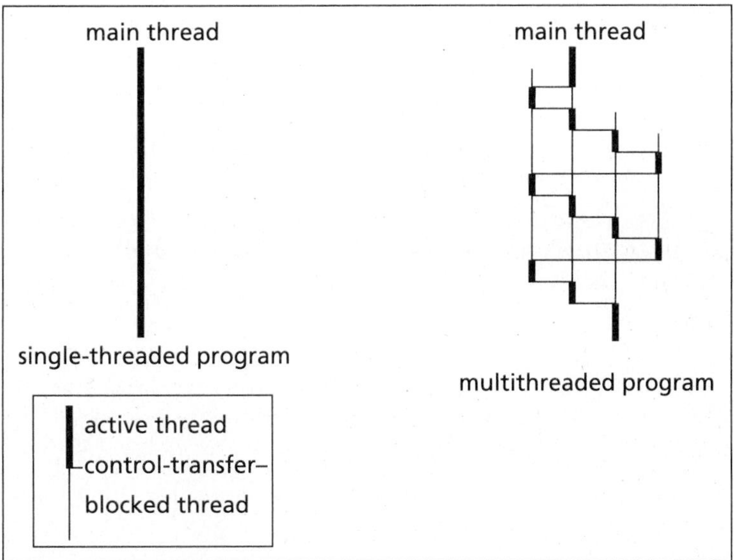

Figure 11-1: Single-threaded and multithreaded programs

How do threads share processing time? The simple story is that they each get a turn at running, and the JVM is in charge of scheduling processor time according to the priorities assigned to the threads. A more complete story depends on whether the native operating system uses preemptive or cooperative multitasking and whether you are running on a single-processor or a multiprocessor machine. Do not assume that threads are dispatched in the same way on all platforms and given the same length of time every time they have an opportunity to run. For example, on a multiprocessor system, the JVM may be able to run more than one thread at the same time on different processors.

When it does not have control, the thread is in a state analogous to suspended animation. Its state does not change except that objects shared with other threads may be modified by other threads or external factors; for example, the state of I/O buffers can change. To the user, it may appear that all threads are running simultaneously, but the reality is more like that depicted on the right side of Figure 11-1.

By default, the JVM tries to distribute control equally to all threads. If you have some threads that require more immediate attention than others, such as threads that encapsulate the user interface and in which response time is very important, you can assign priority values to your threads. Threads with high priority values preempt lower priority threads.

Creating and Running Threads

An object can be run as a thread if it is a Runnable object. In other words, any object that instantiates a class that implements the interface Runnable can be launched as a new thread by the main thread or any other active thread.

Interface	java.lang.Runnable
Purpose	The **Runnable** interface defines the protocol that must be followed by all threads.
Methods	■ **void run()** is the only method in the **Runnable** interface.

You must provide an implementation of the run method in every class that may be instantiated by an object that can run as a thread. This method is the entry point for the thread, and is analogous to main except that all threads, regardless whether they are in applets or applications, must have a run method.

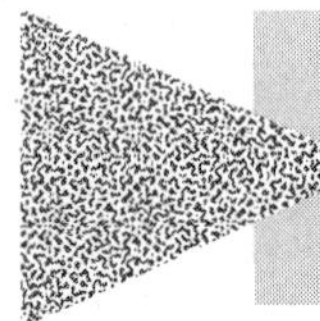

Mini Quiz 11-1

The definition of the run method in the Runnable interface lists no exceptions in its throws clause. What implications does this fact have for exception handling in threads?

The core class Thread implements Runnable, so you can create a thread by instantiating Thread or a subclass of Thread. The Thread class also defines a number of methods that you can use to manage the thread. The next sample program demonstrates extending the Thread class.

Generally, implementing Runnable is considered a better technique than extending Thread, for the following reasons:

- If your class already has a superclass other than Object, extending Thread is not an option.
- A class that implements Runnable inherits less overhead than one that extends Thread. This does not affect the efficiency of the code because you must always have a Thread object for each thread, but does reduce the number of inherited members.

You can always implement Runnable. The only catch is that you must wrap the Runnable object in a Thread object to use it as a thread. Do this by creating a Thread object and passing your Runnable object as an argument of the Thread constructor. When a Thread object is constructed with a Runnable object as input, the Thread object uses the run method of the Runnable object in place of its own run method.

When a class extends Thread, it inherits all the methods and fields required to be manipulated as a separate thread, with one important exception: The Thread class does have a run method, but it is empty. You must override the inherited run method with one from your class if your thread is to accomplish anything.

Class	**java.lang.Thread**
Purpose	The **Thread** class provides the infrastructure for multithreaded programs in the Java platform.
Constructors	■ **Thread()** **Thread(Runnable *object*)** **Thread(Runnable *object*, String *name*)** **Thread(ThreadGroup *group*)** **Thread(ThreadGroup *group*, Runnable *object*)** **Thread(ThreadGroup *group*, String *name*)** **Thread(ThreadGroup *group*, Runnable *object*, String *name*)** When you construct a **Thread** object, you can optionally specify a name for the thread in the argument of type **String**. When you create a thread by instantiating a class that is defined to implement **Runnable**, you must provide the **Runnable** object as an argument of the constructor. Thread groups are discussed later in this chapter.
Methods	■ **String getName()** The **getName** method returns the name of the **Thread** Object.

- **int getPriority()**
  The **int getPriority** method returns the priority of the thread.

- **void interrupt()**
  The interrupt method interrupts the current thread.

- **boolean isDaemon()**
  The **isDaemon** method returns **true** if the **Thread** object is a daemon thread, and **false** otherwise

- **boolean isAlive()**
  The **isAlive** method returns **true** if the thread has been started and has not yet died, and **false** otherwise.

- **void join()**
  void join(long *milliseconds*)
  The **join** method waits for the thread object to terminate. You can optionally specify a maximum number of milliseconds to wait for the lifetime of the thread to end.

- **void resume()**
  The **resume** method resumes a suspended thread. This method is deprecated in version 1.2 of the Java platform.

- **void setDaemon(boolean *on*)**
  The **setDaemon** method determines whether the thread is a daemon thread. When the **boolean** argument has the value **true**, the **Thread** object becomes a daemon. If the argument is **false**, the thread runs as a regular thread.

- **void setPriority(int *priority*)**
  The **setPriority** method sets the priority of a thread to the lesser of the specified value or the maximum allowed for the group to which the thread belongs. Threads with a higher integer priority value can preempt threads with a lower value.

- **void sleep(long *milliseconds*)**
  The **sleep** method makes the thread pause for the specified number of milliseconds.

- **void start()**
  The **start** method causes the thread to begin execution.

- **void stop()**
  The **stop** method forces the thread to stop executing. This method is deprecated in version 1.2 of the Java platform.

- **void suspend()**
  The **suspend** method suspends execution of the thread. This method is deprecated in version 1.2 of the Java platform.

- **void yield()**
  The **yield** method makes the thread pause so another thread can execute.

You do not call the run method to start a thread. After you have created the thread, make it active by calling the start method. The JVM then passes control to the appropriate run method. The thread stays alive until it reaches its normal termination or until you call the stop method. After a thread has started, it can be in a runnable or blocked state. While it is runnable, the thread is either executing or ready to go as soon as the JVM gives it control. The thread can be blocked as the result of a call to suspend, sleep, or object.wait, or because it is waiting for an I/O operation.

Version Watch

Beginning with version 1.2 of the Java platform, the Thread **methods** suspend, resume, **and** stop **are deprecated.**

Use of the stop **method can cause a problem when threads are synchronized. Synchronizing threads is described later in this chapter. Calling the** stop **method has the effect of releasing locks that you set to make sure that only one thread at the same time can access specific objects. If a lock is released when a shared object is in an inconsistent state, using the object can result in unpredictable behavior. The** stop **method is deprecated to avoid this situation.**

The reason that suspend **is deprecated has to do with locks that a thread may be holding at the time of suspension. A JVM implementation will likely have several internal locks that are used to coordinate tasks such as class loading and garbage collection in a multithreaded environment. If a thread is suspended while it holds one of these internal locks, it is very likely that a deadlock will occur when the JVM needs to acquire the same internal lock for another thread.**

The resume **method is deprecated because it has no purpose when** suspend **is deprecated.**

Rather than call the stop **method, let threads complete naturally. There are alternative approaches you can take to calling stop:**

- **Modify a variable to indicate that the target thread should stop running. An example of this approach is demonstrated in the** `Banking` **example later in this chapter.**
- **If the target thread waits for long periods, you can call the** interrupt **method to interrupt the wait.**

The mechanism that terminates a thread is an exception. The JVM throws a ThreadDeath exception when the stop method is invoked for a Thread object. This exception is an unchecked exception, so you do not have to handle it. You can catch the ThreadDeath exception to do cleanup. If you provide a handler for ThreadDeath, be sure to rethrow the exception so that the JVM can delete the threads. Figure 11-2 shows how a thread can change its state during its life cycle.

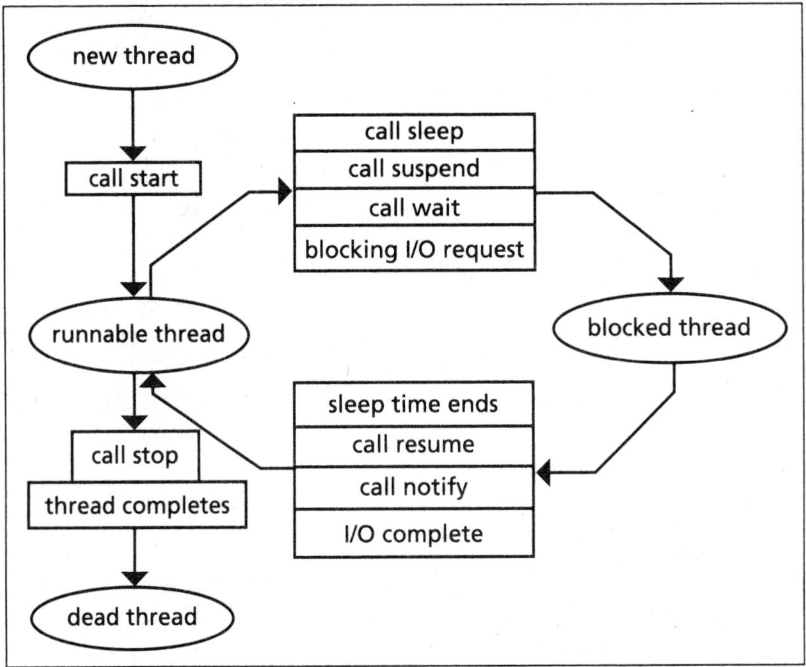

Figure 11-2: How a thread changes state

There are two approaches you can take to creating and running a thread, depending on whether you choose to implement the Runnable interface or extend the Thread class.

For an object that is Runnable but not a Thread:

1. Define a class that implements Runnable.
2. Implement the method run for your class.
3. Instantiate the class to create a Runnable object.
4. Create a Thread object, passing the Runnable object as an argument to the constructor of Thread.
5. Call the start method for the Thread object. Do not call the run method.

For an object that is a Thread:

1. Define a class that extends Thread.
2. Implement the method run for your class.
3. Instantiate the class to create a Thread object.
4. Call the method start for an instance of the class. Do not call the run method.

Here is a simple program that has three threads: a main thread and two threads launched by the main thread. As well as showing how to create and start threads, this program demonstrates the sort of things that can go wrong when you do not synchronize your threads. This program uses the class `RepeatedMessage`. Because `RepeatedMessage` is a public class, it is found in a file called

RepeatedMessage.java. The structure of packages mirrors the file system, so you will find this source code in the java4cpp\threads subfolder of the folder in which you unpacked the JAR file java4cpp.jar.

```
package java4cpp.threads;
/** A class to demonstrate why synchronized methods
  * are needed by showing what can happen when they
  * are not synchronized.
  */
public class RepeatedMessage extends Thread {
   private String message;
   private int pauseTime;
   /** Construct a repeating message
     * @param inputMessage the message to be
     *    repeated
     * @param inputPauseTime the time, in ms,
     *    paused between each letter of the
     *    message
     */
   public RepeatedMessage( String inputMessage,
                           int inputPauseTime ) {
      message = inputMessage;
      pauseTime = inputPauseTime;
   }
   /** Display a repeating message
     * @param rm the message to be repeated
     * @exception InterruptedException if the thread
     *    does not sleep for the full time specified
     */
   public static
          void displayMessage( RepeatedMessage rm )
             throws InterruptedException {
      for( int i=0; i < rm.message.length(); i++ ) {
         System.out.print( rm.message.charAt( i ) );
         sleep( 50 );
      }
      System.out.println();
   }
   /** The workings of the thread
     */
   public void run() {
      try {
         while ( true ) {
            displayMessage( this );
            sleep( pauseTime );
```

```
            }
        } catch( InterruptedException ie ) {
            return;
        }
    }
    /** The test method for the class
      * @param args not used
      */
    public static void main( String[] args ) {
        try {
            RepeatedMessage m1
                = new RepeatedMessage( "bonjour!", 500 );
            m1.start();
            RepeatedMessage m2
                = new RepeatedMessage( "HELLO!", 111 );
            m2.start();
            // pause to let the threads run,
            // then stop them
            sleep( 5000 );
            m1.stop();
            m2.stop();
        } catch( InterruptedException ie ) {
            ie.printStackTrace();
        }
        finally {
            // flush the output buffer
            System.out.println();
        }
    }
}
```

This program allows the output to be scrambled by printing messages one character at a time from different threads, and by pausing between characters. The output may look different on different installations of the Java platform, and may vary from run to run. Here is one possibility:

```
bHoEnLjLoOu!r
!
HELLO!
HbEoLnLjOo!u
r!H
ELLO!
HELbLoOn!j
ouHrE!L
LO!
```

```
HELLbOo!n
joHuErL!L
O!
HELLO!b
onHjEoLuLrO!!
HELLO!
boHnEjLoLuO
```

In this program, two threads are instances of the class `RepeatedMessage`, and the main thread contains the main method of the class `RepeatedMessage`. main instantiates and starts the threads `m1` and `m2`. In these two threads, the run method repeatedly calls `displayMessage` to output a message and sleeps briefly after each call. The sleep method suspends execution for the specified number of milliseconds. Meanwhile, the main thread sleeps.

Notice that the run method is coded as an unending while loop. This looks like terrible programming style, but it is acceptable here because main stops the threads after five seconds, by calling stop. In fact, many event-driven applications rely on similar logic. Threads often loop continuously, monitoring their input buffers or waiting to be notified of an event.

In the code, you see try blocks, catch blocks, and a throws clause for InterruptedException. This exception can occur while sleep is running. The class InterruptedException extends the class Exception, so this is a checked exception. Because run cannot list any exceptions in a throws clause, the exception must be handled within the thread.

Creating Service Threads

Service threads typically are threads that contain a never-ending loop for the sole purpose of receiving and handling requests. You can convert such threads into daemon threads. A **daemon thread** is a thread that runs continuously in the background. Call the setDaemon method for a thread to specify that it is a daemon thread. Call the isDaemon method to determine whether a thread is a daemon thread.

The JVM does not expect daemon threads, unlike regular user threads, to finish. However, a Java application is assumed to be complete when all its threads have terminated. How can a program that starts daemon threads ever end? The JVM can detect when your program reaches a point where only daemon threads are running. The JVM then assumes your application is finished and terminates the daemon threads.

Writing Robust Multithreaded Programs

Creating and running threads is straightforward. Making sure the threads work well together is a far more difficult task. The previous program demonstrates one way in which things can go wrong in multithreaded programs. The Java programming language has two keywords for the specific purpose of eliminating thread-related problems:

- You can qualify variables with the keyword volatile to suppress compiler optimizations that might lose or ignore changes to the variables made by different threads. Changes made to a variable by another thread are called **asynchronous** changes because the flow of control through the current thread does not determine when the changes occur. Asynchronous changes are invisible to the compiler.

  In reality, you rarely need to declare variables to be volatile, because the JVM updates memory frequently, at intervals known as **synchronization points**. However, you should use volatile for shared variables for which you adopt none of the synchronization techniques described in this chapter.
- If you qualify the declaration of a method with synchronized, the method can be run for a particular object or class by only one thread at a time. The Java platform provides features for synchronizing threads. You should use these features to avoid race situations in which threads share variables and the order in which they read or modify shared values can affect the results.

You may be familiar with the volatile **keyword from C++, where it serves the same purpose.**

Deadlock can occur when all threads are in a blocked state, rather like gridlock in road traffic. There is no automatic way of detecting deadlock and resolving it. To avoid deadlock, you can employ a number of design principles that are beyond the scope of this book. However, sometimes a good debugger is your best tool for detecting deadlock.

You are responsible for ensuring that your threads do not interfere with each other and that at least one thread is active until your program is meant to terminate.

Synchronizing Threads

Synchronizing threads involves setting what programmers using the Java programming language call **locks**. You can conceive of locks as flags that indicate whether objects or classes are available for threads to use or are already in use. Sometimes the term **monitor** is used to describe a lock. You can apply locks to methods or blocks of code to prevent them from running simultaneously in more than one thread. You do not have to apply locks to all methods. Use locks for code that requires exclusive access to an object or class while the code is running. Also use locks for code that cannot tolerate changes to fields while it executes.

The concept of locks is similar to that of semaphores, which you may have used in other programming languages for interthread communication. However, a lock is not quite the same thing as a semaphore. There are two kinds of locks:

- **Object locks** apply to instance methods. The lock controls whether a method can be run when it is called for a particular object. Before the method can run, it must acquire the lock on the object, and may have to wait for the lock to become free. The method releases the lock automatically when it ends. Only one thread can have the lock at a time. Therefore, synchronized methods cannot operate on the same object on more than one thread at a time. Other objects of the same class and instance methods that do not require a lock are not affected. All class methods are also unaffected.
- **Class locks** apply to all the class methods. When a thread has the lock for a class, it is the only thread that can execute any of the class methods that require a lock. Class methods that do not require a lock are unaffected. All instance methods are also unaffected.

Syntax

[access_specifier] **synchronized** *[other_qualifiers]*
return_type method_name **(** *argument_list* **)**
*[***throws** *exception_list]*
block

Dissection

- If the method is not declared with the qualifier **static**, the qualifier **synchronized** applies an object lock to the object for which the instance method is called.
- If the method is declared **static**, the qualifier **synchronized** applies a class lock to class methods.

This relatively simple locking mechanism is all that you need in the Java programming language. Just qualify the declaration of methods with the keyword synchronized. You lock classes and objects independently by synchronizing class and instance methods separately.

You do not have to operate on the locks explicitly. The synchronized keyword tells the JVM that the method requires a lock in order to run. The JVM then creates the lock and manages the allocation of the lock to threads during execution, as follows:

- The request for the lock is automatic, and is always satisfied if no other thread has acquired the lock.
- A lock is always available unless a thread has requested and been granted the lock.
- When a synchronized method ends, it releases the lock. If another thread with a synchronized method is waiting for that lock, that thread acquires the lock and can proceed.

Moving from C++

You cannot get a similar effect with features of the C++ language. The C++ standard includes no locks feature for threads. The locks described here are analogous to semaphores, which are an operating system feature. You may have access to semaphores through operating system APIs, C functions, or a C++ class library. In general, using semaphores or equivalent features is trickier than using the locking mechanism provided by the Java programming language.

Synchronized methods are mutually exclusive in the sense that they can be run by only one thread at a time for the locked object. A simple solution to the synchronization problem in the previous sample program is to declare the `displayMessage` method to be synchronized so that the code is as follows:

```
public static synchronized
      void displayMessage ( RepeatedMessage rm )
                    throws InterruptedException {
   for( int i=0; i < rm.message.length(); i++ ) {
      System.out.print( rm.message.charAt( i ) );
      sleep( 50 );
   }
   System.out.println();
}
```

The `displayMessage` method is a class method in this example. As a result, the lock applies to the class `RepeatedMessage`.

You can also indicate that an object lock is required for a single statement or block of code, by using the synchronized statement.

Syntax

synchronized (*object_to_be_locked* **)**
    statement_or_block

Dissection

- When preceding a block or statement, the **synchronized** keyword synchronizes the code for the specified object. You can name any object, and a common technique is to declare a field specifically to act as a lockable object.

Code Example

```
// object used by all instances for its lock
private static Object sharedLock;
public static
      void displayMessage( RepeatedMessage rm )
throws InterruptedException {
   synchronized ( sharedLock ) {
      for( int i=0; i<rm.message.length(); i++ ) {
         System.out.print( rm.message.charAt( i ) );
         sleep( 50 );
      }
      System.out.println();
   }
}
```

Code Dissection An alternative approach to the `displayMessage` problem is to acquire a lock just for the duration of the **for** statement that prints the messages one character at a time. The only reason for creating the object `sharedLock` is to apply its lock to this block of code.

When to Synchronize Code

The most difficult aspect of the synchronized keyword is deciding when to use it. You pay a performance penalty for using synchronized methods. However, ensuring the correct execution of your application is certainly worth the price.

Version 1.2 of the Java platform will deliver many performance enhancements. One of these is a thread-local monitor cache that will enable synchronized methods to run closer to the speed of normal methods.

To determine the level of synchronization that your application requires, consider how the threads within it share classes and objects. You can use one of the following approaches:

- The first and simplest level of synchronization is no synchronization at all. This is acceptable only for single-threaded applications, and for multi-threaded programs where each class containing class methods is used only in a single thread and no objects are shared by threads. (It is worth noting that if none of the class methods modify the objects, no synchronization is required.)
- In the second level of synchronization, all class methods are synchronized to safeguard the integrity of class variables they use. If you adopt this approach, access class variables only by calling synchronized class methods, even from within methods of the same class. In this model, different threads can freely share class variables because they are protected from simultaneous access and modification. This level of synchronization is not adequate when instances of the class may be used by more than one thread.
- In the third level of synchronization, all class methods and instance methods are synchronized to protect the integrity of all fields. This allows different threads to share objects and classes because the fields have been protected from simultaneous access and modification.

Mini Quiz 11-2

Does synchronizing all class methods ensure the integrity of objects of that class in a multi-threaded program?

Never synchronize a constructor. Constructors are used only when an object is created and it is not possible to construct the same object simultaneously on two different threads. Therefore, qualifying a constructor with the keyword synchronized is an error.

When you override a synchronized method, you do not have to synchronize the method in the subclass. The superclass method remains synchronized, even if the subclass method is not synchronized. The Java programming language has no rules about overriding synchronized methods beyond the usual rules about overriding methods.

Mini Quiz 11-3

Can you remember what parts of an overriding method definition must match the equivalent parts of the overridden method?

Synchronizing Methods of Inner Classes

Inner classes can complicate the synchronization of methods. In Chapter 9, you saw that an inner class has access to the fields of the enclosing instances and that several inner class objects can share the same enclosing instance. Therefore, you should design inner class objects in such a way that they do not undermine the synchronization of the methods of the enclosing instances.

There is no special relationship between the synchronized methods of an inner class and its enclosing class. As a result, simply qualifying the methods of the inner and enclosing classes with the synchronized keyword does not provide proper synchronization between them. Using such an approach allows one thread to call a method of the enclosing class while another thread calls a method of the inner class. Potentially, these methods may access and modify the same fields.

The solution is straightforward, if not automatic. The methods of the inner class that access the fields of the enclosing class can use a synchronized statement to obtain a lock on the enclosing instance before accessing or modifying the fields of the enclosing instance.

In the following example, both the inner and enclosing classes have methods for accessing the name field:

```
package java4cpp.threads;
/** Enclosing and inner classes to demonstrate how to
  * synchronize methods between them.
  */
public class Enclosing {
   private String name = "";
   /** get the name value
     * @return the name
     */
```

```
   public synchronized String getName() {
      return name;
   }
   /** set the name value
     * @param s the input name value
     */
   public synchronized void setName( String s ) {
      name = s;
   }
   /** Example inner class
     */
   public class Insider {

      /** convert the name to all upper case
        */
      public void upperCaseName() {
         synchronized( Enclosing.this ) {
            name = name.toUpperCase();
         }
      }
   }
   /** Test method for the class
     * @param args not used
     */
   public static void main( String[] args ) {
      Enclosing enc = new Enclosing();
      enc.setName( "Maria" );
      Insider ins = enc.new Insider();
      ins.upperCaseName();
      System.out.println( enc.getName() );
   }
}
```

In this example, the methods of the inner class use a synchronized statement to obtain a lock on the enclosing instance, `Enclosing.this`, before accessing the name field and changing it.

Do the methods of the inner class need the synchronized qualifier in addition to the synchronized statement? In this simple case, the answer is no, because the inner class does not define any fields of its own and all synchronization is focused on the enclosing class. In general, use the synchronized qualifier to ensure that methods of the inner classes are synchronized when fields of the inner class are used.

When methods of inner and outer classes are both synchronized, the principle of hierarchical locking specifies that the inner class acquires the lock first. **Hierarchical locking** is a design principle that reduces the potential for deadlock.

Communicating Between Threads

In multithreaded programs, you need some form of interthread communication so that threads can notify each other when conditions change. You often want threads to pass messages to each other to wait or to stop waiting because a condition has been satisfied. Some of the methods for interthread communication are built into the Object class.

Class	java.lang.Object
Purpose	The common ancestor class **Object** defines the common behavior of all classes.
Methods	■ **void wait()** **void wait(long** *timeout* **)** **void wait(long** *timeout*, **int** *nanoseconds* **)** The **wait** methods put the current thread object into a blocked state. The method must own the lock when it calls **wait**. This method call releases the lock. If you do not specify a time period, the thread waits until notified by another thread. You can specify a timeout period, in milliseconds, after which the thread stops waiting, regardless of whether it has been notified. You can also specify a number of nanoseconds to add to the wait period. ■ **void notify()** The **notify** method wakes up a single thread that is blocked because it is in a wait state. The thread is put into a ready-to-run state but does not automatically start running. A synchronized method must still wait for the lock on the class or object. ■ **void notifyAll()** The **notifyAll** method sends wake-up messages to all threads waiting for the lock. All the threads go into a runnable state, but only one can actually acquire the lock and start running. So which thread actually gets control? The JVM selects the thread to run. It may be the one that has been waiting longest, but there is no guarantee and you should not base the logic of your application on any assumptions about the order in which the JVM gives locks to threads. The other threads that have been awakened from their **wait** calls will continue as soon as they can reacquire the lock. In other words, there is no need to notify them again unless they call **wait** again.

You can use these methods for objects within single-threaded applications. However, there is no gain unless you are designing a class for use in either single-threaded or multithreaded programs.

The wait, notify, and notifyAll methods are final methods of the **Object** class. You cannot override them and can rest assured that no other class has overridden them. You can call these methods for a particular object only when the current thread has a lock on the object. Otherwise, the JVM throws an IllegalMonitorStateException. In this context, the term **monitor** refers to the locking mechanism.

The following program demonstrates correct and incorrect use of the notifyAll method:

```
package java4cpp.threads;
/** A class to demonstrate the run-time error that
  * occurs if wait, notify, or notifyAll are used
  * when no lock has been obtained.
  */
public class ShowThreadError {
   private int value;
   /** Set the value of an object
     * This method is synchronized
     * @param v the object's new value
     */
   public synchronized void setValue( int v ) {
      value = v;
      doTheNotificationThing();  // okay here
   }
   /** Get the value of the object
     * This method is synchronized
     * @return the object's value
     */
   public synchronized int getValue() {
      return value;
   }
   /** Notify waiting objects of a change
     * This method is not synchronized
     */
   public void doTheNotificationThing() {
      notifyAll();
   }
   /** Test method for the class
     * @param args not used
     */
   public static void main( String[] args ) {
      ShowThreadError t = new ShowThreadError();
      t.setValue( 10 );
      System.out.println( "value has been set to "
                          + t.getValue() );
      // the next statement causes a run-time error
      t.doTheNotificationThing();
   }
}
```

In the following output, some lines have been split and the indenting has been modified to fit on the printed page:

```
value has been set to 10
java.lang.IllegalMonitorStateException:
   current thread not owner
   at
   java4cpp.threads.ShowThreadError.
      doTheNotificationThing(ShowThreadError.java:32)
   at
   java4cpp.threads.ShowThreadError.
       main(ShowThreadError.java:45)
```

This program has only one thread, but can still use the locking mechanism for the `ShowThreadError` object that is created in the main method. If this class is used in a multithreaded application, the accessor method `getValue` and mutator method `setValue` cannot run at the same time on more than one thread.

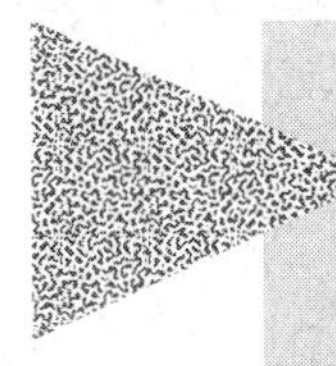

Mini Quiz 11-4

Notice that the method `doTheNotificationThing`, which calls notifyAll, is not synchronized. Why is this method ever allowed to call notifyAll?

Hint: What is different about the methods on the call chain when the call of notifyAll succeeds and when it throws an exception?

Making Threads Wait

The wait method suspends execution of the thread and releases the lock that the thread holds on the object for which wait is called. Call this method when your code must wait for a condition to be satisfied before it can continue. For example, your method may be waiting for input that is not yet available or for a numeric value to reach a certain threshold. For efficiency and to help avoid deadlock, you should call wait to suspend the thread, release the lock that it has on the object, and let other threads run during what otherwise might be wasted processor cycles.

Usually, the thread remains suspended until you call the notify or notifyAll method for the object from another thread. You can call wait with a time-out as an alternative to calling sleep, or use the time-out as a fail-safe measure in case the thread is not always notified as you intended.

Typically you put a call to wait in a loop, in the following form:

```
while  ( condition ) {
  wait();
}
```

Using a loop is the safest approach. The thread may be awakened for many different reasons, and you should not assume that the value of the condition has changed. The while loop gives you an opportunity to check the reason you were waiting every time you regain control, and wait again if the condition is still true.

Threads release locks when they call wait. Take care not to create opportunities for deadlock when you call wait. Consider what can happen when you program to a design that allows access to one class, called (for example) B, only from synchronized methods of another class, called A. Suppose a synchronized method of A calls a synchronized method of B. All is well until the thread in which the method of B runs calls wait. The call of wait releases the lock on the instance of B, but the lock on the instance of A remains. Deadlock can result, because the synchronized methods of A are locked out and no other methods can access B to wake up the blocked thread.

Waking a Single Thread

You can call notify to wake up a thread. You cannot specify which thread should be given control. The JVM decides what thread to notify. This method is most useful when there is only one condition on which threads may be waiting.

Calling notify is more efficient than notifyAll, but has the potential of waking up a thread that should not be given control of the object at that moment while leaving a thread that should have been awakened waiting. When you use notify, be careful that deadlock is not a possible outcome.

Waking All Threads

The notifyAll method wakes up all waiting threads for the object. If different threads are waiting on different conditions, you should call this method rather than notify. The threads should each check their conditions. At least one thread should be able to continue, and threads whose conditions are not yet satisfied should use the wait method to return to the blocked state.

It is important to note that even though more than one thread may be awakened by the notifyAll method, only one can obtain the lock for the object and be allowed to execute.

An Example of Communicating Between Threads

The next example is a relatively long program. Setting up a multithreaded program often involves several classes. The sample program is a simple banking application. For demonstration purposes, it maintains a bank account and performs deposits and withdrawals against the same bank account on separate threads. It uses the wait method to force a withdrawal to wait until there is enough money in an account to maintain a positive bank balance. The program calls notifyAll whenever the bank balance changes so that all threads waiting on that bank account object are informed of the change and can evaluate the situation to determine whether or not they can proceed.

The first of four classes encapsulates a bank account:

```
package java4cpp.threads;
/** A class to demonstrate wait and notify methods
  */
public class BankAccount {
   private int balance = 0;
   private boolean isOpen = true;
   /** The method withdraws an amount from the
     * account. If funds are insufficient, it will
     * wait until the funds are available or the
     * account is closed.
     * @param amount The amount to be withdrawn from
     *    the account
     * @return true if the withdrawal is successful,
     *    false otherwise
     * @exception InterruptedException If another
     *    thread calls the <b>interrupt</b> method
     */
   public synchronized boolean withdraw( int amount )
               throws InterruptedException {
      while ( amount > balance && isOpen() ) {
         System.out.println( "Waiting for "
                             + "some money ..." );
            wait();
      }
      boolean result = false;
      if ( isOpen() ) {
         balance -= amount;
         result = true;
      }
      return result;
   }
   /** The method to deposit an amount into the
     * account, provided that the account is open.
     * When the deposit is successful, it will notify
     * all waiting operations that there is now more
     * money in the account
     * @param amount The amount to be deposited into
     *    the account
     * @return true if the deposit is successful,
     *    false otherwise
     */
```

```
   public synchronized boolean deposit( int amount ) {
      if ( isOpen() ) {
         balance += amount;
         notifyAll();
         return true;
      } else {
         return false;
      }
   }
   /** Check to see if the account is open
     * @return true if it is open, otherwise false
     */
   public synchronized boolean isOpen() {
      return isOpen;
   }
   /** Close the bank account */
   public synchronized void close() {
      isOpen = false;
      notifyAll();
   }
}
```

The BankAccount class has the following characteristics:

- The methods deposit and withdraw are synchronized instance methods. Therefore, the JVM applies a lock to the BankAccount object for which they are called.
- If the account has insufficient funds, the method withdraw calls wait and prints a message. Because withdraw calls wait, an InterruptedException can occur, and must be listed in the throws clause.
- The deposit method calls notifyAll to alert all threads whenever the balance in the account changes.

The methods isOpen and close are also synchronized. isOpen is used simply to check whether transactions are allowed on a BankAccount object, and returns true until the method close is called to close an account. The close method is synchronized so that it can call notifyAll to stop any transactions that are in progress when the account is closed, and to prevent the account from being closed in the middle of a transaction or while another thread is checking to see if it is open.

Here is the thread that makes deposits. It contains a class called Saver that implements Runnable. Saver operates on a BankAccount object that is passed as an argument to the constructor.

```
package java4cpp.threads;
/** A class to demonstrate wait and notify methods
  */
public class Saver implements Runnable {
   private BankAccount account;
   /** Class constructor method
```

```
      * @param ba The bank account where this saver
      *    puts the money
      */
   public Saver( BankAccount ba ) {
      account = ba;
   }
   /** The method the saver uses to put away money */
   public void run() {
      while( account.isOpen() ) {
         try {
            if ( account.deposit( 100 ) ) {
               System.out.println(
               "$100 successfully deposited." );
            }
            Thread.currentThread().sleep( 1000 );
         } catch ( InterruptedException iex ) {
            // display the exception, but continue
            System.err.println( iex );
         }
      }
   }
}
```

The purpose of these classes is to demonstrate how the threads interact, rather than how a banking application should be designed. The run method of the `Saver` class tries repeatedly to deposit $100, as long as the account is open. After making a deposit, run sleeps for a second. The reason for the sleep is to stagger deposits and withdrawal transactions for demonstration purposes. If an InterruptedException is thrown while the thread sleeps, and that exception awakens the thread, the catch block catches but ignores the exception.

The following listing features the thread that makes withdrawals. It contains a class called `Spender` that extends Thread. It also could have implemented Runnable like the `Saver` thread, but extends Thread to demonstrate both techniques. Like the `Saver` class, `Spender` operates on a `BankAccount` object that is passed as an argument to the constructor.

```
package java4cpp.threads;
/** A class to demonstrate wait and notify methods
  */
public class Spender extends Thread {
   private BankAccount account;
   /** Class constructor method
     * @param ba The bank account from which
     *    this spender takes the money
     */
   public Spender( BankAccount ba ) {
      account = ba;
   }
```

```
    /** The method the spender uses
      *  to take out money
      */
    public void run() {
       while( account.isOpen() ) {
          try {
             if ( account.withdraw( 500 ) ) {
                System.out.println(
                "$500 successfully withdrawn." );
             }
             sleep( 1000 );
          } catch ( InterruptedException iex ) {
             // display any interruptions but continue
             System.err.println( iex );
          }
       }
    }
}
```

Like the Saver class, the Spender class is not designed to model realistic banking activity. The run method of the Spender class tries repeatedly to withdraw $500 as long as the account is open. Like a Saver object, a Spender sleeps for a second after each withdrawal, and catches but ignores exceptions thrown during the sleep period.

Here is the test class for the application. The main method creates a BankAccount object, ba. Then it creates and starts a Spender thread named spenderThread for the account ba. A Saver object named aSaver is created for the account ba and put into a Thread object called saverThread. The saver thread is also started.

```
package java4cpp.threads;
/** A class to demonstrate wait and notify methods
  */
public class Banking {
   /** The test method for the class
     * @param args[0] Time in seconds for which
     *    this banking process should run
     */
   public static void main( String[] args ) {
      BankAccount ba = new BankAccount();
      // create the spender thread
      Spender spenderThread = new Spender( ba );
      // create the saver thread which is a two-step
      // process because Saver implements Runnable
      Saver aSaver = new Saver( ba );
      Thread saverThread = new Thread( aSaver );
      spenderThread.start();
      saverThread.start();
```

```
        int time;
        if ( args.length == 0 ) {
           time = 10000;
        } else {
           time = Integer.parseInt( args[0] ) * 1000;
        }
        try {
           Thread.currentThread().sleep( time );
        } catch ( InterruptedException iex ) {
           /* ignore it */
        }
        // close the bank account
        ba.close();
     }
}
```

The threads are preprogrammed to deposit and withdraw money regularly, so the main thread can go to sleep. By default, it sleeps for 10 seconds, but you can specify a different time interval in a command-line argument. Like `deposit` and `withdraw`, main catches and ignores any exceptions that might wake it up during the sleep period.

When the sleep period ends, main wakes up and closes the bank account. This will, in turn, cause the other threads to end.

You can run the program for 12 seconds by issuing the following command:

```
java java4cpp.threads.Banking 12
```

Then, the output may be as follows:

```
Waiting for some money ...
Waiting for some money ...
$100 successfully deposited.
Waiting for some money ...
$100 successfully deposited.
Waiting for some money ...
$100 successfully deposited.
Waiting for some money ...
$100 successfully deposited.
$500 successfully withdrawn.
$100 successfully deposited.
Waiting for some money ...
$100 successfully deposited.
Waiting for some money ...
Waiting for some money ...
$100 successfully deposited.
Waiting for some money ...
$100 successfully deposited.
Waiting for some money ...
$100 successfully deposited.
```

```
$500 successfully withdrawn.
$100 successfully deposited.
Waiting for some money ...
Waiting for some money ...
$100 successfully deposited.
Waiting for some money ...
$100 successfully deposited.
```

Grouping Threads

The Java platform lets you separate or gather (depending on your point of view) your threads into groups. The advantages of creating thread groups are the following:

- Thread objects in separate groups can be protected from each other.
- Some Thread operations are simplified if you perform them on an entire group at once. Do this rather than iterate through a list of threads and perform the same operation on each of them.

For example, you can group sets of threads that load images from files or perform network operations. Then you can assign the same priority to the entire group of threads with one method call, or interrupt all threads involved in an operation when the user clicks a Stop button you include in your GUI.

Most APIs that C++ programmers use for threads have no features equivalent to thread groups. You may find the ability to categorize threads and create groups for different kinds of activities very handy in several situations that occur more often in programs written for the Java platform than in C++ environments.

Use the ThreadGroup class to create and manipulate groups of threads.

Class	java.lang.ThreadGroup
Purpose	A **ThreadGroup** object represents a set of threads. It can include other groups and you can build up a hierarchical structure of thread groups. Each **Thread** object can access information about its own group or its subgroups, but not about the parent groups, if any exist, or any other groups.
Constructors	■ **ThreadGroup(String** *name* **)** **ThreadGroup(ThreadGroup** *parent*, **String** *name* **)** When you create a thread group, you must specify the name of the group as a **String**. You cannot change the name after creating the group. If the new group is to be a subgroup of an existing group, supply the object reference for the parent group as the first argument of the constructor.
Methods	■ **int activeCount()** The **activeCount** method returns an estimate of the number of active threads in the group.

- **int activeGroupCount()**
  The **activeGroupCount** method returns an estimate of the number of groups in the current group.

- **void checkAccess()**
  The **checkAccess** method is a security manager and is called by several other methods in the **ThreadGroup** class. If the thread does not have permission to modify the group, this method throws the exception **SecurityException**.

- **int enumerate(Thread[]** *list* **)**
  int enumerate(Thread[] *list*, **boolean** *recurse* **)**
  int enumerate(ThreadGroup[] *list* **)**
  int enumerate(ThreadGroup[] *list*, **boolean** *recurse* **)**
  The **enumerate** method copies object references for every active thread or thread group into the specified array. You should call **activeCount** or **activeGroupCount** before calling **enumerate,** and pass an array that has enough entries. If you supply a **boolean** argument with the value **true**, all threads or groups in subgroups of the current group are included, recursively. Due to the dynamic nature of threads, it is possible for the number of threads and groups to change between calling **activeCount** or **activeGroupCount** and **enumerate**. It is wise to allocate an array larger than required because the list of threads will be truncated without any error indication if the array is too small.

- **int getMaxPriority()**
  The **getMaxPriority** method returns the highest priority value allowed for the threads in the group.

- **String getName()**
  The **getName** method returns the name of the group.

- **ThreadGroup getParent()**
  The **getParent** method returns an object reference to the group that is the parent of the current group, or **null** if there is no parent group.

- **boolean isDaemon()**
  The **isDaemon** method returns **true** if the group is a daemon thread group, or **false** otherwise.

- **void list()**
  Call the **list** method to output information that is useful for debugging to the stream **System.out**.

- **void resume()**
  The **resume** method resumes all threads in the group.

- **void setDaemon(boolean** *daemon* **)**
  Call the **setDaemon** method with a **boolean** value that establishes whether the group is a daemon group.

- **void setMaxPriority(int *priority*)**
  Call **setMaxPriority** to set the highest priority value allowed for the threads in the group.
- **void stop()**
  The **stop** method stops all threads in the group.
- **void suspend()**
  The **suspend** method suspends all threads in the group.

Beginning with version 1.2 of the Java platform, the ThreadGroup **methods** suspend, resume, **and** stop **are deprecated for the same reasons that the methods with the same names are deprecated in the** Thread **class.**

ThreadGroup objects provide security because a thread is allowed to modify another thread only if both threads are in the same group, or if the modified thread is in a group that is nested within the group of the modifying thread. For example, if a thread calls the setPriority method to lower the priority of a Thread object in another group that is not a subgroup, an exception is thrown.

Every thread belongs to a group. By default, a new thread is placed in the same group as the thread that created it. When you create a thread, you can assign it to a different group by supplying a ThreadGroup reference to the group as an argument to the constructor for the Thread object. After a thread has been created, you cannot change its group.

The next sample program creates two ThreadGroup objects and creates one thread in each group. This program also demonstrates some other features of the Java programming language that you can use in multithreaded programs but which were not used in the earlier examples in this chapter.

```
package java4cpp.threads;
import java.io.*;
/** A class to demonstrate threads and piped streams
  */
public class PlumbingThreads implements Runnable {
   private PipedInputStream pipeIn;
   private PipedOutputStream pipeOut;
   /** Create a PlumbingThreads object to connect with
     * an existing PipedOutputStream
     */
   public PlumbingThreads( PipedOutputStream p ) {
      pipeOut = p;
   }
   /** Create a PlumbingThreads object to connect with
     * an existing PipedInputStream
     */
```

```
public PlumbingThreads( PipedInputStream p ) {
   pipeIn = p;
}
/** Read from standard input and echo
  * the characters to the output pipe
  * @exception IOException general I/O error
  */
public void sendKeystrokes() throws IOException {
   int c;
   while ( ( c = System.in.read() ) != -1 ) {
      pipeOut.write( c );
   }
   pipeOut.close();
}
/** Read characters from the input pipe
  * and echo them to standard out
  * @exception IOException general I/O error
  */
public void receiveKeystrokes() throws IOException {
   int c;
   while ( ( c = pipeIn.read() ) != -1 ) {
      System.out.write( c );
   }
   pipeIn.close();
}
/** The workings of the threads
  */
public void run() {
   try {
      // determine if this is an input or
      // output thread and go to work
      if ( pipeIn != null ) {
         receiveKeystrokes();
      } else if ( pipeOut != null ) {
         sendKeystrokes();
      }
   } catch ( IOException ioe ) {
      System.err.println( ioe );
   }
}
/** The test method for the class
  * @param args not used
  */
public static void main( String[] args ) {
   try {
      // create the input and output pipes
```

```
            PipedInputStream istream
               = new PipedInputStream();
            PipedOutputStream ostream
               = new PipedOutputStream( istream );
            // construct the plumbing threads,
            // specifying the newly created pipes
            PlumbingThreads in
               = new PlumbingThreads( istream );
            PlumbingThreads out
               = new PlumbingThreads( ostream );
            // put the threads into separate groups
            ThreadGroup inputGroup
               = new ThreadGroup( "input thread group" );
            ThreadGroup outputGroup
               = new ThreadGroup( "output thread group" );
            // construct threads with existing
            // plumbing threads
            Thread inputThread
               = new Thread( inputGroup, in,
                             "input pipe" );
            Thread outputThread
               = new Thread( outputGroup, out,
                             "output pipe" );
            // start the threads and let them go!
            inputThread.start();
            outputThread.start();
         } catch ( IOException ioe ) {
            System.err.println( ioe );
         }
      }
   }
```

The class PlumbingThread implements Runnable and does not extend Thread.

PlumbingThread objects communicate through a pipe. If the argument of the constructor is a PipedInputStream object, the thread reads from the pipe. If the argument of the constructor is a PipedOutputStream object, the thread writes to the pipe. Notice how the run method determines which end of the pipe is attached to the PlumbingThread object.

The main method creates two PlumbingThread objects, in and out. Then, main also creates two ThreadGroup objects, inputGroup and outputGroup, and the Thread objects inputThread and outputThread. The constructor of Thread is called with three arguments:

- The ThreadGroup in which to create the thread
- The Runnable object
- A String that becomes the name of the thread

Finally, main starts the two threads. What they actually do is trivial. The input thread reads characters from System.in and puts them into the pipe. The output thread reads characters from the pipe and writes them to System.out.

The only complication that can occur is an IOException, which can be thrown during a read or write operation. The run method of PlumbingThread can catch the exception and print a message.

SUMMARY

This chapter shows how to create threads, and gives some techniques for synchronizing threads and performing interthread communication.

A class can run as a separate thread if it extends the Thread class or implements the Runnable interface. The Thread class provides the full infrastructure for multithreading, and implements Runnable.

All classes that implement Runnable must implement the method run. This method is the entry point for the thread. Your multithreaded program must call Thread.start to launch all but the main thread. The Thread class provides many more methods that you can call to control your threads, including stop, suspend, resume, yield, sleep, and setPriority.

The major part of programming for multithreading is ensuring that your threads do not interfere with each other or go into deadlock by all entering a wait state. The Java programming language has features to help, but you are responsible for that ensuring your threads do not corrupt each other or create deadlock.

You can declare variables to be volatile if other threads may change them. Do this if optimization may generate code that could lose or ignore the changes made to the variables on other threads.

Declare instance methods of a class with the keyword synchronized if only one thread at a time should be able to execute the method against a particular object. The synchronized qualifier on an instance method indicates that a thread must have a lock on the object before it can use the method on the object. While a synchronized method is active, no other synchronized methods defined for the same object can be executed until the lock becomes available.

Declare a class method with synchronized if only one thread at a time should be able to execute the method. In addition, no other synchronized class methods defined for the same class can run while the method is active. Use both the synchronized and static qualifiers to indicate that a thread must have a lock on the class before it can use a method. Object and class locks are independent.

Whether you should choose to synchronize no methods, class methods, or all class and instance methods depends upon how classes and objects are shared between threads.

There is no special relation between the synchronized methods of an inner class and its enclosing class. If a method of an inner class needs to participate in the synchronization of fields in the enclosing class, it should use a synchronized statement to obtain a lock for the enclosing class instance.

You can program one form of interthread communication by calling the methods wait, notify and notifyAll. These are final methods defined in the Object class.

Call the method wait if a thread reaches a condition in which it cannot continue. This method suspends the thread and gives other threads a chance to run. The best way to call wait is in a loop with the following form:

while (*condition*) { wait() }

One thread can wake up another thread waiting for a lock on the same object by calling notify. It is safer to call notifyAll than notify. However, notifyAll is less efficient because it wakes up all threads that are waiting on a particular lock. Each thread can either call wait again or continue processing. Use notifyAll to reduce the risk of deadlock.

For greater security and convenience, you can collect Thread objects into ThreadGroup objects.

This chapter includes three example programs that demonstrate many features of the Java programming language that support multithreading. The last program also used a pipe to transfer data between threads. The sample code shows some common exceptions that can be thrown during multithreaded programs.

QUESTIONS

1. Which of the following qualifiers is applied to a method to indicate that it requires exclusive access to an object or class? Select the best answer.

a. volatile
b. final
c. transient
d. synchronized
e. static

2. Which method is used to initiate the execution of a Thread? Select the best answer.

a. any Thread constructor
b. start
c. go
d. run
e. begin

3. Examine the following code:

```
public class Quiz11_3 {
   // -X-
}
```

Which of the following definitions are valid when placed at the line marked `-X-` ? Select all that apply.

a. `public synchronized Quiz11_3() {}`
b. `private synchronized void b() {}`
c. `public volatile void c() {}`
d. `public static synchronized void d() {}`
e. `public static volatile void d() {}`

4. In which of the following classes are the methods wait, notify, and notifyAll defined? Select all that apply.
   a. Thread
   b. Runnable
   c. ThreadGroup
   d. System
   e. Object

5. Examine the following code:

```
public class Quiz11_5 extends Thread {
   private int limit;
   public Quiz11_5( int l ) {
      limit = l;
   }
   public void run() {
      int i;
      for( i = 0; i <= limit - 1; i++ ) {
         System.out.print( i + ", " );
      }
      System.out.println( i );
   }
   public static void main( String[] args ) {
      Quiz11_5 x = new Quiz11_5( 5 );
      x.run();
   }
}
```

   Which of the following statements are true when the code is compiled and run? Select all that apply.
   a. The compiler rejects the definition of the run method because it does not have the synchronized keyword.
   b. Compilation is successful and the output is

      ```
      0, 1, 2, 3, 4, 5
      ```

   c. The output of the program is written using a different thread than the thread executing the main method.
   d. The compiler rejects the class definition because `Quiz11_5` does not implement the Runnable interface.
   e. The output of the program is written using the same thread as executes the main method.

6. Which of the following methods are defined in the Runnable interface? Select all that apply.
   a. start
   b. run
   c. stop
   d. suspend
   e. resume

7. Examine the following code:

```
public class Quiz11_7 implements Runnable {
   private int limit;
   public Quiz11_7( int l ) {
      limit = l;
   }
   public void run() {
      int i;
      for( i=0; i <= limit - 1; i++ ) {
         System.out.print( i + ", " );
      }
      System.out.println( i );
   }
   public static void main( String[] args ) {
      Quiz11_7 x = new Quiz11_7( 5 );
      Thread t = new Thread( x );
      t.start();
   }
}
```

Which of the following statements are true when the code is compiled and run? Select all that apply.

a. The compiler rejects the definition of the run method because it does not have the synchronized keyword.

b. Compilation is successful and the output is

   `0, 1, 2, 3, 4, 5.`

c. The output of the program is written using a different thread than the one executing the main method.

d. The output of the program is written using the same thread as the one executing the main method.

e. The compiler rejects the expression `new Thread( x )` because the Thread class does not have any constructor that takes a `Quiz11_7` object as a parameter.

8. What kind of thread will the JVM stop if only threads of that kind are running?

9. Examine the following code:

```
public class Quiz11_9 {
   private String name;
   private int count;
   public Quiz11_9( String n, int c ) {
      name = n;
      count = c;
   }
   public static void main( String[] args ) {
      // -X-   }}
```

Which of the following statements are valid synchronized blocks if placed at the line marked `-X-`?

a. `synchronized {}`

b. `synchronized ( String ) {}`

c. `synchronized ( a ) {}`

d. `synchronized ( a.name ) {}`

e. `synchronized ( a.count ) {}`

10. Examine the following code:

```
public class Quiz11_10 {
   public Quiz11_10() throws InterruptedException {
      // A
   }
   public void f1() throws InterruptedException {
      // B
   }
   public static void f2()
                          throws InterruptedException {
      // C
   }
   private void f3() throws InterruptedException {
      // D
   }
   public synchronized void f4()
                          throws InterruptedException {
      // E
      f3();
   }
}
```

Which of the locations marked within the class definition are valid locations from which the wait method can be called?

a. A

b. B

c. C

d. D

e. E

EXERCISES

Debugging

1. Correct all the errors in the following program:

```
package java4cpp.questions.c11;
public class Debug11_1 {
   private int count;
```

```
    public Debug11_1( int c ) {
        count = c;
    }
    public void run() {
        int powerOf2 = 1;
        for( int i=1; i < count; i++ ) {
            powerOf2 = 2*powerOf2;
            System.out.println( powerOf2 );
        }
    }
    public static void main( String[] args ) {
        Debug11_1 x = new Debug11_1( 10 );
        x.start();
    }
}
```

2. Correct all the errors in the following program, but do not change the fact that the class implements the Runnable interface:

```
package java4cpp.questions.c11;
public class Debug11_2 implements Runnable {
    private int count;
    public Debug11_2( int c ) {
        count = c;
    }
    public void run() {
        int powerOf2 = 1;
        for( int i=1; i < count; i++ ) {
            powerOf2 = 2*powerOf2;
            System.out.println( powerOf2 );
        }
    }
    public static void main( String[] args ) {
        Debug11_2 x = new Debug11_2( 12 );
        x.start();
    }
}
```

3. Correct all the errors in the following program without removing the synchronized blocks:

```
package java4cpp.questions.c11;
public class Debug11_3 {
    private double balance = 0.0;
    public void increaseBalance( double increase ) {
        synchronized( balance ) {
            balance += increase;
        }
    }
```

```
   public void decreaseBalance( double decrease ) {
      synchronized( balance ) {
         balance -= decrease;
      }
   }
   public static void main( String[] args ) {
      Debug11_3 x = new Debug11_3();
      x.increaseBalance( 100.75 );
      x.decreaseBalance( 50.50 );
   }
}
```

4. Correct the following program so that all methods of the enclosing class and the inner class are synchronized:

```
package java4cpp.questions.c11;
public class Debug11_4 {
   private String name;
   class HomeAddress {
      private String street;
      private String city;
      public String getStreet() {
         return street;
      }
      public String getCity() {
         return city;
      }
      public void setStreet( String s ) {
         street = s;
      }
      public void setCity( String s ) {
         city = s;
      }
   }
   public synchronized String getName() {
      return name;
   }
   public synchronized void setName( String s ) {
      name = s;
   }
   public static void main( String[] args ) {
      Debug11_4 person = new Debug11_4();
      HomeAddress address = person.new HomeAddress();
      person.setName( "Mike Edotsuc" );
      address.setStreet( "23 Elm Street" );
      address.setCity( "Toronto" );
      System.out.println( person.getName() );
      System.out.println( address.getStreet() );
      System.out.println( address.getCity() );
   }
}
```

5. Correct all the errors in the following program:

```
package java4cpp.questions.c11;
public class Debug11_5 extends Thread {
   private int samples;
   private double average;
   public Debug11_5( int s ) {
      samples = s;
   }
   public synchronized void run() {
      java.util.Random r = new java.util.Random();
      double sum = 0.0;
      for( int i=0; i < samples; i++ ) {
         sum += r.nextDouble();
      }
      average = sum/samples;
   }
   public double getAverage() {
      while ( average == 0.0 ) try {
         wait();
      } catch ( InterruptedException ix ) {
         System.out.println( ix );
      }
      return average;
   }
   public static void main( String[] args ) {
      Debug11_5 x = new Debug11_5( 500000 );
      x.start();
      System.out.println( "Average = "
                          + x.getAverage() );
   }
}
```

Complete the Solution

1. Complete the following class definition by defining the main method to create and start a thread that executes the given run method. The main method should let the thread run long enough to print its message about 10 times. The method then should request that the thread stop.

```
package java4cpp.questions.c11;
public class Complete11_1 implements Runnable {
   private String message;
   private int pause;
   private boolean keepGoing = true;
   public Complete11_1( String m, int p ) {
      message = m;
      pause = p;
   }
```

```
      public void requestStop() {
         keepGoing = false;
      }
      public void run() {
         while ( keepGoing ) {
            System.out.println( message );
            try {
               Thread.currentThread().sleep( pause );
            } catch ( InterruptedException ix ) {
               System.out.println( ix );
            }
         }
      }
      public static void main( String[] args ) {
         // Your code here
      }
   }
```

2. Complete the following class definition by having it extend Thread and by adding a run method that counts characters and outputs the result to the console in a fashion similar to what the main method does in the following code.

```
package java4cpp.questions.c11;
import java.io.*;
public class Complete11_2 {
   private String fileName;
   private int numberOfChars;
   public Complete11_2( String fn ) {
      fileName = fn;
   }
   public void countChars() {
      try {
         InputStream istream
            = new FileInputStream( fileName );
         int c;
         int charCount = 0;
         try {
            while ( ( c = istream.read() ) != -1 ) {
               charCount++;
            }
            numberOfChars = charCount;
         } finally {
            istream.close();
         }
      }
      catch( IOException iox ) {
         System.err.println( iox );
      }
   }
   public int getCharCount() {
      return numberOfChars;
   }
```

```
        public static void main( String[] args ) {
            if ( args.length >= 1 ) {
                Complete11_2 x
                    = new Complete11_2( args[0] );
                x.countChars();
                System.out.println( x.getCharCount() );
            } else {
                System.out.println( "Please give a "
                                    + "filename." );
            }
        }
    }
```

3. Beginning with the code from the previous exercise, complete the solution by having the character counting operation take place on a different thread. But instead of having the package-level class extend Thread, add a method called `backgroundCount` that creates an anonymous inner class that extends Thread. The run method of this anonymous inner class should do the same thing as the run method in question 2.

4. Complete the following class definition by providing a definition for the missing inner class `MessageReader` and by completing the method `addMessage`:

```
package java4cpp.questions.c11;
import java.util.Random;
/** Class representing a message queue with one slot
  * The add and get methods are synchronized
  */
public class MessageQueue {
    private String message;
    private boolean keepGoing = true;
    /** Worker class that continuously writes to the
      * message queue and sleeps for a random period
      * of time.
      */
    class MessageWriter extends Thread {
        /** Continuously write, then sleep */
        public void run() {
            int ms;
            Random r = new Random();
            while( keepGoing ) {
                MessageQueue.this.addMessage(
                    "test message" );
                try {
                    ms = (int)( 100 * r.nextDouble() );
                    Thread.currentThread().sleep( ms );
                } catch ( InterruptedException ix ) {
                    // ignore it
                }
            }
        }
    }
    // Add your MessageReader inner class here
```

```
   /** Add a message to the queue, but wait until it
     * is empty
     * @param m the message being added
     */
   public synchronized void addMessage( String m ) {
      // Your code here
   }
   /** Take a message from the queue, but wait until
     * there is something to take
     * @return the message
     */
   public synchronized String getMessage() {
      while ( message == null && keepGoing ) {
         // wait for a message to be placed
         try {
            System.out.println(
               "Waiting to get..." );
            wait();
         } catch( InterruptedException ix ) {
            // ignore it
         }
      }
      String temp = null;
      if ( keepGoing ) {
         temp = message;
         message = null;
      }
      notifyAll();
      return temp;
   }
   public void requestStop() {
      keepGoing = false;
   }
   /** Test method
     * @param args not used
     */
   public static void main( String[] args )
      throws InterruptedException {
      MessageQueue mq = new MessageQueue();
      MessageReader reader = mq.new MessageReader();
      MessageWriter writer = mq.new MessageWriter();
      reader.start();
      writer.start();
      try {
         Thread.currentThread().sleep( 20000 );
      } finally {
         mq.requestStop();
      }
   }
}
```

5. Complete the following class definition by adding code to the main function that will create in separate threads an instance of both the client and server classes. The main method should give the client enough time to send about 20 messages to the server, and then should end.

```
package java4cpp.questions.c11;
import java.io.*;
import java.net.*;
import java.util.StringTokenizer;
public class Complete11_5 {
   private static final int PORT = 8189;
   private boolean keepGoing = true;
   public class Server extends Thread {
      public void run() {
         try {
            System.out.println(
               "Server starting..." );
            ServerSocket ss
               = new ServerSocket( PORT );
            Socket incoming = ss.accept();
            InputStream is
               = incoming.getInputStream();
            InputStreamReader isr
               = new InputStreamReader( is );
            BufferedReader in
               = new BufferedReader( isr );
            OutputStream os
               = incoming.getOutputStream();
            PrintWriter out = new PrintWriter( os );
            String str = in.readLine();
            while( str != null ) {
               System.out.println( "Received> "
                                   + str );
               str = in.readLine();
            }
            incoming.close();
         }
         catch( IOException iox ) {
            System.out.println( iox );
         }
      }
   }
  public class Client extends Thread {
      public void run() {
         PrintWriter out = null;
         try {
            System.out.println(
               "Client starting..." );
            InetAddress target
               = InetAddress.getLocalHost();
```

```
                Socket client
                   = new Socket( target, PORT );
                OutputStream os
                   = client.getOutputStream();
                out = new PrintWriter( os );
                int count = 1;
                while ( keepGoing ) {
                   out.println( "Message " + count++ );
                   out.flush();
                   Thread.currentThread().sleep( 1000 );
                }
             } catch( Exception x ) {
                System.out.println( x );
             } finally {
                if ( out != null ) {
                   out.close();
                }
             }
          }
       }
       public void requestStop() {
          keepGoing = false;
       }
       public static void main( String[] args ) {
          // Your code here
       }
    }
```

Discovery

1. Create a class called `FileWatcher` that can be given several filenames that may or may not exist. The class should start a thread for each filename. Each thread will periodically check for the existence of its file. If the file appears, the thread will write a message to the console and then end. Put all of the threads within a new ThreadGroup object created by the `FileWatcher` class.
2. Rework the `URLMonitor` class you created in response to Discovery Exercise 2 in Chapter 8, "Input, Output, and Networking," to use threads. Allow the user to specify several URLs to be monitored, and create a thread for each one. Every time a change is detected in the URL, write a message to the console. Call this new class `ThreadedURLMonitor`.

CHAPTER

12

Introduction to Graphical User Interfaces

objectives

In this chapter you will:

- Learn the characteristics of a graphical user interface (GUI).
- Discover how the Abstract Windowing Toolkit (AWT) supports creating GUIs and applets in the Java platform.
- Draw on the application or applet window.
- Design GUIs with layouts that dynamically adjust to screen resolution and window size.
- Include predefined components such as text fields, buttons, and multimedia elements in your GUI.
- See how the AWT provides a framework for interacting with the user in event-driven programs.
- Use the AWT as a bridge between your platform-independent programs and system-specific operating-system services.
- Use rapid application development (RAD) tools such as IBM VisualAge for Java to design GUIs visually and quickly.

Introduction

This chapter explains the main elements of a GUI, gives an overview of the Abstract Windowing Toolkit (AWT), and shows by example how to program a GUI using the core classes in the java.awt package. Use it together with Chapter 13, which presents the detailed descriptions for the classes and interfaces that are provided by the AWT.

Software developers make extensive use of tools for rapid application development (RAD) to create timely solutions for business and other application problems, and to be competitive when bringing software products to market. Building GUIs is particularly well suited to RAD techniques. Many proprietary RAD tools are available that provide different forms of visual design aids and code generators. You may find that in practice you use RAD tools extensively not only to design and generate the GUI portion of your programs, but also for many purposes that are beyond the scope of this book, such as the following:

- Accessing databases
- Creating objects that encapsulate business logic
- Supporting networking and distributed applications

To give you an introduction to the world of RAD tools, this chapter includes a brief tutorial on VisualAge for Java. Follow this tutorial for the experience of designing a GUI-based program visually and using a proprietary code generator to build an application that conforms to Sun's 100% Pure Java™ initiative.

The Challenge of Creating GUIs

Modern computer operating systems include presentation services that provide a user with a GUI. As a result, computer users demand application programs that also provide a GUI. One of the great advantages of the Java platform is that its core classes provide the features for building GUIs. Have you been downloading the sources for Java applets or applications that run in a windowing environment, to learn by understanding existing programs? You may be surprised by how much of the code is concerned with the user interface to the applet or application. When a program has a GUI, a large portion of the code must be devoted to servicing the GUI, even to the point where programming the GUI sometimes becomes the dominant part of the code.

If you want to create applets or applications that have a GUI, you must learn how to use the AWT. The AWT makes up one of the largest sets of classes and interfaces in the Java platform. The Toolkit class is the interface between your platform-independent code and the native operating-system services that a GUI must use. As you move your Java source code from platform to platform, the look and feel of components adjust automatically.

You must display your GUI in graphical form on the screen. Up to this point, most of the sample programs have performed console input and output. In other words, they have been command-line programs with the look and feel of operating systems like DOS. The reason for this is simplicity—many aspects of the Java programming language and the packages in the Java platform are better explained when not obscured by complexities of programming for a GUI. You can continue to use the forms of I/O described in Chapter 8 in a program that has a GUI. Files and networks are available to GUI-oriented applications and applets, with the proviso that applets can use these files and networks in limited ways. Programmers often use stream I/O as an aid to debugging and to trace the activities of their classes during the development stage of a GUI-oriented program.

To program a GUI, you must also master the challenging technique of event-driven programming. GUI-oriented programs tend to be more complex than console-oriented programs because they are event-driven. The user initiates most events by moving and clicking the mouse or pressing keys on the keyboard. Unlike command-line programs that operate in a batch processing mode and perhaps pause occasionally to solicit user input, GUI-based programs must always be responsive to the user and must take direction from the user. A GUI can recognize many more kinds of user activities than typing data.

Moving from C++

You may have encountered and even mastered the complexities of programming a GUI in C or C++. If you have, you know that programming in a windowing environment is a challenging problem.

You probably know that part of the problem in C and C++ is that there are no industry standards for programming GUIs. In C, you probably used the operating system's application programming interface (API). As a result, your program is tied to one platform and to proprietary supporting software. Such programs are not portable and must be rewritten to execute on a new platform. In C++, you can use class libraries; the most popular C++ application development packages include class libraries that support programming GUIs. Depending on which library you choose, you do get a measure of portability. For example, VisualAge for C++ includes the IBM Open Class Library (IOC), which not only lets you write C++ source code that is portable among OS/2, Windows, and AIX, but also can give your program the look and feel of the operating system on each of those platforms.

However, the IOC and most other C++ libraries that support GUIs are huge bodies of software. There are hundreds of classes and thousands of member functions for you to learn! To be fair, the sheer size of these libraries is often an indication of the range of features they support. Some, like the IOC, are extremely powerful. How the classes in these libraries work together can be far from simple to master. You have to climb a very steep learning curve even to begin programming a GUI with them.

Compared to large C++ class libraries and the operating system API, the AWT is a relatively intuitive and manageable software package for programming GUIs. All implementations of the Java platform that claim to be standard must support the AWT. The Java platform can truly make a much stronger claim to being architecture-neutral and portable than most C++ GUI-building tools.

How easy is the AWT to learn? It can claim to provide a flexible set of basic GUI-building features with a minimum of complexity. However, there is always a trade-off between simplicity and features. Many features have been added since the original version of the Java platform, and there is a high probability that the AWT will continue to grow in future releases.

The Main Features and Terminology of a GUI

All interactive output and input should pass through the GUI of your program. Therefore, the GUI consists of what the user sees on the screen. It also contains code to deal with user actions such as clicking with the mouse or typing on the keyboard. It must relate those actions properly to the elements displayed in the GUI and perform the appropriate activities in response.

Programming ▶ tip

A good design principle is to try to separate your program's GUI from the program's processing. This goal is very consistent with object-oriented design. Just as you distinguish between the interface to a class and the implementation of the class, you can design the GUI for a program independently from implementing background processing done by that program and the information that the program handles.

This design pattern, known as Model View Controller (MVC), is a proven way to structure your application effectively. In the MVC design model, all logic for an application is separated from visible elements and the controller controls all interactions between them. Conforming to the principles of MVC is very desirable in all GUI-based programs. A full discussion of MVC is beyond the scope of this book

An example of such structuring is when you run the GUI in one thread to give the user a quick response, at least to acknowledge a user action, and then perform more time-consuming tasks, such as file I/O or number crunching, in other threads. The proportion of the program that is part of the GUI depends on the nature and purpose of the program. For applets, which tend to be short and highly interactive, the GUI often makes up most of the code. For an application, the GUI could be a very simple interface to a complex program.

A major part of a GUI is built of components. In the Java platform, **components** are predefined standard elements such as buttons, text fields, windows, and dialog boxes. From using windowed applications, and perhaps from programming them in C++, you may already be familiar with many elements commonly used in GUIs. The core classes in the AWT provide a large repertoire of components. This chapter mentions only a few of the most commonly used kinds of components.

The display space on the screen is also a component. Like all GUI-based applications, a Java application window is a **frame window** that takes on the look of an application window that is native to the operating system. Frame windows have a title and a border, and buttons for closing, minimizing, and maximizing the window. They can contain a menu bar. The browser or applet viewer you are using controls the display space for an applet. Therefore, applets run in a simpler displayable component called a **panel**.

Controls such as check boxes, labels, scrollbars, text areas, dialog boxes, and list boxes are also components. Some components are used individually, such as a button, but others, called **containers**, can contain other components. For example, a **dialog box** is a window that opens to present information to or receive information from the user. A dialog box is both a component and a container, because it can have buttons, text fields, and other components within it. If you have run applications that let you select or enter a filename in a window, you have used **file dialog boxes**. The Java platform has a class for file dialog boxes. Frame windows and panels are other examples of components that are also containers.

You can use one of the core classes that are called **layout managers** to control how the components are arranged within a container. For each container, you select the layout manager that controls the size and position of components within the container. This separation of container classes from layout manager classes gives you the freedom to select the container you want, and then select a layout manager you want. Containers have no built-in limitations on how you can position components within them.

You can also draw directly onto a window or panel. The term **graphics** refers to drawing in the **graphics context** for a component. You can get the graphics context from a window or panel, and then can call methods to draw entities like lines, text, and images. **Images** are graphical objects, such as pictures or icons, stored in a representation known to your implementation of the Java platform.

Painting is the process of actually displaying components, or refreshing the display of components on the screen. Painting can occur when the GUI for an application or an applet starts, when you call methods to redraw the GUI, or when the application or applet window is resized, moved, or exposed on the screen after being covered. Objects of the component classes handle painting themselves. But when you draw directly to a graphics context, you must also handle the painting.

To ensure that a program does not have to wait for every paint operation to complete, the AWT maintains a separate thread for drawing and forwards all paint requests to that thread, the **AWT thread**.

A most important part of programming a GUI is handling events. **Events** can be actions of the user, such as clicking or moving the mouse or pressing keys on the keyboard. **Action events** occur when the user acts upon components. For example, the user may click a check box, select an item from a list, or type characters into a text field. Components encapsulate not only the look of visual elements of the GUI, but also the set of events that the components generate.

You should structure your user interface so that it is directed by events. You do this by providing handlers that react to events that can occur while your program runs. Chapter 6 introduced the concept of handlers in the discussion of catch clauses for exceptions. However, the AWT supports a much broader use of handlers than is used for exceptions. Exception handlers interrupt the usual flow of control to deal with an error or unexpected situation. In a GUI, event handlers let you pass control of the program to the user, so that your program proceeds by responding to user activities.

The mechanism for event handlers is different from that of exception handlers. This mechanism has also been revised since the original version of the Java platform, and now uses a set of interfaces called **listeners**. Each interface is targeted for a specific type of event, such as mouse events or keystroke events. You create handlers for user-initiated events by defining classes that implement the listener interfaces provided by the AWT. A listener interface is similar in concept to the `java.util.Observer` interface that is explained in Chapter 10. The appropriate listener interface method is called automatically whenever the component generates an event. You establish the relationship between each handler and an event by registering the listener with the component for which the event is generated.

Each listener interface with more than one method has a corresponding adapter class. The **adapters** are classes that implement the interfaces in a trivial way by providing empty methods. Thus, you have a choice between implementing a listener or extending an adapter. The advantage of using an adapter is that you can provide implementations for only the events that are of interest and inherit the trivial handlers for the other events from the adapter class.

Version Watch

Programmers use the term 1.0.2 event model to describe how events were handled in the original version of the Java platform. Listeners and the much-improved event model were introduced in version 1.1 of the Java platform.

Programs that use the 1.0.2 event model can still work, but you should use the new model when you develop code. You should not mix the two event models within a single application. Some programmers continued to code applets for the 1.0.2 event model after the release of version 1.1 of the Java platform but before popular browsers supported the new event model.

When you examine the code for existing applets or applications, you should check whether the applet uses the old or the new Java event model. If any of the event handlers implement an interface with a name that ends with "listener" or extend a class, or with a name that ends with "adapter", it is coded for the new event model. The use of the method handleEvent **indicates that the program uses the old event model.**

When you create a GUI, you usually want to conform to the look and feel of the underlying operating system. One great advantage of the Java platform is that it provides this conformance for you automatically. No special coding is required to make components look and act like the equivalent kinds of components in most other programs that run on the same platform. For example, a frame window takes on the look of a native application window. Your program should also react as users expect similar programs to react to events such as resizing the window.

Version Watch

In version 1.2 of the Java platform, support is added for a pluggable look and feel. This makes it possible to use the same look and feel of one platform across all platforms, or you can create your own look and feel.

The Abstract Windowing Toolkit

To program a GUI-oriented application or an applet, you need extensive support from your application development software. The Java platform provides the AWT in the package java.awt and its subpackages. This book cannot cover all the options of such a large package, and you could spend many weeks learning only the AWT. The goal of this chapter and Chapter 13 is to show you the most commonly used features of the AWT. Another factor to bear in mind is whether you ultimately plan to write code based on the AWT, assemble programs by combining JavaBeans, or use RAD tools. Chapter 15 explains what JavaBeans are and how you can reuse them as building blocks for new programs.

Even without listing every class and method, this book can give you a solid enough understanding of the organization and capabilities of the AWT for you to confidently explore the rest of the package on your own. You can experiment with new features as you require or discover them.

The java.awt package and its subpackages comprise a large number of classes. The classes fall into six major categories, as shown in Figure 12-1.

Category	Description
Graphics	This set of classes in **java.awt** encapsulate fonts, colors, images, polygons, and the like.
Components and containers	This set of classes extends **Component** to provide objects such as buttons, check boxes, labels, scrollbars, and text components. The class **Container** extends **Component** for components that can contain other components, such as windows, panels, and dialog boxes.
Layouts managers	To select a predefined strategy for positioning components in a container, set up an association between a class that extends **LayoutManager** or **LayoutManager2** and a container. You can optionally set a wide range of format controls, and let the layout manager dynamically figure out where to put the components. With layout managers, you do not specify coordinate positions for components. To specify actual screen coordinates would make your program inflexible, probably build in dependence on a platform and screen resolution, and perhaps constrain your ability to translate labels into other languages.
Events	This set of classes in the package **java.awt.event** extends **AWTEvent** to encapsulate the information about a user interaction with the application. For example, some classes are **MouseEvent**, **TextEvent**, and **FocusEvent**. Each kind of event has an associated listener interface.
Listeners and adapters	Listeners and adapters handle events. To create a listener, implement one or more of the listener interfaces in the **java.awt.event** package. If you register an instance of a listener with one or more components, one of the listener methods is called whenever an event is generated by a component with which the event is registered. You can extend an adapter class rather than implement a listener. Extending an adapter can be more efficient because you need to override only the methods that are of interest and do not have to provide your own empty methods for the events to be ignored.
Peers	Peers are classes that implement the elements of a GUI on the platform that is host to your Java platform. You do not use these classes directly. Instead, you use the corresponding subclasses of **Component** classes. For example, a button peer on OS/2 uses an OS/2 Presentation Manager button, and on Solaris uses a Motif button. You create a **Button** object and do not worry about the peer class behind the scenes. When your code runs on a different platform from the development platform, the look of components adjusts automatically.

Figure 12-1: Categories of classes in the AWT

Inside the package java.awt, the AWT encapsulates the platform specifics for the implementation of the AWT in the class Toolkit. This class is the bridge between the platform-dependent AWT classes and their corresponding peers. The class does have some useful methods that provide information on the screen size, screen resolution, available fonts, and the like. The File Browser example program in Chapter 13 uses a Toolkit object to copy data to the system clipboard.

The Event Model

The AWT event model takes advantage of a hierarchy of event classes and associated listener interfaces. You can define any class to be an event handler, regardless of its superclass, by implementing a listener interface. Call a method of a component class to register the listener with the component. Chapter 13 describes how to do so and write the handler. When an event that relates to the component occurs, only the registered listeners are notified and passed a copy of the event. If no listeners are registered, the event is not delivered.

The current event model is more efficient and effective than the event model used in the original version of the Java platform. The current model also is consistent with the JavaBeans interface. JavaBeans facilitate encapsulating GUI components in such a way that developers can easily build GUI-based programs, complete with event handling, by loading JavaBeans into tools and connecting them together.

The current event model is a radical redesign of event handling, and was introduced to the AWT in version 1.1 of the Java platform. The original model had only one class, Event, **to encapsulate all events. Components received all their own events. Each component had to determine the nature of an event by checking the field** Event.id, **and then either handle the event or pass it on to the parent container. The programmer had to define** handleEvent **methods to return a boolean value:** true **if the method handled the event, and** false **otherwise. Each event was propagated and passed up the containment hierarchy regardless of whether any class was interested in the event, until a handler returned** true. **The old event model had some serious shortcomings:**

- **It was not compatible with JavaBeans.**
- **Interrogating the** Event.id **field often led to large, awkward switch statements.**
- **To customize event handling, you had to subclass the component and override its event-handling methods.**
- **You could lose events if a handler did not call superclass handler.**

AWT Programs

An excellent way to get a feel for the AWT is by looking at some small sample programs. The programs in this section introduce some of the most common classes in the AWT. You can start to experiment by writing short programs that are similar to these samples, and expand your knowledge by trying to program variations that use different classes and methods.

The sample programs are applications, not applets. Applets almost always use the AWT, and the AWT is very often described in the context of creating applets rather than applications. Chapter 14 explains that the main difference is that applets extend the java.applet.Applet class, and applications with GUIs extend the java.awt.Frame class. Both Applet and Frame are indirect subclasses of Container. A Web browser displays an applet as a panel within the browser window, so that the applet does not have a title bar or minimize, maximize, or close buttons. Also, applets do not have a main method, but are instead controlled by the browser using an event-driven mechanism that is also explained Chapter 14. Apart from these differences, you can use the AWT classes in an applet just as you can in an application.

A Java "Hello World!" Program

The first sample AWT program is a version of the classic starter program that most programmers write when they first work with a new language or programming environment. This program defines the class `HelloWorld`. Because `HelloWorld` is a public class, it is found in a file called HelloWorld.java. The structure of packages mirrors the file system, so you will find this source code in the java4cpp\windows subfolder of the folder in which you unpacked the JAR file java4cpp.jar. This program displays the string "Hello World!" in a window on the screen. As with most applications, the GUI for this program is contained in a frame window, which is an independent window with its own frame, title, and control boxes.

Although this is a very simple program, the code is longer than a command-line version because it contains a minimal GUI:

```
package java4cpp.windows;
import java.awt.Frame;
import java.awt.Graphics;
import java.awt.Window;
import java.awt.event.WindowListener;
import java.awt.event.WindowAdapter;
import java.awt.event.WindowEvent;
/** An example of a very simple windowed program
  */
public class HelloWorld extends Frame {
   /** Class constructor
     * @param is the title to be used for the window
     */
   public HelloWorld( String titleText ) {
      super( titleText );
      addWindowListener( new WindowAdapter() {
            /** End the program when the user
              * closes the window
              */
```

```
                public void
                windowClosing( WindowEvent event ) {
                    Frame.this.dispose();
                    System.exit( 0 );
                }
            }
        );
        setSize( 300, 100 );
        setVisible( true );
    }
    /** Draws the message in the center of the window
      * @param g the component's graphics context
      */
    public void paint( Graphics g ) {
        g.drawString( "Hello World!", 100, 60 );
    }
    /** The test method for the class
      * @param args not used
      */
    public static void main( String[] args ) {
        new HelloWorld( "Hello World! Sample" );
    }
}
```

The output is very similar on all platforms, but does vary in small ways because the frame takes on the appearance and behavior of the application windows of the native operating system. Therefore, your output may look different from Figure 12-2, particularly in the buttons that are specific to the operating system and the borders of the frame.

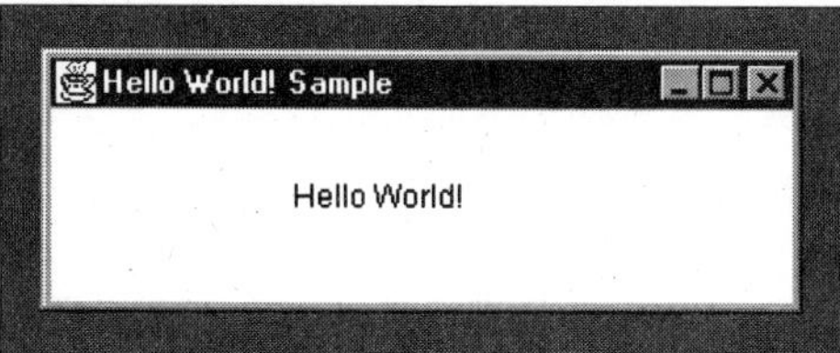

Figure 12-2: Output from the Hello World! program

The Hello World! program is contained in one class, `HelloWorld`. The `HelloWorld` class extends Frame. The Frame class is a component class for frame windows, which are the usual top-level windows in which applications run.

Because it extends Frame, HelloWorld inherits functioning minimize, maximize, and close buttons and a title bar.

```
public class HelloWorld extends Frame {
```

The constructor for HelloWorld has one argument, which is the string to be used in the title bar. It passes the string to the constructor of the superclass Frame so that the string becomes the text in the title bar of the frame window.

```
    public HelloWorld( String titleText ) {
        super( titleText );
```

You do not have to write the code for the event loop that controls a GUI program. The JVM handles that. All you must do is plug in handlers for various events. The next statement is the most involved statement of the Hello World! program, and it deals with the only event of interest to this program: the WINDOW_CLOSING event occurs when the user closes the application window. This event does not automatically terminate execution, but is reported to the Frame object so that the program has an opportunity to close down.

A call of addWindowListener registers an object to listen to window events for the current component. The argument becomes the registered handler for window events. In this call, the handler is an instance of the WindowAdapter class.

```
        addWindowListener( new WindowAdapter() {
                public void
                windowClosing( WindowEvent event ) {
                    Frame.this.dispose();
                    System.exit( 0 );
                }
            }
        );
```

Similar lines of code appear in many GUI-based applications.

Mini Quiz 12-1

What kind of construct is used to create the WindowAdapter object? *Hint:* The object has no name and its class is defined completely within the argument list of the addWindowListener method.

An adapter class is appropriate because this program needs to handle only one of the events for which the WindowListener interface defines handlers. The method windowClosing overrides the default method of the WindowAdapter class to handle the WINDOW_CLOSING event. The method disposes of the current Frame object and then calls System.exit to exit the application.

The constructor of the HelloWorld class also sets the size of its window in pixels, by calling Frame.setSize. The width is 300 pixels and the height 100. The window appears at the upper-left corner of the screen because this constructor does not call Frame.setLocation to override the default location of the Frame object. The constructor must call Frame.setVisible and pass the value true to make the window visible to the user, and to bring the window to the front of other windows.

```
    setSize( 300, 100 );
    setVisible( true );
```

This application must override one method from the Frame class, paint. Use the paint method to draw directly onto a window. Graphical output is actually sent to the graphics context of the window. The paint method provides a context to work with in its argument of type Graphics. The drawing methods are members of the Graphics class.

```
public void paint( Graphics g ) {
   g.drawString( "Hello World!", 100, 60 );
}
```

The Hello World! program never directly calls paint. That is left to the AWT thread. If the window is covered and then exposed while the program is running, the AWT thread automatically calls paint to redisplay of the contents of the window.

Like all drawing methods, drawString is called for the graphics context of the current component. The first argument passes the String object to display, and the second and third arguments specify the position. Positions are expressed in pixels. The first coordinate is the distance in from the leftmost side of the window, and the second is the distance down from the top of the window. Note that (0,0) is the upper-left corner of the window on all platforms. An alternative to using a paint method that calls drawString is to add a label component to the Frame window. No paint method would be required in such a case because the Label object would do its own painting and drawing.

Because the HelloWorld class is an application, it must have a main method. All that main does for this application is create a HelloWindow object and pass the title of the frame window as an argument of the constructor.

```
public static void main( String[] args ) {
   new HelloWorld( "Hello World! Sample" );
}
```

After the Frame object has been created, the application runs until the windowClosing method calls System.exit. The reason is that the JVM creates an AWT thread when the Frame class is instantiated. An application remains active as long as a nondaemon thread is running and the AWT thread is not a daemon thread.

The Three Panels Example

The Hello World! example is about as simple as a GUI program can be. The next program is a bit more complex. It uses layout managers and has buttons and a check box.

The Hello World! program drew directly onto the application Frame window. This program uses a more flexible approach to positioning components on the window than specifying pixel coordinates. It uses Panel objects. The Panel class, like Frame, is subclass of Container, and instances of Panel are the simplest objects that can hold other components. Panels are very widely used to group objects. You can arrange one or more panels within a window using a layout manager.

The next program is called the Three Panels program because it has three Panel objects. The panels are arranged vertically to occupy the top, middle, or bottom slice of a window. Often, event handling deals with user actions such as clicking a button. The Three Panels program demonstrates three buttons and one check box.

Three Panels is a simple application that displays the string "Change the color of this text" across the top panel of the frame window. In the middle panel are three buttons labeled Black, Red, and Green. When the user clicks a button, the sentence above the buttons changes color accordingly. The bottom panel has a check box labeled Disable Changes. The user clicks the check box to disable or enable the buttons.

```
package java4cpp.windows;
import java.awt.*;
import java.awt.event.*;
/** An example class used to demonstrate the basics of
  * creating components such as panels, arranging
  * components using layout objects, and nesting
  * components inside each other.
  */
public class ThreePanels extends Frame {
   private boolean disabled = false;
   private Panel upperPanel, midPanel, lowerPanel;
   private TextField text;
   private Button blackButton, redButton, greenButton;
   private Checkbox disableCheck;
   /** Class constructor method
     * @param titleText Window's title bar text
     */
   public ThreePanels( String titleText ) {
      super( titleText );
      setLayout( new BorderLayout() );
      addWindowListener( new WindowAdapter() {
            /** End the program when the user
              * closes the window
              */
```

```
            public void
            windowClosing( WindowEvent event ) {
               Frame.this.dispose();
               System.exit( 0 );
            }
         }
      );
      ButtonListener aListener = new ButtonListener();
      upperPanel = new Panel();
      upperPanel.setLayout( new BorderLayout() );
      text = new TextField(
         "Change the color of this text" );
      upperPanel.add( text, "Center" );
      midPanel = new Panel();
      midPanel.setLayout( new FlowLayout(
         FlowLayout.CENTER ) );
      blackButton = new Button( "Black" );
      midPanel.add( blackButton );
      blackButton.addActionListener( aListener );
      redButton = new Button( "Red" );
      midPanel.add( redButton );
      redButton.addActionListener( aListener );
      greenButton = new Button( "Green" );
      midPanel.add( greenButton );
      greenButton.addActionListener( aListener );
      lowerPanel = new Panel();
      lowerPanel.setLayout( new FlowLayout(
         FlowLayout.RIGHT ) );
      disableCheck
         = new Checkbox( "Disable changes" );
      lowerPanel.add( disableCheck );
      add( upperPanel, "North" );
      add( midPanel, "Center" );
      add( lowerPanel, "South" );
      pack();
      setVisible( true );
   }
   class ButtonListener implements ActionListener {
      /** Respond to the action events
        * @param evt The window event
        */
      public void actionPerformed( ActionEvent e ) {
         Object source = e.getSource();
         if ( disableCheck.getState() == false ) {
```

```
                if ( source == redButton ) {
                   text.setForeground( Color.red );
                   text.invalidate();
                } else if ( source == greenButton ) {
                   text.setForeground( Color.green );
                   text.invalidate();
                } else if ( source == blackButton ) {
                   text.setForeground( Color.black );
                   text.invalidate();
                }
             }
          }
       }
       /** The test method for the class
         * @param args not used
         */
       public static void main( String[] args ) {
          new ThreePanels( "Three Panels Sample" );
       }
    }
```

The output looks similar to Figure 12-3.

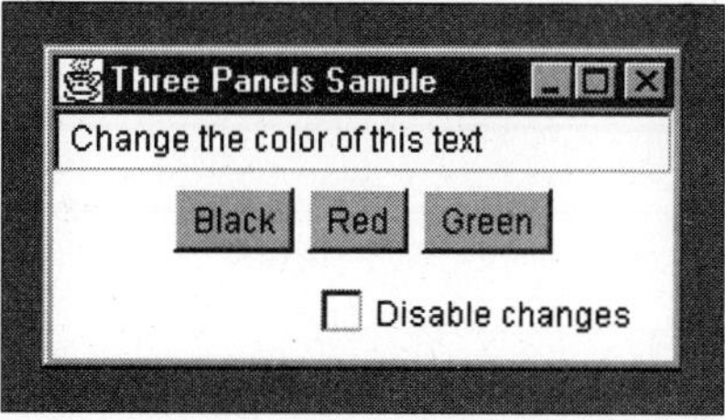

Figure 12-3: Output of the Three Panels application

The class of this application is called `ThreePanels`. Like the Hello World! application, it extends `Frame`. The components used in this application are private fields of the `ThreePanels` class.

```
public class ThreePanels extends Frame {
   private boolean disabled = false;
   private Panel upperPanel, midPanel, lowerPanel;
   private TextField text;
   private Button blackButton, redButton, greenButton;
   private Checkbox disableCheck;
```

Also like the `HelloWorld` class, the constructor of `ThreePanels` passes on the string that becomes the title of the frame window to the constructor of its superclass, Frame. To specify that the layout manager for this class is a border layout, the class calls the setLayout method with a BorderLayout object as the argument.

```
public ThreePanels( String titleText ) {
   super( titleText );
   setLayout( new BorderLayout() );
```

A border layout can contain up to five components arranged as shown on the left in Figure 12-4. This program uses only three components: north, center, and south. Therefore, the west and east drop out, the center component expands, and the arrangement is as shown on the right of Figure 12-4.

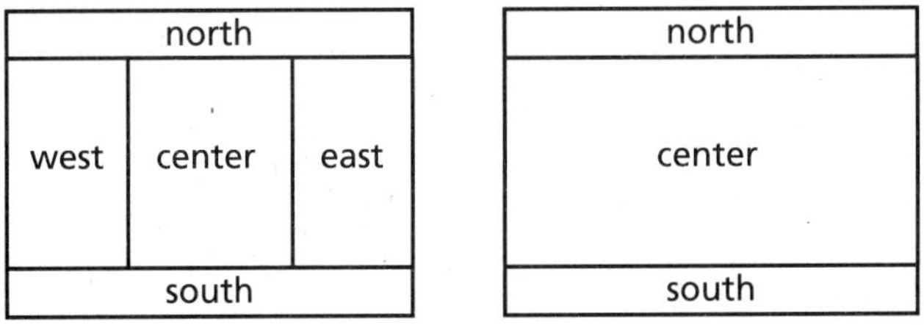

Figure 12-4: Border layouts

The next statement registers and creates a handler for the WINDOW_CLOSING event using the same technique as the Hello World! program:

```
addWindowListener( new WindowAdapter() {
      public void
      windowClosing( WindowEvent event ) {
         Frame.this.dispose();
         System.exit( 0 );
      }
   }
);
```

The next statement creates an instance of the inner class `ButtonListener`, which is defined farther down in the `ThreePanels` class, to handle button-click events. The `ButtonListener` class implements the ActionListener interface.

```
ActionListener aListener = new ButtonListener();
```

The rest of the constructor adds Panel objects to the frame, and components to the panels. First, the constructor assigns one field, `upperPanel`, to a new Panel object, and gives the field a border layout:

```
upperPanel = new Panel();
upperPanel.setLayout( new BorderLayout() );
```

The next object created is a TextField object. The private field `text` is assigned the object reference to the TextField. The TextField class indirectly extends the Component class for objects that hold a single line of text, and the text is passed as a String to the constructor. The method `add` in these lines adds the `text` component to the `upperPanel` container. Here, the argument `"Center"` positions the component in the central area of the upper panel. Because only the center portion of the border layout for the upper panel has contents, the center portion expands to fill the entire area of the upper panel.

```
text = new TextField(
   "Change the color of this text" );
upperPanel.add( text, "Center" );
```

The second of the three panels is assigned to the private field `midPanel`. Unlike the upper panel, `midPanel` has a flow layout. A flow layout places components side by side in the order they are added to the container and wraps onto the next row as required. The argument of the constructor of a FlowLayout object is a constant provided by the FlowLayout class. Here, FlowLayout.CENTER specifies that the rows of components in `midPanel` be centered within the panel:

```
midPanel = new Panel();
midPanel.setLayout( new FlowLayout(
   FlowLayout.CENTER ) );
```

You add most components to containers in a manner similar to the way the three Button objects `blackButton`, `redButton`, and `greenButton` are added to the panel `midPanel` in the following lines. You specify the label that appears on a Button object as the argument of the constructor for the Button object.

To handle button-click events, you must register an ActionListener object with each Button object, by calling the method Button.addActionListener. Here, the `aListener` object of the inner class `ButtonListener` is registered to handle the action events for all three buttons:

```
blackButton = new Button( "Black" );
midPanel.add( blackButton );
blackButton.addActionListener( aListener );
redButton = new Button( "Red" );
midPanel.add( redButton );
redButton.addActionListener( aListener );
greenButton = new Button( "Green" );
midPanel.add( greenButton );
greenButton.addActionListener( aListener );
```

The last of the three panels is assigned to the object reference `lowerPanel`. This panel also has a flow layout, but this flow layout is right-justified. As a result, the Checkbox component labeled "Disable changes" appears on the lower-right of the application frame window.

The Checkbox object `disableCheck` does not need a listener because this application performs no action at the moment the user clicks `disableCheck`.

Instead, the application checks the state of the check box when the user clicks any of the three color buttons.

```
lowerPanel = new Panel();
lowerPanel.setLayout( new FlowLayout(
   FlowLayout.RIGHT ) );
disableCheck
   = new Checkbox( "Disable changes" );
lowerPanel.add( disableCheck );
```

Now that the three panels are complete, the next three statements can add them to the frame window container:

```
add( upperPanel, "North");
add( midPanel, "Center" );
add( lowerPanel, "South");
```

The final statements in this rather long constructor are calls to pack and setVisible. Call pack to give the layout managers a chance to arrange all components for optimal size. When you call pack, the layout managers determine how much space each of the components needs and dynamically adjust the component positions. Call setVisible to make the `ThreePanels` object and all the contained panels and components visible and available for display.

```
pack();
setVisible( true );
```

The `ButtonListener` class implements the ActionListener interface, and implements the actionPerformed method to handle the ActionEvent objects for button clicks. Because the `aListener` object is registered for all the buttons in this application, its actionPerformed method is called automatically when the user clicks any button. The actionPerformed method calls ActionEvent.getSource to get the object reference for the component that is the origin of the event.

```
class ButtonListener implements ActionListener {
   public void actionPerformed( ActionEvent e ) {
      Object source = e.getSource();
```

Mini Quiz 12-2

Can you deduce from this code how many methods the ActionListener interface has?

The method Checkbox.getState returns a boolean value indicating whether the user has clicked the `disableCheck` check box, and an if statement provides the logic to ignore button-click events conditionally. In this case, if statements are also adequate to match the component that is the source of the event to one of the three Button components.

The appropriate action is to set the foreground color for the TextField text by calling the method Component.setForeground. The TextField class inherits this method from the Component class. The class java.awt.Color provides public class variables for many colors, including red, green, and black. Instead of using Color constants, you can alternatively construct a Color object from values for red, green, and blue.

```
if ( disableCheck.getState() == false ) {
   if ( source == redButton ) {
      text.setForeground( Color.red );
      text.invalidate();
   } else if ( source == greenButton ) {
      text.setForeground( Color.green );
      text.invalidate();
   } else if ( source == blackButton ) {
      text.setForeground( Color.black );
      text.invalidate();
   }
}
```

The main method of the ThreePanels class has very little to do. It simply creates a ThreePanels object. This instance of Frame contains all the panels set up in the constructor. The driving force behind the application is the user who triggers events by clicking one of the three color buttons.

```
public static void main( String[] args ) {
  new ThreePanels( "Multiple Panels Sample" );
}
```

Designing a Class Visually

Some proprietary development products include features that can greatly increase your productivity as you develop programs in the Java programming language. Among the most promising tools are those that perform RAD by generating code for you, under your direction. The IBM VisualAge for Java includes a visual Composition Editor that you can use to design your GUI interactively and that generates 100% Pure Java code.

Designing a Class with IBM VisualAge for Java

In the visual Composition Editor, you manipulate classes that conform to the JavaBeans specification. Chapter 15 introduces the concept and usage of JavaBeans. The AWT classes are bean classes, and can use the Composition Editor as a tool for manipulating instances of the AWT classes. You can define your own classes with the Composition Editor in such a way that the generated code also conforms to the JavaBeans specification.

The Composition Editor gives you a palette of beans that encapsulates many of the core classes. You select beans from the palette, drag them with the mouse, and then drop them onto a work surface. VisualAge lets you connect the beans, and represents the connections by drawing arrows between the beans they connect. Connections encapsulate the interactions between the beans.

There are two kinds of beans in the visual Composition Editor:

- **GUI beans** map onto the AWT classes that have graphical representations. These beans represent the components in your GUI. Often, with the Composition Editor, you do not need to do any hand-coding to generate classes based on the AWT.
- **Invisible beans** usually represent logic classes for objects in your program that are not part of the GUI. Use invisible beans for the interface between your GUI and the classes that you create in other ways. For example, if handling the event that occurs when the user clicks a button involves calling a method to process data, you can connect the GUI bean for the button to the invisible bean for a class that does the processing.

In short, you can create whole applets or applications with the Composition Editor. Alternatively, you can create the GUI portion of applications that contains other classes.

Describing the Composition Editor in detail is beyond the scope of this book, but working through a scenario of building a simple application with VisualAge for Java should give you an idea of the power of RAD tools like the Composition Editor.

The Simple Calculator Application

Follow the instructions below to use VisualAge for Java to create a simple calculator application that looks like Figure 12-5.

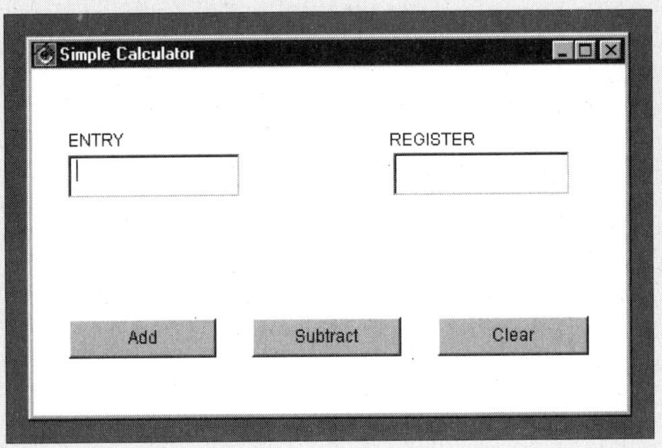

Figure 12-5: The simple calculator application

This simple calculator has one text field, under the label ENTRY, in which users can enter data, and another text field, under the label REGISTER, that displays the result of calculations. The three buttons add the value of contents of the ENTRY field to the value of the REGISTER, subtract the value of the ENTRY field from the value of the REGISTER, or clear the REGISTER by resetting it to zero.

For simplicity, this program uses a number of shortcuts to make this example a brief one. Therefore, the program does not demonstrate the best way to do things with the Composition Editor. The calculator that the program creates works, but is not ideal, for the following reasons:

- The program ignores actions that make no sense, such as clicking Add when there is no number in the ENTRY field, or entering into the ENTRY field a string that is not the representation of a number. A more robust program would provide some feedback to the user in these situations.
- The class produced by following these instructions contains the logic for performing the arithmetic as well as the logic for the GUI. Therefore, the class does not conform to the MVC design pattern. It is better to separate all logic into invisible beans. The resulting program works, but is not designed well enough to be a reusable bean. Creating a separate invisible bean for the processing done inside the calculator is preferable because doing so separates the logic from the GUI. However, such a strategy also adds several steps.
- This program does not use a layout manager. Therefore, the program may not display properly on other screen resolutions and does not adjust when the window is resized. It is quite easy to use a layout manager in the Composition Editor, but doing so adds several steps to the layout stage.
- A design goal is usually to minimize connections. Often you can achieve this goal by connecting events, such as button clicks, to methods rather than to other beans. This program uses connections as much as possible because the goal is to exercise the Composition Editor.
- The resulting class is an application. Creating a class that could be used by either an applet and an application would add a few steps.

Opening the Composition Editor

If you install the version of VisualAge for Java that is available on the CD-ROM that accompanies this book or that can be downloaded from IBM, you can work through this scenario with the actual product. Start by opening the VisualAge for Java Workbench, which is the working environment provided by this product. When VisualAge for Java starts, it presents the SmartGuide, just as it did for the `ShortProgram` in Chapter 1. How you answer some simple questions determines where you enter the Workbench.

To go directly to the Composition Editor:

1. Click **Create a new class/interface** on the **QuickStart** menu.
2. In the SmartGuide, create a class with the name **`SimpleCalc`**.
3. Specify the superclass **java.awt.Frame.**
4. Specify a project called **Learning.**
5. Specify the package **VisualAge.**
6. Select **Design the class visually.**
7. When the window looks like Figure 12-6, click **Finish.** Click **Yes** when you are asked if you want to continue. VisualAge then creates a skeleton application and opens the Composition Editor.

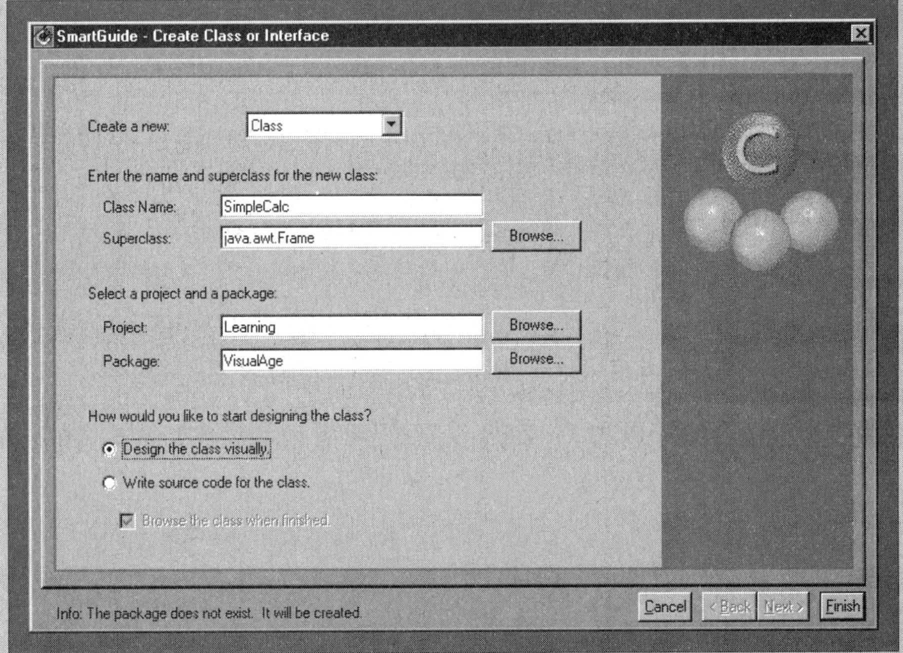

Figure 12-6: The Create Class or Interface SmartGuide

Your starting position for the visual design looks like Figure 12-7.

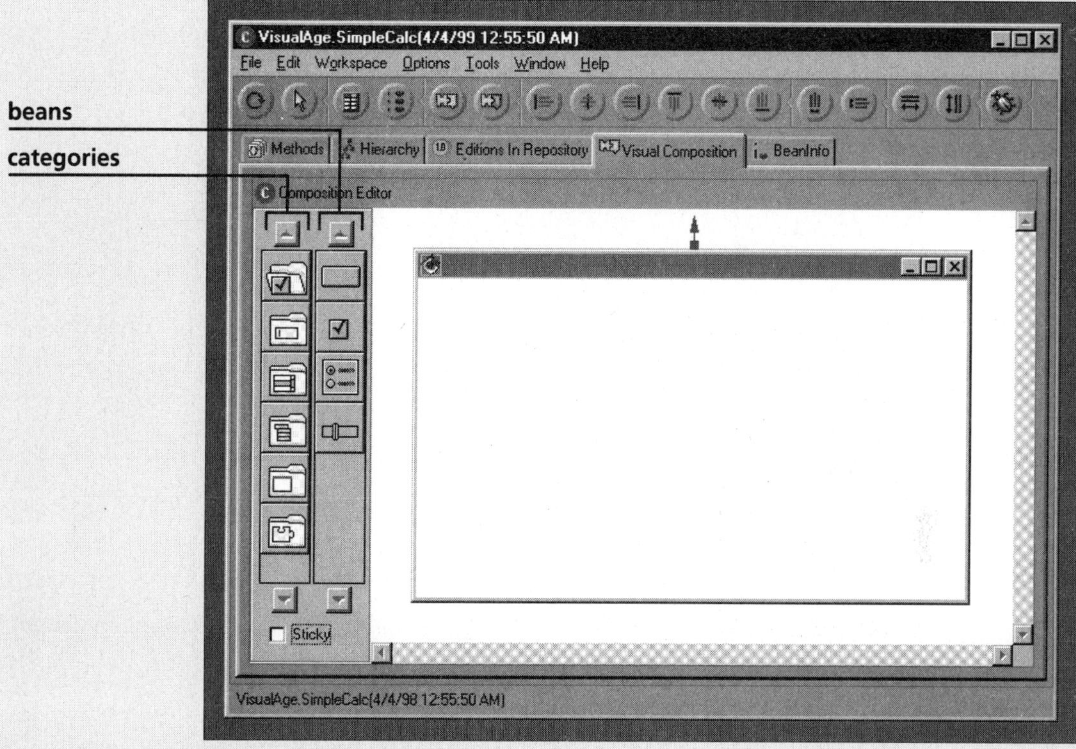

Figure 12-7: Starting to design a class visually

You see what looks like a frame window, and is actually the representation of the GUI bean for a class that extends Frame, drawn on a free-form surface. The arrow from the frame window is a connection. Whether it appears at the top, bottom, or side of the frame depends upon the position of the frame within the free-form surface and does not affect its meaning. This arrow may move if you reposition the frame or resize the Composition Editor window. Connections define how the GUI and invisible beans interact with each other. You can click a connection in the Composition Editor to see a description of the connection in the status line at the bottom of the working window. If you click this arrow, you see that the windowClosing event is connected to the dispose method of the `SimpleCalc` class.

To insert the title in the frame:

1 Right-click inside the frame to display a popup menu. Click **Properties** to open the Properties window that controls the appearance of the bean.

2 Scroll down until the title row is visible in the left column. Type the title **Simple Calculator** into the entry field to the right of the property name title, as shown in Figure 12-8. Close the Properties window. Notice that the title now shows in the frame window.

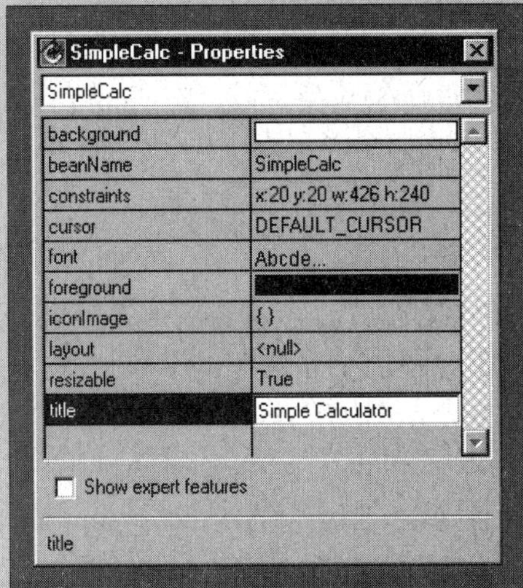

Figure 12-8: Specifying the title of a frame

If you want to use a layout manager, you can select one by setting a property for the frame.

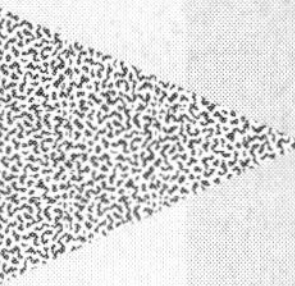

Mini Quiz 12-3

This scenario shows you where to set the layout manager property but accepts the default null layout. Devise a strategy for using layout managers for the simple calculator. You do not actually have to implement your solution. Just list all the containers you would use and the layout managers for each container. You don't need to match Figure 12-8 exactly; just make sure the ENTRY and REGISTER labels appear above the appropriate text areas and arrange the three buttons Add, Subtract, and Clear across the bottom area of the window.

Hint: Look at how the Three Panels program arranges Panel objects in a Frame, and then specifies a different layout manager for each Panel object.

To set the properties for the frame:

1 Reopen the Properties window.
2 In the Layout field, click on the **<null>** text.
3 Click to open the Prompter window. In the Prompter window, click beside the word null to see the list of the available layout managers, shown in Figure 12-9.

Figure 12-9: Selecting a layout manager

To shorten this scenario, you could accept the default null layout and close the Prompter window by clicking **Cancel**.

Because components have fixed sizes and locations in a null layout, you next prevent this window from being resized.

4 Click the **resizable** property, and from the drop-down menu, click the value **false**.

5 Close the Properties window.

Adding Components Visually

The two columns to the left of the Composition Editor are the palette of beans available in the Composition Editor. The first column shows the category and the second column contains the beans in that category. For example, the buttons category is selected by default, as shown in Figure 12-7, and the four kinds of beans in this category (buttons, check boxes, check-box groups, and scrollbars) appear in the right column of the palette. The other categories are data entry, lists, menus, containers, and models. Models are particularly interesting because you can use them to them to represent variables of almost any loaded type, or to create objects dynamically.

The simple calculator uses only a few of the many types of beans supported by the Composition Editor. This simple design uses no invisible beans, which are represented by symbols shaped like jigsaw-puzzle pieces placed outside the frame on the free-form surface.

You are ready to position the labels, buttons, and text fields on the application frame.

To add the ENTRY and REGISTER labels to the frame:

1 Click the **Data Entry** button, the second button from the top in the palette of beans.

2 For the label, click the **Label** bean icon. When you select a bean, the status line at the bottom of the Composition Editor displays the type of the bean.

The cross-hair cursor appears when you move the mouse inside the application frame.

3 Position the cursor roughly where you want the bean to appear. Click to drop the bean in place.

A label appears. The Label bean has the default text label1.

4 To change the label text, hold down the **Alt** key and click the text **label1** to highlight it. Type **ENTRY** and press **Enter**.

The small black boxes in the corners of a component highlight the component when it is selected. You can resize and move a bean by clicking and dragging these boxes. You can always release a selected bean by clicking outside the bean on the free-form surface.

5 In a similar fashion, add the **REGISTER** label.

6 To add the text fields that display the ENTRY and REGISTRY values, click the **TextField** bean icon.

7 Because you are going to drop more than one TextField on the frame, set the sticky flag by clicking the **Sticky** check box that appears below the palette. When this check box is selected, you can drop two TextField components on the frame by simply clicking roughly where you want them to appear, one below each label.

8 Clear the sticky flag by clicking the **Sticky** check box again.

If you accidentally drop more beans than you intended, you can repeatedly choose **Undo** from the **Edit** menu to remove the last beans you dropped on the frame.

9 For the three buttons, click the **Buttons** icon. You can set the sticky flag because there are three buttons to drop.

Click the **Button** bean icon. Drop three buttons below the TextField beans. Clear the **Sticky** flag. Figure 12-10 shows what the screen looks like when you have dropped the last button but not yet released the sticky flag.

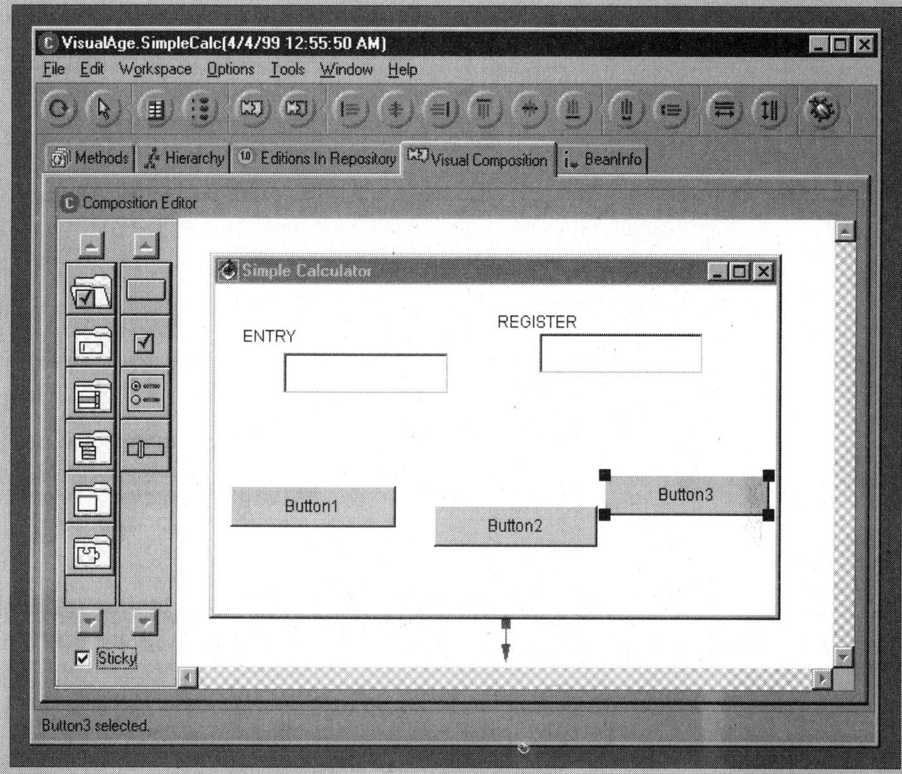

Figure 12-10: Adding beans to a container

10 Change the text on the buttons to **Add, Subtract**, and **Clear** in the same way that you changed the text on the ENTRY and REGISTER labels.

11 The final step in this stage is to prevent users from typing into the REGISTER text field. Double-click the **REGISTER** text field to open its Properties window. Set the editable property to **False.**

12 You can also set the initial text by entering **0** for the text property. Close the **Properties** window.

Arranging the Components Visually

When you use a layout manager, it determines the exact position and size of the beans dynamically at run time. The null layout leaves aligning and sizing the beans up to you and establishes a fixed layout. You can use the visual layout tools provided by the Composition Editor to arrange the beans manually. You can drag and reshape the beans individually with the mouse.

You can also select a group of beans by clicking each one in turn while holding down the Ctrl key. For example, to align the three button beans with the

Add button, hold down the Ctrl key and click Clear, Subtract, and then Add. Little boxes, called **handles**, appear at the corners of the selected components. The component last selected is shown with solid, rather than outlined, handles and becomes the anchor used to arrange the selected components. The toolbar contains buttons to align the selected beans, distribute them evenly, or resize them to matching dimensions. If you pause with the mouse over each button on the toolbar, text pops up to tell you what each button does. It does no harm to experiment with alignment buttons. You can always back out of a change you do not like by choosing Undo from the Edit menu.

To align the buttons:

1 Hold down the **Ctrl** key and select the three buttons, so that Add is the anchor.
2 Click **Distribute Horizontally** [icon], then **Align Bottom** [icon]. Depending on other changes you have made to the arrangement, the screen may look like Figure 12-11.

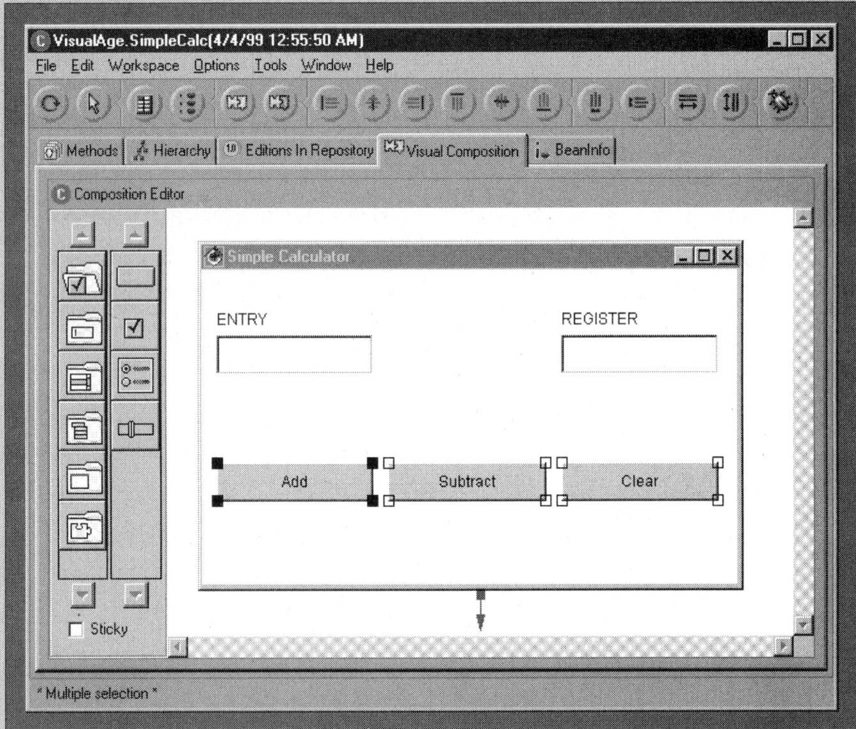

Figure 12-11: Visually arranging the beans

Testing a Program

Now is a good time to run the first test of your application. If you generate code and run at this stage, the application displays the GUI and lets the user enter data into the ENTRY text field, but handles no events. The user can click the buttons, but nothing happens.

To test the bean:

1. Click the **Test** button on the toolbar. This automatically saves your work, generates bytecode, and starts the program.
2. The Command Line Argument window pops up. When a program accepts arguments, you enter them here. In this case, just click **Run**.
3. Allowing for differences in layout, you should see a window similar to Figure 12-5. You can leave the application running in the background (because VisualAge can update a running program) or close it, the same way you close any application window.

Connecting the Components

You can give the beans behavior by connecting them. In the Composition Editor, connections look like arrows. In the generated code, most connections become event handlers or method calls. The direction of the arrow of a connection is significant. The bean at the tail of the arrow is the source bean and the bean at the head of the arrow is the target. They often connect from an event or a change to a property of the source to a property or a method of the target.

The desired effect of the Clear button is to display the string `"0"` in the REGISTER text field. The following steps demonstrate one way to implement the Clear button.

To make the connection between the Clear button and the REGISTER text field:

1. Right-click the **Clear** button to open the shortcut menu of possible actions.
2. Choose **Connect** from the shortcut menu. A submenu opens in which you indicate the source of the connection. Choose **actionPerformed**, which is the handler for the ActionEvent of clicking that button.

3 A dotted line appears. One end is anchored on the Clear button, but the line moves with the mouse and has a spiderlike shape at its moving end. Move the mouse to position the spider over the target bean, as in Figure 12-12.

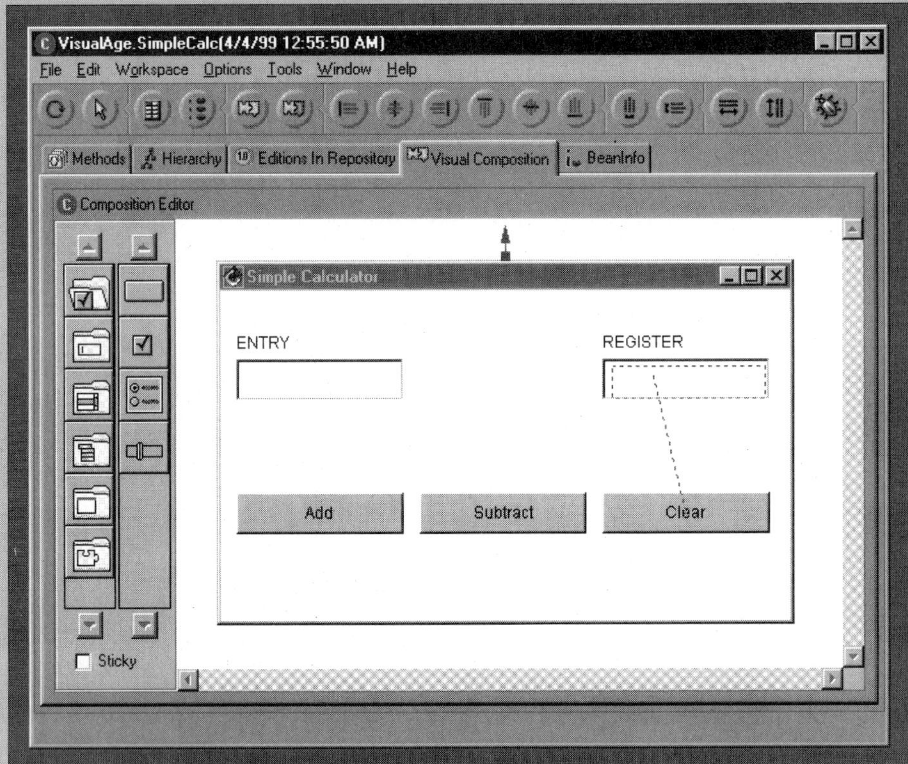

Figure 12-12: Connecting the beans

4 Click the target bean. A menu for the target of the connection opens. Select **text** to connect to the text in the text field.

5 Now the connection is displayed as an arrow. This arrow is dotted because the connection is not complete. The missing element is the string to enter in the text field. In this case, the required string is `"0"`, because the Clear button sets the REGISTER value to the string representation of zero.

6 Right-click the dotted line of the connection.

7 Choose **Properties** from the shortcut menu.

8 In the Property dialog, select **Set parameters**.

9 When the Constant Parameter Value Setting box appears, enter the value `0`, as shown in Figure 12-13.

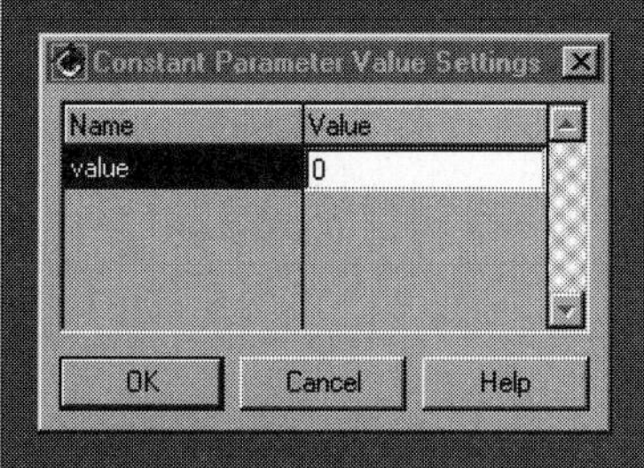

Figure 12-13: Entering properties of a connection

10 Click **OK** in the Constant Parameter Value Setting and Properties windows. The arrow is a solid line. The connection is complete.

11 At any time, you can save the work you have done so far by choosing **Save bean** from the **File** menu, or by taking advantage of the automatic save that occurs when you test the bean.

Connecting with Your Own Methods

The connections from the Add and Subtract buttons are more complicated. They must read the string in the text field under the label ENTRY, and convert the string to a number. They must also convert the string in the REGISTER text field to a number. Then, the connections must add or subtract the values, convert the answer back to a string, and store the result back in the REGISTER field. To do all this, you must write a few lines of code. According to the MVC design model, this code should be in a method of a separate invisible bean. For demonstration purposes, this scenario does as much as possible visually, and adds the code to the GUI bean.

The first step is to consider the overall desired effect of the connection. Therefore the first task is to connect the Add button-click event to the text in the REGISTER text field.

To add connections for the Add button:

1 Make a connection from the actionPerfomed event of the Add button to the REGISTER text field, as in the first stage of connecting the Clear button to this text field. The result is another incomplete connection. The Composition Editor looks like Figure 12-14.

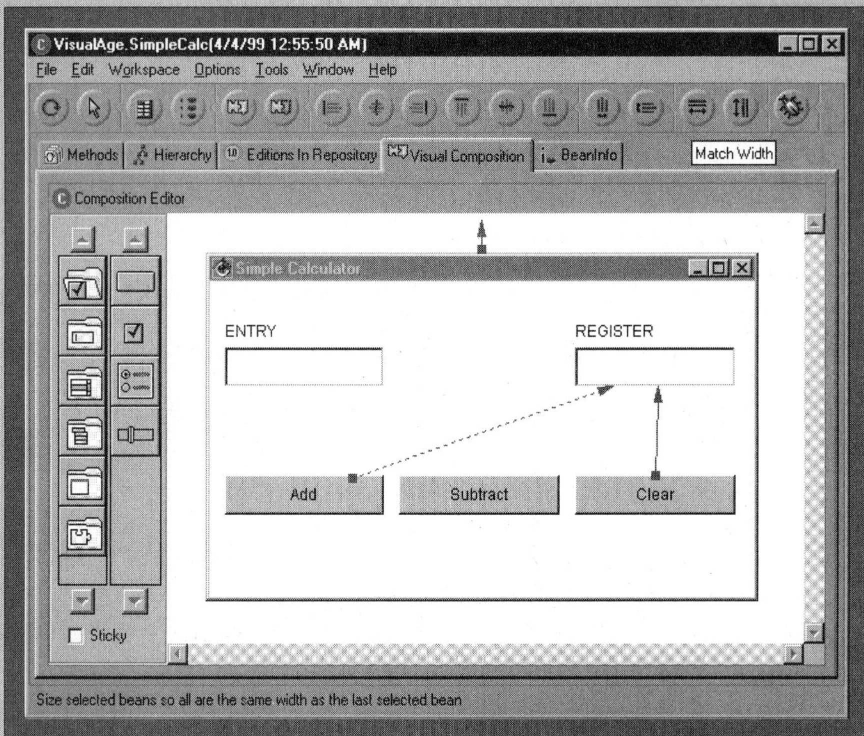

Figure 12-14: The incomplete addition connection

To complete the connection, you need two more connections: one to call a method that performs the addition, and one to get the values to add from the entry fields under the labels ENTRY and REGISTER.

2 Right-click the dotted line of the incomplete connection to open the shortcut menu, then choose **Connect**.

3 In the Connection submenu, choose **value** to pass a value to the REGISTER text field.

Now the spider appears again, but you cannot get the value from a visible bean. Click the free-form space outside the frame. Connecting to the free-form space opens another pop-up menu as shown in Figure 12-15.

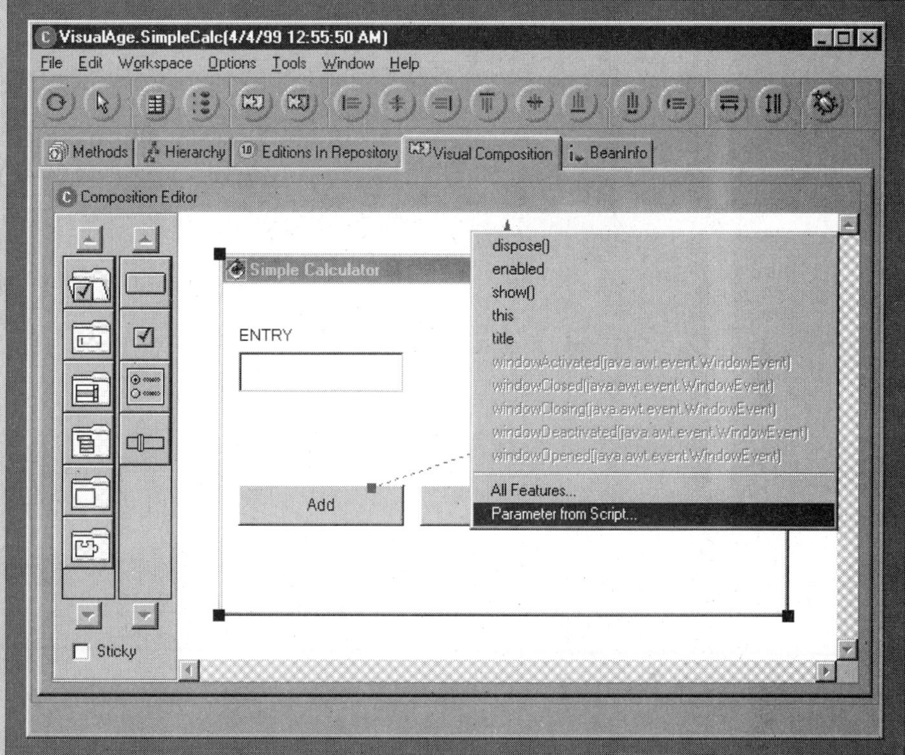

Figure 12-15: The Connect Parameter dialog box

4. To indicate that a method must calculate the value, click **Parameter from Script**. This selection opens the Connect Parameter window.
5. Click **New Method** to open the Create Method dialog box.

6 Fill in the Create Method dialog box as shown in Figure 12-16 to specify that the script is following a new method of the `SimpleCalc` class:

```
String add( String s )
```

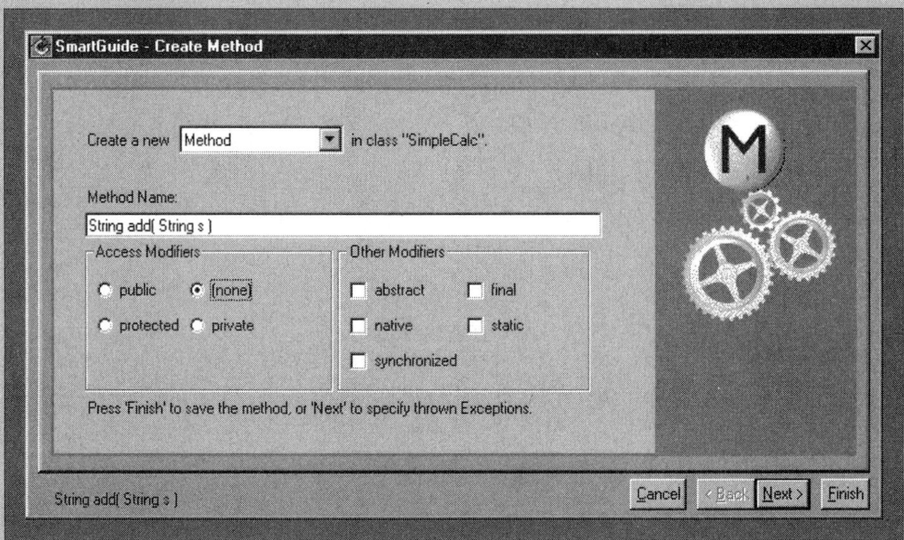

Figure 12-16: The Create Method dialog box

7 Click **Finish** in the Create Method dialog box, then click **OK** in the Connect Parameter window. The new dotted connection appears, as shown in Figure 12-17, and the connection from the Add button to the REGISTER text field is now a solid line, indicating it is complete. You cannot see the skeleton code for the new method that has been added to the `SimpleCalc` class.

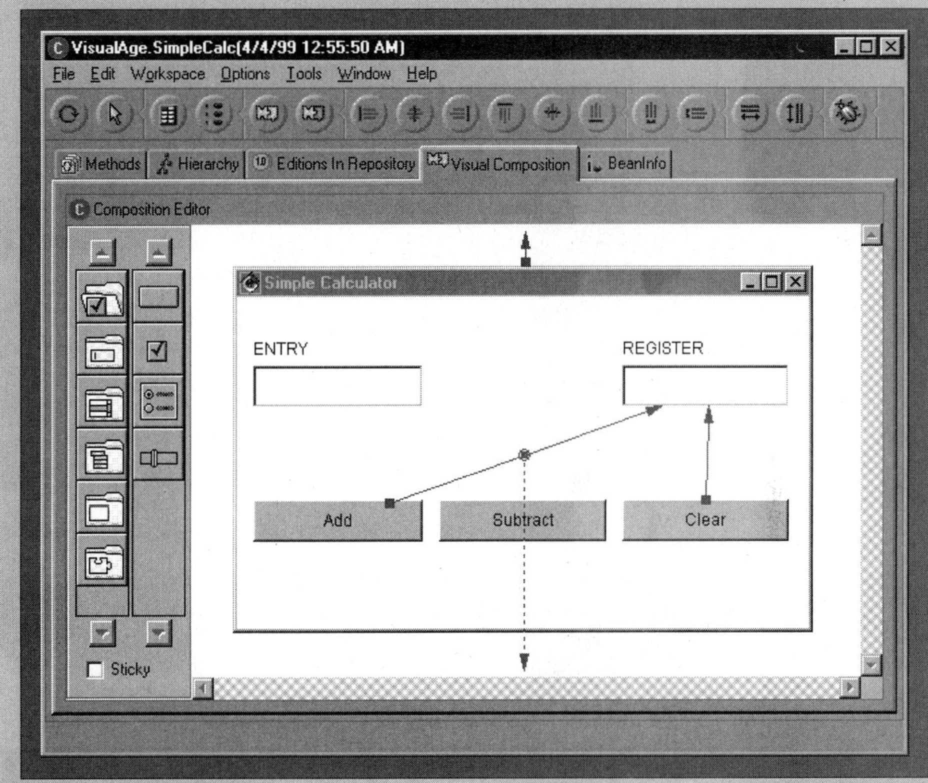

Figure 12-17: Adding a method visually

To complete the new connection, you must get the value of the argument for the `add` method from the ENTRY text field. To get this value, you need another connection.

To create the connection between the `add` method and the ENTRY text field:

1. Right-click the dotted connection to display the shortcut menu, click **Connect**, and then click s, the argument of the `add` method.
2. When the spider appears, move it to the text field under the label ENTRY and click, then select **text** from the pop-up menu. The string in that field now becomes the argument of the `add` method.
3. Now that the set of three connection buttons is complete, the screen looks like Figure 12-18.

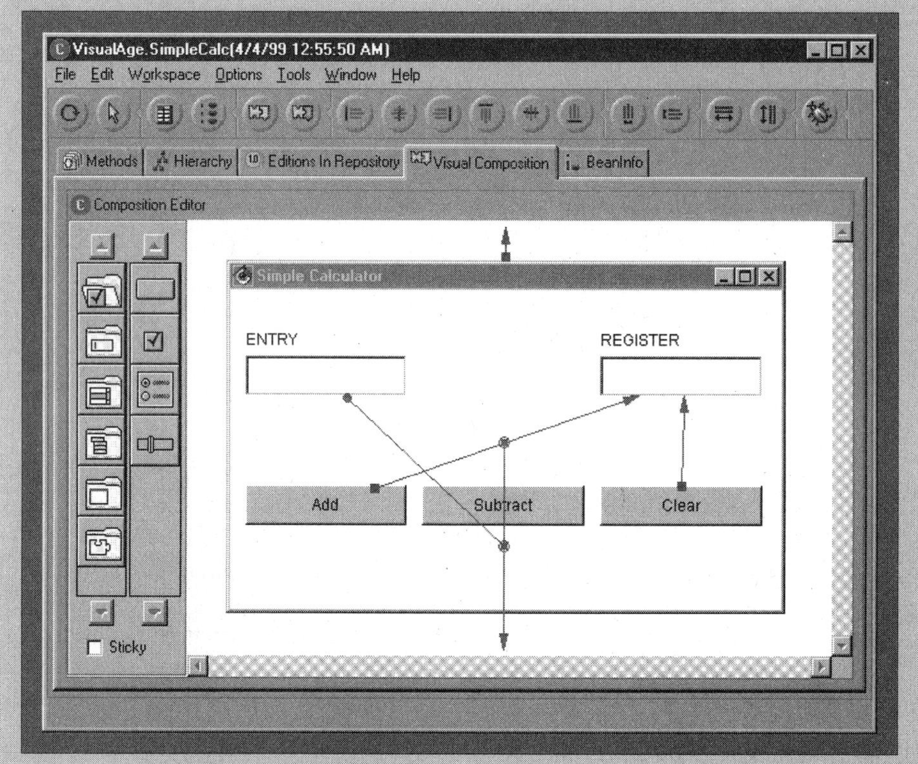

Figure 12-18: The connections for the add method

To recap:

- The first connection joins the Add button to the REGISTER text field.
- The second connection establishes that the value returned by the `add` method is assigned to the text in that entry field.
- The third connection establishes that the argument of the `add` method is the text in the entry field under the label ENTRY.

The only missing element is the body of the `add` method. The Composition Editor generates a skeleton `add` method, but its implementation is empty except for a return statement that returns the value `null`.

Creating the connections for the Subtract button is very much like setting up the Add button, except that the new method you must create is called `subtract` rather than `add`.

To create the connections for the Subtract button:

1 Repeat the steps from the beginning of this section, substituting the `subtract` method wherever the `add` method is specified, and the Subtract button wherever the Add button is specified. When you are in the Create Method dialog box, type the following method:

```
String subtract( String s )
```

Although connections never appear in the working application or applet, you may want to reposition them, or selectively hide and show them, to reduce clutter in the Composition Editor. When you select a connection by clicking it, you see that it has anchor blocks much like the GUI beans. You can change the visual path of a connection by dragging its anchor blocks with the mouse. Figure 12-19 shows the Composition Editor at the end of the visual development stage.

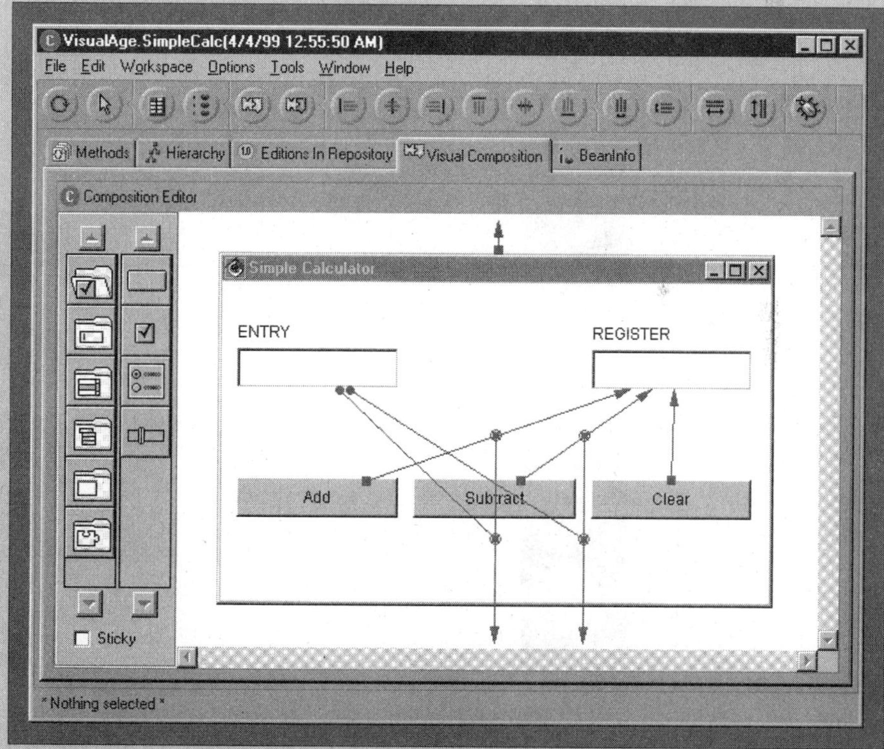

Figure 12-19: A complete set of connections

Coding Methods to Complete the Application

All that remains is to complete the two methods `add` and `subtract`.

To code the `add` and `subtract` methods:

1 Click the **Methods** tab. This action takes you out of the Composition Editor and splits the screen as shown in Figure 12-20, except that a different method might appear at the bottom of the screen.

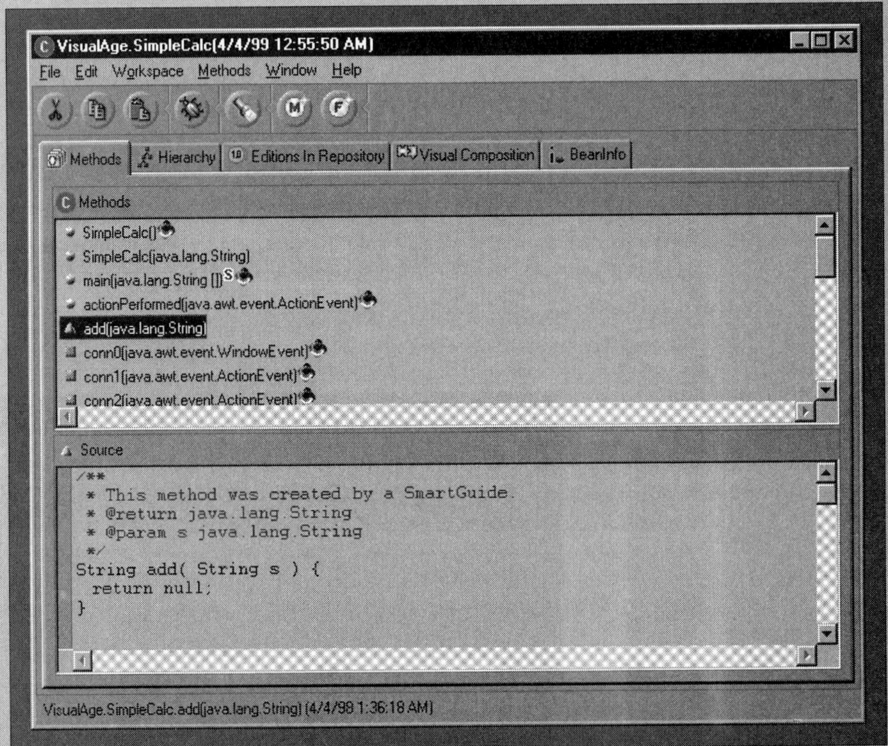

Figure 12-20: Browsing methods in a class

The Methods section of the screen includes a scrolling list of the methods in the `SimpleCalc` class, and in the Source section is an editor window for the code of the selected method.

2 Click **`String add( String )`** in the Methods section. You may have to scroll to find this method. The bottom panel is a text editor. Change the code

```
public String add( String s ) {
   return null;
}
```

to

```
public String add( String s ) {
   double d1 = 0;
   // textField2 is the name of the REGISTER text
   // field
   String register = getTextField2().getText();
   if ( register.length() > 0 ) {
      d1 = ( new Double( register ) ).doubleValue();
   }
   double d2 = ( new Double( s ) ).doubleValue();
   return String.valueOf( d1 + d2 );
}
```

4 Complete the `subtract` method in the same way by entering the code

```
public String subtract( String s ) {
   double d1 = 0;
   // textField2 is the name of the REGISTER TextField
   String register = getTextField2().getText();
   // The REGISTER text field is never empty
   d1 = ( new Double(register) ).doubleValue();
   double d2 = ( new Double( s ) ).doubleValue();
   return String.valueOf( d1 - d2 );
}
```

5 Your work is automatically saved when you click the Test button or leave VisualAge. However, you can explicitly save everything by choosing **Save Workspace** from the **File** menu before you test your code.

6 Test the application by returning to the Composition Editor and clicking the **Test** button.

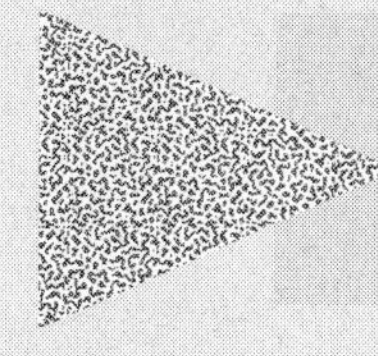

Mini Quiz 12-4

Why does the add method in step 2 introduce the wrapper class Double to convert between String values of the primitive type double?

Now you have a working simple calculator application. The `SimpleCalc` class and the package `VisualAge` that contains it are stored in a repository inside VisualAge. If you want to use the class outside the VisualAge Workbench, export the package.

Before you export the SimpleCalc class, you should add one method call to the connection that closes the frame window when the user clicks the Close button so that the application terminates when GUI shuts down. This action is not automatic because many applications may require additional processing after the user closes the application window and before they terminate.

To add the code to terminate execution when on the window closing event:

1. Return to the Workbench window by clicking it, if it is visible, or by clicking **Workbench** from the **Window** menu.
2. Click the **Packages** tab to open the Packages page of the Workbench.
3. In the top left panel, All Packages, scroll down to VisualAge, which is near the bottom of the alphabetical list of packages. Click **VisualAge**. The SimpleCalc class appears in the middle top window, Classes and Interfaces.
4. Click **SimpleCalc** to display the list of methods in the SimpleCalc class in the top right panel, Methods.
5. Scroll down if necessary, and select the method **conn0(java.awt.event.WindowEvent)** to display the code generated to handle the Window Closing event in the bottom half of the screen, as shown in Figure 12-21.

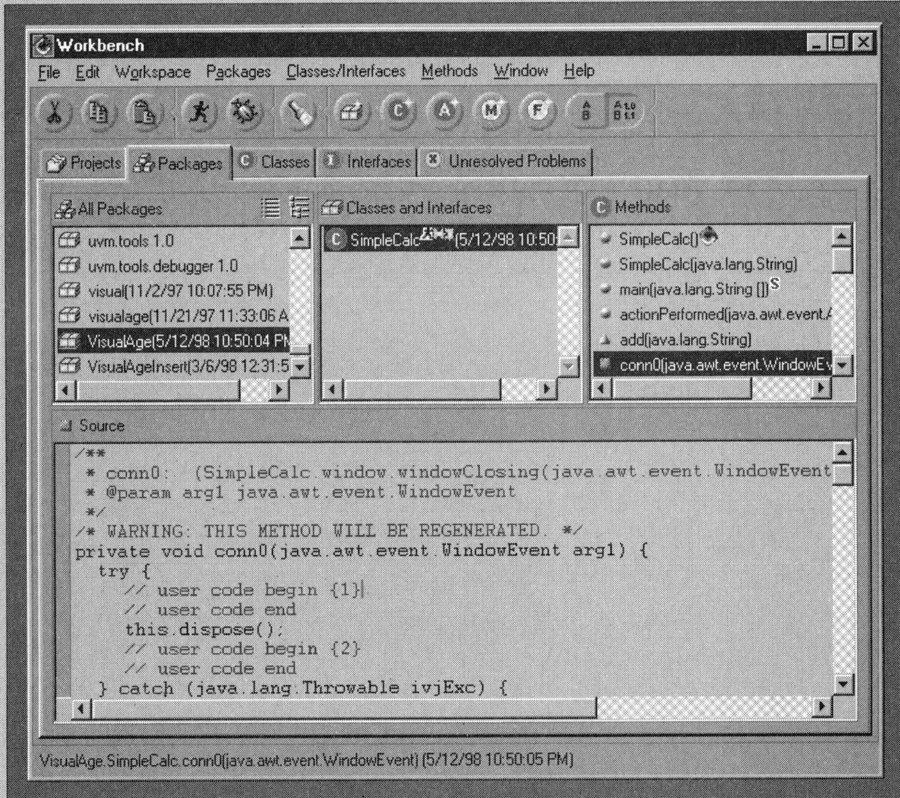

Figure 12-21: The Packages page of the VisualAge Workbench

6 Insert the line shown in bold into the code:

```
try {
// user code begin {1}
// user code end
this.dispose();
// user code begin {2}
System.exit( 0 );
// user code end
```

7 Right-click to bring up the pop-up menu and click **Save** to compile with the new method call.

8 You can test the application again by clicking the **Run** button on the toolbar. When the Command line Argument window pops up, click **Run** in the Command Line Argument window.

9 To export the package, make sure **VisualAge** is highlighted in the All Packages panel of the Packages page, and choose **Export** from the **File** menu.

The Export SmartGuide asks what to export.

10 Select **Both Class and Java files** to export both source and compiled code.

11 Click **Next** to bring up the Export to files SmartGuide. In the SmartGuide, specify the destination folder for the exported code. Usually you want to reflect the package structure you set up in VisualAge.

12 Make sure **Create package subdirectories** is selected.

13 Click **Finish** to complete the export operation.

14 Select **Exit VisualAge** from the **File** menu.

You have completed the simple calculator program in VisualAge for Java. You can run it at any time using the **java** command. If you did not export to a folder that is in your CLASSPATH, go to the folder that you specified as the destination for the export operation before you issue the following command:

```
java VisualAge.SimpleCalc
```

You can now continue with the rest of Chapter 12.

Introducing the Java Foundation Classes

The developers of the Java platform have responded to popular demand and invested considerable effort into providing more powerful and flexible support for creating applications than is available with the AWT alone. Sun Microsystems is meeting developer requirements with the Java Foundation Classes (JFC). The goal of the JFC is to simplify the development of 100% Pure Java programs for network or stand-alone environments. The JFC enables you to design GUIs that reflect the operating system that is host to the JVM, to create your own platform-independent interface, or to use a look and feel that is defined for the Java platform and is common across all implementations of the JVM.

Version Watch

The JFC is included in version 1.2 of the JDK. If you are using the version of the JDK supplied on the CD-ROM that accompanies this book, you can retrofit some parts of the JFC, by first downloading the parts now available and then following the instructions provided by Sun. The URL is as follows:

`http://java.sun.com/products/jfc`

Alternatively, you can upgrade to version 1.2 of the JDK when it becomes available.

The five APIs that make up the JFC are listed in Figure 12-22.

API	Description
Swing	Swing is a code name for an extension of the AWT lightweight UI framework, and is described later in this section.
Abstract Windowing Toolkit	The AWT provides the foundation for the JFC with its support for colors, fonts, graphics, images, and the like.
Java2D	The Java2D API provides a variety of painting styles and features for defining complex shapes and controlling the rendering process.
The Accessibility API	The Accessibility API provides an interface that allows assistive technologies such as screen readers, screen magnifiers, and speech recognition to be easily integrated into applications.
Drag and Drop	The ability to drag and drop between programs created with the Java programming language and applications developed in other languages provides for interoperability between applications.

Figure 12-22: The JFC APIs

Using Lightweight Components

The AWT described in this chapter and Chapter 13 provides a user interface (UI) framework with which you can continue to develop GUIs. The Java platform also includes a lightweight UI framework that the JFC exploits to your advantage.

The AWT in versions of the Java platform prior to 1.2 has some limitations.

To create a new custom component, you have to define a subclass of either java.awt.Canvas or java.awt.Panel. The result was that each new component had its own opaque native window. This one-to-one mapping between components and native windows has disadvantages:

- Native windows can consume a lot of system resources. Therefore, you should create a minimum number of custom components.
- Native windows are handled differently across platforms. Therefore, maintaining a consistent view across varied platforms is difficult and prone to error.

The lightweight UI framework enables you to extend the java.awt.Component and java.awt.Container classes directly. These lightweight components do not have native windows associated with them. Nevertheless, they work with the existing AWT model for painting, layout, and events. They require no special handling or additional APIs.

These components are lightweight because they require no native data structures or peer classes. Because the components do not need native support, you don't have to supply any native code to process them. Therefore, handling lightweight components is 100% Pure Java. The result is common code and complete consistency across platforms.

The Swing API contains 100% Pure Java versions of the AWT components, plus several additional components that are also 100% Pure Java. The Swing API consists of more than 250 classes and 75 interfaces. Over time, these Swing components may replace the peer-based components that were part of the original Java platform. Because Swing does not contain or depend on native code, none of the Swing components are constrained to conform to a single style. Instead, Swing components have a pluggable look-and-feel. As a result, they are adaptable to different operating system platforms or to a custom look and feel. The Swing API consists of the following categories:

- A component named JComponent that extends the AWT class Container and a set of components that are subclasses of JComponent. All of these components have names beginning with the letter *J*.
- Nonvisible support classes provide important services such as event classes and support for the MVC design model. The nonvisible support classes implement the model, or logic, portion of this design model. These classes do not begin with the letter *J*.
- Swing includes a set of related interfaces that are implemented by its component and support classes.

Figure 12-23 lists the components of Swing that have a corresponding AWT component and some of the components that provide functions beyond the existing AWT.

Component	Description
JApplet	Corresponds to **java.applet.Applet**.
JButton	Corresponds to **java.awt.Button**.
JCheckBox	Corresponds to **java.awt.CheckBox**.
JCheckBoxMenuItem	Corresponds to **java.awt.CheckBoxMenuItem**.
JColorChooser	Allows a user to select a color with visual feedback of the color selected.
JComboBox	Combines a text field and drop-down list that lets the user either type in a value or select it from a list that appears in response to a user request. The component provides a superset of the functions provided by **java.awt.Choice**.
JDialog	Corresponds to **java.awt.Dialog**.
JEditorPane	Provides a text pane that lets the user edit content of various kinds.
JFileChooser	Corresponds to **java.awt.FileDialog**.
JFrame	Corresponds to **java.awt.Frame**.
JInternalFrame	Is similar in function to a frame window, but is intended for use within the main frame of an application.
JLabel	Corresponds to **java.awt.Label**.
JList	Corresponds to **java.awt.List**.
JMenu	Corresponds to **java.awt.Menu**.
JMenuBar	Corresponds to **java.awt.MenuBar**.
JOptionPane	Provides a straightforward mechanism for creating simple dialog boxes. For example, use a **JOptionPane** to display a message, ask a yes-no question, or prompt for a single input.
JPasswordField	Lets the user edit a single line of text. Feedback shows that characters are entered but does not display the input characters.
JPopupMenu	Corresponds to **java.awt.PopupMenu**.
JProgressBar	Can be used to indicate the progress of an activity by displaying its percentage of completion.

Figure 12-23: Some Swing components

Component	Description
JRadioButton	Provides a more traditional radio button style that is not a check box.
JRadioButtonMenuItem	Provides a radio button within a menu.
JScrollBar	Corresponds to **java.awt.Scrollbar**.
JScrollPane	Corresponds to **java.awt.ScrollPane**.
JSlider	Lets the user graphically select a value by graphically moving an indicator along a specified range.
JSplitPane	Contains two components, and divides them horizontally or vertically. The user can interactively resize the split between the two components.
JTabbedPane	Lets the user switch from one group of components to another by clicking a tab with a given title or icon.
JTable	Presents data in a two-dimensional table format.
JTextField	Corresponds to **java.awt.TextField**.
JToggleButton	Implements a two-state button. **JToggleButton** is the superclass of both **JRadioButton** and **JCheckBox**.
JToolBar	Displays commonly used actions or controls.
JToolTip	Creates a popup text window that can display a brief textual description of a component.
JTree	Displays a set of hierarchical data as an outline. The display has branches that the user can expand and collapse.
JWindow	Corresponds to **java.awt.Window**.

Figure 12-23: Some Swing components (continued)

Figure 12-23 does not list all the Swing components, but does list all those that correspond to the original AWT components and other notable Swing components.

Using the Swing components is much like using the original AWT components. Swing components use the same layout managers, event objects, and listener interfaces as the AWT components. However, there are some notable differences. In particular, adding components to a JFrame object is not like adding a component to a Frame object. JFrame objects have a content pane in which you must place components. You cannot add components directly to a JFrame object. Instead, call the method getContentPane to obtain a container into which you can add components.

SUMMARY

This chapter and the next are complementary. Chapter 13 builds upon the understanding that you gain in this chapter to provide more comprehensive coverage of the AWT.

In this chapter, you discover that the AWT is part of the Java platform. This toolkit consists of the java.awt package and its subpackages, and contains the classes and interfaces that you use to program a GUI-based application or applet.

The AWT lets you program GUIs and write truly portable code. Internal classes called peers form a bridge between the platform-independent classes that you use and the native operating-system features on which GUIs depend.

The AWT includes classes for the standard elements of GUIs, many of which are components. For example, Button, CheckBox, and TextField are component classes. You build the GUI for your program with components.

Containers are components that can contain other components. For example, Frame, Panel, and Applet are container classes.

To make a class into an application that runs in a top-level window, define your class to extend the class java.awt.Frame. Coding the GUI for an Applet is similar to coding a GUI-based application except that the applet class must extend the class java.applet.Applet and does not have a main method.

You can add components to containers by creating objects of the component class and calling the add method of the container, passing the component as an argument.

Use layout managers to arrange the components in a way that adjusts for screen resolutions and window resizings. Specify a layout manager by calling the setLayout method for the container.

You can also draw directly onto the graphics context of a component. When you do so, you are responsible for coding the paint method to produce the required output. Then you can leave the drawing of components to the AWT. Do not call paint explicitly.

An equally important aspect of programming GUIs is responding when the user moves the mouse, clicks the mouse, or types on the keyboard. These kinds of user input are events. Each component class supports a number of events that are appropriate to its type of component.

To handle an event, define a class to implement the appropriate listener interface. Call a method for the component to register the listener with the component. The methods in the listener interface are automatically called when events occur, and receive an event object as an argument. Therefore, the listener can interrogate and handle the event.

You can use adapter classes that implement the interfaces to reduce the number of methods you must implement to just the events of interest.

You can code for the AWT manually or use RAD tools to program much more productively. A variety of proprietary development environments with RAD features are available.

VisualAge for Java from IBM provides an integrated development environment that includes a visual Composition Editor. You can use the Composition Editor to design the visual elements of your program and to connect the visual elements to nonvisual elements.

You can create complete programs with the VisualAge for Java Composition Editor, entering a minimum of code manually. VisualAge for Java generates 100% Pure Java code. You can develop, test, and debug within the VisualAge environment and then export packages for use in other implementations of the Java platform.

Upcoming releases of the Java platform will extend the facilities for creating GUIs. Version 1.2 introduces the JFC. The feature of the JFC known as Swing includes a set of components that contain no native code and let you customize the look and feel of a GUI.

QUESTIONS

1. Which of the following major groups of the java.awt package is responsible for the strategy of placing GUI elements within an interface? Select the best answer.

a. Graphics
b. Components
c. Layout managers
d. Events
e. Listeners and adapters

2. Which class in the java.awt package is the superclass of all events generated by AWT components?

3. Which of the following are subpackages of the java.awt package? Select all that apply.

a. java.awt.components
b. java.awt.event
c. java.awt.image
d. java.awt.graphics
e. java.awt.peer

4. Which classes are superclasses of all applets? Select all that apply.

a. java.lang.Object
b. java.awt.Frame
c. java.awt.Panel
d. java.applet.Applet
e. java.awt.Window

5. What method must a class override if it needs to draw in its own graphics context?

6. Which components in a BorderLayout stretch horizontally as the container stretches? Select all that apply.

a. North
b. South
c. Center
d. East
e. West

7. Which components in a BorderLayout stretch vertically as the container stretches? Select all that apply.
   a. North
   b. South
   c. Center
   d. East
   e. West
8. What interface must a class implement if it needs to handle the event that occurs when a user clicks a push button?
9. What class in the java.awt.event package implements all of the methods defined in the WindowListener interface?
10. Which method is used to set the position of a window on the desktop?

EXERCISES

Debugging

1. Correct all the errors in the following program:

```
package java4cpp.questions.c12;
import java.awt.*;
import java.awt.event.*;
public class Debug12_1 {
   public Debug12_1( String titleText ) {
      addWindowListener( new WindowAdapter() {
            public void
            windowClosing( WindowEvent event ) {
               Frame.this.dispose();
               System.exit( 0 );
            }
         }
      );
      setSize( 300, 100 );
      setVisible( true );
   }
   public void paint( Graphics g ) {
      g.drawString( "Debug Question", 100, 60 );
   }
   public static void main( String[] args ) {
      new Debug12_1( "Hello World! Sample" );
   }
}
```

2. Correct all the errors in the following program:

```
package java4cpp.questions.c12;
import java.awt.*;
import java.awt.event.*;
public class Debug12_2 extends Frame {
   public Debug12_2( String titleText ) {
      super( titleText );
      addWindowListener( new WindowAdapter() {
            public void
            windowClosing( WindowEvent event ) {
               Frame.this.dispose();
               System.exit( 0 );
            }
         }
      );
   }
   public void paint( Graphics g ) {
      g.drawString( "Debug Question", 100, 60 );
   }
   public static void main( String[] args ) {
      new Debug12_2( "Hello World! Sample" );
   }
}
```

3. Correct all the errors in the following program:

```
package java4cpp.questions.c12;
import java.awt.*;
import java.awt.event.*;
public class Debug12_3 extends Frame {
   public Debug12_3( String titleText ) {
      super( titleText );
      addWindowListener( new WindowAdapter() {
            public void
            windowClosing( WindowEvent event ) {
               Frame.this.dispose();
            }
         }
      );
      setSize( 300, 100 );
      setVisible( true );
   }
   public void paint( Graphics g ) {
      g.drawString( "Debug Question", 100, 60 );
   }
   public static void main( String[] args ) {
      new Debug12_3( "Hello World! Sample" );
   }
}
```

4. Correct all the errors in the following program so that a single button appears in the middle of the frame window:

```
package java4cpp.questions.c12;
import java.awt.*;
import java.awt.event.*;
public class Debug12_4 extends Frame {
   private Button debugButton;
   public Debug12_4( String titleText ) {
      super( titleText );
      addWindowListener( new WindowAdapter() {
            public void
            windowClosing( WindowEvent event ) {
               Frame.this.dispose();
               System.exit( 0 );
            }
         }
      );
      setLayout( new BorderLayout() );
      add( debugButton, "Center" );
      pack();
      setVisible( true );
   }
   public static void main( String[] args ) {
      new Debug12_4( "Debug Question" );
   }
}
```

5. Correct all the errors in the following program so that the three buttons appear within the frame in a single row:

```
package java4cpp.questions.c12;
import java.awt.*;
import java.awt.event.*;
public class Debug12_5 extends Frame {
   private Button blackButton, redButton, greenButton;
   public Debug12_5( String titleText ) {
      super( titleText );
      addWindowListener( new WindowAdapter() {
            public void
            windowClosing( WindowEvent event ) {
               Frame.this.dispose();
               System.exit( 0 );
            }
         }
      );
      blackButton = new Button( "Black" );
      add( blackButton );
      redButton = new Button( "Red" );
      add( redButton );
      greenButton = new Button( "Green" );
```

```
      add( greenButton );
      pack();
      setVisible( true );
   }
   public static void main( String[] args ) {
      new Debug12_5( "Debug Question" );
   }
}
```

Complete the Solution

1. Complete the following class definition by adding a paint method that writes the string, “I completed the solution!”

```
package java4cpp.questions.c12;
import java.awt.*;
import java.awt.event.*;
public class Complete12_1 extends Frame {
   public Complete12_1( String titleText ) {
      super( titleText );
      addWindowListener( new WindowAdapter() {
            public void
            windowClosing( WindowEvent event ) {
               Frame.this.dispose();
               System.exit( 0 );
            }
         }
      );
      setSize( 300, 100 );
      setVisible( true );
   }
   // your paint method goes here
   public static void main( String[] args ) {
      new Complete12_1( " Complete the Solution" );
   }
}
```

2. Complete the following class definition by adding a TextField that can hold 40 characters in the center of the frame window:

```
package java4cpp.questions.c12;
import java.awt.*;
import java.awt.event.*;
public class Complete12_2 extends Frame {
   public Complete12_2( String titleText ) {
      super( titleText );
      addWindowListener( new WindowAdapter() {
            public void
            windowClosing( WindowEvent event ) {
               Frame.this.dispose();
```

```
                System.exit( 0 );
            }
        }
    );
    // put your code to add a TextField here
    pack();
    setVisible( true );
}
public static void main( String[] args ) {
    new Complete12_2( "Complete the Solution" );
}
}
```

3. Complete the following class definition by creating a Panel object and a CheckBox object. Put the check box into the center of the panel and put the panel into the North section of the frame window.

```
package java4cpp.questions.c12;
import java.awt.*;
import java.awt.event.*;
public class Complete12_3 extends Frame {
   public Complete12_3( String titleText ) {
      super( titleText );
      addWindowListener( new WindowAdapter() {
            public void
            windowClosing( WindowEvent event ) {
               Frame.this.dispose();
               System.exit( 0 );
            }
         }
      );
      // put your code for the Panel
      // and the check box here
      pack();
      setVisible( true );
   }
   public static void main( String[] args ) {
      new Complete12_3( "Complete the Solution" );
   }
}
```

4. Complete the following class definition by adding code to the actionPerformed method that will change the label of the button to "Thanks!" when the user clicks it:

```
package java4cpp.questions.c12;
import java.awt.*;
import java.awt.event.*;
public class Complete12_4 extends Frame {
   public Complete12_4( String titleText ) {
      super( titleText );
      addWindowListener( new WindowAdapter() {
            public void
```

```
            windowClosing( WindowEvent event ) {
               Frame.this.dispose();
               System.exit( 0 );
            }
         }
      );
      Button grateful
         = new Button( "Please click me" );
      grateful.addActionListener(
                          new ActionListener() {
            public void
            actionPerformed( ActionEvent e ) {
               // add your action-handling code here
            }
         }
      );
      add( grateful, "Center" );
      pack();
      setVisible( true );
   }
   public static void main( String[] args ) {
      new Complete12_4( "Complete the Solution" );
   }
}
```

5. Complete the following class definition by putting a check box in the middle of the window. When the check box is selected, its text should be green; when the check box is not selected, the text should be red.

```
package java4cpp.questions.c12;
import java.awt.*;
import java.awt.event.*;
public class Complete12_5 extends Frame {
   public Complete12_5( String titleText ) {
      super( titleText );
      addWindowListener( new WindowAdapter() {
            public void
            windowClosing( WindowEvent event ) {
               Frame.this.dispose();
               System.exit( 0 );
            }
         }
      );
      // put your code for the check box
      // and its handler here
      pack();
      setVisible( true );
   }
   public static void main( String[] args ) {
      new Complete12_5( "Complete the Solution" );
   }
}
```

Discovery

1. Create a special-purpose calculator that finds only square roots. The user interface for this calculator should have an entry field where the user enters the input number for the calculation, and a second entry field that displays the answer. Put two buttons in the window: one called Calculate that causes the square root to be calculated and displayed, and another called Cancel that ends the program.
2. Add a user interface to the `JUnzip` class described in the Discovery questions in Chapter 10. The user interface should display the files contained in a zip file and provide two buttons: one to unzip the file and the other to end the program. The name of the zip file is passed as a command line argument.

CHAPTER 13

Programming Windows and Events

objectives

In this chapter you will:

- **Create a GUI for your application or applet.**
- **Write code that uses the** setVisible, setEnabled, getSize, setForeground, **and** setBackground **methods of the** java.awt.Component **class.**
- **Construct a** java.awt.TextArea **or** java.awt.List **to display a specified number of rows.**
- **Construct a** java.awt.TextArea **or** java.awt.TextField **to display a specified number of columns.**
- **State the significance of a column where one of the text components uses a proportional pitch font or a fixed-pitch font.**
- **Identify the** drawString, drawLine, drawRect, drawImage, drawPolygon, drawArc, fillRect, fillPolygon, **and** fillArc **methods of the** Graphics **class.**
- **Demonstrate the use of the** add(Component) **and** add(String, Component) **methods of the** java.awt.Container **class and recognize which classes in the** java.awt **and** java.lang **packages are valid arguments to these methods.**
- **Distinguish between Abstract Windowing Toolkit (AWT) classes that are directly responsible for determining component layout and those responsible for implementing that layout.**
- **Write code to change the layout scheme associated with an AWT container.**
- **Use** BorderLayout, FlowLayout, **and** GridLayout **to achieve the required dynamic resizing behavior of a component.**
- **Write a nonabstract class that implements a specified** Listener **interface, given the interface definition.**
- **Select methods from the classes in the** java.awt.event **package that identify the affected component, mouse position, nature, and time of the event.**
- **Demonstrate correct uses of the listener methods in the** Component, TextArea, **and** TextField **classes.**
- **For any listener in the** java.awt.event **package, state the argument type and return type of a specified listener method, given the name of the interface that declares the method and the name of the method itself.**
- **Identify the sequence of** Component **methods involved in redrawing areas of an AWT graphical user interface (GUI) under exposure and programmed redraw conditions.**
- **Distinguish between methods invoked by the user thread and those normally invoked by an AWT thread.**
- **Write code to implement the** paint **method of a** java.awt.Component.

Programming with the AWT

After you have mastered the basics of the Java programming language, the part of the Java platform that you are likely to spend the most time learning is the AWT. The AWT consists of the set of classes that supports programming a GUI, and programming a GUI is not a trivial task. This chapter builds upon the introduction to writing GUI-based applications and applets given in Chapter 12. Comprehensive coverage of the AWT is beyond the scope of this book. The approach here is to describe the classes that implement the concepts introduced in Chapter 12 and to demonstrate how to use many of them in the file browser program that ends the chapter. The AWT does not get more difficult or complex as you explore its many classes and methods. It just gets bigger, although it never reaches the level of complexity or size of comparable C++ class libraries.

This chapter covers the classes and specific tasks related to the AWT that are mentioned in the objectives of the Sun Java Programmer Certification Exam. The exception is that some classes, such as Image, that are used mostly in applets and are covered in Chapter 14. The exam has questions on four categories drawn from the AWT:

- Components and facilities
- Layouts
- Event handling
- Painting

You do not have to use the AWT if you are programming only for console I/O, but users of applications usually demand GUI operation, and the very nature of applets mandates that you program for a windowing environment. Therefore, many, if not all, of your programs are likely to use the AWT.

Another factor to consider is whether you will be using only the AWT classes to build your GUI. The AWT has been available since the original Java platform, although the event-handling model was radically redesigned for version 1.1 of the Java platform. When version 1.2 of the Java platform is available, you can use the Java Foundation Classes (JFC). As explained in Chapter 12, the JFC is composed of a number of frameworks, one of which is the AWT. The framework called Swing provides additional 100% Pure Java features for creating GUIs, a facility for pluggable look and feel, and includes many classes that have corresponding classes in the AWT and classes that support additional features.

One of the great advantages of the Java platform is that the support for creating a GUI is provided in core classes and interfaces. Learning the AWT is analogous to mastering a class library or the system API you use to create a GUI in C++. One important difference is that in the Java platform you are learning a portable and standard set of programming features.

The AWT is contained in the core package java.awt and the following subpackages as shown in Figure 13-1.

Subpackage of **java.awt**	Description
java.awt.datatransfer	The classes in **java.awt.datatransfer** support data transfer between applications. For example, you can give users access to the operating system clipboard and let them perform cut–and-paste operations to and from the clipboard.
java.awt.event	Some classes in **java.awt.event** encapsulate the various kinds of user activities. Other classes and interfaces provide the framework within which you create customized handlers for the events.
java.awt.image	Classes that support different color models and image filters for image processing are in **java.awt.image**. The **Image** class itself is part of the **java.awt** package, not this package.
java.awt.peer	The peer classes that form the bridge between the AWT classes that you do use and implementations that are dependent on the native operating system. Usually, you do not use the classes in this package directly. The Swing classes from the JFC in version 1.2 of the Java platform do not use peers and have no native code. One of the advantages of Swing is greater flexibility in designing the look and feel of a GUI than is possible with the AWT.

Figure 13-1: Subpackages of java.awt

Components

The Java platform provides a set of classes for the most common visual components of GUIs. These components are standard elements of most GUIs, such as buttons, check boxes, text areas, and windows themselves. There is no need to design your own classes for standard buttons and the like. Just instantiate a component class to get an object that is not only ready and easy to use, but also performs and looks like what your users expect on whatever operating system is host to the Java Virtual Machine (JVM).

Components know how to draw themselves. For example, if you create an instance of the Button class and add it to a container, the button appears fully rendered on the screen when the object is displayed. Components also perform the very large job of supporting the framework for user interaction that is appropriate for the component. For example, the Button class can generate events when the user clicks a Button object. The AWT component classes do all this for you. Most GUI applications and applets make heavy use of component classes provided by the JDK.

Figure 13-2 shows a class hierarchy diagram of the component class and its subclasses. Shaded boxes represent abstract classes.

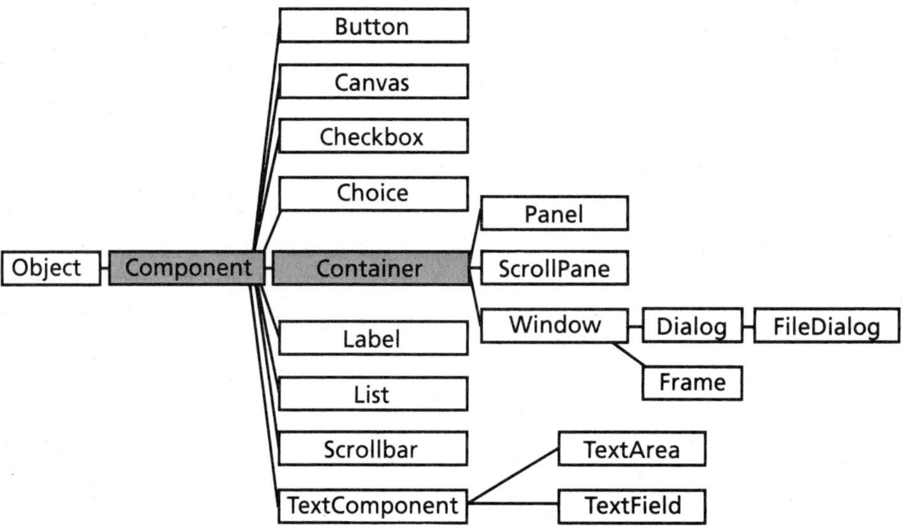

Figure 13-2: The component classes

All the classes in Figure 13-2 are in the package java.awt, except Object, which belongs to java.lang. Component and Container are abstract classes. You can create instances of all the other kinds of components.

A major benefit of components is that they take on the look and feel of equivalent components supported by the native operating system that is the host of the JVM. The AWT achieves this by using peer classes internally. You do not have to worry about platform implementation differences, apart from being aware that your applications and applets may look slightly different when run on different native operating systems.

The Component class is the superclass of all visual classes except for the menu-related classes, which are described later in this chapter. You have already seen Button objects, a Checkbox, and a TextField in the Three Panels program of Chapter 12. The following are the most commonly used component classes.

Class	java.awt.Label
Purpose	A **Label** object is a single line of read-only text. A common use of **Label** objects is to position descriptive text above or beside other components.
Constructors	■ **Label()** **Label(String *text*)** **Label(String *text*, int *alignment*)**

The constructor with no arguments creates a left-justified, empty **Label**. Use the **String** argument to specify the contents of the **Label**. The alignment is an integer, and you can specify one of the fields **Label.LEFT**, **Label.CENTER**, or **Label.RIGHT**.

Code Example	`Label greetings = new Label( "Hello World" );`
Code Output	Hello World
Code Dissection	The actual appearance of the label when it is painted depends upon the current font and the foreground and background colors.

You have already seen Button objects, a Checkbox, and a TextField in the Three Panels program of Chapter 12.

Class	**java.awt.Button**
Purpose	A **Button** object is a push button with a text label.
Constructors	■ **Button()** **Button(String *label*)** When you create a button, you can specify the text that appears on the button as a **String** argument of the constructor.
Code Example	`Button okButton = new Button( "OK" );`
Code Output	OK

You can create individual check boxes or group mutually exclusive check boxes.

Class	**java.awt.Checkbox**
Purpose	A **Checkbox** object is a check box with a text label.
Constructors	■ **Checkbox()** **Checkbox(String *label*)** **Checkbox(String *label*, boolean *state*)** **Checkbox(String *label*, boolean *state*, CheckboxGroup *group*)** The **String** contains the text that labels the check box. The **boolean** indicates whether the check box is on or off, and is set to off, or **false,** by default. You can also create groups of check boxes. A **CheckboxGroup** is a set of **Checkbox** objects from which the user can check only one box in the group at a time. To combine a **Checkbox** with others in a group, specify a **CheckboxGroup** object as the third parameter of the constructor. Check boxes in a **CheckboxGroup** are mutually exclusive, which means that when the user selects one, all others in the same group are automatically deselected.

Code Example	`Checkbox select = new Checkbox( "Selected Only" );`
Code Output	☐ Selected Only

A user cannot edit a list, but can select single or multiple items from the list.

Class	**java.awt.List**
Purpose	A **List** object displays a list of strings.
Constructors	■ **List()** **List(int *rows*)** **List(int *rows*, boolean *multipleMode*)** You can specify the number of rows to show in the **List** object. When *multipleMode* is set to **true**, the user can select more than one item in the list at a time. Otherwise, the user can select only one line at a time from the list, because the default is **false**.

Code Example	`List months = new List( 4, false );`
	`months.addItem( "Apple" );`
	`months.addItem( "Banana" );`
	`months.addItem( "Orange" );`
	`months.addItem( "Pear" );`

Code Output	Apple Banana Orange Pear

A user can enter text in a TextField.

Class	**java.awt.TextField**
Purpose	A **TextField** can display a single line of text, and lets the user enter or edit the text.
Constructors	■ **TextField()** **TextField(String *text*)** **TextField(int *columns*)** **TextField(String *text*, int *columns*)** If you supply an initial text string, it is displayed in the **TextField**. Otherwise, the **TextField** is initially empty. The **int** argument is the width of the **TextField** expressed as the number of characters that can be displayed. For a fixed-pitch or monospace font, the width is equivalent to the number of columns of characters that fit on the line. For a variable-pitch or proportional font,

the width is an approximation based on letters of medium size. You may see more letters if the string contains several occurrences of narrow letters such as *l* or *i*, but fewer characters if the string contains several occurrences of wide letters such as *m* or *w*. If you do not specify a width, the **TextField** is wide enough to display either the specified **String** object or a minimum of one character.

Code Example

```
TextField entry = new TextField( 12 );
```

Code Output

Code Dissection

This example displays the cursor for text entry. The cursor appears when the user clicks in the **TextField** area. The cursor indicates to the user that this entry field is ready to accept input.

A TextArea can be edited by the user, and can have scrollbars.

Class **java.awt.TextArea**

Purpose A TextArea is a region that can contain several lines of text.

Constructors

- **TextArea()**
  TextArea(int *rows*, int *columns*)
  TextArea(String *text*)
  TextArea(String *text*, int *rows*, int *columns*)
  TextArea(String *text*, int *rows*, int *columns*, int *scroll*)

You can specify the size of the **TextArea** in terms of the number of rows and the number of characters or columns that are displayable at once. As with a **TextField**, the number of columns is exact for a fixed-pitch font and approximate for a variable-pitch font. If you specify a string to the constructor, the content of the string is displayed when the **TextArea** is displayed. The optional fourth integer argument indicates what scrollbars you require. You can set this argument to one of the following:

TextArea.SCROLLBARS_BOTH
TextArea.SCROLLBARS_VERTICAL_ONLY
TextArea.SCROLLBARS_HORIZONTAL _ONLY
TextArea.SCROLLBARS_NONE

By default, you get both horizontal and vertical scrollbars.

Code Example

```
TextArea story = new TextArea( "My text", 7, 17 );
```

Code Output

In addition to their overloaded constructors, the various subclasses of the **Component** class inherit a number of methods that establish the common behavior of all components. The following description of the **Component** class does not list all the methods, but does list several of the most frequently used ones. For each mutator method listed for the **Component** class, there is an accessor method. For example, you can call **setSize** and pass a **Dimension** object to specify the exact size of a component in pixels. To find out the size of a component, call **getSize**, which returns a **Dimension** object.

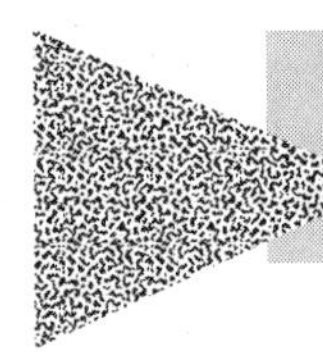

Mini Quiz 13-1

With what layout strategy is setSize useful?

Class	**java.awt.Component**
Purpose	The **Component** class is the abstract superclass for all components.

Methods

- **void setBackground(Color *c*)**

  Call **setBackground** to set the background color. For the argument, you can use one of the constants defined in the class **java.awt.Color**. Several color constants are available, including **red**, **green**, **blue**, **yellow**, **black**, and **white**. You can also specify colors as 24-bit values in which the first eight bits are the intensity of red, the middle eight bits are the intensity of green, and the last eight bits are the intensity of blue. To do that, use **Color** objects created by passing integer values in the range 0 to 255 for the red, green, and blue integer arguments to the **Color** constructor.

- **void setEnabled(boolean *b*)**

  Call **setEnabled(true)** to enable the component to respond to user input and generate events. Components are enabled by default. When the argument is **false**, the component is not enabled.

- **void setFont(Font *f*)**

  Call **setFont** to specify the font for all textual data in the component. The argument should be an instance of the class **java.awt.Font**. When you create a **Font** object, you specify the name of the font, the style, and the point size in arguments of the constructor. The File Browser program later in this chapter demonstrates creating and modifying **Font** objects.

- **void setForeground(Color *c*)**

  Call **setForeground** to set the foreground color. Specify the argument exactly like you specify the argument to the method **setBackground**.

- **void setSize(Dimension *d*)**

  Call **setSize** to set the size of a component in pixels. The argument should be an instance of the class **java.awt.Dimension**. You can create a **Dimension** object with an **int** argument for width, followed by an **int** argument for height, or just one argument or a square shape.

- **void setVisible(boolean *b*)**

  Call **setVisible** and pass the value **true** to show the component. Pass **false** to hide it.

- **void paint(Graphics *context*)**

  The **paint** method actually paints components. It directs output to the specified graphics context. The JVM provides the graphics context, which is available for use inside the method. You can override this method to draw onto the graphics context of a component, but do not call **paint** directly to display the component. Graphics and painting are described later in this chapter.

- **void repaint()**
  void repaint(long *tm*)

  You can call the **repaint** method to have the current component repainted. If you do not supply a parameter, the **repaint** request is sent immediately to the AWT thread. You can schedule the repainting operation by specifying that the repaint begins in ***tm*** milliseconds.

- **void update(Graphics *context*)**

  The default implementation of **update** clears the background of the component by filling it with the background color, and then calls **paint** to repaint the component completely. You can override this method, but do not call it directly.

- **void add*xxx*Listener(*xxx*Listener *object*)**

  This is a set of methods, in which the name of each method begins with the word **add** and ends with **Listener**. Each registers a listener of a different type with the component. Use listeners to handle user-initiated events that relate to the component. Different listeners handle different types of events. The ***xxx*** in the method name varies, depending on the type of the listener. Events and listeners are discussed later in this chapter.

- **void print(Graphics *g*)**

  The **print** method prints this component. Printing components is described later in this chapter.

- **void printAll(Graphics *g*)**

  The **printAll** method prints this component and all its subcomponents.

The following lines are an example of using the mutator methods for a TextField object. They create an entry box in which the user can type white characters on a blue background:

```
TextField entry = new TextField( 12 );
entry.setBackground( Color.blue );
entry.setForeground( Color.white );
```

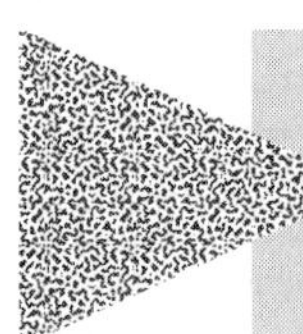

Mini Quiz 13-2

For each of the mutator methods in the Component class listed in this section, what is the associated accessor method? *Hint:* The names of mutator methods all start with "set" and the names of accessor methods all start with "get."

Containers

Containers are a type of component. Containers are designed to hold other components. A container can also hold other containers because every container is also a component. The ability to nest components within containers, and containers within containers, gives you flexibility to create an enormous variety of designs for your user interface. The abstract class Container extends the abstract class Component. Creating a Container is as easy as creating any other Component. Adding a component to the container simply involves calling the method add for the container object and passing the Component object as the argument of add. There are six nonabstract subclasses of Container.

Class	**java.awt.Window**
Purpose	**Window** objects are empty windows that have no title or menu bar. They are typically used as the basis for creating custom components. By default, the layout manager for a **Window** object is a **BorderLayout.**
Constructors	■ **Window(Frame *parent*)** You usually specify the **Frame** for your application as the parent of a **Window** object. In this context, the parent is the owner of the window. When a parent window is closed, its child windows are also closed automatically. The parent-child relationship does not place any constraints on the positioning of child windows as it does in some windowing systems.

Before the PopupMenu **class was added to the AWT in version 1.1 of the Java platform,** Window **objects were commonly used for popup menus.**

Frame objects are top-level application windows that are often called **frame windows**.

Class	java.awt.Frame
Purpose	The **Frame** class extends **Window**. A **Frame** object is a window with borders and a title bar. It can also have a menu bar. All the sample programs in this and the previous chapter are created and displayed as **Frame** objects. By default, the layout manager for a **Frame** object is a **BorderLayout**.
Constructors	■ **Frame()** **Frame(String *title*)** If you pass a **String** object to the constructor, the content of the string appears in the title bar of the frame window.

Use dialog boxes to display messages for the user or to receive input from the user.

Class	java.awt.Dialog
Purpose	The **Dialog** class extends **Window**. By default, the layout manager for a **Dialog** object is a **BorderLayout.**
Constructors	■ **Dialog(Frame *parent*)** **Dialog(Frame *parent*, boolean *modal*)** **Dialog(Frame *parent*, String *title*)** **Dialog(Frame *parent*, String *title*, boolean *modal*)** A **Dialog** object must have a parent window, which usually is the **Frame** for your application. By default, **Dialog** windows are not modal. If you want to prevent the user from interacting with other windows while the **Dialog** is visible, include the **boolean** argument with the value **true.** To give the **Dialog** a title, specify it with **String** argument.

The File Browser program later in this chapter uses a FileDialog container to specify the file for reading and writing.

Class	java.awt.FileDialog
Purpose	The **FileDialog** class extends **Dialog**. Use a file dialog box to let your users browse the file system and select a file.

Constructors	■ **FileDialog(Frame *parent*)** **FileDialog(Frame *parent*, String *title*)** **FileDialog(Frame *parent*, String *title*, int *mode*)** As with a **Dialog**, you must specify a parent **Frame**, and can optionally supply a **String** to be the title of the **Dialog**. If you want to use the file dialog box in a file-load or file-save scenario, you should take advantage of the **int** argument. Specify the value **FileDialog.LOAD** to open the file for reading or **FileDialog.SAVE** to open the file for writing.

Use Panel objects when you want to place a container within a container.

Class	java.awt.Panel
Purpose	The **Panel** class extends **Container**, not **Window**. A **Panel** object does not have its own window and is almost always contained in a window. You can add several panels to a window to divide the area of the window into regions, as you did in the Three Panels program in Chapter 12. You can use layout managers and nested panels to create almost any arrangement of components on the screen that you can imagine. By default, a **Panel** object uses a **FlowLayout** layout manager.
Constructors	■ **Panel()** **Panel(LayoutManager *layout*)** If you do not want the default arrangement of components on a panel, specify a **LayoutManager**.

The Applet class in the package java.applet extends Panel. One of the main differences between an application and an applet is that for an application you must create a Frame to be the top-level window for the GUI of an application. For an applet, the browser or applet viewer tool is considered to be the top-level window and displays the Panel for your applet in that window.

Class	java.awt.ScrollPane
Purpose	Use a **ScrollPane** object when you have a container with contents that are likely to exceed the container's visible area. The **ScrollPane** class can add scrollbars to containers and automatically control all scrolling operations. Like the **Panel** class, **ScrollPane** extends **Container** directly. A **ScrollPane** object does not have its own window and is almost always contained in a window. Unlike the other container classes, objects of the **ScrollPane** have a null **LayoutManager** when they are created. You must specify a **LayoutManager** using the **setLayout** method.

Constructors	■ **ScrollPane()** **ScrollPane(int *scrollbarDisplayPolicy*)** By default, scrollbars are included as needed to make it possible to view the entire container by scrolling. You can also specify an integer representing the scrollbar display policy. The ***scrollbarDisplayPolicy*** value should be one of **ScrollPane.SCROLLBARS_ALWAYS**, **ScrollPane.SCROLLBARS_AS_NEEDED**, or **ScrollPane.SCROLLBARS_NEVER**.

Version Watch

In the original version of the Java platform, the programmer was responsible for adding scrollbars and controlling the scrolling when a container was too big for its visible area. The ScrollPane **class was added in version 1.1 to eliminate this inefficient and error-prone limitation.**

Generally, windows, frames, and panels are not interesting to the user in their own right. They are just the drawing surfaces on which other components are placed. However, these containers are very important for programmers because containers organize and, with the help of layout managers, establish the visual design of a GUI.

Class	**java.awt.Container**
Purpose	The **Container** class provides a number of methods to add and remove components or to work with layouts.
Methods	■ **void add(Component *comp*)** **void add(Component *comp*, Object *constraint*)** The **add** method adds the specified component to the container using default placement rules. For some layout managers, you should specify an object that constrains where the layout manager places the component. For example, if your container has a border layout, specify the area in which to put the component as a **String** in the second argument of the **add** method. Some overloaded **add** methods return the object reference passed as an argument to the method. ■ **Component[ ] getComponents()** The **getComponents** method returns an array containing all the components within the container. ■ **LayoutManager getLayout()** The **getLayout** method returns the layout manager for the container. ■ **void remove(Component *comp*)** The **remove** method removes the component from the container.

- **void setLayout(LayoutManager *mgr*)**

  The **setLayout** method determines which layout manager controls the arrangement of components as they are added to the container.

If you want to pass information to the layout manager when you are adding a component to a container, you should use the method add(Component, Object). **The method** add(Component, Object) **was added to the Java platform in version 1.1. The method** add(String, Component) **is a legacy from the original version of the Java platform, and should not be used in any new code.**

Menus

A set of classes in the AWT supports the menu bars that many applications include in the frame windows. These classes are subclasses of the abstract class MenuComponent. MenuComponent is not a subclass of Component and is a direct subclass of Object, as shown in Figure 13-3. Shaded boxes represent abstract classes.

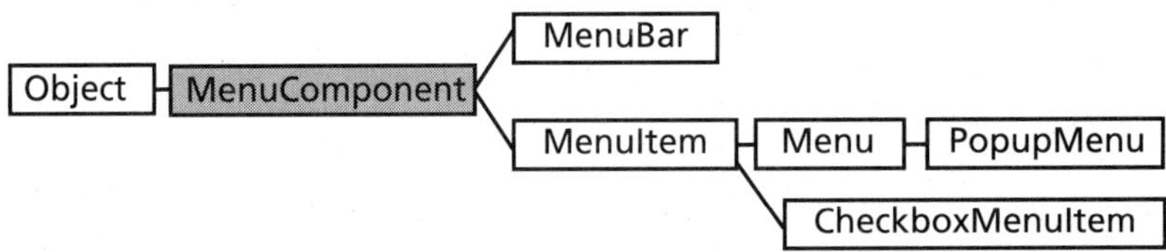

Figure 13-3: Menu classes in java.awt

All the classes in Figure 13-3 are in the package java.awt, except Object, which belongs to java.lang. MenuComponent is an abstract class. The File Browser program later in this chapter uses MenuBar and MenuItem objects. Objects of the subclasses of MenuComponent can look quite different on different platforms, but they behave in the same way on all platforms. You can create instances of all the following classes and combine them into menus:

- To create a main menu for an application, use a MenuBar object. Use the add method to add menus to the menu bar.
- For a menu that is associated with a component and pops up when the user clicks a component, create a PopupMenu object.
- For every item in a menu, use an instance of MenuItem or a subclass of MenuItem.
- To nest menus, use Menu objects. A Menu object is a MenuItem that is itself a menu.
- For a menu item that is also a check box, use a CheckboxMenuItem object.

Class	java.awt.MenuBar
Purpose	The **MenuBar** encapsulates the sort of menu bars you often see directly under the title of the **Frame** for an application. Items in the menu are arranged side by side starting on the left. Often each item is itself a pull-down menu.

Constructors	■ **MenuBar()**
	
	A **MenuBar** object must be bound to a **Frame** object. To create a a **MenuBar** and associate it with a **Frame**, use the method **Frame.setMenuBar**.
	
	`MenuBar mainMenu = new MenuBar();`
	`setMenuBar( mainMenu );`

Methods	■ **Menu add(Menu *m*)** The **add** method adds a **Menu** object to a **MenuBar**, and returns an object reference for the added **Menu**. ■ **void remove(MenuComponent *item*)** The **remove** method removes a menu component from a menu bar.

Every item in a menu must be an instance of MenuItem or a subclass of MenuItem.

Class	java.awt.MenuItem
Constructors	■ **MenuItem()** **MenuItem(String *label*)** **MenuItem(String *label*, MenuShortcut *accelerator*)** Usually, you give every item a label so users can identify the menu item. You pass the label to the constructor as a **String**. If you want to set up a shortcut or accelerator key, such as Ctrl+O for Open, create an object of the class **java.awt.MenuShortcut** and specify the object also as an argument of the constructor.
Methods	■ **void setEnabled(boolean *b*)** By default, all menu items are enabled. You can disable an item by calling **setEnabled** with an argument that evaluates to **false**, and enable it again by calling **setEnabled** with an argument that evaluates to **true.** ■ **void setShortcut(MenuShortcut *s*)** After a menu item has been created, you can create a **MenuShortcut** object that encapsulates a keyboard accelerator key for the menu item. Set the shortcut for a menu item by calling the **setShortcut** method.

Every item in a Menu must be an object of MenuItem or a subclass of MenuItem.

Class	**java.awt.Menu**
Purpose	A **Menu** object is a **MenuItem** that is itself a pull-down menu from a **MenuBar**.
Constructors	■ **Menu()** **Menu(String *label*)** **Menu(String *label*, boolean *tearoff*)** The **String** is the label of the **Menu** in the **MenuBar** or other **Menu** of which this object is a submenu. By default, **Menu** objects disappear when the user releases the mouse button. If your native operating system supports **tear-off menus**, which are pulldown menus that can be dragged from the menu bar and positioned elsewhere for convenient access, you can create a tear-off menu by setting the **boolean** argument to **true**.
Methods	■ **MenuItem add(MenuItem *item*)** The **add** method adds a **MenuItem** to the menu and returns an object reference for the added **MenuItem**. ■ **void addSeparator()** The **addSeparator** method adds a separator line, or a hyphen, to the menu at the current position. ■ **void remove(MenuComponent *item*)** The **remove** method removes a menu component from a menu.

Another type of menu is a PopupMenu.

Class	**java.awt.PopupMenu**
Purpose	A **PopupMenu** object is a menu that is not tied to the menu bar and can appear at a dynamically determined position within a component.
Constructors	■ **PopupMenu()** **PopupMenu(String *name*)** When you create a **PopupMenu**, you can optionally give it a specific name by supplying a **String** argument to the constructor. Associate a popup menu with a component by calling the following method: `Component.add( PopupMenu popup )` The **add** method of **Component** class adds the specified **PopupMenu** object to the component.

Methods	■ **void PopupMenu.show(Component *origin*, int *x*, int *y*)** The **show** method makes a **PopupMenu** object appear, positioned *x* pixels to the right of and *y* pixels down from the origin of the specified **Component**.

To create a check box, you use the **CheckboxMenuItem** object.

Class	**java.awt.CheckboxMenuItem**
Purpose	A **CheckboxMenuItem** object is a **MenuItem** object that takes the form of a check box.
Constructors	■ **CheckboxMenuItem()** **CheckboxMenuItem(String *label*)** **CheckboxMenuItem(String *label*, boolean *state*)** When you create a **Checkbox MenuItem**, you can optionally specify the label to appear beside the check box. The **boolean** argument indicates whether the check box is initially checked. Include this argument with the value **true** to override the default state, in which the check box is not checked.

Layout Managers

You use layout managers to automate the process of positioning components within containers. They free you from the tricky task of figuring out how much space each component requires, and at what pixel coordinates to position it. Usually, you do not care about the exact position of components, but you do want to arrange them tidily. For example, you probably want components such as button and labels to be aligned, and not to overlap or crowd into one area of the screen.

Layout managers make optimal use of space and automatically align buttons and the like. Moreover, they adjust for factors such as different screen resolutions, platform-to-platform variations in the appearance of components, and font sizes. You would find it very difficult to program a GUI if you could not depend on layout managers to figure out the best layout on the target platform at run time.

In the JDK, two interfaces, LayoutManager and LayoutManager2, are the base for all the layout manager classes. As its name implies, the LayoutManager2 interface is an extension of LayoutManager. It adds additional layout management methods to support layout constraints that are typically used in the more complicated layout managers.

These interfaces define the methods necessary for arranging Component objects inside Container objects. The relationship between the layout manager interfaces and classes that implement them is shown in Figure 13-4. Ovals represent interfaces.

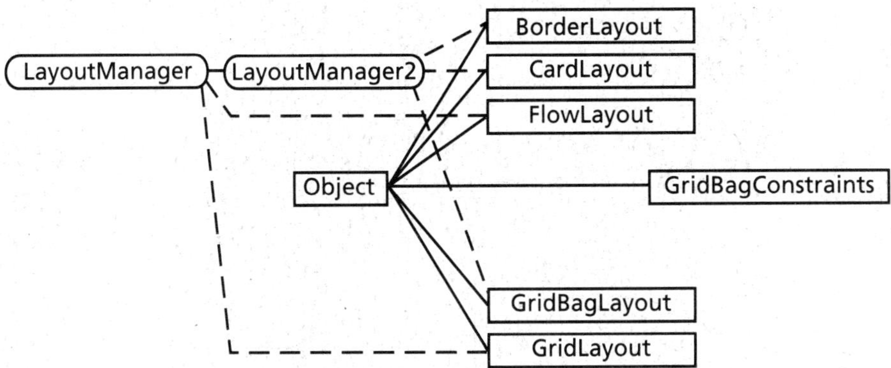

Figure 13-4: Layout managers and related interfaces

Each layout manager supports a different strategy for arranging components within a container. Of course, the individual components can in turn be containers, which gives you the option of nesting layout managers within layout managers. You can nest a layout of one kind within a layout of a different kind, which means you can create an amazing variety of effects by manipulating just a few layout manager classes.

When you create a new Container object, you should call the method Container.setLayout(LayoutManager *manager*) for it, specifying an object of one of the classes that implement LayoutManager. Each container class has a default layout manager, but the defaults are not the same for all types of containers. Therefore, it is best to set the layout manager for a container explicitly.

The AWT provides five layout manager classes to give you five different layout strategies. You can also create your own layout manager class by defining a class that implements the LayoutManager interface.

Border Layouts

The class BorderLayout class implements the LayoutManager2 interface to support a container that holds as many as five components. The components are sized to fill the entire area of the container, and arranged as shown in Figure 13-5. The relative sizes of the areas are determined at run time from the contents of each position. If you do not fill all positions, the empty ones collapse so that they take up no space, and the other areas expand to fill the window.

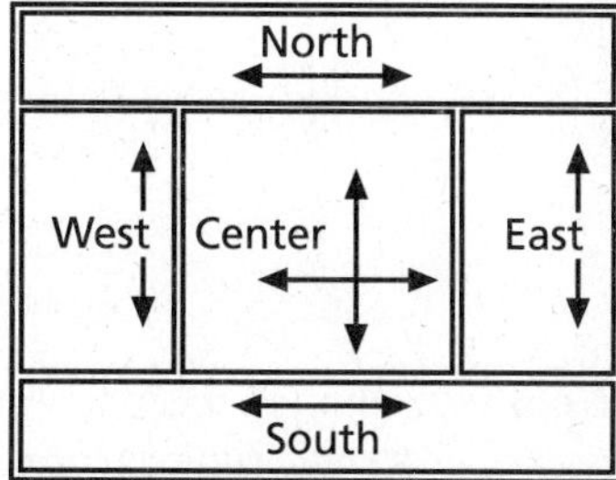

Figure 13-5: The BorderLayout strategy

When a window containing BorderLayout is resized to be wider or narrower, the north and south regions change in width, but the sizes of the west and east regions do not change. When the window is stretched vertically, the west and east regions get taller or shorter, but the north and south regions do not change. The central region can expand and contract in both directions.

When you add a component, you specify in which area of the layout to place the component, using the area names North, South, East, West, and Center. Use the form of the add method for which the first argument is a reference to the component and the second argument is an Object indicating the position constraint. This layout manager requires that the position constraint object be a String object. For example, the following lines of code give a container a border layout and add a component called newPanel to the center of the layout.

```
setLayout( new Borderlayout() );
add( newPanel, "Center" );
```

You can put only one component into each area, and the size of the component adjusts to fill the area. This is not as restrictive as it might seem, because each component can also be a container. That container can have its own layout manager and can hold any number of components. When the window is displayed, the border layout manager investigates the component in each area to see how much space it needs. If the component is a container, the sizing algorithm recursively determines how much space the components within the container need. As a result, border layouts give you great flexibility to group components and create a wide variety of arrangements.

By default, the Window, Frame, and Dialog containers have border layouts.

Flow Layouts

The class FlowLayout implements the LayoutManager interface to support flow layouts. If the container uses a flow layout, components are arranged in a row across the area of the container. When you add a component, it is added to the right. If there is not enough room, the row wraps so that the new component starts a new row. Figure 13-6 shows one possible effect of positioning four buttons in a container with a flow layout, with alignment set to FlowLayout.CENTER.

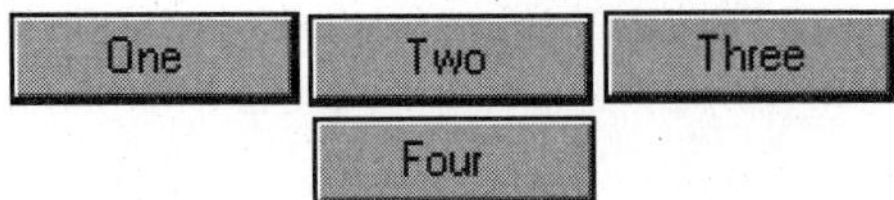

Figure 13-6: A FlowLayout

When you create a FlowLayout object, you can specify with an argument to the constructor whether components are centered, right-justified, or left-justified. By default the components are centered. The following line of code gives a container a centered flow layout, and adds a button to the container:

```
setLayout( new FlowLayout( FlowLayout.CENTER ) );
add( new Button( "Cancel" ) );
```

Unlike in a border layout, where a component expands to fill the area in which it is placed, in a flow layout components retain their natural size. Resizing the window does not change the size of the components in a flow layout, but may adjust their positions.

By default, Panel objects, which include applets, have flow layouts.

Grid Layouts

The class GridLayout implements the LayoutManager2 interface to support grid layouts. This layout manager divides the area of the container into a grid of equally sized rows and columns. When you add a component to the container, it goes automatically into the next cell in the grid. Components are put into cells in row order, as shown in Figure 13-7.

One	Two
Three	Four
Five	Six

Figure 13-7: A GridLayout

When you set up a grid layout, you specify the number of rows and columns as arguments to the constructor. You can specify zero to mean an unlimited number. You cannot specify a row or column position when you add a component to the container. Components are automatically put into the next cell, filling the current row before moving on to the first cell in the next row. You cannot leave a cell empty, or insert a component before a filled cell. The following lines of code give a container a grid layout of three rows and two columns, and add six Button objects to the container, as in Figure 13-7:

```
setLayout( new GridLayout( 3, 2 ) );
add( new Button( "One" ) );
add( new Button( "Two" ) );
add( new Button( "Three" ) );
add( new Button( "Four" ) );
add( new Button( "Five" ) );
add( new Button( "Six" ) );
```

When the user resizes a window that has a grid layout, the cells in the grid change size, and the appearance of components in those cells adjusts accordingly.

Grid-Bag Layouts

The class GridBagLayout implements the LayoutManager2 interface to support grid-bag layouts. This layout manager is more flexible than a grid layout because components can be put in any cell and can span more than one cell. A grid-bag layout is based on a rectangular grid, like a grid layout, but also uses a helper class, GridBagConstraints, to specify how each component should be located within the grid. You can create effects such as the arrangement shown in Figure 13-8.

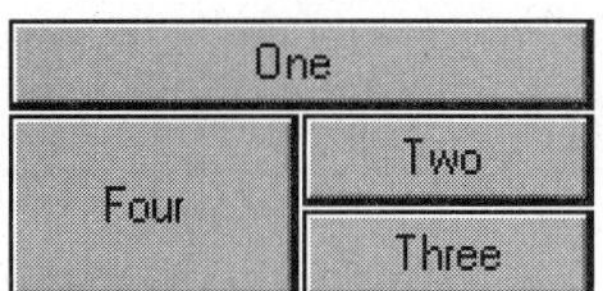

Figure 13-8: A GridBagLayout

Using a grid-bag layout is not as simple as using a grid, border, or flow layout. You should create a GridBagConstraints object for each component that you put in the container. In the GridBagConstraints object, you set fields to indicate factors such as the following:

- How many vertical or horizontal cells to span
- Where to position the component in the container, and whether that position should be relative to that of the previous component
- Where to orient the component if it does not fill its display area
- How to display a component that is too big for its display area

The JDK documentation describes the full set of methods for the GridBagLayout class and fields in the GridBagConstraints class. You must do some extra work to take advantage of the power of a grid-bag layout.

Card Layouts

The class CardLayout implements the LayoutManager2 interface to support card layouts. If a container has a card layout, the components are stacked on top of each other, like a deck of cards, so that only one component is visible at a time. This layout is not frequently used, but you may find it suitable in situations where you want users to be able to view the components in a container one component at a time and in order. The CardLayout class provides the methods first, last, and next that you can call to make a component visible.

Positioning Components Manually

If you want to position components manually, you can suppress the layout manager with the following method call:

```
setLayout( null );
```

If you turn off the layout manager, you are responsible for positioning and shaping all the components in the container. The Component class provides methods for doing this. In particular, you can call setBounds to specify the height, width, and upper-left corner of a component. You can use the setLocation method to reposition a component, and setSize to resize a component. There are two reasons you may want undertake the considerable effort of arranging components:

- To gain more precise control than an available layout manager gives you
- As part of creating a layout manager of your own

Painting

Painting is the act of producing the graphics image of windows and everything that they contain on the screen. This is a different task from making a window visible by calling the setVisible method. A window can be fully rendered, or painted, but not visible because it is minimized or hidden behind another window. Painting occurs every time the display is updated. For example, when the window is resized or covered by another window and then uncovered, it must be repainted.

All paint operations are performed by a central thread, which is often called the AWT thread. When your code requests that a component be painted or repainted, the JVM passes the request to the AWT thread. Your code then continues to execute in its own thread while the AWT thread does the actual painting.

All objects that are instances of subclasses of Component handle their own painting. Unless your application has special requirements for graphics, such as drawing directly on the graphics context or performing animation, you do not have to implement the paint method. Generally, it is better to let the Java platform use its own methods for the painting of components.

Three key methods are involved in painting components:

- The method of the component class that actually renders components for display is the following:

  void paint(Graphics *context*)

  The paint method draws the entire component automatically when the component is first displayed, exposed after being covered, resized, or scrolled into view. Do not call paint directly. Only the AWT thread schedules the painting of objects, to make sure that painting operations always complete and do not have unpredictable results such as leaving half of a window on the screen while the application does something else.
- To make sure a component is painted, you can call the following method:

  void repaint(long *time*)

  When you call repaint, the JVM calls update and then paint for the current component. Unlike paint, repaint can be called directly. You can call the overloaded version of the repaint method with no arguments to start the repaint immediately. Because painting occurs on a separate AWT thread, specifying a time interval in milliseconds before the next paint is to begin can give better performance than tying up the processor by repainting frequently in a tight loop.
- The third essential painting method is the following:

  void update(Graphics *context*)

  Unlike paint, which must be able to render the entire component, update can be used to update selective areas. One reason to override update is to create smooth animations. The default implementation can produce a flickering image because it floods the entire area of the component with the background color before calling paint. An example of an animated applet in Chapter 14 demonstrates this technique.

When you override paint **or** update **methods, make sure your code can execute very quickly. Include all the statements you need for painting, but no more. For example, try to remove all calculations and retain only the drawing statements. You do not want to slow down the AWT thread by making it perform any operations that you can do elsewhere. If the** paint **method for one component hogs time, it can prevent other components from being painted in a timely fashion and potentially cause a situation in which the display for a program does not match its internal state.**

Graphics

Many programs produce graphical output. Lines, characters, and any shapes drawn directly onto a component's display area make up graphical output. Graphical output can be part of your GUI. The AWT provides the class Graphics, which includes many methods you can use for drawing. This class is one of many utility classes that reside in the package java.awt.

The drawing methods are instance methods of the Graphics class, and each instance of Graphics is the **graphics context** for a component. The paint and update methods provide a Graphics object as an argument of the method for you to use when you override the method. For example, the Hello World program of Chapter 12 contains the following lines:

```
public void paint( Graphics g ) {
   g.drawString( "Hello World!", 100, 60 );
   // lines of code omitted
}
```

The next sample program, the `Drawings` class, provides a more extensive demonstration of using the methods of the **Graphics** class.

Drawing in the graphics context of a component is a very different process than adding a component to a container. In the preceding example, drawing the **String** "Hello World!" produces output that looks like a **Label** containing "Hello World!" in a container, but it is produced with lower-level constructs. The main differences are the following:

- No core Java platform layout manager class can work with graphics, and you must specify coordinates. For example, the **String** "Hello World!" in the preceding example is drawn starting at 100 pixels to the right and 60 pixels down from the upper-left corner of the component.
- Components automatically redraw themselves when the window in which they appear is displayed, resized, or uncovered on the screen. You must redraw graphical output as required. Usually, you effect redraw operations by including in the **paint** method the method calls for drawing.
- If your program uses only components and never draws to the graphics context, there is no need to implement **paint**.

Class	**java.awt.Graphics**
Purpose	The **Graphics** class provides a number of methods for drawing onto a component.
Methods	■ **void drawString(String *str*, int *x*, int *y*)** The **drawString** method draws the string provided by the first argument so that the lower-left corner of the first character is at pixel coordinate **(*x*, *y*)**. The characters appear in the current font and color, which you can set with other methods of the **Graphics** class. ■ **void drawLine(int *x1*, int *y1*, int *x2*, int *y2*)** The **drawLine** method draws a line from **(*x1*, *y1*)** to **(*x2*, *y2*)**, in the coordinates of the graphics context. ■ **void drawRect(int *x*, int *y*, int *width*, int *height*)** The **drawRect** method draws the outline of a rectangle from **(*x*, *y*)** to **(*x+width*, *y+height*)**. ■ **void drawPolygon(int[] *xPoints*, int[] *yPoints*, int *nPoints*)**

The **drawPolygon** method draws the closed polygon defined by the arrays of ***x*** and ***y*** coordinates. It is also possible to create an instance of the **Polygon** class and use the version of **drawPolygon** with a single **Polygon** parameter.

- **void drawArc(int *x*, int *y*, int *width*, int *height*,**
  int *startAngle*, int *arcAngle*)

  The **drawArc** method draws an arc of an ellipse or circle bounded by the coordinates ***x*** and ***y*** and the specified ***width*** and ***height*** arguments. The arc rotates counterclockwise from ***startAngle*** degrees to ***startAngle*** + ***arcAngle*** degrees.

- **boolean drawImage(Image *img*, int *x*, int *y*,**
  ImageObserver *observer*)

  The **drawImage** method draws an image at the coordinates specified. The **Image** class is defined in **java.awt** for GIF files, JPEG files, and URLs. Images are most frequently used in applets, and the **Image** and **ImageObserver** classes are described in Chapter 14 along with other applet topics. Loading an image can take some time. Therefore, the method returns without waiting, and a return value of **false** indicates the image is not completely loaded. The **ImageObserver** object is notified when the operation is complete. Chapter 14 describes how to display **Image** objects.

- **void fillRect(int *x*, int *y*, int *width*, int *height*)**
  void fillPolygon(int *xPoints*[], int *yPoints*[], int *nPoints*)
  void fillArc(int *x*, int *y*, int *width*, int *height*,
  int *startAngle*, int *arcAngle*

  These methods of the **Graphics** class fill areas of the screen with color rather than draw outlines. The result of a draw or fill operation depends upon various settings that you can specify by calling the following methods of the **Graphics** class.

- **void setColor(Color *c*)**

  The **setColor** method sets the color used for subsequent drawing and fill coloring.

- **void setFont(Font f)**

  This method sets the font for subsequent text operations.

- **void setPaintMode()**
  void setXORMode(Color c)

  The **setPaintMode** and **setXORMode** methods set alternatives paint modes. Call **setPaintMode** to overwrite whatever is already drawn on the screen. Call **setXORMode** to display pixels in the color that results from an EXCLUSIVE OR

(XOR) operation between the current color and the color specified in the argument. Predicting the resulting colors from XOR mode is very difficult, and this mode can create bizarre effects. However, the colors are reversible, and you can restore pixels to the original color by drawing twice.

It is important to note that the values set for a particular Graphics object used in a paint method are lost at the end of the paint method. This is because each paint method gets a fresh Graphics object with which to work. To make such changes stick, you should make them to the Component object.

Although the Graphics class is useful, it does have limitations. For example, you cannot specify the width of a line or use a fill pattern.

The JFC in version 1.2 of the Java platform includes Java 2D API. This API provides a framework for using device- and resolution-independent graphics that are more powerful than the AWT. The Java 2D API builds on the graphics and imaging classes defined by java.awt to make it easy to incorporate two-dimensional graphics, text, and images in Java applications and applets. The API provides a two-dimensional imaging model for line art, text, and images that uniformly addresses color, spatial transformations, and compositing.

Here is a program that exercises several methods of the Graphics class. It also demonstrates using the java.awt.Font class to set the size of characters to draw, and working with the java.awt.Color class. The program does not have much meaning, pretense to art, or even amusing output. But it does exercise a representative sample of the methods in the Graphics class. As with the other sample programs for the AWT, a breakdown of this code follows the output.

This program defines the class `Drawings`. Because `Drawings` is a public class, it is found in a file called Drawings.java. The structure of packages mirrors the file system, so you will find this source code in the java4cpp\windows subfolder of the folder in which you unpacked the JAR file java4cpp.jar.

```
package java4cpp.windows;
import java.awt.*;
import java.awt.event.*;
/** An example class used to demonstrate various
  * drawing techniques including text, lines,
  * shapes, and filled shapes.
  */
public class Drawings extends Frame {
   /** Class constructor method
     * @param titleText Name to be put in the
     *    window's title bar
     */
   public Drawings( String titleText ) {
      super( titleText );
      addWindowListener( new WindowAdapter() {
```

```
            /** Exit when the window closes */
            public void
            windowClosing( WindowEvent event ) {
               Frame.this.dispose();
               System.exit( 0 );
            }
         }
      );
      setSize( 500, 500 );
      setBackground( Color.white );
      setVisible( true );
   }
   /** Draws the text, lines, and shapes in the
     * specified graphics context
     * @param g the component's graphics context
     */
   public void paint( Graphics g ) {
      g.drawString( "Hello World!", 100, 60 );
      Font cFont = g.getFont();
      Font newFont = new Font( cFont.getName(),
                               cFont.getStyle(),
                               cFont.getSize() + 20 );
      g.setFont( newFont );
      g.drawString( "Here I am!", 200, 80 );
      g.drawLine( 50, 50, 100, 200 );
      g.setColor( Color.blue );
      g.drawRoundRect( 150, 300, 100, 125, 15, 15 );
      g.setColor( Color.red );
      g.fillOval( 400, 200, 50, 180 );
   }
   /** The test method for the class
     * @param args not used
     */
   public static void main( String[] args ) {
      new Drawings( "Drawings Sample" );
   }
}
```

Allowing for differences in operating systems, the output should be similar to Figure 13-9.

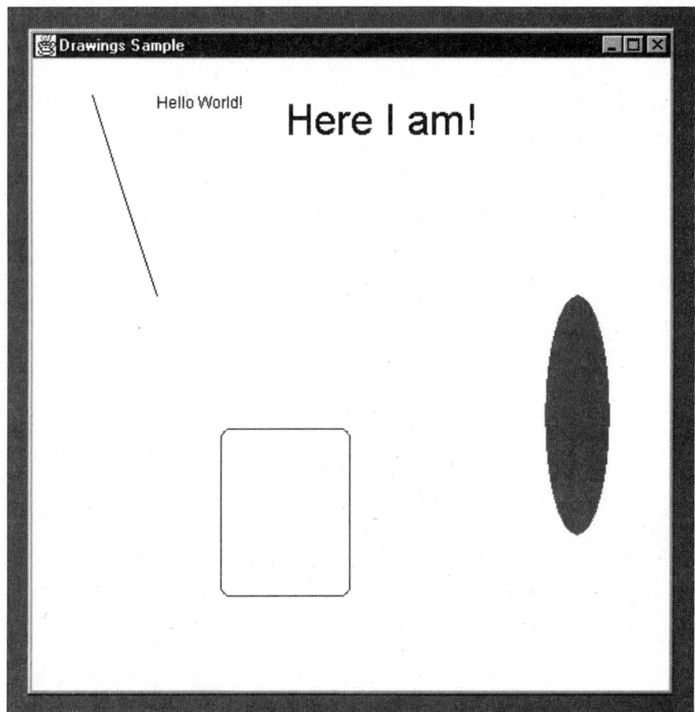

Figure 13-9: Output of the Drawings class

The class encapsulating the drawing program is called `Drawings`. The constructor, as usual, begins by passing the title for the Frame to the constructor of the Frame superclass.

```
public Drawings( String titleText ) {
   super( titleText );
```

As in the sample programs in Chapter 12, an anonymous inner class extends WindowAdapter and overrides the windowClosing method to handle the event generated when the user closes the application frame window. This method disposes of the resources used by the window and exits the program. One statement in the `Drawings` constructor creates an instance of the inner class and registers it as the event handler by calling addWindowListener:

```
   addWindowListener( new WindowAdapter() {
         /** Exit when the window closes */
         public void
         windowClosing( WindowEvent event ) {
```

```
                Frame.this.dispose();
                System.exit( 0 );
            }
        }
    );
```

The last statements of the constructor call two methods that are inherited from the Component class. The first sets the size of the Frame, in pixels. The second sets the background color, using a constant defined in the Color class. Finally, the Frame is displayed by a call to setVisible. The setVisible method is implemented in the Component class to make the component visible, and overridden in the Window class also to bring the window to the front of the display if other windows are displayed on top of it:

```
    setSize( 500, 500 );
    setBackground( Color.white );
    setVisible( true );
}
```

This application just draws some shapes, so most of the action occurs in the paint method:

```
public void paint( Graphics g ) {
```

The paint method draws two strings, "Hello World!" and "Here I am!," at different sizes. The "Hello World!" string is drawn in the default font. To be bigger than "Hello World!," "Here I am!" must be drawn with a different font. The Font class is a utility class in java.awt that encapsulates fonts, and the Font constructor has arguments for the name, style, and size of the required font. Here, the new font is a variation on the default font because only the size changes, so the paint method creates a Font object and specifies it as the font for the graphics context, as follows:

- Obtain an object reference for the current font of the graphics context, by calling Graphics.getFont.
- Interrogate the current Font object to determine its name, style, and size by calling Font.getName, Font.getStyle, and Font.getSize. The name of a font is specified in a String. You can call the method Toolkit.getFontList to get the names of the fonts available on your installation of the Java platform. The possible styles are Font.PLAIN, Font.BOLD, and Font.ITALIC. The size is expressed in points.
- Use the new keyword to create a new Font object with the same characteristics as the current font except that the size is increased by 20 points.
- Call Graphics.setFont to set the new font as the current font for the current graphics context.

```
public void paint( Graphics g ) {
    g.drawString( "Hello World!", 100, 60 );
    Font cFont = g.getFont();
```

```
   Font newFont = new Font( cFont.getName(),
                            cFont.getStyle(),
                            cFont.getSize() + 20 );
   g.setFont( newFont );
   g.drawString( "Here I am!", 200, 80 );
```

The remaining lines of the paint method draw a line in the default foreground color, a rounded rectangle in blue, and a solid oval shape in red:

```
   g.drawLine( 50, 50, 100, 200 );
   g.setColor( Color.blue );
   g.drawRoundRect( 150, 300, 100, 125, 15, 15 );
   g.setColor( Color.red );
   g.fillOval( 400, 200, 50, 180 );
}
```

The main method for the Drawings class simply creates a Drawings object and passes the title bar text as the parameter for the constructor.

```
public static void main( String[] args ) {
   new Drawings( "Drawings Sample" );
}
```

Events

Creating a user interface involves more than displaying components and graphics. An interface is not just output. Programming to interact with the user input is a very important part of developing any user interface. In a GUI for a Java application, **events** are objects that encapsulate changes in state initiated by the user. Generally, the user triggers events by pressing and releasing keys on the keyboard, or moving and clicking with the mouse. Some events, such as button clicks or text entry, have meaning only for specific components in your GUI. Others, such as resizing a window or moving focus from window to window, are also recognized by the native operating system.

The AWT includes a package java.awt.event. Figure 13-10 shows the classes, which encapsulate the events that relate to the GUI components in your application or applet.

The Object class is in java.lang, and EventObject, the superclass for all events, is in the package java.util. The abstract class AWTEvent is in the package java.awt.event. The events you actually handle are all objects of classes in java.awt.event. Apart from AWTEvent, only one class, InputEvent, is abstract, because user input is represented as consisting of either KeyEvent or MouseEvent objects.

A large part of programming a GUI involves providing handlers for events. In the Java programming language, this task is fairly straightforward because you create event handlers by implementing predefined listener interfaces or extending predefined adapter classes. Listeners and adapters are described later in this chapter. Shaded boxes represent abstract classes.

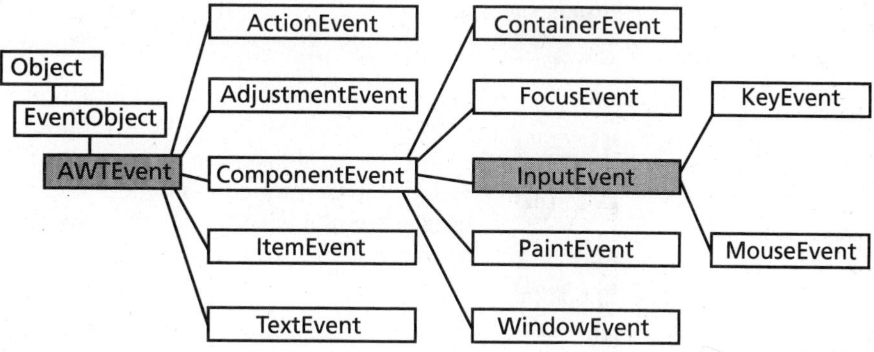

Figure 13-10: Event classes

To catch and handle events, you adopt the "Hollywood model" of programming: "Don't call us, we'll call you." In other words, you do not poll the environment looking for events. When an event occurs, the AWT thread calls you. In parts of your code not directly related to events, you can ignore events. Like different threads in a multithreaded application, these parts of your code just carry on with their usual business. When events occur, the JVM or your Web browser receives messages from the operating system. The classes in java.awt.event determine the nature of the event and identify the appropriate component. The JVM calls the object that implements the Listener interface registered for the event. Through listeners, events call you. The types of events are listed in Figure 3-11.

Event class	Description
ActionEvent	Action events relate to the components that users click, such as buttons, check boxes, and menu items.
AdjustmentEvent	Adjustment events indicate a change to an object of a class that implements the **Adjustable** interface. The **Scrollbar** class is an example of an **Adjustable** class of objects.
ComponentEvent	Component events occur when a component has been moved, resized, shown, or hidden. The AWT thread typically handles such events.
ContainerEvent	Container events occur when the contents of a container have changed or when a component has been added or removed. Use this event as notification only, because the AWT thread handles these events.

Figure 13-11: Description of the event classes

Event class	Description
FocusEvent	Multitasking operating systems let a user have more than one window open simultaneously, but only one window at a time can be highlighted and brought to the foreground. The foreground window is said to have **focus**, and the user usually brings a window into focus by clicking the mouse over it. A focus event occurs when a component gets or loses focus.
InputEvent	This **InputEvent** class is the superclass for both keyboard and mouse events. It has no corresponding listener interface.
ItemEvent	Item events occur when the state of an item within a component that implements the **ItemSelectable** interface has changed. **Checkbox**, **Choice**, and **List** are examples of selectable components.
KeyEvent	A key event occurs when the user releases a key on the keyboard.
MouseEvent	The vents encapsulated by this class are pressing the mouse button, releasing the button, dragging the mouse, and moving the mouse.
PaintEvent	Paint events indicate that a component should have its **update** method invoked. The AWT thread handles these events automatically.
TextEvent	When the user edits the text value in a **TextField** or **TextArea**, a text event occurs.
WindowEvent	User actions relating to windows generate instances of this event class.

Figure 13-11: Description of the event classes (continued)

Each event object contains the appropriate data for the event. You can call methods of the event classes to access this information. Figure 13-12 shows some methods you can call to get information about an event in an event handler.

Class	Method	Description
AWTEvent	**int getID()**	The superclass method returns the type of the current event.

Figure 13-12: Some methods of the event classes

Class	Method	Description
ComponentEvent	**Component getComponent()**	This method returns the component involved in the event.
ItemEvent	**Object getItem()**	This method returns the object that was either selected or deselected.
ItemEvent	**int getStateChange()**	The return value is **ItemEvent.SELECTED** or **ItemEvent.DESELECTED**. A method to indicate the change of state is required because the only handler in the **ItemListener** interface, **itemStateChanged**, does not make this distinction.
KeyEvent	**int getKeyChar()**	This method returns the Unicode character that was typed.
MouseEvent	**int getClickCount()**	This method distinguishes between single and double mouse clicks.
InputEvent	**int getModifiers()**	The return value indicates which mouse button is involved. Different operating systems support one, two, or three mouse buttons.
MouseEvent	**Point getPoint()**	This method returns the location for the mouse event.
PaintEvent	**Rectangle getUpdatedRect()**	This method returns the rectangle representing the area to be painted.
WindowEvent	**Window getWindow()**	This method returns the window that is the source of the event.

Figure 13-12: Some methods of the event classes (continued)

To make the method AWTEvent.getID easier to use, each event subclass defines named integer constants for events associated with the class. For example, the FocusEvent class defines the two constants FOCUS_GAINED and FOCUS_LOST. Very often the context of each event handler gives you the same information as the getID method, so you do not have to call this method. For example, there are two handlers for FocusEvent objects in the FocusListener interface: focusGained and focusLost.

Version Watch

The original version of the Java platform used a very different event model. There was only one class for events, java.awt.Event, **and not the hierarchy of classes that was introduced in version 1.1.**

Listeners and Adapters

The AWT defines a set of interfaces called listeners. Each kind of event has a listener interface, and each listener has methods for every event that can occur in its event class. For example, the TextListener interface corresponds to the TextEvent class. The only thing a user can do to a TextField or TextArea object is change the contents of the text component, so the only method in the TextListener interface is textValueChanged.

Use listener interfaces to create handlers for events. Basically, you must complete two steps to create a handler for an event:

- Define a class that implements the appropriate listener interface. Your class provides the handler by implementing the methods that are declared in the interface.
- Register an instance of the class with the component affected by the event.

Class	***any component class***
Methods	■ **void addxxxListener(xxxListener *object*)** The **add*xxx*Listener** methods register a listener with a component; they all return **void**. The ***xxx*** is the type of the listener. All components have the methods **addComponentListener, addFocusListener, addMouseListener**, and **addMouseMotionListener**.

Code Example	<pre>class myHandler implements TextListener {
	   public void textValueChanged(TextEvent e) {
	      // implementation of textValueChanged omitted
	   }
	}
	TextListener tl = new myHandler();
	TextArea t = new TextArea();
	t.addTextListener(tl);</pre>

Code Dissection	These lines of code are excerpts from a program that handles text events.

The structure of the listener interfaces is very regular and predictable. All the methods of all the interfaces follow the same form.

Interface	***xxx*Listener**
Dissection	Each event class has an associated listener interface.The **xxx** represents the name of an event class.
Methods	■ **void *xxxEvent*(xxxEvent *E*)** All listener methods have return type **void.** All listener methods take one argument, an object of an event class. All listener methods begin with the same word as the listener. For example, all the methods in the **ComponentListener** interface begin with **component**, have an argument of type **ComponentEvent**, and return **void**. The methods in a **ComponentListener** are **componentMoved, componentShown**, and **componentHidden**. Mouse events are the one exception to this pattern. Mouse event handlers are split over two interfaces: **MouseListener** and **MouseMotionListener**. The methods in these two interfaces all begin with **mouse** and all take a single **MouseEvent** object as a parameter. The **MouseListener** methods are **mouseClicked, mousePressed, mouseReleased, mouseEntered**, and **mouseExited**. The **MouseMotionListener** methods are **mouseDragged** and **mouseMoved**.

You can implement a listener interface directly. For listener interfaces with more than one method, you can alternatively implement the listener indirectly by extending its adapter class. The AWT provides several adapter classes that implement listener interfaces for you. The adapters provide empty implementations of all the methods in the interface. The advantage of the adapter classes is that classes that extend them can implement only the handlers of interest, and inherit the empty implementations of all other methods.

The adapter classes follow a similar naming pattern to the listener interfaces, except that the names are *xxx*Adapter rather than *xxx*Listener, where *xxx* is the type event for which the interface is listening.

Generally, extending adapter classes is preferable when a minority of the methods in the interface are of interest. Using an adapter simplifies the coding, but does not change the mechanism. The example programs in Chapter 12 and this chapter use adapter classes.

The set of listener interfaces and adapter classes is shown in Figure 13-13. Ovals represent interfaces.

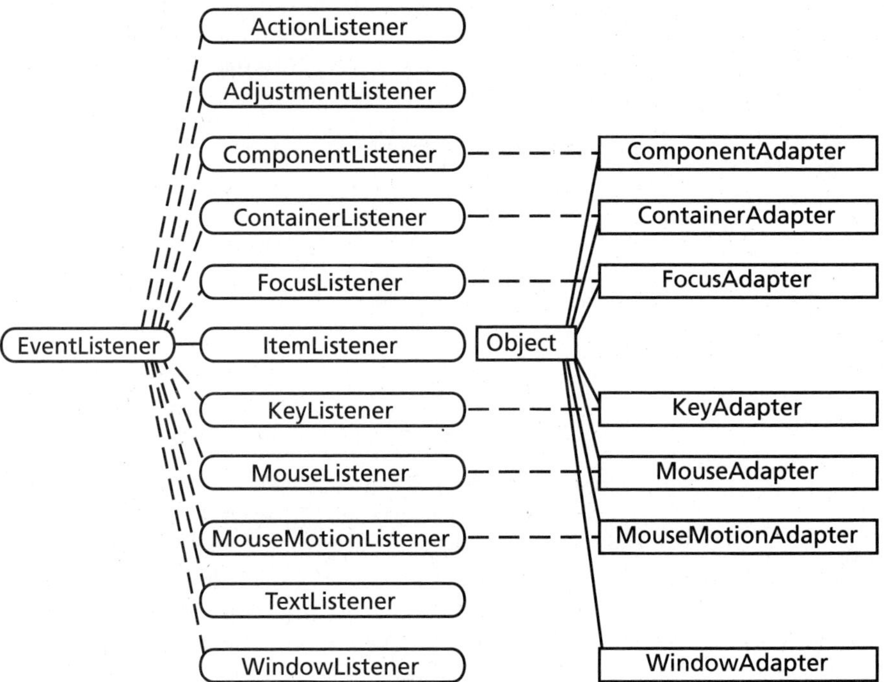

Figure 13-13: Listener interfaces and adapter classes

The listener interfaces in java.awt.event all extend the interface EventListener from the package java.util, just as the adapter classes extend Object from java.lang. The predefined adapter classes for listeners are all abstract classes.

Any class can handle events, not just GUI components; all a class needs to do is to implement the appropriate interface and register itself with the object that generates the events.

Printing

The Java platform provides rudimentary support for printing in the form of two classes in the AWT: java.awt.PrintGraphics and java.awt.PrintJob. The PrintGraphics class extends the Graphics class. The PrintGraphics class was made distinct from the Graphics class so that you can easily handle the drawing commands differently for display and print purposes, if necessary.

You can print components as well as display them. There are several steps you must follow to print. In simplified pseudocode, the process is as follows:

1. Obtain a PrintJob object from a Toolkit object.
2. Obtain a Graphics objects using PrintJob.getGraphics().
3. Print a page into the Graphics object using the existing methods for Graphics objects.
4. Call the Graphics.dispose() method to flush the page
5. Repeat steps 2 through 4 for all the pages in the job.
6. Call PrintJob.dispose() to end the print job.

There are several methods in the PrintJob class that provide information about the page size, resolution, and page ordering.

The Component class defines methods for print operations:

- voidprint(Graphics *g*)
  The print method prints the specified component. Override this method for components that must do special processing before being printed or that should be printed differently than they are painted. By default, this method calls the paint method.
- voidprintAll(Graphics *g*)
  The printAll method prints the specified component and all its subcomponents. This method is used in the File Browser program later in this chapter.

Version Watch

The original version of the Java platform had no support for printing, and users were left on their own to find alternative solutions. Version 1.1 introduced the classes PrintJob **and** PrintGraphics **and support for printing components.**

Using the Clipboard

You can use the classes in the package java.awt.datatransfer to cut or copy to the system Clipboard or to paste from the Clipboard. The java.awt.datatransfer package supports generic data transfer between applications, of which the Clipboard cut, copy, and paste operations are just three examples.

Version Watch

In version 1.2 of the Java platform, you will be able to drag and drop information using support that will be added as part of the Java Foundation Classes (JFC).

Objects of a class can be transferred to or from the Clipboard only if the class implements the interface Transferable. This interface is provided by the java.awt.datatransfer package, and includes the methods that a class must implement to support Clipboard operations on objects of the class. Clipboard operations often operate on String objects. Therefore, the Java platform provides a convenience class, java.awt.datatransfer.StringSelection, that implements Transferable. The StringSelection class is a concrete class designed for the specific purpose of cutting, copying, and pasting String objects to and from the Clipboard.

The File Browser program later in this chapter demonstrates how to copy data to the system Clipboard.

Class	java.awt.datatransfer.Clipboard
Purpose	The **Clipboard** class in the **java.awt.datatransfer** package supports cut, copy, and paste operations for the system Clipboard.
Constructors	■ **Clipboard(String *name*)** Applications can create their own **Clipboard** objects for data transfer within the application. When you create a **Clipboard** object, supply a name as the argument of the constructor. You can also access the system Clipboard by using the method **Toolkit.getSystemClipboard**. Using the system Clipboard is a common way to transfer data between applications.
Methods	■ **void setContents(Transferable *content*, ClipboardOwner *owner*)** This method cuts or copies a **Transferable** object to the Clipboard. The **ClipboardOwner** object is notified when the transfer is complete. ■ **Transferable getContents(Object *requestor*)** This method requests the contents of the Clipboard. Use this method in paste operations.

For performance reasons, the AWT reserves the right to defer data transfer to the Clipboard until a consumer requests the data from the Clipboard. Therefore, you must create a ClipboardOwner object that you use to determine when you actually lose ownership of the data transferred and can safely destroy it.

Interface	java.awt.datatransfer.ClipboardOwner
Purpose	The **ClipboardOwner** interface contains one method.
Methods	■ **void lostOwnership(Clipboard *clipboard*, Transferable *contents*)** This method informs the **ClipboardOwner** object that ownership of data has been transferred to the Clipboard. You should attempt to keep the data available until this method is called.

The java.awt.datatransfer **package was introduced in version 1.1 of the Java platform. The original version had no support for the Clipboard.**

Applets are not allowed to access the native system Clipboard because the information contained within it may be sensitive. However, applets can still create other Clipboard objects for their own internal use.

The File Browser Program

Here is an example application that demonstrates the use of dialog boxes and a number of other components, including event handlers. It shows some file I/O and exception handling, and many of the features of the Java programming language that are covered in earlier chapters. The program is fairly long for a sample, so a breakdown of the more interesting parts of the code follows the listing and output.

This application is a simple file browser. It lets the user specify a filename in a file dialog box. The application then reads the contents of that file and displays them in a text area that occupies the larger part of a border layout with only two components. A status line occupies the bottom of the window.

This application contains a menu bar with three menus labeled File, Edit and Options. The File menu has three items: File open, Print and Exit. The only item on the Options menus is Font. When the user clicks Font, a dialog box appears in which the available fonts are listed and the current font is selected. The user can select a different font and press one of two buttons: Apply or Cancel. If the user applies the selected font, the program redraws the contents of the file in the new font. The Edit menu has only the item Copy all. Copy all puts the entire contents of the file onto the clipboard.

Here is the top-level class of the application, `FileBrowser`:

```
package java4cpp.windows;
import java.awt.*;
import java.awt.event.*;
import java.awt.datatransfer.*;
import java.io.*;
/** An example class used to demonstrate the
  * use of menus, dialog boxes, printing, and
  * the system Clipboard
  */
public class FileBrowser extends Frame {
   private FontDialog fontDialog;
   private TextField  statusLine;
   private TextArea   text;
   /** Class constructor
     * @param titleText Title bar text
     */
   public FileBrowser( String titleText ) {
      super( titleText );
      addWindowListener( new WindowAdapter() {
            /** Exit when the window closes */
            public void
            windowClosing( WindowEvent event ) {
               Frame.this.dispose();
               System.exit( 0 );
            }
         }
      );
      setLayout( new BorderLayout() );
      setMenuBar( buildMenuBar() );
      text = new TextArea();
      text.setEditable( false );
```

```
      text.setBackground( Color.white );
      add( text, "Center" );
      statusLine = new TextField();
      add( statusLine, "South" );
      pack();
      setVisible( true );
   }
   /** Present a dialog box to have the user select
     * the file for browsing */
   public void loadFile() {
      FileDialog fileDialog
         = new FileDialog( this, "File Open",
                           FileDialog.LOAD );
      fileDialog.setVisible( true );
      if ( fileDialog.getFile() != null ) try {
         FileReader fr = new FileReader(
            fileDialog.getDirectory() +
            fileDialog.getFile() );
         text.setText( "" );
         text.setVisible( false );
         setCursor( Cursor.getPredefinedCursor(
            Cursor.WAIT_CURSOR ) );
         char[] charBuffer = new char[4096];
         int charsRead = fr.read( charBuffer, 0,
                                  charBuffer.length );
         while ( charsRead != -1 ) {
            text.append( new String( charBuffer, 0,
                                     charsRead ) );
            charsRead = fr.read( charBuffer, 0,
                                 charBuffer.length );
         }
         text.setVisible( true );
         setCursor( Cursor.getDefaultCursor() );
      } catch( IOException ioe ) {
         statusLine.setText( ioe.toString() );
      }
      fileDialog.dispose();
   }
   /** Build the menu bar, menus, and menu items for
     * the file browser */
   public MenuBar buildMenuBar() {
      MenuBar menuBar = new MenuBar();
      Menu fileMenu = new Menu( "File" );
      Menu editMenu = new Menu( "Edit" );
      Menu optionsMenu = new Menu( "Options" );
      MenuItem exitItem = new MenuItem( "Exit" );
```

```
MenuItem fileOpenItem
   = new MenuItem( "File open..." );
MenuItem printItem
   = new MenuItem( "Print..." );
MenuItem copyAllItem
   = new MenuItem( "Copy all" );
MenuItem fontsItem
   = new MenuItem( "Fonts..." );
fileOpenItem.setShortcut(
   new MenuShortcut( KeyEvent.VK_O ) );
printItem.setShortcut(
   new MenuShortcut( KeyEvent.VK_P ) );
fontsItem.setShortcut(
   new MenuShortcut( KeyEvent.VK_F ) );
fileOpenItem.addActionListener(
   new ActionListener() {
      public void
      actionPerformed( ActionEvent event ) {
         loadFile();
      }
   }
);
printItem.addActionListener(
   new ActionListener() {
      public void
      actionPerformed( ActionEvent event ) {
         printText();
      }
   }
);
exitItem.addActionListener(
   new ActionListener() {
      public void
      actionPerformed( ActionEvent event ) {
         dispose();
         System.exit( 0 );
      }
   }
);
copyAllItem.addActionListener(
   new ActionListener() {
      public void
      actionPerformed( ActionEvent event ) {
         copyAllToClipboard();
      }
```

```
            }
        );
        fontsItem.addActionListener(
            new ActionListener() {
                public void
                actionPerformed( ActionEvent event ) {
                    updateFont();
                }
            }
        );
        menuBar.add( fileMenu );
        menuBar.add( editMenu );
        menuBar.add( optionsMenu );
        fileMenu.add( fileOpenItem );
        fileMenu.add( printItem );
        fileMenu.addSeparator();
        fileMenu.add( exitItem );
        editMenu.add( copyAllItem );
        optionsMenu.add( fontsItem );
        return menuBar;
    }
    /** Print the current contents of the text area */
    public void printText() {
        Toolkit tk = getToolkit();
        PrintJob pjob = tk.getPrintJob( this,
                        "File Print Job",
                        null );
        if ( pjob != null ) {
            Graphics pg = pjob.getGraphics();
            if ( pg != null ) {
                text.printAll( pg );
                pg.dispose();
            }
            pjob.end();
        }
    }
    /** Allow font selection and update */
    public void updateFont() {
        fontDialog = new FontDialog( this,
                                     text.getFont() );
        Font f = text.getFont();
        String chosenFont = fontDialog.getFontName();
        if ( chosenFont != null ) {
            text.setFont( new Font( chosenFont,
                                    f.getStyle(),
```

```
                                   f.getSize() ) );
      }
   }
   /** Copy file contents to system Clipboard */
   public void copyAllToClipboard() {
      Toolkit tk = getToolkit();
      Clipboard sysClip = tk.getSystemClipboard();
      StringSelection ss
         = new StringSelection( text.getText() );
      sysClip.setContents( ss, new ClipboardOwner() {
            public void
            lostOwnership( Clipboard c,
                           Transferable t ) {
               /* do nothing */
            }
         }
      );
   }
   /** The test method for the class
     * @param args not used
     */
   public static void main( String[] args ) {
      new FileBrowser( "File Browser Sample" );
   }
}
class FontDialog extends Dialog {
   private List fontChoices;
   private String fontName;
   /** Class constructor
     * @param parent The dialog box's parent window
     *    ( the main browser window )
     * @param currentFont Font being used in
     *    the main browser window
     */
   public FontDialog( Frame parent,
                      Font currentFont ){
      super( parent, "Fonts", true );
      addWindowListener( new WindowAdapter() {
            /** Exit when the window closes */
            public void
            windowClosing( WindowEvent event ) {
               Dialog.this.dispose();
            }
         }
      );
```

```
setLayout( new BorderLayout() );
final Button okay = new Button( "Apply" );
okay.setEnabled( false );
okay.addActionListener(
   new ActionListener() {
      public void
      actionPerformed( ActionEvent event ) {
         fontName
            = fontChoices.getSelectedItem();
         dispose();
      }
   }
);
final Button cancel = new Button( "Cancel" );
cancel.addActionListener(
   new ActionListener() {
      public void
      actionPerformed( ActionEvent event ) {
         fontName = null;
         dispose();
      }
   }
);
String[] availableFonts
   = getToolkit().getFontList();
fontChoices = new List( availableFonts.length,
                        false );
for ( int i=0; i<availableFonts.length; i++ ) {
   fontChoices.add( availableFonts[i] );
   if ( availableFonts[i].equals(
        currentFont.getName() ) ) {
      fontChoices.select( i );
   }
}
fontChoices.addItemListener(
   new ItemListener() {
      public void
      itemStateChanged( ItemEvent event ) {
         if ( event.getStateChange() ==
               ItemEvent.SELECTED ) {
            fontName =
               fontChoices.getSelectedItem();
            okay.setEnabled( true );
         }
      }
```

```
         }
      );
      add( new Label( "Font name choices:" ),
                      "North" );
      add( fontChoices, "Center" );
      Panel buttonPanel = new Panel();
      buttonPanel.add( okay );
      buttonPanel.add( cancel );
      add( buttonPanel, "South" );
      Insets i = getParent().getInsets();
      setLocation( i.left, i.top );
      pack();
      setVisible( true );
   }
   /** Retrieve the font name selected by the user
     * @return The name of the font selected
     */
   public String getFontName() {
      return fontName;
   }
}
```

Allowing for platform variations, the output appears as shown in the following figures. In Figure 13-14, the source file for the `FileBrowser` class is displayed in Helvetica font, and the file menu is shown.

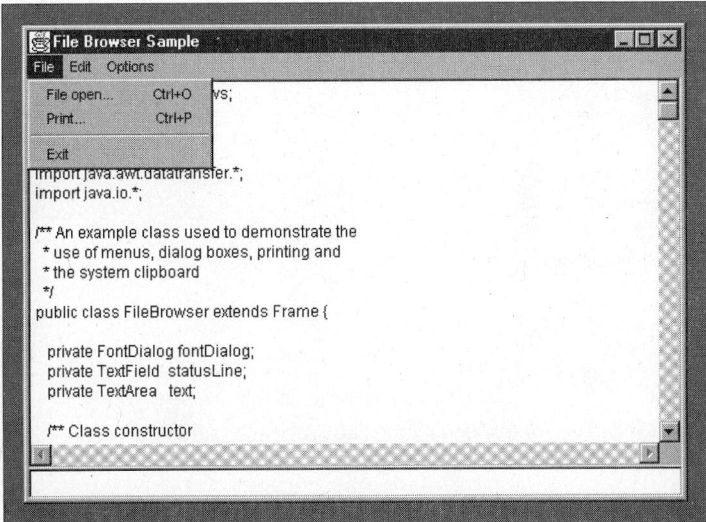

Figure 13-14: Possible output of the File Browser program

Figure 13-15 shows part of the same file appears in Courier font, and the Options menu, of which the Font menu is a submenu.

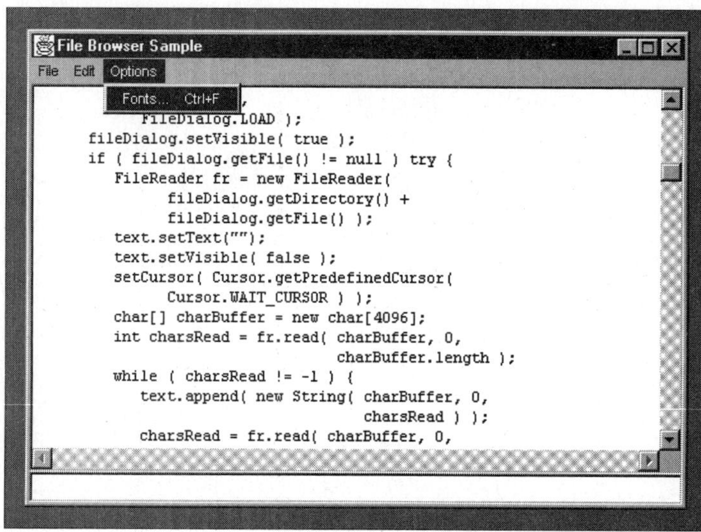

Figure 13-15: More possible output of the File Browser program

Figure 13-16 shows the Fonts menu that lists the fonts available on one implementation of the Java platform. This menu may have different entries when you run this program.

Figure 13-16: The Fonts menu of the File Browser program

Breakdown of the File Browser Program

The File Browser program begins much like all the sample programs in Chapter 12 and this chapter. The first three statements call the superclass constructor, register a handler for window events, and set the layout manager.

```
public class FileBrowser extends Frame {
   private FontDialog fontDialog;
   private TextField  statusLine;
   private TextArea   text;
   /** Class constructor
     * @param titleText Title bar text
     */
   public FileBrowser( String titleText ) {
      super( titleText );
      addWindowListener( new WindowAdapter() {
            /** Exit when the window closes */
            public void
            windowClosing( WindowEvent event ) {
               Frame.this.dispose();
               System.exit( 0 );
            }
         }
      );
      setLayout( new BorderLayout() );
```

The next statement calls the `buildMenuBar` method of the `FileBrowser` class to create and set the menu bar for the application:

```
      setMenuBar( buildMenuBar() );
```

Here is the `buildMenuBar` method. It begins by creating all of the objects that are used in the menu. These include the MenuBar object, three Menu objects, and five MenuItem objects:

```
   public MenuBar buildMenuBar() {
      MenuBar menuBar = new MenuBar();
      Menu fileMenu = new Menu( "File" );
      Menu editMenu = new Menu( "Edit" );
      Menu optionsMenu = new Menu( "Options" );
      MenuItem exitItem = new MenuItem( "Exit" );
      MenuItem fileOpenItem
         = new MenuItem( "File open..." );
      MenuItem printItem
         = new MenuItem( "Print..." );
      MenuItem copyAllItem
         = new MenuItem( "Copy all" );
      MenuItem fontsItem
         = new MenuItem( "Fonts..." );
```

After the objects have been created, shortcuts are defined and set for three of the menu items. Keystroke constants in the KeyEvent class specify the shortcut key. The triggering of shortcut keys is platform-dependent. For example, on Windows platforms, the specified key is combined with the Ctrl key. The result is that

Ctrl+O is the shortcut for the File open item, Ctrl+P is the shortcut for the Print item, and Ctrl+F is the shortcut for the Fonts item.

```
fileOpenItem.setShortcut(
   new MenuShortcut( KeyEvent.VK_O ) );
printItem.setShortcut(
   new MenuShortcut( KeyEvent.VK_P ) );
fontsItem.setShortcut(
   new MenuShortcut( KeyEvent.VK_F ) );
```

The next statement defines an anonymous inner class that implements the ActionListener interface method actionPerformed for the File open menu item. An object of this class is created and registered to handle the action event for the menu item. This handler is called every time the user selects a File open menu item, and it invokes the `loadFile` method each time:

```
fileOpenItem.addActionListener(
    new ActionListener() {
       public void
       actionPerformed( ActionEvent event ) {
          loadFile();
       }
    }
 );
```

Similarly, the next three statements create and register handlers for the Print, Exit, Copy all, and Fonts menu items. The Print handler calls the `printText` method of the `FileBrowser` class. This method begins by retrieving the current Toolkit object and creating a PrintJob object. From the PrintJob object, a Graphics object is obtained and the contents of the text area are printed to the Graphics object. Calling the Graphics.dispose method prints the page, and calling the PrintJob.dispose method ends the print job.

```
public void printText() {
   Toolkit tk = getToolkit();
   PrintJob pjob = tk.getPrintJob( this,
                   "File Print Job",
                   null);
   if ( pjob != null ) {
      Graphics pg = pjob.getGraphics();
      if ( pg != null ) {
         text.printAll( pg );
         pg.dispose();
      }
      pjob.end();
   }
}
```

The `Exit` handler disposes of the window resources and terminates the application.

The `Copy all` handler calls the `FileBrowser.copyAllToClipboard` method. This method uses the current Toolkit object to get a reference to the system Clipboard object. A StringSelection object is created as a wrapper around the contents of the text area and is then put into the system clipboard. The second parameter of the setContents method requires an object that implements the ClipboardOwner interface. For this simple example, you do not need to know at what point you lose ownership of the clipboard because String objects are immutable, and because the strings put on the clipboard will not be garbage-collected as long as they are on the clipboard and thus will always be available. The program defines an anonymous inner class to implement the interface with an empty version of the lostOwnership method:

```
public void copyAllToClipboard() {
   Toolkit tk = getToolkit();
   Clipboard sysClip = tk.getSystemClipboard();
   StringSelection ss
      = new StringSelection( text.getText() );
   sysClip.setContents( ss, new ClipboardOwner() {
         public void
         lostOwnership( Clipboard c,
                        Transferable t ) {
            /* do nothing */
         }
      }
   );
}
```

The `Fonts` handler calls the `FileBrowser`.`updateFont` method. This method creates an instance of the class `FontDialog`. This dialog box is defined to be always modal, so this handler waits for the `FontDialog` object to be dismissed. The method `FontDialog.getFontName` returns the name of a font and, provided the String reference containing the name is not null, `updateFont` changes the font of the TextArea. The remainder of the method adds the menus to the menu bar, adds the menu items to the menus, and then returns the completed MenuBar object:

```
public void updateFont() {
   fontDialog = new FontDialog( this,
                                text.getFont() );
   Font f = text.getFont();
   String chosenFont = fontDialog.getFontName();
   if ( chosenFont != null ) {
      text.setFont( new Font( chosenFont,
                              f.getStyle(),
                              f.getSize() ) );
   }
}
```

Back in the `FileBrowser` constructor, the text area where the file will be displayed is created and set to be read-only. Its background color is set to white and is placed in the center of the frame window's container. A TextField is created for use as a status line and put at the bottom of the frame window. The program then lays out the container by calling pack and makes the container visible by calling show.

```
    text = new TextArea();
    text.setEditable( false );
    text.setBackground( Color.white );
    add( text, "Center" );
    statusLine = new TextField();
    add( statusLine, "South" );
    pack();
    setVisible( true );
}
```

The `loadFile` method of this class begins by opening a file selection dialog box. This dialog box is modal, so the method waits for the dialog box to be dismissed. When this happens, the program creates a FileReader object for the concatenated folder and filename, provided that it is not null.

```
public void loadFile() {
   FileDialog fileDialog
      = new FileDialog( this, "File Open",
                        FileDialog.LOAD );
   fileDialog.setVisible( true );
   if ( fileDialog.getFile() != null ) try {
      FileReader fr = new FileReader(
         fileDialog.getDirectory() +
         fileDialog.getFile() );
```

At this point, the program throws an exception if the file cannot be located, so the code can proceed with the assumption that all is well. The text area is initialized to a null string. The program makes the text area invisible for the duration of the file loading to prevent flickering as the file contents are read. Since the read operation may take time, the program sets the cursor to be a wait cursor.

```
      text.setText( "" );
      text.setVisible( false );
      setCursor( Cursor.getPredefinedCursor(
         Cursor.WAIT_CURSOR ) );
```

The program creates a character array as a buffer for reading in the file and executes the first read operation. The method enters a loop for as long as some number of characters are read. In each iteration, the contents of the character buffer are appended to the contents of the TextArea object. When the loop exits, the program makes the text area visible again and restores the cursor to its default state.

```
        char[] charBuffer = new char[4096];
        int charsRead = fr.read( charBuffer, 0,
                                 charBuffer.length );
        while ( charsRead != -1 ) {
           text.append( new String( charBuffer, 0,
                                    charsRead ) );
           charsRead = fr.read( charBuffer, 0,
                                charBuffer.length );
        }
        text.setVisible( true );
        setCursor( Cursor.getDefaultCursor() );
```

The catch block near the end of the method handles I/O exceptions by writing the text of the exception to the status line. The last line disposes of the dialog box resources.

```
      } catch( IOException ioe ) {
         statusLine.setText( ioe.toString() );
      }
      fileDialog.dispose();
   }
```

The main method of the `FileBrowser` class simply creates an instance of the `FileBrowser` class to get the application started:

```
      public static void main( String[] args ) {
         new FileBrowser( "File Browser Sample" );
      }
   }
```

The second class inside the source file is defined to handle the font selection dialog box. The class requires a reference to the current frame window and a reference to the current font. The first statement calls the superclass constructor with the frame window reference, the title bar text, and the modality setting. The modality is always set to true so that the dialog box is the focus of all input events while it is active. Just like the `FileBrowser` class, the `FontDialog` class registers an object of an anonymous inner class to handle its window events. Notice that the handler does not call System.exit, since that would end the entire application, not only the dialog box. The third statement selects a border layout strategy for this class.

```
class FontDialog extends Dialog {
   private List fontChoices;
   private String fontName;
   public FontDialog( Frame parent,
                      Font currentFont ){
      super( parent, "Fonts", true );
      addWindowListener( new WindowAdapter() {
            public void
            windowClosing( WindowEvent event ) {
```

```
                Dialog.this.dispose();
            }
        }
    );
    setLayout( new BorderLayout() );
```

The next group of statements declares the button to use to apply a font change. The initial state of this button is disabled since the initial selection is the current font. If the user selects a different font, this button is enabled. The handler for this button saves the currently selected font item and disposes the dialog box.

```
    final Button okay = new Button( "Apply" );
    okay.setEnabled( false );
    okay.addActionListener(
        new ActionListener() {
                public void
                actionPerformed( ActionEvent event ) {
                fontName
                    = fontChoices.getSelectedItem();
                dispose();
            }
        }
    );
```

Mini Quiz 13-3

Why must the Button object okay be declared final?

The declaration and use of the Cancel button are very similar to those of the Apply button. The only difference is that the `fontName` field is set to null to indicate that no selection was made.

```
    final Button cancel = new Button( "Cancel" );
    cancel.addActionListener(
        new ActionListener() {
            public void
            actionPerformed( ActionEvent event ) {
                fontName = null;
                dispose();
            }
        }
    );
```

Next, the list of available font names is obtained from the Toolkit and a List object is created and populated with the names. Notice that the size of the list is set to the number of choices so that all are visible at once. This works because there are typically a small number of available fonts.

```
String[] availableFonts
   = getToolkit().getFontList();
fontChoices = new List( availableFonts.length,
                        false );
for ( int i=0; i<availableFonts.length; i++ ) {
   fontChoices.add( availableFonts[i] );
   if ( availableFonts[i].equals(
      currentFont.getName() ) ) {
      fontChoices.select( i );
   }
}
```

The next statement defines an anonymous inner class to act as the handler for the List object. Notice that the interface implemented here differs from the one implemented for the Button handlers. In this case, the interface is ItemListener. This handler saves the name of the newly selected item and enables the Apply button.

```
fontChoices.addItemListener(
   new ItemListener() {
      public void
      itemStateChanged( ItemEvent event ) {
         if ( event.getStateChange() ==
            ItemEvent.SELECTED ) {
            fontName
               = fontChoices.getSelectedItem();
            okay.setEnabled( true );
         }
      }
   }
);
```

The list requires a label, so the program creates one and places it at the top-center of the dialog box's container.

```
add( new Label( "Font name choices:" ),
                "North" );
add( fontChoices, "Center" );
```

The program creates a panel to collect the two buttons together. Because you can put only one component in each area of a border layout, the program uses a single Panel to contain both Button objects. The Panel is put at the bottom of the dialog box container.

```
Panel buttonPanel = new Panel();
buttonPanel.add( okay );
buttonPanel.add( cancel );
add( buttonPanel, "South" );
```

Mini Quiz 13-4

What layout manager controls the arrangement of the `okay` and `cancel` buttons in the `buttonPanel`?

The next lines position the dialog box so that it does not cover up the title bar and menu bar of the frame window, and so that it is inside the frame of the frame window. The program retrieves insets for the parent frame window so that the inset from the top and the inset from the left can be used to position the top-left corner of the dialog box. Every Container object has an Insets object that can be queried to find out where the client area of the container begins.

```
Insets i = getParent().getInsets();
setLocation( i.left, i.top );
```

Lastly, the constructor packs the components in its container and makes the dialog box visible:

```
pack();
setVisible( true );
```

There is one other method in this class. The parent frame window uses the `getFontName` method to find out which font the user actually selected:

```
public String getFontName() {
   return fontName_;
}
```

S U M M A R Y

The AWT is provided by the package java.awt and its subpackages.

Most GUIs consist of components. The abstract class Component has the subclasses Label, Button, Checkbox, List, TextField, and TextArea that you instantiate to create components to add to your GUI.

Components that are containers hold other components. The classes Window, Frame, Dialog, FileDialog, ScrollPane, and Panel are subclasses of the abstract class Container, which in turn is a subclass of Component.

An application runs in a Frame object. An applet runs in a Panel. You build a GUI adding containers and components to the Frame of an application or the Panel of an applet.

The AWT components adopt the look and feel of the native operating system components. They automatically repaint themselves as required, and generate events in response to user actions.

Each container has a layout manager that arranges components dynamically. Standard layout managers include BorderLayout, FlowLayout, GridLayout, GridBagLayout, and CardLayout. You can nest components and layout managers for flexible arrangements. Panel objects are very useful containers for this purpose.

Use the classes MenuBar, MenuItem, Menu, PopupMenu, and CheckboxMenuItem to add menus to your GUI.

Painting is the act of drawing onto the graphics context of a component. Usually, you call drawing methods of the Graphics class in overloaded paint and update methods of a component. The graphics context is a Graphics object passed as an argument to these methods. Do not call paint or update directly. You can call repaint, which calls update, and then call paint.

The AWT contains a hierarchy of event classes for kinds of user-initiated events, such as ComponentEvent, MouseEvent, KeyEvent, ItemEvent, TextEvent, and ActionEvent.

Create handers for the various kinds of events by instantiating classes that implement listener interfaces. The listener interfaces are named *xxx*Listener, where *xxx* is the kind of event. Register a listener with a component by calling the component method add*xxx*Listener, where *xxx* is the kind of event.

For most listeners, there is an associated adapter class. Often, it is more convenient to extend the adapter class than to implement the interface.

The AWT provides some support for printing and data transfer to and from Clipboard objects, including the system Clipboard.

The AWT will continue to work with the JFC and new features being added to the Java platform.

QUESTIONS

1. Which of the following classes are subclasses of java.awt.Component? Select all that apply.

a. Button
b. Graphics
c. Frame
d. Choice
e. MenuItem

2. Which method of the Component class allows a component to respond to user input and generate events? Select the best answer.

a. setVisible
b. setEnabled
c. setReady
d. addListener
e. setActive

3. Which of the following classes are subclasses of java.awt.Container? Select all that apply.
   a. Canvas
   b. Window
   c. Dialog
   d. List
   e. ScrollPane
4. Which of the following statements construct a TextArea object that can display 20 lines of text of approximately 60 characters each? Select all that apply.

```
a. TextArea t = new TextArea( 60, 20 );
b. TextArea t = new TextArea( 20, 60 );
c. TextArea t = new TextArea( "Sales Projections:",
                              60, 20 );
d. TextArea t = new TextArea( "Sales Projections:",
                              20, 60 );
e. TextArea t = new TextArea( 60, 20,
                              "Sales Projections:" );
```

5. Which of the following classes implement the LayoutManager interface? Select all that apply.
   a. Container
   b. Canvas
   c. FlowLayout
   d. GridBagLayout
   e. GridLayout
6. Which of the following classes is the default LayoutManager class for the Panel class? Select the best answer.
   a. BorderLayout
   b. CardLayout
   c. FlowLayout
   d. GridBagLayout
   e. There is no default.
7. Which of the following method definitions can be used to override the update method of the Component class? Select all that apply.
   a. protected void update( ) { }
   b. protected boolean update( ) { return false; }
   c. public boolean update( ) { return false; }
   d. public void update( ) { }
   e. protected void update( ) throws Throwable { }

8. Assuming that g is a Graphics object, what does the following statement do when executed? Select the best answer.

```
g.drawString( "Hello!", 100, 60 );
```

a. It writes the string Hello into g in an area 100 pixels wide by 60 pixels high.
b. It writes the string Hello into g in an area 60 pixels wide by 100 pixels high.
c. It writes the string Hello into g in an area 60 pixels from the top edge of the area and 100 pixels from the left edge of the area.
d. It writes the string Hello into g in an area 100 pixels from the top edge of the area and 60 pixels from the left edge of the area.
e. It writes the string Hello into g in an area 100 pixels from the top edge of the area and 60 pixels from the right edge of the area.

9. Which of the following statements draws a horizontal line 100 pixels long into a Graphics object g? Select all that apply.

a. `g.drawLine( 50, 50, 150, 50 );`
b. `g.drawLine( 50, 50, 100 );`
c. `g.drawLine( 100 );`
d. `g.drawLine( 50, 50, 50, 150 );`
e. `g.drawLine( 100, 50, 50 );`

10. What is the return type of all methods defined in the ContainerListener interface? Select the best answer.

a. void
b. boolean
c. ContainerEvent
d. ContainerListener
e. Container

11. What is the parameter type of all methods defined in the KeyListener interface? Select the best answer.

a. These methods have no parameters.
b. boolean
c. KeyEvent
d. KeyListener
e. KeyAdapter

 **E X E R C I S E S**

Debugging

1. Correct all the errors in the following program so that the text in the label is green when the window appears.

```
package java4cpp.questions.c13;
import java.awt.*;
import java.awt.event.*;
```

```
public class Debug13_1 extends Frame {
   public Debug13_1( String titleText ) {
      super( titleText );
      addWindowListener( new WindowAdapter() {
            public void
            windowClosing( WindowEvent event ) {
               Frame.this.dispose();
               System.exit( 0 );
            }
         }
      );
      Label l = new Label( "Debug question" );
      l.setColor( green );
      add( l, "Center" );
      setSize( 300, 100 );
      setVisible( true );
   }
   public static void main( String[] args ) {
      new Debug13_1( "Debug Question" );
   }
}
```

2. Correct all the errors in the following program so that when the frame window appears it contains a text area with 80 columns and 25 rows.

```
package java4cpp.questions.c13;
import java.awt.*;
import java.awt.event.*;
public class Debug13_2 extends Frame {
   public Debug13_2( String titleText ) {
      super( titleText );
      addWindowListener( new WindowAdapter() {
            public void
            windowClosing( WindowEvent event ) {
               Frame.this.dispose();
               System.exit( 0 );
            }
         }
      );
      TextArea ta
         = new TextArea( 80, 25, "Sample Text" );
      add( ta, "Center" );
      setVisible( true );
   }
   public static void main( String[] args ) {
      new Debug13_2( "Debug Question" );
   }
}
```

3. Correct all the errors in the following program so that the nine buttons are displayed in a three-by-three grid no matter how the frame window is resized.

```
package java4cpp.questions.c13;
import java.awt.*;
import java.awt.event.*;
public class Debug13_3 extends Frame {
   public Debug13_3( String titleText ) {
      super( titleText );
      addWindowListener( new WindowAdapter() {
            public void
            windowClosing( WindowEvent event ) {
               Frame.this.dispose();
               System.exit( 0 );
            }
         }
      );
      Button[] buttons = new Button[9];
      for( int i=0; i<buttons.length; i++ ) {
         buttons[i]
            = new Button( String.valueOf( i+1 ) );
         add( buttons[i] );
      }
      pack();
      setVisible( true );
   }
   public static void main( String[] args ) {
      new Debug13_3( "Debug Question" );
   }
}
```

4. Correct all the errors in the following program so that the handler defined for the TextField converts any lowercase character entered to uppercase.

```
package java4cpp.questions.c13;
import java.awt.*;
import java.awt.event.*;
public class Debug13_4 extends Frame {
   public Debug13_4( String titleText ) {
      super( titleText );
      addWindowListener( new WindowAdapter() {
            public void
            windowClosing( WindowEvent event ) {
               Frame.this.dispose();
               System.exit( 0 );
            }
         }
      );
      final TextField tf = new TextField( 40 );
      tf.addListener( new Listener() {
            public void valueChanged( TextEvent e ) {
```

```
                String s = tf.getText();
                char lastChar
                   = s.charAt( s.length() - 1 );
                if ( Character.isLowerCase(
                                         lastChar ) ) {
                   tf.setText( s.toUpperCase() );
                   tf.setCaretPosition( s.length() );
                }
             }
          }
       );
       add( tf, "North" );
       pack();
       setVisible( true );
    }
    public static void main( String[] args ) {
       new Debug13_4( "Debug Question" );
    }
}
```

5. Correct all the errors in the following program so that the pattern of alternating black and white squares begins with a black square in the upper-left corner of the window.

```
package java4cpp.questions.c13;
import java.awt.*;
import java.awt.event.*;
// extend the Frame class
public class Debug13_5 extends Frame {
   public Debug13_5( String titleText ) {
      // add call to superclass
      super( titleText );
      addWindowListener( new WindowAdapter() {
            public void
            windowClosing( WindowEvent event ) {
               Frame.this.dispose();
               System.exit( 0 );
            }
         }
      );
      setSize( 500, 300 );
      setVisible( true );
   }
   public void paint( Graphics g ) {
      int squareSize = 30;
      Dimension d = getSize();
      g.setColor( Color.black );
      for( int y=0; y<d.height; y+=squareSize*2 ) {
         for( int x=0; x<d.width; x+=squareSize*2 ) {
            g.fillRect( x, y,
                        squareSize, squareSize );
         }
```

```
      }
   }
   public static void main( String[] args ) {
      new Debug13_5( "Debug Question" );
   }
}
```

Complete the Solution

1. Complete the following class definition by defining the class `CheckboxHandler`. Objects of this class will handle events generated by the `disableCheck` object. When `disableCheck` is selected, all the `Button` objects should be disabled.

```
package java4cpp.questions.c13;
import java.awt.*;
import java.awt.event.*;
public class Complete13_1 extends Frame {
   private Panel upperPanel, midPanel, lowerPanel;
   private TextField text;
   private Button blackButton, redButton, greenButton;
   private Checkbox disableCheck;
   public Complete13_1( String titleText ) {
      super( titleText );
      setLayout( new BorderLayout() );
      addWindowListener( new WindowAdapter() {
            public void
            windowClosing( WindowEvent event ) {
               Frame.this.dispose();
               System.exit( 0 );
            }
         }
      );
      ButtonListener aListener
         = new ButtonListener();
      CheckboxHandler cbHandler
         = new CheckboxHandler();
      upperPanel = new Panel();
      upperPanel.setLayout( new BorderLayout() );
      text = new TextField(
         "Change the color of this text" );
      upperPanel.add( text, "Center" );
      midPanel = new Panel();
      midPanel.setLayout( new FlowLayout(
         FlowLayout.CENTER ) );
      blackButton = new Button( "Black" );
      midPanel.add( blackButton );
      blackButton.addActionListener( aListener );
      redButton = new Button( "Red" );
      midPanel.add( redButton );
```

```
            redButton.addActionListener( aListener );
            greenButton = new Button( "Green" );
            midPanel.add( greenButton );
            greenButton.addActionListener( aListener );
            lowerPanel = new Panel();
            lowerPanel.setLayout( new FlowLayout(
               FlowLayout.RIGHT ) );
            disableCheck = new Checkbox( "Disable changes" );
            disableCheck.addItemListener( cbHandler );
            lowerPanel.add( disableCheck );
            add( upperPanel, "North" );
            add( midPanel, "Center" );
            add( lowerPanel, "South" );
            pack();
            setVisible( true );
         }
         class ButtonListener implements ActionListener {
            public void actionPerformed( ActionEvent e ) {
               Object source = e.getSource();
               if ( source == redButton ) {
                  text.setForeground( Color.red );
                  text.invalidate();
               } else if ( source == greenButton ) {
                  text.setForeground( Color.green );
                  text.invalidate();
               } else if ( source == blackButton ) {
                  text.setForeground( Color.black );
                  text.invalidate();
               }
            }
         }
         // put your CheckboxHandler class definition here
         public static void main( String[] args ) {
            new Complete13_1( "Complete the Solution" );
         }
      }
```

2. Complete the following class definition by adding statements that create a label, a list, and a panel with two buttons. Put the label in the north position of the frame, the list in the center position, and the button panel in the south position. It isn't necessary to add any event handlers for these components.

```
package java4cpp.questions.c13;
import java.awt.*;
import java.awt.event.*;
public class Complete13_2 extends Frame {
   public Complete13_2( String titleText ) {
      super( titleText );
      addWindowListener( new WindowAdapter() {
            public void
            windowClosing( WindowEvent event ) {
```

```
                  Frame.this.dispose();
                  System.exit( 0 );
               }
            }
         );
         // Add code for the label, list, panel,
         // and buttons here
         pack();
         setVisible( true );
      }
      public static void main( String[] args ) {
         new Complete13_2( "Complete the Solution" );
      }
   }
```

3. Complete the following class definition by adding statements to the empty `centerOnDesktop` method so that the method centers the window on the user's desktop. Look to the Toolkit class for methods that provide information about the desktop.

```
package java4cpp.questions.c13;
import java.awt.*;
import java.awt.event.*;
public class Complete13_3 extends Frame {
   public Complete13_3( String titleText ) {
      super( titleText );
      addWindowListener( new WindowAdapter() {
            public void
            windowClosing( WindowEvent event ) {
               Frame.this.dispose();
               System.exit( 0 );
            }
         }
      );
      setSize( 300, 200 );
      centerOnDesktop();
      setVisible( true );
   }
   public void centerOnDesktop() {
      // your code goes here
   }
   public void paint( Graphics g ) {
      g.drawString( "Please center this window.",
                    65, 100 );
   }
   public static void main( String[] args ) {
      new Complete13_3( "Complete the Solution" );
   }
}
```

4. Complete the following class definition by writing a paint method that draws a chessboard pattern of eight rows and eight columns of black and white squares with a black outline around the entire board.

```
package java4cpp.questions.c13;
import java.awt.*;
import java.awt.event.*;
public class Complete13_4 extends Frame {
   public Complete13_4( String titleText ) {
      super( titleText );
      addWindowListener( new WindowAdapter() {
            public void
            windowClosing( WindowEvent event ) {
               Frame.this.dispose();
               System.exit( 0 );
            }
         }
      );
      setSize( 500, 300 );
      setVisible( true );
   }
   // your paint method to draw the chessboard
   // pattern goes here
   public static void main( String[] args ) {
      new Complete13_4( "Complete the Solution" );
   }
}
```

5. Complete the following class definition by adding a MouseEvent handler that responds to mouse clicks and puts their locations into either the `singleClicks` or the `doubleClicks` Vector object depending upon whether or not they are single or double clicks. The definition provides a paint method that draws blue dots (for single clicks) and green dots (for double clicks) at the click location.

```
package java4cpp.questions.c13;
import java.awt.*;
import java.awt.event.*;
import java.util.Vector;
import java.util.Enumeration;
public class Complete13_5 extends Frame {
   private Vector singleClicks = new Vector();
   private Vector doubleClicks = new Vector();
   public Complete13_5( String titleText ) {
      super( titleText );
      addWindowListener( new WindowAdapter() {
            public void
            windowClosing( WindowEvent event ) {
               Frame.this.dispose();
               System.exit( 0 );
            }
         }
```

```
      );
      // add your mouse handler here
      setSize( 500, 300 );
      setVisible( true );
   }
   public void paint( Graphics g ) {
      final int dotRadius = 5;
      // show single clicks by drawing blue dots
      Enumeration e = singleClicks.elements();
      g.setColor( Color.blue );
      while ( e.hasMoreElements() ) {
         Point p = (Point) e.nextElement();
         g.fillOval( p.x - dotRadius, p.y - dotRadius,
                     dotRadius * 2, dotRadius * 2 );
      }
      // show double clicks by drawing green dots
      e = doubleClicks.elements();
      g.setColor( Color.green );
      while ( e.hasMoreElements() ) {
         Point p = (Point) e.nextElement();
         g.fillOval( p.x - dotRadius, p.y - dotRadius,
                     dotRadius * 2, dotRadius * 2 );
      }
   }
   public static void main( String[] args ) {
      new Complete13_5( "Complete the Solution" );
   }
}
```

Discovery

1. Create a class called `ColoredScribble` that lets the user click, drag, and release with the mouse to draw lines in a window. Include menu items that let the user select the color of the line to be drawn, save the drawing to a file, retrieve the drawing from a file, and print the drawing. (*Hint:* Use object serialization for saving and retrieving the drawing.)
2. Create a class called `Chat` that implements a simple point-to-point chat program that lets two users send and receive messages over a TCP/IP connection. Provide a TextField where the user can enter messages to be sent and a TextArea that displays a history of messages that have been sent and received.
3. Continue the enhancement of your `JUnzip` class from the previous chapter's Discovery questions to allow the user either to extract all files or extract files selectively from the Zip archive.

CHAPTER 14

Applets

objectives

In this chapter you will:

- **Learn what applets are and how they are different from Java applications.**
- **Use the core class** Applet.
- **Invoke applets from HTML documents.**
- **Pass information between a Web browser and an applet, and between applets in the same HTML document.**
- **Add special effects such as animation and sound clips to applets.**
- **Learn what you cannot do in an applet and why these limitations are beneficial for security reasons.**
- **Use .jar (Java archive) files, to reduce data transmission time when loading applets and related files over a network.**
- **Write code to obtain a suitable** Graphics **object from an** Image.
- **Distinguish between situations that require the use of an** Image **object from those that require the use of a** Graphics **object.**

Introduction

This chapter teaches you how to write and run Java applets. The Sun Java Programmer Certification Exam concentrates on the Java programming language as a general-purpose programming language, to the extent of seeming to ignore the important topic of programming applets. The certification exam asks no questions about applet security, or what you can and cannot do in an applet. In part, this may be because some aspects of applets, such as calling them from HTML documents, do not involve the Java programming language at all. HTML provides all the control you need to tell a Web browser how to embed a compiled applet into a Web page. No feature of the Java programming language is exclusively for use in applets. In fact, the opposite is true: Some features cannot be used in applets and are only for use in applications.

Some core classes and interfaces of the Java platform are most frequently used in applets, including the **Applet** class itself. Some of the features of in the Abstract Windowing Toolkit (AWT) belong in this category, and are described in this chapter.

> **tip**
>
> **Can you start with this chapter without plowing through all the preceding chapters? The answer to that question is a qualified maybe.**
>
> **Experimenting with applets is a fun way of exploring the Java platform. With some knowledge of C++, a copy of the Java Developer's Kit (JDK) documentation, and some sample applets, you may manage to write some handy or amusing applets. What you can do in applets is a subset of what you can do in a Java application, so you certainly do not have to know all aspects of the Java platform in depth before you start coding applets.**
>
> **If you want to program applets well, you do need grounding in the Java programming language and some of the core classes. Most applets have a large visual component, so you should become familiar with the** java.awt **package very early in your applet-writing career. Even within the AWT, you cannot use every feature, because the** Applet **class extends the class** Panel **rather than the class** Frame**. Perhaps you can take your understanding of the implications of this last sentence as an indication of whether you are ready to start programming applets. You may decide first to review at least Chapters 2, 3, 4, 5, 12, and 13, which cover the essentials the Java programming language and the** java.awt **package.**

What Are Applets?

Java applets are Java programs designed to be run from HTML documents in the context of a Web browser. Usually, an applet is small piece of code that performs a very specific task. Unlike applications, applets must have a graphical user interface (GUI) because they always run in a graphical environment. In terms of class definitions and inheritance, an applet is a class that extends the core class **Applet** from the package **java.applet**. Instead of using the method **main** as an entry point, an applet is initialized, started, and stopped when its methods are called by the browser that is displaying the HTML document. Applets can do most of things that applications can do, but are limited by some security restrictions that are described later in this chapter. However, these restrictions are outweighed in many cases by the ease of distributing a program on a Web page to large audience that does not have to do anything more than view an HTML document in order to run the program. No installation of any kind is required, and updates made by the programmer are automatically available the next time the HTML document is opened. This is true for HTML documents on both the Internet and a company's own intranet.

Moving from C++

Applets are a concept that is new with the Java programming language. The C++ language and C++ class libraries have nothing similar to applets. The Java programming language is quite unique in having a feature that is intended for use with Web browsers and HTML Web pages.

Viewing HTML Documents

When you browse the World Wide Web, each Web page that you look at is an HTML document. An HTML document is a text file that contains a mixture of ordinary text and tags that control how text and other elements appear. The **tags** are character sequences enclosed in angle brackets. For example, <hr> inserts a horizontal line. Other tags come in on-off pairs; for example, the HTML coding to display "some text" in italics is the following:

```
<i>some text</i>
```

Many tags have attributes. For example, in the pair of tags that enclose hypertext links, <a> and </a>, the attribute `href` must be assigned a value that represents the location to which to link, usually a URL. The following HTML excerpt defines link to the IBM home page that the user activates by clicking the phrase "the IBM home page":

```
<a href="http://www.ibm.com">the IBM home page</a>
```

If you have used the World Wide Web, or a private corporate intranet, you probably have used some applets, quite possibly without knowing it, because your Web browser loads applets from the Internet and runs them on your workstation. Part of the great business potential for applets comes from the fact that they require no expertise of the user, and are easily accessible by everyone who has learned to surf the Web. As rule of thumb, an applet is usually running in the following situations:

- You are viewing a Web page that contains more extensive animation than an image that moves through a relatively small number of prerecorded frames. Images such as rotating balls and flickering lights can be stored in files called **animated GIFs** and do not require applets.
- You are reading a table of data on a Web page that appears to be updated in real time.
- A Web page that you are viewing lets you complete some interactive sequence other than filling in a form.

However, you cannot always be sure that an applet is running. The Web page may contain code that is written in an interpreted language called **JavaScript**, which has superficial similarities to the Java programming language. One of the differences between applets and JavaScript is that the code that makes up an applet is not stored in the HTML document. Your Web browser starts and loads applets when you view the HTML document. JavaScript code must be available as source statements that are typically embedded in tags in the HTML document. The Web browser interprets the JavaScript statements when the HTML document is loaded.

Another alternative to applets is a mechanism called the **Common Gateway Interface (CGI)**. CGI is a standard for interfacing external applications with information servers, and is commonly used to provide features such as forms processing. Essentially, a CGI program runs when a Web server treats a URL not as the name of a file to be sent back to the client, but as the name of a program to run on the server. The output of the CGI program is then sent to the client Web browser for display. CGI programs are often written using the programming languages Perl or Tcl, or command processor shell scripts, but can be written in any language, including C++.

Nevertheless, in such situations, the chance that a Java applet is involved is high, and is likely to become higher in the future. Programming Java applets is an increasingly popular way to make Web pages dynamic, interactive, and customizable.

Running Applets

For many people, the most compelling reason for learning the Java programming language is to add applets to Web pages. To add an applet to a Web page, you need to know how to create an HTML document. The HTML tags for applets are described after the first sample applet in this chapter, so that the `SimplestApplet` class can serve as an example.

The HTML tags are recognized by all browsers, including Netscape Navigator, Microsoft Internet Explorer, and HotJava from Sun. Before proceeding with this chapter, you should check the configuration of your browser to make sure that all the settings that enable applets are selected. Most browsers provide an Enable Java or similar setting in a Preferences or Options menu. If you can find no such settings, you may have an old browser and should consider updating it.

You can run applets without a Web browser. Here are two other ways to run an applet:

- Load the HTML document that invokes one or more applets into the appletviewer program supplied with the JDK. The appletviewer ignores all HTML tags except for the applet tags and displays only the applet. This is an excellent way to test applets because of the simplicity of the environment.
- Test your applet in the proprietary Java development package that you use to develop it. VisualAge for Java, the Sun Java Workshop, and most other proprietary Java development packages provide features for loading, running, and debugging applets without requiring an HTML document.

Creating Applets

There are two main steps to producing an applet and distributing it through Web pages:

- Use the package java.applet and define a class that extends the class Applet.
- Insert applet tags in an HTML document. The tags instruct the browser to load the applet bytecode, embed the applet in the Web page, and run the applet.

To pass security checks, use only the features of the Java platform that are permitted in applets. Generally, what you can do in applets is a very large subset of what you can do in Java applications.

One of the potential problems you may encounter when programming applets for the World Wide Web is that Web browsers may not support the same level of Java platform that you use to develop your applet. To work for a wide range of users, who might have different Web browsers or use old versions, you may have to restrict your usage of the very latest classes and methods.

Also consider that your applet may be loaded over the network. To reduce transmission time, you should try to minimize the size of the applet and the amount of data it downloads.

Future versions of the Java platform may become available for use in browsers much more quickly than the early versions did. Sun has released the "Java Plug-in", formerly known as Project Java Activator, to let users specify that browsers use Sun's implementation of the Java Runtime Environment (JRE) in Internet Explorer 3.02 or later, and Netscape Navigator 3.0 or later instead of the browser's default JVM.

Running a Simple Applet

Here is an example of a very simple applet. It shows the structure of an applet and the Web page that contains it, but has very limited functionality. This program defines the class `SimplestApplet`. Because `SimplestApplet` is a public class, it is found in a file called SimplestApplet.java. The structure of packages mirrors the file system, so you will find this source code in the java4cpp\applet subfolder of the folder in which you unpacked the file java4cpp.jar. This applet draws the string "Simplest Applet" into the graphics context of the applet panel. The HTML and sample output follow:

```
package java4cpp.applet;
import java.applet.Applet;
import java.awt.Graphics;
/** A class to demonstrate how simple an applet can be
  */
public class SimplestApplet extends Applet {
   public void paint( Graphics g ) {
      g.drawString( "Simplest Applet", 100, 50 );
   }
}
```

To run an applet with a Web browser or the JDK appletviewer, you must create an HTML document. Be careful where you put the HTML document. By default, browsers look for files used by applets in the location from which the browser loaded HTML document. Therefore, you can create your HTML document in the same folder as the top-level package that contains the applet. Many browsers and the appletviewer also use the CLASSPATH environment variable to find applet files. If you are using such a browser and make sure that the CLASSPATH includes the parent folder of the top-level package containing your applet, you can put the HTML document anywhere on your file system.

All the files required to run the `SimplestApplet` and other applets in this chapter are included in the .jar file java4cpp.jar on the CD-ROM that accompanies this book. The multimedia applets use sound and image files. Therefore, the easiest way to run all the sample applets is from the java4cpp folder that is created when you unpack the .jar file. Before you try any of the applets, do the following:

To prepare to try an applet:

1. Unpack the **java4cpp.jar** file, if you have not done so already. Instructions for unpacking the .jar file are in the ReadMe file on the CD-ROM.
2. Make sure the CLASSPATH environment variable lists the parent folder of the java4cpp subfolder.

Once you have prepared an applet you should test it.

To test the SimplestApplet class:

1. Open the folder **java4cpp\applet**. The file **TestSimplestApplet.html** contains the following HTML document. You can edit it to add additional text and tags to the HTML, or use this minimal Web page to run the applet.

```
<html>
<applet code="java4cpp.applet.SimplestApplet.class"
        width=300 height=100>
</applet>
</html>
```

2. Either load the file **TestSimplestApplet.html** into your Web browser or issue the following command:

```
appletviewer TestSimplestApplet.html
```

3. If you used the appletviewer utility, you should see a window that looks like Figure 14-1. (If this is the first time you have used **appletviewer**, you will need to first click to accept the copyright notice.) Close the appletviewer window the same way you close any window. If you used a Web browser,

the output includes any extra text that you added to the HTML document. Close the applet by closing the browser or moving to another page.

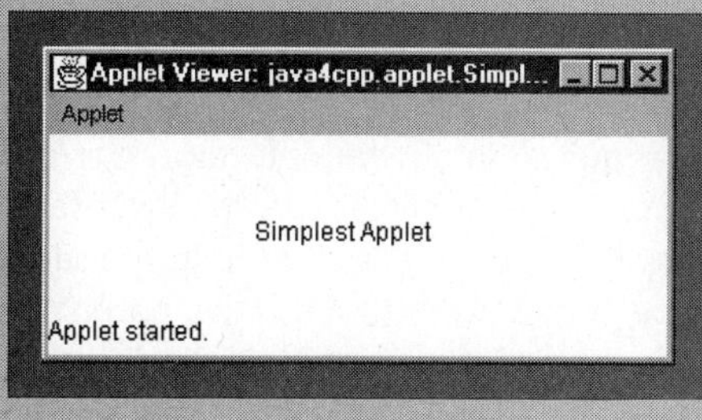

Figure 14-1: Output of SimplestApplet

If the applet does not display in your browser, the problem may be one of the following:

- The browser may not be configured to enable applets. Check the browser settings.
- The browser may not support the Java platform. This is most likely with older browsers. The only solution is to get a new browser.
- The browser may not find the applet because it does not use the CLASSPATH environment variable. In this case, copy the HTML document into the parent folder of java4cpp and try loading the copy into the browser.

Using HTML Applet Tags

The very simple HTML page TestSimplestApplet.html contains only two pairs of HTML tags, <html> </html> and <applet> </applet>. Like all HTML documents, TestSimplestApplet.html begins with <html> and ends with </html>. These tags identify an HTML document and are required regardless of whether the page contains applets.

To include an applet in an HTML document, use the tag pair <applet> and </applet>. You can control how the browser handles the applet by including attributes in the <applet> tag. The simple applet page shows the three attributes that are not optional. For every applet, you must specify include attributes code, width, and height. You can also specify parameters for the browser to pass to the applet with the <param> tag.

HTML Tag	**<applet *attributes*>*alternative content*</applet>**
Purpose	The start and end tags for an applet are **<applet>** and **</applet>**, respectively. You can insert alternative content for browsers that do not support applets, by inserting any valid HTML after the **<applet>** tag and before the **</applet>** tag. Web browsers ignore tags they do not understand. Therefore, browsers that do not recognize the applet tags skip over them, but do process whatever comes between the tags. The alternative content is also used when a browser that

recognizes the applet tags does not display the applet. This can happen for a number of reasons. For example, some browsers do not have graphics facilities (some produce alternative forms of output such as Braille), and sometimes the user has set options to turn graphics off.

Attributes

- **code = "*appletFile*"**

  The **code** attribute is required in all **<applet>** tags. It specifies the name of the .class file that contains the applet bytecode. By default, the browser assumes that the compiled bytecode is in a file in the same folder as the HTML file. You can prefix the file with a relative path. You can also specify a different folder with the **codebase** attribute. Enclosing the filename in double quotation marks is required only if the filename contains spaces, punctuation, or characters other than letters and digits. However, the safest approach is always to include the quotation marks.

- **width = *pixels***

  The **width** attribute is required in all **<applet>** tags. It sets the horizontal size of the panel occupied by the applet, in pixels. The author of the HTML document, rather than the creator of the applet, controls the viewable area of the applet with the **width** and **height** attributes.

- **height = *pixels***

  The **height** attribute is required in all **<applet>** tags. It sets the vertical size of the panel occupied by the applet, in pixels.

- **codebase = "*codebaseURL*"**

  The optional **codebase** attribute specifies a folder in which the browser should look for the applet bytecode. You use this attribute if the applet files reside in a different folder from the HTML file, and if the folder cannot be specified in the **code** attribute with the relative folder name.

- **alt = "*string*"**

  The **alt** attribute is used by browsers that recognize the **<applet>** tag but do not load and run the applet. The **alt** tag specifies the text to appear in place of the applet. Typically, the text is a message to inform users that the page contains an applet they cannot view. You can supply only a simple string. For more flexible alternative content, you can include any valid HTML between the **<applet>** and **</applet>** tags.

- **name = *name***

  The **name** attribute assigns a name to the applet. Include this attribute if two or more applets that run from the same HTML document may try to communicate with each other. If an applet has a name, other applets can ask, and be told, the name. JavaScript statements can also use names specified by this attribute for communicating with the applets.

- **vspace =** ***pixels***

  The **vspace** attribute specifies the depth of borders above and below the applet. Specify the number of pixels that the browser should leave empty between the surrounding elements in the HTML document and the applet panel.

- **hspace =** ***pixels***

  The **hspace** attribute specifies the width of borders to the left and right of the applet. Specify the number of pixels that the browser should leave empty between the surrounding elements in the HTML document and the applet panel.

- **align = left | right | top | texttop | middle | absmiddle | baseline | bottom | absbottom**

  Use the **align** attribute when an applet occupies less screen space than the HTML file gives it. Include this attribute and specify one of the alignment values to control the positioning of the applet within the space provided.

  If the applet requires more space than it is given, the panel is clipped and no errors result.

- **archive = "*JARfilename*"**

  The **archive** tag identifies an archive file that stores all the files required by the applet. The value is the URL identifying the archive, and usually specifies a .zip or .jar file. Creating a .jar file is an excellent way to package for distribution the .class files and other files used by the applet.

There is an interaction between the code **and** codebase **attributes and the** CLASSPATH **environment variable. Chapter 1 describes this environment variable. If your applets do not run as expected and your browser is configured to run applets, the problem may be that the browser does not find the applet because it is not searching the folder in which the applet resides. When you are running applets from the local file system, the search for files checks every folder listed in the** CLASSPATH**. The file and path specified in the** code **attribute and the folders specified in the** codebase **attribute are treated as relative to the folders listed in your** CLASSPATH**. It is always a good idea to include the current folder, specified by a simple dot, in the** CLASSPATH.

To pass parameters to an applet, include <param> tags after the <applet> tag and before the </applet> tag. The use of <param> tags is optional. You can have none, one, or several of them.

HTML Tag	**<param *attributes*>**
Purpose	Include one **<param>** tag for each parameter to be passed from the browser or applet viewer to the applet.

Attributes

- **name = "*parameter name*"**

  You must include the **name** attribute. It specifies the name of a parameter of the applet. Double quotation marks around the parameter name are required only when the name contains embedded blanks, but it is safest always to include the quotation marks.

- **value = "*parameter value*"**

  You must include the **value** attribute. It assigns a value to the parameter named in the same **<param>** tag. Double quotation marks around the value are required only when the value contains embedded blanks, but it is safest always to include the quotation marks. The value is always passed to the applet as a **String** object.

Using the java.applet Package

The package java.applet supports writing applets. This package has only the class Applet and three interfaces. Figure 14-2 shows how the applet class is related to other Java classes. Shaded boxes represent abstract classes and ovals represent interfaces.

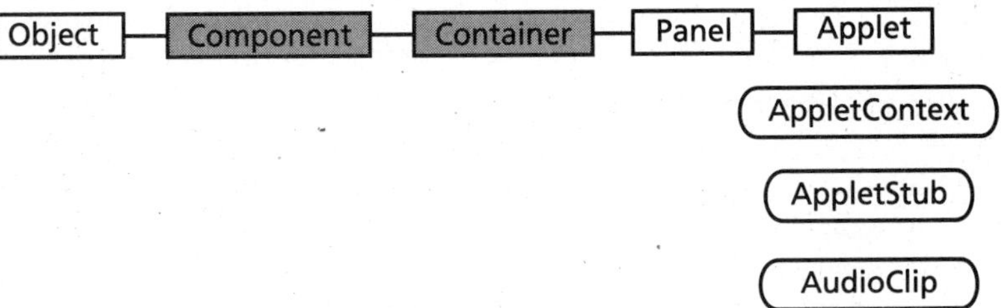

Figure 14-2: The java.applet package

The superclasses Panel, Container, and Component of the Applet class are in the package java.awt. AppletContext, AppletStub, and AudioClip are interfaces in the java.applet package.

The class Applet extends the class Panel from the package java.awt. Therefore, an applet is a container, but not a frame. The fact that an applet is a Panel object is a very significant design criterion. An applet is intended to look like part of an HTML page, and not like a stand-alone application. The size of the applet window is fixed, and set by the height and width attributes of the HTML <applet> tag. This gives HTML authors control over the layout of their pages, but puts considerable restraints on the developers of applets. Because an applet is not a Frame object, you can do less with it than you can in most GUIs. For example, you cannot add a menu bar.

Security is a very important issue when it comes to loading applets from the Internet. By extending Panel rather than Frame, the Applet class prevents mischievous or malicious programmers from **spoofing** users. For example, if a particular applet is a **Frame**, it could be made to resemble an application that resides on the client systems. A user might be tricked into entering data that the applet could transmit back to its host system.

Nevertheless, you can create a frame window from an applet by instantiating the **Frame** class in your applet. The safety measure is that the browser adds a warning message to a frame window opened by a Java applet in order to foil spoofing. The form of the warning varies from browser to browser. Such a warning may be enough to deter unsophisticated users, and warn others about the activities of the applet.

The life cycle of an applet is unlike that of a Java application. Because **Applets** are **Panel** objects, they can respond to events, but cannot take the initiative. They do not have a **main** method to drive them. Instead, they live within the Web page and are under the control of a browser or an applet-viewer utility, to which they must respond. The class **Applet** provides the methods you need to make applets work in the required way.

Extending the Applet Class

To create an applet, define a class that extends the **Applet** class and override some or all of the methods of the **Applet** class. Usually you accept the default, no-argument constructor for your applet class. However, you can define a constructor if you want to make your class useable in some other way than as an applet. If you provide a constructor that has one or more arguments, make sure that you also explicitly provide a constructor that has no arguments.

Class	**java.applet.Applet**
Purpose	The applet class provides all the methods that you need to program an applet.
Constructors	■ **Applet()** To create an applet class, you extend, rather than instantiate, the **Applet** class.
Methods	■ **void init()** The browser or applet-viewer utility calls **init** after loading the applet and before the first call of **start**. There is a default **init** method, but you usually override it to set up objects used by your applet. You should use **init** rather than the constructor to initialize your applet. If you define a constructor for your applet class, the constructor runs before **init**. ■ **void start()** The browser or applet viewer calls **start** to tell the applet to start processing. There may be a time interval between the call to **init** and the call to **start**. In this method, code the applet to do its job. ■ **void stop()** The **stop** method tells the applet to stop processing. This method may be called because the page that contains the applet has been replaced by another page or the **destroy** method is about to be called. The browser also

calls **stop** when the user scrolls up or down the page so that the applet is no longer visible. Usually, you want to suspend processing to avoid wasting CPU cycles when the applet is outside the viewing area. For example, there is no point in maintaining an animation that the user cannot see.

- **void destroy()**

  The **destroy** method gives the applet an opportunity deallocate resources before it is destroyed. For example, you can use this method to close a socket that had been opened for communication purposes and is no longer required. Usually you do not need to implement this method, but it is available in case you have objects that you want to clean up. The browser calls **destroy** after **stop**, but not necessarily after every call to **stop**. If you depend upon the **destroy** method, you should allow for the fact that not all browsers use it in the same way. Some browsers call **destroy** for all loaded applets when they are shutting down or unloading a page that contains applets.

- **String getAppletInfo()**

  The **getAppletInfo** method is called by the browser and gives you an opportunity to return the name of the author, copyright information, the version number, and the like for your applet. Return the information in a **String** object. The format and content of the string are up to you.

- **String getParameter(String *parameterName*)**

  If your applet has parameters, you call the **getParameter** method to access the parameter values specified in the **<param>** tag in the HTML markup. You supply the name of a parameter as a **String** object. If the string matches the value of the **name** attribute in a **<param>** tag, the return value is the contents of the **value** attribute of the **<param>** tag. Typically, this method is used in the **init** method. Do not try to call **getParameter** in the constructor because the parameters are not yet available when the constructor for the applet runs.

- **String[][] getParameterInfo()**

  The browser can call the **getParameterInfo** method. If your applet has any parameters, you can override the **getParameterInfo** method to provide the user with documentation about the parameters of the applet. Return the name, the type, and a description of each parameter in a two-dimensional array of strings as shown in Figure 14-3.

- **AudioClip getAudioClip(URL *url*)**
  AudioClip getAudioClip(URL *url*, String *name*)

  The **getAudioClip** method returns an **AudioClip** object. Use the object to add sound to your applet, as described later in this chapter. The audio clip is retrieved from a URL specified by an object of type **java.net.URL**. You can also supply a **String** object that contains the location of the audio clip relative to the URL.

- **URL getDocumentBase()**

  The **getDocumentBase** method returns the **URL** object that represents the URL of the HTML document in which the applet is used. If the document resides in the local file system, the URL consists of a filename and a path name.

- **Image getImage(URL *url*)**

  Image getImage(URL *url*, String *name*)

  The **getImage** method returns an **Image** object. You can display the image in your applet, as described later in this chapter. The image is retrieved from a URL specified by an object of type **java.net.URL**. You can also supply a **String** object that contains the location of the image file relative to the URL.

String appletParameterInfo [ ] [3]

Parameters of an Applet			
position	name	value	description
1			
2			
3			
. . .			

Figure 14-3: Applet parameter information

The methods **init**, **start**, **stop**, and **destroy** control the life cycle of the applet. During the life cycle of the applet, **start** and **stop** may be called several times as the user moves up and down the page or back and forth between pages. Structure the logic of your **start** and **stop** methods accordingly.

The methods **getAppletInfo**, **getParameterInfo**, and **getParameter** pass information between the applet and the browser. The default implementation of these methods returns **null**. Use **getParameter** to obtain the parameter values specified in the HTML document that embeds the applet. Implementing the other two methods is optional. You can override **getAppletInfo** to provide general information about the applet to the user and **getParameterInfo** to document the parameters of the applet. How users access the applet and parameter information varies from browser to browser. The JDK **appletviewer** displays this information when you choose Info from the Applet menu.

Mini Quiz 14-1

How can you use getParameter to determine the values of parameters when values have types other than String, such as int and double?

You can use parameters to generalize an applet so that you can use it in many different Web pages. For example, the sample applet `TickerMessage` below demonstrates receiving a parameter from the HTML document. The content of the message to display is a parameter of the applet.

Because applets extend the Panel class, which in turn extends Component, you can also override the methods of the Component class in your applet. Creating animations is an extremely popular use for applets. To create animations, use the painting methods of the Component class. The `TickerMessage` example demonstrates how to use the painting methods in an applet. The following is a review of the painting methods that are described in Chapter 13.

Class	java.awt.Component
Methods	■ **void paint(Graphics *context*)** The AWT thread automatically calls **paint** to display your applet on the screen. If your applet contains only **Component** objects, you can accept the default **paint** method. For other graphics output, you should override this method. You can call methods of the **Graphics** class to draw on the applet area, using the **Graphics** object that the **Component** class passes to the argument of this method. ■ **void update(Graphics *context*)** The default **update** method floods the applet area with the background color and then calls **paint** to update the applet display. In animation, repeated clearing and redrawing can result in flicker. For smoother animation, override **update** to avoid clearing the background between each frame and to keep the amount of redrawing to a minimum. Applets that do not perform animation usually accept the default **update** method. ■ **void repaint()** **void repaint(long *milliseconds*)** Do not call the **update** method for your applet directly. Instead, call the **repaint** method to request that the AWT thread call **update**. The **repaint** method calls **update** for you. You can use **repaint** to create frame-by-frame animation in this way. To control the speed of animation, you can pass an argument to **repaint** in which you specify a time interval to pause before repainting.

The Ticker Message Applet

This sample applet creates a fairly simple but very common form of animation. Like a ticker tape, it prints a message on the screen, and animates the message by moving it from right to left across the panel occupied by the applet.

The HTML required to run the applet and some of the interesting points in the code are described after the full code example.

```
package java4cpp.applet;
import java.applet.*;
import java.awt.*;
/** A class to demonstrate how an applet can use
  * a thread and parameters specified in HTML
  */
public class TickerMessage extends Applet
                           implements Runnable {
   private String message;
   private int delay;
   private int stringWidth, x, y;
   private Thread scrollingThread;
   private static final Color backgroundColor =
      Color.lightGray;
   private static final Color textColor =
      Color.black;
   /** Initialize the applet and prepare to start
     */
   public void init() {
      Dimension mySize = getSize();
      // get the message and period parameter values
      // from the HTML file
      message = getParameter( "message" );
      if ( message == null ) {
         message = "missing parameter 'message'";
      }
      String p = getParameter( "period" );
      int period;
      if ( p == null ) {
         period = 20;
      } else {
         period = Integer.parseInt( p );
      }
      // Calculate the delay between repaints based
      // on the size and specified period.  This
      // calculation is only very approximate because
      // the time needed to do the painting is not
      // accurately accounted for.  Dividing the delay
      // by an adjustment factor is a simple attempt.
```

```
        delay = ( 1000 * period / mySize.width ) / 2;
        // Set the font and calculate the width and
        // height using the font's metric information
        Font f = new Font( "Helvetica", Font.BOLD, 18 );
        setFont( f );
        FontMetrics fm = getFontMetrics( f );
        stringWidth = fm.stringWidth( message );
        y = mySize.height / 2 + fm.getHeight() / 2;
        x = 0;
    }
    /** Start the ticker applet running, creating a
      * new thread as necessary
      */
    public void start() {
        if ( scrollingThread == null ) {
            scrollingThread = new Thread( this );
            scrollingThread.start();
        }
    }
    /** Stop the ticker applet running
      */
    public void stop() {
        if ( scrollingThread != null ) {
            scrollingThread.stop();
            scrollingThread = null;
        }
    }
    /** Run the ticker.  This method repaints
      * the message repeatedly, which will cause it
      * to move across the display.  To save CPU,
      * it will sleep between repaint operations.
      */
    public void run() {
        while ( true ) {
            repaint();
            try {
                Thread.sleep( delay );
            } catch ( Exception e ) {
                // ignore it
            }
        }
    }
    /** Paint the display area.  This is
      * called whenever the ticker starts
      * or restarts.
      */
    public void paint( Graphics g ) {
```

```
      g.setColor( backgroundColor );
      g.fillRect( 0, 0,
                  getSize().width,
                  getSize().height );
   }
   /** Update the ticker on the display by
     * "erasing" it at its current position
     * and redrawing it at its new position,
     * moved slightly to the left.
     */
   public void update( Graphics g ) {
      g.setColor( backgroundColor );
      g.drawString( message, x, y );
      g.setColor( textColor );
      x--;
      if ( x < -stringWidth ) {
         x = getSize().width;
      }
      g.drawString( message, x, y );
   }
   /** A very brief description of the applet
     * @return the applet description
     */
   public String getAppletInfo() {
      return "Demonstration applet";
   }
   /** Provide information about the applet
     * parameters
     * @return a two-dimensional array containing
     *    parameter names, types, and
     *    descriptions
     */
   public String[][] getParameterInfo() {
      return new String[][] {
         { "message",
           "String",
           "The message to be displayed"
         },
         { "period",
           "int",
           "The time (in sec) to display the message"
         }
      };
   }
}
```

Here is the HTML page that runs the Ticker applet:

```
<html>
<applet code="java4cpp.applet.TickerMessage.class"
       width=400 height=90>
<param name=message value="Your Message Here!">
<param name=period value="10">
</applet>
</html>
```

To run the Ticker applet, use the same method you used to run the simple applet earlier. Either load the file `java4cpp\applet\TestTickerMessage.html` into your Web browser, or make the subfolder java4cpp\applet the current folder and issue the following command:

```
appletviewer TestTickerApplet.html
```

At one point during execution, the output looks like Figure 14-4.

Figure 14-4: Output of the TickerMessage applet

The first thing you may notice is that the class `TickerMessage` implements Runnable. Running in a separate thread is desirable for animations, because you can use the features of multithreading to ensure that they do not take up a lot of processor time.

```
public class TickerMessage extends Applet
                           implements Runnable {
```

The next notable part of the applet is the init method. This is where the parameters are read. One parameter is the text of the message, and a default message is available. A second parameter controls the animation speed, and the default period for the message to cross the screen is 20 seconds. The delay between repaints is calculated based on the period parameter and the width of the applet area.

```
public void init() {
   Dimension mySize = getSize();
   message = getParameter( "message" );
   if ( message == null ) {
      message = "missing parameter 'message'";
   }
```

```
    String p = getParameter( "period" );
    int period;
    if ( p == null ) {
       period = 20;
    } else {
       period = Integer.parseInt( p );
    }
    delay = ( 1000 * period / mySize.width ) / 2;
```

To set the font for the message, it is necessary to create an appropriate Font object to pass to the setFont method that the applet inherits from Container. The class java.awt.FontMetrics provides information about the rendering of a font on a specific screen. Here, the method FontMetrics.stringWidth returns the number of pixels required to display the message. The value of y is calculated to position the message exactly halfway down the applet panel. The value of x is set to 0, to display first the message starting at the left edge of the panel.

```
    Font f = new Font( "Helvetica", Font.BOLD, 18 );
    setFont( f );
    FontMetrics fm = getFontMetrics( f );
    stringWidth = fm.stringWidth( message );
    y = mySize.height / 2 + fm.getHeight() / 2;
    x = 0;
}
```

The methods start and stop override start and stop of the Applet class. Here, the animation thread is launched in start and terminated in stop. The if statements check whether scrollingThread is a running thread, using the value of the object reference as a flag.

```
public void start() {
   if ( scrollingThread == null ) {
      scrollingThread = new Thread( this );
      scrollingThread.start();
   }
}
public void stop() {
   if ( scrollingThread != null ) {
      scrollingThread.stop();
      scrollingThread = null;
   }
}
```

Mini Quiz 14-2

Why does the program pass this to the constructor of Thread? *Hint:* Does the class `TickerMessage` extend the class Thread?

The run method is the entry point of the thread. This method repaints continually, relying on the overloaded update method to modify the drawing and create the effect of animation. Here, the call to sleep controls the speed of the animation, but that is not the only reason for calling sleep between repeated calls of repaint. The repaint method is asynchronous, which means it returns without waiting for the paint operation that it requests to complete. It is possible to keep the CPU so busy scheduling paint requests that the AWT thread is not given a chance to keep up. The sleep method gives the AWT thread, as well as other threads in your program, a chance run.

```
public void run() {
   while ( true ) {
      repaint();
      try {
         Thread.sleep( delay );
      } catch ( Exception e ) {
         // ignore it
      }
   }
}
```

Mini Quiz 14-3

Why is the sleep method in a try block? What exception might the catch clause handle?

The paint method is not called by the overridden update method and has no role in the animation except to prepare the background when the applet is first displayed.

```
public void paint( Graphics g ) {
   g.setColor( backgroundColor );
   g.fillRect( 0, 0,
               getSize().width,
               getSize().height );
}
```

The update method creates the animation effect. First the method writes the message in the old position in the background color, effectively erasing the message. The method decrements x to reposition the start of the message one pixel to the left, and then draws the message again in the foreground color. When the value of **x** is less than zero, the message is clipped at the left edge of the applet area. When the message disappears completely, the value of **x** is reset so that the message reappears at the right of the applet area.

```
public void update( Graphics g ) {
   g.setColor( backgroundColor );
   g.drawString( message, x, y );
   g.setColor( textColor );
   x--;
   if ( x < -stringWidth ) {
      x = getSize().width;
   }
   g.drawString( message, x, y );
}
```

Mini Quiz 14-4

Why does an implementation of the repaint method, which this class uses, not appear in the program listing?

The last two methods provide information about the applet and its parameters so that a browser can retrieve on demand:

```
public String getAppletInfo() {
   return "Demonstration applet";
}
/** Provide information about the applet
  * parameters
  * @return a two-dimensional array containing
  *    parameter names, types, and
  *    descriptions
  */
public String [][] getParameterInfo() {
   return new String [][] {
      { "message",
        "String",
        "The message to be displayed"
      },
      { "period",
        "int",
        "The time (in sec) to display the message"
      }
   };
}
```

If you run this applet in the **appletviewer**, and choose Info from the Applet menu, you see the information displayed in Figure 14-5.

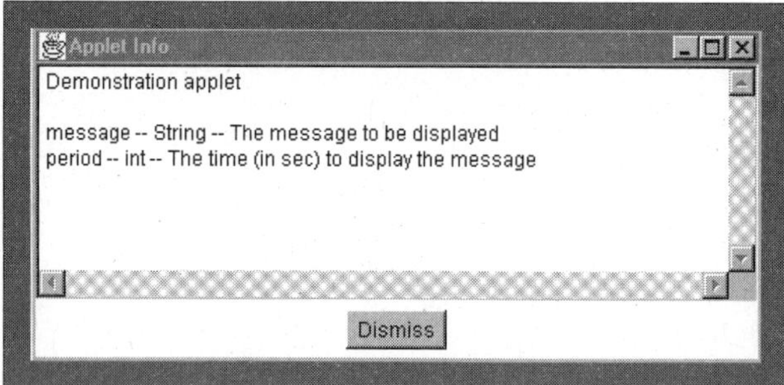

Figure 14-5: TickerMessage applet information

Adding Multimedia to Applets

Adding multimedia to applets is an extremely popular programming exercise. Many people include applets in their Web pages for the very purpose of adding sound or images, the most common elements of multimedia. By combining multimedia and animation, you can create some appealing special effects.

Of course, a Java application can also use sound and images. These topics are presented in this chapter because they are most frequently used in applets, but the features described here work also in applications.

Version 1.2 of the Java platform enhances the support for sound. New features include playback support for MIDI files and the full range of wav, aiff, and au files. The sound quality is also much improved. For a simpler way of obtaining an audio clip, applications can call a new class method in the java.applet.Applet **class.**

Adding Sound

Adding sound to an applet is very simple. Simply call the method getAudioClip of the Applet class to get an object that implements the interface java.applet.AudioClip. The support for audio clips is available only from the java.applet package. Java applications can use this support too, but must create at least one Applet object to do so.

Interface	java.applet.AudioClip
Methods	■ **AudioClip getAudioClip(URL *url*)** **AudioClip getAudioClip(URL *url*, String *name*)** These methods retrieve an **AudioClip** object from the specified URL. The method returns immediately, regardless of whether the audio clip exists. You can use the methods of this interface for the audio clip in your applet.

- **void play()**

  The **play** method plays an audio clip, or restarts a playing audio clip from the start. If the data for the audio clip is not yet loaded, it is loaded after you call this method.

- **void loop()**

  The **loop** method plays the audio clip repeatedly in a loop.

- **void stop()**

  The **stop** method stops playing the audio clip.

Here is a very simple applet that loads an audio clip from the folder in which the HTML document resides, and plays the audio clip once. The name of the audio clip file is a parameter of the applet called sound.

```
package java4cpp.applet;
import java.applet.*;
/** An example applet that loads and plays an audio clip
  */
public class SoundApplet extends Applet {
   private AudioClip sound;
   public void init() {
      sound = getAudioClip( getDocumentBase(),
                            getParameter( "sound" ) );
   }
   public void start() {
      sound.play();
   }
   public void stop() {
      sound.stop();
   }
   public String getAppletInfo() {
      return "Demonstration applet";
   }
   public String[][] getParameterInfo() {
      String pInfo[][] = {
         { "sound", "String",
           "The file containing the sound clip" }
      };
      return pInfo;
   }
}
```

Here is the HTML document that runs the SoundApplet class:

```
<html>
<applet code="java4cpp.applet.SoundApplet.class"
        width=300 height=300>
<param name=sound value="youthink.au">
</applet>
</html>
```

The audio clip for this applet, youthink.au, is included in the java4cpp\applet folder. To run the applet, either load the file java4cpp\applet\TestSoundApplet.html into your browser or go to the subfolder java4cpp\applet and issue the following command:

```
appletviewer TestSoundApplet.html
```

When this applet runs in the applet viewer, you see an empty applet viewer window. In a browser, you see an empty Web page. However, if your workstation is enabled for sound, you should hear a few bars of guitar music while the audio clip is playing.

Adding Images

Use the Image class to work with pictorial data stored in a known graphics format. For example, the source for an image can be a GIF or JPEG file that you load into your application from a file, or any data that you download into your applet from a URL on the Web. The Image class is in the package java.awt.

Version Watch

The original version of the Java platform accepted files in GIF format only. Support for JPEG files was added in version 1.1.

Adding images to applets is very similar to adding sound clips. As with AudioClip, you cannot simply create an Image object, because Image is an abstract class. Instead, call a method that returns an Image object. You can call a getImage method of the Applet or Toolkit class. The Applet class provides two methods for getting an image from a URL:

- Image getImage(URL *url*)
- Image getImage(URL *url*, String *name*)

You can also call instance methods of the Toolkit class. In an applet, the Applet.getImage methods are usually more convenient because you do not have to create a Toolkit object. But in an application, you can use the Toolkit methods.

Class	java.awt.Toolkit
Purpose	The **Toolkit** class contains the methods that join the platform-independent classes of the AWT with the platform-specific implementations of peer classes. This class has many methods, but usually you do not call them directly. However, the **Toolkit** methods are useful in some specific circumstances, such as when you want to load an image from a file. To get the **Toolkit** object for a component, use the **Component.getToolkit** method. The **getToolkit** method has no argument and returns a **Toolkit** object. You can then use the **Toolkit** object to call instance methods of the **Toolkit** class, including **getImage**.
Methods	■ **Image getImage(String *filename*)** **Image getImage(URL *url*)** The **getImage** method returns an **Image** object. You can specify the location of the image as either a URL encapsulated in a **URL** object, or a filename in a **String**.
Code Example	`Image babycats = getToolkit().getImage( "kittens.gif" );`
Code Dissection	This statement accesses the file kittens.gif.

To display the image in a graphics context, use one of the drawImage methods of the Graphics class. There are several overloaded drawImage methods. The simplest is the following:

```
boolean drawImage( Image img,
                   int x, int y,
                   Color bgcolor,
                   ImageObserver observer )
```

The image is drawn so that its upper-left corner is at the specified coordinates. If the image contains transparent pixels, they are drawn in the color specified by the Color argument. Images can take time to load. The ImageObserver objects are objects that are notified about the progress of drawing an image. You can also use objects of the java.awt.MediaTracker class to monitor the loading of several images with a single object. Using a MediaTracker is much more convenient than using several ImageObserver objects.

Here is a sample applet that retrieves and displays an image that is frequently used in demonstrations of Java technology:

```
package java4cpp.applet;
import java.awt.*;
import java.applet.Applet;
/** An example applet that loads and displays an image
  */
public class ImageApplet extends Applet {
   private Image image;
   public void init() {
      image = getImage( getDocumentBase(),
                        getParameter( "image" ) );
   }
   public void paint( Graphics g ) {
      g.drawImage( image , 0, 0, this );
   }
   public String getAppletInfo() {
      return "Demonstration applet";
   }
   public String[][] getParameterInfo() {
      String pInfo[][] = {
         { "image", "String",
           "The file containing the image." }
      };
      return pInfo;
   }
}
```

You use the following HTML document to test the applet:

```
<html>
<applet code="java4cpp.applet.ImageApplet.class"
        width=300 height=300>
<param name=image value="Juggler0.gif">
</applet>
</html>
```

The image file for this applet, Juggler0.gif, is included in the java4cpp\applet folder. To run the applet, either load the file java4cpp\applet\TestImageApplet.html into your browser or go to the subfolder java4cpp\applet and issue the following command:

```
appletviewer TestImageApplet.html
```

The output looks like Figure 14-6.

Figure 14-6: Output of the image applet

Buffering Drawing with Off-screen Images

You can improve the quality of animations that involve displaying images by using a technique called double buffering. Each Image object has its own Graphics object that can be drawn off the screen. Drawing an image in its own graphics context creates an off-screen image. The graphics context acts as a buffer to hold the image. After the Graphics object has been drawn off screen, it can be drawn onto the screen with a single method. The technique of first drawing the image in a buffer and then copying it to the screen is a form of double buffering. Displaying the image on the screen is reduced to a single operation of transferring a prepared image from one buffer to the other buffer. As a result, the repaint is quicker than when the image must be rendered directly onto the screen. The benefit is reduced flickering and what appears to be much smoother movement.

Mini Quiz 14-5

What is the role of a Graphics object when drawing in a component? *Hint:* You may need to combine your knowledge of applets with what you learned in Chapters 12 and 13.

You can call the following method of the Component to create an off-screen image:

Image createImage(int *width*, int *height*)

The Image returned can only be used as an off-screen image for double buffering.

The arguments specify the size of the image, in pixels.

Use the following method of the Image class to get a Graphics object for an Image object:

Graphics getGraphics( )

This method returns a graphics context for an off-screen image. You cannot use this method for an image that is displayed on the screen.

The next sample program uses this technique to improve the scrolling animation of the TickerMessage class.

Using Off-screen Images

To convert the TickerMessage applet to the BufferedTickerMessage applet, you need only change the name of the class, some comments, and the update method. If you compare the code in this applet with the TickerMessage class, you may notice that really only the update method has changed. Here is a shortened listing of the BufferedTickerMessage class. A breakdown of the update method follows the listing.

```
package java4cpp.applet;
import java.applet.*;
import java.awt.*;
/** A class to demonstrate how an applet can use
  * a thread and parameters specified in HTML
  */
public class BufferedTickerMessage extends Applet
                                implements Runnable {
/*************************************************/
/* omitting code identical to TickerMessage      */
/* field definitions                             */
/*************************************************/
   private Dimension offDim;
   private Image offImage;
   private Graphics offGraphics;
/*************************************************/
/* public void init()                            */
/* public void start()                           */
/* public void stop()                            */
/* public void run()                             */
/* public void paint(Graphic g)                  */
/*************************************************/
   public void update( Graphic g )
   // set up the off-screen Graphics object
      Dimension d = getSize();
      if ( offGraphics == null
           || offDim.width != d.width
           || offDim.height != d.height ) {
         offDim = d;
```

```
            offImage = createImage( d.width,
                                    d.height );
            offGraphics = offImage.getGraphics();
         }
         // clear the off-screen Graphics object
         offGraphics.setColor( backgroundColor );
         offGraphics.fillRect( 0, 0,
                               d.width, d.height );
         offGraphics.setColor( textColor );
         x--;
         if ( x < -stringWidth ) {
            x = getSize().width;
         }
         offGraphics.drawString( message, x, y );
         // paint the image onto the screen
         g.drawImage( offImage, 0, 0, this );
      }
/****************************************************/
/* public String getAppletInfo()                    */
/* public String[][] getParameterInfo()             */
/****************************************************/
}
```

Here is the update method in more detail. It begins by getting the size of the current applet. Because the scrolling message takes up the entire space of the applet, the current applet's size is the size of the drawing area.

```
public void update( Graphics g ) {
   Dimension d = getSize();
```

Next, the method checks the `offGraphics` object to see if it is valid, and creates a new one if the graphics context is not usable:

```
   if ( offGraphics == null
        || offDim.width != d.width
        || offDim.height != d.height ) {
      offDim = d;
      offImage = createImage( d.width,
                              d.height );
      offGraphics = offImage.getGraphics();
   }
```

The update method clears the `offGraphics` context by filling it with the background color. Next it sets the text color and redraws the string at the new position.

```
   offGraphics.setColor( backGroundColor );
   offGraphics.fillRect( 0, 0,
                         d.width, d.height );
   offGraphics.setColor( textColor );
```

```
    x--;
    if ( x < -stringWidth ) {
          x = getSize().width;
       }
       offGraphics.drawString( message, x, y );
```

Now, the off-screen graphics context is ready, and can be drawn onto the current graphics context all at once with a single method:

```
   // paint the image onto the screen
   g.drawImage( offImage, 0, 0, this );
}
```

The HTML file to test the `BufferedTickerMessage` class is as follows:

```
<html>
<applet
    code="java4cpp.applet.BufferedTickerMessage.class"
    width=400 height=90>
<param name=message value="Your Message Here!">
<param name=period value="10">
</applet>
</html>
```

To run the applet, either load the file java4cpp\applet\TestBufferedTickerMessage.html into your browser or go to the subfolder java4cpp\applet and issue the following command:

```
appletviewer TestBufferedTickerMessage.html
```

The output looks like that of the `TickerMessage` applet in Figure 14-4. These two applets are so simple that you may have to run them side by side to see that the double-buffered version has less flashing and flickering. The buffered animation is smoother because its images are drawn onto the display only after they have been completely prepared.

Providing Applet Security

Security is a very serious concern, because many applets are designed to be loaded from the World Wide Web. They may come through firewalls to run on your personal computer. A **firewall** is software barrier that many companies set up to prevent access to their intranets from the outside. Because applets are executable code, the worry about viruses and other unwanted side effects is very valid. The JVM puts many restrictions on applets, which limit severely what they can do. Nevertheless, most users welcome the limitations as good safety precautions.

When you load an HTML document from the Web into your Web browser, you are operating in a client-server environment. Your browser that displays the page is the client. The host from which the Web page is accessed is the server. The client and server can both be on the same workstation or thousands of miles apart on the Internet. Generally, security is an issue only when you are running applets that have been downloaded from other sites.

By default, bytecode files for applets loaded over the network are passed through the bytecode verifier, which makes sure that the bytecode conforms to the Java virtual machine specification. The verifier reduces the chance that a saboteur can hand-code bytecode and trick the JVM into performing actions it would not otherwise allow. The verifier is not called for applets loaded from local disk storage unless the user specifically requests the verifier.

During execution, the applet security manager enforces applet security restrictions. All browsers define their own subclass of the java.lang.SecurityManager to enforce their security policy, as does the appletviewer that comes with the JDK. The SecurityManager class provides many methods with names that start with the word check. Each check method corresponds to an action that can possibly be disallowed. For example, every time a user attempts to delete a file, the method checkDelete is called. You can set arguments that determine whether the method decides to allow or disallow the operation by throwing a java.lang.SecurityException object. Because different browsers implement the check methods differently, sometimes the same applet may execute without an error within one browser but trigger a security exception within another browser.

Security managers typically impose the following restrictions:

- An applet cannot read and write files on the client file system. However, it can read and write files on the system on which the applet originated. Some browsers do let applets use certain folders. Exactly what files your applet can access vary from client to client.
- An applet can access only a subset of the system property values returned by the method System.getProperty.
- An applet may make network connections only with sockets on the computer from which the applet was loaded. This restriction prevents applets from becoming "Trojan horse" attackers. For example, an applet cannot move inside a firewall and then set up connections on the intranet where the applet would otherwise not be allowed to establish connections.
- An applet cannot start other programs on the client.
- An applet cannot shut down the Web browser by calling the System.exit method.
- The System class defines the method loadLibrary, which is used to bring in a shared code library. This method is not available to applets.
- An applet cannot use native methods. Native methods are used to run code written in other languages than the Java programming language that run outside the JVM. Appendix A describes how to create native methods. Native methods are considered unsafe because there is no way to know what they have been programmed to do.
- Applets cannot provide their own versions of classes from any package that begins with "java". For example, an applet cannot create its own version of java.lang.String and have it downloaded to the client system.

Signed Applets

Many people find the preceding security restrictions limiting and wish there was a way around some of them. Of course, if there were a way around them, then it would be more of a security hole than a feature. But what if you knew that someone you trust wrote a certain applet?

The purpose of signed applets is to let you relax the security rules for applets that are signed by people you trust. The signature is a digital signature that is applied to a .jar file. A browser that supports signed applets recognizes the digital signature and allows the applet special privileges.

The JDK includes a tool called **javakey** that is intended to help generate and manage digital signatures. Unfortunately, at this time, the support for this technology in popular browsers is immature. But keep an eye on this technology, because it is bound to be very important in the future. In particular, companies with their own intranets may want to use applets as applications and give the applets special privileges on employee workstations.

Version 1.2 of the Java platform will introduce policy-based, configurable, fine-grained access control with the concepts of permission and policy. Code will be assigned permissions based on the security policy currently in effect. Each permission **specifies a permitted access to a particular resource (such as read and write access to a specified file or folder, connect access to a given host and port, and so on.). The** policy, **specifying which permissions are available for code from various signers and or locations, can be initialized from an external configurable policy file. Unless a permission is explicitly granted to code, the program cannot access the resource that is guarded by that permission. These new concepts of permission and policy enable the Java platform to offer fine-grain, configurable, and extensible access control for all Java code, not just applets.**

Packaging Applets in .jar Files

Files with a .jar extension are intended to provide a packaging mechanism for Java applets and JavaBeans. For applets, the files address the inefficiencies that come from the fact that each bytecode file, image file, and sound file is downloaded separately in its own HTTP request. By bundling everything that an applet needs into a single file, a .jar file ensures that only one HTTP request is needed.

The .jar files can be compressed files that use the same format as the zip files. You can create a .jar file with **jar** tool that comes with the JDK.

Syntax	jar *options [manifest] destination file_list*
Dissection	■ Control the activities of the **jar** utility with options. The fields you include in a **jar** command depend upon the actions to be performed. ■ When you specify more than one option, concatenate them into one token. ■ The optional manifest file holds information about the .jar file. A default manifest is included in the .jar file if you do not specify one of your own. Usually the default manifest is adequate.

- You can use the wild-card characters * and **?** when listing files. You can also specify folder names.
- The **jar** command recursively processes subfolders when the input file is a folder.
- Options of the jar command are the following:

  The option **c** creates a new or empty .jar file.

  Include option **f** to indicate that the .jar file to create is named on the command line. Without this option, the command sends the output to standard output. When combined with the x or **t** options, option **f** indicates that the second field on the command line is the name of an existing .jar file to process.

  To include information from an existing manifest, include the **m** option and list the manifest file on the command line.

  If you do not want a manifest file, include option **m** to suppress creation of a manifest.

  The option **t** lists the table of contents for the archive.

  The option **v** generates additional output, such as the size of files and when they were created.

  The option **x** extracts the files named on the command line, or all files if no specific files are listed.

  The **0** (digit zero) option tells the **jar** utility to store the files only when creating a .jar file, and not to apply any compression

Code Examples

```
jar cf mystuff.jar *.class *.au *.gif *.jpg

jar cmf mymanifest.txt mystuff.jar *.class

jar tf newjar.jar
```

Code Dissection

The first command creates a .jar file called mystuff.jar and adds to the .jar file all files in the current folder with the extension .class, .au, .gif or .jpg.

The second command creates a .jar file called mystuff.jar, using an existing manifest mymanifest.txt, and adds all .class files in the current folder to the .jar file.

The third command lists all the files in the .jar file newjar.jar.

SUMMARY

Applets are small programs that can run from HTML Web pages. Applets run only in Web browsers, application development environments, or special utilities such as the **appletviewer** of the JDK.

To run an applet from an HTML document, you specify the name of the applet and its size in an <applet> tag. Use the <param> tag to pass parameters to the applet.

The java.applet package supports applets. It contains the Applet class, which all applets must extend, and which extends java.awt.Panel. Because applets are panels, they are containers and have graphics contexts that can be drawn on. However, they cannot have all the characteristics of Frame objects, such as a menu bar or a title bar with a system menu button and window-manipulation buttons.

Use methods of the Applet class to initialize, start, and stop your applet, and to pass parameters between the applet and the browser.

Most applets are small and many have a high graphics content, such as animation, images, and multimedia objects. Therefore, applet programming usually makes heavy use of the AWT. You can use the repaint and update methods to achieve animation by redrawing on the panel.

Use the AudioClip interface for sound.

Use the Image class for pictures stored on file. Creating off-screen images and writing to their graphics context is an effective way to save drawing time and to achieve smooth animation.

Applications can do everything that applets can do. To access the methods of the Applet class, an application must create an Applet object.

Security is such a major concern with applets that most people welcome the restrictions put on applets for protection against viruses, spoofing, and other forms of malicious code. Applet code downloaded from a network is verified, the security manager prevents a downloaded applet from accessing the local file system, and more limitations apply.

Applets that originate locally and signed applets have relaxed security limitations. The security technology is in its infancy, and tools such as **javakey** are being developed for managing signatures.

The **jar** tool compresses and packages files into .jar files, which are a convenient and efficient way to distribute sets of files required by applets.

QUESTIONS

1. Which of the following classes cannot be part of an applet's user interface? Select all that apply.

a. Button

b. MenuBar

c. List

d. Choice

e. TextField

2. Which method of the Applet class is called when the applet is loaded? Select the best answer.
   a. init
   b. start
   c. begin
   d. play
   e. load

3. Which methods of the Applet class are called when the HTML page on which an applet is defined is removed from the browser's window and then brought back again? Select the best answer.
   a. init
   b. start
   c. destroy
   d. stop
   e. load

4. Which of the following HTML tags load the applet class Hello? Select all that apply.
   a. `<applet code=Hello.class>`
   b. `<applet code=Hello.class width=300 height=100>`
   c. `<applet code=Hello width=300 height=100>`
   d. `<applet code=Hello>`
   e. `<applet code=Hello.class width=300 height=100 name=Hello>`

5. Which of the following are valid attributes for the <applet> HTML tag? Select all that apply.
   a. param
   b. archive
   c. vspace
   d. alt
   e. value

6. Examine the following HTML statements:

```
<applet code="TickerTape.class" width=400 height=90>
<param name=speed value="1">
</applet>
```

   Which of the following Java statements successfully retrieve the specified parameter for the class `TickerTape`? Select all that apply.
   a. `String speed = getParameter( "speed" );`
   b. `String speed = getParameter( speed );`
   c. `String speed = getValue( "speed" );`
   d. `int speed = getParameter( "speed" );`
   e. `int speed = getValue( "speed" );`

7. In which of the following situations is the update method called for a component? Select all that apply.
   a. The component is resized.
   b. A method of the component calls the repaint method without any arguments.
   c. A method of the component calls the repaint method with an int argument.
   d. The component is constructed and made visible.
   e. A method of the component calls the paint method.
8. Which class of the java.applet package is used to manipulate sound?
9. What does the following statement do when executed within an applet? Select the best answer.

```
getImage( getDocumentBase(), "duke.jpg" );
```

   a. Returns an Image object called duke.jpg, located at the same URL as the applet, that can be painted in a Graphics object.
   b. Returns a Graphics object called duke.jpg, located at the same URL as the current HTML document, that can be painted in an Image object.
   c. Returns an Image object called duke.jpg, located at the same URL as the current HTML document, that can be painted in a Graphics object.
   d. Returns a Graphics object called duke.jpg, located at the same URL as the applet, that can be painted in an Image object.
   e. Displays an image called duke.jpg, located at the same URL as the HTML document.
10. Given that `img` is a valid Image object and `g` is a valid Graphics object, which of the following statements draw the image 20 pixels from the top edge of the container and 30 pixels from the left edge of the container? Assume that the method is called from within an instance method of an applet. Select all that apply.
   a. `g.drawImage( img, 30, 20, this );`
   b. `g.drawImage( img, 20, 30, this );`
   c. `g.drawImage( img, 30, 20 );`
   d. `g.drawImage( img, 30, 20, 100, 100, this );`
   e. `g.drawImage( img, 20, 30, 100, 100, this );`
11. True or False: The drawImage method returns only after the Image object has been drawn.

EXERCISES

Debugging

1. Correct any errors in the following HTML document:

```
<html>
<applet code="java4cpp.questions.c14.Debug14_1.class"
        width=300 height=100>
</applet>
</html>
```

Also correct any errors in the following class definition:

```
package java4cpp.questions.c14;
public class Debug14_1 {
   public void paint( java.awt.Graphics g ) {
      g.drawString( "Debug question.", 100, 50 );
   }
}
```

2. Correct any errors in the following HTML document:

```
<html>
<applet code="java4cpp.questions.c14.Debug14_2.class"
        width=300 height=100>
</applet>
</html>
```

Also correct any errors in the following class definition:

```
package java4cpp.questions.c14;
import java.awt.*;
import java.applet.*;
public class Debug14_2 extends Applet {
   public void init( Graphics g ) {
      Label l = new Label( "Label text" );
      add( l );
   }
}
```

3. Correct any errors in the following HTML document:

```
<html>
<applet code="java4cpp.questions.c14.Debug14_3.class"
        width=500 height=600>
</applet>
</html>
```

Also correct any errors in the following class definition:

```
package java4cpp.questions.c14;
import java.awt.*;
import java.applet.*;
public class Debug14_3 extends Applet {
   public void init() {
      Label l = new Label( "TextArea Label" );
      TextArea ta = new TextArea( 25, 40 );
      add( ta, "Center" );
      add( l, "North" );
   }
}
```

4. Correct any errors in the following HTML document:

```
<html>
<applet code="java4cpp.questions.c14.Debug14_4.class"
        width=400 height=400>
<param Choice1="pepperoni">
<param Choice2="extra cheese">
<param Choice3="sweet peppers">
<param Choice4="hot peppers">
<param Choice5="mushrooms">
<param Choice6="tomatoes">
<param Choice7="sausage">
<param Choice8="black olives">
</applet>
</html>
```

Also correct any errors in the following class definition:

```
package java4cpp.questions.c14;
import java.awt.*;
public class Debug14_4 extends java.applet.Applet {
   public void init() {
      Label label = new Label( "Please choose your "
                              + "pizza toppings:" );
      List list = new List( 10, true );
      Panel buttonPanel = new Panel();
      Button order = new Button( "Order Pizza" );
      Button cancel = new Button( "Cancel Order" );
      buttonPanel.add( order );
      buttonPanel.add( cancel );
      int index = 1;
      String choice = getParameter( Choice + index );
      while ( choice != null ) {
         list.add( choice );
         ++index;
         choice = getParameter( Choice + index );
      }
      setLayout( new BorderLayout( 10, 10 ) );
      add( label, "North" );
      add( list, "Center" );
      add( buttonPanel, "South" );
      setSize( 200, 300 );
   }
}
```

5. Correct any errors in the following HTML document:

```
<html>
<applet code="java4cpp.questions.c14.Debug14_5.class"
        width=500 height=300>
</applet>
</html>
```

Also correct any errors in the following class definition so that the animation sequence is displayed properly. The animation sequence uses the 10 files T1.gif to T10.gif that are located in the same folder as the HTML file and the Java source file.

```
package java4cpp.questions.c14;
import java.awt.*;
import java.applet.*;
public class Debug14_5 extends Applet
                       implements Runnable {
   private static final int NUM_IMAGES = 10;
   private static final int ID_VALUE = 0;
   private static final int PAUSE_MS = 250;
   private Image[] images = new Image[NUM_IMAGES];
   private int currentImage = 0;
   boolean keepGoing;
   Thread  animate;
   public void init() {
      MediaTracker tracker = new MediaTracker( this );
      for ( int i=0; i < NUM_IMAGES; i++ ) {
         images[i] = getImage( getDocumentBase(),
                               "T" + (i+1) + ".gif" );
         tracker.addImage( images[i], ID_VALUE );
      }
      try {
         tracker.waitForAll();
      } catch ( InterruptedException ix ) {
         System.out.println( ix );
      }
   }
   public void start() {
      keepGoing = true;
      animate = new Thread( this );
      animate.start();
   }
   public void stop() {
      keepGoing = false;
   }
   public void paint( Graphics g ) {
      Insets insets = getInsets();
      currentImage = 0;
      g.drawImage( images[currentImage],
                   insets.left, insets.top, this );
   }
   public void update( Graphics g ) {
      Insets insets = getInsets();
      ++currentImage;
      g.drawImage( images[currentImage],
                   insets.left, insets.top, this );
   }
   public void run() {
```

```
            while ( keepGoing ) {
               repaint( PAUSE_MS );
            }
         }
      }
```

Complete the Solution

1. Complete the class `Debug14_5` defined in the last exercise (after you've fixed the errors in it) by adding support for three parameters that can be passed from the HTML document into the applet. The first parameter, `fileroot`, is the part of the image filename that comes before the number. The second parameter, `fileext`, is the extension of all the image files. The third parameter, `numfiles`, is the number of image files in the sequence. The default values for these parameters should be `"T"`, `".gif"`, and `10`.
2. Complete the following HTML document:

```
<html>
<applet
    code="java4cpp.questions.c14.Complete14_2.class"
    width=300 height=200>
</applet>
</html>
```

Also complete the following class definition by defining an anonymous inner class that extends MouseAdapter and creating an object of this class called ml. The class definition should override the mouseEntered and mouseExited methods so that the label text changes to red when the mouse moves over the labels. The labels are arranged in a single column to give the appearance of a menu of choices, and the color feedback lets the user know which choice is active.

```
package java4cpp.questions.c14;
import java.awt.*;
import java.awt.event.*;
import java.applet.Applet;
public class Complete14_2 extends Applet {
   public void init() {
      Label c1 = new Label( "Choice 1" );
      Label c2 = new Label( "Choice 2" );
      Label c3 = new Label( "Choice 3" );
      Label c4 = new Label( "Choice 4" );
      Label c5 = new Label( "Choice 5" );
      Label c6 = new Label( "Choice 6" );
      Label[] labels = { c1, c2, c3, c4, c5, c6 };
      // put your anonymous class definition here
      // and define an object of that class called ml
      setLayout( new GridLayout( 0, 1 ) );
      for ( int i=0; i<labels.length; i++ ) {
         add( labels[i] );
```

```
            labels[i].addMouseListener( ml );
        }
        setSize( 75, 100 );
    }
}
```

3. Complete the following HTML document:

```
<html>
<applet
    code="java4cpp.questions.c14.Complete14_3.class"
    width=300 height=200>
</applet>
</html>
```

Also complete the following class definition by providing ActionEvent handlers for the two buttons. This applet converts measurements between feet and meters. One button converts the value entered from feet to meters, and the other converts from meters to feet. After the conversion operation is complete, the focus should return to the entry field and the value in the field should be selected so that it is easy for the user to enter another value. Make sure that your conversion operations can gracefully handle cases where the user enters a string that is not a number.

```
package java4cpp.questions.c14;
import java.awt.*;
import java.awt.event.*;
import java.applet.Applet;
public class Complete14_3 extends .Applet {
   public void init() {
      // arrange the components in a single column
      setLayout( new GridLayout( 0, 1 ) );
      add( new Label(
                  "Please enter a measurement:" ) );
      final TextField value = new TextField( "0.0" );
      add( value );
      Panel lowerPanel = new Panel();
      Button f2m = new Button( "Feet to Meters" );
      Button m2f = new Button( "Meters to Feet" );
      // create your button event handlers here and
      // attach them to the buttons f2m and m2f
      lowerPanel.add( f2m );
      lowerPanel.add( m2f );
      add( lowerPanel, "South" );
      setSize( 200, 100 );
   }
}
```

4. Complete the following HTML document:

```
<html>
<applet
    code="java4cpp.questions.c14.Complete14_4.class"
    width=400 height=400>
<param name=clip1 value="beep.au">
<param name=clip2 value="yahoo1.au">
<param name=clip3 value="that.hurts.au">
<param name=clip4 value="tiptoe.thru.the.tulips.au">
<param name=clip5 value="gong.au">
<param name=clip6 value="spacemusic.au">
<param name=clip7 value="joy.au">
<param name=clip8 value="return.au">
<param name=clip9 value="thin.bell.au">
</applet>
</html>
```

Also complete the following class definition by adding an ActionEvent handler for the `playSound` button that retrieves the selected audio clip and plays it. You also need to add code that reads the names of the audio clips from the parameters in the HTML document and puts the names into the list box, where the user can select them.

```
package java4cpp.questions.c14;
import java.awt.*;
import java.awt.event.*;
import java.applet.*;
public class Complete14_4 extends Applet {
   public void init() {
      Label label
         = new Label( "Select an audio clip:" );
      final List list = new List( 10, false );
      Panel buttonPanel = new Panel();
      final Button playSound = new Button( "Play" );
      buttonPanel.add( playSound );
      // put your ActionEvent handler here to play
      // the selected sound
      // read in the names of the sound clips from
      // the HTML file here
      setLayout( new BorderLayout( 10, 10 ) );
      add( label, "North" );
      add( list, "Center" );
      add( buttonPanel, "South" );
      setSize( 200, 300 );
   }
}
```

5. Complete the following HTML document:

```
<html>
<applet
    code="java4cpp.questions.c14.Complete14_5.class"
    width=600 height=600>
</applet>
</html>
```

Also complete the following class definition by completing the start, stop, and run methods so that the simple animation of an expanding circle runs:

```
package java4cpp.questions.c14;
import java.awt.*;
import java.applet.*;
public class Complete14_5 extends Applet
                          implements Runnable {
   private static final int MAX_DIAM = 150;
   private int diameter;
   public void init() {
      setSize( 450, 450 );
   }
   public void start() {
      // your code here
   }
   public void stop() {
      // your code here
   }
   public void paint( Graphics g ) {
      diameter = 10;
      g.fillOval( 200, 200, diameter, diameter );
   }
   public void update( Graphics g ) {
      // erase by drawing in
      // the background color
      g.setColor( getBackground() );
      g.fillOval( 200, 200, diameter, diameter );
      // draw the new shape
      g.setColor( Color.blue );
      diameter += 10;
      if ( diameter > MAX_DIAM ) {
         diameter = 10;
      }
      g.fillOval( 200, 200, diameter, diameter );
   }
   public void run() {
      // your code here
   }
}
```

Discovery

1. Create a class called `SpyApplet` that lets the user enter the name of a Java class and can display a list of that class's fields, constructors, and methods in a text area. (You will need to use the Reflection API to get this class information.) Use a set of check boxes to let the user select whether to display the fields, constructors, or methods.
2. Create a class called `SpreadSheetApplet` that implements a very basic spreadsheet consisting of 10 rows, A to J, and 10 columns, 1 to 10. Cell names are identified by their row and column, as in B7. Cells in this spreadsheet can contain a string inside double quotes, a number, or a formula. Formulas are distinguished from strings because they are not enclosed in quotes. To keep the class really simple, allow only addition operations in the formulas.

CHAPTER

JavaBeans

15

objectives

In this chapter you will:

- **Learn what the JavaBeans component model is.**
- **Create your own JavaBean components.**
- **Learn how beanboxes consume beans.**
- **Learn the characteristics of a JavaBean, including how to define the properties, methods, and events for your own beans.**
- **Add custom event types to your beans.**
- **Use JavaBeans information classes to make all features available to beanboxes that operate on your beans.**
- **Provide customized editors so that properties of your beans can be edited in a beanbox.**

Introduction

A grounding in JavaBeans can help you create better software, because it forces you to think and design in a very modular fashion. Two groups of Java programmers need to understand the JavaBeans architecture:

- Programmers who create **beanboxes**, which are the tools that consume JavaBeans and allow them to be connected together.
- Developers who create the actual JavaBeans.

This chapter focuses on the latter group because they are the far bigger portion of programmers. Much of the discussion centers on using the Java programming language and the core classes and interfaces in the package java.beans to create beans. Because understanding how beans are used to create applications is essential for designers of beans, this chapter includes an introduction to the Beans Development Kit (BDK) and BeanBox from Sun.

The JavaBeans Component Model

For many years, software developers have been striving to achieve modularity and reusability of software components. The goal to is make the integration of software components a reality, so that software developers can build applications from existing parts, much like electronic circuit designers do when they create the Integrated Circuit (IC) packages that are commonly known simply as chips. Electronic circuit designers can refer to books that list thousands of chips and document all the characteristics and connections of the chips. Integrated circuit designers can lay out complex circuit boards one step at a time by connecting the output of one chip to the input of another.

The goal of the software IC is coming closer to reality through the development of software component models. The Java platform's designers have taken a bold step forward by proposing the platform's own component model, called JavaBeans. The JavaBeans component model provides a framework for creating reusable, embeddable software components. Increasingly, Integrated Development Environments (IDEs) for the Java platform, such as Sun's Java Workshop and Java Studio and IBM's VisualAge for Java, are being designed to accept JavaBean components. These packages provide environments in which the programmer can easily connect one JavaBean component to another, much like an electronic circuit designer can wire together chips, slowly building up complex software applications. It is in such IDEs that JavaBeans really shine. For a good example, see the section "Designing a Class Visually" in Chapter 12. When you use a visual development environment, the distinguishing feature of components like JavaBeans becomes clear: The components are manipulated at design time as binary executables. You are not modifying source statements or working with the Java platform APIs.

By no means is JavaBeans the first component model, but it is the first component model for the Java platform. Recognizing that other component models are in use, the creators of the JavaBeans component model designed the model for interoperability with other component frameworks. For example, the ActiveX bridge, which is available on 32-bit Windows platforms, can turn a bean into an ActiveX control for embedding in ActiveX-aware software such as Lotus WordPro.

Conforming to the specification of the JavaBeans component model can be compatible with other Java programming models. For example, you can create a class that can function both as an applet and as a JavaBean. Indeed, you may already be more familiar with the JavaBeans specification than you realize. All of the AWT components that are described in Chapter 13 are JavaBeans.

What Makes a Class a Bean

The core classes and interfaces in the package java.beans provide the support for creating JavaBeans. However, there is no JavaBean superclass that all JavaBeans extend, and no interface that all JavaBeans implement. Creating a class of JavaBeans largely involves adhering to the standards of the JavaBeans component model.

Version Watch

Support for the JavaBeans component model was added to the Java platform with version 1.1.

Many AWT method names were changed between versions 1.0 and 1.1 to follow the JavaBeans convention. The original event model was deprecated and the current model was introduced to make JavaBeans possible. The original event-handling model relied on the inheritance hierarchy of AWT components to control the flow of events. Therefore, programmers could not apply the model in situations where objects with no inheritance relationship were connected together and expected to notify each other of events. JavaBeans use listeners, just as the AWT component classes do.

Creating a reusable, embeddable piece of software like a JavaBean requires some planning. Enough of the workings of the JavaBean must be exposed to make it useful, but not so much that the user is overwhelmed with its complexity or becomes hopelessly dependent on the details of the bean's inner workings. Each item of a JavaBean interface falls into one of the three categories listed in Figure 15-1:

A full description of the JavaBeans specification is beyond the scope of this book. The programming conventions are summarized in Figure 15-2 at the end of this section, and the full specifications are available from the Sun Web site at the following URL:

```
http://java.sun.com/beans/spec.html
```

Element	Description
Methods	A method represents some action that can be executed against the JavaBean. For example, a JavaBean that contains an animation may have methods to start and stop the animation.
Properties	A property represents an attribute of the JavaBean, such as its color or font. The property does not have to be a visible attribute. For example, a property can be an abstract quality, such as a **boolean** flag that indicates whether a component is enabled for input. Properties can be single entities or indexed elements of a set. They can be passive or bound. A **passive** property cannot initiate any activity. A **bound** property can notify other beans when they change. If a property is **constrained**, other beans can prevent it from changing value.
Events	JavaBean objects use events to notify other JavaBean objects that some event has occurred. These objects use the same event-handling mechanism as components in the AWT. JavaBeans that must be aware of a certain event register as a listener with the JavaBean that generates the event. Listener JavaBeans must implement the interface that corresponds to the event class of interest. Source JavaBeans provide registration methods for the event. When the event occurs, the source JavaBean sends a copy of the event to each registered listener. Many of the events generated by beans are **PropertyChangeEvent** objects, but you can define custom events.

Figure 15-1: Elements of a JavaBean interface

Some of the main characteristics of JavaBeans are the following:

- If a bean has a property named X, it can have public methods named setX or getX, to assign and return the value of the property X. A variation on this convention is allowed for properties of type boolean, for which the methods are named setX and isX. A read-only or write-only property has only one method of the pair. A read-only property is not necessarily constant; a change to another property might change a read-only property indirectly.
- If a bean can generate events of the class *Y*Event, it should have public methods of the following forms:

```
void addYListener( YEvent )
void removeYListener( YEvent )
```

- Other public methods of the class are actions that the JavaBean can execute.
- All beans should have a constructor that takes no arguments, because most beanboxes call this constructor. When the superclass constructor has required arguments, the bean constructor must call the superclass constructor and pass literal constants as arguments.
- A JavaBean class must implement the marker interface Serializable because beanboxes use serialization to save the state of beans. (Chapter 9 describes object serialization.) As a result, fields that are instances of classes that do not support serialization must be qualified with the keyword **transient**. In general, attributes that depend on system-specific features such as font sizes should also be qualified with **transient** so that they can be recalculated when the bean is deserialized.

Figure 15-2 gives a more complete list of the programming conventions for declarations in a bean.

Element of the Bean	Form of Declaration
Property X of type C	
Accessor	**public C getX()**
Mutator	**public void setX(C *value*)**
Boolean property X	
Accessor	**public boolean getX()**
	or **public boolean isX()**
Mutator	**public void setX(boolean *value*)**
Indexed property X of type C[ ]	
Group accessor	**public C[] getX()**
Group mutator	**public void setX(C[] *value*)**
Element accessor	**public C getX(int *index*)**
Element mutator	**public void setX(int *index*, C *value*)**
Bound property X of type C	
Accessor	**public C getX()**
Mutator	**public void setX(C *value*)**
Listener registration	**public void addPropertyChangeListener(PropertyChangeListener *listener*)**
Listener removal	**public void removePropertyChangeListener(PropertyChangeListener *listener*)**

Figure 15-2: Programming conventions for JavaBeans

Element of the Bean	Form of Declaration
Constrained property X of type	
Accessor	**public C[] getX()**
Mutator	**public void setX(C[]** ***value*** **)** **throws PropertyVetoException**
Listener registration	**public void addVetoableChangeListener(** **VetoableChangeListener** ***listener*** **)**
Listener removal	**public void** **RemoveVetotableChangeListener(** **VetoableChangeListener** ***listener*** **)**
Event Y	
Class name	**YEvent**
Listener name	**YListener**
Listener registration	**public void addYListener(YListener** ***listener*** **)**
Listener removal	**public void removeYListener(YListener** ***listener*** **)**
BeanInfo class for class JB	
Class name	**JBBeanInfo**
Property editor for type C	
Class name	**CEditor**
Constructor	Must have a no-argument constructor.
Customizer for class JB	
Class name	Any, but **JBCustomizer** is common.
Superclass	Must be **java.awt.Component** or a subclass, usually **Panel**.
Constructor	One constructor must have no arguments.

Figure 15-2: Programming conventions for JavaBeans (continued)

Bean Development Environments

When you are creating JavaBeans, it is very helpful to have an understanding of how development environments operate on JavaBeans. To that end, Sun created a demonstration development environment called the **BeanBox**. This book uses this capitalized term when referring to this specific environment to distinguish it from a generic beanbox environment. The BeanBox is part of the BDK that has been included on the CD-ROM that accompanies this book. You can download the most recent version from the Sun Web site. Because the BDK is freely available, it is used as the reference point for the JavaBean examples in this chapter. When using the BeanBox, keep in mind that it is not a production IDE and that you should not use it to create JavaBean applications. You should do production development using tools such as Sun Java Workshop and Sun Java Studio or IBM VisualAge for Java.

You can load beans into the Sun BeanBox directly from a JAR file. You create and manipulate these files using the **jar** utility, as described Chapter 14. A JAR file should contain all the class files that the bean needs. The manifest file indicates which of these class files contain a JavaBean class. A single JAR file can have more than one JavaBean class.

In general, a beanbox uses the classes of the java.lang.reflect package to analyze the classes contained within the JAR file. This package supports run-time type information, as described in Chapter 7. If the beanbox finds public methods of the form setX, getX, or isX, it assumes that X is a property of the JavaBean. If the beanbox finds public methods of the form addYListener and removeYListener, both of which return void and take a single argument of type YEvent, it assumes that the JavaBean fires events of the class YEvent. Some beanboxes, including the version of the Sun BeanBox described in this chapter, have a limitation that prevents them from handling other methods, unless the methods take no arguments and return void. This restriction is not part of the JavaBeans specification.

Using the Sun BeanBox

To follow the examples in this chapter, install the Sun BeanBox by following the instructions in the ReadMe file in the BDK folder on the CD-ROM.The installation program asks you to specify a target folder into which the program then installs the BDK files.

To start the BeanBox:

1. Open a command-line window and go to the folder in which you installed the BDK.
2. Make the subfolder **beanbox** the current folder.
3. Enter **run**.

The **run** command executes a batch file that sets up the environment for the BDK, loads the JVM, and loads the BeanBox Java application. When the BeanBox starts, you see three windows similar to those shown in Figure 15-3, Figure 15-4, and Figure 15-5.

The Toolbox window serves as a palette of the available beans. Beans are loaded when the BeanBox automatically opens and processes all JAR files that reside in the reserved subfolder called jars. If you start with only the files supplied with the BDK, the Toolbox window lists the demonstration beans included with the BDK.

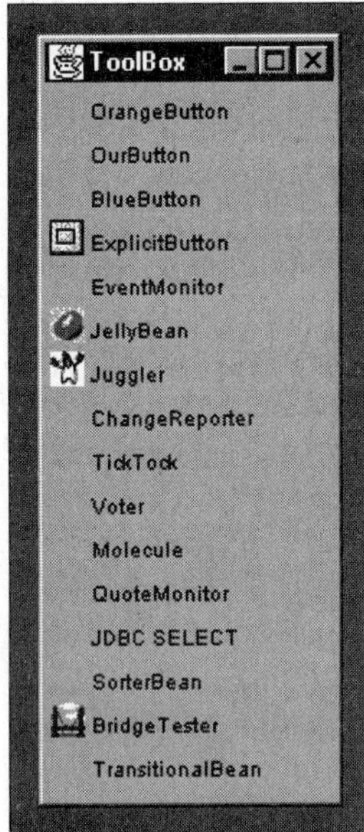

Figure 15-3: The BDK BeanBox Toolbox window

The window labeled BeanBox is the Composition window in which you can arrange and connect the beans. You can load a JAR file into the Toolbox window after the BeanBox has started by choosing Load Jar from the File menu of this window.

Figure 15-4: The BDK BeanBox composition window

The Properties window, shown in Figure 15-5, lists the properties of a selected bean and lets you edit them.

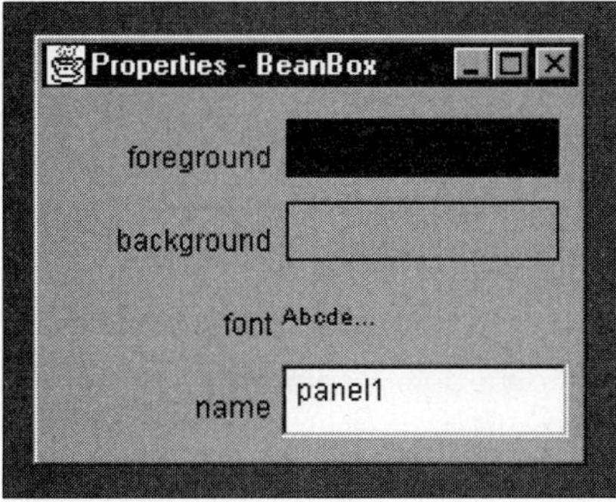

Figure 15-5: The BDK BeanBox Properties window

Before developing this chapter's example bean, try positioning a demonstration bean in the Composition window and then removing the bean.

To position a demonstration bean in the Composition window:

1. Select the OrangeButton bean from the Toolbox window by clicking the word **OrangeButton** with the mouse. The crosshair cursor appears.
2. Position the cross-hair cursor on the BeanBox window. Click the **BeanBox** window, and the OrangeButton bean drops into place.

   The bean is surrounded by a hatched black and gray border. This border indicates the bean is selected. When a bean is selected, its properties are displayed and editable in the Properties window.
3. Try changing some properties. Click the **background** box in the Properties window. The window called sun.beans.editors.ColorEditor pops up. Figure 15-6 shows the ColorEditor window.

Figure 15-6: A BeanBox Property Editor window

4. Change the color of the bean by selecting a color by name from the drop-down list on the right of the window, or by changing the red, green, or blue intensity values in the middle of the window. The color on the left of the ColorEditor and the color of the bean in the BeanBox window change immediately.

Now you are ready to remove the bean from the BeanBox window.

To remove the bean from the BeanBox window:

1 Make sure the bean is selected.

2 Click **Edit** from the BeanBox menu bar, then click **Cut**.

3 Click **File** from the BeanBox menu bar, then click **Exit** to close the BeanBox window.

The BeanBox comes with its own documentation in a web of HTML documents, including more complete instructions for using the BeanBox than this chapter can include. To read the BeanBox documentation, load the file README.html from the folder in which you installed the BeanBox into your Web browser. You can experiment with the BeanBox until you have a feel for how it works.

When a bean is instantiated in a beanbox, the bean's methods are called in the following order:

- The constructor with no arguments is called to set up the bean.
- The preferredSize method, which you encounter again later in this chapter, returns the display dimensions of the bean.
- The paint method draws the bean on the BeanBox window.

Creating a JavaBean Class

As a programmer, you may be expected to build beans that other developers load into a beanbox and use to build an application. An example JavaBean is developed throughout this chapter. The purpose of this bean is to display an image on a panel. The first version is a class called `ImageBean1`. It extends the class Panel and manipulates an object of type Image. The default image is a GIF file that is provided by the Sun BeanBox and that contains the same picture loaded by the `ImageApplet` of Chapter 14, the familiar juggler.

The `ImageBean1` bean has three properties:

- The properties `fileName` and `fillColor` have mutator methods `setFileName` and `setFillColor`, and accessor methods `getFileName` and `getFillColor`. They are read-write properties.
- `ImageBean1` has a getPeferredSize method but no setPreferredSize method. The property `preferredSize` is a read-only property of the bean.

If the image chosen is smaller than the panel, the empty space is painted using a specified fill color.

Here is the complete source code for the `ImageBean1` JavaBean. Because `ImageBean1` is a public class, it is found in a file called ImageBean1.java. The structure of packages mirrors the file system, so you will find this source code in the java4cpp\beans subfolder of the folder in which you unpacked the file java4cpp.jar.

```
package java4cpp.beans;
import java.awt.*;
import java.io.*;
import java.awt.image.ImageObserver;
/** A very simple JavaBean class that displays an image
  * and allows the user to specify the file containing
  * the image and the fill color to be used if the
  * image is smaller than the panel
  */
public class ImageBean1 extends Panel {
   private String fileName = "";
   private transient Image image;
   private int width = 200;
   private int height = 150;
   private Color fill = Color.lightGray;
   /** No-argument constructor; sets the filename to a
     * default value.
     */
   public ImageBean1() {
      setFileName( "..\\demo\\sunw\\demo\\juggler\\"
                   + "Juggler0.gif" );
   }
   /** Accessor for the filename property.
     * @return The current image's filename
     */
   public String getFileName() {
      return fileName;
   }
   /** The preferred size of the panel
     * @return The size of the current image
     */
   public Dimension getPreferredSize() {
      return new Dimension( width, height );
   }
   /** Accessor for the fillColor property
     * @return The current fill color
     */
   public Color getFillColor() {
      return fill;
   }
   /** Method for monitoring the progress of the
     * loading of the current image.
     */
   public boolean imageUpdate( Image img,
                               int infoflags,
                               int x, int y,
                               int w, int h ) {
```

```
      if ( (infoflags & ImageObserver.ALLBITS) != 0 ) {
         width = img.getWidth( null );
         height = img.getHeight( null );
         repaint();
         return false;
      } else {
         return true;
      }
   }
   /** Paint the fill color if the panel is bigger than
     * the image and then draw the image.
     * @param g the panel's graphics context
     */
   public void paint( Graphics g ) {
      Dimension panelSize = getSize();
      if ( panelSize.width > width ||
           panelSize.height > height ) {
         g.setColor ( fill );
         g.fillRect ( 0, 0, panelSize.width,
                      panelSize.height );
      }
      if ( image != null ) {
         g.drawImage( image, 0, 0, this );
      }
   }
   /** Deserialization method called for the JavaBean.
     * This is necessary because Image objects can be
     * serialized and must be regenerated manually.
     * @exception IOException if an error occurs
     *            reading the serialized JavaBean.
     * @exception ClassNotFoundException if the
     *            serialized JavaBean can't be found.
     */
   private void readObject( ObjectInputStream ois )
         throws IOException, ClassNotFoundException {
      ois.defaultReadObject();
      image = getToolkit().getImage( fileName );
      repaint();
   }
   /** Mutator method for the fillColor property.
     * @param c the new fill color value
     */
   public void setFillColor( Color c ) {
      fill = c;
      repaint();
   }
   /** Mutator method for the fileName property.
```

```
      * @param fn the new image filename
      */
   public void setFileName( String fn ) {
      fileName = fn;
      image = getToolkit().getImage( fileName );
      repaint();
   }
}
```

Breakdown of the ImageBean1 Class

The `ImageBean1` class is in the package `java4cpp.beans`. The `ImageBean1` class uses several classes in the packages java.awt and java.io, as well as the ImageObserver class in the package java.awt.image.

```
package java4cpp.beans;
import java.awt.*;
import java.io.*;
import java.awt.image.ImageObserver;
```

The class `ImageBean1` inherits its serialization behavior from its superclass, Panel. Therefore, `ImageBean1` does not have to declare explicitly that it implements the interface Serializable.

```
public class ImageBean1 extends Panel {
```

The fields of the `ImageBean1` class record the state of the JavaBean. They are all given default values except for the Image instance. Note that the `image` instance variable is qualified as transient. The Image class does not implement the interface Serializable. Therefore, the `image` field cannot be serialized with the other fields in an `ImageBean1` object. Because the Image class is not serializable, any attempt to serialize an Image object results in an exception.

```
private String fileName = "";
private transient Image image;
private int width = 200;
private int height = 150;
private Color fill = Color.lightGray;
```

Mini Quiz 15-1

The majority of core classes implement Serializable. Some do not for a good reason. Can you name at least two core classes, other than Image, that do not implement Serializable?

The `ImageBean1` has a constructor with no arguments. The beanbox calls this constructor when an object of this class is dropped on the beanbox canvas. This constructor initializes the `fileName` property of the JavaBean. The default filename has a relative path, ..\demo\sunw\demo\juggler\juggler0.gif, and is set on the assumption that a JAR file containing the `ImageBean1` class is in the jars subfolder of the folder in which the BDK is installed. You can edit the **`fileName`** property to point to any other valid file containing an image.

```
public ImageBean1() {
   setFileName( "..\\demo\\sunw\\demo\\juggler\\"
                + "Juggler0.gif" );
}
```

The next three methods are accessor methods that return the current values of the three properties of the JavaBean: `fileName`, `preferredSize`, and `fillColor`.

```
public String getFileName() {
   return fileName;
}
public Dimension getPreferredSize() {
   return new Dimension( width, height );
}
public Color getFillColor() {
   return fill;
}
```

The imageUpdate method is part of the ImageObserver interface that all AWT components implement. When a method is called to draw an image, the method may return before the image is fully available. For this reason, the methods to draw images take a reference to an ImageObserver object. Periodically, the bean's imageUpdate method is called to update the status of the image. As long as imageUpdate returns true, the updates continue.

This implementation of imageUpdate waits until the information flags have the ALLBITS flag set on. When that condition indicates that the entire image is drawn, the actual width and height of the image are requested and the image is repainted. The method returns false to indicate that no further updates are required.

```
public boolean imageUpdate( Image img,
                            int infoflags,
                            int x, int y,
                            int w, int h ) {
   if ( (infoflags & ImageObserver.ALLBITS) != 0 ) {
      width = img.getWidth( null );
      height = img.getHeight( null );
      repaint();
      return false;
   } else {
      return true;
   }
}
```

The paint method for this JavaBean compares the size of the panel to the size of the image. If the panel is bigger, the paint operation begins by filling the panel with the specified fill color. Then, if the image is not null, it is drawn starting in the upper-left corner of the panel.

```
public void paint( Graphics g ) {
   Dimension panelSize = getSize();
   if ( panelSize.width > width ||
        panelSize.height > height ) {
      g.setColor ( fill );
      g.fillRect ( 0, 0, panelSize.width,
                   panelSize.height );
   }
   if ( image != null ) {
      g.drawImage( image, 0, 0, this );
   }
}
```

The instance variable `image` must be qualified with the transient keyword so that the image is not saved when the bean is serialized and not restored when the bean is deserialized. The consequence is that the image must be reloaded from the GIF file when this bean is deserialized. Deserializing the bean is accomplished using the readObject method.

```
private void readObject( ObjectInputStream ois )
      throws IOException, ClassNotFoundException {
   ois.defaultReadObject();
   image = getToolkit().getImage( fileName );
   repaint();
}
```

Mini Quiz 15-2

Why is the readObject method a suitable place to reload the image, and why does the readObject method call defaultReadObject first? *Hint:* Review the description of the Serializable interface in Chapter 9.

The last two methods of the JavaBean class are the mutator methods that allow the read-write properties `fileName` and `fillColor` to be changed. Both of these methods trigger a repaint operation. A change of the filename also causes a new image to be loaded, which may cause the `preferredSize` property to change.

```
public void setFillColor( Color c ) {
   fill = c;
   repaint();
}
```

```
    public void setFileName( String fn ) {
        fileName = fn;
        image = getToolkit().getImage( fileName );
        repaint();
    }
}
```

The ImageBean1 Class Used in a Beanbox

Before you can access a JavaBean in a beanbox, you must put it in a JAR file. There is an additional requirement: The JAR file must include a manifest that specifies which .class files in the JAR file are JavaBeans. To do this, you simply set the Java-Bean property in the manifest to be "True" for the JavaBean class.

To load this example bean into the BeanBox window of the BDK:

1 Create a minimal manifest file for the bean `ImageBean1`. In a text editor, create a flat text file that contains the following two lines. Spaces are significant: Make sure both lines start in the first character position of each line.

```
Name: java4cpp/beans/ImageBean1.class
Java-Bean: True
```

2 Save the file with filename **ImageBeans.manifest** in the folder that is the parent of the folder that contains the package `java4cpp`.

3 Make sure the current folder is the one that contains the file ImageBeans.manifest and the java4cpp folder. Type the following command on one line to create a JAR file named ImageBeans.jar:

```
jar cfm ImageBeans.jar ImageBeans.manifest
                       java4cpp\beans\*.class
```

4 Copy the file **ImageBeans.jar** into the **jars** subfolder of the folder in which you installed the BDK.

5 To start the beanbox, make the subfolder **beanbox** the current folder and enter the command **`run`**.

When the three windows appear, you should see `ImageBean1` listed in the Toolbox window, as in Figure 15-7.

6 Using the same method described earlier in this chapter, load the **`ImageBean1`** bean into the BeanBox ToolBox window.

7 Select the ImageBean1 bean from the Toolbox window by clicking the word **ImageBean1** with the mouse. The crosshair cursor appears. (Note that the position of ImageBean1 in the list may not be exactly as shown in Figure 15-7.)

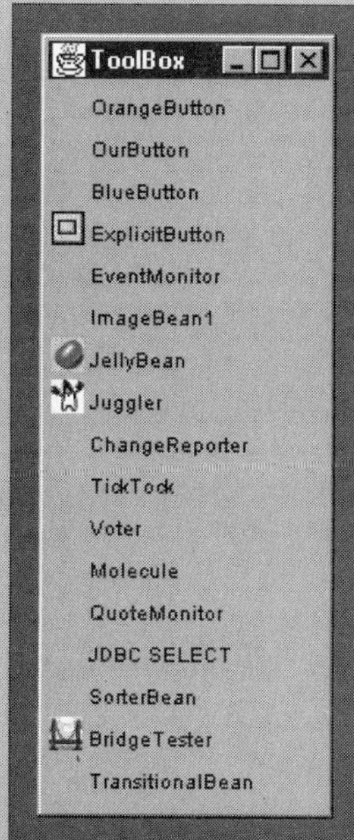

Figure 15-7: The ImageBean1 in the Toolbox window

8 Position the crosshair cursor on the BeanBox window. Click the **BeanBox** window and the ImageBean1 bean drops into place so that it looks like Figure 15-8.

Figure 15-8: The ImageBean1 in the BeanBox window

The Properties window for the `ImageBean1` bean looks like Figure 15-9 and shows six fields, although the `ImageBean1` class defines only two read-write properties. The properties foreground, background, font, and name are inherited from the superclass, Panel. In the Properties window, you can enter different values for the `fillColor` and the `fileName` properties of the JavaBean. Try this, and see the changes immediately reflected in the BeanBox window.

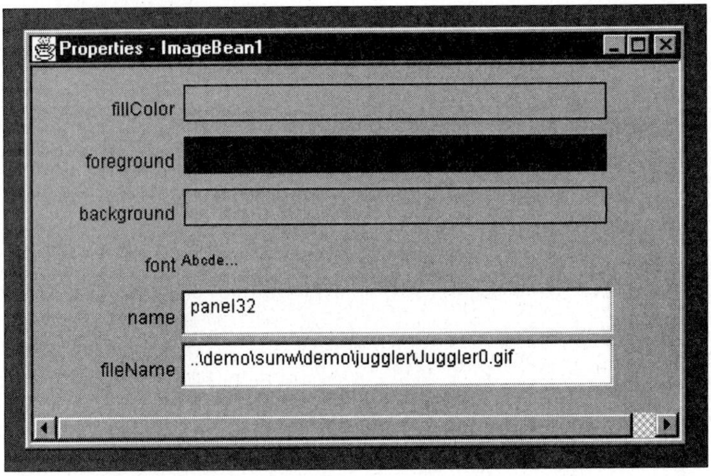

Properties - ImageBean1

fillColor

foreground

background

font Abcde...

name panel32

fileName ..\demo\sunw\demo\juggler\Juggler0.gif

Figure 15-9: The Properties window for the ImageBean1 bean

You can bind a property of the `ImageBean1` bean to a property of another bean, if the properties have the same type.

To tie a property from the JellyBean JavaBean to the ImageBean1 JavaBean:

1 The BeanBox ships a `JellyBean` JavaBean that has a color property. Select the **`JellyBean`** bean from the Toolbox window, then drop the bean on the BeanBox composition window.

2 The `JellyBean` should be surrounded by a hatched black and gray border to indicate it is selected. If it is not, click the **`JellyBean`** to select it.

3 Click **Edit** on the menu bar of the BeanBox window, then click **Bind property.**

4 The PropertyNameDialog box appears, as shown in Figure 15-10. It lists properties of the `JellyBean`. Select **color** and click **OK** to close the dialog box.

5 A red line appears. One end of the line is attached to the `JellyBean` and the other end follows the mouse. Drag the moving end of the line over the `ImageBean1` bean and click.

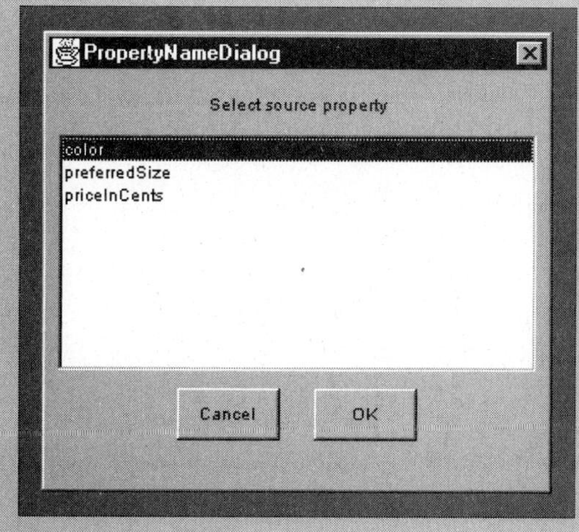

Figure 15-10: The PropertyNameDialog box

6 The PropertyNameDialog box appears again, now showing the properties of the `ImageBean1` bean. Select **fillColor** and click **OK**.

The `ImageBean1` is selected, and its fill color is the same as the color of the `JellyBean`.

If you select the `JellyBean` and change its color using the Properties window, the fill color of the `ImageBean1` changes to match. The reason is that the `color` property of the `JellyBean` is now **bound** to the `fillColor` property of the `ImageBean1` bean.

You cannot do much more with the `ImageBean1` bean. It is limited to being a passive participant in a beanbox. Enabling this bean to be wired more actively to other components involves adding events and more methods. The next version of this bean, `ImageBean2`, can be a more active participant in an application or applet.

Exploring More Property Types

The bean `ImageBean1` has the simplest type of property. For more flexibility, you can use properties that are indexed, bound, or constrained.

Indexed Properties

Properties are not limited to individual values. They can be indexed under a single name with an integer index value. For example, to alter the `ImageBean1` to display an animated sequence, you might have to supply several filenames for the sequence of images. In that case, `fileName` must become an **indexed property**. In addition to providing the methods for reading and writing the entire indexed property, you can provide methods for reading and writing individual elements of the property.

Syntax	***property_type* get*property_name*(int *index*)** **void set*property_name*(*property_type* x, int *index*)**
Dissection	■ The mutator and accessor methods for an indexed property must have the arguments, names, and return types shown here. Beanboxes also recognize method signatures with these patterns and add them to the list of properties for the JavaBean. To be usable, the methods must be public.
Code Example	`myBean.setFileName( "Juggler0.gif", 0 );` `String fn = myBean.getFilename( 0 );`
Code Dissection	■ These are the accessor and mutator methods for an indexed property called `fileName` of type **String**.

Bound Properties

Bound properties provide notification when they change so that other JavaBeans can listen for these changes and act accordingly. For example, the properties of the `ImageBean1` class are passive but are tied to the bound properties of a demonstration JavaBean of the `JellyBean` class. The `fillColor` property of the `ImageBean1` class is not bound. However, the `color` property of the `JellyBean` class is bound.

The package java.beans includes a class for use with bound properties.

Class	**java.beans.PropertyChangeSupport**
Purpose	You can create an instance of this class for a JavaBean class and delegate to it the tasks of maintaining a list of interested listeners and sending **java.beans.PropertyChangeEvent** objects.
Constructors	■ **PropertyChangeSupport(Object *sourceBean*)** You can create a **PropertyChangeSupport** object for a JavaBean.
Methods	■ **void addPropertyChangeListener(PropertyChangeListener *listener*)** The **addPropertyChangeListener** method adds the specified object to the list of listeners for the bean. ■ **void firePropertyChange(String *propertyName*, Object *oldValue*, Object *newValue*)** The **firePropertyChange** method informs all listeners of a change to a bound property. The method generates no event if the new value equals the old value.

- **void removePropertyChangeListener(PropertyChangeListener *listener*)**
  The **removePropertyChangeListener** method removes the specified object from the list of listeners for the bean.

The next example program shows how these methods are typically used:

- A class defines its own addPropertyChangeListener and removePropertyChangeListener methods that do little more than pass the PropertyChangeListener parameter they receive along to the PropertyChangeSupport instance.
- The set methods for the properties are modified to call the firePropertyChange method to indicate that the value has changed.

Constrained Properties

The JavaBeans component model allows for the possibility that one or more of the listening objects might not allow some changes to the value of a property. This variation is known as a **constrained property**. In this case, each listener can veto a change and stop it from happening.

The difference between implementing support for a constrained property and a bound property is mostly in the support class that is chosen. To implement a constrained property, a JavaBean class should use a VetoableChangeSupport object.

Class	**java.beans.VetoableChangeSupport**
Purpose	Use a **VetoableChangeSupport** object for constrained properties much like you use a **PropertyChangeSupport** object for bound properties.
Constructors	■ **VetoableChangeSupport(Object *sourceBean*)** You can create a **VetoableChangeSupport** object for a JavaBean.
Methods	■ **void addVetoableChangeListener(PropertyChangeListener *listener*)** The **addVetoableChangeListener** method adds the specified object to the list of listeners for the bean. ■ **void firePropertyChange(String *propertyName*, Object *oldValue* Object *newValue*)** The **firePropertyChange** method informs all listeners of a change to a bound property. The method generates no event if the new value equals the old value. Listeners can veto the change by throwing a **java.beans.PropertyVetoException** object. When this happens, the

VetoableChangeSupport object catches this exception, renotifies the other listeners that the property is reverting back to its original value, and then rethrows the exception.

- **void removeVetoableChangeListener(PropertyChangeListener *listener*)** The **removeVetoableChangeListener** method removes the specified object from the list of listeners for the bean.

The event object type is PropertyChangeEvent for both constrained and bound properties, because the information contained in the event object is the same. Only the mechanism for delivering the event differs. Write the set method for a constrained property to catch the PropertyVetoException object and undo the change.

Adding Custom Event Types

JavaBeans are not limited to just the PropertyChangeEvent event type. They can use any event type, even custom event types. Unfortunately, implementing custom event types requires more work because there is no core class analogous to PropertyChangeSupport to support such events.

To create and use a custom event:

1. Define the event class that extends java.util.EventObject or one of its subclasses. The rest of this discussion refers to this class as class X.
2. Define the interface, XListener, that the event listeners must implement. This interface should extend the marker interface java.util.EventListener. The methods of this interface are the event handlers. They should return void and take one parameter of type X. They have the following form:

   void handleX(X event)

   The JavaBean class that can fire the event should define the methods addXListener and removeXListener, both taking a single parameter of type XListener. An instance of the Vector class can be used to hold the list of registered listeners updated by these two methods.
3. The JavaBean class should define a method, fireX, that goes through the list of registered listeners and calls the handleX method, passing an X object, for each of them.

   Follow these conventions so that a beanbox can detect the presence of the custom event type and allow it to be connected to other JavaBeans. The `ImageBean2` class that follows contains an example of a custom event type called `FillColorEvent`.

Creating a JavaBean Class with Events

The second JavaBean class, `ImageBean2`, is an enhancement of the `ImageBean1` class. This class converts all the properties into bound properties, and adds a custom event type, `FillColorEvent`. The code for the `FillColorEvent` follows the discussion of the `ImageBean2` class.

The class adds two methods, `makeFillGreen` and `makeFillRed`, as conveniences to the users of the JavaBean. In a beanbox, it is very simple to add a button JavaBean and then connect the button's click action to one of these methods.

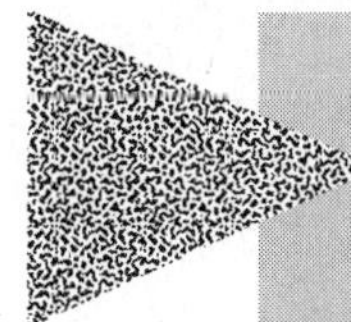

Mini Quiz 15-3

What conventions for the arguments and return type must be used to enable a beanbox to recognize the two new methods, `makeFillGreen` and `makeFillRed`, and add them to the list of available methods?

Much of the following code is identical to the Java source `ImageBean1`. Therefore, the changes are highlighted in boldface.The details of the changes made from `ImageBean1` to `ImageBean2` are described in the breakdown after the complete source code.

```
package java4cpp.beans;
import java.awt.*;
import java.io.*;
import java.util.*;
import java.awt.image.ImageObserver;
import java.beans.*;
/** A very simple JavaBean class that displays an image
  * and allows the user to specify the file containing
  * the image and the fill color to be used if the
  * image is smaller than the panel
  */
public class ImageBean2 extends Panel {
   private String fileName;
   private transient Image image;
   private int width = 200;
   private int height = 150;
   private Color fill = Color.lightGray;
   private PropertyChangeSupport
      myListeners = new PropertyChangeSupport( this );
   private Vector fillColorListeners = new Vector();
   /** No-argument constructor; sets the filename to a
     * default value.
     */
   public ImageBean2() {
```

```
   setFileName( "..\\demo\\sunw\\demo\\juggler\\"
                +"Juggler0.gif" );
}
/** Send an event to all registered listeners */
public void fireFillColorEvent( FillColorEvent e ) {
   Vector snapshot
      = (Vector) fillColorListeners.clone();
   Enumeration cursor = snapshot.elements();
   while( cursor.hasMoreElements() ) {
      FillColorListener fcl
         = (FillColorListener) cursor.nextElement();
      if ( e.getID()
                == FillColorEvent.COLOR_CHANGE ) {
         fcl.fillColorChange( e );
      }
   }
}
/** Accessor for the filename property.
  * @return The current image's filename
  */
public String getFileName() {
   return fileName;
}
/** The preferred size of the panel
  * @return The size of the current image
  */
public Dimension getPreferredSize() {
   return new Dimension( width, height );
}
/** Accessor for the fillColor property
  * @return The current fill color
  */
public Color getFillColor() {
   return fill;
}
/** Method for monitoring the progress of the
  * loading of the current image.
  */
public boolean imageUpdate( Image img,
                            int infoflags,
                            int x, int y,
                            int w, int h ) {
   if ( (infoflags & ImageObserver.ALLBITS) != 0 ) {
      int oldWidth = width;
      int oldHeight = height;
      width = img.getWidth( null );
```

```
         height = img.getHeight( null );
         if ( oldWidth != width
              || oldHeight != height ) {
            myListeners.firePropertyChange(
               "preferredSize",
               new Dimension( oldWidth, oldHeight ),
               new Dimension( width, height ) );
         }
         repaint();
         return false;
      } else {
         return true;
      }
   }
   /** Set the image fill color to green.  The Sun
     * BeanBox recognizes only methods without
     * parameters that return void.
     */
   public void makeFillGreen() {
      setFillColor( Color.green );
   }
   /** Set the image fill color to red.  The Sun
     * BeanBox recognizes only methods without
     * parameters that return void.
     */
   public void makeFillRed() {
      setFillColor( Color.red );
   }
   /** Paint the fill color if the panel is bigger than
     * the image and then draw the image.
     * @param g the panel's graphics context
     */
   public void paint( Graphics g ) {
      Dimension panelSize = getSize();
      if ( panelSize.width > width
           panelSize.height > height ) {
         g.setColor ( fill );
         g.fillRect ( 0, 0,
                      panelSize.width,
                      panelSize.height );
      }
      if ( image != null ) {
         g.drawImage( image, 0, 0, this );
      }
   }
   /** Deserialization method called for the JavaBean.
```

```
   * This is necessary because Image objects can be
   * serialized and must be regenerated manually.
   * @exception IOException if an error occurs
   *            reading the serialized JavaBean.
   * @exception ClassNotFoundException if the
   *            serialized JavaBean can't be found.
   */
private void readObject( ObjectInputStream ois )
        throws IOException, ClassNotFoundException {
   ois.defaultReadObject();
   image = getToolkit().getImage( fileName );
   repaint();
}
/** Mutator method for the fillColor property.
  * @param c the new fill color value
  */
public void setFillColor( Color c ) {
   Color oldFill = fill;
   fill = c;
   myListeners.firePropertyChange( "fillColor",
                                   oldFill,
                                   fill );
   fireFillColorEvent( new FillColorEvent( this,
                       FillColorEvent.COLOR_CHANGE,
                       c ) );
   repaint();
}
/** Mutator method for the fileName property.
  * @param fn the new image filename
  */
public void setFileName( String fn ) {
   String oldFileName = fileName;
   fileName = fn;
   image = getToolkit().getImage( fileName );
   myListeners.firePropertyChange( "fileName",
                                   oldFileName,
                                   fileName );
   repaint();
}
/** Add a listener interested in FillColorEvent
  * objects
  */
public void
addFillColorListener( FillColorListener l ) {
   fillColorListeners.addElement( l );
}
```

```
   /** Add a listener interested in property change
     * events
     */
   public void addPropertyChangeListener(
      PropertyChangeListener l ) {
      myListeners.addPropertyChangeListener( l );
   }
   /** Remove a listener no longer interested in
     * FillColorEvent objects
     */
   public void removeFillColorListener(
      FillColorListener l ) {
      fillColorListeners.removeElement( l );
   }
   /** Remove a listener no longer interested in
     * property change events
     */
   public void
   removePropertyChangeListener(
      PropertyChangeListener l ) {
      myListeners.removePropertyChangeListener( l );
   }
}
```

Breakdown of the ImageBean2 Class

The two new fields support the handling of events. The field `myListeners` provides the support for creating bound properties. The field `fillColorListeners` is the list of listeners registered to receive `FillColorEvent` objects.

```
public class ImageBean2 extends Panel {
   private String fileName;
   private transient Image image;
   private int width = 200;
   private int height = 150;
   private Color fill = Color.lightGray;
   private PropertyChangeSupport
      myListeners = new PropertyChangeSupport( this );
   private Vector fillColorListeners = new Vector();
```

The method `fireFillColorEvent` is used to send a FillColorEvent object to all registered listeners. It begins by cloning the list of registered listeners to avoid any problems that could arise if the list changed while the events were being delivered. Using an Enumeration object, the program visits all items in the list and calls the handler method `fillColorChange` for each one.

```
public void fireFillColorEvent( FillColorEvent e ) {
   Vector snapshot
      = (Vector) fillColorListeners.clone();
   Enumeration cursor = snapshot.elements();
   while( cursor.hasMoreElements() ) {
      FillColorListener fcl
         = (FillColorListener) cursor.nextElement();
      if ( e.getID()
         == FillColorEvent.COLOR_CHANGE ) {
         fcl.fillColorChange( e );
      }
   }
}
```

The methods for accessing the properties have not changed. But the imageUpdate method has changed to fire a PropertyChangeEvent if the image loaded has a size different from the previous image. The method also saves the old width and height at the beginning of the method so that the old and new values can be put into the event object. Because the `preferredSize` property is returned as a Dimension object, two Dimension objects are created to hold the old and new values.

```
public boolean imageUpdate( Image img,
                            int infoflags,
                            int x, int y,
                            int w, int h ) {
   if ( (infoflags & ImageObserver.ALLBITS) != 0 ) {
      int oldWidth = width;
      int oldHeight = height;
      width = img.getWidth( null );
      height = img.getHeight( null );
      if ( oldWidth != width
           || oldHeight != height ) {
         myListeners.firePropertyChange(
            "preferredSize",
            new Dimension( oldWidth, oldHeight ),
            new Dimension( width, height ) );
      }
      repaint();
      return false;
   } else {
      return true;
   }
}
```

The convenience methods makeFillGreen and makeFillRed simply call the setFillColor method and pass the appropriate constant value. These do not set the field fillColor directly because that would bypass the property-change reporting that has been added to this class.

```
public void makeFillGreen() {
   setFillColor( Color.green );
}
public void makeFillRed() {
   setFillColor( Color.red );
}
```

The painting and deserialization methods do not change, but the mutator methods are altered to add change reporting. Both methods now begin by saving the old value of the property before changing it to the new value. After the change is made, the firePropertyChange method is used to fire the PropertyChangeEvent. The setFillColor method not only reports a property change event, but it also fires a FillColorEvent with an ID value of COLOR_CHANGE.

```
public void setFillColor( Color c ) {
   Color oldFill = fill;
   fill = c;
   myListeners.firePropertyChange( "fillColor",
                                   oldFill,
                                   fill );
   fireFillColorEvent( new FillColorEvent( this,
                       FillColorEvent.COLOR_CHANGE,
                       c ) );
   repaint();
}
public void setFileName( String fn ) {
   String oldFileName = fileName;
   fileName = fn;
   image = getToolkit().getImage( fileName );
   myListeners.firePropertyChange( "fileName",
                                   oldFileName,
                                   fileName );
   repaint();
}
```

The last four methods of the class are for adding and removing event listeners. The method addFillColorListener puts the given listener object into the Vector of listeners.

```
public void
addFillColorListener( FillColorListener l ) {
   fillColorListeners.addElement( l );
}
```

The addPropertyChangeListener method delegates to the PropertyChangeSupport object, `myListeners`, the handling of the bound property listeners.

```
public void addPropertyChangeListener(
   PropertyChangeListener l ) {
   myListeners.addPropertyChangeListener( l );
}
```

To remove themselves from the list, listeners no longer interested in FillColorEvent objects use the method `removeFillColorListener`. This method then removes the element from the Vector holding the list.

```
public void removeFillColorListener(
   FillColorListener l ) {
   fillColorListeners.removeElement( l );
}
```

The method removePropertyChangeListener delegates to the PropertyChangeSupport object the removal of the specified PropertyChangeListener object from the list.

```
   public void
   removePropertyChangeListener(
      PropertyChangeListener l ) {
      myListeners.removePropertyChangeListener( l );
   }
}
```

The Custom Event Class for the ImageBean2 Bean

A separate class defines the custom event used in the `ImageBean2` class. The constructor takes three inputs: a reference to the object that is the source of the event, an integer constant that is the event identifier, and the color associated with the event. The source reference is passed along to the superclass constructor, EventObject. The other methods of the class are defined so that the receiving objects can extract information from the event. Here is the class:

```
package java4cpp.beans;
import java.awt.Color;
import java.util.EventObject;
/** A user-defined event class
  */
public class FillColorEvent extends EventObject {
   /** event type identifier */
   public static final int COLOR_CHANGE = 0;
   private int id;
   private Color color;
   /** Construct an event object
     * @param source the object initiating the event
     * @param id the event identifier
```

```
      * @param c the color for the event
      */
    public FillColorEvent( Object source, int id,
                           Color c ) {
       super( source );
       id = id;
       color = c;
    }
    /** Return the color associated with the event
      * @return The color
      */
    public Color getColor() {
       return color;
    }
    /** Return the event identifier
      * @return The event identifier
      */
    public int getID() {
       return id;
    }
}
```

The Listener Interface for the Custom Event Class

The last piece of code needed for this example is the definition of the `FillColorListener` interface. It adds just one empty method to the EventListener interface.

```
package java4cpp.beans;
import java.util.EventListener;
public interface FillColorListener
   extends EventListener {
   /** The method called when a FillColor change occurs
     */
   public void fillColorChange( FillColorEvent e );
}
```

The ImageBean2 Used in a BeanBox

You can test the bean, or change roles from that of a bean provider to an application developer who uses predefined beans, by loading the bean into a beanbox. To load the `ImageBean2` JavaBean into the BDK BeanBox, follow the same process you used for `ImageBean1`.

To load ImageBean2 into the BDK BeanBox:

1. Add lines to the ImageBeans.manifest file in the folder into which you unpacked the java4cpp.jar file, so that the file lists both `ImageBean1` and `ImageBean2`. One JAR file can list any number of beans. The BDK BeanBox requires a blank line between the entries for each bean. The manifest file should now look like the following:

   ```
   Name: java4cpp/beans/ImageBean1.class
   Java-Bean: True

   Name: java4cpp/beans/ImageBean2.class
   Java-Bean: True
   ```

2. Type the following command, on one line, from the parent folder of the java4cpp folder to create a JAR file ImageBeans.jar:

   ```
   jar cfm ImageBeans.jar ImageBeans.manifest
                          java4cpp\beans\*.class
   ```

3. Copy the file **ImageBeans.jar** into the **jars** subfolder of the folder in which you installed the BDK.
4. Start the BeanBox. See that `ImageBean2` is now listed in the Toolbox window.

   You can have a little fun with this bean. Try the following.

5. Drag an `ImageBean2` bean onto the BeanBox window.
6. Drag two `BlueButton` beans on to the BeanBox window and position them near but not on top of the `ImageBean2`. These beans look like buttons labeled "press."
7. Change the background property of one `BlueButton` to red and of the other `BlueButton` to green. Use the Properties window and ColorEditor the same way as when you changed the color of a `JellyBean` object earlier in this chapter.
8. Click the **red** button. While it is selected, click **Edit** menu on the menu bar, and then click **Events**. From the cascading menus, select **button push** and then **action performed.**

   A red line appears from the bean to the current mouse position.

9. Move over the area of the ImageBean2 bean and click.
10. The EventTargetDialog appears, inviting you to select a target method. Click makeFillRed, then **OK**. Briefly, a message box appears saying that an adaptorclass is being generated and compiled.
11. Now try clicking the **red** button. The fill color of the `ImageBean2` should turn red.

12 In a similar fashion, make the green button change the fill color of the `ImageBean2` to green.

Depending on how you arrange the beans, your BeanBox window may look similar to Figure 15-11.

Figure 15-11: The ImageBean2 in the BDK BeanBox

Now see how you can use the bound properties of the `ImageBean2`.

13 Drag a JellyBean onto the BeanBox window.

14 Select the **`ImageBean2`**. Click **Edit** from the menu bar and then **Bind property**. When the PropertyNameDialog pops up, select **fillColor** and then **OK**.

15 Connect the red line from the `ImageBean2` to the `JellyBean`. When the PropertyNameDialog pops up, select **color** and then **OK**.

16 Now click the **red** and **green** buttons and see what happens. Feel free to experiment further.

Supplying Additional JavaBean Information

Beanboxes generally can use the Reflection API to determine what they need to know about a JavaBean. But some pieces of information cannot be deduced from the definition of a JavaBean, and in some cases the programming conventions that beanboxes depend on cannot be followed. For these reasons, the JavaBeans specification allows for the definition of additional information classes to accompany a JavaBean class: BeanInfo classes. BeanInfo classes are used only when beans are being connected together in a beanbox. They have no role when the bean is executing, so you do not have to include them in the JAR file when you package JavaBeans into an application. The BeanInfo classes implement the java.beans.BeanInfo interface.

A beanbox finds the information classes in the following way:

- For each JavaBean class, the beanbox looks for a class with a name formed by appending the suffix **BeanInfo** onto the name of the JavaBean class. For example, if the JavaBean class is named `JB`, the beanbox looks for class `JBBeanInfo`.
- If a class satisfies the naming convention, the beanbox next checks whether the class implements the **BeanInfo** interface. For example, the beanbox accepts the following class:

```
class JBBeanInfo implements java.beans.BeanInfo
```

- If a class satisfies these requirements, the beanbox can call its methods to collect detailed information about the JavaBean. Some of the information is encapsulated in instances of other classes in the **java.beans** package that are listed in Figure 15-12.

Class	Description
FeatureDescriptor	**FeatureDescriptor** is the superclass for all the other descriptor classes. It contains methods for reading and writing information that is common to all features of a JavaBean, such as **name**, **shortDescription**, and **value**.
BeanDescriptor	The **BeanDescriptor** class contains high-level information for the entire JavaBean class.
EventSetDescriptor	The **EventSetDescriptor** class provides detail about the set of events that are gathered under a single listener interface. Each listener interface supported by the JavaBean can have its own **EventSetDescriptor** object.
MethodDescriptor	The **MethodDescriptor** class describes one of the methods supported by a JavaBean.
ParameterDescriptor	**ParameterDescriptor** objects are associated with **MethodDescriptor** objects. Each **ParameterDescriptor** describes one arguments of a method
PropertyDescriptor	A PropertyDescriptor object describes a single property of a JavaBean. If your bean has a property for which the read and write methods do not follow the JavaBeans naming convention, use the **PropertyDescriptor** object to identify the read and write methods.
IndexedPropertyDescriptor	The **IndexedPropertyDescriptor** class extends **PropertyDescriptor** and adds additional methods for the indexed read and write methods.

Figure 15-12: JavaBean information classes

Class	java.beans.BeanInfo
Purpose	You can optionally define a class that implements this interface, to provide information about the methods, events, properties, and other characteristics of your JavaBean class. Development tools that consume JavaBean classes may use the classes that implement this interface. Programs that use the JavaBean class do not use BeanInfo classes.
Methods	■ **BeanInfo[] getAdditionalBeanInfo()** Implement the **getAdditionalBeanInfo** method to specify an array of additional **BeanInfo** objects that provide information about the JavaBean. ■ **BeanDescriptor getBeanDescriptor()** Implement **getBeanDescriptor** to return general information in a **BeanDescriptor** object. ■ **int getDefaultEventIndex()** Implement **getDefaultEventIndex** to tell the beanbox which element in the **EventSetDescriptor** array to treat as the default event when a user interacts with the JavaBean. ■ **int getDefaultPropertyIndex()** Implement the **getDefaultPropertyIndex** method to tell the beanbox which element in the **PropertyDescriptor** array to treat as the default when a user interacts with the JavaBean. ■ **EventSetDescriptor[] getEventSetDescriptors()** Implement **getEventSetDescriptors** to return an array of **EventSetDescriptor** objects that describes the events generated by this bean. ■ **Image getIcon(int *iconKind*)** Implement the **getIcon** method to return an icon that can be used to represent the JavaBean in toolbars and the like. The argument specifies the kind of icon required. ■ **MethodDescriptor[] getMethodDescriptors()** Implement the **getMethodDescriptors** method to return an array of **MethodDescriptor** objects that describe the externally visible methods of the JavaBean. ■ **PropertyDescriptor[] getPropertyDescriptors()** Implement the **getPropertyDescriptors** method to return an array of **PropertyDescriptor** objects that describe the properties of the JavaBean.

You can define a class that implements the BeanInfo interface and supply implementations of all the BeanInfo methods. A simpler approach is to define a class that extends the class java.beans.SimpleBeanInfo. This class implements the BeanInfo interface and provides methods in which the return values indicate that no information is available. You can extend the SimpleBeanInfo class and override selected methods. For example, if an icon can represent your JavaBean class, you can implement the BeanInfo.getIcon method to return the icon. Some of the classes in the java.beans package that provide information about JavaBean classes are listed in Figure 15-12.

Providing a Custom Property Editor

Beanboxes can provide property editors for several different types of properties, including String, Font, and Color. However, a programmer who creates JavaBeans must provide a property editor for other kinds of properties. All property editors must implement the interface java.beans.PropertyEditor. Property editors must keep track of all objects that are interested in the property and notify all these objects when a property changes.

The class java.beans.PropertyEditorSupport provides a trivial property editor. For many cases, all you must do to create a custom property editor is extend this class and override a few of its methods. For example, if all the editor needs to do is present a list of valid choices for the property value, the support provided by PropertyEditorSupport is sufficient. The next example program demonstrates a customized editor class that takes this approach.

For cases requiring something more complex, a class that directly implements the PropertyEditor interface and provides implementation of all its methods may be more appropriate.

Beanboxes usually provide a dialog box containing a list of all the JavaBean properties and a field for editing each one. Often this dialog box is sufficient. Nevertheless, a complex JavaBean may require that you efficiently customize a specialized user interface. A special-purpose customizer can treat the JavaBean as a whole, because it can understand the dependencies between fields and makes sure that they are respected.

A customizer class must meet the following criteria:

- The class must implement the java.beans.Customizer interface.
- An instance of the class must be an AWT component that can be embedded in a dialog box. Typically, you define a customizer class to extend the Panel class.
- The class must have a constructor that has no arguments.

When you create a customizer class, you must also provide the method getBeanDescriptor in the BeanInfo class associated with the JavaBean. The BeanDescriptor associates the customizer class with a particular JavaBean. To instantiate the BeanDescriptor class, use the form of the constructor that has two arguments, so that you can specify both the JavaBean object and the customizer object.

Syntax	**BeanDescriptor myBeanDescriptor** **= new BeanDescriptor(** ***beanClass, customizerClass*** **);**
Dissection	■ The first argument of the constructor is the **Class** object for the JavaBean class. ■ The second argument of the constructor is the **Class** object for the customizer class.

Creating a JavaBean Class with a BeanInfo Class

The third and final version the example JavaBean, the `ImageBean3` class, is expanded further by the addition of another property, `scaling`, which allows the image to appear at its original size or scaled to fit the panel that contains it. This property has only two allowable values, the constants `ORIGINAL_SIZE` and `SCALED_TO_FIT`, both of which are defined in the class. A custom property editor is created for this property that lets the user choose between these two values without having to know the integer values used within the class.

`ImageBean3` also has an accompanying **BeanInfo** class. Following the prescribed naming convention, this class is called `ImageBean3BeanInfo`. The source for the `scaling` property editor class and the `ImageBean3BeanInfo` class follow the breakdown of the `ImageBean3` class.

Here is the complete source code for this third version of the `ImageBean` example. The differences between this version and the previous version are highlighted in boldface and described in detail after the source code.

```
package java4cpp.beans;
import java.awt.*;
import java.io.*;
import java.util.*;
import java.awt.image.ImageObserver;
import java.beans.*;
/** A very simple JavaBean class that displays an image
  * and allows the user to specify the file containing
  * the image and the fill color to be used if the
  * image is smaller than the panel. There is also a
  * scaling property that allows the image to be shown
  * in its original size or scaled to fit in the panel.
  */
public class ImageBean3 extends Panel {
   private String fileName;
   private transient Image image;
   private int width = 200;
   private int height=150;
   private Color fill = Color.lightGray;
   private PropertyChangeSupport
```

```
   myListeners = new PropertyChangeSupport( this );
private Vector fillColorListeners = new Vector();
/** Specify how the image is drawn, must be one of
  * the constants defined below */
private int scaling;
/** Draw the image in its original size */
public static final int ORIGINAL_SIZE = 0;
/** Scale the image to fit in the panel */
public static final int SCALED_TO_FIT = 1;
/** No-argument constructor; sets the file name to a
  * default value.
  */
public ImageBean3() {
   setFileName( "..\\demo\\sunw\\demo\\juggler\\"
                + "Juggler0.gif" );
}
/** Send an event to all registered listeners */
public void fireFillColorEvent( FillColorEvent e ) {
   Vector snapshot
      = (Vector) fillColorListeners.clone();
   Enumeration cursor = snapshot.elements();
   while( cursor.hasMoreElements() ) {
      FillColorListener fcl
         = (FillColorListener) cursor.nextElement();
      if ( e.getID()
         == FillColorEvent.COLOR_CHANGE ) {
         fcl.fillColorChange( e );
      }
   }
}
/** Display the image at its original size.  The Sun
  * BeanBox recognizes only methods without
  * parameters that return void.
  */
public void displayOriginalSize() {
   setScaling( ORIGINAL_SIZE );
}
/** Display the image scaled to fit the panel.  The
  * Sun BeanBox recognizes only methods without
  * parameters that return void.
  */
public void displayScaledToFit() {
   setScaling( SCALED_TO_FIT );
}
/** Accessor for the filename property.
  * @return The current image's filename
  */
```

```
public String getFileName() {
   return fileName;
}
/** Accessor for the fillColor property
  * @return The current fill color
  */
public Color getFillColor() {
   return fill;
}
/** The preferred size of the panel
  * @return The size of the current image
  */
public Dimension getPreferredSize() {
   return new Dimension( width, height );
}
/** How the image is drawn within the panel
  */
public int getScaling() {
   return scaling;
}
/** Method for monitoring the progress of the
  * loading of the current image.
  */
public boolean imageUpdate( Image img,
                            int infoflags,
                            int x, int y,
                            int w, int h ) {
   if ( (infoflags & ImageObserver.ALLBITS) != 0 ) {
      int oldWidth = width;
      int oldHeight = height;
      width = img.getWidth( null );
      height = img.getHeight( null );
      if ( oldWidth != width
           || oldHeight != height ) {
         myListeners.firePropertyChange(
            "preferredSize",
            new Dimension( oldWidth, oldHeight ),
            new Dimension( width, height ) );
      }
      repaint();
      return false;
   } else {
      return true;
   }
}
/** Set the image fill color to green.  The Sun
  * BeanBox recognizes only methods without
```

```
      * parameters that return void.
      */
    public void makeFillGreen() {
       setFillColor( Color.green );
    }
    /** Set the image fill color to red.  The Sun
      * BeanBox recognizes only methods without
      * parameters that return void.
      */
    public void makeFillRed() {
       setFillColor( Color.red );
    }
    /** Paint the fill color if the panel is bigger than
      * the image and the image will be displayed
      * original size.  Then draw the image according to
      * the selected scaling type.
      * @param g the panel's graphics context
      */
    public void paint( Graphics g ) {
       Dimension panelSize = getSize();
       if ( scaling == ORIGINAL_SIZE &&
          ( panelSize.width > width
            panelSize.height > height ) ) {
          g.setColor ( fill );
          g.fillRect ( 0, 0,
                       panelSize.width,
                       panelSize.height );
       }
       if ( image != null ) {
          if ( scaling == SCALED_TO_FIT ) {
             g.drawImage( image, 0, 0,
                          panelSize.width,
                          panelSize.height,
                          fill, this );
          } else {
             g.drawImage( image, 0, 0, this );
          }
       }
    }
    /** Deserialization method called for the JavaBean.
      * This is necessary because Image objects can be
      * serialized and must be regenerated manually.
      * @exception IOException if an error occurs
      *            reading the serialized JavaBean.
      * @exception ClassNotFoundException if the
      *            serialized JavaBean can't be found.
```

```
   */
private void readObject( ObjectInputStream ois )
        throws IOException, ClassNotFoundException {
   ois.defaultReadObject();
   image = getToolkit().getImage( fileName );
   repaint();
}
/** Mutator method for the fillColor property.
  * @param c the new fill color value
  */
public void setFillColor( Color c ) {
   Color oldFill = fill;
   fill = c;
   myListeners.firePropertyChange( "fillColor",
                                   oldFill,
                                   fill );
   fireFillColorEvent( new FillColorEvent( this,
                       FillColorEvent.COLOR_CHANGE,
                       c ) );
   repaint();
}
/** Mutator method for the fileName property.
  * @param fn the new image filename
  */
public void setFileName( String fn ) {
   String oldFileName = fileName;
   fileName = fn;
   image = getToolkit().getImage( fileName );
   myListeners.firePropertyChange( "fileName",
                                  oldFileName,
                                  fileName );
   repaint();
}
/** Mutator method for the image-scaling property
  * used to specify how the image should be drawn
  * within the panel.
  * @param s the scaling type, either ORIGINAL_SIZE
  *         or SCALED_TO_FIT
  */
public void setScaling( int s ) {
   int oldScaling = scaling;
   scaling = s;
   myListeners.firePropertyChange( "scaling",
      new Integer( oldScaling ),
      new Integer( scaling ) );
}
/** Add a listener interested in FillColorEvent
```

```
         * objects
         */
        public void
        addFillColorListener( FillColorListener l ) {
           fillColorListeners.addElement( l );
        }
        /** Add a listener interested in property change
         * events
         */
        public void addPropertyChangeListener(
           PropertyChangeListener l ) {
           myListeners.addPropertyChangeListener( l );
        }
        /** Remove a listener no longer interested in
         * FillColorEvent objects
         */
        public void removeFillColorListener(
           FillColorListener l ) {
           fillColorListeners.removeElement( l );
        }
        /** Remove a listener no longer interested in
         * property change events
         */
        public void
        removePropertyChangeListener(
           PropertyChangeListener l ) {
           myListeners.removePropertyChangeListener( l );
        }
    }
```

Breakdown of the ImageBean3 Class

The `ImageBean3` class is the last variation on `ImageBean1` class.

```
public class ImageBean3 extends Panel {
```

Three fields are added to the class. One is the field for holding the scaling, `scaling`, and the other two are the constant values to be assigned to the `scaling` field.

```
private int scaling;
public static final int ORIGINAL_SIZE = 0;
public static final int SCALED_TO_FIT = 1;
```

Two more convenience methods are added for changing the scaling of the image. Because they return no value and take no input, they are very easy to connect to the events of other JavaBeans.

```
public void displayOriginalSize() {
   setScaling( ORIGINAL_SIZE );
}
public void displayScaledToFit() {
   setScaling( SCALED_TO_FIT );
}
```

An accessor method for the scaling property is added.

```
public int getScaling() {
   return scaling;
}
```

The paint method is changed to handle the choices of image scaling. If the scaling property has the value `ORIGINAL_SIZE`, the image is drawn as before. If the value is `SCALED_TO_FIT`, a different version of the drawImage method is used. This version takes the size that the image should become, which is the size of the panel.

```
public void paint( Graphics g ) {
   Dimension panelSize = getSize();
   if ( scaling == ORIGINAL_SIZE &&
      ( panelSize.width > width
        panelSize.height > height ) ) {
      g.setColor ( fill );
      g.fillRect ( 0, 0,
                   panelSize.width,
                   panelSize.height );
   }
   if ( image != null ) {
      if ( scaling == SCALED_TO_FIT ) {
         g.drawImage( image, 0, 0,
                      panelSize.width,
                      panelSize.height,
                      fill, this );
      } else {
         g.drawImage( image, 0, 0, this );
      }
   }
}
```

A mutator method for the scaling type has been added.

```
public void setScaling( int s ) {
   int oldScaling = scaling;
   scaling = s;
   myListeners.firePropertyChange( "scaling",
      new Integer( oldScaling ),
      new Integer( scaling ) );
}
```

None of the other methods in the `ImageBean3` class are new or have been updated. However, this class uses two additional classes:

- The property editor class
- The bean information class

The Property Editor Class for the ImageBean3 Class

The scaling property of the `ImageBean3` class requires a customized editor, and the `ScalingEditor` class provides it. This simple property editor only needs to present a list of two choices for users. Therefore, the `ScalingEditor` can be defined as a subclass of PropertyEditorSupport and can use most of the inherited method implementations.

```
package java4cpp.beans;
import java.beans.*;
/** This class provides the editing support for the
  * scaling property of the ImageBean3 class.
  */
public class ScalingEditor
   extends PropertyEditorSupport {
   /** Provide the names of the allowable values.
     * Don't put spaces in these tags
     * for the Sun BeanBox, ensure that no
     * spaces appear in these tags.
     * @return An array of strings containing the
     *         allowable values
     */
   public String[] getTags() {
      return new String[] { "original_size",
                            "scaled_to_fit" };
   }
   /** Convert a tag string into a tag name into a
     * value.  The default is to set the value to
     * the ORIGINAL_SIZE value.
     * @param s The tag string
     */
   public void setAsText( String s ) {
      if ( s.equals( "scaled_to_fit" ) ) {
         setValue( new Integer(
                   ImageBean3.SCALED_TO_FIT) );
      } else {
         setValue( new Integer(
                   ImageBean3.ORIGINAL_SIZE) );
      }
   }
   /** For a given property value, return a string
     * that can be used for code generation.  The
```

```
     * default value returned is the string for the
     * ORIGINAL_SIZE value.
     * @return The string put into the generated code
     */
   public String getJavaInitializationString() {
      switch( ( (Number) getValue() ).intValue() ) {
         default:
         case ImageBean3.ORIGINAL_SIZE:
            return "java4cpp.beans.ImageBean3."
                  +"ORIGINAL_SIZE";
         case ImageBean3.SCALED_TO_FIT:
            return "java4cpp.beans.ImageBean3."
                  +"SCALED_TO_FIT";
      }
   }
}
```

The `ScalingEditor` class overrides three methods of the PropertyEditorSupport class that relate to the names and values of the allowable choices. The getTags method returns the names of the value `scaling` for the property.

```
public String[] getTags()
```

The setAsText method is overridden to convert the tag strings into the actual integer values they represent.

```
public void setAsText( String s )
```

The getJavaInitializationString method returns a string in a form suitable for putting into a class definition. This method is used when a beanbox is generating a class definition and is preparing Java statements for inclusion in the class.

```
public String getJavaInitializationString()
```

The Information Class for the ImageBean3 Class

To make the `ImageBean3` class usable as a bean, a BeanInfo class is required. The primary reason to create this class is to associate the `ScalingEditor` class with the scaling property of `ImageBean3`. Here is the complete source code for the `ImageBean3BeanInfo` class. Following the listing is a detailed breakdown of the code.

```
package java4cpp.beans;
import java.beans.*;
import java.lang.reflect.Method;
/** The class contains information about the ImageBean3
  * class in a format that is understood by JavaBean
  * builder programs like Sun's BeanBox
  */
```

```
public class ImageBean3BeanInfo
   extends SimpleBeanInfo {
   /** Create an array of PropertyDescriptor objects
     * representing each of the class's properties
     * @return The array of PropertyDescriptor objects
     */
   public PropertyDescriptor[]
      getPropertyDescriptors() {
      PropertyDescriptor[] pds = null;
      try {
         pds = new PropertyDescriptor[] {
            new PropertyDescriptor( "fillColor",
                                    ImageBean3.class ),
            new PropertyDescriptor( "fileName",
                                    ImageBean3.class ),
            new PropertyDescriptor( "scaling",
                                    ImageBean3.class ),
            new PropertyDescriptor( "preferredSize",
                                    ImageBean3.class,
                                    "getPreferredSize",
                                    null )
         };
         pds[0].setShortDescription(
            "The fill color around the image" );
         pds[1].setShortDescription(
            "The file containing the image" );
         pds[2].setShortDescription(
            "How the image should be drawn" );
         pds[3].setShortDescription(
            "The preferred size of the panel" );
         // all properties of this bean are bound
         for ( int i = 0; i < pds.length; i++ ) {
            pds[i].setBound( true );
         }
         pds[2].setPropertyEditorClass(
            ScalingEditor.class );
      } catch( IntrospectionException ix ) {
         System.out.println( ix );
         return super.getPropertyDescriptors();
      }
      return pds;
   }
   /** Indicate that the fileName property is the
     * default property to be updated by returning
     * its index in the PropertyDescriptor array
     * obtained from the method
```

```
      * getPropertyDescriptors
      * @return The index of the fileName array
      *          element
      */
     public int getDefaultPropertyIndex() {
        return 1;    // the filename property index
     }
}
```

Breakdown of the ImageBean3BeanInfo Class

The first method of the class, getPropertyDescriptors, returns an array of objects in which each element describes a different property of the `ImageBean3` class.

```
public class ImageBean3BeanInfo extends SimpleBeanInfo {
   public PropertyDescriptor[] getPropertyDescriptors() {
```

The method begins by declaring the array and then initializing it using an anonymous array that has the descriptor objects in it. The descriptor objects must be created inside a try block because their constructor may throw an IntrospectionException that can be caught and handled. The minimum constructor arguments required are the name of the property and the class to which the property belongs. These constructor arguments suffice for all of the properties except `preferredSize`. Because `preferredSize` is a read-only property, additional arguments of the constructor are specified for the methods that read and write `preferredSize`. The null indicates that the property has no write method.

```
   PropertyDescriptor[] pds = null;
      try {
         pds = new PropertyDescriptor[] {
            new PropertyDescriptor( "fillColor",
                                    ImageBean3.class ),
            new PropertyDescriptor( "fileName",
                                    ImageBean3.class ),
            new PropertyDescriptor( "scaling",
                                    ImageBean3.class ),
            new PropertyDescriptor( "preferredSize",
                                    ImageBean3.class,
                                    "getPreferredSize",
                                    null )
         };
```

The next group of statements sets the short descriptions for the properties. Not all beanboxes make use of these short descriptions, but they can be helpful.

```
         pds[0].setShortDescription(
            "The fill color around the image" );
         pds[1].setShortDescription(
```

```
      "The file containing the image" );
   pds[2].setShortDescription(
      "How the image should be drawn" );
   pds[3].setShortDescription(
      "The preferred size of the panel" );
```

The for loop marks each property as a bound property.

```
   for ( int i = 0; i < pds.length; i++ ) {
      pds[i].setBound( true );
   }
```

Mini Quiz 15-4

Why is the variable pds declared outside the try block in the `getPropertyDescriptors` method?

The method setPropertyEditorClass makes the association between the scaling property and its editor class. In the `pds` array, the scaling property has the index value two.

```
pds[2].setPropertyEditorClass(
   ScalingEditor.class );
```

The catch block is required to handle any errors that may occur because the introspection process could not be completed for the JavaBean. This catch clause recovers by printing a message to the console and returning the default list of property descriptors as determined by the superclass, SimpleBeanInfo. If no errors occur, the array calculated in this method is returned.

```
   } catch( IntrospectionException ix ) {
      System.out.println( ix );
      return super.getPropertyDescriptors();
   }
   return pds;
}
```

The other method in this BeanInfo class is used to indicate the default property for the JavaBean. It does this by returning the index of a property in the array prepared by getPropertyDescriptors. It is assumed that the beanbox will give this property some sort of preferential treatment. Returning a value of –1 indicates that there is no default. In this case, the default property is the filename for the image file.

```
public int getDefaultPropertyIndex() {
   return 1;   // the filename property index
}
```

To load the `ImageBean3` JavaBean into the BDK BeanBox, follow the same process you used for `ImageBean1` and `ImageBean2`.

To load the ImageBean3 into the BeanBox:

1. Add lines to the ImageBeans.manifest file in the folder into which you unpacked the java4cpp.jar file, so that the manifest file lists all three image beans, as follows:

```
Name: java4cpp/beans/ImageBean1.class
Java-Bean: True

Name: java4cpp/beans/ImageBean2.class
Java-Bean: True

Name: java4cpp/beans/ImageBean3.class
Java-Bean: True
```

2. Issue the following command, on one line, from the parent folder of the java4cpp folder to create a JAR file named ImageBeans.jar:

```
jar cfm ImageBeans.jar ImageBeans.manifest
                        java4cpp\beans\*.class
```

3. Copy the file ImageBeans.jar into the jars subfolder of the folder in which you installed the BDK.
4. Start the beanbox. See that the Toolbox window now lists `ImageBean3`.

   The interesting feature of this bean is the `scaling` property and the customized property editor, `ScalingEditor`.
5. Drag an `ImageBean3` bean onto the BeanBox window and make sure that the bean is selected.
6. You may have to resize the Properties window to see all of it. Click the **down arrow** ▾ beside the scaling property or on the scaling entry field. The drop-down menu that is shown in Figure 15-13 appears.
7. Select **scaled_to_fit**, and see the image in the bean expand to fill the dimensions of the bean. Select **original_size** and the image is redrawn at the original size.

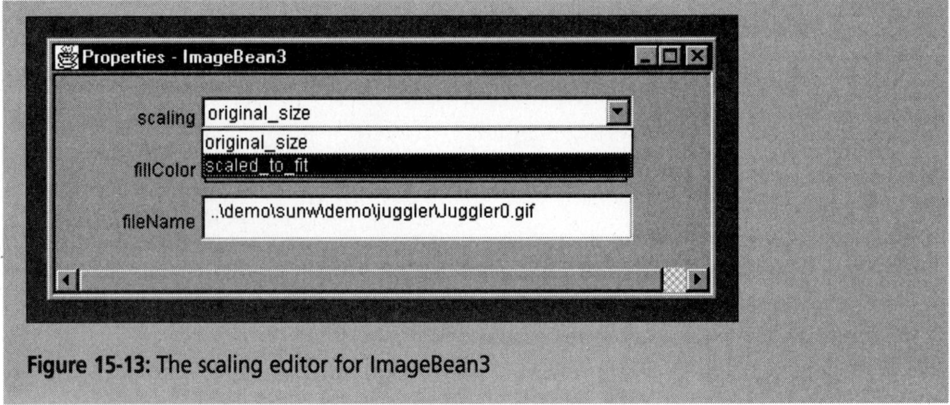

Figure 15-13: The scaling editor for ImageBean3

Feel free to explore the BeanBox, trying other demonstration beans, before you close the BeanBox window and proceed to Chapter 16.

SUMMARY

The JavaBeans component model is a framework for creating reusable Java classes. Classes that conform to the JavaBeans specification can be loaded into development tools called beanboxes, with which developers can create applications by positioning and connecting beans. This new and emerging technology may become the dominant software technique in the future.

- The interface to a JavaBean consists of methods, properties, and events.
- The package java.beans provides the core classes and interfaces that support beans.
- A bean must implement the interface java.io.Serializable, because beanboxes use object serialization.
- A bean must have a constructor that has no arguments. You must make provisions to pass arguments, if necessary, to the superclass of a bean.
- Beanboxes use the Reflection API in the package java.lang.reflect to interrogate a bean.
- Properties are the attributes of a bean, commonly implemented as the fields of a Java class.
- Properties may be single entities or indexed properties, which are arrays of values.
- Bound properties can notify other beans when their value changes. Use the class PropertyChangeSupport to implement support for bound properties.
- Constrained properties are bound properties with the additional characteristic that other listeners can prevent a change in value from occurring. Use the class VetoableChangeSupport to implement support for constrained properties.
- Event handling follows the same model as event handling for components in the AWT. If a bean can generate an event Y, the class for the event is YEvent. A listener class YListener should handle YEvent objects.
- Changes to properties trigger events of the class PropertyChangeEvent objects. You can add custom events for other kinds of events.

- If the Reflection API cannot provide all the information that a beanbox needs about a bean, you can supply an additional information class that implements the interface BeanInfo. In simple cases, you can extend the class SimpleBeanInfo rather than implementing the interface.
- Beanboxes provide property editors for String, Font, and Color properties. You can provide customized editors for other kinds of properties, by defining a class that extends PropertyEditorSupport or implements the PropertyEditor interface.
- If the property editor dialog box of the beanbox is not adequate, you can provide a customizer class for the bean.

QUESTIONS

1. Which of the following represent a major category of the JavaBeans interface? Select all that apply.
   a. Properties
   b. Events
   c. Menus
   d. Methods
   e. Streams
2. Which of the following describe a category of JavaBeans events? Select all that apply.
   a. restrained
   b. indexed
   c. bound
   d. controlled
   e. reversible
3. If a JavaBean has a property called `X` with type `T`, which of the following are possible mutator methods for that property in the absence of any other information? Select all that apply.
   a. `T isX( )`
   b. `void setXValue( T` *`newValue`* `)`
   c. `T getX( )`
   d. `void setX( T` *`newValue`* `)`
   e. `void putX( T` *`newValue`* `)`
4. Which class can be used as the basis for supporting bound properties in a JavaBean?
5. If a JavaBean has a property called `X` with type `T`, which of the following are possible accessor methods for that property in the absence of any other information? Select all that apply.
   a. `T isX( )`
   b. `void getXValue( T` *`newValue`* `)`
   c. `T getX( )`
   d. `void setX( T` *`newValue`* `)`
   e. `T getX( int` *`index`* `)`

6. For a JavaBean class named `A`, which of the following would be the name of its associated BeanInfo class? Select the best answer.
   a. `BeanInfo`
   b. `SimpleBeanInfo`
   c. `ABeanInfo`
   d. `AInfo`
   e. `ASimpleBeanInfo`
7. Which of the following are classes that can be used to describe features of a JavaBean? Select all that apply.
   a. ParameterDescriptor
   b. IndexedPropertyDescriptor
   c. MethodDescriptor
   d. ConstructorDescriptor
   e. EventSetDescriptor
8. What class can be used to provide a basic editor for a JavaBean property with values that must be chosen from a list?
9. Which interface must all JavaBeans implement? Select the best answer.
   a. Runnable
   b. Beanable
   c. Cloneable
   d. Serializable
   e. PropertyChangeListener
10. How does a listener object veto a proposed property change?

EXERCISES

Debugging

1. Correct all the errors in the following JavaBean class to create a bean that draws a square of a specified size:

```
package java4cpp.questions.c15;
import java.awt.*;
import java.io.Serializable;
public class Debug15_1 extends Panel
                       implements Serializable {
   private String sideLength = "10";
   private static final Point START
      = new Point( 20, 20 );
   void setSideLength( String sideLength ) {
      this.sideLength = sideLength;
   }
   String getSideLength() {
      return sideLength;
   }
```

```
   public Dimension getPreferredSize() {
      return new Dimension( 100, 100 );
   }
   public void paint( Graphics g ) {
      int sl = Integer.parseInt( sideLength );
      g.drawRect( START.x, START.y, sl, sl );
   }
}
```

Use the following entry in the manifest file Debug15_1 of your JAR file:

```
Name: java4cpp/questions/c15/Debug15_1.class
Java-Bean: True
```

Then execute the following command (entered on a single line) from the parent folder of the java4cpp folder to create the JAR file:

```
jar cfm0 java4cpp/questions/c15/Debug15_1.jar
         java4cpp/questions/c15/Debug15_1.manifest
         java4cpp/questions/c15/Debug15_1.class
```

2. Correct all the errors in the following JavaBean class to create a bean that draws a circle of a specified radius:

```
package java4cpp.questions.c15;
import java.awt.*;
import java.io.Serializable;
public class Debug15_2 extends Panel
                       implements Serializable {
   private String radius = "25";
   private static final Point START
      = new Point( 20, 20 );
   public void radius( String radius ) {
      this.radius = radius;
   }
   public String radius() {
      return radius;
   }
   public Dimension getPreferredSize() {
      return new Dimension( 100, 100 );
   }
   public void paint( Graphics g ) {
      int r = Integer.parseInt( radius );
      g.fillOval( START.x, START.y, r, r );
   }
}
```

Use the following entry in the manifest file Debug15_2 of your JAR file:

```
Name: java4cpp/questions/c15/Debug15_2.class
Java-Bean: True
```

Then execute the following command (entered on a single line) from the parent folder of the java4cpp folder to create the JAR file:

```
jar cfm0 java4cpp/questions/c15/Debug15_2.jar
         java4cpp/questions/c15/Debug15_2.manifest
         java4cpp/questions/c15/Debug15_2.class
```

3. Correct all the errors in the following JavaBean class to create a bean that draws the given text and provides notification when the text changes:

```
package java4cpp.questions.c15;
import java.awt.*;
import java.beans.*;
import java.io.Serializable;
public class Debug15_3 extends Panel
                       implements Serializable {
   private String text = "Default text";
   private static final Point START
      = new Point( 20, 20 );
   private PropertyChangeSupport listeners
      = new PropertyChangeSupport( this );
   public void setDrawText( String text ) {
      this.text = text;
   }
   public String getDrawText() {
      return text;
   }
   public Dimension getPreferredSize() {
      return new Dimension( 100, 40 );
   }
   public void paint( Graphics g ) {
      g.drawString( text, START.x, START.y );
   }
   public void addPropertyChangeListener(
            PropertyChangeListener l ) {
      listeners.addPropertyChangeListener( l );
   }
   public void removePropertyChangeListener(
            PropertyChangeListener l ) {
      listeners.removePropertyChangeListener( l );
   }
}
```

Use the following entry in the manifest file Debug15_3 of your JAR file:

```
Name: java4cpp/questions/c15/Debug15_3.class
Java-Bean: True
```

Then execute the following command (entered on a single line) from the parent folder of the java4cpp folder to create the JAR file:

```
jar cfm0 java4cpp/questions/c15/Debug15_3.jar
         java4cpp/questions/c15/Debug15_3.manifest
         java4cpp/questions/c15/Debug15_3.class
```

4. Correct all the errors in the following JavaBean class to create a bean that draws ovals and provides vetoable notification when the height or width of the oval changes:

```
package java4cpp.questions.c15;
import java.awt.*;
import java.io.Serializable;
public class Debug15_4 extends Panel
                       implements Serializable {
   private String ovalHeight = "25";
   private String ovalWidth = "50";
   private static final Point START = new Point( 20, 20 );
   public void setOvalHeight( String ovalHeight ) {
      try {
         listeners.fireVetoableChange( "ovalHeight",
                                       this.ovalHeight,
                                       ovalHeight );
         this.ovalHeight = ovalHeight;
      } catch ( PropertyVetoException pve ) {
         // change was vetoed, nothing to do
      }
   }
   public String getOvalHeight() {
      return ovalHeight;
   }
   public void setOvalWidth( String ovalWidth ) {
      try {
         listeners.fireVetoableChange( "ovalWidth",
                                       this.ovalWidth,
                                       ovalWidth );
         this.ovalWidth = ovalWidth;
      } catch ( PropertyVetoException pve ) {
         // change was vetoed, nothing to do
      }
   }
   public String getOvalWidth() {
      return ovalWidth;
   }
   public Dimension getPreferredSize() {
      return new Dimension( 100, 100 );
   }
   public void paint( Graphics g ) {
      int h = Integer.parseInt( ovalHeight );
      int w = Integer.parseInt( ovalWidth );
      g.fillOval( START.x, START.y, w, h );
   }
}
```

Use the following entry in the manifest file Debug15_4 of your JAR file:

```
Name: java4cpp/questions/c15/Debug15_4.class
Java-Bean: True
```

Then execute the following command (entered on a single line) from the parent folder of the java4cpp folder to create the JAR file:

```
jar cfm0 java4cpp/questions/c15/Debug15_4.jar
         java4cpp/questions/c15/Debug15_4.manifest
         java4cpp/questions/c15/Debug15_4.class
```

5. Correct all the errors in the following JavaBean class and its associated BeanInfo and editor classes to create a bean that draws a rectangle with either sharp or rounded corners:

```
package java4cpp.questions.c15;
import java.awt.*;
import java.io.Serializable;
public class Debug15_5 extends Panel
                       implements Serializable {
   public static final int SHARP = 0;
   public static final int ROUNDED = 1;
   private String sideLength = "60";
   private int corners = SHARP;
   private static final Point START
      = new Point( 20, 20 );
   private static final int ROUNDING = 20;
   public void setCorners( int corners ) {
      this.corners = corners;
   }
   public int getCorners() {
      return corners;
   }
   public Dimension getPreferredSize() {
      return new Dimension( 100, 100 );
   }
   public void paint( Graphics g ) {
      int sl = Integer.parseInt( sideLength );
      if ( corners == SHARP ) {
         g.drawRect( START.x, START.y, sl, sl );
      } else {
         g.drawRoundRect( START.x, START.y, sl, sl,
                          ROUNDING, ROUNDING );
      }
   }
}
package java4cpp.questions.c15;
import java.beans.*;
public class Debug15_5BeanInfo extends SimpleBeanInfo {
   public PropertyDescriptor[]
   getPropertyDescriptors() {
```

```
        PropertyDescriptor[] pds = null;
        try {
           pds = new PropertyDescriptor[] {
              new PropertyDescriptor( "corners",
                                      Debug15_5.class ),
           };
           pds[0].setShortDescription(
              "The shape of the rectangle's corners" );
           pds[0].setBound( false );
        } catch( IntrospectionException ix ) {
           ix.printStackTrace();
           return super.getPropertyDescriptors();
        }
        return pds;
     }
}
package java4cpp.questions.c15;
import java.beans.*;
public class Debug15_5Editor
   extends PropertyEditorSupport {
   public String[] getTags() {
      return new String[] { "sharp", "rounded" };
   }
   public String getJavaInitializationString() {
      switch( ( ( Number ) getValue() ).intValue() ) {
         default:
         case Debug15_5.SHARP:
            return "java4cpp.questions.c15.Debug15_5."
                   +"SHARP";
         case Debug15_5.ROUNDED:
            return "java4cpp.questions.c15.Debug15_5."
                   +"ROUNDED";
      }
   }
}
```

Use the following entry in the manifest file Debug15_5 of your JAR file:

```
Name: java4cpp/questions/c15/Debug15_5.class
Java-Bean: True
```

Then execute the following command (entered on a single line) from the parent folder of the java4cpp folder to create the JAR file:

```
jar cfm0 java4cpp/questions/c15/Debug15_5.jar
         java4cpp/questions/c15/Debug15_5.manifest
         java4cpp/questions/c15/Debug15_5*.class
```

Complete the Solution

1. Complete the following JavaBean class definition by adding another property, `messageFont`, that defines the font used to display the message:

```
package java4cpp.questions.c15;
import java.awt.*;
import java.awt.event.*;
import java.io.Serializable;
public class Complete15_1 extends Panel
                              implements Serializable {
   private Label msg = new Label( "Default message" );
   public Complete15_1() {
      setLayout( new BorderLayout() );
      add( msg, "North" );
      Button okay = new Button( "OK" );
      okay.addActionListener( new ActionListener() {
            public void
            actionPerformed( ActionEvent e ) {
               // disappear when the button is clicked
               Panel.this.setVisible( false );
            }
         }
      );
      Panel p = new Panel();
      p.setLayout( new FlowLayout( FlowLayout.CENTER ) );
      p.add( okay );
      add( p, "South" );
   }
   public void displayMessage() {
      setVisible( true );
   }
   public void setMessage( String message ) {
      msg.setText( message );
   }
   public String getMessage() {
      return msg.getText();
   }
   public Dimension getPreferredSize() {
      return new Dimension( 200, 75 );
   }
}
```

Use the following entry in the manifest file Complete15_1 of your JAR file:

```
Name: java4cpp/questions/c15/Complete15_1.class
Java-Bean: True
```

Then execute the following command (entered on a single line) from the parent folder of the java4cpp folder to create the JAR file:

```
jar cfm0 java4cpp/questions/c15/Complete15_1.jar
         java4cpp/questions/c15/Complete15_1.manifest
         java4cpp/questions/c15/Complete15_1*.class
```

2. Beginning with the JavaBean class shown in the preceding exercise, change the message property so that it is a bound message that provides notification when it changes.

3. Complete the following class definition for a progress bar JavaBean by adding the methods required to make the current position and upper limit into properties that the user can customize:

```
package java4cpp.questions.c15;
import java.awt.*;
import java.awt.event.*;
import java.beans.*;
import java.io.Serializable;
public class Complete15_3 extends Canvas
                        implements Serializable {
   private String lowerLimit = "0";
   private String upperLimit = "100";
   private String position = "0";
   private static final int LENGTH = 200;
   private static final int WIDTH = 20;
   private static final int VSPACE = 20;
   private static final int HSPACE = 10;
   private static final int PROG_INSET = 2;
   private PropertyChangeSupport listeners
      = new PropertyChangeSupport( this );
   public void paint( Graphics g ) {
      // get the font metrics for the graphics context
      FontMetrics fm = g.getFontMetrics();
      // get the height of the font in use
      int fontHeight = fm.getHeight();
      // put the start label on the progress bar
      g.drawString( lowerLimit, HSPACE, VSPACE );
      // put the end label on the progress bar so that
      // the end of the text lines up with the end of
      // the progress bar
      int upperLen = fm.stringWidth( upperLimit );
      g.drawString( upperLimit,
                    HSPACE + LENGTH - upperLen,
                    VSPACE );
      // draw the outline of the progress bar
      g.drawRect( HSPACE, VSPACE + fontHeight,
                  LENGTH, WIDTH );
      // fill in the appropriate amount of the bar
      // based upon the current position
      int ul = Integer.parseInt( upperLimit );
      int ll = Integer.parseInt( lowerLimit );
      int pos = Integer.parseInt( position );
      double progress = (double)(pos - ll) /
                        (double)(ul - ll);
      int progressLength = (int) (progress * LENGTH);
      g.setColor( Color.red );
      g.fillRect( HSPACE + PROG_INSET,
                  VSPACE + fontHeight + PROG_INSET,
```

```
                        progressLength - PROG_INSET*2,
                        WIDTH - PROG_INSET*2 );
   }
   public Dimension getPreferredSize() {
      // determine the font height for the font in use
      int fontHeight
         = getFontMetrics(getFont()).getHeight();
      // set the size so that the progress bar, its
      // labels and the spacing between them and around
      // them is taken into account
      return new Dimension( LENGTH + 2*HSPACE,
                            HEIGHT + 3*VSPACE
                                   + fontHeight );
   }
}
```

Use the following entry in the manifest file Complete15_3 of your JAR file:

```
Name: java4cpp/questions/c15/Complete15_3.class
Java-Bean: True
```

Then execute the following command (entered on a single line) from the parent folder of the java4cpp folder to create the JAR file:

```
jar cfm0 java4cpp/questions/c15/Complete15_3.jar
         java4cpp/questions/c15/Complete15_3.manifest
         java4cpp/questions/c15/Complete15_3*.class
```

4. Beginning with the JavaBean class shown in the preceding exercise, add the support needed to make the position and upper limit properties into constrained properties.
5. Beginning with the JavaBean class shown in Exercise 3, add a corresponding BeanInfo class that gives short descriptions of the properties, indicates that the properties are constrained, and identifies the position property as the default property for customization.

Discovery

1. Create a JavaBean class called `Prompter` that displays a prompting message and provides an entry field where users can enter their response to the prompt. This bean should also include a button, OK, that users can use to indicate they are finished entering their response.
2. Create a JavaBean class called `Counter` that counts upwards from 0 to some limit. The increment and the interval between ticks should be properties of this bean, and the actual count should be a bound property. Try connecting this bean to the progress bar bean from the Complete the Solution exercises so that the count and the progress bar move in unison to the same upper limit.
3. Create a JavaBean class called `BarGraph` that draws a simple bar graph for the data given as five separate bar height properties.

CHAPTER 16

Internationalization

objectives

In this chapter you will:

- Create Java programs that take on the characteristics of the cultural environment in which they run.
- Learn about the Unicode character-encoding scheme.
- Learn how locales encapsulate operations that depend on the current cultural environment.
- Write code that uses objects of the classes InputStreamReader and OutputStreamWriter to translate between Unicode and either the platform-default or ISO 8859-1 character encodings.
- Distinguish between conditions under which you should use platform-default encoding conversion and conditions under which you should use a specific conversion.
- Use resource bundles to separate data that requires translation for different cultural environments into files from your Java source code.

Programming for the International Market

After gaining confidence in your ability to program in the Java programming language and creating several useful Java applications and applets, you are ready to share or sell your programs. There is no advantage in limiting your market to those who live in the same country or use the same cultural environment as you. One of the strengths of the Java platform is that it includes some core classes that can make it relatively easy to provide your programs worldwide. You may be creating applets for the World Wide Web, programming for international networks such as the Internet, or creating applications that run in a Java Virtual Machine (JVM). In all cases, you can create programs that people all over the world can run in their own language, using their own customs.

Programming for the international market takes some foresight. Unfortunately, many programmers overlook the world outside their own country and code in such a way that adapting the programs for other cultural environments is very difficult. Indeed, all the examples so far in this book have this failing. Historically, a huge body of existing C and C++ programs share this shortcoming, even though the concept of locales, upon which many of the internationalization and localization features of the Java platform are based, were introduced for C and even expanded in C++. You can avoid this pitfall from the start. This chapter shows you how.

The most common impediment to internationalizing a program is text that is embedded in the source code. For example, the following statement is really only addressing the English-speaking portion of the world:

```
System.out.println( "Hello World!" );
```

Adapting programs with embedded text for other languages is a time-consuming process. You must create a copy of the source code for each target language. Then you must check every source statement to locate and translate every occurrence of displayable text. This approach is also extremely error prone. At a minimum, you must test the program again to make sure that none of the changes affect the operation of the program.

Another common problem comes from the fact that the format of dates, times, currency values, and numbers varies from country to country. For example, the Americans and the British write the number *one thousand* as *1,000,* but the French read that number as 1, accurate to 3 decimal digits. In the United States, the compact date format for September 1, 1998 is 09/01/1998, but in Canada that compact date expands into January 9, 1998. These are just two examples of the enormous potential for misunderstanding and errors that can undermine your internationalization ambitions.

The key to making your program adaptable for other cultural environments is to separate the functionality of your program from the elements that depend on language and customs. This process is called **internationalization,** a term often abbreviated as **I18N**, because *internationalization* is a long word that begins with *I*, ends with *N*, and has 18 characters in between. The complementary process of adapting the program for a particular country or region is called **localization.**

To a programmer, a cultural environment has several facets, including the following:

- How characters are encoded. The number of bytes required and the bit pattern used to represent different characters determine how data is interpreted.
- The **collating sequence** for ordering and sorting characters. The collating sequence defines the alphabetic order of letters, and extends to cover digits, punctuation, and all characters represented in the current encoding scheme.
- How dates and times are formatted.
- How currency values, percentages, and other numbers are formatted.

In the original version of the Java platform, support for internationalization and localization was incomplete. However, since its inception, Java technology has been successful around the world. The result was a great initial demand for true support for the international market. The demand is largely met by features for internationalization that have been available since version 1.1.

Understanding Unicode Character Encoding

To present text to users in their own language, you must be able to represent all the characters in the alphabet of that language. You may also need accented characters and a different set of digits that you do not use in your own cultural environment. This may sound obvious, but the fact is that most programming languages explicitly accept only a subset of characters used by the English-speaking world.

You may be familiar with a limited, but very widely used, character set: seven-bit ASCII (American Standard Code for Information Interchange). Seven bits allow for 128 character mappings: 32 control characters, 26 lowercase letters, 26 uppercase letters, 10 digits, and some punctuation characters. A character set defined by the International Organization for Standardization (ISO) is Latin-1, also known as ISO-8859-1. Latin-1 supports 256 characters by using all eight bits of each byte for character encoding. The Latin-1 character set includes the 128 ASCII characters plus many of the symbols and accented letters required for western European languages. Latin-1 is adequate for much of the western world, but the character set fails to accommodate languages for which the script is not based on the Latin alphabet, such as Russian, Greek, and most Asian and Middle Eastern languages.

The Unicode encoding scheme allows for a much larger character set by letting individual characters occupy more than one byte. ISO also defines Unicode standards. Unicode characters can take different forms. The Java platform uses the **canonical form,** in which each character occupies two bytes of Unicode 2 for its internal representation of characters. Using two bytes rather than one creates a potential of 65,536 different character mappings. Unicode 2 supports 38,885 distinct characters taken from 25 scripts. The scripts include characters used by many of the principal languages of the world, including Arabic, Cyrillic, Greek, Gujurati, Han (logographic characters for Chinese, Japanese, and Korean), Hebrew, and many more. The Latin-1 characters are a subset of Unicode 2.

Version Watch

Originally the Java platform used Unicode version 1.1. Version 1.1 and later versions of the Java platform use Unicode version 2. Unicode 2 includes more scripts than the Unicode version 1. Future versions of Unicode will support even more scripts.

Characters in Java Source Code

Any Unicode character can be used within a Java program as part of a string or an identifier. Few, if any, commonly available text editors support Unicode as fully as the Java platform does. Therefore, the Java platform provides a special escape sequence for entering Unicode characters with the form **\u***dddd*, where *dddd* is the hexadecimal number assigned to the character by Unicode. For the full set of escape sequences used in the Java platform, see the section "Escape Sequences" in Chapter 3.

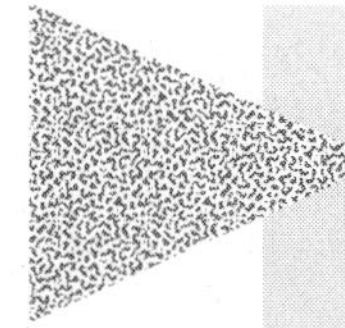

Mini Quiz 16-1

Recall from Chapter 3 that the escape sequence for the newline control character is \n, and that the Unicode escape sequence for a newline is \u000a. Can you use the literal strings `"X\nY"` and `"X\u000aY"` interchangeably in your source code? Why or why not?

Moving from C++

It is interesting to note that C++ has faced similar pressure to support a wide range of characters. In contrast to the achievements of the Java programming language's designers, the changes required to meet this demand in C++ add considerable complexity to the language. The fact that a char occupies one byte in C++ is far too entrenched to change. Therefore, the C++ standard has introduced a new fundamental type, wchar_t, for characters that occupy more than one byte. As a result, the standard redefines the input and output stream classes, the iostream classes, as a library of template classes that programmers can instantiate for types char or wchar_t. The C++ solution is powerful, but is complicated and poses a real problem for C++ programmers migrating existing code to compilers that support the new standard. Compared to C++, the Java programming language is better designed for the international market because it uses Unicode 2 character encoding internally.

The latest C++ standard also lets you represent Unicode characters in your source much like you can in the Java programming language. Here is a case where the Java programming language is ahead of its parent language. Programmers have been able to use Unicode in the Java programming language for some time. C++ compilers that support Unicode characters are just coming on the market.

Characters in Data Files

The compiler and other tools in the Java Development Kit (JDK) process files, but can only handle files that use the Latin-1 or Unicode character-encoding schemes, or a mixture of the two. If your native platform uses ASCII characters, your files are compatible with Latin-1. But what if you receive a source file from another country, or are working on a Japanese, Chinese, or other operating system with a character-encoding scheme that is not Unicode or Latin-1? The JDK includes a tool to convert files between any known encoding scheme and Unicode. The tool is a command-line program called **native2ascii**. To convert a file, run **native2ascii** and specify the character-encoding scheme and the name of the input file, followed by a name for the converted output file on the command line. For example, the following command converts a file called in.dat containing Japanese Extended Unix Code (EUC) characters to a Unicode file called out.dat:

```
native2ascii -encoding EUCJIS in.dat out.dat
```

A program running in the JVM operates on Unicode characters internally. Few operating systems currently support Unicode as the character-encoding scheme for the file system. The Java platform includes input/output (I/O) classes that you can use in your programs to translate between the native character encoding of the operating system and Unicode. When you are performing file I/O, you should use the character-oriented Reader and Writer classes. These classes are sensitive to the character-encoding scheme used by the native file system and translate properly to and from Unicode. The byte-oriented stream classes that extend InputStream and OutputStream are adequate only for files in which all characters conform to Latin-1 encoding. The byte-oriented stream classes truncate each character to a single byte before determining its Unicode equivalent. Chapter 9 describes how to use the stream I/O classes.

Version Watch

The initial version of the Java platform had only the byte-oriented streams. The character-oriented streams were one of the many features added in version 1.1 to meet the needs of the international community.

The character encoding used by the file system is available as the system property file.encoding. The following small program shows how you can access this property. This example contains a class called `GetEncoding`. It is a public class, and therefore is found in a file called GetEncoding.java. The structure of packages mirrors the file system, so you will find this source code in the java4cpp\i18n subfolder of the folder in which you unpacked the file java4cpp.jar.

```
package java4cpp.i18n;
/** Class to demonstrate how to determine the default
  * file encoding for a platform
  */
public class GetEncoding {
   /** Test method for the class
     * @param args not used
     */
   public static void main( String[] args ) {
      String fe
         = System.getProperty( "file.encoding" );
      System.out.println( fe );
   }
}
```

If you unpacked the java4cpp.jar file into a folder that is listed in your **CLASSPATH** environment variable, you can run this program from the command line by entering the following command:

```
java java4cpp.i18n.GetEncoding
```

The following is one possible output when you run this example:

```
8859_1
```

The encoding 8859_1 represents ISO8859-1, or Latin-1. The JDK documentation includes a full list of the encoding schemes available on the Java platform.

You can create objects that automatically convert characters between Unicode and different encoding schemes when you perform stream I/O.

Class	**java.io.InputStreamReader**
Dissection	The class **InputStreamReader** extends **Reader**. Instances of this class can be used wherever a **Reader** can be used.
Constructors	■ **InputStreamReader(InputStream *in*)** **InputStreamReader(InputStream *in*, String *encoding*)** Specify an **InputStream** object in the first argument of the constructor. You can supply a **String** object specifying the character-encoding scheme in the second argument, or use a one-argument version of the constructor to specify implicitly the default system-encoding scheme.

Class	**java.io.OutputStreamWriter**
Purpose	The class **OutputStreamWriter** extends **Writer**. Instances of this class can be used wherever a **Writer** can be used.
Constructors	■ **OutputStreamWriter(OutputStream *out*)** **OutputStreamWriter(OutputStream *out*, String *encoding*)** Specify an **OutputStream** object in the first argument of the constructor. You can supply a **String** object specifying the character-encoding scheme in the second argument, or use the one-argument version of the constructor to specify implicitly the default system-encoding scheme.

Converting Character Encoding in a File

The next example program takes advantage of the classes that support character-encoding schemes to convert a file from one encoding scheme to another. The program reads from the input file stream using the default encoding, and writes to the output file stream using the Cyrillic encoding scheme, ISO8859-5. The Cyrillic character set is used in Russian and several other Eastern European languages.

```
package java4cpp.i18n;
import java.io.*;
/** A class to convert a file from one
  * character-encoding scheme to another
  */
public class ChangeEncoding {
   /**
     * @param args Two parameters are required for
     *             identifying the input and output
     *             filenames
     */
   public static void main( String[] args ) {
      if ( args.length < 2 ) {
         System.out.println( "Please provide an input "
                            + "and output filename." );
      } else try {
         FileInputStream fileIn
            = new FileInputStream( args[0] );
         FileOutputStream fileOut
            = new FileOutputStream( args[1] );
         String encoding
            = System.getProperty( "file.encoding" );
         String cyrillic = "8859_5";
         InputStreamReader isr
            = new InputStreamReader( fileIn,
                                     encoding );
         OutputStreamWriter osr
            = new OutputStreamWriter( fileOut,
                                      cyrillic );
         BufferedReader br = new BufferedReader( isr );
         PrintWriter pw = new PrintWriter( osr );
         String nextLine = br.readLine();
         while ( nextLine != null ) {
            pw.println( nextLine );
            nextLine = br.readLine();
         }
         pw.close();
         br.close();
      } catch( Exception x ) {
         System.out.println( x );
      }
   }
}
```

The only construct in this program that you have not seen in earlier examples in this book is the construction of the InputStreamReader object `isr`, and the OutputStreamWriter object `osr`. The stream `isr` is created for the default encoding scheme recorded in the system property table. The stream `osr` is given the Cyrillic encoding scheme.

```
String encoding
   = System.getProperty( "file.encoding" );
String cyrillic = "8859_5";
InputStreamReader isr
   = new InputStreamReader( fileIn,
                            encoding );
OutputStreamWriter osr
   = new OutputStreamWriter( fileOut,
                             cyrillic );
```

To run this program, you need an input file. In an ASCII environment, you cannot create a file that contains characters that map onto characters only in the Cyrillic script. If you test this program on an ASCII text file, it runs but creates an output file that is identical to the input file.

Performing Other Character Conversions

Input and output operations are not the only ones that are sensitive to character-encoding schemes. Some operations can perform translation between **String** objects and character information in its raw byte form. The **String** and **ByteArrayOutputStream** classes provide methods with this capability.

Class	java.lang.String
Constructors	■ **String(byte[]** ***bytes*****, String** ***encoding*** **)** **String(byte[]** ***bytes*****, int** ***first*****, int** ***last*****, String** ***encoding*** **)** Use one of these constructors to create a **String** object from an array of **byte** objects. Specify the character-encoding scheme in the argument of type **String**. The optional integer arguments specify the first and last elements of the **byte** array to include.
Methods	■ **byte[] getBytes(String** ***encoding*** **)** The **getBytes** method returns an array of **byte** objects representing the same set of characters as the **String** object. Specify the character-encoding scheme as a **String** argument.

Class	java.io.ByteArrayOutputStream
Methods	■ **String toString(String** ***encoding*** **)** The **toString** method converts the contents of a buffer to a **String,** using the character-encoding scheme specified in the argument of type **String**.

The methods that convert between arrays of byte objects and String objects have other overloaded forms that omit the String argument and use the default encoding scheme. If the String argument does not contain the name of a valid character-encoding scheme, these methods throw a checked exception, java.io.UnsupportedEncodingException.

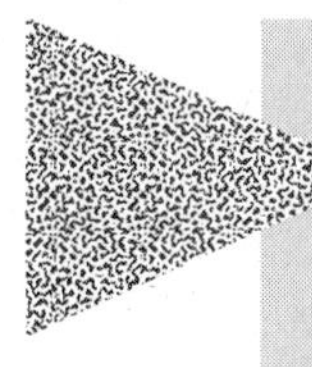

Mini Quiz 16-2

To specify a character-encoding scheme with one of these methods, you must pass the scheme's name as a String argument. Can you think of how the developers of the Java platform could have designed a more elegant interface that would let you check the validity of the encoding scheme before calling one of the conversion methods?

Using Locales

For a way to handle cultural environments, the developers of the Java programming language looked back not only to its parent language, C++, but to the grandparent language, C. In the mid 1980s, a solution to the problem of how to best represent local customs was proposed for use with C. The solution involves creating locale structures for different languages, countries, and regions. **Locales** are composed of **facets**, and each facet contains data to represent one particular custom such as numeric formatting. A facet may have several fields; for example, the facet for representing numbers includes the character separator between thousands and the character that separates the whole number part from the fractional part of a real number.

The Java platform has adopted the same approach and provides the equivalent to C locales with the class java.util.Locale. It is interesting to note that until recently, C++ programmers simply used the C locales. With the latest standard, C++ has finally acquired a Locale class of its own.

Locale objects are not the means by which the Java platform achieves internationalization. Instead, they provide the information that classes that are sensitive to locales need to support localization. Many locales are built into the Java platform as nonpublic data classes that are in a subpackage of the java.text package. Later, this chapter explores how you can create classes that are sensitive to locale information and how the support for these classes is provided.

The first version of the Java platform lacked support for internationalization. This shortcoming quickly became apparent as great interest in Java technology spread worldwide. The Locale **class, like character-oriented I/O streams, was a major enhancement introduced to support the international market. Version 1.1 of the Java platform added the** Locale **class and all locale-sensitive classes and methods that use the class.**

There is a default locale, which is usually initially set to match your host system. The most common default locale is U.S. English. If you do not specify a locale, all operations that can be locale-sensitive use the default locale.

Class	java.util.Locale
Purpose	To set the locale for a locale-sensitive operation, you need a **Locale** object.
Constructors	■ **Locale(String *language*, String *country*)** **Locale(String *language*, String *country*, String *variant*)** You can create a **Locale** object with either of these constructors. The **String** arguments contain abbreviations that follow international conventions.
Methods	■ **Locale getDefault()** The **getDefault** class method returns an object encapsulating the current default locale. ■ **void setDefault (Locale *newLocale*)** The **setDefault** class method changes the default locale to the locale encapsulated in the specified **Locale** object.

Language abbreviations are specified in lowercase and country abbreviations are specified in uppercase. For example, the following statements create three different locales:

```
// English as written in the United States
Locale usa = new Locale( "en", "US" )
// English as written in Canada
Locale canadaE = new Locale( "en", "CA" )
// French as written in Canada
Locale canadaF = new Locale( "fr", "CA" )
```

As a convenience, many of the commonly used Locale objects are available as public static final members of the Locale class. For example, the three Locale objects defined in the preceding statements correspond to the objects Locale.US, Locale.CANADA, and Locale.CANADA_FRENCH.

When you create a Locale object, do not rely on an exception to be thrown if you request a combination of language, country, and variant that does not exist. Any combination is accepted. However, the actual locale used may be very different from what you intended, because of the way locales are organized into a hierarchy. The locale selected is the available locale that best matches the arguments of the constructor. The first in the following set of criteria to be satisfied determines which locale is used:

- The language, country, and variant match exactly.
- The language and country match.
- The language matches.
- Nothing matches. In this case, the default locale is used.

For example, if you ask for a locale supporting French as spoken in the Canadian province of New Brunswick, you may have to settle for the locale that supports French as spoken in Canada. If that is not available, the next best match is the default French locale. Failing even that, the default locale is used.

There are times when a particular locale is needed only briefly and changing the default locale is inappropriate. For such situations, many methods take a **Locale** object as input to override the default locale with the specified locale for the duration of the method.

Comparing and Collating Strings

An important application of locales is providing the proper context for comparing and sorting character information. The **String** class does provide **equals** and **compareTo** methods that work well for the English language, but they are not locale-sensitive. As a result, they do not always provide the expected answer when applied to strings containing words and phrases of languages other than English. For example, the characters *e* and *é* should be considered equal in alphabetic order in a French locale, but they have different Unicode values, and *e* comes before *é* according to the **String.equals** and **String.compareTo** methods.

The **Collator** class from the **java.text** package provides locale-sensitive methods for comparing strings.

Class	**java.text.Collator**
Purpose	If you obtain the **Collator** object for a specific locale, you can use the object's methods to perform string comparisons correctly for that locale.
Fields	■ **PRIMARY** The class variable **PRIMARY** is a constant that you can use when specifying the minimum distinction between characters to be treated as a significant difference. The interpretation depends on the current locale. Typically, you set **PRIMARY** to distinguish only when the base letters are different. For example, there is a primary difference between *a* and *b*, but not between *a* and *â* or *a* and *A*. ■ **SECONDARY** The class variable **SECONDARY** is a constant that you can use when specifying the minimum distinction between characters to be treated as a significant difference. The interpretation depends on the current locale. Typically, you can set **SECONDARY** to distinguish between different accented forms of the same letter. For example, there is a secondary difference between *a* and *â* but not between *a* and *A*. ■ **TERTIARY** The class variable **TERTIARY** is a constant that you can use when specifying the minimum distinction between characters to be treated as a significant difference. The interpretation depends on the current locale. Typically, you set **TERTIARY** to distinguish between uppercase and lowercase. For example, there is a tertiary difference between *a* and *A*. ■ **IDENTICAL** The class variable **IDENTICAL** is a constant that you can use when specifying the minimum distinction between characters to be treated as a significant

	difference. The interpretation depends on the current locale. Typically, you set **IDENTICAL** to distinguish all differences in Unicode spelling.
Constructors	■ **Collator()** The **Collator** class is an abstract class. Use the class method **Collator.getInstance** to get a **Collator** object.
Methods	■ **int compare(String *source*, String *target*)** The **compare** method compares the specified **String** objects according to the collation rules for this **Collator** object. The return value is less than zero if the source argument comes before the target argument, zero if the strings are equal, and greater than zero if the source comes after the target. ■ **boolean equals(String *source*, String *target*)** The **equals** method compares the specified **String** objects according to the collation rules for this **Collator** object. The return value is **true** if the source argument is equal in value to the target, and **false** otherwise. ■ **CollationKey getCollationKey(String *source*)** The **getCollationKey** method returns a **CollationKey** object for the specified source string. If the same string is involved in many comparisons, comparing **CollationKey** objects is more efficient than comparing **String** objects. ■ **Collator getInstance()** **Collator getInstance(Locale *locale*)** The **getInstance** method returns a **Collator** object for a locale. You can specify the locale as an argument of type **Locale**, or provide no argument to this method and accept the default locale. ■ **Collator setStrength(int *strength*)** The **setStrength** method sets a property of the **Collator** class that determines the minimum level of difference that is significant in a comparison. You can use one of the constant fields defined in this class as the strength argument.

The Collator class has a companion class, java.text.CollationKey, that you can use to speed comparisons. There is some overhead in creating a CollationKey object for a particular string, but this investment pays off if the string is used in many comparison operations.

Class	**java.text.CollationKey**
Purpose	A **CollationKey** object represents a **String** as a set of bits that can be compared more quickly than **String** objects can be compared.
Constructors	■ **CollationKey()** The **CollationKey** class is an abstract class. Use the method **Collator.getCollationKey** to get a **CollationKey** object.

Methods

- **int compareTo(CollationKey *target*)**
  The **compareTo** method compares the current **CollationKey** object to the specified target, according to the current collation rules of the **Collator** object from which this **CollationKey** object is created. The return value is less than zero if the current **CollationKey** value is less than that of the target argument, zero if the keys are equal, and greater than zero if the target has the lower **CollationKey** value.

- **boolean equals(Object *target*)**
  The **equals** method compares the current **CollationKey** object to the specified target, according to the current collation rules of the **Collator** object from which this **CollationKey** object is created. The return value is **true** if the keys have the same value, and **false** otherwise.

Version Watch

The initial version of the Java platform did not include either the Collator **class or the** CollationKey **class. Both classes became available in version 1.1.**

Sorting Strings Using Collation Keys

The next example program implements the bubble sort algorithm for strings using both a Collator object and an array of CollationKey objects. The CollationKey array is created, and then filled with a collation key value for each element in the array of strings being sorted. Comparisons operate on the CollationKey objects to speed the sort because each string is used in many comparison operations. Note how the sorting order is independent of the case of the characters in the strings.

```
package java4cpp.i18n;
import java.util.Locale;
import java.text.Collator;
import java.text.CollationKey;
/** A class to demonstrate the use of Collator
  * and CollationKey classes
  */
public class BubbleSorter {
   /** main entrypoint - starts the application
     * @param args not used
     */
   public static void main( String[] args ) {
      String[] data = { "Washington", "Cairo",
                        "paris", "london",
                        "Ottawa", "Madrid" };
      System.out.println( "Before:" );
      for( int i = 0; i < data.length; i++ ) {
         System.out.println( "\t" + data[i] );
```

```
        }
        sort( data );
        System.out.println( "After:" );
        for( int i = 0; i < data.length; i++ ) {
           System.out.println( "\t" + data[i] );
        }
     }
     /** Sort the input array of strings
       * @param input the array to be sorted
       */
     public static void sort( String[] input ) {
        // get collator for the default locale
        Collator c
          = Collator.getInstance( Locale.CANADA_FRENCH );
        // build up the array of collation keys
        CollationKey[] ckeys
           = new CollationKey[input.length];
        for ( int i = 0; i < input.length; i++ ) {
           ckeys[i] = c.getCollationKey( input[i] );
        }
        // do the bubble sort
        CollationKey tempKey;
        for ( int i = 1; i < ckeys.length; i++ ) {
           for ( int j = 0; j < ckeys.length-i; j++ ) {
              if ( ckeys[j].compareTo( ckeys[j+1] )
                   > 0 ) {
                 // swap values
                 tempKey = ckeys[j];
                 ckeys[j] = ckeys[j+1];
                 ckeys[j+1] = tempKey;
              }
           }
        }
        // recover the sorted array from the sorted
        // CollationKey objects
        for ( int i = 0; i < input.length; i++ ) {
           input[i] = ckeys[i].getSourceString();
        }
     }
  }
```

You can run this program from the command line by entering the following command:

```
java java4cpp.i18n.BubbleSorter
```

The output is as follows:

```
Before:
        Washington
        Cairo
        paris
        london
        Ottawa
        Madrid
After:
        Cairo
        london
        Madrid
        Ottawa
        paris
        Washington
```

This example uses a Collator object for the Canadian French locale to show how to specify the locale as the input to the Collator.getInstance method. The data to be sorted does not have any non-ANSI characters, so the choice of locale is unlikely to have any effect on the outcome of the sort operation in this case.

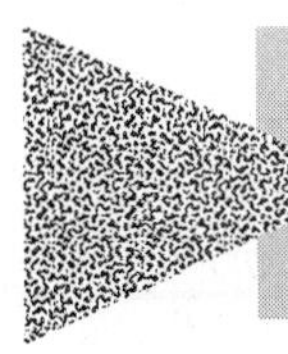

Mini Quiz 16-3

You can improve the efficiency of the BubbleSorter algorithm by adding a test to break out of one of the loops. Can you see the place where you would make this change?

Manipulating Date and Time Data

Of course, there is a lot more to local customs than language. The formats of date and time information also vary widely from place to place. The Java platform provides two abstract classes for working with dates and times, Calendar and TimeZone, and corresponding concrete classes GregorianCalendar and SimpleTimeZone. These classes belong to the java.util package and are introduced in Chapter 10.

The initial version of the Java platform had only the Date class for working with date and time information. The additional classes became available with support for locales in version 1.1. As a result, some methods of the Date class are deprecated, and replaced with methods of the Calendar class.

Class	**java.util.Calendar**
Purpose	The **Calendar** class is an abstract class that you can use to convert a **Date** object into locale-sensitive representations for the year, month, day, and the like. To get a **Calendar** object, call the class method **getInstance**.

Methods	■ **Calendar getInstance( )** **Calendar getInstance(TimeZone *zone*)** **Calendar getInstance(Locale *locale*)** **Calendar getInstance(TimeZone *zone*, Locale *locale*)** The **getInstance class** method returns a reference to an instance of a subclass of **Calendar**. If you do not specify a **Locale** object, you get a **Calendar** for the default locale. Specify an object of the **java.util.TimeZone** class to ensure that the method sets the proper offset from Greenwich Mean Time (GMT).

The Date class contains a number of methods that have been deprecated and moved to the Calendar class since the original release of the Java platform. When looking for methods and constants for processing date and time information, look first to the Calendar class.

Use the DateFormat class to format date and time information in a locale-sensitive manner.

Class	**java.text.DateFormat**
Purpose	The **DateFormat** class is an abstract class that provides methods you can use to parse and format date and time information according to a locale.
Fields	■ **DEFAULT** The class variable **DEFAULT** is a constant you can use to specify that date and time be formatted with the default style. For an example of this style, see the output of the next sample program. ■ **FULL** The class variable **FULL** is a constant you can use to specify the full style pattern for formatting date and time data. For an example of this style, see the output of the next sample program. ■ **LONG** The class variable **LONG** is a constant you can use to specify a long style pattern for formatting date and time data. For an example of this style, see the output of the next sample program. ■ **MEDIUM** The class variable **MEDIUM** is a constant you can use to specify a medium-length style pattern for formatting date and time data. For an example of this style, see the output of the next sample program. ■ **SHORT** The class variable **SHORT** is a constant you can use to specify a short style pattern for formatting date and time data. For an example of this style, see the output of the next sample program.

Constructors	■ **DateFormat()** To get a **DateFormat** object, call one of the class methods, depending on the format of information you require.
Methods	■ **DateFormat getDateInstance()** **DateFormat getDateInstance(int *style*)** **DateFormat getDateInstance(int *style*, Locale *locale*)** The **getDateInstance class** method returns a reference to a date formatter object. You can optionally specify the style pattern to control the formatting, by supplying a constant that is defined in this class. You can also specify a locale or accept the current default locale. ■ **DateFormat getDateTimeInstance()** **DateFormat getDateTimeInstance(int datestyle, int timestyle)** **DateFormat getDateInstance(int *datestyle*, int *timestyle*, Locale *locale*)** The **getDateTimeInstance class** method returns a reference to a date and time formatter object. You can optionally specify the style patterns to control the formatting of the date and time values independently, by supplying constants that are defined in this class. You can also specify a locale or accept the current default locale. ■ **DateFormat getTimeInstance()** **DateFormat getTimeInstance(int *style*)** **DateFormat getTimeInstance(int *style*, Locale *locale*)** The **getTimeInstance** class method returns a reference **to** a time formatter object. You can optionally specify the style pattern to control the formatting, by supplying a constant that is defined in this class. You can also specify a locale or accept the current default locale.

Formatting Dates and Times

The following example program demonstrates how you can use the Calendar and DateFormat classes with different locales and formats. In this case, the program prints the current date for both the default and Italian locales in all of the supported styles.

```
package java4cpp.i18n;
import java.text.DateFormat;
import java.util.Calendar;
import java.util.Date;
import java.util.Locale;
/** Class to demonstrate the use of the Calendar
  * class and date formatting
  */
public class DateFormatter {
   /** main entrypoint - starts the application
     * @param args not used
     */
```

```
    public static void main( String[] args) {
       Calendar calDefault = Calendar.getInstance();
       Date today = calDefault.getTime();
       test( "DEFAULT style",
             DateFormat.DEFAULT, today );
       test( "FULL style", DateFormat.FULL, today );
       test( "LONG style", DateFormat.LONG, today );
       test( "MEDIUM style", DateFormat.MEDIUM, today );
       test( "SHORT style", DateFormat.SHORT, today );
    }
    /** Common test routine
      * @param label the label for the test
      * @param style the DateFormat style to be used
      * @param date the date to be formatted
      */
    static void test( String label, int style,
                      Date date ) {
       System.out.println( label );
       DateFormat df
          = DateFormat.getDateInstance( style );
       System.out.print( "\tDefault locale:   " );
       System.out.println( df.format( date ) );
       df = DateFormat.getDateInstance( style,
                                        Locale.ITALY );
       System.out.print( "\tLocale for Italy: " );
       System.out.println( df.format( date ) );
    }
}
```

You can run this program from the command line by entering the following command:

```
java java4cpp.i18n.DateFormatter.
```

When you run the program on March 30, 1998, the output is as follows:

```
DEFAULT style
        Default locale:   30-Mar-98
        Locale for Italy: 30-mar-98
FULL style
        Default locale:   Monday, March 30, 1998
        Locale for Italy: marted_ 30 marzo 1998
LONG style
        Default locale:   March 30, 1998
        Locale for Italy: 30 marzo 1998
MEDIUM style
        Default locale:   30-Mar-98
        Locale for Italy: 30-mar-98
```

```
SHORT style
        Default locale:    3/30/98
        Locale for Italy: 30/03/98
```

Working with Time Zones

Use the TimeZone class to obtain time zone information.

Class	java.util.TimeZone
Purpose	The **TimeZone** class is an abstract class that encapsulates the time offset from GMT. It also corrects for daylight savings time. To get a **TimeZone** object, call a class method of this class.
Methods	■ **String[] getAvailableIDs()** **String[] getAvailableIDs(int *offset*)** The **getAvailableIDs** class method returns a list of available time zone identifiers. If an offset is specified, all identifiers for time zones with the specified offset from GMT are returned. If no offset is specified, all supported time zone identifiers are returned. ■ **TimeZone getDefault()** The **getDefault** class method returns a reference to a subclass of **TimeZone** that represents the default time zone for the system. ■ **TimeZone getTimeZone(String *zone*)** The class method **getTimeZone** returns a reference to a **TimeZone** object for the specified time zone.

The next sample program retrieves all of the supported time zone identifiers and displays the current time in each of them. To format the time information, the program uses a DateFormat object returned by the getTimeInstance method with the default style. The time zone information is associated with a DateFormat object; when formatting the time, the program calculates the appropriate offset from the local time.

```
package java4cpp.i18n;
import java.text.DateFormat;
import java.util.Calendar;
import java.util.Date;
import java.util.Locale;
import java.util.TimeZone;
/** Class to demonstrate the use of the TimeZone
  * class and time formatting
  */
public class TimeFormatter {
```

```
    /** Test method for the class
      * @param args not used
      */
    public static void main( String[] args ) {
       Calendar calDefault = Calendar.getInstance();
       TimeZone tzDefault = calDefault.getTimeZone();
       Date currentTime = calDefault.getTime();
       String[] timezones = TimeZone.getAvailableIDs();
       DateFormat df = DateFormat.getTimeInstance(
                  DateFormat.DEFAULT, Locale.GERMAN );
       for( int i = 0; i < timezones.length; i++ ) {
          TimeZone tz
             = TimeZone.getTimeZone( timezones[i] );
          df.setTimeZone( tz );
          System.out.print( timezones[i] + ": " );
          System.out.println( df.format(currentTime) );
       }
    }
}
```

For a bit of variety, the program formats the time for the German Locale object. Note that the DateFormat object df controls the look of the time data, but not the names of the time zones. There is no worldwide standard for time zone names, and the Java platform uses the set of names that are recognized in North America. The program returns the array of time zone identifiers sorted, beginning with GMT and progressing around the world to the east.

You can run this program from the command line by entering the following command:

```
java java4cpp.i18n.TimeFormatter
```

The output depends on when you run the program, but looks similar to the following:

```
GMT: 22:27:40
ECT: 23:27:40
EET: 01:27:40
ART: 00:27:40
EAT: 01:27:40
MET: 01:57:40
NET: 02:27:40
PLT: 03:27:40
IST: 03:57:40
BST: 04:27:40
VST: 05:27:40
CTT: 06:27:40
JST: 07:27:40
ACT: 07:57:40
```

```
AET: 08:27:40
SST: 09:27:40
NST: 10:27:40
MIT: 11:27:40
HST: 12:27:40
AST: 13:27:40
PST: 14:27:40
PNT: 15:27:40
MST: 15:27:40
CST: 16:27:40
EST: 17:27:40
IET: 17:27:40
PRT: 18:27:40
CNT: 18:57:40
AGT: 19:27:40
BET: 19:27:40
CAT: 21:27:40
```

Formatting Percentages, Currency, and Numbers

Just as date and time information can be formatted in a locale-sensitive way, so can currency values and numbers.

Class	**java.text.NumberFormat**
Purpose	**NumberFormat** is an abstract class for formatting and parsing currency values, percentages, and numbers according to a locale. To obtain a **NumberFormat** object, call a class method of this class.
Methods	■ **NumberFormat getNumberInstance()** **NumberFormat getNumberInstance(Locale *locale*)** **The getNumberInstance** class method returns a **NumberFormat** object for general-purpose numbers. If you do not specify a locale, the method uses the current default locale. ■ **NumberFormat getCurrencyInstance()** **NumberFormat getCurrencyInstance(Locale *locale*)** The **getCurrencyInstance** class method returns a **NumberFormat** object for monetary value numbers. If you do not specify a locale, the method uses the current default locale. ■ **NumberFormat getPercentInstance()** **NumberFormat getPercentInstance(Locale *locale*)** The **getPercentInstance** class method returns a **NumberFormat** object for percentage values. If you do not specify a locale, the method uses the current default locale.

- **NumberFormat getInstance()**
  NumberFormat getInstance(Locale *locale*)
  The **getInstance** class method returns the default format for numeric values. The default format can be the format of general-purpose numbers, currency values, or percentages depending on the locale. If you do not specify a locale, the method uses the current default locale.

Formatting Numeric Values

The next sample program applies the three kinds of number formatting for two locales, the default of U.S. English and the locale for Germany, to the same value. One thing that should be obvious, but probably still bears pointing out, is that the currency formatting does not apply exchange rates to convert between monetary values. The formatter merely controls the formatting of the provided number.

```
package java4cpp.i18n;
import java.text.NumberFormat;
import java.util.Locale;
/** Class to demonstrate the use of the NumberFormat
  * class for currency and other numbers
  */
public class NumberFormatter {
   /** Test program for the class
     * @param args not used
     */
   public static void main( String[] args ) {
      double x = 100000000.12345;
      NumberFormat nfDefault
         = NumberFormat.getInstance();
      NumberFormat nfGermany
         = NumberFormat.getInstance( Locale.GERMANY );
      test( "Default number format",
            nfDefault, nfGermany, x );
      nfDefault.setMaximumFractionDigits( 6 );
      nfGermany.setMaximumFractionDigits( 6 );
      test( "Default number format, more precision",
            nfDefault, nfGermany, x );
      double y = 0.12345;
      NumberFormat nfDefaultPc
         = NumberFormat.getPercentInstance();
      NumberFormat nfGermanyPc
         = NumberFormat.getPercentInstance(
                                       Locale.GERMANY );
      test( "Percent format",
            nfDefaultPc, nfGermanyPc, y );
```

```
        double z = 12345.6789;
        NumberFormat nfDefaultCr
           = NumberFormat.getCurrencyInstance();
        NumberFormat nfGermanyCr
           = NumberFormat.getCurrencyInstance(
                                         Locale.GERMANY );
        test( "Currency format",
              nfDefaultCr, nfGermanyCr, z );
     }
     /** Test method
       * @param label the name of the test
       * @param defNf the NumberFormat object for the
       *    default locale
       * @param gerNf the NumberFormat object for the
       *    GERMANY locale
       * @param value the value to be formatted.
       */
     public static void test( String label,
                              NumberFormat defNf,
                              NumberFormat gerNf,
                              double value ) {
        System.out.println( label );
        System.out.println( "\tdefault locale: "
                            + defNf.format( value ) );
        System.out.println( "\tGerman locale:  "
                            + gerNf.format( value ) );
     }
}
```

You can run this program from the command line by entering the following command:

```
java java4cpp.i18n.NumberFormatter
```

The program's output is as follows:

```
Default number format
        default locale: 100,000,000.123
        German locale:  100.000.000,123
Default number format, more precision
        default locale: 100,000,000.12345
        German locale:  100.000.000,12345
Percent format
        default locale: 12%
        German locale:  12%
Currency format
        default locale: $12,345.68
        German locale:  12.345,68 DM
```

Creating and Using Resources

So far, you have seen how to take advantage of localization support and use a variety of classes to make sure that your program properly encodes and sorts character information and presents all date, time, currency, and numeric information according to the local customs. An equally important aspect of internationalization concerns the display of textual information. You cannot avoid the need to translate into the user's language the words that appear in your graphical user interface (GUI) and output.

The way to make translation as painless as possible is to organize properly the text that appears in your program. You should to treat all textual elements as resources, and not imbed any literal strings in your source code. In this context, a resource is a single entity, such as a text message, that your program can access and use. The important characteristic of resources is that they are stored outside the source code, and therefore can be objects that your program can manipulate. For this purpose, the Java platform provides the class java.util.ResourceBundle. Use this class to collect resources together into one manageable object. The resources can then reside in a separate file called a **properties file** or in a class definition created expressly for the purpose of holding resources.

If you have used resource files in C++, you know the C++ language has no provision for resources. You have to use tools provided by the native operating system or your application development environment to create resource source files, compile them, and bind the resulting compiled resources to your executable file. As a result, in C++, resources are often not portable between operating systems, and there is no standard way to work with them. Unlike C++, the Java platform not only understands this important programming consideration, but gives you a standard and portable methodology.

Using resources to internationalize your program essentially involves three steps:

- Create a properties file that contains all of the textual elements that appear in your program and that require translation. Alternatively, you can supply a separate class definition that extends ListResourceBundle. You can include other resources such as images and audio clips if you create a subclass of ListResourceBundle.
- Have the text elements of the properties file or ListResourceBundle translated. The result is a set of properties files or class definitions, one for each locale. Following the required naming conventions, give each properties file or class definition a name that begins with your choice of base name and a suffix that identifies the locale for which file or class definition is used.
- Modify your program to use the ResourceBundle class or its subclasses to load resources by using the ResourceBundle class method getBundle.

Removing locale-specific literals from your code achieves the goal of internationalizing your code. Dynamically loading the locale-specific elements as required at run time achieves the goal of localizing your program for the cultural environment of the user.

Using Resource Bundles

This section describes how to use existing resources in a properties file or a class that extends the class ListResourceBundle. The following section describes properties files in detail and how to create them. The final section of this chapter tells you how to use properties files not only for static text, but also for messages that can be formulated dynamically at run time.

To access resources in a Java class, you need a ResourceBundle object.

Class	**java.util.ResourceBundle**
Purpose	This abstract class **ResourceBundle** encapsulates resources that are loaded from a properties file or from a class that extends **ListResourceBundle**.
Constructors	■ **ResourceBundle()** To acquire an instance of this abstract class, you should call the class method **getBundle**.
Methods	■ **ResourceBundle getBundle(String *basename*)** **ResourceBundle getBundle(String *basename*, Locale *locale*)** The final class method **getBundle** returns a **ResourceBundle**. Call it to load resources into a program from a properties file. You must specify a base name for the file. You can optionally specify a locale or accept the current default locale. The full name of the resource file is formed by combining the base name of the properties file and letters identifying the locale. ■ **Enumeration getKeys()** The abstract method **getKeys** returns an **Enumeration** object that you can use to access keys in a **ResourceBundle**. ■ **Object getObject(String *key*)** The final method **getObject** returns the object that is the value of the resource specified by the key argument. ■ **String getString(String *key*)** The final method **getString** returns a **String** that is the value of a resource that is specified by the key argument. Use this convenience method when the object with the given key is known to be a **String**, to avoid casting. ■ **String[] getStringArray(String *key*)** The final method **getStringArray** returns an array of **String** objects that is the value of the resource specified by the key argument. Use this convenience method when the object with the given key is known to be a **String** array, to avoid casting. ■ **Object handleGetObject(String *key*)** The abstract method **handleGetObject** returns the value of resource from a **ResourceBundle**. The argument is a key for a resource that you can acquire by calling the **getKeys** method.

The usual way to get a PropertyResourceBundle object is by calling the ResourceBundle.getBundle method. The next two sample programs demonstrate how to do this. The getBundle method locates either a .class file or a .properties file, parses the file, and then creates a ResourceBundle object containing the resource information. You can then call methods of the ResourceBundle class, such as getString, to get the value individual resources as need them in your program.

ResourceBundle has two subclasses, ListResourceBundle and PropertyResourceBundle, that provide implementations for ResourceBundle's abstract methods. The class ListResourceBundle is an abstract class with an abstract method of its own, getContents, which returns resources to your program as a two-dimensional Object array. For resources that have other types than String, you should use the class ListResourceBundle and include an implementation of getContents. When your resources all are strings, creating a properties file is a convenient way to work with resources.

Class	java.util.ListResourceBundle
Purpose	The abstract class **ListResourceBundle** is a subclass of **ResourceBundle** that provides methods to extract resources from a resource bundle. This class is commonly extended to create a class definition used to hold program resources. To specify the language associated with a **ListResourceBundle**, append an underscore to the class name followed by the standard abbreviation for the language. Specifying the language is optional. To specify a country, append another underscore after the language's abbreviation and append the standard abbreviation for the country. Specifying the country is optional, and is allowed only if you specify the language.
Constructors	■ **ListResourceBundle()** The **ListResourceBundle** class is an abstract class that you must extend to use.
Constructors	■ **Object[][] getContents()** When you extend the **ListResourceBundle** class, you must implement the **getContents** method to access resources. This method must return an array of pairs of objects in which each resource is a key and value pair. The key must be a **String** object. The value can be anything, including an **Image** or **AudioClip** object. The next sample program demonstrates this method.

Class	java.util.PropertyResourceBundle
Purpose	You can use the **PropertyResourceBundle** subclass of **ResourceBundle** as an interface to a properties file.
Constructors	■ **PropertyResourceBundle(InputStream *is*)** When you create a **PropertyResourceBundle** object, you must specify an input stream for the properties file to be read.

Methods

- **Object handleGetObject(String *key*)**
  The **handleGetObject** method implements the abstract method of the **ResourceBundle** class to return the value of the resource from a **ResourceBundle**. The argument is a key for a resource that you can acquire by calling the **getKeys** method.

- **Enumeration getKeys()**
  The **getKeys** method implements the abstract method of the **ResourceBundle** class to return an **Enumeration** object that you can use to access keys in a **ResourceBundle**.

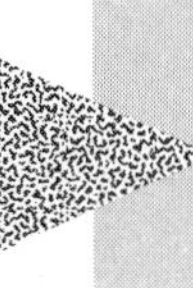

Mini Quiz 16-4

What methods are available for use with the Enumeration object returned by getKeys? *Hint*: You may want to review how Enumeration objects are used in Chapter 10.

Here is an example that demonstrates the use of the ListResourceBundle class. This example consists of two files: MyBundle_en_CA and TestMyBundle. The resources are not stored in a properties file, but are set up in the body of the method getContents in the public class `MyBundle_en_CA` that extends ListResourceBundle.

```
package java4cpp.i18n;
import java.util.ListResourceBundle;
/** A class to demonstrate how to extend the
  * ListResourceBundle class
  */
public class MyBundle_en_CA
   extends ListResourceBundle {
   /** This method must be overridden by this class
     * @return Object[][] containing the key and
     * resource pairs
     */
   protected Object[][] getContents() {
      Object[][] myContents = {
                       { "count", new Integer(6) },
                       { "weight", new Double(4.56) },
                       { "name", "Edgar" },
                       { "relationship", "neighbour" }
      };
      return myContents;
   }
}
```

The class TestMyBundle uses the method getBundle, providing the name of the MyBundle class and specifying the locale for Canada. Because the language code for the Locale.CANADA object is en and the country code is CA, the JVM searches the CLASSPATH for the file MyBundle_en_CA.class and loads the file when it finds it. The rest of the TestMyBundle class prints out the contents of the bundle.

```
package java4cpp.i18n;
import java.util.ResourceBundle;
import java.util.Enumeration;
import java.util.Locale;
public class TestMyBundle {
   /** Test method for the class
     * @param args not used
     */
   public static void main( String[] args ) {
      ResourceBundle rb;
      String bundleName = "java4cpp.i18n.MyBundle";
      rb = ResourceBundle.getBundle( bundleName,
                                     Locale.CANADA );
      print( "CANADA Locale:", rb );
   }
   /** Print the contents of a resource file
     * @param label the label given to the output
     * @param rb the ResourceBundle object to print
     */
   public static void print( String label,
                             ResourceBundle rb ) {
      System.out.println( label );
      Enumeration e = rb.getKeys();
      String key;
      while( e.hasMoreElements() ) {
         key = (String) e.nextElement();
         System.out.println( "\t" + key + " = "
                             + rb.getObject( key ) );
      }
   }
}
```

You can run this program from the command line by entering the following command:

```
java java4cpp.i18n.TestMyBundle
```

The output is as follows:

```
CANADA Locale:
        relationship = neighbour
```

```
weight = 4.56
count = 6
name = Edgar
```

Using Resource Properties Files

The attraction of using properties files instead of classes that extend ListResourceBundle is that you can use simple text-editing tools to create and maintain properties files, and thus don't have to know the syntax of the Java programming language. Use properties files as a way to simplify greatly the task of translating into other languages the text that your program uses. All you have to do is to create the master version of the properties file as a text file and then give the file to a person or service that can create a translated version. The translator does not need to know anything about Java technology. Translation involves making a copy of the file and then using a text editor to translate all the strings.

Syntax

 # comment

key=value

Dissection

- A properties file is a line-oriented text file. You should create it with an editor that inserts no formatting codes into the text.
- A properties file can have any base filename allowed on your operating system. Often, it is convenient to give the file the same name as the class that uses it. Matching class names and properties filenames is a helpful convention but not a requirement.
- To specify the language used in a properties file, append an underscore to the base filename followed by the standard abbreviation for the language.
- To specify a country, append another underscore after the language and append the standard abbreviation for the country.
- The file extension is .properties.
- Specify one resource on each line. Each resource is a key and value pair. The key is the name used by a program to identify and extract the resource. The value is the definition of the resource and is the information returned to the program. The value can have embedded spaces and is not enclosed in quotation marks or other delimiting characters.
- You can insert comments. Comments can occupy a full line or follow resource information on the same line. Either way, start a comment with character # (which goes by many names but is officially known as an **octothorpe**). Comments end at the end of the line.
- Single quotation marks are treated as special characters within the file. If you want to put a single quote in a text value, use two consecutive single quotes.

- To indicate that a resource definition continues onto the next line, end the line with a backslash character, \.
- Placeholders for substitution strings provided by the program are represented by **{*n*}**.

  The value of ***n*** is 0 for the first substitution in the line, 1 for the second, and so on. Substitution strings are described later in this chapter.

Here is a sample properties file. It is used in the next sample program. It could be called IntlPanels_en.properties. Because English is the default, this file is simply named IntlPanels.properties.

```
# IntlPanels.properties
# This file contains the string used in the IntlPanels
# example.  The default is to display English text.
buttons.black.label=Black
buttons.red.label=Red
buttons.green.label=Green
checkboxes.disable.label=Disable changes
textfield.sample=Change the color of this text
window.title=Multiple Panels Sample
messages.missing_resource=Couldn''t find resource "{0}"
```

You can also create a properties file for a particular language as spoken in a particular country. For example, Canadian English has a different spelling of the word *color*: *colour*. For the example here, you need a file IntlPanels_en_CA.properties, named by appending first the language abbreviation, and then the country abbreviation to the default properties filename. Here is the entire file:

```
# IntlPanels_en_CA.properties
# This file contains the string used in the IntlPanels
# example when the locale is English for Canada.  Note
# the spelling of color has been changed to colour.
textfield.sample=Change the colour of this text
```

Notice that this file does not repeat all of the English messages in the default properties file, only the one that is different. The JVM can provide this convenience because of the way that it looks for resources in the resource bundles. The search always begins with the bundle for the specific country and language. If the JVM fails to find the resource there, the search continues in the bundle for the language. If that search also fails, the JVM uses the default bundle. For example, if you request the locale for French as spoken in Canada, the file search order is as follows:

- `IntlPanels_fr_CA.properties`
- `IntlPanels_fr.properties`
- `IntlPanels.properties.`

If the JVM does not find the key and value pair for the resource in any resource bundle, the program throws the exception MissingResourceException.

Using a Properties File

Here is a simple application that has had its textual information stripped from the source code and placed into a properties file. You may recognize the program as a variation of the `ThreePanels` class from Chapter 12. The following resources are stored in the file IntlPanels.properties:

- The string displayed in the text field
- Labels on the three buttons
- Label on the check box
- Error messages

The following is the code for the application. Following the code is a breakdown of the lines that have changed since the version in Chapter 12.

```
package java4cpp.i18n;
import java.awt.*;
import java.awt.event.*;
import java.util.Locale;
import java.util.MissingResourceException;
import java.util.ResourceBundle;
import java.text.MessageFormat;
/** An example class used to demonstrate the basics
  * of internationalizing an application by taking
  * all textual information and separating it into
  * a properties file that is then accessed via
  * a ResourceBundle object.
  */
public class IntlPanels extends Frame {
   private Panel upperPanel, midPanel,
                 lowerPanel;
   private TextField text;
   private Button blackButton, redButton,
                  greenButton;
   private Checkbox disableCheck;
   private ResourceBundle rb;
   /** Class constructor method
     * @param rb The resource bundle for the frame
     */
   public IntlPanels( ResourceBundle inputBundle ) {
      try {
         rb = inputBundle;
         setTitle( rb.getString( "window.title" ) );
         setLayout( new BorderLayout() );
```

```
// use an anonymous inner class to handle the
// window closing event
addWindowListener( new WindowAdapter() {
      /** End the program when the user
        * closes the window
        */
      public void
      windowClosing( WindowEvent e ) {
         Frame.this.dispose();
         System.exit( 0 );
      }
   }
);
ButtonListener aListener
   = new ButtonListener();
upperPanel = new Panel();
upperPanel.setLayout( new BorderLayout() );
text = new TextField(
   rb.getString( "textfield.sample" ) );
upperPanel.add( text, "Center" );
midPanel = new Panel();
midPanel.setLayout( new FlowLayout(
                    FlowLayout.CENTER ) );
blackButton =
   new Button( rb.getString(
               "buttons.black.label" ) );
midPanel.add( blackButton );
blackButton.addActionListener( aListener );
redButton =
   new Button( rb.getString(
               "buttons.red.label" ) );
midPanel.add( redButton );
redButton.addActionListener( aListener );
greenButton =
   new Button( rb.getString(
               "buttons.green.label" ) );
midPanel.add( greenButton );
greenButton.addActionListener( aListener );

lowerPanel = new Panel();
lowerPanel.setLayout( new FlowLayout(
                      FlowLayout.RIGHT ) );
disableCheck =
   new Checkbox( rb.getString(
      "checkboxes.disable.label" ) );
lowerPanel.add( disableCheck );
add( upperPanel, "North" );
```

```
         add( midPanel, "Center" );
         add( lowerPanel, "South" );
         pack();
         setVisible( true );
      } catch ( MissingResourceException mrx ) {
         String message;
         try {
            message = rb.getString(
                      "messages.missing_resource" );
         } catch ( MissingResourceException ignore ) {
            message
               = "Couldn''t find resource \"{0}\"";
         }
         MessageFormat mf
            = new MessageFormat( message );
         Object[] messageArgs = { mrx.getKey() };
         System.out.println(
            mf.format( messageArgs ) );
      }
   }
   class ButtonListener implements ActionListener {
      /** Respond to the action events in which this
        * application is interested
        * @param e The window event
        */
      public void actionPerformed( ActionEvent e ) {
         Object source = e.getSource();
         if ( disableCheck.getState() == false ) {
            if ( source == redButton ) {
               text.setForeground( Color.red );
            } else if ( source == greenButton ) {
               text.setForeground( Color.green );
            } else if ( source == blackButton ) {
               text.setForeground( Color.black );
            }
         }
      }
   }
   /** The test method for the class
     * @param args Input parameters.  Only the first
     * two parameters are used.  The first is assumed
     * to identify the language (e.g. en, fr, it) and
     * the second will identify the country (e.g. US,
     * FR, CA, IT).
     */
   public static void main( String[] args ) {
```

```
      String language, country;
      language = args.length < 1 ? "default" : args[0];
      country  = args.length < 2 ? "default" : args[1];
      Locale.setDefault( new Locale( language,
                                     country ) );
      ResourceBundle rb
         = ResourceBundle.getBundle( "IntlPanels" );
      IntlPanels myWindow = new IntlPanels( rb );
   }
}
```

The main method accepts two optional parameters, `language` and `country`, which are used to identify the locale. If less than two parameters are provided, the program uses a placeholder string that will be ignored. When the locale is set, the program can retrieve the ResourceBundle by passing the base name of the file, IntlPanels.

```
public static void main( String[] args ) {
   String language, country;
   language = args.length < 1 ? "default" : args[0];
   country  = args.length < 2 ? "default" : args[1];
   Locale.setDefault( new Locale( language,
                                  country ) );
   ResourceBundle rb
      = ResourceBundle.getBundle( "IntlPanels" );
   IntlPanels myWindow = new IntlPanels( rb );
}
```

The constructor of the `IntlPanels` class receives ResourceBundle as an argument. The first thing that the new object does is extract its title from the bundle using the getString method with the input `"window.title"` and pass the title to the Frame superclass constructor.

```
public IntlPanels( ResourceBundle inputBundle ) {
   try {
      rb = inputBundle;
      setTitle( rb.getString( "window.title" ) );
```

All statements in this program that included string literals in the version in Chapter 12 have been changed to use the getString method with a key value for the particular string required. For example, the program previously creates the check box as follows:

```
   disableCheck = new Checkbox( "Disable changes" );
```

In this version, the program creates the check box as follows:

```
   disableCheck =
      new Checkbox( rb.getString(
                    "checkboxes.disable.label" ) );
```

Notice the try block and catch clause for objects of the class MissingResourceException. If the program uses a key that cannot be found within the bundle, an exception of this class is thrown. The handler of this exception simply displays a message indicating which exception could not be found. In a nested try block, this handler attempts to retrieve the message from the bundle so it can be translated, too. Because this retrieval may also fail, the inner catch phrase resorts to a string literal. In such a case, it is better to pop up a message in a foreign language than no message at all!

```
      catch ( MissingResourceException mrx ) {
         String message;
         try {
            message = rb.getString(
                         "messages.missing_resource" );
         } catch ( MissingResourceException ignore ) {
            message
               = "Couldn''t find resource \"{0}\"";
         }
```

The last lines of the outer catch clause are a sneak preview to the topic of message retrieval and formatting, which follows this example.

```
      MessageFormat mf
         = new MessageFormat( message );
      Object[] messageArgs = { mrx.getKey() };
      System.out.println(
                        mf.format( messageArgs ) );
   }
```

Mini Quiz 16-5

A MissingResourceException is a RuntimeException. Is it a checked exception? *Hint:* Review the discussion of exceptions in Chapter 6.

This program requires properties files to run. The folder java4cpp\i18n supplies three properties files:

- IntlPanels.properties is the default properties file. It is listed earlier in this chapter and is set up for the U.S. English locale.
- IntlPanels_en_CA.properties is the properties file for English as written in Canada. It is also listed earlier in this chapter.
- IntlPanels_fr.properties is a French locale. Here is a listing:

```
# IntlPanels_fr.properties
# This file contains the string used in the IntlPanels
# example when the selected locale is French
buttons.black.label=Noir
```

```
buttons.red.label=Rouge
buttons.green.label=Vert
checkboxes.disable.label=Ne permit pas des changes
textfield.sample=Changez la couleur de ce texte.
window.title=Example des Panneaux Multiples
# note the Unicode escape sequence \u00E9 in the
# next message to give the letter e with acute accent
messages.missing_resource=La ressource "{0}" n''est\
 pas trouv\u00E9e.
```

To run this program, either go to the folder into which you unpacked the java4cpp.jar file and then to subfolder java4cpp\i18n, or copy the properties files from the java4cpp\i18n folder into your current folder. Try running in different locales, by entering the following commands:

- `java java4cpp.i18n.IntlPanels`
- `java jav4cpp.i18n.IntlPanels en CA`
- `java java4cpp.i18n.IntlPanels fr`

Figure 16-1 shows the output when you run the program in a French locale.

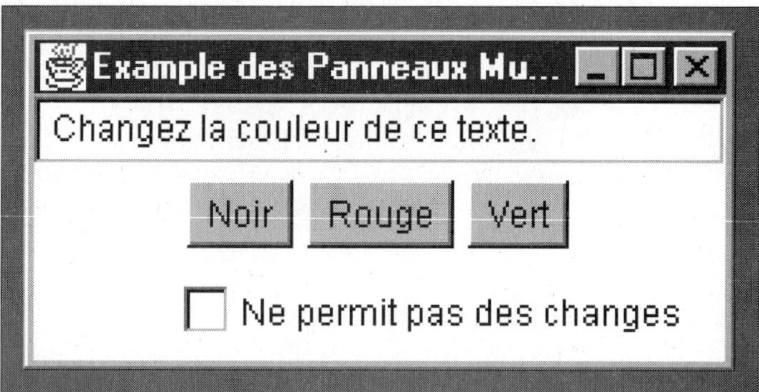

Figure 16-1: The ThreePanels program run in a French locale

Retrieving and Formatting Messages

The final step in separating textual information into a properties file is to extend the process to messages. If the entire message is a literal string, you can treat it like any other resource. Sometimes, you cannot know parts of a message when you create the properties file. In such cases, you must insert substitute text into the message as the program runs. In fact, the previous sample program does exactly that when it uses the following line from the IntPanels.properties file:

```
messages.missing_resource=Couldn''t find resource "{0}"
```

In this case, the `{0}` is a placeholder for the name of the resource that could not be found. To handle the substitution, wrap an object of the class **java.text.MessageFormat** around the message retrieved from the resource bundle. Declare an array of type

Object[] to hold the substitution arguments for the message. This example uses only the key from the MissingResourceException object, so the array has only one element. The array is passed to the format method of the MessageFormat object and the result is the final message.

```
MessageFormat mf
   = new MessageFormat( message );
Object[] messageArgs = { mrx.getKey() };
System.out.println( mf.format( messageArgs ) );
```

When more than one element must be substituted, the program gives those elements sequential values `{0}`, `{1}`, `{2}`, and so on. The symbols are matched to the contents of the Object[] array in order. However, these symbols can appear within the message in any order. For example, the following line might define a legitimate message in a properties file:

```
messages.example=Error {2}:Item {0} in container {1}
```

The flexibility of positioning substitution symbols in messages allows for the different grammatical structures of different languages. What may be the first substitution element in an English sentence may be the last in the same sentence translated into French. For example, "an unknown name" in French is a "un nom inconnu." The French word for unknown, *inconnu,* is the last word in this phrase, not the second word, as in English.

You can include additional information within the substitution symbol to specify how it should be formatted. For example, if the substitution value 0 should be formatted as a time value using the long style, include the string `time, long` within the substitution symbol, as follows:

```
{ 0, time, long }
```

Other format types that can be specified are date, number, and choice. Each of these can also have a format style specified to control the output format more precisely.

This book cannot cover all the possibilities of message formatting. In general, the Java platform provides many more classes, interfaces, methods, fields, and options than this book can contain. However, reading this book should have given you some insight into the capabilities of Java technologies and enough details for you to begin programming full-fledged applications and applets. A wealth of more information about Java technology is available on the World Wide Web. Appendix D lists some of the more useful Web sites. You can also look in the documentation supplied with the JDK from Sun Microsystems and in the help or documentation provided with your choice of application development software. Java technology is expanding and improving constantly and at an unprecedented pace, even for the computer industry. Perhaps the best way to keep up is simply to start programming and try new tools as they become available.

SUMMARY

In this chapter, you learned how to prepare your Java applications and applets for the international market. Internationalization is now such an important issue that the word has been given an abbreviation, I18N.

- The JVM stores all characters internally as Unicode characters. Unicode is an international character set defined by the ISO. The JVM uses a form in which each character is 16 bits.
- The character-oriented input and output streams not only support Unicode, but also can convert between various character-encoding schemes and Unicode. You can use the classes InputStreamReader and OutputStreamWriter to convert data between the native operating system encoding and Unicode.
- The byte-oriented I/O streams allow only one byte for a character and assume the coding scheme is Latin-1, otherwise known as ISO8859-1.
- Locales encapsulate the many facets that make up a cultural environment. The class Locale supports locales. Many locales are available in the JVM. You can specify a locale for a language, a language and a country, or a language-country-variant combination. The default locale is usually U.S. English.
- Localizing your code involves using locales whenever you perform an operation that is sensitive to the cultural environment.
- Use the Collator and CollationKey classes to sort strings according to the collation sequence for a specified locale.
- To manipulate date and time data, use the classes Calendar, TimeZone, subclasses of these classes, and Date. Use the class DateFormat to format date and time data as specified in a locale.
- Use the NumberFormat for locale-sensitive formatting of currency values, percentages, and other numbers.
- An important aspect of internationalizing your code is isolating textual elements that require translation from your code. Replace literal strings with resources that can be loaded at run time.
- Resource bundles are a mechanism for working with text, images, audio clips, and other resources that are stored in separate files from your program. Use the class ResourceBundle and optionally the subclasses ListResourceBundle and PropertyResourceBundle to access resources at run time.
- Resources are stored in properties files. Properties files are simple text files that can be translated into different languages with a text editor.
- You can also store the messages that your program outputs in properties files. Your program can alter the content of the message at run time by using substitution strings that can also be resources.

QUESTIONS

1. Where are Unicode escape sequences allowed? Select all that apply.
   a. class names
   b. field names
   c. comments
   d. string literals
   e. method names
2. Which JDK tool converts a system's native character encoding into ASCII encoding with Unicode escape sequences?
3. Which system property contains the encoding scheme currently in use by the system?
4. What does the following statement do? Choose the best answer.

```
new InputStreamReader( System.in, "8859_1" );
```

   a. Creates an object that reads bytes from the console and converts them to Unicode characters from ASCII Latin-1 encoding.
   b. Creates an object that reads Unicode characters from the console and converts them from Unicode to ASCII Latin-1 encoding.
   c. Creates an object that reads bytes from the console and converts them from Unicode to ASCII Cyrillic encoding.
   d. Creates an object that reads Unicode characters from the console and converts them to ASCII Latin-1 encoding.
   e. Creates an object that reads bytes from the console and converts them to Unicode characters from ASCII Cyrillic encoding.
5. Which of the following are valid statements for constructing a Locale object? Select all that apply.
   a. `Locale();`
   b. `Locale( "en" );`
   c. `Locale( "US" );`
   d. `Locale( "en", "CA" );`
   e. `Locale( "fr", "CA" );`
6. Which of the following methods are locale-sensitive? Select all that apply.
   a. String.equals
   b. String.compareTo
   c. Collator.compare
   d. Collator.equals
   e. CollationKey.compareTo
7. Which of the following are abstract classes? Select all that apply.
   a. Collator
   b. GregorianCalendar
   c. SimpleTimeZone
   d. TimeZone
   e. Date

8. Which of the following have formats that can be controlled by a NumberFormat object? Select all that apply.
   a. integers
   b. floating-point numbers
   c. percentage values
   d. currency values
   e. dates

9. Examine the following statements:

```
Locale.setDefault( new Locale( "fr", "FR" ) );
ResourceBundle rb;
rb = ResourceBundle.getBundle( "MyApp" );
```

   Which of the following files will be used for the resource bundle? Select the best answer.
   a. MyApp.properties
   b. MyAppfrFR.properties
   c. MyApp_fr.properties
   d. MyApp_FR.properties
   e. MyAppen.properties

10. Examine the following entry in the file Quiz16.properties file:

```
messages.example=Error {2}: Item {0} in container {1}
```

   What will be the output when the following class definition is compiled and run?

```
import java.util.ResourceBundle;
import java.text.MessageFormat;
public class Quiz16_10 {
   public static void main( String[] args ) {
      ResourceBundle rb
         = ResourceBundle.getBundle( "Quiz16" );
      String message
         = rb.getString( "messages.example" );
      MessageFormat mf = new MessageFormat( message );
      Object[] messageArgs = { "parts", "stock",
                               "2-45674" };
      System.out.println( mf.format( messageArgs ) );
   }
}
```

   Select the best answer:
   a. `messages.example=Error {2}: Item {0} in container {1}`
   b. `Error {2}: Item {0} in container {1}`
   c. `Error parts: Item stock in container 2-45674`
   d. `Error {stock}: Item {2-45674} in container {parts}`
   e. `Error 2-45674: Item parts in container stock`

EXERCISES

Debugging

1. Correct all the errors in the following class definition so that it will correctly use the system's file-encoding scheme for converting the bytes read from the console input:

```
package java4cpp.questions.c16;
import java.io.*;
class Debug16_1 {
   public static void main( String[] args )
         throws UnsupportedEncodingException {
      InputStreamReader isr
         = new InputStreamReader( System.in,
                                  "file.encoding" );
   }
}
```

2. Correct all the errors in the following class definition so that the default locale is set properly for Japan:

```
package java4cpp.questions.c16;
import java.util.Locale;
class Debug16_2 {
   public static void main( String[] args ) {
      setDefault( JAPAN );
   }
}
```

3. Correct all the errors in the following class definition:

```
package java4cpp.questions.c16;
import java.text.Collator;
class Debug16_3 {
   public static void main( String[] args ) {
      String s1 = "Smith, John";
      String s2 = "Smith, Joan";
      Collator c = new Collator();
      int result = c.compareTo( s1, s2 );
      switch( result ) {
         case -1:
            System.out.println( s1 + " < " + s2 );
            break;
         case 0:
            System.out.println( s1 + " == " + s2 );
            break;
         case 1:
            System.out.println( s1 + " > " + s2 );
            break;
      }
   }
}
```

4. Correct all the errors in the following class definition so that the program displays today's date correctly for France in its long format:

```
package java4cpp.questions.c16;
import java.util.Calendar;
import java.util.Date;
import java.util.Locale;
public class Debug16_4 {
   public static void main( String[] args ) {
      Calendar cal = Calendar.getInstance();
      Date today
         = cal.getTime( LONG, Locale.FRANCE );
      System.out.println( today );
   }
}
```

5. Correct all the errors in the following class definition so that a ResourceBundle subclass is correctly defined and its data is displayed:

```
package java4cpp.questions.c16;
import java.util.ResourceBundle;
import java.util.ListResourceBundle;
public class Debug16_5 {
   protected Object[] getContents() {
      Object[] myContents = {
         "price", new Double( 3.79 ),
         "name", "Shimmer floor wax"
      };
      return myContents;
   }
   public static void main( String[] args ) {
      ResourceBundle rb = new Debug16_5();
      String key = "price";
      System.out.println( key + " = "
                          + rb.getObject( key ) );
      key = "name";
      System.out.println( key + " = "
                          + rb.getObject( key ) );
   }
}
```

Complete the Solution

1. Complete the following class definition so that the bytes read from the console input are explicitly converted to Unicode using ISO 8859-1 character encoding:

```
package java4cpp.questions.c16;
import java.io.*;
class Complete16_1 {
   public static void main( String[] args ) {
      try {
         InputStreamReader isr
            = new InputStreamReader( System.in );
         FileWriter fw
            = new FileWriter( "Complete16_1.out" );
         char[] buffer = new char[128];
         int count = isr.read( buffer );
         while ( count != -1 ) {
           fw.write( buffer, 0, count );
           count = isr.read( buffer );
         }
         isr.close();
         fw.close();
      } catch( UnsupportedEncodingException uee ) {
         uee.printStackTrace();
      } catch( IOException ioe ) {
         ioe.printStackTrace();
      }
   }
}
```

2. Complete the following class definition by adding support for comparing the given strings using methods that are locale-sensitive:

```
package java4cpp.questions.c16;
class Complete16_2 {
   public static void main( String[] args ) {
      String[] fruit = {
         "kiwi",
         "strawberry",
         "peach",
         "plum",
         "apple",
         "grape",
         "pear",
         "apricot",
         "raspberry"
      };
      String first = fruit[0];
      int result;
      for( int i = 1; i < fruit.length; i++ ) {
         result = fruit[i].compareTo( first );
         if ( result < 0 ) {
```

```
                first = fruit[i];
            }
        }
        System.out.println( "Alphabetically, the first "
                            + "fruit is " + first );
    }
}
```

3. Complete the following class definition by adding support so that the calculated percentage is output with two decimal places and is in a format appropriate for Italy:

```
package java4cpp.questions.c16;
import java.text.NumberFormat;
import java.util.Locale;
public class Complete16_3 {
   public static double calcDiscount(
               double origPrice, double newPrice ) {
      return ( origPrice - newPrice ) / origPrice;
   }
   public static void main( String[] args ) {
      double discount = calcDiscount( 34.99, 29.99 );
      System.out.println( "The discount is "
                          + discount*100 + "%" );
   }
}
```

4. Complete the following class definition by creating a properties file containing all of the needed messages. The content of the messages can be whatever you like.

```
package java4cpp.questions.c16;
import java.awt.*;
import java.awt.event.*;
import java.util.ResourceBundle;
import java.util.MissingResourceException;
class Complete16_4 extends Frame {
   private ResourceBundle rb;
   public Complete16_4()
                  throws MissingResourceException {
      // get the resource bundle for the class.  A
      // hyphen is used in place of an underscore so
      // that _4 is not interpreted as a language
      // identifier.
      rb = ResourceBundle.getBundle( "Complete16-4" );
      setTitle( rb.getString( "title.text" ) );
      // create and register the object used for
      // closing the window
      addWindowListener( new WindowAdapter() {
            public void
            windowClosing( WindowEvent e ) {
               Frame.this.dispose();
               System.exit( 0 );
            }
```

```
            }
         );
         Label l
            = new Label( rb.getString( "label.text" ) );
         add( l, "North" );
         add( new TextArea( 12, 60 ), "Center" );
         Button okay
            = new Button( rb.getString( "okay.text" ) );
         Button cancel
            = new Button( rb.getString( "cancel.text" ) );
         Panel buttonPanel = new Panel();
         buttonPanel.add( okay );
         buttonPanel.add( cancel );
         add( buttonPanel, "South" );
         pack();
         setVisible( true );
      }
      public static void main( String[] args ) {
         new Complete16_4();
      }
   }
```

5. Complete the following class definition by removing all of the displayed text strings from the program and putting them into a properties file:

```
package java4cpp.questions.c16;
import java.awt.*;
import java.awt.event.*;
public class Complete16_5 extends Frame {
   public Complete16_5() {
      setTitle( "Ice Cream Sundae Orders" );
      // create and register the object used for
      // closing the window
      addWindowListener( new WindowAdapter() {
            public void
            windowClosing( WindowEvent e ) {
               Frame.this.dispose();
               System.exit( 0 );
            }
         }
      );
      Label label = new Label( "Please choose your "
                               + "sundae toppings:" );
      List list = new List( 10, true );
      Panel buttonPanel = new Panel();
      Button order = new Button( "Order Sundae" );
      Button cancel = new Button( "Cancel Order" );
      buttonPanel.add( order );
      buttonPanel.add( cancel );
      list.add( "chocolate sauce" );
      list.add( "strawberries" );
      list.add( "sprinkles" );
```

```
            list.add( "shaved coconut" );
            list.add( "sliced bananas" );
            list.add( "candied cherries" );
            list.add( "butterscotch sauce" );
            list.add( "crushed cookies" );
            list.add( "raspberries" );
            setLayout( new BorderLayout( 10, 10 ) );
            add( label, "North" );
            add( list, "Center" );
            add( buttonPanel, "South" );
            pack();
            setVisible( true );
        }
        public static void main( String[] args ) {
            new Complete16_5();
        }
    }
```

Discovery

1. Create a class called `WorldClock` that lets users choose from a list of cities around the world and displays the current time and date in that city. You'll need to do a bit of homework for each city by determining its time zone in advance. When the user selects a city, use its time zone information to get the current date and time.
2. Take the `FileBrowser` example from Chapter 14 and enable it for internationalization by extracting all of its displayable text strings and putting them into a properties file.

APPENDIX A

Native Methods

This appendix is a high-level introduction to the Java Native Interface (JNI). It explains how classes can use code that is local to the workstation and outside the Java Virtual Machine (JVM). The feature of the Java programming language that supports the JNI is **native methods**. Native methods are a mechanism you can use to access code that is written using other programming languages from a Java class.

Programs that you write in the Java programming language run in the JVM, but you cannot always ignore the real platform that is hosting the Java platform. Sometimes you need a bridge from the JVM to the native environment.

The following are some reasons to use native methods:

- To leverage existing code that has been developed and proven robust, but is not written in the Java programming language.
- To let your application access a system-specific facility that is not accessible through the JVM.
- To enhance performance by running code that has been compiled into machine code.

Consider carefully before deciding that using a native method is the best way to meet a requirement. Native methods have some serious disadvantages, including the following:

- A native method can do anything, including infect its host with a virus.
- You cannot define native methods in applets loaded from an untrusted source. Java technology has been widely accepted for the World Wide Web in part because of the security guaranteed to applets. In general, an applet cannot define methods that access code outside the virtual machine and you are not allowed to declare native methods in applets. For more on applet security, see Chapter 14.
- Native methods undermine portability. Clearly, if you use them to call system-specific APIs, you are creating an application that runs only on a platform that supports those APIs. When you introduce native methods, you reduce the portability of your class to the portability of the non-Java libraries on which your native method relies. Even if you avoid system-specific APIs, you must know (and be able to compile for) every platform your application will run on. This is a distribution and maintenance headache even if the native code is fairly portable.
- The argument for improved performance is not as clear-cut as it at first may seem. Evaluating performance requirements often involves balancing issues such as development effort and even robustness of code against user demand and real improvements that are detectable by users. The equation is constantly changing as tools, such as Just in Time (JIT) compilers, become available.

Ultimately, the decision to rely on non-Java code depends on your circumstances. Developers who create in-house applications for a particular company may have a more reduced requirement for cross-platform portability than a software development organization that sells its products to the general public.

Even if you do not use native methods, you should be aware that your applications and applets do use native code indirectly. All implementations of the JVM depend upon a considerable amount of native code, and many of the core classes contain platform-specific code that is not written in the Java programming language.

The details of the loading and linking with non-Java code depend on your operating system, the language to which you are linking, and other factors that are specific to your individual circumstances. Therefore, this discussion cannot attempt to give comprehensive coverage of this very large topic. It concentrates on one common scenario: calling C functions from a dynamic link library on Windows platforms. Because the way that you use native methods depends on many factors outside the Java platform, native methods are not included in the objectives of the certification exam.

Defining Native Methods

You can define a method that is a wrapper for, or an interface to, code that is not written in the Java programming language and that runs outside the JVM. Use the keyword `native` to indicate that a method is just a stub for code that runs in the native operating system.

Syntax	*[access_specifier] [qualifiers]* **native** *return_type method_name(argument_list)* **[throws** *exception_list]*;
Dissection	■ The qualifier **native** on a method indicates that the method is a wrapper for code that runs outside the JVM, in the native operating system. ■ You do not supply the body of a native method, because the implementation is provided by code outside the JVM. ■ The function for which the native method is a stub may throw an exception. If that is possible, list the exceptions in a **throws** clause, as explained in Chapter 6.
Code Example	`public static native int increment( int input );`
Code Dissection	■ This is the declaration of the native method called by the sample program in this appendix.

You call the native method just like you call other methods. However, that is not the whole story. Unlike Java classes, native methods are not automatically available in the JVM. The next section tells you how to link to a native method.

Calling a C function from the Java platform is more complicated than it is from C++. This should not be surprising, because C is a subset of C++ but an entirely different language from the Java programming language. All the C++ programmer has to do to call a C function is declare it with extern "C", **and link in the usual manner. The keyword** native **may be as easy to use as** extern "C" **in C++, but providing the body of the C function and linking to it requires more work.**

The Java programming language included the keyword native **from the start. However, the implementation of native methods has improved considerably since the Java platform was first introduced, and the usage of native methods did not stabilize until version 1.1 of the Java platform.**

Linking to Code Outside the JVM

To be accessible from programs that run in the JVM, native code must be in a library that can be loaded at run time. On OS/2 and Windows platforms, you must build a dynamic link library (DLL) that holds the implementations of your native methods. On UNIX platforms, you can use a shared library.

Often the native code is compiled from source code written in the C language. That is because system-specific features are usually supported by a C API. Also, C is often the language of choice when performance is the highest priority.

The following example demonstrates linking to a C DLL. In this example, a very simple native method receives an integer as an argument, increments the value of the argument, and returns the incremented value. If you have access to application development tools with which you can compile C code and create a DLL, you may be able to follow the steps listed here to complete the sample scenario.

The files used in this example are included in the java4cpp.jar file. If you unpacked the .jar file as described at the beginning of this book, the following files are in the folder java4cpp:

- The file NativeExample.java contains the source code for the class listed in step 1 of this scenario.
- The file NativeExample.class contains the bytecode for the `NativeExample` class created when the class is compiled in step 2 of this scenario.
- The file NativeExample.h is the header files created by running the **javah** tool as described in step 3 of this scenario.
- The file NativeExample.c contains the C function listed in Step 5 of the following scenario.
- The file NativeExample.dll is a DLL that contains the C function called by the native method in this example. You can use it on 32-bit Windows operating systems if you do not have facilities to create your own library in Step 6 of the following scenario.

In general, you can use the following method as a guideline for connecting to a DLL.

To connect to a DLL:

1 Define the class that contains the native methods. Add a static initialization block in which you call the method **System.loadLibrary** to load the library containing the C code. As a result, the library is loaded when the class is loaded. Static initialization blocks are described in Chapter 4. The **loadLibrary** method adds any required prefix or suffix to the library, as required by the operating system. On Windows and OS/2 platforms, the .dll extension is added; on Solaris a "lib" prefix and a .so suffix is added.

Here is the class for the example:

```
/** A class that uses a native method
  * This class is assigned to the default package
  */
public class NativeExample {
   /** the method increment is a wrapper for a C
     * function that resides in NativeExample.dll
     * @param input an int value that the C
     *    function increments
     */
   public static native int increment( int input );
   /** test main method passes the value 4
     * to the native method and prints incremented
     * value returned by the native method
     * @param args not used
     */
```

```
    public static void main( String[] args ) {
       System.out.println( increment( 4 ) );
       System.out.println(
          "Native method called successfully" );
    }
    static {  // static initialization block
       System.loadLibrary ( "NativeExample" );
       System.out.println (
          "Library Loaded Successfully" );
    }
}
```

2 Compile the class in the normal way. This class can be compiled with the following command:

```
javac NativeExample.java
```

3 Run the **javah** tool. Supply the NativeExample.class file as input. Specify the option **–jni** to create a C header file containing required function prototypes. The command is

```
javah -jni NativeExample
```

4 The output is a header file with a name that is the concatenation of all the package names and the class name. Underscores are substituted for dots in the concatenation. The `NativeExample` class is not in a package, so the resulting file is NativeExample.h. The contents of NativeExample.h are as follows:

```
/* DO NOT EDIT THIS FILE - it is machine generated */
#include <jni.h>
/* Header for class NativeExample */

#ifndef _Included_NativeExample
#define _Included_NativeExample
#ifdef __cplusplus
extern "C" {
#endif
/*
 * Class:      NativeExample
 * Method:     increment
 * Signature: (I)I
 */
JNIEXPORT jint JNICALL Java_NativeExample_increment
  (JNIEnv *, jclass, jint);

#ifdef __cplusplus
}
#endif
#endif
```

5 Create a C source file. Include the .h file output by **javah** and provide implementations for the native methods. The file NativeExample.c contains the simple increment method:

```
#include "NativeExample.h"
/*
* Class:     NativeExample
* Method:    increment
* Signature: (I)I
*/
JNIEXPORT jint JNICALL Java_NativeExample_increment
   (JNIEnv * e, jclass c, jint i)
{
   return ++i;
}
```

6 Using C application development software obtained separately from the JDK, compile the C source file and build a dynamic link library that contains it. In addition to supplying the source files NativeExample.c and NativeExample.h, you must supply system header files from the JDK to resolve symbols in the JNI interface. You can find these files in a system-specific subfolder of the include subfolder of the folder in which you installed the JDK. In this case, jni.h and jni_md.h must be available to the C compiler.

7 To test the application in the JVM, enter the command **java NativeExample.**

The output is as follows:

```
Library loaded successfully
5
Native method called successfully
```

Passing Parameters to Native Methods

The simple example native method passed one parameter of type int to the C code. Did you notice that the parameter and return type in the .java source file are mapped to the type jint in the C files? The JNI makes extensive use of C **typedef** statements to map the primitive types of the Java programming language onto C types. Figure A-1 shows the mappings used on Intel platforms.

Java Type	Native Type	Description
boolean	jboolean	unsigned 8 bits
byte	jbyte	signed 8 bits
char	jchar	unsigned 16 bits
short	jshort	signed 16 bits
int	jint	signed 32 bits
long	jlong	signed 64 bits
float	jfloat	32 bits
double	jdouble	64 bits
void	void	N/A

Figure A-1: Mapping primitive types to C types

The Bigger Picture

There is much more for you to learn if you are going to exploit native methods more substantially than this simple example does. The following are some questions you should consider:

- How do you pass arguments of reference types?
- How do you handle exceptions across the language boundary?

As well, there is also the entire subject of how the JNI allows native code to initiate calls to Java code. Such an approach is usually required when a JVM is embedded in an application written in C or C++. For example, many popular browsers available today are written in C and C++ and embed a JVM for running applets.

An in-depth examination of the JNI is beyond the scope of this book. You can find more details in the JDK documentation.

APPENDIX

Comparing C++ and the Java Platform

objectives

In this appendix you will:

- **Compare the keywords recognized in C++ with those of the Java programming language**
- **Learn how the Java programming language manages without a preprocessor**

Comparing the Keywords

The bulk of this book provides an in-depth discussion of many features of the Java programming language, pointing out similarities and differences from C++ throughout. At first sight, the set of keywords in the C++ language in Figure B-1 may seem to be very similar to keywords in the Java programming language. Each language has some unique keywords, but many keywords do appear in both languages. Sometimes the usage is almost identical, but equally often there is only a similarly of purpose, not of syntax or semantics.

C++ Keyword	Java Keyword	Usage in the Java Programming Language	See
	abstract	The qualifier **abstract** identifies an abstract method, not the notation **=0;** classes can also be abstract.	Chapter 5
asm	**native**	The Java platform provides no interface to inline assembly language, but native methods are wrappers for code outside the Java Virtual Machine (JVM).	Appendix A
auto		Primitive types are placed on the stack. The JVM manages dynamic memory for objects.	Chapter 3
bool	**boolean**	This primitive type specifies true or false values.	Chapter 3
break	**break**	**break** alters the flow of control in **for**, **if**, or **switch** statements. Unlike C++, you can break to a label.	Chapter 2
	byte	A byte is an eight-bit signed integer. The **byte** keyword is not interchangeable with type **char**.	Chapter 3
case	**case**	Use **case** in a selection clause in switch statement.	Chapter 2
catch	**catch**	This keyword begins an exception handler.	Chapter 6
char	**char**	**char** specifies the character type. Characters are stored in 16-bit Unicode, not bytes.	Chapter 3
class	**class**	This keyword begins a class definition.	Chapter 4
const	**final**	This qualifier prevents modification of variables, overriding of methods and extending of classes.	Chapter 2 Chapter 5
const_cast		Operations on pointers and references, apart from simple assignment to object references, are not available in the Java programming language.	

Figure B-1: A comparison of keywords

C++ Keyword	Java Keyword	Usage in the Java Programming Language	See
continue	**continue**	This keyword alters the flow of control in a for statement. Unlike C++, you can continue a label.	Chapter 2
default	**default**	**default** is the selection clause in a switch statement when no other clauses apply.	Chapter 2
delete		Objects of the Java platform cannot be explicitly deleted.	Chapter 3
do	**do**	This keyword begins an iterative statement.	Chapter 2
double	**double**	**double** specifies a high-resolution floating-point type.	Chapter 3
dynamic_cast		Operations on pointers and references, apart from simple assignment to object references, are not available in the Java programming language. All casts on object references in the Java programming language are just like **dynamic_cast** in C++	
else	**else**	This keyword begins the optional else clause in an **if** statement.	Chapter 2
enum		The Java programming language does not have enumeration types. The **Enumeration** class is used to iterate through aggregate objects.	Chapter 10
explicit		Usual rules of argument type checking and implicit casts always apply to constructors.	
	extends	A subclass extends a superclass with the keyword **extends**, not with a colon **(:)**	Chapter 5
extern		This keyword is not required in the Java programming language. All fields and methods are class members. Access specifiers control whether other classes can use members.	

Figure B-1: A comparison of keywords (continued)

C++ Keyword	Java Keyword	Usage in the Java Programming Language	See
false	**false**	**false** is a boolean value. This is actually a literal rather than a keyword.	Chapter 3
	finally	This keyword begins a clause that is always executed at the end of a try block.	Chapter 6
float	**float**	**float** specifies a floating-point type.	Chapter 3
for	**for**	This keyword begins an iterative statement.	Chapter 2
friend		The Java programming language does not require **friend**. By default, classes can access members of all classes in the same package.	Chapter 4
goto	**goto**	This keyword is not used in the Java programming language, but it remains a reserved word.	Chapter 2
if	**if**	**if** begins a conditional statement.	Chapter 2
	implements	A class implements an interface with this keyword.	Chapter 5
	import	**import** specifies a package to search for unqualified class names. It is similar to C++ using declarations and using directives.	Chapter 4
inline		The compiler decides what methods to inline.	
	instanceof	This operator indicates whether an object is an instance of a class or subclass of that class.	
int	**int**	int specifies a 32-bit signed integer type.	Chapter 3
	interface	This keyword begins the definition of an interface. C++ does not have interfaces.	Chapter 5
long	**long**	**long** specifies a 64-bit signed integer type.	Chapter 3

Figure B-1: A comparison of keywords (continued)

C++ Keyword	Java Keyword	Usage in the Java Programming Language	See
mutable		A class cannot be declared constant. A nonfinal field can be modified.	
namespace		This keyword is not required. Class names are qualified by the name of the package to which they belong, which achieves a similar effect.	Chapter 4
new	new	**new** creates objects of reference types.	Chapter 3
operator		This keyword is not available. The Java programming language does not have function notation for operators or operator overloading.	
	package	**package** begins a file in which classes that belong to the named package belong.	Chapter 4
private	**private**	This keyword specifies the most restrictive access.	Chapter 5
protected	**protected**	**protected** is an access specifier.	Chapter 5
public	**public**	This keyword specifies the least restrictive access.	Chapter 5
register		**register** is not available in the Java programming language.	
reinterpret_cast		Operations on pointers and references, apart from simple assignment to object references, are not available in the Java programming language. Casting of primitive types in the Java programming language is similar to the C++ **reinterpret_cast**.	
return	**return**	This keyword ends a method and optionally specifies a return value.	Chapter 2
short	**short**	**short** specifies a 16-bit signed integer type.	Chapter 3
signed		All integer types are signed.	

Figure B-1: A comparison of keywords (continued)

C++ Keyword	Java Keyword	Usage in the Java Programming Language	See
sizeof		This keyword is not required. For arrays, use the **length** field; for strings, use the **length** method.	Chapter 3
	super	**super** calls a method or constructor of the superclass.	Chapter 5
static	**static**	This keyword qualifies a member to pertain to the class rather than an instance. **static** makes an enclosed class a nested top-level rather than an inner class.	Chapter 2 Chapter 4 Chapter 9
static_cast		Operations on pointers and references, apart from simple assignment to object references, are not available in the Java programming language. Casting of primitive types in the Java programming language is similar to the C++ **static_cast**.	
struct		The Java programming language does not have structures, but a public class with public fields can be used like a C++ **struct**.	Chapter 4
switch	**switch**	This keyword begins a selection statement.	Chapter 2
	synchronized	**synchronized** prevents more than one thread from operating on the same object at once.	
template		The Java programming language does not support class or method templates.	
this	**this**	This keyword is an object reference for the current object. **this** can represent a constructor call.	Chapter 4
	transient	**transient** excludes a field from read or write operations during object serialization.	Chapter 8
throw	**throw**	Use this keyword to throw an exception.	Chapter 6

Figure B-1: A comparison of keywords (continued)

C++ Keyword	Java Keyword	Usage in the Java Programming Language	See
throw	throws	These keywords begin an exception specification in a method declaration.	Chapter 6
true	true	**true** is a boolean value. This is actually a literal rather than a keyword.	Chapter 3
try	try	This keyword begins a clause in which code is monitored for exceptions.	Chapter 6
typedef		The Java programming language does not allow definition of types names, apart from class definitions.	
typeid		RTTI is provided by the **Class** class, the **instanceof** operator and the Reflection API.	Chapter 7
typename		RTTI is provided by the **Class** class, the **instanceof** operator and the Reflection API.	Chapter 7
union		Different types cannot share units of storage.	
unsigned		All integer types are signed.	Chapter 3
using		Packages serve part of the purpose of namespaces.	Chapter 4
virtual		The Java programming language does not require this keyword. Instance methods are dynamically bound by default.	Chapter 5
void	void	**void** specifies a primitive type.	Chapter 3
volatile	volatile	This keyword prevents optimizations that may lose changes to variables made from other threads.	Chapter 11
wchar_t	char	All characters are stored in Unicode.	Chapter 16
while	while	This keyword begins an iterative statement.	Chapter 2

Figure B-1: A comparison of keywords (continued)

Working without a Preprocessor

Have you noticed the lack of preprocessor directives in the sample programs in this book? Did you wonder why none of the sample programs or end-of-chapter exercises includes a preprocessing stage? Perhaps you have already come to the true explanation: There is no preprocessor in the Java platform.

In C++, you must use a preprocessor to prepare C++ source code for the C++ compiler. Often the compiler calls the preprocessor automatically, so you do have to include an explicit preprocessing stage in your makefile or a set of build commands. Nevertheless, you cannot program in C++ without understanding the preprocessor, and almost every C++ source file contains preprocessor directives. A C++ programmer uses the preprocessor for the following purposes:

- To replace tokens in the source with replacement values, usually to define constants. For this purpose, you define macros with #define directives.
- To imbed source code from other files, typically header files. Almost every C++ source file contains #include directives.
- To exclude sections of source code depending on the build environment. Programmers achieve conditional compilation with a set directives including #ifdef, #ifndef, and #endif.

Is the preprocessor really necessary, even in C++? Please consider the opinion of the creator of C++, Bjarne Stroustrup:

> Among the facilities, techniques, and ideas C++ inherited from C was the C preprocessor, Cpp. I didn't like Cpp at all, and I still don't like it. The character and file orientation of the preprocessor is fundamentally at odds with a programming language designed around the notions of scopes, types, and interfaces. (From Stroustrup, *The Design and Evolution of* C++, Addison Wesley, 1994. Page 423.)
>
> I'd like to see Cpp abolished. However, the only realistic and responsible way of doing that is first to make it redundant, then encourage people to use the better alternatives, and *then*—years later—banish Cpp into the program development environment with the other extra-linguistic tools where it belongs. (From Stroustrup, *The Design and Evolution of* C++, Addison Wesley, 1994. Page 426.)

If you are a C++ programmer used to relying heavily on the preprocessor, you may have an adjustment to make. However, you may be able to find all the facilities you require within the Java platform.

Programming without Preprocessor Macros

The C++ programming language provided a way to define constants that was new to C programmers: the keyword const. But C++ programmers can also use #define preprocessor directives, and many still continue to do so. One can argue that using the preprocessor to create constants is unnecessary in C++, and may even be poor style. Surely it is better to code as much as possible in the C++ language, and reduce dependencies on exterior programs, such as the preprocessor, to a minimum.

The Java programming language has introduced a keyword, final, to identify constants. There are several differences between final and the C++ keyword const, but the most important difference is that there is no alternative method to create constants.

The preprocessor approach involves macro expansion through token replacement. The approach can be a source of errors, and can produce constructs that are not what you intended. For example, consider the macro MAX defined in the following directive:

```
#define MAX( (a), (b) ) ( (a) > (b) ? (a) : (b) )
```

You can use this macro in a statement like the following:

```
c = MAX( ++a, ++b );
```

Even though the arguments of the macro are enclosed in parentheses to reduce the chance of misinterpretation, the preprocessor expands the macro into a statement in which either a or b is incremented twice.

```
c = (++a) > (++b) ? (++a) : (++b);
```

The result may be that c is not assigned the value you intended, even though the code is syntactically correct.

Because the C++ compiler and debugger do not see preprocessor macros, the diagnostics they produce can be misleading. For example, the compiler cannot check whether you are using types properly when you define a replacement string in the preprocessor directive.

Programming without Included Files

To compare the use of included files, you must consider the programming environment. The most common use for an included file in C++ is to bring in header files that contain class definitions and other global declarations on which the source code depends. Dependence on the preprocessor to include header files is an inherent characteristic of most C++ compilers.

The Java programming language has a very different environment. The Java compiler searches, using the CLASSPATH environment variable, for bytecode files as it needs them during compilation. Also, the bytecode files are interpreted by the JVM, which loads classes dynamically while a program is running. This is very different from C++ on platforms where all references to symbols must be satisfied when you build an executable file, before run time. The JVM can always find classes because the Java compiler puts each compiled class definition into its own bytecode file with a filename that matches the name of the class.

All elements of Java programs must be contained within classes. There is no global scope and no global declarations to include. All told, there is need for included files in the Java platform.

The Java programming language does have an import statement that is described in Chapter 4. The similarity between import and #include is very superficial. The import keyword registers a package name so that you do not have to include it, like a path, every time you refer to the names of classes from that package. The import keyword gives access to a name, but imports no code. If you are willing to code the full name of classes, you never have to import classes.

Programming without Conditional Compilation

The third common use for the C++ preprocessor is to exclude some source code from compilation depending on a condition.

As with #include, some situations where conditional compilation is used do not apply to the JVM. For example, conditional compilation is often used in C++ to prevent recompiling the same header file every time it is included in another source.

In C++, you often have to code one way for one platform and a slightly different way for another, Therefore, you may use conditional compilation for different target or development platforms. The primary goal of the Java platform is platform-independence, as stated in the catch phrase, "Write once, run anywhere." Generally, you should try not to take advantage of, or code around, platform-specific quirks in various implementations of the Java platform. Always try to write portable code, because platform-specific variations are subject to change.

If your code must contain statements that you want the compiler to ignore, the best you can do is to enclose the statements in an if statement. This is not true conditional compilation, because the compiler itself must process the conditional statements. Here is an example:

```
if ( false ) {
   // code to be ignored
}
```

In this example, code to be ignored is guaranteed never to execute. The bytecode should be optimized so that no code is generated for the conditional statement. Of course, if you want to use the statements in other circumstances, you must modify the source code. To be more flexible, the condition should be a run-time expression. You can program for some platform differences by calling the method getProperty of the System class for answers to questions such as, "What platform is this?" and, "What is the end-of-line character?"

APPENDIX

Java Platform Implementation Notes

C

Some creative solutions are required to allow for naming files and packages on the wide variety of native operating systems that can be host to the Java Virtual Machine (JVM). The problem is particularly critical because applets and applications written in the Java programming language are expected to run on all implementations of the Java platform.

Applying Conventions for Unique Names

How does the JVM find Java source or compiled bytecode when it must compile and load a class? Chapter 1 explained that searches for .class files are based on the assumption that filenames match class names and that folder names match package names. Therefore, you must follow naming conventions and put only one public class in a source file. Of course, you must make sure that filenames, including the path portion of the name, are unique.

Within one workstation, maintaining unique class names, and therefore unique filenames, should not be difficult. All names must be unique within one folder. What happens when the files are not in the current working folder, and you do not explicitly give the absolute or relative path to the files? The answer may depend on your implementation of the JVM. On many platforms, the JDK and Web browsers use an environment variable named CLASSPATH and search for local files in paths relative to the folders listed in CLASSPATH. The CLASSPATH is discussed in Chapter 1 of this book. All versions of the **java** command have a **-classpath** argument which can also be used.

The Internet does complicate the hunt for unique names. You may be making your packages available on the World Wide Web, or downloading packages. Can you imagine the potential for different institutions to duplicate package and class names, especially if the institutions are developing packages for similar purposes and trying to use mnemonic names based on English? The following convention is proposed to ensure unique package names on an Internet-wide basis:

- Package names begin with the domain name of the institution where the package is developed.
- The domain name is reversed.

For example, developers at the IBM laboratory in Toronto, domain torolab.ibm.com, should start package names with com.ibm.torolab.

Understanding How the JDK Stores the Core Classes

The Java Development Kit (JDK) contains a very large number of classes divided into many packages. Have you looked in the folder in which you installed the JDK for subfolders named lang, awt, or any of the core API package names? Are you puzzled that you cannot find them?

The standard packages of the Java platform are gathered into one archive file named classes.zip on Windows and OS/2 platforms. This makes for very convenient distribution of the JDK. The JVM can load classes directly from this archive file, just as it can from a .jar file. The files in the archive are not compressed, so there is no performance overhead from combining all the core classes into one file.

Apart from convenience, there is a great advantage in combining all the core classes into one archive file. The file can reside on operating systems that do not support long filenames. Inside the archive, the folders have their full names, but the native operating system sees only the archive filename. Therefore, Java programs can run on operating systems that support only disks formatted for traditional file allocation tables (FAT), such as DOS. You cannot develop new classes on a native operating system that cannot handle names with more than eight characters or extensions with more than three characters. But you can run existing programs. In particular, users with old machines can run programs written in the Java programming language.

Another advantage is that having one large archive file will often require less hard disk space than hundreds of individual files. This is because some file systems allocate space for files in blocks. Any unused storage in the block at the end of the file cannot be reallocated to other files and becomes wasted space. On average, each file wastes half a block of storage. If you have one huge file, your system will never waste more than one block of space.

Working in FAT File Systems

Did you notice that the file extensions for class source and bytecode files, .java and .class, do not conform to the 8.3 file naming restrictions of some file systems? You cannot truncate these file extensions to three characters or supply alternative extensions. The JVM insists that these extensions must be either .java and .class. Moreover, File Allocation Table (FAT) filenames cannot contain more than one dot, and the FAT file system does not distinguish between uppercase and lowercase letters. In short, FAT file systems simply cannot comply with the conventions required of the Java platform the way that UNIX-based file systems that easily handle long filenames can.

You can download and run Java applets and applications on FAT drives because the file classes.zip does conform to FAT file naming conventions.

You can develop Java applications on FAT partitions on Windows 95 and Windows NT because these operating systems have added support for long filenames on FAT. On Windows NT, you may prefer working in NT File System (NTFS)-formatted disk partitions.

If your platform is OS/2, you must install your implementation of the Java platform on a High Performance File System (HPFS)-formatted disk partition. The HPFS file system, like NTFS and UNIX-based file systems, can fully support all conventions required by the Java platform for filenames.

APPENDIX

D

Web Resources for the Java Platform

The World Wide Web offers abundant resources to help you get the most out of the Java platform. This appendix lists the URLs for a few of the sites that offer these useful resources. All URLs listed in this appendix should be read and entered as one line. Some are split here simply to fit on the printed page. Continuation lines in URLs are indented.

Web sites are always subject to change. You may find that some of these URLs are no longer available or direct you to more current pages.

Getting the Latest Version of the JDK

As well as providing downloadable versions of the JDK, the sites listed in Figure D-1 have links to much more information about Java technology and related technologies.

Accessing General Information

A wealth of other information is available on the World Wide Web. Figure D-2 lists a few key sites from which you can start your exploration.

Platform	Download Site
For Win32 and Solaris; contact Sun Microsystems	`http://java.sun.com/products/jdk`
For OS/2, AIX, OS/390, and AS/400; contact the IBM Centre for Java Technology	`http://ncc.hursley.ibm.com/javainfo/hurindex.html`
For a listing of Java platform ports for other operating systems	`http://java.sun.com/cgi-bin/java-ports.cgi`

Figure D-1: JDK download sites

Topic or Site	URL
Coding conventions for the Java programming language	`http://java.sun.com/docs/codeconv/html/codeConventions.doc.html`
Education and certification from Sun Microsystems	`http://suned.sun.com/suned/`
Gamelan: the Official Directory for Java for sample programs and much more	`http://www.developer.com/directories/pages/dir.java.html`
Glossary of terms related to Java technology	`http://www.javasoft.com/docs/glossary.html` or `http://www.javasoft.com/docs/glossary.print.html`
Java Foundation Classes	`http://java.sun.com/products/jfc/`
JavaBeans	`http://java.sun.com/beans`
JavaWorld online magazine	`http://www.javaworld.com/javaworld`
Main IBM Java Web site	`http://www.ibm.com/java/`
Official Java Web site	`http://java.sun.com/`
Tools for testing applets and applications	`http://www.sun.com/suntest/`
Unicode home page	`http://www.unicode.org`
VisualAge for Java home page	`http://www.software.ibm.com/ad/vajava/`

Figure D-2: URLs for additional information

MINI QUIZ ANSWERS

Mini Quiz 1-1

The `FirstProgram` class depends on correct user input. Methods of core classes that this program uses throw exceptions to indicate that they cannot complete the requested operation due to conditions that arise at run time. The following exceptions cause `FirstProgram` to end:

- If you enter a blank line or a line with less than two tokens, the method StringTokenizer.nextToken throws the exception NoSuchElementException. In Chapter 2, you learn how to prevent this exception from happening by calling StringTokenizer.hasMoreTokens before calling nextToken.
- If you enter a string when a number is expected, the Float.valueOf method throws a NumberFormatException.

The program has no problem with less than three lines of data. This condition is indicated by the value returned by BufferedReader.readLine and is detected by the condition that ends the while loop in which data is read.

Chapter 6 discusses the important topic of exception handling. One of the strengths of the Java platform is that it deals with most errors or unexpected conditions by throwing exceptions. By including exception handling in your code, you can build in a recovery mechanism. For example, you can modify this program to inform the user of the problem and continue running.

Mini Quiz 2-1

A logical right shift, >>>, is required to shift bit patterns to the right and introduce a 0 on the left for every bit position shifted to the right. The >> operator performs an arithmetic shift, which propagates the sign bit by introducing a 1 on the left for negative values. An arithmetic right shift does not convert negative integral values into positive values. In the case of a left shift, a logical and an arithmetic shift are identical because in both cases the operator introduces a 0 bit on the right for every position shift to the left. In a left shift, the sign bit is not affected until the value represented overflows the storage unit being shifted.

Mini Quiz 2-2

Expressions are evaluated from left to right unless operator priority or associativity dictates otherwise. In this case, the expression `"x + y = " + x` is evaluated first. Therefore, the first + operator performs string concatenation, and the result is `"x + y = 1"`. Then `"x + y = 1" + y` is evaluated, producing `"x + y = 12"`. To print the value of the sum of `x` and `y`, you must insert parentheses, as in `"x + y = " + (x + y)`, so that the expression `(x + y)` is evaluated before string concatenation takes place.

Mini Quiz 2-3

More than one solution is possible. To minimize the amount of code to change, simply convert the labeled continue into an unlabeled continue. The effect is to skip the print statement whenever an element of the array has a value equal to zero, but to continue processing the current row of elements. You should also delete the label search: because it is not used. Here is a listing:

```
public class Findit2 {
   public static void main( String[] args ) {
      int row = 0, col = 0;
      int a[][] = { {7,4,0}, {0,5,0}, {2,0,6} };
```

```
        for( row = 0; row < 3; row++ ) {
            for( col = 0; col < 3; col++ ) {
                if ( a[row][col] == 0 ) {
                    continue;
                }
                System.out.println( a[row][col] + " at ("
                    + row + "," + col +")" );
            }
        }
    }
}
```

Mini Quiz 2-4

No. When all parentheses are removed, operator priority determines the order of execution. The subtraction operator, -, has higher priority than the left shift, <<, which in turn has higher priority than |.

In the expression `flag | ( mask << ( position-1 ) )`, the parentheses are not necessary because they do not alter the order of evaluation, but including these parentheses is still good style because they do make the code easier to read.

Mini Quiz 2-5

No. A program can have only one entry point, but that entry point is determined by which class you tell the Java Virtual Machine (JVM) to run. Only the main method of the top-level class for an application is run, and any methods named main in other classes are ignored unless called explicitly during execution. There is no ambiguity of names because the fully qualified name of every method includes the class name.

Mini Quiz 3-1

In the declaration `short x = 123;`, `123` is a short value and no casting is required. The Java programming language allows implicit casts from types that can store a narrower range of values to types that can store a wider range of values, but not the other way around. The reason is to prevent an unintentional loss of information. Therefore, the compiler does not allow the cast from int to short in `short x = i;`, even though the actual value of the `i` can be accurately represented in an `x`. You can fix the statement with an explicit cast, as in the following example:

```
short x = (short) i;
```

Mini Quiz 3-2

This swap method is an attempt to swap the values of two integers by passing object references for two instances of the Integer wrapper class to the method swap. In fact, Integer objects are immutable, and this approach cannot work. The first line in the swap method looks good, and creates a third Integer object to use during the swap. However, the second and third lines simply reassign the object references and do not change the values stored in the Integer wrappers. The object references themselves are passed by value, so that after the method returns, the object references are not changed. In other words, this method achieves nothing.

Mini Quiz 3-3

Arrays are objects, just like instances of the core classes and your own classes, and are stored on the heap. If no object references refer to an array, it is no longer accessible and there is no way to use it again. The array becomes a candidate for garbage collection.

Mini Quiz 3-4

The main method of the ArrayTypes class has two for loops, which begin as follows:

```
for ( int i = 0; i < a.length; i++ )
for ( int i = 0; i < b.length; i++ )
```

In both cases, the variable i is local to the for statement and ceases to exist when the for statement ends. You can use the same identifier repeatedly for the counter in any number of for loops that are not nested within each other.

Mini Quiz 3-5

The method ArrayReturn.returnsArray declares the arrays array1 and array2. Like all arrays, these arrays are created on the heap, and the object reference for each of them is a local object. The method returns an object reference for one array, so that the calling method can access one of the arrays. After the method returns, no object references are left for the other array, which then may be destroyed by garbage collection.

The argument flag is of the primitive type boolean. Therefore, true or false is passed by value

The type of x is ArrayReturn.

The type of x.returnsArray is int[], an array of integers.

This class contains doc comments, or comments in **javadoc** notation. The /** sequence begins a doc comment. The **javadoc** tool recognizes the tag @param in a doc comment as the start of a description of a parameter of the following method, and the tag @returns as the start of a description of the return value.

Mini Quiz 3-6

The declaration creates five objects and five object references. The array object seasons and four String objects are stored on the heap. The object references for the String objects "winter", "spring", "summer", and "fall" are stored in the array seasons, which is on the heap. If the declaration of seasons appears in a method, the object reference for seasons is a local variable and stored on the stack until the method ends.

Mini Quiz 4-1

The Java programming language does not allow any declarations, except of classes, at file or global scope. Therefore, you cannot declare a method outside a class, and all methods are members. Similarly, you cannot declare a variable outside a class. All declarations of data elements declare fields of classes or local variables inside methods.

Mini Quiz 4-2

When you issue the **java** command, you must supply the name of a public class that has a main method. The main method of that class is the entry point for the program. In all proprietary integrated development environments (IDEs), you also specify which class to run.

Mini Quiz 4-3

Figure MQ 4-3 uses arrows to show the flow of control between the main method and the constructor, and uses rounded boxes to highlight the lines that produce output.

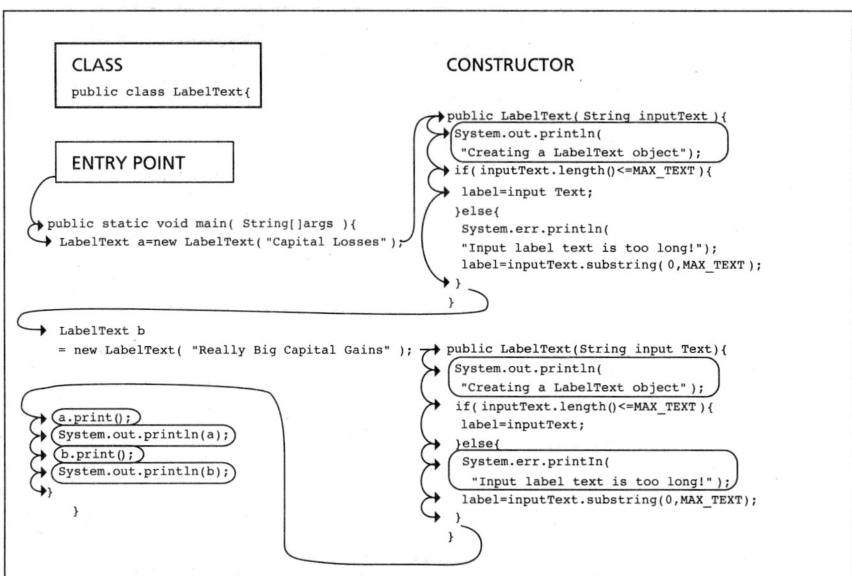

Figure MQ 4-3: Tracing the execution of an application

Mini Quiz 4-4

The scope operator, ::, is defined in C++ but not in the Java programming language where the dot operator separates package, subpackage, and class names, just as it separates class or instance names and member names.

Mini Quiz 4-5

The following statement sets the class variable `alpine` in the `Pine` class to true from within `Pine.main`:

```
alpine = true;
```

The following statement sets the class variable `Pine` to true from another class in the same package:

```
Pine.alpine = true;
```

The following statement sets the class variable `Pine` to true from within a class that is in a subpackage other than the subpackage `conifers`:

```
conifers.Pine.alpine = true;
```

Mini Quiz 5-1

There is no one right answer for this question. The most important principle to follow is that each subclass is more specific and has more characteristics than the superclass. If you know about birds, you may be able to apply knowledge from the problem domain and improve on the chart shown in Figure MQ 5-1. The chart shows a solution that assumes that song birds, birds of prey, and waterfowl are mutually exclusive categories and that all birds in these categories can fly. Therefore, the method `fly` is a member of the `FlyingBirds` class. To force each instance of `Birds` to belong to one of the four categories, make `Birds` and `FlyingBirds` abstract classes.

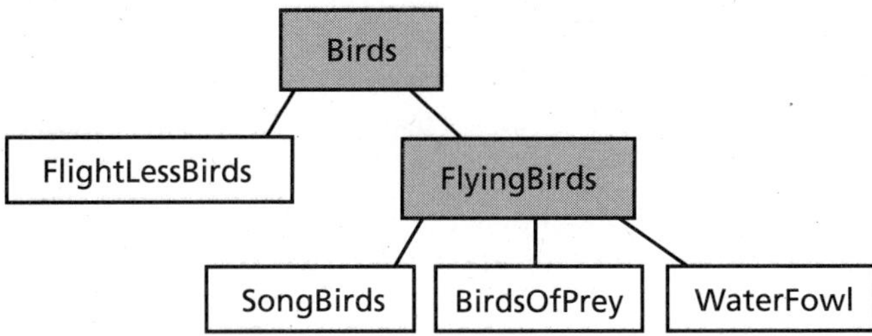

Figure MQ 5-1: A class hierarchy for birds

Mini Quiz 5-2

Methods that are either final or static do not use dynamic binding. The particular method to be used is determined statically at compile time. The whole point of defining an interface is to create methods that must be overridden, which requires dynamic binding.

Mini Quiz 5-3

An interface cannot contain the implementations of methods. Therefore, it cannot implement another interface. However, an interface can extend another interface. If an interface could extend a class, it would inherit the methods of that class. This situation also breaks the rule that an interface cannot contain only method declarations and no implementations.

Mini Quiz 5-4

The `super` object reference works because every class except Object has one direct superclass. Unlike C++, the Java programming language does not support multiple inheritance. In a multiple inheritance situation, the object reference `super` would be ambiguous. In the C++ language, an equivalent for `super` would have to resolve to null or be undefined for classes that do not have base classes, and would be adequate for classes with one base class, but ambiguous for classes with multiple base classes.

Mini Quiz 5-5

You do not call finalizers explicitly, with the exception that a subclass finalize method can, and should, call the finalize method of the superclass. The JVM calls finalizers, and is not bound by the access specifiers. Because superclass finalizers can be called by subclasses, which may not always be in the same package, private and default package access are too restrictive. Protected or public access would work, but public access is unnecessary and would force all subclasses to grant public access also to their finalizer methods.

Finalizers run before objects are destroyed by garbage collection. If the garbage collector never runs, your finalizers may never run either. To make sure finalizers run before your program ends, call System.runFinalizersOnExit. You can also call System.runFinalization to request that the JVM run the finalizers for objects that are ready for garbage collection and have not yet been finalized.

Mini Quiz 5-6

Syntactically, you can include a main method in an abstract class. Because main is a class method, you can run it. However, including an entry point in an abstract class makes little sense. Only the class methods would be available, and the proper use of an abstract class is as the superclass of a class that provides implementations of the abstract methods.

Mini Quiz 6-1

```
throws Throwable
```

Mini Quiz 6-2

The argument of a catch clause is never a primitive type, so only object references are ever the arguments of a catch clause. In no case can the caught object reference be changed if it is declared final. If the argument is a reference to an object of an immutable class, the object cannot be changed. However, if the reference is to an object of a class that defines mutator methods, the object may be changed.

Mini Quiz 7-1

The clone method is declared in the class Object, where the only possible return type is Object. An overriding method cannot change the return type. Therefore, all implementations of clone methods must have the return type Object.

Mini Quiz 7-2

The way to force a subclass to implement a method is to provide an abstract method that is inherited by the subclass. Any class that contains at least one abstract method must itself be declared abstract.

Any class that inherits an abstract clone method must provide an implementation of the clone method to be able to create instances of that class. Otherwise, the subclass must also be abstract.

An overriding method cannot throw an exception unless that exception type, or one of its supertypes, is listed in the throws clause of the overridden method. The example superclass contains an abstract clone method but no throws clause. Therefore, it forces the subclass to implement clone in a way that generates no uncaught exceptions.

Mini Quiz 7-3

The class field is public so that any class can access it, static because it pertains to the entire class and not to individual objects, and final so that no programmer can change it. It is important that the class field be universally accessible and trustworthy.

Mini Quiz 7-4

If you supply any constructor for a class, the Java compiler does not generate the default, no-argument, constructor. Therefore, any class that has a constructor that takes arguments will not have a no-argument constructor unless the programmer defines one.

The forName method is unique in that it returns a Class object when given the name of a class. forName must be a class method because the caller may have no instance of Class with which to call this method. The other methods return information pertaining to a particular Class object and are therefore instance methods.

Mini Quiz 7-5

In the example, the following statements are true of the class `java4cpp.rtti.CreateByName`:

- The Class.newInstance method can throw an InstantiationException or an IllegalAccessException.
- The Class.forName method can throw a ClassNotFoundException.

Mini Quiz 7-6

RuntimeException objects are not checked exceptions. The Java compiler does not check the throws clause of a method for unchecked exceptions. RuntimeException is a direct subclass of Exception. All other subclasses of Exception are checked exceptions. Programmers often list Exception in the throws clause of a method to cover all checked exceptions, and as a result include exceptions that are RuntimeException objects. Listing unchecked exceptions in a throws clause does no harm but is not necessary and has no advantage except as a programming convenience.

Mini Quiz 7-7

The Modifier class has a constant for every modifier that can be applied to a member of a class, and a method that indicates whether a specific modifier is applied to a specific member of a class. The argument of the method must be an int returned by Class.getModifiers and is a value in which all which the modifiers of a member are encoded. The following are the 11 fields and associated methods:

- The field ABSTRACT is checked by the following method:

  boolean isAbstract(int *value*)

- The field FINAL is checked by the following method:

  boolean isFinal(int *value*)

- The field INTERFACE is checked by the following method:

  boolean isInterface(int *value*)

- The field NATIVE is checked by the following method:

  boolean isNative(int *value*)

- The field PRIVATE is checked by the following method:

  boolean isPrivate(int *value*)

- The field PROTECTED is checked by the following method:

  boolean isProtected(int *value*)

- The field PUBLIC is checked by the following method:

  boolean isPublic(int *value*)

- The field STATIC is checked by the following method:

  boolean isStatic(int *value*)

- The field SYNCHRONIZED is checked by the following method:

  boolean isSynchronized(int *value*)

- The field TRANSIENT is checked by the following method:

  boolean isTransient(int *value*)

- The field VOLATILE is checked by the following method:

  boolean isVolatile(int *value*)

Mini Quiz 7-8

In a wrapper class, the field TYPE is an object reference for the Class object of the wrapped primitive type. TYPE is also a static final field. In other words, it is a constant object reference and, following the convention for constants, has a name that is all uppercase.

On the other hand, the class field does not appear in the class definition. It is created by the JVM for each class, when the class is loaded and is available as a convenient way to access the Class object for a specific named class.

Mini Quiz 8-1

Because these objects are declared static, they are class variables and you do not have to create a System object to use them. Because they are final, they cannot be modified by you or any other programmer. Therefore, you know that they conform to the standard behavior. Because they are public, you can use them from any class, regardless of the package to which the class belongs.

Mini Quiz 8-2

The write method must convert from an internal Unicode character to a byte that can be output. Unicode characters require 16 bits, and therefore do not fit into a byte. Why is the argument a 32-bit int rather than a 16-bit short? Unlike the value of a short, Unicode character encoding does not include a sign bit and requires 17 bits to be represented as a signed integral value.

Mini Quiz 8-3

If you look carefully at the source of the CaseMixer class, you see that the catch clause that handles the IOException catches only exceptions thrown in the try block. As a result, only exceptions thrown while reading from a FileInputStream or writing to a FileOutputStream are handled inside the main method. An IOException could also occur during the creation of the FileInputStream and FileOutputStream objects, before the try block. Therefore, failure opening the files can cause an uncaught IOException. This is a checked exception, so the throws clause must list it.

Mini Quiz 8-4

The StreamTokenizer class is a wrapper class that can be used with the byte-oriented stream InputStream or the character-oriented stream Reader. To be sure each character is correctly converted into Unicode, you should convert a byte-oriented stream to a character-oriented stream before tokenizing it, as shown for an InputStream is in the following lines:

```
Reader r
   = new BufferedReader( new InputStreamReader( is ) );
StreamTokenizer st = new StreamTokenizer( r );
```

Since version 1.1 of the Java platform, this practice has been encouraged by the deprecation of the StreamTokenizer constructor that takes an InputStream object as the argument.

Mini Quiz 8-5

As in all client-server relationships, the AdditionClient client program must open the connection to the AdditionServer server program. The server waits passively for a client to make contact, and then the ServerSocket.accept method returns an input stream. The server cannot know when a connection is attempted but fails. On the other hand, the constructor of the client end of the socket throws an exception if it cannot connect to the specified host.

Mini Quiz 9-1

The dot notation is used to separate packages, subpackages, classes, inner or nested classes, and members. The answer to this question is no, but coding conventions give a strong clue. Usually only class names start with an uppercase letter and otherwise consist of lowercase letters. Therefore, you should suspect that both Graph1 and Node are classes, which implies that the definition of Node is nested inside the definition of Graph1. For the compiler, the name is not ambiguous because the context determines the meaning.

Mini Quiz 9-2

The enclosing class has full access to the fields of all inner classes. In the Computer class, a separate variable size is a member of every HardDrive object for which an object reference is stored in the array drives. Therefore, the qualifier is necessary to specify which HardDrive to consider.

Mini Quiz 9-3

Yes. The following example works because the member class `Inner` itself uses the default constructor. The constructor of `SubInner` has no need to call super because there are no arguments to the constructor of `Inner`.

```
import java.io.*;
public class Test {
   public static void main ( String[] args ) {
      Test t = new Test();
      SubInner s = t.new SubInner();
      System.out.println( "Success" + s.innerField
          + s.subInnerField );
   }
   class Inner {
      int innerField = 1;
   }
   class SubInner extends Inner {
      int subInnerField = 2;
   }
}
```

Mini Quiz 9-4

If a method and local variables are used in a local inner class, their argument must be declared final. For primitive types, the values of these variables cannot change within the method. Local variables become constants. The value of an argument is held constant only locally, and no restriction applies to the calling method.

The same is true of object references in their own right. You cannot assign null or references to other objects to these final references. But you can always use the references to access the object, and you can modify the objects unless they are immutable for other reasons.

Mini Quiz 9-5

The output of the `java4cpp.inner.Equation1` program is calculated in the following statement:

```
return (double) input1/input2 - equationInput
   + localVar[2] - normalField;
```

With actual values inserted, the expression becomes the following:

```
33.0D / 5 - 10 - 0 - 2
```

This expression evaluates to –5.4.

Although the object reference for the array `localVar` cannot be changed, you can perform all the usual operations on the elements of the array.

Mini Quiz 10-1

The classes `Buzzer` and `Valve` are not declared static. Therefore, they are inner classes.

Mini Quiz 10-2

A `Buzzer` object is an Observer. Therefore, the JVM calls `Buzzer's` update method when the Observable object, in this case an instance of `Valve`, calls the method notifyObservers.

The output from running the `java4cpp.observe.Pump` class is:

```
Buzzer on
Buzzer off
```

Mini Quiz 10-3

Collections hold object references only, not variables of the primitive types. The strict answer is no. However, you can create collections of the wrapper classes Integer, Float, and so on. Therefore, the practical answer is yes, you can use the wrapper classes for the primitive types. Indeed, if the individual elements are declared to be of type Object, you can indirectly store variables of different primitive types in a collection or an array.

Mini Quiz 10-4

The method `listPoints` in the class `java4cpp.collections.Line` outputs a string representation of the `Point` objects stored in the `Vector` points in the following code line:

```
ps.println( e.nextElement() );
```

The method nextElement of the enumeration e returns an object reference to an Object. The println method calls toString for its argument, which by dynamic binding becomes a call to the toString method of the Point class.

Mini Quiz 10-5

The method nextElement of an Enumeration has the return type Object, regardless of the type of the objects stored in the collection. In the `sysProps` collection, each element is a String, but the compiler cannot detect that fact at compile time. The following line, which creates a String object to hold the name of a property, must explicitly cast from type Object to type String because you cannot implicitly cast from a more general type to a more specific type. The compiler would reject the following line if the explicit cast were removed:

```
String propName = (String) e.nextElement();
```

Mini Quiz 11-1

Each thread that you launch in a program, except the main thread, must handle all checked exceptions that are thrown as a result of the execution of the thread. Because no uncaught checked exceptions can leak out of the original declaration of run, no uncaught checked exceptions are allowed in methods that override run. A run method directly or indirectly calls all your code that runs in a thread other than the main thread.

Mini Quiz 11-2

Synchronizing all methods is a very crude way of ensuring object integrity, and you can do it if you think your class may be used in a multithreaded program. Synchronization avoids situations in which a change made to an object in one thread affects either an operation involving that object on another thread or the state of the object when the threads end. However, synchronization is meaningful only for methods that use objects that may also be used by the same method or other methods running on other threads. Similarly, you need not synchronize methods that share objects if none of them modify any of the shared objects. In general, you should minimize the constraints that your code places on the JVM, and synchronize only the methods that benefit from synchronization.

Mini Quiz 11-3

An overriding method must exactly match the method it overrides in the following:

- The method name
- The number, type, and order of arguments
- The return type

In addition, the overriding method must not do either of the following:

- Add new types of exceptions to the throws clause
- Grant less restrictive access than the overridden method

Mini Quiz 11-4

A method can call notify and notifyAll only when at least one method on the call chain is synchronized. Note that `doTheNotificationThing` is called by `setValue`, which is synchronized. When called on this path through execution, `doTheNotificationThing` acquires the lock from `setValue`, and can call notifyAll.

Mini Quiz 12-1

Here, WindowAdapter is an instance of an anonymous inner class. Using inner classes in this way is convenient, but not necessary. You could also define a top-level WindowAdapter class outside the `HelloWorld` class. Then you would have to instantiate a WindowAdapter inside the `HelloWorld` class, and pass an object reference for the WindowAdapter to the addWindowListener method.

Mini Quiz 12-2

A class that implements an interface must provide implementations for all methods defined in the interface. You can deduce that ActionListener has only one method, actionPerformed, from the fact that the working `ButtonListener` class implements ActionListener and has only the actionPerformed method.

Mini Quiz 12-3

There are many possible correct answers to this question. Figure MQ 12-3 shows one possibility based on assigning a border layout to the application frame. Two panels positioned in the center and south areas expand to fill the frame. The center panel has a grid layout in which the labels occupy two cells in the first row and the text fields occupy two of the cells in the second row. The south panel has a flow layout in which the three buttons are centered.

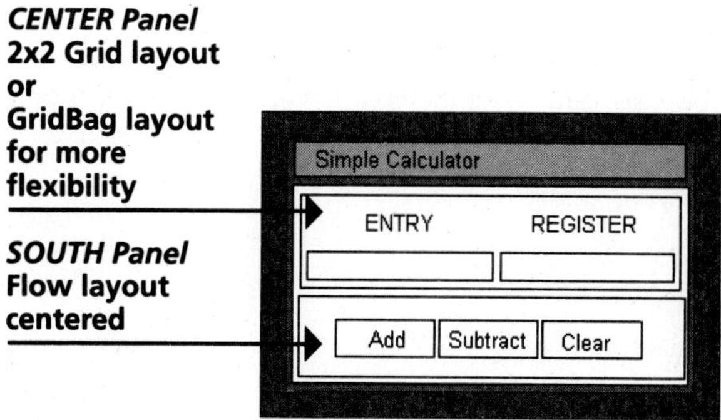

Figure MQ 12-3: A layout scheme for the simple calculator

Mini Quiz 12-4

The `add` and `subtract` methods of the `SimpleCalc` class must perform arithmetic operations on numeric values for which only stored representations are **String** objects. The **String** class has no methods that return values of primitive types represented by a **String** object. But each wrapper class for a primitive type, including **Double**, has a constructor that takes a **String** argument and a method that returns the value in the associated primitive type. Therefore, the easiest way to convert from **String** to **double** is to use the **Double** class.

Note: A better implementation of the simple calculator would use an invisible bean to perform the arithmetic. Inside the invisible bean the numeric values could be stored as properties of type **Double**. Such a solution conforms to the MVC design pattern and eliminates the need for the **Double** wrapper objects.

Mini Quiz 13-1

If you set the size of a component, you may not want a layout manager to stretch or compress the component. The only standard layout manager in which components retain their size is the flow layout manager.

Mini Quiz 13-2

To find out the background color of a component, call the following method:

```
Color getBackground()
```

To find out whether a component is enabled for events, call the following method:

```
boolean isEnabled()
```

To find out what font is set for a component, call the following method:

```
Font getFont()
```

To find out the foreground color of a component, call the following method:

```
Color getForeground()
```

To find out the size of a component, call the following method:

```
Dimension getSize()
```

To find out whether a component is visible, call the following method:

```
boolean isVisible()
```

Mini Quiz 13-3

In the constructor of the FontDialog class of the file browser sample program, the listener for action events is an instance of an anonymous inner class that implements ActionListener. The OK button object is declared final so that the inner class can use the button.

Mini Quiz 13-4

The buttonPanel object is a Panel object in the FontDialog class of the file browser sample program. The code specifies no layout manager, so the program uses the default manager for the Panel object. This Panel has a flow layout.

Mini Quiz 14-1

The value of an applet parameter is always expressed as a String when returned from the Applet.getParameter method. The string can represent a value of another type. To get the value, you can use the conversion methods of the wrapper classes for the primitive type as in the following statements:

```
// get an integer parameter
int number = ( new Integer(
   getParameter( "number" ) ) ).intValue;
// get a double parameter
double ratio = ( new Double(
   getParameter( "ratio" ) ) ).doubleValue;
```

Mini Quiz 14-2

The TickerMessage class implements Runnable. Therefore, a separate Thread object is required to support this Runnable class. When the start method of TickerMessage creates the Thread object, the method must specify the current instance of TickerMessage to indicate that the current instance of TickerMessage is the Runnable object for the new Thread object.

Mini Quiz 14-3

An InterruptedException may interrupt any sleeping thread. To make sure the exception does not terminate your program, you usually enclose a call to sleep in a try block and provide a catch clause that catches an InterruptedException. You can program the catch clause to ignore the exception or take any other action.

Mini Quiz 14-4

The TickerMessage class uses the default paint method, which is the inherited Component.repaint method. The run method calls repaint repeatedly to achieve the animation, and repaint calls update automatically. In the TickerMessage applet, all the drawing work of the animation is performed by the update method, which is implemented in this class.

Mini Quiz 14-5

When you draw directly onto a component, you must draw onto its graphics context. The AWT gives every component a graphics context, encapsulated in an object of the Graphics class. The AWT gives you access to the graphics context by passing it as an argument to the paint and repaint methods. In paint and repaint, you can call methods of the Graphics class, such as drawLine or fillRect, to draw in the display space of the component.

Mini Quiz 15-1

Any two of Math, Process, Runtime, SecurityManager, System, Thread, ThreadGroup, and Void are appropriate answers. The nature of these classes makes serializing them inappropriate, as Chapter 8 explains. There are many classes in other packages that are not serializable, including the I/O stream classes.

Mini Quiz 15-2

The purpose of the readObject method is to retrieve a serialized object and make it ready for use after deserialization. Therefore, this method is the best place to deal with transient fields and perform any other specialized work required to reconstitute the object. Reloading an image is very typical of the activities of readObject.

The readObject method does not actually perform object deserialization. The method defaultReadObject does that. You do not override defaultReadObject, but you are responsible for ensuring that it is called. You must implement readObject to deserialize an object and should implement it to start by calling defaultReadObject.

Mini Quiz 15-3

A beanbox recognizes methods that satisfy these criteria:

- The access specifier is public. Although not stated in the question, this is a requirement of methods in a bean.
- The return type is void.
- For the BDK BeanBox, the method has no arguments.

Mini Quiz 15-4

In the `ImageBean3BeanInfo` class, the method getPropertyDescriptors returns `pds`, an object reference to an array of property descriptors for the `ImageBean3` class. The array is set up inside a try block, to give the method a chance to recover if an IntrospectionException occurs. To be available outside the try block, `pds` must be declared outside the try block. Otherwise, `pds` would be local to the try block and not available for the return statement.

Mini Quiz 16-1

Unicode escape sequences are handled differently from other escape sequences. Unicode characters are inserted at the start of compilation, before the syntax-checking stage. Therefore, the string `"X\u000aY"` becomes a string that spans two lines:

```
"X
Y"
```

In the Java programming language, the opening and matching closing quotation marks must be on the same line, so the compiler rejects this string as a syntax error. On the other hand, the compiler accepts the literal `"X\nY"` in its unaltered form.

Mini Quiz 16-2

The Java platform has many precedents for passing specific types of information in a form that can be checked for validity before it is used. The key is to provide a class that encapsulates the type of information. Either of the following approaches, and maybe others you can think of, could give the programmer a chance to make sure the encoding scheme is valid before calling a method to convert characters.

One approach is to supply constructors that check whether the programmer has correctly specified the data to construct the object. For example, the constructor of the URL class creates a URL object if its arguments specify a properly formed URL, and throws an exception otherwise.

The Font class demonstrates another approach. Before you create a Font object, you can call the method Toolkit.getFont to find out what fonts are available on your implementation of the Java platform.

Mini Quiz 16-3

The following lines are an excerpt from an improved `BubbleSorter.sort` method. The new lines are shown in boldface:

```
// do the bubble sort
CollationKey tempKey;
for ( int i=1; i < ckeys.length; i++ ) {
   int numberOfSwaps = 0;
   for ( int j=0; j < ckeys.length-i; j++ ) {
      if ( ckeys[j].compareTo( ckeys[j+1] > 0 ) {
         // swap values
         numberOfSwaps++;
         tempKey = ckeys[j];
         ckeys[j] = ckeys[j+1];
         ckeys[j+1] = tempKey;
      }
  if ( numberOfSwaps == 0 ) break; }
}
```

Mini Quiz 16-4

The Enumeration interface provides two methods:

- You can call one method to determine whether more elements are available:

  boolean hasMoreElements()

- If hasMoreElements returns true, you can call the following method to retrieve the next element:

  Object nextElement()

Mini Quiz 16-5

RuntimeException objects are not checked exceptions, but they are Throwable objects. Therefore, you can throw and catch them, as shown in the `IntlPanels` class. Usually, wrapping a try block around code that extracts resources from a ResourceBundle is advantageous because it gives you a chance to recover if there is a problem with the properties file. There is only one implication of the fact that MissingResourceException is unchecked: The compiler does not force you either to handle the exception or list it in the throws clauses of methods that get properties from ResourceBundle objects.

Index

A

B

C

D

G

H

I

N

O

Q

R

S

T

U

V

License Agreement for IBM* VisualAge* for Java** Professional for Windows**, Version 1.0 ("Program")

PLEASE READ THIS AGREEMENT CAREFULLY BEFORE USING THE PROGRAM. IBM WILL ONLY LICENSE THE PROGRAM TO YOU IF YOU FIRST ACCEPT THE TERMS OF THIS AGREEMENT BY USING THE PROGRAM. IF YOU DO NOT AGREE TO THE TERMS OF THIS AGREEMENT, DO NOT INSTALL THE PROGRAM.

The Program is owned by International Business Machines Corporation or one of its subsidiaries (IBM) or an IBM supplier, and is copyrighted and licensed, not sold. IBM grants you a nonexclusive, nontransferable license for the Program. The term "Program" means the original program and all whole or partial copies of it, including portions merged into other programs. A Program consists of machine-readable instructions, audio/visual content (such as images, text, recordings, or pictures), and related licensed materials.

1. License. Use Of The Program. You may use the Program on only one machine at any one time. You agree to ensure that anyone who uses the Program (accessed either locally or remotely) does so only for your authorized use and complies with the terms of this Agreement. A Program is considered to be in use when it resides in memory or is otherwise stored on a machine. A Program stored on a network server solely for the purpose of being distributed to other machines is not considered to be in use. For a Program managed by a license management tool, copies may be made and stored on machines under control of that tool, but your use may not exceed the total number of users or amount of resource authorized. You may 1) copy the Program for backup and 2) merge the Program into another program. You must reproduce the copyright notice and any other legend of ownership on each copy, or partial copy, of the Program. You may not: 1) use, copy, merge, or transfer the Program except as provided in this Agreement; 2) reverse assemble, reverse compile, or otherwise translate the Program except as specifically permitted by law without the possibility of contractual waiver; or 3) sublicense, rent or lease the Program.

Transfer of Rights and Obligations. You may not transfer your rights and obligations under a license for a Program to another party.

2. Limited Warranty. IBM warrants that when the Program is used in the specified operating environment, it will conform to its published specifications found in IBM manuals. IBM does not warrant uninterrupted or error-free operation of a Program. The warranty period for a Program expires when its Program services are no longer available. During the warranty period warranty service is provided, without charge, through defect-related Program services. Program services will be available until December 31, 1998. IBM provides defect support through Program Services. A defect related problem means the Program does not conform to specifications and could be either a code or documentation error. For information on how you may access Program Services, or other fee-based support services, please contact IBM or its reseller from whom you acquired this Program.

THESE WARRANTIES REPLACE ALL OTHER WARRANTIES OR CONDITIONS, EXPRESS OR IMPLIED, INCLUDING, BUT NOT LIMITED TO, THE IMPLIED WARRANTIES OR CONDITIONS OF MERCHANTABILITY AND FITNESS FOR A PARTICULAR PURPOSE.

These warranties give you specific legal rights, and you may also have other rights which vary from jurisdiction to jurisdiction. Some jurisdictions do not allow the exclusion or limitation of implied warranties, so the above exclusion or limitation may not apply to you. In that event such warranties are limited in duration to the warranty period. No warranties apply after that period.

3. Patents and Copyrights. If a third party claims that a Program IBM provides to you infringes that party's patent or copyright, IBM will, at its expense, defend you against that claim and pay all costs, damages, and attorney's fees that a court finally awards, provided that you 1) promptly notify IBM in writing of the claim and 2) allow IBM to control, and cooperate with IBM in, the defense and any related settlement negotiations. If such a claim is made or appears likely to be made, you agree to permit IBM to enable you to continue to use the Program, or to modify it, or replace it with one that is at least functionally equivalent. If IBM determines that none of these alternatives is reasonably available, you agree to return the Program to IBM on IBM's written request. IBM will then give you a credit for a one-time charge Program, provided its total charges have been fully paid. This is IBM's entire obligation to you regarding any claim of infringement. IBM has no obligation regarding any claim based on any of the following: 1) your modification of a Program; 2) the combination, operation, or use of a Program with any programs, data, or apparatus that IBM did not provide; or 3) infringement by a non-IBM Program.

4. Limitation of Liability. Regardless of the basis on which you may be entitled to recover damages from IBM, for any claim (including fundamental breach, negligence, misrepresentation or other tort), IBM's liability will only be for 1) payments referred to in the patents and copyrights terms described above; 2) bodily injury (including death), and damage to real property and tangible personal property; and 3) the amount of any other actual direct damages or loss, up to the greater of the equivalent of U.S. $10,000 in your local currency or IBM's then generally available license charge for the Program.

IBM WILL NOT BE LIABLE FOR ANY SPECIAL, INCIDENTAL, OR INDIRECT DAMAGES OR FOR ANY ECONOMIC CONSEQUENTIAL DAMAGES (INCLUDING LOST PROFITS OR SAVINGS), EVEN IF IBM, OR ITS RESELLER, HAS BEEN ADVISED OF THE POSSIBILITY OF SUCH DAMAGES. SOME JURISDICTIONS DO NOT ALLOW THE EXCLUSION OR LIMITATION OF INCIDENTAL OR CONSEQUENTIAL DAMAGES, SO THE ABOVE LIMITATION OR EXCLUSION MAY NOT APPLY TO YOU.

IBM will not be liable for 1) loss of, or damage to, your records or data or 2) any damages claimed by you based on any third party claim. This limitation of liability also applies to any developer of a Program supplied to IBM. It is the maximum for which we are collectively responsible.

5. General. You may terminate your license at any time. If you do so, all your license rights to the Program are terminated. You may keep a copy of the Program in your archives. IBM may terminate your license if you fail to comply with the terms of this Agreement. If IBM does so, all your license rights to the Program are terminated and you must destroy all your copies of it. You agree to comply with all applicable export laws and regulations. Neither party may bring a legal action under this Agreement more than two years after the cause of action arose. This Agreement is governed by the laws of the country in which you acquired the Program. In the United States, this agreement is governed by the laws of the State of New York. In Canada, this agreement is governed by the laws of the Province of Ontario. U.S. Government Users Restricted Rights - Use, duplication, or disclosure restricted by the GSA ADP Schedule Contract with the IBM Corporation. Any other documentation with respect to this licensed program, including any such documentation referenced herein, is provided for information purposes only and does not extend or modify the material contained in the License Information.

* Trademark of IBM Corp.

** Java is a trademark of Sun Microsystems, Inc.
Windows is a trademark of Microsoft Corp.

Java™ Development Kit Version 1.1.5 and BDK Version 1.0 Combined Binary Code License

This binary code license ("License") contains rights and restrictions associated with use of the accompanying software and documentation ("Software"). Read the License carefully before installing the Software. By installing the Software you agree to the terms and conditions of this License.

1. Limited License Grant. Sun grants to you ("Licensee") a non-exclusive, non-transferable limited license to use the Software without fee for evaluation of the Software and for development of Java compatible applets and applications. Licensee may make one archival copy of the Software. Except for the foregoing, Licensee may not re-distribute the Software in whole or in part, either separately or included with a product. Refer to the Java Runtime Environment Version 1.1 binary code license (http://java.sun.com/products/JDK/1.1/index.html) for the availability of runtime code which may be distributed with Java compatible applets and applications.

2. Redistribution of Demonstration Files. Sun grants Licensee the right to use, modify and redistribute the Beans example and demonstration code, including the Bean Box ("Demos"), in both source and binary code form provided that (i) Licensee does not utilize the Demos in a manner which is disparaging to Sun; and (ii) Licensee indemnifies and holds Sun harmless from all claims relating to any such use or distribution of the Demos. Such distribution is limited to the source and binary code of the Demos and specifically excludes any rights to modify or distribute any graphical images contained in the Demos.

3. Java Platform Interface. Licensee may not modify the Java Platform Interface ("JPI", identified as classes contained within the "java" package or any subpackages of the "java" package), by creating additional classes within the JPI or otherwise causing the addition to or modification of the classes in the JPI. In the event that Licensee creates any Java-related API and distributes such API to others for applet or application development, Licensee must promptly publish an accurate specification for such API for free use by all developers of Java-based software.

4. Restrictions. Software is confidential copyrighted information of Sun and title to all copies is retained by Sun and/or its licensors. Licensee shall not modify, decompile, disassemble, decrypt, extract, or otherwise reverse engineer Software. Software may not be leased, assigned, or sublicensed, in whole or in part. Software is not designed or intended for use in online control of aircraft, air traffic, aircraft navigation or aircraft communications; or in the design, construction, operation or maintenance of any nuclear facility. Licensee warrants that it will not use or redistribute the Software for such purposes.

5. Trademarks and Logos. This License does not authorize Licensee to use any Sun name, trademark or logo. Licensee acknowledges that Sun owns the Java trademark and all Java-related trademarks, logos and icons including the Coffee Cup and Duke ("Java Marks") and agrees to: (i) comply with the Java Trademark Guidelines at http://java.sun.com/trademarks.html; (ii) not do anything harmful to or inconsistent with Sun's rights in the Java Marks; and (iii) assist Sun in protecting those rights, including assigning to Sun any rights acquired by Licensee in any Java Mark.

6. Disclaimer of Warranty. Software is provided "AS IS," without a warranty of any kind. ALL EXPRESS OR IMPLIED REPRESENTATIONS AND WARRANTIES, INCLUDING ANY IMPLIED WARRANTY OF MERCHANTABILITY, FITNESS FOR A PARTICULAR PURPOSE OR NON-INFRINGEMENT, ARE HEREBY EXCLUDED.

7. Limitation of Liability. SUN AND ITS LICENSORS SHALL NOT BE LIABLE FOR ANY DAMAGES SUFFERED BY LICENSEE OR ANY THIRD PARTY AS A RESULT OF USING OR DISTRIBUTING SOFTWARE. IN NO EVENT WILL SUN OR ITS LICENSORS BE LIABLE FOR ANY LOST REVENUE, PROFIT OR DATA, OR FOR DIRECT, INDIRECT, SPECIAL, CONSEQUENTIAL, INCIDENTAL OR PUNITIVE DAMAGES, HOWEVER CAUSED AND REGARDLESS OF THE THEORY OF LIABILITY, ARISING OUT OF THE USE OF OR INABILITY TO USE SOFTWARE, EVEN IF SUN HAS BEEN ADVISED OF THE POSSIBILITY OF SUCH DAMAGES.

8. Termination. Licensee may terminate this License at any time by destroying all copies of Software. This License will terminate immediately without notice from Sun if Licensee fails to comply with any provision of this License. Upon such termination, Licensee must destroy all copies of Software.
9. Export Regulations. Software, including technical data, is subject to U.S. export control laws, including the U.S. Export Administration Act and its associated regulations, and may be subject to export or import regulations in other countries. Licensee agrees to comply strictly with all such regulations and acknowledges that it has the responsibility to obtain licenses to export, re-export, or import Software. Software may not be downloaded, or otherwise exported or re-exported (i) into, or to a national or resident of, Cuba, Iraq, Iran, North Korea, Libya, Sudan, Syria or any country to which the U.S. has embargoed goods; or (ii) to anyone on the U.S. Treasury Department's list of Specially Designated Nations or the U.S. Commerce Department's Table of Denial Orders.
10. Restricted Rights. Use, duplication or disclosure by the United States government is subject to the restrictions as set forth in the Rights in Technical Data and Computer Software Clauses in DFARS 252.227-7013(c) (1) (ii) and FAR 52.227-19(c) (2) as applicable.
11. Governing Law. Any action related to this License will be governed by California law and controlling U.S. federal law. No choice of law rules of any jurisdiction will apply.
12. Severability. If any of the above provisions are held to be in violation of applicable law, void, or unenforceable in any jurisdiction, then such provisions are herewith waived to the extent necessary for the License to be otherwise enforceable in such jurisdiction. However, if in Sun's opinion deletion of any provisions of the License by operation of this paragraph unreasonably compromises the rights or increases the liabilities of Sun or its licensors, Sun reserves the right to terminate the License and refund the fee paid by Licensee, if any, as Licensee's sole and exclusive remedy.

LICENSE AGREEMENT TO EVALUATE Java WorkShop™ 2.0

If customer is using the software for evaluation purposes only, customer agrees to be bound by the following terms and conditions:
1. License to Use for Evaluation Purposes. Customer is granted a non-exclusive and non-transferable license ("License") to use the accompanying binary software in machine-readable form, together with accompanying documentation ("Software"), internally for the purposes of evaluation and demonstration. No license is granted to Customer for any other purpose. Customer shall not distribute the Software, in whole or in part, to any third party. This License expires thirty (30) days after the date of installation.
2. No Support of Evaluation Software. SOFTWARE USED FOR EVALUATION PURPOSES IS LICENSED "AS IS." SUN DISCLAIMS ALL WARRANTIES CONCERNING SUCH EVALUATION SOFTWARE, EXPRESS OR IMPLIED, INCLUDING ANY IMPLIED WARRANTY OF MERCHANTABILITY, FITNESS FOR A PARTICULAR PURPOSE OR NON-INFRINGEMENT.
3. Restrictions. Software is copyrighted and title to all copies is retained by Sun and/or its licensors. Customer shall not make copies of Software, other than a single copy of Software for archival purposes and, if applicable, Customer may, for its internal use only, print the number of copies of on-line documentation for which the applicable fee has been paid, in which event all proprietary rights notices on Software shall be reproduced and applied. Except as specifically authorized elsewhere in this Agreement or unless enforcement of this provision is prohibited by applicable law, Customer shall not modify, decompile, disassemble, decrypt, extract, or otherwise reverse engineer Software, and Customer shall not use, copy or distribute any Sun icons in any Customer-developed programs. Software is not designed or licensed for use in on-line control equipment in hazardous environments such as operation of nuclear facilities, aircraft navigation or control, or direct life support machines.
4. Confidentiality. Software is confidential and proprietary information of Sun and/or its licensors. Customer agrees to take adequate steps to protect Software from unauthorized disclosure or use.
5. Limitation of Liability. IN NO EVENT WILL SUN BE LIABLE FOR ANY LOST REVENUE, PROFIT OR DATA, OR FOR SPECIAL, INDIRECT, CONSEQUENTIAL, INCIDENTAL OR PUNITIVE DAMAGES HOWEVER CAUSED AND REGARDLESS OF THE THEORY OF LIABILITY ARISING OUT OF THE USE OF OR INABILITY TO USE SOFTWARE, EVEN IF SUN HAS BEEN ADVISED OF THE POSSIBILITY OF SUCH DAMAGES. In no event shall Sun's liability to Customer, whether in contract, tort (including negligence), or otherwise, exceed the license fee paid by Customer for Software. The foregoing limitations shall apply even if the above stated warranty fails of its essential purpose.
6. Termination. This License is effective until terminated. Customer may terminate this License at any time by destroying all copies of Software including any documentation. This License will terminate immediately without notice from Sun if Customer fails to comply with any provision of this License. Upon termination, Customer must destroy all copies of Software.
7. Export Regulations. Software, including technical data, is subject to U.S. export control laws, including the U.S. Export Administration Act and its associated regulations, and may be subject to export or import regulations in other countries. Customer agrees to comply strictly with all such regulations and acknowledges that it has the responsibility to obtain licenses to export, re-export, or import Software.
8. U.S. Government Restricted Rights. If Customer is acquiring Software including accompanying documentation on behalf of the U.S. Government, the following provisions apply. If Software is supplied to the Department of Defense ("DOD"). Software is subject to "Restricted Rights", as that term is defined in the DOD Supplement to the Federal Acquisition Regulations ("DFAR") in paragraphs 252.227-7015 (b)(6/95) and 227.7202-3(a). If Software is supplied to any unit or agency of the United States Government other than DOD, the Government's rights in Software will be defined in paragraphs 52.227-14(g)(2)(6/87) and 52.227-19(6/87) of the Federal Acquisition Regulations ("FAR"). Use, duplication, reproduction or disclosure by the Government is subject to such restrictions or successor provisions. Contractor/Manufacturer is: Sun Microsystems, Inc., 901 San Antonio Road, Palo Alto, CA 94303.
9. Governing Law. This Agreement is made under, shall be governed by and construed in accordance with the laws of the State of California, U.S.A., excluding its choice of law provisions.
10. Severability. If any of the above provisions are held to be in violation of applicable law, void, or unenforceable in any jurisdiction, then such provisions are herewith waived or amended to the extent necessary for the License to be otherwise enforceable in such jurisdiction, However, if in Sun's opinion deletion or amendment of any provisions of the License by operation of this paragraph unreasonably compromises the rights or liabilities of Sun or its licensors, Sun reserves the right to terminate the License and refund the fee paid by Customer as Customer's sole and exclusive remedy.
11. Integration. This Agreement (including any supplementary terms) is the entire agreement between Customer and Sun relating to Software and: (i) supersedes all prior or contemporaneous oral or written communications, proposals and representations with respect to its subject matter; and (ii) prevails over any conflicting or additional terms of any quote, order, acknowledgment, or similar communication between the parties during the term of this Agreement. No modification to the Agreement will be binding, unless in writing and signed by a duly authorized representative of each party.
Supplemental Terms and Conditions for Java WorkShop. These terms and conditions for Java WorkShop supplement the terms and conditions of the Binary Code License ("BCL"). Capitalized terms not defined herein shall have the meanings ascribed to them in the BCL. These terms and conditions shall supersede any inconsistent or conflicting terms and conditions in the BCL.
1. Java Platform Interface. Customer may not modify the Java Platform Interface ("JPI", identified as classes contained within the "java" package or any subpackages of the "java" package), by creating additional classes within the JPI or otherwise causing the addition to or modification of the classes in the JPI. In the event that Customer creates any Java-related API and distributes such API to others for applet or application development, Customer must promptly publish broadly, an accurate specification for such API for free use by all developers of Java-based software.
2. Trademarks and Logos. This License does not authorize Customer to use any Sun name, trademark or logo. Customer acknowledges that Sun owns the Java trademark and all Java-related trademarks, logos
including the Coffee Cup and Duke ("Java Marks") and agrees to comply with the Java Trademark Guidelines at http://java.sun.com/trademarks.html; (iii) not do anything harmful to or inconsistent with Sun's rights in the Java Marks; and (iv) assist Sun in protecting those rights, including assigning to Sun any rights acquired by Customer in any Java Mark.